THE EMPIRE CITY

A TREASURY OF NEW YORK

Collected and Edited by

Alexander Klein

Essay Index Reprint Series

BOOKS FOR LIBRARIES PRESS
FREEPORT, NEW YORK

LAMAR UNIVERSITY LIBRARY

Copyright © 1955 by Alexander Klein

Reprinted 1971 by arrangement

INTERNATIONAL STANDARD BOOK NUMBER:
0-8369-2236-0

LIBRARY OF CONGRESS CATALOG CARD NUMBER:
75-152184

PRINTED IN THE UNITED STATES OF AMERICA

TO JUDY ANN, MANCI AND MARTIN

ACKNOWLEDGMENTS

Grateful appreciation is expressed herewith to all authors, publishers, periodicals and agents who courteously granted permission to include copyrighted material:

Donald L. Alderton for "The City of My Dreams" and "The City Awakes" from *The Color of a Great City* by Theodore Dreiser, Copyright, 1923, by Boni & Liveright, Inc., Copyright renewed, 1951, by Mrs. Theodore Dreiser

Roger Angell and *Holiday* for "Everything Money Can Buy," Copyright, 1949, by The Curtis Publishing Company

Herbert Asbury and *Holiday* for "Exotic Chinatown," Copyright, 1952, by The Curtis Publishing Company

Brooks Atkinson for "The Fabulous Port of New York," Copyright, 1951, by The New York Times Company

William Barrett for "Greenwich Village: New Designs in Bohemia," Copyright, 1950, 1954, by The New York Times Company

B. T. Batsford Ltd., London, England, for "The Unreal City" from *Portrait of New York*, by Cecil Beaton

Lucius Beebe and *Holiday* for "21: New York's Most Glamorous Restaurant," Copyright, 1952, by The Curtis Publishing Company

Meyer Berger for "Preface," Copyright, 1953, by The New York Times Company, and for "Lindy's: Sturgeon Saga of the Main Stem," Copyright, 1949, by The New York Times Company

Meyer Berger and *Holiday* for "The Finest," Copyright, 1949, by The Curtis Publishing Company

ACKNOWLEDGMENTS

Brandt & Brandt for "Contest" by Francis Steegmuller, Copyright, 1945, by Francis Steegmuller. Originally published in *The New Yorker*

Gene M. Brown for "Wall Street: Men and Money," Copyright, 1952, by Park Magazine, Inc.

George T. Bye and Company for "Jimmy Walker: The Dream Prince" from *Night Club Era* by Stanley Walker, Copyright, 1933, by Stanley Walker

Melville H. Cane for "That Was New York and That Was Me," by Sinclair Lewis, Copyright, 1937, by The New Yorker Magazine, Inc.

Allen Churchill for "Sins and Secrets of Times Square," Copyright, 1951, by Park Magazine, Inc., and for "Ross and The New Yorker," Copyright, 1948, by The American Mercury, Inc.

Russel Crouse for "That Was New York: Jim Fisk," Copyright, 1928, by The New Yorker Magazine, Inc.

Arthur Daley and *The New York Times* for "The Fabulous Yankees Through Fifty Years," Copyright, 1952, by The New York Times Company

The John Day Company, Inc. and Methuen & Company, Ltd., London, England, for selections from *The Silent Traveller in New York* by Chiang Yee

Doubleday & Company, Inc. for "The Metropolitan Milieu" by Lewis Mumford, from *America and Alfred Stieglitz*, edited by Waldo Frank, Copyright, 1934, by Doubleday & Company, Inc.; for an excerpt from *The Voice of the City* by O. Henry, Copyright, 1910, by Doubleday & Company, Inc.; and for "I Go Adventuring in the Metropolis" from *Midstream* by Helen Keller, Copyright, 1929, by Helen Keller

E. P. Dutton & Co., Inc. for selections from *The Story of Old New York*, by Henry Collins Brown, Copyright, 1934, by E. P. Dutton & Co., Inc.; and from *Brownstone Fronts and Saratoga Fronts*, by Henry Collins Brown, Copyright, 1935, by E. P. Dutton & Co., Inc.

George Frazier and *Esquire* for "Elegance by the Mile: Fifth Avenue," by George Frazier, Copyright, 1953, by Esquire, Inc.

Librairie Gallimard, Paris, France, and *Town & Country* for "Manhattan: Great American Desert," by Jean-Paul Sartre, Copyright, 1946, by Hearst Magazines, Inc. All rights reserved by Librairie Gallimard

ACKNOWLEDGMENTS

Lewis Gannett for "The Wilderness of New York," Copyright, 1925, by The Century Company

Jack Gaver and Dave Stanley for "Brooklyn, The Forty-Ninth State," Copyright, 1948, by *The American Mercury*

Harcourt, Brace and Company, Inc. for "The Place of Sacrifice" from *Collected Edition of Heywood Broun*, Copyright, 1941, by Heywood Hale Broun; for "Statue of Liberty" and "Savage Sunsets" from *Once Around the Sun* by Brooks Atkinson, Copyright, 1951, by Brooks Atkinson; and for "The Fairy Catastrophe" from *When the Cathedrals Were White* by Le Corbusier, translated from the French by Francis E. Hyslop, Jr., Copyright, 1947, by Harcourt, Brace and Company, Inc.

Harper & Brothers, for "The Typical New Yorker" from *20,000 Leagues Under the Sea*, by Robert Benchley, Copyright, 1928, by Harper & Brothers; for selections from *The American Scene* by Henry James, Copyright, 1907, by Harper & Brothers, Copyright, 1935, by Henry James; for *Here Is New York* by E. B. White, Copyright, 1949, by The Curtis Publishing Company; for "Enchanted City" from *The Web and the Rock* by Thomas Wolfe, Copyright, 1939, by Maxwell Perkins as Executor; and for "The Sex in New York" from *Mark Twain's Travels with Mr. Brown*

Mel Heimer for selections from *The Big Drag*, Copyright, 1944, by Mel Heimer

Fannie Hurst for "Harlem, Known and Unknown," Copyright, 1946, by The New York Times Company

Alfred Kazin and *Harper's Bazaar* for "Brooklyn Bridge," by Alfred Kazin, Copyright, 1946, by Hearst Magazines, Inc.

Helen Keller for "A Romantic Edifice"

Alfred A. Knopf, Inc. for "Big Wind from Kansas: Carrie Nation vs. John L. Sullivan," from *All Around the Town* by Herbert Asbury, Copyright, 1933, 1934, by Alfred A. Knopf, Inc.; for "When the Negro Was In Vogue" from *The Big Sea* by Langston Hughes, Copyright, 1940, by Alfred A. Knopf, Inc.; for "There Are Parts for All in the *Totentanz*" from *Prejudices, Sixth Series*, by H. L. Mencken, Copyright, 1927, by Alfred A. Knopf, Inc.; for "New York Women" from *Salsette Discovers America* by Jules Romains, translated from the French by Lewis Galantière, Copyright, 1942, by Alfred A. Knopf, Inc.; and for "The Sex in New York" from *Mark Twain's Travels with Mr. Brown*

Helen Lawrenson and *Esquire* for "New York: The Crack-up City," Copyright, 1953, by Esquire, Inc.

Littauer and Wilkinson for "Nether World" by Richard Gehman, Copyright, 1951, by Park Magazine, Inc., and for "Manhattan's Wonderful Cab Drivers" by George Weinstein, Copyright, 1952, by Park Magazine, Inc.

Dwight Macdonald for "Action on Fifty-Third Street," Copyright, 1953, by The New Yorker Magazine, Inc.

Richard Maney for "The Empire Theatre," Copyright, 1953, by The New York Times Company

Meta Markel, Executrix of the Estate of Irwin Edman, for "The Spirit Has Many Mansions," by Irwin Edman, Copyright, 1953, by The New York Times Company

Massachusetts Historical Society for the selection from *The Education of Henry Adams* by Henry Adams, Copyright, 1918, by The Massachusetts Historical Society, Copyright, 1931, by The Modern Library, Inc.

Carson McCullers, Floria V. Lasky and The Condé Nast Publications, Inc. for "Brooklyn Is My Neighborhood," Copyright, 1941, by The Condé Nast Publications, Inc.

Mavis McIntosh-Elizabeth McKee for "New York's Brownstone Girl" by Robert Lowry, Copyright, 1951, by The American Mercury, Inc.

McIntosh and Otis, Inc. for "The Making of a New Yorker," by John Steinbeck, Copyright, 1953, by The New York Times Company

William Morris Agency for the selection from *Tallulah* by Tallulah Bankhead, Copyright, 1952, by Tallulah Bankhead; and for "The City Where Nobody Lives," by Joe Alex Morris, Copyright, 1949, by The Curtis Publishing Company

New Directions and Harold Ober Associations for "My Lost City" from *The Crack Up* by F. Scott Fitzgerald, edited by Edmund Wilson, Copyright, 1945, by New Directions, Copyright, 1951, by Frances Scott Fitzgerald Lanahan

George Sessions Perry and *The Saturday Evening Post* for "Look, Ma—Real Grass," by George Sessions Perry, Copyright, 1947, by The Curtis Publishing Company

Prentice-Hall Inc. for "Capital of the World" and "Urban Jungle" from *New York Today*, by Agnes Rothery, Copyright, 1951, by Agnes Rothery

Random House, Inc. for selections from *Local Color* by Truman Capote, Copyright, 1946, 1947, 1948, 1949, 1950, by Truman Capote; and for selections from *Incredible New York* by Lloyd Morris, Copyright, 1951, by Lloyd Morris

ACKNOWLEDGMENTS xi

Jo Ranson for "Coney by the Sea," Copyright, 1951, by Park Magazine, Inc.

Rinehart & Company, Inc. for the selection from *The Vicious Circle* by Margaret Case Harriman, Copyright, 1951, by Margaret Case Harriman

Charles J. Rolo and *Flair* for "Blue Blood and Printer's Ink," by Charles J. Rolo, Copyright, 1950, by Cowles Magazines, Inc.

Sydney A. Sanders Literary Agency for "Fire Raid on New York City," by Herbert Ravenel Sass, Copyright, 1949, by The Curtis Publishing Company

Budd Schulberg for "Joe Docks," Copyright, 1952, by The New York Times Company

Sheridan House and A. J. Liebling for "Tummler" from *Back Where I Came From*, by A. J. Liebling, Copyright, 1938, by A. J. Liebling. Originally published in *The New Yorker*

Simon & Schuster, Inc, for "Sidewalk Fisherman" and "The Capuchins" from *The Eight Million* by Meyer Berger, Copyright, 1942, by Meyer Berger; and for the selection from *A Child of the Century* by Ben Hecht, Copyright, 1954, by Ben Hecht

Edward Stanley and *Holiday* for "Broadway," by Edward Stanley, Copyright, 1951, by The Curtis Publishing Company

Time, Inc. for "Billion-Dollar Baby," Copyright, 1949, by Time, Inc.; and for "Columbia University," Copyright, 1954, by Time, Inc.

University of Chicago Press for "The Fashionable Life," by James Kirke Paulding; "The Big Town, Circa 1837," by Asa Greene; "Bowery Boy vs. Broadway Fop," by "A South Carolinian," from *Mirror for Americans*, edited by Warren S. Tryon

Hy Turkin and *Coronet* for "Those Daffy Dodgers," by Hy Turkin, Copyright, 1952, by Esquire, Inc.

The Viking Press, Inc. for the selection from *Father, Dear Father*, by Ludwig Bemelmans, Copyright, 1953, by Ludwig Bemelmans; and for the selection from *Going to Pieces* by Alexander Woollcott, Copyright, 1928, by Alexander Woollcott

A. P. Watt & Son, and Hodder & Stoughton, London, England, and Miss D. E. Collins for "A Meditation in Broadway" from *What I Saw in America* by G. K. Chesterton

Weidenfeld & Nicolson, Ltd. and Cyril Connolly, London, England, for the selection from *Ideas and Places* by Cyril Connolly

Walter Winchell and the New York *Mirror* for "Waiting for Lepke" by Walter Winchell, Copyright, 1939, by the New York *Mirror*

Frank Lloyd Wright for the selection from *The Disappearing City*, by Frank Lloyd Wright, Copyright, 1932, by William Farquhar Payson

Thanks are also extended to *The American Mercury, Coronet, Esquire, Flair, Harper's Bazaar, Holiday, The New York Times Magazine, The New Yorker, Park East, The Saturday Evening Post* and *Town & Country* for their permission to reprint those articles mentioned above which first appeared in their publications.

CONTENTS

Preface · *Meyer Berger* — xviii
Introduction · *Alexander Klein* — xxi

I *Bird's-Eye View*

Here Is New York · *E. B. White* — 3
The Metropolitan Milieu · *Lewis Mumford* — 20

II *Grand Tour: This Is New York*

Statue of Liberty · *Brooks Atkinson* — 33
Broadway: World's Most Exciting Street · *Edward Stanley* — 35
The City Where Nobody Lives (Rockefeller Center) · *Joe Alex Morris* — 43
Elegance by the Mile: Fifth Avenue · *George Frazier* — 52
Exotic Chinatown · *Herbert Asbury* — 57
Wall Street: Men and Money · *Gene M. Brown* — 65
Look, Ma—Real Grass! (Central Park) · *George Sessions Perry* — 69
Empire State Building
    A Romantic Edifice · *Helen Keller* — 76
    The Optical Center · *Chiang Yee* — 76
Sins and Secrets of Times Square · *Allen Churchill* — 79
Lindy's: Sturgeon Saga of the Main Stem · *Meyer Berger* — 83

Action on West Fifty-Third Street (Museum of Modern Art) · *Dwight Macdonald*	89
Greenwich Village: New Designs in Bohemia · *William Barrett*	97
The Fabulous Port of New York · *Brooks Atkinson*	105
Everything Money Can Buy · *Roger Angell*	109
Places of Worship · *Chiang Yee*	117
Of Scholarship and Peace (Public Library) · *Chiang Yee*	120
Man's Right to Knowledge (Columbia University) · *from* Time	122
Harlem, Known and Unknown · *Fannie Hurst*	126
21: New York's Most Glamorous Restaurant · *Lucius Beebe*	131
The Met · *Chiang Yee*	137
Nether World · *Richard Gehman*	140
Urban Jungle (Bronx Zoo) · *Agnes Rothery*	144
Brooklyn Bridge · *Alfred Kazin*	148
In Defense and Praise of Brooklyn · *Truman Capote*	155
· *Ludwig Bemelmans*	156
Brooklyn Is My Neighborhood · *Carson McCullers*	157
Brooklyn, The Forty-Ninth State · *Jack Gaver and Dave Stanley*	160
Coney by the Sea · *Jo Ranson*	166
Capital of the World (United Nations) · *Agnes Rothery*	170

III *Those Were the Days*

Early New York: Fascinating Little Wench · *Henry Collins Brown*	175
The Fashionable Life, 1828 · *James Kirke Paulding*	177
The Big Town, Circa 1837 · *Asa Greene*	179
Traffic, Dirt and Cholera	179
Riots Galore: Doctors, Anti-Abolition, Flour	181
The Great Fire of 1835	183
A Jaundiced View · *Charles Dickens*	185
Bowery Boy vs. Broadway Fop · *"A South Carolinian"*	192
The Fire Raid on New York City · *Herbert Ravenel Sass*	194
High, Wide and Handsome · *Lloyd Morris*	203
The Sex in New York · *Mark Twain*	206
Boss Tweed: What Are You Going to Do About It? · *Lloyd Morris*	207

CONTENTS xv

Pleasures Gone By · *Henry Collins Brown*	216
All the Perfumes of Arabia	216
Red Flannels to the Rescue	216
That Was New York: Jim Fisk · *Russel Crouse*	217
Private Joys Through Public Notices · *James D. McCabe, Jr.*	222
Floral Tributes and Midnight Suppers · *Henry Collins Brown*	224
In the Broadway Cars · *Stephen Crane*	226
Dr. Parkhurst Investigates · *Lloyd Morris*	229
Meet Me at the Waldorf · *Lloyd Morris*	233
Carry Nation vs. John L. Sullivan · *Herbert Asbury*	236
Cosmopolis Under the El · *Lloyd Morris*	239
Paint, Protest and Parties · *Lloyd Morris*	243
The Vicious Circle · *Margaret Case Harriman*	250
Don Juan in New York · *Ben Hecht*	262
When the Negro Was in Vogue · *Langston Hughes*	265
Jimmy Walker, the Dream Prince · *Stanley Walker*	269
Waiting for Lepke · *Walter Winchell*	272
The Empire Theatre: Shrine and Symbol · *Richard Maney*	276

IV *It Takes All Kinds: People, Places, Things*

New York Women: A French View · *Jules Romains*	283
Sidewalk Fisherman · *Meyer Berger*	288
The Capuchins · *Meyer Berger*	295
Every Day a Jubilee · *Chiang Yee*	297
Tummler · *A. J. Liebling*	300
New York's Brownstone Girl · *Robert Lowry*	305
Manhattan's Wonderful Cab Drivers · *George Weinstein*	311
Joe Docks · *Budd Schulberg*	316
Ross and *The New Yorker* · *Allen Churchill*	323
Billion-Dollar Baby · *From* Time	332
The Typical New Yorker · *Robert Benchley*	338
Hothouse Flower on the Big Drag · *Mel Heimer*	342
The Finest · *Meyer Berger*	348

Blue Blood and Printer's Ink · *Charles J. Rolo*	*354*
The Wildness of New York: How Nature Persists in the Metropolis *Lewis S. Gannett*	*360*
The Giants and Me · *Tallulah Bankhead*	*364*
Fabulous Yankees Through Fifty Years · *Arthur Daley*	*366*
Those Daffy Dodgers · *Hy Turkin*	*371*
Big Drag Vignettes · *Mel Heimer*	*375*
The Ham What Am: At Sardi's and Environs	*375*
The Night-Life Blues	*377*
The Crack-Up City · *Helen Lawrenson*	*379*
Contest · *Francis Steegmuller*	*382*
The Spirit Has Many Mansions · *Irwin Edman*	*385*
Savage Sunsets · *Brooks Atkinson*	*389*

V *Perspectives: The City and the Dream*

WALT WHITMAN · *Crossing Brooklyn Ferry (1856–1885)*	*391*
· *Mannahatta*	*394*
SINCLAIR LEWIS · *That Was New York—and That Was Me (1903)*	*395*
HENRY ADAMS · *No Constantine in Sight (1904)*	*399*
O. HENRY · *The Voice of the City (1905)*	*400*
HENRY JAMES · *New York Revisited (1907)*	*404*
G. K. CHESTERTON · *A Meditation in Broadway (1921)*	*410*
THEODORE DREISER · *The Color of a Great City (1903–1923)* · *The City of My Dreams* · *The City Awakes*	*412*
H. L. MENCKEN · *There Are Parts for All in the "Totentanz" (1927)*	*416*
ALEXANDER WOOLLCOTT · *No Yesterdays (1928)*	*420*
HELEN KELLER · *I Go Adventuring (1929)*	*421*
F. SCOTT FITZGERALD · *My Lost City (July, 1932)*	*425*
FRANK LLOYD WRIGHT · *The Disappearing City (1932)*	*433*
THOMAS WOLFE · *Enchanted City (1925–1935)*	*437*
LE CORBUSIER · *The Fairy Catastrophe (1936)*	*442*
HEYWOOD BROUN · *The Place of Sacrifice (1938)*	*449*

CONTENTS

JEAN-PAUL SARTRE · *Manhattan: the Great American Desert* (*1946*) ... *451*
CECIL BEATON · *The Unreal City* (*1938-1948*) ... *457*
TRUMAN CAPOTE · *The Diamond Iceberg* (*1950*) ... *461*
CYRIL CONNOLLY · *Notes on Today's Supreme Metropolis* (*1953*) ... *464*
JOHN STEINBECK · *The Making of a New Yorker* (*1953*) ... *469*

PREFACE

by
Meyer Berger

In February, 1653, a little group of leathern-breeched, ponderous, pipe-smoking Dutch burghers in absurd high-crowned headgear met as the first City Fathers in an ill-lighted tavern at the foot of Manhattan Island, at the southern tip of the living map that glows a quarter-mile below the turret window of the Empire State Building tonight, a map drawn in running fire and with spangles and jewels from The Battery to Westchester.

The island was a sweet-scented paradise then. Vagrant breezes carried the heady perfume of its dense stands of primitive woods and of its massed blossoms far out to sea. Wild things crept through its forests—bear, foxes, deer, wolves, beaver, chattering squirrels and screaming panthers. In autumn its skies filled with honking, strident migratory flocks.

If there had been an Empire State tower in 1653 it would have looked out not only on the molten silver ribbons that flank the island shores and on the broad mirrors that are its southern bays but on hundreds of streams, brooks, falls and estuaries now all pavement-smothered yet silently coursing around subway walls, around skyscraper foundations, diverted but undying.

The community administered by the schnapps-swilling first City Fathers held only around eight hundred souls in some one hundred twenty crude dwellings close to the southern shore. It huddled behind high tree-trunk palisades and locked wooden gates, and its little mullioned windows went dark soon after sundown.

That village site is screened from even the Empire State tower tonight by massed steel-and-concrete structures that reach for the stars with weird, ethereal beauty—buildings studded with lambent moonstones; offices flooded with incandescent and fluorescent light. The cow track and cart road that led out of that tiny city behind the tree-trunk wall is the string of lighted pearls that runs from the island's tip to its northernmost reach—and beyond. It was their bravely named Great Highway, a rut through the hills and the thick woods. Now it is Broadway.

The ground area of the first one hundred years' growth does not show up much from this tower tonight. You see only the tops of the huge buildings that leap up from it, and the twinkling street lights deep down in man-made canyons. Under the first City Fathers the Dutch did not push much beyond Maiden Lane, but as they moved they stripped away the greenery and the forests, like human locusts. They laid the first street armor in a lane between Broad and Whitehall Streets and named it Stone Street because they used stone for the uppermost layer.

The first formal municipal administration lasted only thirty-one years. Then the English came and changed to English forms—aldermen, sheriff, and the like—and the Britons were locusts, too. They stripped away more trees and laid more paving. By 1753 they had fashioned a sort of vest-pocket London between The Battery and Canal Street. At the end of the first hundred years New York had twenty-five hundred buildings and its population was fifteen times what the first City Fathers ruled in 1653. Even at the end of two hundred years, the city had crept only as far as Fourteenth Street, to the blob of blurred lights one mile south of Empire State tower that is Union Square Park.

New York's population has increased ten thousand-fold since the first City Fathers were named in 1653. To these eight millions, and to the millions more who visit it, or see pictures of it, or read of it, what does this aggregate of stone and steel, this city which has become the world's first, mean?

Each man reads his own meaning into New York. To one it means the great art center, the world's greatest concentration of theatres, music halls, museums, libraries, galleries.

To the average tourist it is a huddle of frightening skyscrapers, gangster hideouts, untidy Chinatown, The Bowery, the slums and Wall Street. He carries home that picture.

The visiting buyer from Eugene, Oregon, knows it for its hot spots, for its plush hotels, its top-price eating places, its glittering bars.

For countless thousands who have fled the prying eyes and the clacking tongues of small-town neighbors, it is the perfect hiding place. It is the ultimate goal for the boy or girl eager for a big spot in the theatre, in radio, in opera, in the ballet, in business.

To each of these, depending on their defeat or on their success, New York has different meaning. To many it becomes a second home and takes on additional meaning. The defeated go down in it, embittered, or flee from it and curse it.

Moving among The City's slums, you could weep for the poor who dwell in them except that you know that hundreds will struggle up, one day, to the richest mansions on Park Avenue and to the quiet dignity of Sutton Place.

You will find comfort in the thought that wiser City Fathers are aware of the tragedies that grow out of the slums, and that they have built or sponsored the building of cleaner and better housing centers.

Standing off from the city in the Brooklyn and Staten Island ferries, or coming in from the sea, your eyes will widen and your heart will soften at what the rising sun does to the soaring towers that look down on the spot where the first Dutch settlers built.

Then the eye picks out the cluster of new United Nations buildings, a ghostly group on East River shore at midtown, and sudden warmth comes aflame inside. You think that this glittering island, grown from wilderness to great metropolis in three hundred years, holds that one hope for mankind's ultimate realization of peace—reason enough for the existence of New York, even if there were no other.

INTRODUCTION

New York City has laid claim to being first in so many things that it has been derisively dubbed the Capital of Everything. But the derision cannot obscure the fact that this is almost literally true; for the best pours in to enrich the metropolis—along with the worst and all shades between. Even by the latest measure of a city's stature, the number of bombs required to raze it, New York maintains its leadership.

More than a century ago James Fenimore Cooper wrote: "New York is essentially national in interest, position, pursuits. No one thinks of the place as belonging to a particular state, but to the United States." Recently I watched a child draw his concept of the earth. First he drew a circle, then within it a recognizable outline map of the United States, and, finally, jutting out of the northeast corner, what looked to me like a dunce cap. "What's that?" I asked, puzzled. "Empire State Building!" he replied, scornful of my ignorance, and he added more height to his representation so that it protruded well beyond the globe-circle to the edge of the paper.

And essentially the child was right. Today the towers of Manhattan cast their shadows not only over the entire nation but everywhere on the globe. For New York City has become the crucible and nerve center, the focus and symbol of man's civilization on earth.

There are some who would say with passion that the only real advantage of living in New York is that all its residents ascend to heaven directly after their deaths, having served their full term in purgatory right on Manhattan island. Others love the city, pridefully. But, loved or hated, soul-destroying or life-giving, New York City concededly adds up to the greatest show on earth—both literally and in terms of the archetypes it has come to embody for hundreds of millions all over the world. Every facet of man in all his glory and shame finds its expression in the eight million current inhabitants of the city and the relatively brief, three-hundred-odd years of its history. Thus a portrait of New York is, perforce, a portrait of man and his works, and of the imponderables of existence as muddled through in what E. B. White has called "the greatest human concentrate on earth." Viewed in this light, the accounts collected in this book will, I believe, form a more meaningful pattern and, individually, prove more rewarding reading.

Youngest of the great cities of the world, New York is probably the most written about of all of them. There have been many accounts by individual authors—tours of main attractions, personal tributes or impressions, histories. But, repeatedly, writers about New York have stressed its immense scope and the need for varied points of view to present a rounded experience of the city. Although it is struggling to maintain its present mold, great changes appear to be in the making. As Frank Lloyd Wright points out, modern technology has made great density of population unnecessary, and he envisions the Broadacre City of tomorrow. On the other hand, Le Corbusier points the way to a functional use of vertical space to create free horizontal space that could mean an even larger metropolis. Perhaps New York in its present form, inherited from previous epochs, has already passed the crest of the wave; if so, it is hardly perceptible as yet. It seems fitting that while the city as we have known it is still in its heyday, this composite portrait of it should be put together.

The alternating rhythm of the book's sections is from long-shot to close-up and back again to the long view. After the superb, complementary bird's-eye views of White and Mumford, comes the *Grand Tour,* intensive explorations of the city's highlights today. Many of these are known by name around the world—how little *truly* known, readers, including long-time residents of the city, will, I think, be surprised to discover. This freshness is not only a matter of physical details and anecdotes. A new awareness also emerges of the facets of man reflected by those landmarks, running the gamut from the nobility and tragedy of the Statue of Liberty (rescued from its grave of overfamiliarity by Brooks Atkinson) through the struggles and postures of Greenwich Village's new "bohemia," the intrigue and conflicts of Wall Street, to the courage, whimsy and practicality embodied in the history and daily drama of Rockefeller Center or Brooklyn Bridge or

INTRODUCTION   xxiii

the UN Building. For the authors of these accounts—whether their subject is the high jinks at 21 or Lindy's, the shame and splendor of Harlem or Broadway or the Port of New York, or the improbable phenomena, both pleasant and sinister, of Chinatown, Central Park, the Bronx Zoo or the human zoo of Coney Island—always reveal not only the physical façade of those landmarks but also the hidden human drama, current and past, that swirls around them.

Withal, tourist highlights are, of course, hardly the whole city. Admittedly no single volume about New York could claim encyclopedic completeness, but I have selected accounts of other representative metropolitan phenomena to deepen, broaden and vivify the reader's experience of the city. In the next section, *Those Were The Days*, we move back for some historical perspective. This is in no sense intended as a history, although the pieces, arranged in chronological order, begin with a fascinating glimpse of seventeenth century New York and end in the 1950's. Rather, this section presents some of the side lights and high points, the low life and high life, as well as some of the physical aspects, of the developing city as viewed both by contemporary authors who write from firsthand knowledge and by later and current reporters who had the advantage of historical distance.

Some of these accounts detail developments of major, often national import, such as the rise of Greenwich Village, the ferment of the lower East Side during the early decades of this century and the cultural reign of the Algonquin Round Table. Others are bits of nostalgia that recreate the flavor of a bygone era (*e.g.* the risqué "personals" flaunted on the front page of the *Tribune;* Stephen Crane's description of the hazards of a Broadway car) or dramatic episodes and scandals that have become a part of the city's legend (*e.g.* the rise and fall of men like Fisk, Boss Tweed, Jimmy Walker and Lepke Buchalter; the Confederate plot that almost burned the city to ashes). The last one hundred years has been favored and certain decades predominate—1850–1870, the 1890's and 1920's—because they offered the most interesting material.

In the following section, *It Takes All Kinds*, we return to current facets of the city's million-ring circus. Here contrast is particularly in evidence, both of subjects and of writers' points of view. Jules Romains, for instance, gives us a French view of New York women, while Chiang Yee provides a refreshing, cosmopolitan Chinese experience of the subway rush, and native Meyer Berger pauses in the peaceful oasis of a monastery right in the heart of the concrete jungle.

Irwin Edman focuses on the city's cultural life, while Helen Lawrenson deftly sketches the neurotic results of the city's get-ahead-or-else, dog-eat-dog compulsions. As they share the confined space of the metropolis, so they share the pages of this book: Budd Schulberg's dockworkers rub shoulders with the editors of the *New Yorker;* Charles Rolo's new, blue-blood bohemians and their darlings with the highly touted New York cab drivers who speed them on their errands of culture and ego; Mel Heimer's sharp Broadwayites with Benchley's midwestern "typical New Yorkers."

In the final section, *The City and the Dream,* we shift back again to the longer view. Here all the authors—with the exception of Whitman whose approach is timeless—are from the twentieth century, with the last two decades predominating, so that, by and large, it is the modern city we view through the lens of each writer's consciousness. And here again contrast is the rule, a different city with each writer. Compare, for example, Henry Adams' jeremiad (it could have been written this morning) with O. Henry's sentimental search for the voice of the city and Henry James' aesthetic-moral review, all written within a three year period; or the current impressions of Sartre, Beaton, Cyril Connolly, Steinbeck and, to come full circle, E. B. White. Different cities and yet all one city, with recognizable physical and human patterns emerging from all these diverse perspectives.

Each man, as Meyer Berger has phrased it, finds his own meaning in New York. Similarly, each reader will find his own way about this book and discover his own emphases. Some comments on a few of the touchstones I found in these accounts may prove suggestive.

Take the theme of the young man's coming to the great city. The narratives of Sinclair Lewis, Steinbeck and Thomas Wolfe bear vivid witness to the fact that for many people there have been two birth traumas, the second on the day they arrived in New York. Other accounts, of course, tell of another typical advance upon the city: gleefully, as if it were a vast, star-spangled, year-round Christmas stocking, overstuffed for plundering. But nearly all the reports show it to be a difficult city in which to feel at home. Nowhere else can one feel quite so triumphant or so lonely, nor are the two feelings mutually exclusive. (F. Scott Fitzgerald recalls that when his wife, Zelda, was about to give birth to their baby, they felt so lost and lonesome that they fled back to St. Paul. And this was after Fitzgerald's first novel had appeared, while he was being feted and hailed, in Fitzgerald's words, "as the arch type of what New York wanted.") Yet, as Steinbeck reveals, New York did become the ideal home for him, as it continues to become for millions, including many who can choose to live wherever they please.

Another recurring theme is ambition. Basically, the accounts in this volume describe two ways of meeting the challenge of the city—licking it or joining it. Of the millions who fail to conquer the city, to win its adulation or at least its attention, some join it, adopt it as an extension of themselves, the way the cab drivers and Dodger fans sketched by Turkin and Weinstein do, so that the ball club they may never get to see in action is *their* team, its stars their friends, Central Park their own back yard, the night clubs they have never visited their personal pleasure palaces. But there is a very large group—their members make several appearances in these pages—who can never fully join the city in this sense, who remain psychologically in the camp of the would-be conquerors nearly all their lives. For them—if despite Capote's warnings they stay—the city offers, in addition to the illusory nearness of the goal as spur, three anodynes: anonymity, distractions, and an audience (of friends, acquaintances, even casual ones like the elevator man) for whom the coveted role can be acted out. And, sometimes, in the city the lucky moment does belatedly arrive.

As E. B. White points out there are thousands of people for whom New York functions as a sort of gigantic, man-made womb—people who, in George Orwell's phrase, find living in New York the best means of getting "inside the Whale," of insulating themselves from all shock, while being nourished continually by the city's infinite supply of distractions. But they cannot escape the sobering and challenging thought that the Capital of Distractions is also the world's number one bomb target. For in New York, where the personal and the local events are forever cheek-by-jowl with national and international ones, hardly anyone is immune from the feeling that he has no control whatsoever over his own destiny. At the same time, as reflected in so many of these narratives, nearly everyone in New York has the paradoxical feeling—stronger, perhaps, and more frequently than elsewhere—that he is participating in large and majestic, even if terrible, events.

Inevitably, the subject of the advantages and disadvantages of living in the big city appears repeatedly in this volume. Traditionally, metropolitan living is supposed to dull one's senses, and city folk are always setting out for the country for rejuvenation. Granting that adjustment to the city involves considerable desensitizing, to noise and other overplentiful urban phenomena, many of the accounts I have included offer evidence that the city man's talents and sensitivities are also sharpened by the very limitations and complexities of his special environment. It is no trick at all to love one's fellow man out in the country where he is but a rare speck on the landscape. But to love one's fellow man in New York where he is encountered daily as the major obstacle in the city's course—in the form, say, of a coalesced mass of two hundred in a subway car (where, Richard Gehman reports, humor and love both manage to flourish)—is a fear of quite another order.

As for sensitivity to nature, Agnes Rothery, in taking us for a visit to the Bronx Zoo, notes how city children see marvels in a cow or sheep to which country youngsters have long since become insensible. And Lewis Gannett, chronicling the tenaciousness of nature in the metropolis, portrays also the persistence with which city dwellers, harried and confined, prove the greenness of their thumbs. (Conversely, I can remember mornings at Bar Harbor or Peterborough, after I had been some weeks in residence, when the flutterings and songs of a hundred birds outside the window failed to make my eyes rise from their work. But one morning, not long ago, as I was sitting at my desk in our eleventh-floor New York apartment, I glanced up and noticed a bird—it looked like a sandpiper—climbing slowly, steadily up the sheer wall of the building. I stopped my work and watched with fascination, even stepping out on the fire escape to cheer him silently all the way to the roof garden.)

Again and again—in the pieces by White, Sartre, Perry and Bemelmans, for example—we find evidence that in the very center of the works of man, the works of nature have a heightened poignancy and beauty. Nowhere, Sartre implies, does one turn to the sky more often than in New York, and nowhere does the sky seem to promise so much. Of course, the New Yorker's particular interest in the sky is partly due to his reaction to the feeling of being buried in the city's canyons. (A couple I know who live in what is euphemistically called "a garden apartment" used to discover each morning what sort of a day it was by bending down low, head nearly touching the floor, to catch a glimpse through the window of a telltale patch of sky. Now they no longer have to crane their necks; they've put a mirror outside the bedroom window, strategically inclined so they can see the sky's reflection right from their bed. For about two hours each day the mirror also reflects sunlight into the room.) But Sartre is right, the buildings which create the special need for the sky also carry the eye upward and provide a frame, supply form and added meaning.

The insistence with which so unurban a theme as nature repeatedly thrust itself into the accounts in this volume is one index to the thematic richness of New York City as a subject. However, the themes and the approaches to the book touched on here are but random soundings. Each reader will, I trust, discover for himself the lineaments of this portrait of a city and of man which these accounts join in fashioning.

I owe thanks for helpful suggestions to Hollis Alpert, William Barrett, Martin Fass, Jay Leyda, Lewis Mumford, Gunther Pohl of the New York Public Library Local History Division, and Robert Rahtz. To Charles Neider I owe particular thanks for his valuable counsel. I am especially grateful to Theodore S. Amussen and Robert D. Loomis of Rinehart and Company for their encouragement and suggestions. Above all I want to express my gratitude to my wife, Virginia Copeland Klein, for her understanding and patience and her gracious and invaluable aid.

ALEXANDER KLEIN

New York
February 11, 1955

The Empire City

A TREASURY OF NEW YORK

I

In old age, lame and sick, pondering for years on many a doubt and danger for this republic of ours—fully aware of all that can be said on the other side—I find in this visit to New York, and the daily contact and rapport with its myriad people, on the scale of the oceans and tides, the best, most effective medicine my soul has yet partaken—the grandest physical habitat and surroundings of land and water the globe affords . . .

—WALT WHITMAN

HERE IS NEW YORK

E. B. WHITE

On any person who desires such queer prizes, New York will bestow the gift of loneliness and the gift of privacy. It is this largess that accounts for the presence within the city's walls of a considerable section of the population; for the residents of Manhattan are to a large extent strangers who have pulled up stakes somewhere and come to town, seeking sanctuary or fulfillment or some greater or lesser grail. The capacity to make such dubious gifts is a mysterious quality of New York. It can destroy an individual, or it can fulfill him, depending a good deal on luck. No one should come to New York to live unless he is willing to be lucky.

New York is the concentrate of art and commerce and sport and religion and entertainment and finance, bringing to a single compact arena the gladiator, the evangelist, the promoter, the actor, the trader, and the merchant. It carries on its lapel the unexpungeable odor of the long past, so that no matter where you sit in New York you feel the vibrations of great times and tall deeds, of queer people and events and undertakings. I am sitting at the moment in a stifling hotel room in ninety-degree heat, halfway down an air shaft, in midtown. No air moves in or out of the room, yet I am curiously affected by emanations from the immediate surroundings. I am twenty-two blocks from where Rudolph Valentino lay in state, eight blocks from where Nathan Hale was executed, five blocks from the publisher's office where Ernest Hemingway hit Max Eastman on the nose, four miles from where Walt Whitman sat sweating out editorials for the *Brooklyn Eagle*, thirty-four blocks from the street Willa Cather lived in when she came to New York to write books about Nebraska, one block from where Marceline used to clown on the boards of the Hippodrome, thirty-six blocks from the spot where the historian Joe Gould kicked a radio to pieces in full view of the public; thirteen blocks from where Harry Thaw shot Stanford White, five blocks from where I used to usher at the Metropolitan Opera, and only a hundred and twelve blocks from the spot where Clarence Day the Elder was washed of his sins in the Church of the Epiphany (I could continue this list indefinitely); and for that matter I am probably occupying the very room that any number of exalted and somewise memorable characters sat in, some of them on hot, breathless afternoons, lonely and private and full of their own sense of emanations from without.

When I went down to lunch a few minutes ago I noticed that the man sitting next to me (about eighteen inches away along the wall) was Fred Stone, the actor. The eighteen inches were both the connection and the separation that New York provides for its inhabitants. My only connection with Fred Stone was that I saw him in *The Wizard of Oz* around the beginning of the century. But our waiter felt the same stimulus from being close to a man from Oz, and after Mr. Stone left the room the waiter told me that when he (the waiter) was a young man just arrived in this country and before he could understand a word of English, he had taken his girl for their first theater date to *The Wizard of Oz*. It was a wonderful show, the waiter recalled—a man of straw, a man of tin. Wonderful! (And still only eighteen inches away.) "Mr. Stone is a very hearty eater," said the waiter thoughtfully, content with this fragile participation in destiny, this link with Oz.

New York blends the gift of privacy with the excitement of participation; and better than most dense communities it succeeds in insulating the individual (if he wants it, and almost everybody wants or needs it) against all enormous and violent and wonderful events that are taking place every minute. Since I have been sitting in this miasmic air shaft, a good many rather splashy events have occurred in town. A man shot and killed his wife in a fit of jealousy. It caused no stir outside his block and got only small mention in the papers. I did not attend. Since my arrival, the greatest air show ever staged in all the world took place in town. I didn't attend and neither did most of the eight million other inhabitants, although they say there was quite a crowd. I didn't even hear any planes except a couple of west-bound commercial airliners that habitually use this air shaft to fly over. The biggest ocean-going ships on the North Atlantic arrived and departed. I didn't notice them and neither did most other New Yorkers. I am told this is the greatest seaport in the world, with six hundred and fifty miles of water front, and ships calling here from many exotic lands, but the only boat I've happened to notice since my arrival was a small sloop tacking out of the East River night before last on the ebb tide when I was walking across the Brooklyn Bridge. I heard the *Queen Mary* blow one midnight, though, and the sound carried the whole history of departure and longing and loss. The Lions have been in convention. I've seen not one Lion. A friend of mine saw one and told me about him. (He was lame, and was wearing a bolero.) At the ballgrounds and horse parks the greatest sporting spectacles have been enacted. I saw no ballplayer, no race horse. The governor came to town. I heard the siren scream but that was all there was to that—an eighteen-inch margin again. A man was killed by a falling cornice. I was not a party to the tragedy, and again the inches counted heavily.

I mention these merely to show that New York is peculiarly constructed to absorb almost anything that comes along (whether a thousand-foot liner out of the East or a twenty-thousand-man convention out of the West) without inflicting the event on its inhabitants; so that every event is, in a sense, optional, and the inhabitant is in the happy position of being able to choose his spectacle and so conserve his soul. In most metropolises, small and large, the choice is often not with the individual at all. He is thrown to the Lions. The Lions are overwhelming; the event is unavoidable. A cornice falls, and it hits every citizen on the head, every last man in town. I sometimes think that the only event that hits every New Yorker on the head is the annual St. Patrick's Day parade, which is fairly penetrating—the Irish are a hard race to tune out, there are five hundred thousand of them in residence, and they have the police force right in the family.

The quality in New York that insulates its inhabitants from life may simply weaken them as individuals. Perhaps it is healthier to live in a community where, when a cornice falls, you feel the blow; where, when the governor passes, you see at any rate his hat.

I am not defending New York in this regard. Many of its settlers are probably here merely to escape, not face, reality. But whatever it means, it is a rather rare gift, and I believe it has a positive effect on the creative capacities of New Yorkers—for creation is in part merely the business of forgoing the great and small distractions.

Although New York often imparts a feeling of great forlornness or forsakenness, it seldom seems dead or unresourceful; and you always feel that either by shifting your location ten blocks or by reducing your fortune by five dollars you can experience rejuvenation. Many people who have no real independence of spirit depend on the city's tremendous variety and sources of excitement for spiritual sustenance and maintenance of morale. In the country there are a few chances of sudden rejuvenation—a shift in weather, perhaps, or something arriving in the mail. But in New York the chances are endless. I think that although many persons are here from some excess of spirit (which caused them to break away from their small town), some, too, are here from a deficiency of spirit, who find in New York a protection, or an easy substitution.

There are roughly three New Yorks. There is, first, the New York of the man or woman who was born here, who takes the city for granted and accepts its size and its turbulence as natural and inevitable. Second, there is the New York of the commuter—the city that is devoured by locusts each day and spat out each night. Third, there is the New York of the person who was born somewhere else and came to New York in quest of something. Of these three trembling cities the greatest is the last—the city of final destination, the city that is a goal. It is this third city that accounts for New York's high-strung disposition, its poetical deportment, its dedication to the arts, and its incomparable achievements. Commuters give the city its tidal restlessness; natives give it solidity and continuity; but the settlers give it passion. And whether it is a farmer arriving from Italy to set up a small grocery store in a slum, or a young girl arriving from a small town in Mississippi to escape the indignity of being observed by her neighbors, or a boy arriving from the Corn Belt with a manuscript in his suitcase and a pain in his heart, it makes no difference: each embraces New York with the intense excitement of first love, each absorbs New

York with the fresh eyes of an adventurer, each generates heat and light to dwarf the Consolidated Edison Company.

    The commuter is the queerest bird of all. The suburb he inhabits has no essential vitality of its own and is a mere roost where he comes at day's end to go to sleep. Except in rare cases, the man who lives in Mamaroneck or Little Neck or Teaneck, and works in New York, discovers nothing much about the city except the time of arrival and departure of trains and buses, and the path to a quick lunch. He is desk-bound, and has never, idly roaming in the gloaming, stumbled suddenly on Belvedere Tower in the Park, seen the ramparts rise sheer from the water of the pond, and the boys along the shore fishing for minnows, girls stretched out negligently on the shelves of the rocks; he has never come suddenly on anything at all in New York as a loiterer, because he has had no time between trains. He has fished in Manhattan's wallet and dug out coins, but has never listened to Manhattan's breathing, never awakened to its morning, never dropped off to sleep in its night. About four hundred thousand men and women come charging onto the Island each week-day morning, out of the mouths of tubes and tunnels. Not many among them have ever spent a drowsy afternoon in the great rustling oaken silence of the reading room of the Public Library, with the book elevator (like an old water wheel) spewing out books onto the trays. They tend their furnaces in Westchester and in Jersey, but have never seen the furnaces of the Bowery, the fires that burn in oil drums on zero winter nights. They may work in the financial district downtown and never see the extravagant plantings of Rockefeller Center—the daffodils and grape hyacinths and birches of the flags trimmed to the wind on a fine morning in spring. Or they may work in a mid-town office and may let a whole year swing round without sighting Governor's Island from the sea wall. The commuter dies with tremendous mileage to his credit, but he is no rover. His entrances and exits are more devious than those in a prairie-dog village; and he calmly plays bridge while his train is buried in the mud at the bottom of the East River. The Long Island Rail Road alone carried forty million commuters last year; but many of them were the same fellow retracing his steps.

    The terrain of New York is such that a resident sometimes travels farther, in the end, than a commuter. The journey of the composer Irving Berlin from Cherry Street in the lower East Side to an apartment uptown was through an alley and was only three or four miles in length; but it was like going three times around the world.

A poem compresses much in a small space and adds music, thus heightening its meaning. The city is like poetry: it compresses all life, all races and breeds, into a small island and adds music and the accompaniment of internal engines. The island of Manhattan is without any doubt the greatest human concentrate on earth, the poem whose magic is comprehensible to millions of permanent residents but whose full meaning will always remain illusive. At the feet of the tallest and plushiest offices lie the crummiest slums. The genteel mysteries housed in the Riverside Church are only a few blocks from the voodoo charms of Harlem. The merchant princes, riding to Wall Street in their limousines down the East River Drive, pass within a few hundred yards of the gypsy kings; but the princes do not know they are passing kings, and the kings are not up yet anyway—they live a more leisurely life than the princes and get drunk more consistently.

New York is nothing like Paris; it is nothing like London; and it is not Spokane multiplied by sixty, or Detroit multiplied by four. It is by all odds the loftiest of cities. It even managed to reach the highest point in the sky at the lowest moment of the depression. The Empire State Building shot twelve hundred and fifty feet into the air when it was madness to put out as much as six inches of new growth. (The building has a mooring mast that no dirigible has ever tied to; it employs a man to flush toilets in slack times; it has been hit by an airplane in a fog, struck countless times by lightning, and been jumped off of by so many unhappy people that pedestrians instinctively quicken step when passing Fifth Avenue and 34th Street.)

Manhattan has been compelled to expand skyward because of the absence of any other direction in which to grow. This, more than any other thing, is responsible for its physical majesty. It is to the nation what the white church spire is to the village—the visible symbol of aspiration and faith, the white plume saying that the way is up. The summer traveler swings in over Hell Gate Bridge and from the window of his sleeping car as it glides above the pigeon lofts and back yards of Queens looks southwest to where the morning light first strikes the steel peaks of mid-town, and he sees its upward thrust unmistakable: the great walls and towers rising, the smoke rising, the heat not yet rising, the hopes and ferments of so many awakening millions rising—this vigorous spear that presses heaven hard.

It is a miracle that New York works at all. The whole thing is implausible. Every time the residents brush their teeth, millions of gallons of water must be drawn from the Catskill mountains and the hills of Westchester. When a young man in Manhattan writes a letter to his girl in Brooklyn, the love message gets blown to her through a pneumatic tube—*pfft*—just like that. The subterranean system of telephone cables, power lines, steam pipes, gas mains, and sewer pipes is reason enough to abandon the island to the gods and the weevils. Every time an incision is made in the pavement, the noisy surgeons expose ganglia that are tangled beyond belief. By rights New York should have destroyed itself long ago, from panic or fire or rioting or failure of some vital supply line in its circulatory system or from some deep labyrinthine short circuit. Long ago the city should have experienced an insoluble traffic snarl at some impossible bottleneck. It should have perished of hunger when food lines failed for a few days. It should have been wiped out by a plague starting in its slums or carried in by ships' rats. It should have been overwhelmed by the sea that licks at it on every side. The workers in its myriad cells should have succumbed to nerves, from the fearful pall of smoke-fog that drifts over every few days from Jersey, blotting out all light at noon and leaving the high offices suspended, men groping and depressed, and the sense of world's end. It should have been touched in the head by the August heat and gone off its rocker.

Mass hysteria is a terrible force, yet New Yorkers seem always to escape it by some tiny margin: they sit in stalled subways without claustrophobia, they extricate themselves from panic situations by some lucky wisecrack, they meet confusion and congestion with patience and grit—a sort of perpetual muddling through. Every facility is inadequate—the hospitals and schools and playgrounds are overcrowded, the express highways are feverish, the unimproved highways and bridges are bottlenecks; there is not enough air and not enough light, and there is usually either too much heat or too little. But the city makes up for its hazards and its deficiencies by supplying its citizens with massive doses of a supplementary vitamin—the sense of belonging to something unique, cosmopolitan, mighty, and unparalleled.

To an outlander a stay in New York can be and often is a series of small embarrassments and discomforts and disappointments: not understanding the waiter, not being able to distinguish between a sucker joint and a friendly saloon, riding the wrong subway, being slapped down by a bus driver for asking an innocent question, enduring sleepless nights when the street noises fill the bedroom. Tourists make for New York, particularly in summertime—they swarm all over the

Statue of Liberty (where many a resident of the town has never set foot), they invade the Automat, visit radio studios, St. Patrick's Cathedral, and they window shop. Mostly they have a pretty good time. But sometimes in New York you run across the disillusioned—a young couple who are obviously visitors, newlyweds perhaps, for whom the bright dream has vanished. The place has been too much for them; they sit languishing in a cheap restaurant over a speechless meal.

The oft-quoted thumbnail sketch of New York is, of course: "It's a wonderful place, but I'd hate to live there." I have an idea that people from villages and small towns, people accustomed to the convenience and the friendliness of neighborhood over-the-fence living, are unaware that life in New York follows the neighborhood pattern. The city is literally a composite of tens of thousands of tiny neighborhood units. There are, of course, the big districts and big units: Chelsea and Murray Hill and Gramercy (which are residential units), Harlem (a racial unit), Greenwich Village (a unit dedicated to the arts and other matters), and there is Radio City (a commercial development), Peter Cooper Village (a housing unit), the Medical Center (a sickness unit) and many other sections each of which has some distinguishing characteristic. But the curious thing about New York is that each large geographical unit is composed of countless small neighborhoods. Each neighborhood is virtually self-sufficient. Usually it is no more than two or three blocks long and a couple of blocks wide. Each area is a city within a city within a city. Thus, no matter where you live in New York, you will find within a block or two a grocery store, a barbershop, a newsstand and shoeshine shack, an ice-coal-and-wood cellar (where you write your order on a pad outside as you walk by), a dry cleaner, a laundry, a delicatessen (beer and sandwiches delivered at any hour to your door), a flower shop, an undertaker's parlor, a movie house, a radio-repair shop, a stationer, a haberdasher, a tailor, a drugstore, a garage, a tearoom, a saloon, a hardware store, a liquor store, a shoe-repair shop. Every block or two, in most residential sections of New York, is a little main street. A man starts for work in the morning and before he has gone two hundred yards he has completed half a dozen missions: bought a paper, left a pair of shoes to be soled, picked up a pack of cigarettes, ordered a bottle of whisky to be dispatched in the opposite direction against his homecoming, written a message to the unseen forces of the wood cellar, and notified the dry cleaner that a pair of trousers awaits call. Homeward bound eight hours later, he buys a bunch of pussy willows, a Mazda bulb, a drink, a shine—all between the corner where he steps off the bus and his apartment. So complete is each neighborhood, and so strong the sense of neighborhood, that many a New Yorker spends a lifetime within the confines of an area smaller than a country village. Let him walk two blocks from his corner and he is in a strange land and will feel uneasy till he gets back.

Storekeepers are particularly conscious of neighborhood boundary lines. A woman friend of mine moved recently from one apartment to another, a distance of three blocks. When she turned up, the day after the move, at the same grocer's that she had patronized for years, the proprietor was in ecstasy—almost in tears—at seeing her. "I was afraid," he said, "now that you've moved away I wouldn't be seeing you any more." To him, *away* was three blocks, or about seven hundred and fifty feet.

I am, at the moment of writing this, living not as a neighborhood man in New York but as a transient, or vagrant, in from the country for a few days. Summertime is a good time to re-examine New York and to receive again the gift of privacy, the jewel of loneliness. In summer the city contains (except for tourists) only die-hards and authentic characters. No casual, spotty dwellers are around, only the real article. And the town has a somewhat relaxed air, and one can lie in a loincloth, gasping and remembering things.

I've been remembering what it felt like as a young man to live in the same town with giants. When I first arrived in New York my personal giants were a dozen or so columnists and critics and poets whose names appeared regularly in the papers. I burned with a low steady fever just because I was on the same island with Don Marquis, Heywood Broun, Christopher Morley, Franklin P. Adams, Robert C. Benchley, Frank Sullivan, Dorothy Parker, Alexander Woollcott, Ring Lardner, and Stephen Vincent Benét. I would hang around the corners of Chambers Street and Broadway, thinking: "Somewhere in that building is the typewriter that archy the cockroach jumps on at night." New York hardly gave me a living at that period, but it sustained me. I used to walk quickly past the house in West 13th Street between Sixth and Seventh where Franklin P. Adams lived, and the block seemed to tremble under my feet—the way Park Avenue trembles when a train leaves Grand Central. This excitation (nearness of giants) is a continuing thing. The city is always full of young worshipful beginners—young actors, young aspiring poets, ballerinas, painters, reporters, singers—each depending on his own brand of tonic to stay alive, each with his own stable of giants.

New York provides not only a continuing excitation but also a spectacle that is continuing. I wander around, re-examining this spectacle, hoping that I can put it on paper. It is Saturday, toward the end of the afternoon. I turn through West 48th Street. From the open windows of the drum and saxophone parlors come the listless sounds of musical instruction, monstrous insect noises in the brooding field of summer. The Cort Theater is disgorging its matinee audience. Suddenly the whole block is filled with the mighty voice of a street singer. He approaches, looking for an audience, a large, cheerful Negro with grand-opera contours, strolling with head thrown back, filling the canyon with uninhibited song. He carries a long cane as his sole prop, and is tidily but casually dressed—slacks, seersucker jacket, a book showing in his pocket.

This is perfect artistic timing; the audience from the Cort, where Sartre's *The Respectful Prostitute* is playing, has just received a lesson in race relations and is in a mood to improve the condition of the black race as speedily as possible. Coins (mostly quarters) rattle to the street, and a few minutes of minstrelsy improves the condition of one Negro by about eight dollars. If he does as well as this at every performance, he has a living right there. New York is the city of opportunity, they say. Even the mounted cop, clumping along on his nag a few minutes later, scans the gutter carefully for dropped silver, like a bird watching for spilt grain.

It is seven o'clock and I re-examine an ex-speakeasy in East 53rd Street, with dinner in mind. A thin crowd, a summer-night buzz of fans interrupted by an occasional drink being shaken at the small bar. It is dark in here (the proprietor sees no reason for boosting his light bill just because liquor laws have changed). How dark, how pleasing; and how miraculously beautiful the murals showing Italian lake scenes —probably executed by a cousin of the owner. The owner himself mixes. The fans intone the prayer for cool salvation. From the next booth drifts the conversation of radio executives; from the green salad comes the little taste of garlic. Behind me (eighteen inches again) a young intellectual is trying to persuade a girl to come live with him and be his love. She has her guard up, but he is extremely reasonable, careful not to overplay his hand. A combination of intellectual companionship and sexuality is what they have to offer each other, he feels.

In the mirror over the bar I can see the ritual of the second drink. Then he has to go to the men's room and she has to go to the ladies' room, and when they return, the argument has lost its tone. And the fan takes over again, and the heat and the relaxed air and the memory of so many good little dinners in so many good little illegal places, with the theme of love, the sound of ventilation, the brief medicinal illusion of gin.

Another hot night I stop off at the Goldman Band concert in the Mall in Central Park. The people seated on the benches fanned out in front of the band shell are attentive, appreciative. In the trees the night wind stirs, bringing the leaves to life, endowing them with speech; the electric lights illuminate the green branches from the under side, translating them into a new language. Overhead a plane passes dreamily, its running light winking. On the bench directly in front of me, a boy sits with his arm around his girl; they are proud of each other and are swathed in music. The cornetist steps forward for a solo, begins, "Drink to me only with thine eyes . . ." In the wide, warm night the horn is startlingly pure and magical. Then from the North River another horn solo begins—the *Queen Mary* announcing her intentions. She is not on key; she is a half tone off. The trumpeter in the bandstand never flinches. The horns quarrel savagely, but no one minds having the intimation of travel injected into the pledge of love. "I leave," sobs Mary. "And I will pledge with mine," sighs the trumpeter. Along the asphalt paths strollers pass to and fro; they behave considerately, respecting the musical atmosphere. Popsicles are moving well. In the warm grass beyond the fence, forms wriggle in the shadows, and the skirts of the girls approaching on the Mall are ballooned by the breeze, and their bare shoulders catch the lamplight. "Drink to me only with thine eyes." It is a magical occasion, and it's all free.

On week ends in summer the town empties. I visit my office on a Saturday afternoon. No phone rings, no one feeds the hungry IN-baskets, no one disturbs the papers; it is a building of the dead, a time of awesome suspension. The whole city is honeycombed with abandoned cells—a jail that has been effectively broken. Occasionally from somewhere in the building a night bell rings, summoning the elevator —a special fire alarm ring. This is the pit of loneliness, in an office on a summer Saturday. I stand at the window and look down at the batteries and batteries of offices across the way, recalling how the thing looks in winter twilight when everything is going full blast, every cell lighted, and how you can see in pantomime the puppets fumbling with their slips of paper (but you don't hear the rustle), see them pick up their phone (but you don't hear the ring), see the noiseless, ceaseless moving about of so many passers of pieces of paper: New York, the capital of memoranda, in touch with Calcutta, in touch with Reykjavik, and always fooling with something.

In the café of the Lafayette, the regulars sit and talk. It is busy yet peaceful. Nursing a drink, I stare through the west windows at the Manufacturers Trust Company and at the red brick fronts on the north side of Ninth Street, watching the red turning slowly to purple as the light dwindles. Brick buildings have a way of turning color at the end of the day, the way a red rose turns bluish as it wilts. The café is a sanctuary. The waiters are ageless and they change not. Nothing has been modernized. Notre Dame stands guard in its travel poster. The coffee is strong and full of chicory, and good.

Walk the Bowery under the elevated railway at night and all you feel is a sort of cold guilt. Touched for a dime, you try to drop the coin and not touch the hand, because the hand is dirty; you try to avoid the glance, because the glance accuses. This is not so much personal menace as universal—the cold menace of unresolved human suffering and poverty and the advanced stages of the disease alcoholism. On a summer night the drunks sleep in the open. The sidewalk is a free bed, and there are no lice. Pedestrians step along and over and around the still forms as though walking on a battlefield among the dead. In doorways, on the steps of the savings bank, the bums lie sleeping it off. Standing sentinel at each sleeper's head is the empty bottle from which he drained his release. Wedged in the crook of his arm is the paper bag containing his things. The glib barker on the sightseeing bus tells his passengers that this is the "street of lost souls," but the Bowery does not think of itself as lost; it meets its peculiar problem in its own way—plenty of gin mills, plenty of flophouses, plenty of indifference, and always, at the end of the line, Bellevue.

A block or two east and the atmosphere changes sharply. In the slums are poverty and bad housing, but with them the reassuring sobriety and safety of family life. I head east along Rivington. All is cheerful and filthy and crowded. Small shops overflow onto the sidewalk, leaving only half the normal width for passers-by. In the candid light from unshaded bulbs gleam watermelons and lingerie. Families have fled the hot rooms upstairs and have found relief on the pavement. They sit on orange crates, smoking, relaxed, congenial. This is the nightly garden party of the vast Lower East Side—and on the whole they are more agreeable-looking hot-weather groups than some you see in bright canvas deck chairs on green lawns in country circumstances. It is folksy here with the smell of warm flesh and squashed fruit and fly-bitten filth in the gutter, and cooking.

At the corner of Lewis, in the playground behind the wire fence, an open-air dance is going on—some sort of neighborhood affair, probably designed to combat delinquency. Women push baby carriages in and out among the dancers, as though to exhibit what dancing leads to at last. Overhead, like banners decorating a cotillion hall, stream the pants and bras from the pulley lines. The music stops, and a beautiful Italian girl takes a brush from her handbag and stands under the street lamp brushing her long blue-black hair till it shines. The cop in the patrol car watches sullenly.

The Consolidated Edison Company says there are eight million people in the five boroughs of New York, and the company is in a position to know. As in every dense community, virtually all races, all religions, all nationalities are represented. Population figures are shifty—they change almost as fast as one can break them down. It is safe to say that about two million of New York's eight million are Jews—roughly one in four. Among this two million who are Jewish are, of course, a great many nationalities—Russian, German, Polish, Rumanian, Austrian, a long list. The Urban League of Greater New York estimates that the number of Negroes in New York is about 700,000. Of these, about 500,000 live in Harlem, a district that extends northward from 110th Street. The Negro population has increased rapidly in the last few years. There are half again as many Negroes in New York today as there were in 1940. There are about 230,000 Puerto Ricans living in New York. There are half a million Irish, half a million Germans. There are 900,000 Russians, 150,000 English, 400,000 Poles, and there are quantities of Finns and Czechs and Swedes and Danes and Norwegians and Latvians and Belgians and Welsh and Greeks, and even Dutch, who have been here from away back. It is very hard to say how many Chinese there are. Officially there are 12,000 but there are many Chinese who are in New York illegally and who don't like census takers.

The collision and the intermingling of these millions of foreign-born people representing so many races, creeds and nationalities, make New York a permanent exhibit of the phenomenon of one world. The citizens of New York are tolerant not only from disposition but from necessity. The city has to be tolerant, otherwise it would explode in a radio-active cloud of hate and rancor and bigotry. If the people were to depart even briefly from the peace of cosmopolitan intercourse, the town would blow up higher than a kite. In New York smolders every race problem there is, but the noticeable thing is not the problem but the inviolate truce. Harlem is a city in itself, and being a city Harlem symbolizes segregation; yet Negro life in New York lacks the more conspicuous elements of Jim Crowism. Negroes ride subways and buses on terms of equality with whites, but they have not yet found that same equality in hotels and restaurants. Professionally, Negroes get on well in the theater, in music, in art, and in literature; but in many fields of employment the going is tough. The Jim Crow principle lives chiefly in the housing rules and customs. Private owners of dwellings legally can, and do, exclude Negroes. Under a recent city ordinance, however, apartment buildings that are financed with public moneys or that receive any tax exemption must accept tenants without regard to race, color, or religion.

To a New Yorker the city is both changeless and changing. In many respects it neither looks nor feels the way it did twenty-five years ago. The elevated railways have been pulled down, all but the Third Avenue. An old-timer walking up Sixth past the Jefferson Market jail misses the railroad, misses its sound, its spotted shade, its little aerial stations, and the tremor of the thing. Broadway has changed in aspect. It used to have a discernible bony structure beneath its loud bright surface; but the signs are so enormous now, the buildings and shops and hotels have largely disappeared under the neon lights and letters and the frozen-custard façade. Broadway is a custard street with no frame supporting it. In Greenwich Village the light is thinning: big apartments have come in, bordering the Square, and the bars are mirrored and chromed. But there are still in the Village the lingering traces of poesy, Mexican glass, hammered brass, batik, lamps made of whisky bottles, first novels made of fresh memories—the old Village with its alleys and ratty one-room rents catering to the erratic needs of those whose hearts are young and gay.

Grand Central Terminal has become honky-tonk, with its extra-dimensional advertising displays and its tendency to adopt the tactics of a travel broker. I practically lived in Grand Central at one period (it has all the conveniences and I had no other place to stay) and the great hall seemed to me one of the more inspiring interiors in New

York, until advertisements for Lastex and Coca-Cola got into the temple.

All over town the great mansions are in decline. Schwab's house facing the Hudson on Riverside is gone. Gould's house on Fifth Avenue is an antique shop. Morgan's house on Madison Avenue is a church administration office. What was once the Fahnestock house is now Random House. Rich men nowadays don't live in houses; they live in the attics of big apartment buildings and plant trees on the setbacks, hundreds of feet above the street.

There are fewer newspapers than there used to be, thanks somewhat to the late Frank Munsey. One misses the *Globe,* the *Mail,* the *Herald;* and to many a New Yorker life has never seemed the same since the *World* took the count.

Police now ride in radio prowl cars instead of gumshoeing around the block swinging their sticks. A ride in the subway costs fifteen cents, and the seats are apt to be dark green instead of straw yellow. Men go to saloons to gaze at televised events instead of to think long thoughts. It is all very disconcerting. Even parades have changed some. The last triumphal military procession in Manhattan simply filled the city with an ominous and terrible rumble of heavy tanks.

The slums are gradually giving way to the lofty housing projects —high in stature, high in purpose, low in rent. There are a couple of dozen of these new developments scattered around; each is a city in itself (one of them in the Bronx accommodates twelve thousand families), sky acreage hitherto untilled, lifting people far above the street, standardizing their sanitary life, giving them some place to sit other than an orange crate. Federal money, state money, city money, and private money have flowed into these projects. Banks and insurance companies are in back of some of them. Architects have turned the buildings slightly on their bases, to catch more light. In some of them, rents are as low as eight dollars a month a room. Thousands of new units are still needed and will eventually be built, but New York never quite catches up with itself, is never in equilibrium. In flush times the population mushrooms and the new dwellings sprout from the rock. Come bad times and the population scatters and the lofts are abandoned and the landlord withers and dies.

New York has changed in tempo and in temper during the years I have known it. There is greater tension, increased irritability. You encounter it in many places, in many faces. The normal frustrations of modern life are here multiplied and amplified—a single run of a crosstown bus contains, for the driver, enough frustration and annoyance to carry him over the edge of sanity: the light that changes always an instant too soon, the passenger that bangs on the shut door, the truck that blocks the only opening, the coin that slips to the floor, the question asked at the wrong moment. There is greater tension and there is greater speed. Taxis roll faster than they rolled ten years ago —and they were rolling fast then. Hackmen used to drive with verve; now they sometimes seem to drive with desperation, toward the ultimate tip. On the West Side Highway, approaching the city, the motorist is swept along in a trance—a sort of fever of inescapable motion, goaded from behind, hemmed in on either side, a mere chip in a mill-race.

The city has never been so uncomfortable, so crowded, so tense. Money has been plentiful and New York has responded. Restaurants are hard to get into; businessmen stand in line for a Schrafft's luncheon as meekly as idle men used to stand in soup lines. (Prosperity creates its bread lines, the same as depression.) The lunch hour in Manhattan has been shoved ahead half an hour, to twelve or twelve thirty, in the hopes of beating the crowd to a table. Everyone is a little emptier at quitting time than he used to be. Apartments are festooned with No Vacancy signs. There is standing-room-only in Fifth Avenue buses, which once reserved a seat for every paying guest. The old double-deckers are disappearing—people don't ride just for the fun of it any more.

At certain hours on certain days it is almost impossible to find an empty taxi and there is a great deal of chasing around after them. You grab a handle and open the door, and find that some other citizen is entering from the other side. Doormen grow rich blowing their whistles for cabs; and some doormen belong to no door at all—merely wander about through the streets, opening cabs for people as they happen to find them. By comparison with other less hectic days, the city is uncomfortable and inconvenient; but New Yorkers temperamentally do not crave comfort and convenience—if they did they would live elsewhere.

The subtlest change in New York is something people don't speak much about but that is in everyone's mind. The city, for the first time in its long history, is destructible. A single flight of planes no bigger than a wedge of geese can quickly end this island fantasy, burn the towers, crumble the bridges, turn the underground passages into lethal chambers, cremate the millions. The intimation of mortality is part of New York now: in the sound of jets overhead, in the black headlines of the latest edition.

All dwellers in cities must live with the stubborn fact of annihilation; in New York the fact is somewhat more concentrated because of the concentration of the city itself, and because, of all targets, New York has a certain clear priority. In the mind of whatever perverted dreamer might loose the lightning, New York must hold a steady irresistible charm.

It used to be that the Statue of Liberty was the signpost that proclaimed New York and translated it for all the world. Today Liberty shares the role with Death. Along the East River, from the razed slaughterhouses of Turtle Bay, as though in a race with the spectral flight of planes, men are carving out the permanent headquarters of the United Nations—the greatest housing project of them all. In its stride, New York takes on one more interior city, to shelter, this time, all governments, and to clear the slum called war. New York is not a capital city—it is not a national capital or a state capital. But it is by way of becoming the capital of the world. The building, as conceived by architects, will be cigar boxes set on end. Traffic will flow in a new tunnel under First Avenue, 47th Street will be widened (and if my guess is any good), trucks will appear late at night to plant tall trees surreptitiously, their roots to mingle with the intestines of the town. Once again the city will absorb, almost without showing any sign of it, a congress of visitors. It has already shown itself capable of stashing away the United Nations—a great many of the delegates have been around town during the past couple of years, and the citizenry has hardly caught a glimpse of their coattails or their black Homburgs.

This race—this race between the destroying planes and the struggling Parliament of Man—it sticks in all our heads. The city at last perfectly illustrates both the universal dilemma and the general solution; this riddle in steel and stone is at once the perfect target and the perfect demonstration of nonviolence, of racial brotherhood, this lofty target scraping the skies and meeting the destroying planes halfway, home of all people and all nations, capital of everything, housing the deliberations by which the planes are to be stayed and their errand forestalled.

A block or two west of the new City of Man in Turtle Bay there is an old willow tree that presides over an interior garden. It is a battered tree, long suffering and much climbed, held together by strands of wire but beloved of those who know it. In a way it symbolizes the city: life under difficulties, growth against odds, sap-rise in the midst of concrete, and the steady reaching for the sun. Whenever I look at it nowadays, and feel the cold shadow of the planes, I think: "This must be saved, this particular thing, this very tree." If it were to go, all would go—this city, this mischievous and marvelous monument which not to look upon would be like death.

THE METROPOLITAN MILIEU

LEWIS MUMFORD

Before the Civil War, New York shared its intellectual distinction with Boston, its industrial place with Philadelphia, and its commercial supremacy with Baltimore and New Orleans. Though it had become the mouth of the continent, thanks to the Erie Canal, it was not yet the maw. After the Civil War, despite the energetic rise of Chicago, New York City became an imperial metropolis, sucking into its own whirlpool the wealth and the wreckage of the rest of the country and of the lands beyond the sea.

When Dickens first visited America, voracious pigs rooted in the streets of Manhattan. Less than a generation later, through the holy transmutation of war, most of them were turned into financiers and industrial enterprisers, and they confined their operations to Wall Street, where the troughs were deep and the wallow good. Poets became stockbrokers; Pan took a flier in railroad securities; satirical humorists hobnobbed with millionaires and turned the lance of their satire against purely legendary kings, instead of driving their steel through the middle of the real kings, the Cooks, the Vanderbilts, the Rogerses, the Rockefellers. New York had become the center of a furious decay, which was called growth and enterprise and greatness. The decay caused foul gases to form; the gases caused the physical body of the city to be distended; the distention was called Progress.

So the city grew. Brownstone mansions, often grotesquely scratched with Eastlike ornament, wheeled into position along Fifth Avenue; and brownstone houses, in solid speculative rows, lined the side streets as the city stumbled rapidly northward. On either side of them, in the cheaper quarters, were the new tenements, with common toilets in the halls, and dusty vestibules where, in the 'seventies, a row of pitchers would be exposed through the night, to be filled with milk in the morning. The crosstown traffic became less important, as the rivers ceased to provide the main entrances to the city; but the tangle of wheels on the avenues thickened: shafts interlocked, hubs scraped, horses reared, presently a bridge was built over Broadway for the pedestrian. The vivacious dangers of congestion had all appeared: exasperated drivers exchanged oaths as deadly as bullets, and gangsters, lining up for fights on the dingier side streets, exchanged bullets as lightly as oaths. Respectable folk hunched their shoulders, lowered their heads, and hypnotized themselves into somnolence by counting sheep: at all events the population was increasing.

Beer saloons, four to as many corners in most parts of the city, brought together in their more squalid forms the ancient forces of hunger and love and politics: "free lunch," "ladies' entrance," and the political boss and his underlings. The main duty of the latter was to protect vice and crime and to levy a constant tax upon virtue in whatever offensive form it might take—as justice, as public spirit, as intelligence. Whisky and beer ruled the wits and the emotional life of the city: whisky for aggressiveness and beer for good-natured befuddlement. Barber shops specialized, until the present century, in painting out black eyes that did not yield to the cold iron of the lamppost. The swells of course drank their wine convivially at Martin's or Delmonico's; but that was as far from the beer saloon as Newport or Narragansett were from Coney Island. In the 'nineties Messrs. McKim, Mead, and White began to make over the city for the more polished classes: they designed the Century Club, Gorham's, Tiffany's, Delmonico's, and many mansions in the city for the new Borgias and Sforzas. But these cultured architects of course remained aloof from the principal buildings of the populace, the tenement and the saloon. The dingy brown front of the saloon, with the swinging doors and the sawdust floors and the slate carrying the day's menu and the soap-decorated mirrors, remained unchanged by fashion for two generations or more, obeying the biological law that the lowest organisms tend to remain stable.

In the 'seventies, elevated railroads were built; and for miles and miles, on each side of these ill-designed iron ways, which contrasted so unfavorably with those Berlin built only slightly later, tenement houses were planted. Thousands of people lived under the shadow of the elevated, with the smoke of the old-fashioned locomotives puffing into their windows, with the clank and rattle causing them to shout in daily conversation to overcome the roar outside. The obliviousness to low sounds, the indifference to cacophony which makes the ideal radio listener of present-day America, was part of the original acquisition of Manhattan in the Brown Decades. This torment of noise-troubled sleep, lowered waking efficiency, depleted vitality; but it was endured as if it were an irremediable fact of nature. In the lull of the elevated's thunder, the occasional tinkle of the cowbells of the ragman on a side street, or the solemn *I—I—I—I cas' clo's* of the second-hand clothing buyer, would have an almost pastoral touch; while *Carmen*, on an Italian's clanking hand organ, could splash the sky with color.

Within the span of a generation, the open spaces and the natural vistas began to disappear. The older beer gardens, like Niblo's Garden, gardens that had frequently preserved the trees and open space of a whole block, were wiped out: only in the further reaches of the city did they remain, like Unter den Linden on upper Broadway, and like the roadhouses which dotted the more or less open country that remained on the West Side above 125th Street until the end of the century. The rocky base of Manhattan, always unkind to life, steadily lost its filament of soil. The trees in the streets became more infrequent as the city grew; and their leaves grew sear before autumn came. Even the great Boulevard above Sixty-fifth Street, which the ignoble Tweed had planted along Broadway for his own pecuniary benefit, sacrificed its magnificent trees to the first subway; while only the ailanthus tree, quick growing and lean living, kept the back yards occasionally green, to gladden the lonely young men and women from the country, who faced their first year in the city from hall bedrooms on the top-floor rear of unamiable boardinghouses. And as the city grew, it grew away from its old markets: one of the last of these, to prove more reminiscent of the old than anticipatory of the new, was the Jefferson Market, with its medieval German tower, at Eighth Street. Vanishing from the consciousness of most Manhattanites were the open markets that had once brought the touch of the sea and the country to its streets, connecting farmstead and city home by means of little boats that plied the Hudson and Long Island Sound.

The waterfront kept a hold on the city, modifying its character, longer than the countryside did. The oyster stands remained on South and West streets; and "mast-hemmed Mannahatta," was still an accurate description up to the end of the 'nineties: Alfred Stieglitz has indeed recorded for us the bowsprit of an old sailing vessel, thrust like a proud harpoon into the side of our *Leviathan*. But most of the things that had made life pleasant and sane in the city, the old houses, red brick, with their white doorways and delicate Georgian fanlights, the friendly tree-lined streets, the salty lick and lap of the sea at the end of every crosstown street, as Melville described it in the opening pages of Moby Dick—all these things were disappearing from the eye, from the nose and touch, and so from the mind.

The water and the soil, as the prime environment of life, were becoming "immaterial," that is to say, they were of no use to the canny minds that were promoting the metropolis, unless they could be described in a legal document, appraised quantitatively, and converted ultimately into cash. A farm became for the speculator a place that might be converted into building lots: in that process, indeed, lay the meaning of this feverish growth, this anxious speculation, this reckless transformation of the quick into the dead. People staked out claims on the farther parts of the city in the way that prospectors stake out claims in a gold rush. There was always the chance that some negligible patch of earth might become, in the course of the city's growth, a gold mine. That was magic. In the atmosphere of magic, the desire to get something for nothing, a whole population hoped and breathed and lived. That in reality the environment was becoming unfit for human habitation in the process did not concern the midas-fingered gentlemen who ruled the city, nor did it affect the dull-fingered million who lacked that golden touch: their dreams were framed within the same heaven. Lacking the reality, they fed on the gilded lubricities of Mr. Bennett's, Mr. Pulitzer's, and Mr. Hearst's newspapers.

The ledger and the prospectus, the advertisement and the yellow journal, the world of paper, paper profits, paper achievements, paper hopes, and paper lusts, the world of sudden fortunes on paper and equally grimy paper tragedies, in short, the world of Jay Cook and Boss Tweed and James Gordon Bennett, had unfolded itself everywhere, obliterating under its flimsy tissues all the realities of life that were not exploitable, as either profits or news, on paper. Events happened to fill the paper that described them and to provide the daily titillation that relieved a commercialized routine. When they came reluctantly, they were manufactured, like the Spanish-American War, an event to which Newspaper Row contributed rather more than statesmanship did.

Behold this paper city, buried in its newspapers in the morning, intent through the day on its journals and ledgers and briefs and Dear-sir-in-reply-to-yours-of-even-date, picking at its newly invented typewriters and mimeographs and adding machines, manifolding and filing, watching the ticker tape flow from the glib automatons in Broad Street, piling its soiled paper into deep baskets, burying its dead paper in dusty alphabetical cemeteries, binding fat little dockets with red tape, counting the crisp rolls and bank notes, cutting the coupons of the gilt-edged bonds, redeemable twenty years hence, forty years hence, in paper that might be even more dubious than the original loan issue. At night, when the paper day is over, the city buries itself in paper once more: the Wall Street closing prices, the Five Star Sporting Extra, with the ninth inning scores, the Special Extra, *All-about-the-big-fight*, all about the anarchist assassination in St. Petersburg—or Pittsburgh.

The cult of paper brings with it indifference to sight and sound: print and arithmetic are the Bible and the incense of this religious ritual. Realities of the world not included in this religion become dim and unreal to both the priests and the worshipers: these pious New Yorkers live in a world of Nature and human tradition, as indifferent to the round of the seasons and to the delights of the awakened senses and the deeper stores of social memory as an early Christian ascetic, occupied with his devotions amid the splendid temples of a Greek Acropolis. They collect pictures as they collect securities; their patronage of learning is merely a premature engraving of their own tombstones. It is not the images or the thoughts, but the reports of their munificence in the newspaper, that justifies their gifts. The whole social fabric is built on a foundation of printed paper; it is cemented together by paper; it is crowned with paper. No wonder the anarchists, with more generous modes of life in mind, have invented the ominous phrase: "Incinerate the documents!" That would wreck this world worse than an earthquake.

Beneath this arid ritual, life itself, attenuated but real, starved but still hungry, goes on. Lovers still become radiant and breathless; honest workers shave wood, rivet steel beams, dig in the earth, or set type with sure hands and quiet satisfaction; scholars incubate ideas, and now and again a poet or an artist broods by himself in some half-shaded city square. In rebellion against this arid and ugly new environment, some country-bred person, a William Cullen Bryant or a Frederick Law Olmsted, would attempt to preserve faltering rural delights: a picnic grove here, a park there. Just before the Civil War the building of Central Park began; and despite the raids of political gangsters, despite the brazen indecent robbery of the Tweed gang—so malodorously like the political gangs of our own day—a stretch of green was carved out, not merely carved out, but actually improved, from barren goat pasture and shantydom into a comely park.

Meanwhile, the city as a whole became progressively more foul. In the late 'seventies the new model tenement design, that for the so-called dumbbell apartment, standardized the habitations of the workers on the lowest possible level, encouraging for twenty years the erection of tenements in which only two rooms in six or seven got direct sunlight or a modicum of air. Even the best residences were grim, dreary, genteelly fusty. If something better was at last achieved for the rich in the eighteen nineties, on Riverside Drive and West End Avenue, it remained in existence scarcely twenty years and was replaced by mass congestion.

During the period we are looking at, the period of Alfred Stieglitz's birth and education and achievement, we are confronted with a city bent on its own annihilation. For New York used its intense energy and its taut, over-quickened life to produce meaner habitations, a more constricted environment, a duller daily routine, in short, smaller joys, than it had produced during the modest provincial period. By denying itself the essentials of a fine human existence, the city was able to concentrate more intently upon its paper figments. It threw open its doors to the Irish of the 'forties, to the Germans of the 'fifties and 'sixties, later to the Italians, and to the Russians and Jews of eastern Europe: the outside world, contemptuous but hopeful, sneering but credulous, sent many of its finest children to New York. Some of them pushed on, to the cornlands, the wheatlands, the woodlands, the vinelands, to the iron mines, the coal mines, the copper mines; while those that remained were forced to huddle in utmost squalor. But the congested East Side, for all its poverty and dirt, was not the poorest part of the city: it still had its open markets with their color, its narrow streets with their sociability and their vivid common life and neighborly help, its synagogues with at least the dried remnants of a common vision.

This New York produced the elevator apartment house at the end of the 'sixties, and the tall building, called the skyscraper after the topmost sail of its old clipper ships, a little later; and it used these new utilities as a means of defrauding its people of space and light and sun, turning the streets into deep chasms, and obliterating the back yards and gardens that had preserved a humaner environment even when people drank their water, not from the remote Croton River, but from the Tea-water Pump.

The spirit of pecuniary pride was reckless and indiscriminate; it annihilated whatever stood in the path of profit. It ruined the ruling classes as well as their victims. As time went on it became ever more positive in its denial of life; so that in more elegant parts of the East Side today there are splendid "modern" mansions that are practically built back to back, even worse in some respects than the vilest slums on Cherry Street. This negative energy, this suicidal vitality, was the very essence of the new city that raised itself after the Civil War, and came to fullest bloom in the decade after the World War. Beholding it in its final manifestations, a German friend of mine wrote: *Dies ist die Hölle, und der Teufel war der Baumeister.* Men and women, if they survived in this environment, did so at the price of some sort of psychal dismemberment or paralysis. They sought to compensate themselves for their withered members by dwelling on the material satisfactions of this metropolitan life: how fresh fruits and vegetables came from California and Africa, thanks to refrigeration, how bathtubs and sanitary plumbing offset the undiminished dirt and the growing tendency toward constipation, how finally the sun lamps that were bought by the well-to-do overcame the lack of real sunlight in these misplanned domestic quarters. Mechanical apparatus, the refinements of scientific knowledge and of inventive ingenuity, would stay the process of deterioration for a time: when they failed, the jails, the asylums, the hospitals, the clinics, would be multiplied. Were not these thriving institutions too signs of progress, tokens of metropolitan intelligence and philanthropy?

But in the end, the *expectation* of health and wholeness, like the expectation of honesty and justice, tended within the great metropolis to disappear. In the course of its imperialistic expansion the metropolis, as Patrick Geddes put it, becomes a megalopolis, concentrating upon bigness and abstract magnitude and the numerical fictions of finance; megalopolis becomes parasitopolis, dominated by those secondary pecuniary processes that live on the living; and parasitopolis gives way to patholopolis, the city that ceases effectively to function and so becomes the prey of all manner of diseases, physical, social, moral. Within such a town, graft and corruption are normal processes; the greater part of the population shares the animus of the criminal, applauds him when he "gets away with it," and condones his crime when he is caught red-handed. The city that has good words for its Commodore

Vanderbilts and Tweeds and Crokers, to say nothing of contemporary gamblers and shysters who have practised on an even larger scale, which multiplied these antisocial types a thousand times, is a city in which a deteriorated social life, without elementary probity or public spirit, has become normalized into the accepted routine.

So every profession has its racket; every man his price. The tonsil snatcher and the ambulance chaser and the insurance fixer and the testimonial writer have their counterparts in the higher reaches of the professions. The more universal forms of dishonor become honorable, and graft and shakedowns, like the private toll exacted for automobile and marriage licenses, become so common that they even escape notice. Those who actively oppose these customary injustices and these systematic perversions of law and decency are looked upon as disappointed men who have set their own price too high. Force, fraud, lying, chicane, become commonplaces; the law is enforced by illegal methods, the constitution protected by unconstitutional practices; vast businesses are conducted in "peace" by judicious connivance with armed thugs—now passive blackmailers, now active strikebreakers—whose work proceeds under the amiable eyes of the very agents supposed to combat it. No one believes that the alternative to living with honor is to die with honor: it is easier, it is more comfortable, to live sordidly, accepting dishonor.

In such a city, an honest man looms high. He is a lighthouse on a low and treacherous coast. To attain even a human level becomes, in this megalopolitan environment, an arduous, almost a superhuman, task.

Any fair picture of New York must confess the underlying sordidness of a large part of its preoccupations and activities. It is not that manufacture and shipping and the exchange of goods are necessarily antivital or antisocial processes: quite the contrary. But when these activities become central to life, when they are themselves perverted to serve chiefly as instruments in an abstract accountancy of profit and power, the human hierarchy of values is displaced; and, as in some perversion of the physiological functions, the head becomes cretinous, and the subordinate members become gigantic *and useless*. What I have elsewhere called a purposeless materialism became the essential principle of the city's life.

One must not flinch, then, from recognizing the dark elements of the picture. But one would have no true image, in fact, no image at all, if one forgot to add the light that defines and relieves the blackest shape; and even at its worst, these elements were always present. There is, to begin with, the physical magnificence of the scene: the sweep and curve of the bay, the grand spaciousness of the river, the rhythm of the tides that encircle it, the strike of its mica-gleaming schists as they crop out in the park or the temporary excavation, and finally, the proud upthrust of the Palisades themselves. In the very shape of the island is something tight, lean, athletic: a contrast to the glacial till of Long Island, with its fat Dutch landscape, its duckponds, its feathery asparagus beds. The skyscrapers, despite their disorder, have not diminished those positive lines in their stalagmitic upthrust: they are almost as geometric as gypsum crystals. And before the skyscrapers were built, from Brooklyn Heights, from the Palisades, from the Belvedere in Central Park, from Morningside Heights, one could see and feel the hard flanks of Manhattan.

Above all, there is the sky; pervading all these activities is the weather. The sharp crystalline days of early autumn, with intense blue sky and a few curls of cloud, drifting through space like the little jets of steam that were once such characteristic outlets of the older skyscrapers: the splendors of sunset on the waters, over the Palisades, crossing the Brooklyn Ferry, looking toward the Jersey shore from the Brooklyn Bridge; the swift, whiplike changes from heat to cold, from fog to clarity, from the sharp jeweled contours of John Bellini to the soft tones of Whistler and Fuller. Occasionally, too, the sulphurous hell of the dog days, to whip up appetite for the dank clouds in the west and the brave crackle of lightning and the drenching showers. At the other extreme the benignity and quiet of a city quenched by snow: the jingle of sleighbells in the eighteen nineties, the cold flash of electricity on the elevated tracks twenty years later.

The niggling interests of the day might lead to a neglect of these fundamental beauties; but they could not obliterate them. Nature remained, ready to nourish the first person who opened his eyes and breathed in the air—the clear, slightly salt-laden air, grey wings swooping and circling through it. This clear air and this intense sunlight are no small encouragements to the photographer. And the landscape as a whole has definition, a disciplined line: the rocks run as due north and south as the points of the compass, and the very sides of the island, once scraggly, have been shaped by the hands of man into sharp lines, like the margin of a Dutch canal. No matter how great the confusion on the surface, beneath it all, in the rocks themselves is order: no matter how shifty man's top layer, the foundations are solid. If the streets are dingy, there is the dazzle of the sky itself: if the alleys and streets are foul, heavy with ancient dirt, with the effluvia of the sewers or the factories, there is the sanative taste of salt in the first wind that blows from the Atlantic. The cold sea fog in spring, sweeping inland in the midafternoon, calls one to the ocean as imperatively as the proud, deep-throated roar of the steamer, claiming the channel as she passes out to sea. So the ocean and the sky and the rivers hold the city in their grip, even while the people, like busy ants in the cracks and crevices, are unconscious of these more primal presences, save when they read a report in the morning paper, and reach for an umbrella, an overcoat, a fan.

Along with its great landscape, New York has had its men. Even in the worst periods of the city's deterioration, there has always been a saving remnant, that handful of honest souls whose presence might have saved the Biblical cities of the plain.

There was, for one, Walt Whitman himself, "of Mannahatta a son," whose visits to the city, with even occasional public appearances, continued after the Civil War, and whose brief pictures of the city are precious records of its life. Whitman, who had rambled about every part of the city, who knew it coming inward from his native Huntington, from Coney Island when that spot was just a fishing hamlet, from the rocky wilds of the upper part of the island, where he would go walking with Bryant—Whitman knew the city at its best. While he realized the evil significance of so much of its vitality, and the impoverishment of its wealth—see his description of the fashionable parade in Central Park in 'seventy-nine—he was nourished by it and fed steadily on it, opera, theater, bookstalls, libraries, lecture halls; above all, the million-headed throng on the streets.

Drinking at Pfaff's, loafing on the Fifth Avenue stages with the coach drivers, crossing the Brooklyn Ferry, Whitman had caught something in the common life that was dear and permanent. He who really touches the soil of Manhattan and the pavement of New York touches, whether he knows it or not, Walt Whitman. Beneath the snobbery of the commercial élite there was in New York a genuinely cosmopolitan spirit. In those who, like Whitman and Melville, were well rooted in the provincial soil, this spirit was capable of reaching out for elements that were still foreign to the new country—the philosophy of Hegel and Schopenhauer, the criticism of Carlyle and Ruskin, the vision of Michelet and Hugo—and transporting them to our unfinished landscape. Melville, who had been a common sailor, and Whitman, a common printer and carpenter, were not caught by the bourgeoisie and debased into accepting their prudent paper routine. Both of them were capable of a passionate aristocracy that reserved for the spirit its primacy in the affairs of men. Whitman's democracy was the prelude to a broader-rooted aristocracy, and none knew that fact better than he.

The Roeblings were in New York, too, during the 'sixties, and Washington remained on, though an invalid, until the Brooklyn Bridge was finally completed in 1883. Not alone did they compose the poem of granite and steel that is the Brooklyn Bridge, one of the first of those grand native works of art that Whitman had demanded of the sayers and delvers, but they brought that arduous habit of intellectual exertion, that capability for heroic sacrifice on behalf of immaterial things, that strict obligation to self-discipline, which came directly from the great Germany of Kant and Goethe and Hegel, a Germany the elder Roebling—who was a pupil of Hegel's—so well knew. It was right for a New Yorker who was interested in science or engineering to seek Berlin during this period; so that even though Stieglitz was unaware of the fact that he was following in the footsteps of the great engineer who built the bridge, it was as natural for him to go to Berlin as it was for Louis Sullivan, a little earlier, to follow the footsteps of Richardson to the Ecole des Beaux Arts in Paris.

Though none of the new buildings in New York could compare in beauty with the High Bridge, in its original stone form, or with the Brooklyn Bridge, there was a stir in architecture in the 'eighties and 'nineties, due chiefly to the work of Richardson, whose influence remained even though he changed his residence from Staten Island to Boston. Beginning with the De Vinne Building on Lafayette Street, an excellent structure created for a scrupulous and craftsmanlike master of printing, the finest works of New York architecture were the series of loft and factory and storage buildings that arose in the 'eighties: buildings whose round arches, solid stone courses, and subtle brickwork set a mark that few later buildings have surpassed. These buildings, moreover, were better than the very best Europe could show in this department at the same period; and contemporary European travelers of discernment noted and admitted this.

Finally, there was Albert Pinkham Ryder, the most sensitive, the most noble mind that appeared in New York after the war, a worthy companion in the spirit to that other post-war recluse, the author of Moby Dick. If the bold sunlight of Broadway made its sheet-iron buildings look flimsy and unreal, the moonlight of Ryder's inner landscape gave body to reality: Ryder with his intuitions of human destiny, Death Riding around a Racetrack, with his wistful melodies of love, the vision of Perette, Siegfried and the Rhine Maidens, with his presentation of fate in the little boats with a tiny sheet of sail on a broad moonlit sea, to which he so often returned, this mystic had a strength and a purpose that the ephemeral activities of the outer world did not possess. A benign figure, ranging up and down the streets after dark, penetrating life in its stillness and peace more bravely than those who flung themselves into the noisiest corners of the battlefield, Ryder also became part of the soil of Manhattan. No one can be aware of the rich vitality of the city who does not know its Ryder as well as its Whitman. He needed little from the city; he gave back much.

II

Grand Tour: This Is New York

STATUE OF LIBERTY

BROOKS ATKINSON

On this day in 1886 the Statue of Liberty was unveiled on Bedloe's Island in the Bay. Like the Hudson River and the Palisades, it is now accepted as one of the natural glories of New York. We who are used to it seldom see it consciously, but it is in our souls and governs our attitude towards the contemporary world. It is a work of art beyond criticism now, for no one knows how deeply it has penetrated into the life of America and of the world, nor how much it has strengthened the ideal of liberty by standing there year after year and holding a lighted torch in the sky. The Constitution is no more explicit than this silent colossus that rises three hundred and five feet, eleven inches above low water in our harbor and greets every ship that steams through the Narrows.

Now that it has become part of our heritage, it is difficult to realize that once it was planned deliberately. Edouard René de Laboulaye, a friend of America, called together a group of French artists and writers at Versailles in 1865 to consider some way of commemorating the first century of freedom in America. Author of a number of political studies of America, he had once written: "The folly of love and the madness of ambition are sometimes curable, but no one was ever cured of a mania for liberty." This perceptive statement shows how genuinely he understood the American principle. The men meeting in his house decided to give America a huge statue of Liberty as a gesture of friendship from the French people. Frédéric Auguste Bartholdi, the sculptor, drew the sketches and chose the setting on Bedloe's Island (then Fort Wood). He wanted to design the largest statue in the world, but harmonize it so completely with the harbor that the size would not be conspicuous.

In the course of years more than a million francs were raised by popular subscription in France. It was not easy to raise the whole amount, but in time the people gave it, and the Statue of Liberty is genuinely a gift from the French people. It took the United States nine years to collect three hundred thousand dollars to build the pedestal. An immigrant to America, Joseph Pulitzer, raised a large part of that sum through an active campaign in his newspaper, the *World*. More than 80 per cent of the money raised came in contributions of less than one dollar. Like Laboulaye, Pulitzer fully understood the truth of the project, and perhaps also foresaw what it would mean to the world. The inspired sonnet by Emma Lazarus, a pioneer Zionist, was contributed to the *World* as part of the campaign, and is now inscribed on the statue:

> *Not like the brazen giant of Greek fame,*
> *With conquering limbs astride from land to land;*
> *Here at our sea-washed, sunset gates shall stand*
> *A mighty woman with a torch, whose flame*
> *Is the imprisoned lightning, and her name*
> *Mother of Exiles. From her beacon hand*
> *Glows world-wide welcome; her mild eyes command*
> *The air-bridged harbor that twin cities frame.*
> *"Keep, ancient lands, your storied pomp!" cries she*
> *With silent lips. "Give me your tired, your poor,*
> *Your huddled masses yearning to breathe free,*
> *The wretched refuse of your teeming shore.*
> *Send these, the homeless, tempest-tost to me,*
> *I lift my lamp beside the golden door."*

Everything about the Statue of Liberty is enlightened, honest and noble. It has become everything it was intended to be. It is the Statue of "Liberty Enlightening the World," to use Bartholdi's original title for his heroic work. Out of good will and imagination some French people created a statue that has become one of the most priceless of our natural resources.

BROADWAY:
World's Most Exciting Street

EDWARD STANLEY

BROADWAY

What hurrying human tides, or day or night!
What passions, winnings, losses, ardors, swim thy waters!
What whirls of evil, bliss and sorrow, stem thee!
What curious questioning glances—glints of love!
Leer, envy, scorn, contempt, hope, aspiration!
Thou portal—thou arena—thou of the myriad long-drawn
 lines and groups!
(Could but thy flagstones, curbs, façades, tell their inimitable
 tales;
Thy windows rich, and huge hotels—thy side-walks wide;)
Thou of the endless sliding, mincing, shuffling feet!
Thou, like the parti-colored world itself—like infinite,
 teeming, mocking life!
Thou visor'd, vast, and unspeakable show and lesson!

—WALT WHITMAN

Broadway stands for an idea—a romantic identification with the gay and sophisticated world which touches everybody everywhere. In terms of the responses it commands, Broadway is the greatest of all the evocative avenues, *the* street which the world holds in common.

Robust, monumentally vulgar, and durable is Broadway. Like humanity, it survives, swinging its earthy hips athwart the neat geometry of Manhattan, twisting along the hard high backbone of the island from one corner to the other. Almost barren of graces, and with none of the endearing intimacies of other famous streets, yet it produces a bizarre nostalgia of its own.

And it has its lyric moments: unexpected, unfamiliar vistas, so unlike the views taught the eye by right-angled streets. Columbus Circle in the summer twilight, or the whirling snow. The foot of Wall Street on a Saturday afternoon, where Broadway tips its hat to Trinity, that dowager of churches, so self-possessed among the banks. And for some, the furious cacophony of sound and color and multitudes around Times Square holds a barbaric magic that amounts to poetry.

For all its gaudy grossness, Broadway is a street about which songs are written—demonstration, surely, that it is held in affection.

Eighteen miles long in Manhattan, Broadway is the only street which runs the length of the island. For some blocks, from Bowling Green to Astor Place, Broadway runs straight enough. But then, in a manner that can only be described as catawampus, it angles wildly across the city to the far northwest corner of Manhattan, where it leaps the Harlem River Ship Canal and as U.S. No. 9 runs up the eastern bank of the Hudson.

Broadway was an Indian pathway, following the ridges of dry land in the swampy meadows of lower Manhattan, long before Giovanni da Verrazzano (an Italian sailing for the French) pushed the first European vessel inquisitively into the harbor in 1524, and that was nearly a century before Henry Hudson (an Englishman sailing for the Dutch) sailed in and left his name on the river. The Indians who came cautiously and apprehensively down to the tip of the island in the summer of 1611, to trade their furs for Adriaen Block's trinkets, may well have come down this pathway, down Broadway. Block was there on behalf of the Dutch West India Company, and in 1613 built the first house on the site of 41 Broadway, then quite a way out of town. Fifty years later, when the British took over, Broadway was only 550 yards long. Whatever the Indians called their trail, the name which persisted came from the Dutch, who called it the Broad Wagon Way.

An imaginative man walking up Broadway would find himself taking a stroll through time, walking through much of America's history. He would have to walk *up* Broadway, because that was the way the street grew, save a few feet which were added by dumping refuse at the tip of Manhattan in the island's first land-fill operation. A British governor, fearing an attack by the French fleet in 1693, ordered the fill, and a gun platform was erected. The French never came, but Battery Park had made its debut.

Lord Cornbury, the nervous governor, also had the habit of appearing on Broadway wearing women's clothing. In two and a half centuries, Broadway has learned to tolerate almost anything; but back then the solid and startled burghers found his conduct scandalous.

In the decade following the Revolution the Battery was the fashionable evening promenade, lined with elms, the social center of the city, which had about fifty thousand inhabitants.

For many years the fine residences in the city were grouped at the lower end of Broadway, but as the area grew commercial they moved

BROADWAY 37

farther up the street. By 1850 the fashionable world had departed. The men who made great fortunes out of Broadway real estate—the Astors, Goelets and Wendels—had a rule of thumb that Broadway moved north ten blocks every ten years.

Lots along Broadway, when first sold by the Dutch, brought fifty dollars, and the house and lot at No. 11 sold for fifteen thousand dollars in the depression which followed the panic of 1837. The corner of Wall and Broadway is assessed at more than that a front foot today.

Until about twenty years ago, Broadway was New York's favorite avenue for parades. So many tremendous and historic processions have moved along it that the list reads like an index to our past. There were gay parades—Macy's annual Thanksgiving Day parade for kids is such a one—but most of them have been solemn, and often sad: The Seventh Regiment, marching off to the Civil War in the April sunshine, expecting to be gone for a month. The doughboys bound for World War I, singing a Broadway song, *Over There*. And funeral processions for many Presidents and generals and statesmen—Monroe, Harrison, Taylor, Grant, Clay and Webster. Saddest of all was the slow procession for Lincoln, and not for eighty years was Broadway to know again such deep bewildered grief for a President.

Up near 77th Street, around the time of the Civil War, lived Fernando Wood, who if not the worst mayor New York ever had is certainly a strong candidate for the title. His corruption was notorious. Under his regime (he was Tammany then) the Bowery and Five Points gangs flourished. In 1857, when the state legislature abolished New York's municipal police and set up a new Metropolitan Police District under state control, Wood refused to disband the local force, which was practically his private army. Aldermen and magistrates took sides, and the gangs had a carnival, going so far as to rob stage coaches on Broadway in broad daylight. Eventually the Seventh Regiment was called out to oust Wood.

His eclipse was engineered by Boss Tweed, whose name has become a synonym for municipal looting. In Tweed's day Broadway made its greatest single leap northward, along the old Bloomingdale Road, which ran roughly from 59th Street to Kingsbridge.

Nandy Wood's crime-infested administration, and the monstrous Tweed era which followed, probably created the wilderness of vice known as the Tenderloin, which flourished without letup for half a century. Roughly, it stretched from 24th to 40th Streets, and from

Fifth to Seventh Avenues. Broadway twisted through the heart of the blight. Police captains of the day prized the assignment there; one of them, in fact, is credited with having given the area its name when he was transferred there. He had been living on pigs' ears in one of the barren outlying precincts, but now, as he put it, he would be having "some of the tenderloin."

The Tenderloin drew many Broadway tourists, as well as slummers. A contemporary guidebook gave them these warnings:

BEWARE—Of the good-natured civilities of persons you have never seen before.

BEWARE—Of Panel Houses. A sliding panel is let into the walls of some double houses, through which thieves enter unperceived and have you at their mercy.

BEWARE—Of Saloons with "Pretty Waiter Girls." They are among the most dangerous in the city.

BEWARE—Of visiting fashionable gambling houses "just to see what is going on."

BEWARE—Especially in the evening, of persons who ask you what time it is. They have designs on your watch.

BEWARE—Of even the *orderly* "Dance Houses." A sadder story of New York life cannot be written than that connected with these places.

For all its wickedness, the Tenderloin seems to have contributed nothing to Broadway but a bad name. Even knockout drops were an innovation from San Francisco. No writers, no artists, no dances, no theater—burlesque and its bawdy ways has origins older by far. One might expect a few remarkable individuals, but out of all the swarming anthill there is hardly one.

There was gambling, of course, in the Tenderloin—Oscar Wilde was clipped in a card game for simpletons called banco and stopped payment on a check for fifteen hundred dollars once he realized he had been had. Serious gambling, however, centered in the Roaring Forties, which were quieter and where the distractions of the Tenderloin would not take a man's mind off a good hand.

The big and open gambling came to an end about the time of World War I, and for a point in time, the murder of the gambler Herman Rosenthal at 2 A.M., July 16, 1912, is probably it. Rosenthal had given an affidavit naming Police Lieutenant Becker, and was shot for his trouble. Becker was executed, along with four gangsters. You may remember their names: Gyp the Blood, Lefty Looie, Dago Frank and Whitey Lewis. Today, save for a floating crap game or so, Broadway's gambling is concentrated on efforts to improve the breed of Thoroughbred horses, an unbelievably resistant strain. No servants in livery, no fancy vittles. But far, far more money changes hands.

The theater had a hard time getting started in New York. Plays and players were regarded as immoral in the sobersided 1780's and for years along Broadway the tea gardens were its centers of amusement, featuring acrobats, magicians, and, of course, music.

The first theater built for the purpose was the Park, in Park Row, which opened in 1798.

Plays of the time included works by Shakespeare and Sheridan. But often the entertainment was a variety program, frequently including a singer who imitated dogs. The performance has been out of style for more than a century, but the tradition of imitation persists on Broadway. A few years ago a man who cleverly imitated wallpaper was a great success.

Museums and circuses were popular—and still are—but this phase of Broadway, busy as it must have been, seems to have been sleeping until P. T. Barnum leased the American Museum at Ann Street and Broadway in 1840. He had been traveling about exhibiting a Negro woman, who, he claimed, was 160 years old and had been George Washington's nurse. (When she died she was found to be only seventy.) He had a tremendous success with Tom Thumb, and a greater one with Jenny Lind, engaged to sing 150 concerts at one thousand dollars each. Barnum worked hard at his museum, where he installed a ferocious brass band, and he brought to Broadway the technique of extravagant exploitation which it follows to this day.

In the decade before the Civil War, Negro minstrels became the most popular entertainment, with as many as fifty companies running on Broadway at the same time. Christy's was perhaps the most famous, and it was at his theater that a song written by Daniel Emmett was presented as a fill-in because they were short a tune. It was lively and exciting, it made men's blood tingle, and it became the campaign song of all political parties that fall. The year was 1859 and the song was *Dixie*.

The music world moved to Broadway in 1883, when the Metropolitan Opera House was opened, largely because the old Academy of Music on 14th Street had grown too small. The Met was in financial difficulties from the start, and was made available for affairs as varied as the flower show and wrestling.

The golden age of Broadway as the center of the theatrical world lasted fifty years—until the talkies, actually. The theatrical section moved steadily uptown through Union Square (the south side was the haunt of unemployed actors in the '80's and '90's) to Times Square at the turn of the century, and might have continued northward had not the talking picture intervened. However this may have altered the theater's future, it does seem to have stabilized the industry in the Times Square area, and today, despite the shooting galleries and penny arcades, the Square remains the center of the amusement world.

The famous Astor House, between Vesey and Barclay Streets, was the first of the great New York hotels, and from 1836 onward it maintained its dominance for half a century as a meeting place for celebrities, long after the center of social life had moved north. Andrew Jackson was a guest there, Sam Houston, Daniel Webster, Henry Clay, Lincoln. And, of course, Jenny Lind. Edgar Allan Poe, when he edited the *Broadway Journal*, may have known its Rotunda restaurant, the smart luncheon place, half restaurant, half bar, where a man could keep his silk hat on while he ate and drape the tails of his frock coat over the stool, thus preserving both dignity and press.

The first of the really sumptuous hotels on Broadway was the Imperial, built by the Goelets in 1890. Its magnificence led a visiting Englishman to assert that he was afraid to leave his boots in the hallway to be polished: "I'm afraid I'd find them gilded in the morning." The Imperial startled the Astors into building the Waldorf around the corner and launched the modern era in the city's luxury hotels.

Until the turn of the century, the crossroads formed by the intersections of Broadway and Seventh Avenue and 42nd and 50th Streets was known informally as Long Acre. Then the New York *Times* moved its plant uptown, and suggested that the triangle might be called Times Square. The name was adopted officially. The upper triangle was long known as Long Acre, but was renamed Duffy Square in honor of Father Duffy, the 69th Regiment's chaplain in World War I, a beloved Broadway personality.

Even after the theatrical world began to take over the area, it was the carriage and harness-making center—the name Long Acre came from the London carriage center—and until 1910 the American Horse Exchange stood on the present site of the Winter Garden. The tradition remains in Broadway's "automobile row," which runs from Columbus Circle almost to Times Square.

World War I changed the character of Times Square, bringing greater surges of humanity than it had ever known, and the experience was enlarged in World War II. Walking up one side of Times Square and back on the other, was something a soldier could do without spending a dime. Times Square crowds a great part of the time seem to be doing nothing more than walking and talking. Many are tourists on week-end all-expense trips, and Times Square is one of the sights of the city. It's probably what people have in mind when they say, "New York is a wonderful place to visit, but I wouldn't want to live there." Yet I lived one winter in a hotel which overlooked Times Square, and which was quiet, almost subdued, and served a handsome farmer-style breakfast.

The feeling exists that during the depression the main stem lost caste when the circus-midway type of enterprise got house room. But property values have not been harmed. While Broadway has always been an entertainment street in the public mind, the fact is that it has always beeen greater as a business street.

The tremendous garment center, the largest New York industry, runs from 34th Street to 42nd, and occupies much of the area once held by the roistering Tenderloin. This is nearly a five-billion-dollar industry, employing more than two hundred thousand people. With its thousands of out-of-town buyers, it brings solid support to the theatrical industry just above it on Broadway, and fills the big hotels nearby.

The garment center is a traffic-locked area, the worst in the city, with handcarts and rolling dress racks competing for gangway with huge trucks. At noontime it is hard to see where the sidewalk ends and the street begins, and jaywalking is accomplished with a mass nonchalance. Once predominantly Jewish, the industry is at least 50 per cent Italian now, with a heavy sprinkling of Puerto Ricans. The noonday floods of humanity, warm with gesticulation and hubbub, may be a legacy of ancient Oriental bazaars, but whatever its origins, the center is a part of the Broadway pattern.

Union Square, after its period of high fashion, was taken over by soapbox orators. Henry George, the great single-taxer, was one of them, and after the spectacular success of his book *Progress and Poverty*, he became the anti-Tammany candidate for mayor and might well have been elected. Unfortunately, he died of an apoplectic stroke after an impassioned speech in Union Square.

Traffic has always been Broadway's headache, and despite the fact that it is no longer the street of primary communication, it is still heavily clogged from Columbia University at 116th Street, to the Battery. Three subways converge on Times Square, plus a shuttle from Grand

Central and various surface lines. The big traffic problem is to get the theater crush safely across the Square. For all the opportunity, however, a serious accident is rare. A pedestrian may get bumped, but the Broadway breed has a high survival quotient, and the victim usually walks away, leaving a few words he has been saving for such an occasion.

It was the same when Broadway traffic moved by horsepower. There were private rigs of infinite variety and elegance, as well as heavy drays, wagons, carts, and that peril of the streets, the two-wheeled butcher cart. Broadway stores had awnings, and the street was pleasantly tree-lined, but the drivers of the horse-drawn buses were of the same perverse stock that handles today's motor coaches. When ruts in the road were too bad, or the street too crowded, they simply put a couple of wheels on the sidewalk. But in winter, while the snow lasted, the buses were superseded by omnibus sleighs, each pulled by twelve horses equipped with bells, and they gave the whole city an air of frolic.

However magnificent a contribution to civilization the subway may be, it is a miserable way to meet Broadway for the first time, to come up suddenly out of the moisty damp and into the whirl and lights. Broadway is a ganglion of energy and light and emotion almost tactile in its impact on the senses, and no one ought to be thrust into it suddenly, with no time to watch and wonder.

It has been a long time now, half my life, since I checked in at the Pennsylvania (now the Statler) and asked the doorman, "Where is Broadway from here?"

"Right down there." He pointed.

This was early evening, in the spring, and the world was very young then, with almost no hint of the terrors to come. Early evening in New York, if the season be soft and the day right, can bring an amethyst twilight, all pinks and blues. Into such a promising twilight, layer on layer of gossamer, I walked up Broadway. The lights began to come on, and up ahead the big signs began to play. I didn't know a soul in town and it was wonderful.

It didn't seem a very long walk, and suddenly I was across 42nd Street, past the Times building, and there it was, all magic, all true, bigger than life, fourteen hundred miles due east, just under the 41st parallel of latitude, from Aurora, Nebraska.

I stood there a long time, and nobody asked me to move along. I suppose country boys from every degree of latitude have been coming to look at Broadway for two centuries. I saw a show called *Hit the*

Deck, walked back down Broadway and caught a train west next morning. One good look was as much as I could handle, then.

Well, of course, the mystery and the magic have worn off and I am able to see the warts and wens. But I never ride on Broadway, or even cross it, without realizing that I am on the greatest street in the world.

THE CITY WHERE NOBODY LIVES
(Rockefeller Center)

JOE ALEX MORRIS

The most magnificent city in America is an irregular block of limestone, steel, glass and masonry snugly set into a dozen acres of solid rock, with its foundations anchored sixty-eight feet below the surface and its towers rising eight hundred fifty feet toward—and frequently into—the clouds. Nobody lives there.

This one-hundred-twenty-five-million-dollar construction project is known as Rockefeller Center, and actually it is a city within the city of New York. Inside the inlaid brass lines that mark its boundaries on the sidewalks, there are all of the material requirements for a secure and pleasant existence from babyhood to old age.

The Center's big plaza is about as close as New York can come to a village green, and the public not only takes an interest in what goes on there but assumes the right to criticize in a loud voice. This attitude is largely the result of a series of outdoor community events staged in the plaza, including Easter music and Christmas carols by a volunteer chorus in front of the most lavish seasonal decorations that can be devised by the mind of man. A Christmas wreath to be recognized as a Christmas wreath at Rockefeller Center should be sixteen feet across, and a Christmas tree should be ninety feet tall.

In the fifteen buildings of the Center itself, there are twenty-six restaurants, three radio broadcasting companies, a hospital, a big employee and community gymnasium, a six-story garage, a volunteer fire department, a police force and a post office. There are many scores of shops and stores along about two miles of outdoor streets, indoor streets, mezzanine streets and elaborate underground streets.

There are eight handsome gardens and an eighty-foot brook that babbles with professional happiness across a rooftop eleven floors above the street. There is the world's largest indoor theater, the Radio City Music Hall, atop which the famous Rockette precision dancers acquire a midsummer sun tan with professional indifference to stares from hundreds of adjacent office windows. There is an outdoor skating pond that attracts a constantly changing audience ranging up to one thousand persons; there is a private street, and there are about one hundred heroic murals, sculptures and mosaics that may or may not be classed as works of art.

In view of such elegance and enterprise, it is a remarkable fact that Rockefeller Center has no population at all. These are office buildings, and the management ruled out all living quarters—even the apartments that originally were planned for the building superintendents.

There are, however, about 32,000 persons who work in the Center, and it is estimated that some 130,000 others visit it daily on business or just to look around, so that the floating population is believed to be about 162,000. There are only fifty-five cities in the United States with a population of more than 160,000.

Rockefeller Center, in contrast to its present planned commercial magnificence, came into being partly by chance and partly as the result of a major national catastrophe. The element of chance was that John D. Rockefeller, Jr., who learned to play the violin in his youth, just happened to get involved in a project for the encouragement of grand opera.

Back in the late 1920's when things were booming along, Rockefeller joined in plans for building a new home for the Metropolitan Opera Company. He agreed to an arrangement whereby he would lease an area between 48th and 51st streets and Fifth Avenue and the Avenue of the Americas (it was then Sixth Avenue), a development of which the opera was to be the center. This land had once been part of a public botanic garden which was operated by Dr. David Hosack, of Columbia College, but he sold it to the state in 1811 and it was turned over to Columbia College three years later. In 1823, the college received rent of $125 a year from the land. One hundred years later, conditions were somewhat changed, and the deal Rockefeller made was to pay Columbia University a rental of $3,300,000 a year on the land under a lease which, with options, runs until 2015, at which time the land and the buildings on it revert to the university.

After the lease had been signed, catastrophe in the form of the 1929 stock-market collapse ended plans for the new opera house. The Metropolitan's angels fled for cover and left Rockefeller holding a bag that contained some of the most expensive rock and 229 of the most dilapidated old brownstone houses in New York City. Rockefeller was paying almost twice the normal rent for that area on which he was losing some three million dollars a year, plus taxes of more than one million dollars. He had no intention of breaking his word, but he had to do something, and almost the only thing he could do was to defy the depression. This he did with a great deal of courage and—despite outbursts of criticism and even ridicule—a great deal of vision.

Laying grand opera gently away in moth balls, he arranged for the firms of Todd, Robertson, Todd Engineering Corporation and Todd and Brown, Inc., to construct and operate for him a strictly commercial office-building development. These managers picked out radio as the fastest-growing industry in the country and decided to create a "radio city" as the keystone in the enterprise. An arrangement was made to lease one million square feet of office space and four theaters to the Radio Corporation of America, the National Broadcasting Company and Radio-Keith-Orpheum Corporation for a total of three million dollars a year. This deal was later modified, but it was enough to enable the builders to start excavation for the first four buildings of the Center in July of 1931.

At this point, when it was freely predicted that the enterprise would be a colossal flop, the builders got a couple of breaks. The depression brought building costs down to about half of what they had been before the stock-market collapse. Furthermore, the architects were able to take advantage of new ideas and mechanical developments that came along after the first World War and were being perfected in the late '20's.

In addition to mechanical marvels, Rockefeller always kept firmly in mind the idea of providing a place in which to focus community activities and community attention—a sort of hang-over from the days when he had been interested in a new opera house.

At one point, Hugh S. Robertson, now a member of the board of directors, developed the idea of a fashionable shopping center that would have prestige of the kind enjoyed by Bond Street in London or the Rue de la Paix in Paris. To do this, he created an entirely new street through the middle of the project and, although it never became known for its shops, it achieved fame as Rockefeller Plaza, a privately owned street. Once every year, with proper ceremony, including the news photographers, the three-block-long street is closed to the public for twelve hours, and all doors—they are largely those of financial institutions—opening on it are locked. This is to prevent the street from becoming public property under the law that provides that any road open to passers-by for a full year becomes a public way.

As building progressed in the 1930's, the Center was operating at a deficit of about four million dollars a year, and the huge skyscrapers were mortgaged for forty-five million dollars. Conditions generally, particularly in 1937, were so discouraging to business that some timid souls discussed abandonment of plans to construct the last three buildings. It was fairly obvious, however, that the only chance of ever making an operating profit was to complete the project, and Rockefeller never wavered from that goal. He just kept on signing checks and insisting on perfection to the last detail.

It was not until the early 1940's that Rockefeller Center broke out of the red on an operating basis. Today Rockefeller Center, Inc., in which the Rockefellers are the only stockholders, has a gross income of more than twenty million dollars a year and has just about lifted the mortgage on the old homestead. The buildings are fully occupied by about eleven hundred tenants, and there are some fifteen hundred names on a list of firms which at one time or another have requested space.

This situation reflects the general postwar space shortage, but it is also a result of the over-all planning and operation of Rockefeller Center, including the remarkable architectural contributions of such men as Raymond Hood, Wallace Harrison, Andrew Reinhard, Harvey W. Corbett, J. André Fouilhoux and Henry Hofmeister. For the first time in the history of city planning a group of skyscrapers was built in a manner that created a sense of order in the relationship of one building to another, and with 10 to 15 per cent of the land left vacant to permit proper spacing of the buildings for light and air. Rockefeller Center is architecturally unique, but its basic influence has been felt everywhere in city planning.

The British Empire Building and La Maison Française, adjacent to the International Building, are the smallest in the Center, only six stories. They face Fifth Avenue, and a flower-lined promenade, popularly called the Channel, runs between them to form a main entrance to the Center and give the visitor a striking first glimpse of the soaring RCA Building in the background.

The Channel leads into the lower plaza, a huge rectangular pit 125 feet by ninety-five feet and some seventeen feet below the street level. This was originally supposed to be a fashionable shopping area that would lead on into an underground avenue of shops stretching entirely across the Center. As such, however, it flopped. There was considerable anguish about this costly waste of space, and the management finally decided to get what they could out of it by putting in two restaurants and making the plaza into a colorful and quaint Skating Pond in the shadow of New York's skyscrapers. This started off rather calmly, but ice skating seemed to bring out the ham in everybody who tried it, and the pond soon became one of the Center's main attractions.

One of the brightest spots in the Center is a display of the flags of the United Nations around the lower plaza. The Flags are a permanent display, but the Channel and the plaza are elaborately refurbished a number of times each year in keeping with the seasonal changes, including ten or a dozen complete changes of plantings between the lavish display of Easter lilies and the final sunburst of October's chrysanthemums. All these changes, which attract big crowds to the Center, are planned six months or a year in advance by Aart M. van den Hoek, the horticultural director, who worries mightily about bringing the flowers to a bloom on exactly the right day. If necessary, he puts them in cold storage or forces them, in order to be sure that Nature keeps in line with the Center's timetable.

Van den Hoek's greatest foe is the wind, which is inclined to whistle violently through the plaza most of the time because the tall buildings form a sort of chimney with a strong draft. This is likely to shake a lily to pieces in a few moments and make a wreck of many weeks of work and planning by the director and his seven gardeners. Extremes of climate, exhaust gases, soot and the pigeons—which go for begonias —also complicate the landscaping problem.

The eight elm trees, some fifty feet high, planted on Fifth Avenue and fed with injections of chemicals, have a life expectancy of only ten years, after which they are replaced. This is an expensive way to provide shade and beauty—almost two hundred dollars per tree per year— but the management figures they are worth the effort and the money.

In addition to the flower displays, the function of the plaza as a sort of glorified village green is demonstrated by large crowds that attend occasional dog shows, fashion shows and such events of general interest as the televised presentation of election returns on a mammoth screen. The outstanding event, however, is the Christmas season, when scouts scour the countryside for a towering tree, and Robert Carson, architect and director of display, rigs up a spectacular lighting arrangement.

The origin of the Center's Christmas tree is attributed to a group of workmen who set up a tiny pine and strung a few lights on it while they were excavating for the first buildings back in the early 1930's. The management decided to carry on their sentimental gesture by putting up a handsome tree in the plaza each Christmas. The development of this enterprise over the last fifteen years has been a little frightening and may be significant to students of such phenomena. In 1934, the tree was sixty feet tall and draped with 1200 colored lights. In 1935 it was seventy feet tall and the lights numbered 1700. In 1936 the tree was up to eighty feet and there were 4000 lights. The war years slowed down this frenzied progression, but only for the duration. By 1948 the tree was ninety feet tall and required seven miles of wiring and 7500 lights, with the future entirely unpredictable.

All these things, of course, are merely the window dressing. The real business of Rockefeller Center, Inc., is keeping the tenants happy, a task that requires 1500 hourly wage earners and an administrative and clerical staff of about 300. The nerve center is a huge and complicated switchboard on the second floor of the RCA Building, called the control room, which has never been closed since the first tenant moved in.

The control board shows every time a watchman or guard turns his key in a time clock—or if he fails to turn the key at the proper time. It is the center of an elaborate fire-and-burglar-alarm system, and it automatically records the presence of any person attempting to leave a building by the fire stairs in time to permit a guard to intercept him and determine whether he has merely lost his way or is trying to escape notice.

The operator of the control board can establish a telephone connection with any one of the 215 elevators in the Center or carry on a conversation with any of the one hundred patrolmen and watchmen whose equipment includes a portable telephone. If there is a fire or a flood—and the Center has had both on a small scale—the warning sounds first in the control room, automatically starting a series of alarms designed to handle the emergency without help from the outside, if possible.

The control board and its related service department handle almost three hundred calls a day. Five girls take the calls during normal working hours and type out memos for everything from knocking down a partition to opening an office door for some tenant who forgot his key.

One woman, working at night in her office, complained that a hall light on the thirty-eighth floor of a building across the street annoyed her. The control board turned it off. A worried wife called at one A.M. to say that her husband had failed to show up for dinner, and that the telephone in his office didn't answer. The control board found him in a quiet poker game in the next-door office. Once the control board demonstrated its remarkable sensitivity to what is going on by coming to the aid of a girl whom a guard found sobbing in the lobby of the RCA Building. She had a date to meet a soldier in the lobby, but she couldn't find him. The control board merely queried the patrolmen in all the lobbies, described the soldier and produced him from another lobby in time to save the day for romance and the United States Army.

The nerve system of intricate wires that reaches out from the control room shows only the outline of the mechanical and human operation required to run Rockefeller Center. There are four underground levels where men and machines work day and night to provide water, heat, air conditioning, electricity and all kinds of supplies for the offices, shops and twenty-six restaurants on the upper floors.

At the very bottom of the RCA Building is the central trucking space. Every day some seven hundred delivery trucks circle down a ramp into this huge underground parking space, check in at the main gate and are directed to the platform nearest the building to which their goods are consigned. The exhaust fumes from the procession of trucks —it mounts to more than one thousand a day at Christmas time—would soon make the trucking space a death chamber except for big pipes that suck the air out through grilles in the ceiling and at the base of the big concrete columns, and finally release it harmlessly several floors above the sidewalks.

Along almost a dozen miles of passageways in the other basement levels of the Center are whole platoons of pumps, motors, fans, generators, switchboards, refrigerators and recording devices that automatically go about the business of making tenants comfortable. Here, too, are the great pipes through which steam under tremendous pressure comes from the New York Steam Corporation and is filtered down into smaller conduits, and finally into the twisting network of water, steam, electric, sewage and air-conditioning pipes—each a different color—that reaches to every corner and spire of the Center.

All these automatic operations create a feeling that robots run the place, until you get a look at some of the eighteen hundred persons busily performing duties for Rockefeller Center, Inc. These include, besides engineers and electricians and carpenters, a number of specialists, such as the two porters who do nothing but clean chewing gum off the floors and sidewalks, the two who pick up cigarette butts, and a crew that, for an extra two dollars a week per man, was assigned to the specialized job of cleaning cuspidors after the regular cleaning women balked two years ago. At that time, the management was surprised to find that they had one thousand cuspidors around the place, some in tobacco-company offices and some in the offices of oil-company big shots who acquired the tobacco-chewing habit during their early days, when they were not allowed to smoke while working around oil wells.

Covering the wall of the cleaning headquarters on one of the lower levels is a huge chart, sprinkled with floor numbers, firm names and gaily covered pins to show just what has been done to each office, lobby and corridor since the first of the month and what remains to be done before month's end. In adjoining rooms are batteries of huge vacuum cleaners, floor-washing machines, waxing machines, buffing machines and a tractor snow shovel for the sidewalks. There are also rows of ordinary mops, brooms and dustcloths. Together, these cover the 5,500,000 square feet of floor space, from the maple flooring of the gymnasium to the travertine Italian marble of the lobbies, five nights a week, at speeds varying from 300 to 10,000 square feet an hour.

The cleaners, who spread 2800 pounds of soap, 500 gallons of wax and 110 gallons of brass polish over a period of one month, assemble each evening like a small army collecting equipment and rations.

There is also a special crew for bronze polishing, which covers certain spots each night and works over the bigger areas, such as the huge statue of Atlas on Fifth Avenue, once a week. The Center is very careful about preserving its works of art and at one time worked itself into a dither over the big wood statue of Man and Nature which Carl Milles carved for the lobby of the Time and Life Building. The statue shows a man on horseback listening to a singing bird perched on a tree above his head. The bird really moves its wings and sings once every hour, assisted by a concealed phonograph record of a Mexican nightingale.

The Center's experts are unusually proud of the result—if you ever tried to get a Mexican nightingale to sing for a recording machine you would understand why—and were distressed when the statue began to acquire a coating of dust and dirt. They finally wrote to Milles at his Michigan home and asked him how to clean it. The return letter from the temperamental sculptor, by air mail and four pages long, threatened lawsuits and perhaps mayhem against any cleaning woman who dared remove the patina of age from his statue. He finally ended up by telling the Center's experts that, if they simply had to do something, they might try blowing the dust off with a bellows. They did.

The cleaning department also has learned to be careful about wastepaper baskets. All wastepaper is gathered into sacks that are tagged with the office number and the floor number, and the whole lot, amounting to some eight hundred bags, is withheld from final disposal for two days. That two days is a margin of safety for recovery of valuables that tenants are constantly losing on the floor or in the wastebasket. Jewelry, watches and documents can be and are regularly recovered from the tagged sacks or from the vacuum cleaners, which are also tagged and remain unemptied for twelve hours. The biggest recovery was eighty thousand dollars in diamonds which had been misplaced in the trash of a jewelry shop.

In addition to all this concern about the welfare and property of the tenants, the Center devotes considerable time and money to cultivating the good will of the public. Nelson Rockefeller, who is now president of the corporation, once told how his father stopped to watch a steam shovel in operation during the early construction days and was told by a guard to "move along, buddy." Rockefeller moved along, but he didn't like it, and he assumed that thousands of other passers-by wouldn't like it either. So he had special openings cut in the board fences for anyone who wanted to watch without interference. This led to one of the town's best public-relations stunts, in which each spectator was presented with a card certifying that he was a member of the Sidewalk Superintendents' Club.

The Center has remained sensitive ever since to the public attitude and, in turn, the public has taken a sort of proprietary interest in what goes on around Rockefeller Plaza. When architects published plans to erect an oval building on Fifth Avenue, the public wrote letters of protest until the idea was dropped. When luncheon-hour idlers in the Channel complained that they had to stand up while loafing, benches were installed. During the war, when Victory gardens were in vogue, tomatoes were planted around the wall of the lower plaza. They were a great success and everybody seemed pleased until one day when Rockefeller got a letter complaining bitterly that no salt or pepper was provided to go with the ripe tomatoes. He sent the letter to Horticulturist van den Hoek without any comment, but sometimes the builder of Rockefeller Center feels that even the public can carry things a little too far.

ELEGANCE BY THE MILE:
Fifth Avenue

GEORGE FRAZIER

If Fifth Avenue, the scant seven miles which bisect New York City socially as well as geographically, is the stateliest and most elegant street in the world, it is also the most contradictory—on the one hand, for example, inflexibly inaccessible to bootblacks, parking lots, panhandlers and movie theatres, and, on the other, expansive enough to welcome the lusty St. Patrick's Day parade by applying a coat of green paint to the white traffic line that runs down its middle. It is a further incongruity of what was once a trout stream and is now, according to its more fervent admirers, "a national symbol," that while it is lined with posh shops amenable to selling a diamond necklace for $275,000, toys at $300 each, or the mellowed paneling from an English manor for $3500, it has but one place, and that up at 110th Street, where one can buy a gallon of gas. It is the site of the tallest building ever erected —the Empire State, which has 102 stories, rises 1472 feet into the sky, and was once hit by an airplane—but it has never provided the convenience of a funeral parlor in which to embalm what remained of those who used to plunge from the building's cloud-wreathed crest. What's more, it is the residence of "the world's richest girl," Doris Duke, and at the same time the mailing address for the members of Little Puerto Rico, one of the most ill-fed, ill-clothed, and ill-housed of all communities. Notwithstanding such disparities, though, Fifth Avenue is, at least for three-or-so miles, not without a measure of consistency. Between 34th Street, where the great department stores begin, and 90th Street, where the mausoleum-like mansions end, it possesses a beauty, grandeur, gentility, and profusion of riches that can be found on no other street.

For one thing, it is unquestionably the most aristocratic thoroughfare in New York City. As a matter of fact, the old guard of Manhattan society regards Park, which is over the underground tracks of the New York Central Railroad, as impudently *nouveau riche* and utterly devoid of the patrician heritage and entrenched wealth that are so intrinsically part of Fifth.

Fifth Avenue, by and large, also has no equal among shopping centers anywhere in the world. On Fifth Avenue it is enough merely to window-shop. About its window displays there is always a shiny splendor, a changing excitement, an exquisite imagination, and an altogether breath-taking suspense.

Christmas, of course, is the resplendent time on Fifth Avenue. The windows become even more of a beckoning fairyland then than at any other season, and everywhere there is a sense of peace on earth to men of good will and at every turn something evocative of the sugarplum magic of a childhood peopled with Donner and Blitzen and dedicated to a willful and persistent trust in the efficacy of a stocking hung over the mantel on the night before Christmas.

In the wintry dusk the strains of *Silent Night*, plaintive and devout, or of *King Wenceslas*, resonant and hearty, waft out over the frosty air from the throats of a papier-mâché choir posted on the second floor front of Saks Fifth. Beside the skating rink in Rockefeller Plaza a giant tree spirals like a cluster of diamonds against the darkening sky. At Bonwit Teller's and Saks' cocktails are served free of charge to males in quest of gifts for their ladies. At 58th Street, where Bergdorf Goodman's one Christmas contributed an air of utter swank by blowing simulated champagne bubbles around their windows, pretty girls, their cheeks flushed with the cold, turn in toward the old-world charm of the Plaza Hotel.

Everywhere on the Avenue is the spirit of Christmas—the firs glowing in the dark outside the churches hard by Washington Square, where Fifth begins; the lighted wreaths around the necks of the massive, haughty stone lions flanking the entrance to the Public Library at 42nd Street; people—a little tipsy, a little lipstick-smeared—weaving homeward from office parties; the huge wreaths in the windows of the vast and elegant National City Bank at 51st Street; and then the sudden hush on the afternoon of December 24, with the Avenue deserted, until finally the new day is born and in St. Patrick's Cathedral there is the solemn beauty of Midnight Mass and the simple dignity of the Gospel according to St. Luke.

But it is one of the major assets of Fifth Avenue that its enchantment is not confined to any one season or any single part of the day. It is lovely at dawn, with the sharp sunlight glinting on the shop windows and the pigeons gathering on the steps of St. Patrick's and the whole sweep of the Avenue, from Washington Square to 110th Street, where Little Puerto Rico begins, touched with magnificence. At noon, it is lovely too, but different—crowded now with women all so impeccably groomed that shop girl is indistinguishable from Social Registerite, and bustling with bright and purposeful young men from the shiny buildings in Rockefeller Center. And then there is the softness of the early dark, with the skyscrapers debouching their hordes into the crepuscular rush, with people hurrying to cocktails at the Stork (to the east on 53rd) or "21" (west on 52nd) or the luxury hotels like the Plaza, the St. Regis, the Pierre, the Savoy-Plaza, and the Sherry-Netherland, all of them unmistakably of the Avenue, and always, of course, with the stenographers and file clerks and receptionists and all the others homeward bound for the Bronx or Brooklyn or Staten Island or wherever.

Like the different hours of the day, all the seasons—not Christmas alone—are pregnant with beauty or rapture or perhaps even the bittersweet loneliness of the hot Friday afternoon when Anson Hunter, the rich boy in Scott Fitzgerald's short story, strolled up the deserted Avenue to the Plaza, where he suddenly came upon Paula Legendre, the only girl he had ever truly loved. As John O'Hara has pointed out, there are still people who wander into the Plaza on a summer's afternoon expecting to see Anson and Paula—and, funny thing, they do see them, at least in a way, because Fifth Avenue is like that, always changing but somehow always the same. Every day there are people just like Anson Hunter and Paula Legendre in the Plaza. Indeed, over the 129 years since it was opened as a public thoroughfare, Fifth Avenue has suffered only one major change which might be termed detrimental. That was the disappearance a few years ago of the open-top two-decker buses.

It is only fair, however, to concede that not all the Avenue is glitter. From Washington Arch (which commemorates the inauguration of George Washington in New York City on April 30, 1789, and is the only arch in the world erected by private funds to observe a historical event) to around 12th Street there is an air of fading gentility. Once, of course, it was irreproachably fashionable. It was on the corner of Eighth Street, for example, that in 1855 John Taylor Johnston built the first marble residence in the city. Now the elegance is departed—the gaiety that was Delmonico's when it occupied a site near 14th Street in the 1860's—and all that remains is the expiring charm, like something out of the pages of Henry James, of sidewalk cafés and snug churches.

From there to 34th Street things take a frankly commercial turn, but one without any of the imaginativeness to be found further up the Avenue; mostly, it is an area of wholesale houses. In bygone years, though, it was the location of the original Fifth Avenue Hotel, which was the greatest hostelry of its time. There for two and a half dollars one could get a room with a fireplace and four meals a day.

Starting at 34th Street, Fifth Avenue begins to assume its true grandeur. Between there and 59th Street are some of the most exciting stores anywhere in the world. Here too are some of the most distinguished churches in North America—St. Patrick's Cathedral, which cost four million dollars to build; the Fifth Avenue Presbyterian; St. Thomas', and others.

In 1841, the strip of Fifth Avenue between 40th and 86th Streets was appraised at $397,000; in 1924, at $259,611,000. What is extraordinary about this is not so much the fantastic rise in values as the fact that such a prodigiously expensive parcel of land could remain so decorative.

At the Grand Army Plaza, a lovely, tree-shaded park with a splashing fountain and the densest concentration of pigeons in the city, Fifth Avenue takes on another aspect. The Plaza, between 58th and 60th on the west side of the Avenue, marks the end of the shopping district and the beginning of "New York's Great Back Yard," Central Park, which runs some two-and-half-miles to 110th Street, a point, incidentally, which many people erroneously regard as the end of Fifth Avenue, though it actually extends to 142nd Street where the Harlem River is located.

To the residents of upper Fifth Avenue, Central Park is where the governesses take children when they have returned them from such neighboring private schools as Miss Hewitt's Classes and Brearley. Sitting by the playgrounds in the warm sunlight, the "nanas" and "mam'selles" discuss the innermost secrets of their employers, who live in the towering apartment houses that line the east side of the Avenue. Unfortunately, the possibilities for gossip are somewhat less extensive than they were in the years when upper Fifth Avenue was lined with sumptuous mansions. The Frick house at 70th Street, which had 110 rooms, is now the excellent Frick Collection; the Carnegie mansion at 91st has become the New York School of Social Work. Generally speaking, upper Fifth Avenue, except for its apartment houses, is a blend of the religious, medical and educational. It has three superb hospitals—Mt. Sinai, Flower, and Fifth Avenue; four superlative museums—the Metropolitan, the Frick, the Museum of the City of New York and the Guggenheim; and the largest synagogue in the world—Temple Emanu-El, which is at 65th Street.

But there is little likelihood that upper Fifth Avenue will ever perish as a select residential district. The view out over Central Park, with its lakes sparkling in the sunlight, is magnificent. And, there is the ever-increasing spaciousness and luxury of the apartment houses, many of which shot up into the sky almost as soon as the multimillionaires decided to shutter their palaces, thus committing what Oliver Wendell Holmes liked to refer to as "intentional domicide."

If the attractiveness of Fifth Avenue can be attributed to any single factor, it must be to the vigilance of the merchants who constitute the Fifth Avenue Association. It is they who, by policing themselves, have banned panhandlers, billboards, bootblacks, parking lots, gas stations, funeral parlors, projecting signs, and moving window displays (except during the Christmas season) from the Avenue. At the same time, by awarding prizes for the best-looking windows, they have inspired stores to imaginative heights. During the Easter season, for example, one store is done in a woodland motif, and to reach the main rooms of the establishment one has to cross a bridge that arches a stream flowing through the floor.

The climax of the season arrives, of course, with the parade on Easter Sunday. A tradition that grew out of the custom of carrying flowers from St. Thomas' to the patients at St. Luke's, the Easter Parade suffered a serious loss of prestige one year when the presence of television converted what had always been a dignified performance into the most crass sort of commercial display. But the next year the Fifth Avenue Association stepped in and adamantly restored the procession to its pristine integrity, with the result that once again the Avenue displayed the muffled beauty of the Irving Berlin song.

That, indeed, is one of the glories of Fifth Avenue—the loyalty to basic values, the deep sense of *noblesse oblige*, the respect for beauty and tradition. It is apparent almost everywhere—in the horse carriages and their top-hatted drivers drowsing in the splash of sunlight in the Plaza; in the vast apartment houses, like the one at 60th Street in which each partner in the House of Morgan occupied a whole floor, or the one at 92nd Street in which Mrs. Joseph Davies, the wife of the former U.S. Ambassador to Russia, had quarters for which she paid more than one million dollars in advance for five years' rental; in the innumerable travel bureaus and their bright promise of the lure of faraway places; in the haunting memory of the Vanderbilt mansion, now razed, and of stately dinners on evenings long vanished; in the appearance of the celebrities who are to be seen at every turn; in the icy-blue freshness of beauty salons like Hudnut's or Arden's or Rubinstein's as well as in the cool, haughty loveliness of the women who patronize them; in the marquee lights that flash on and off to summon taxis or in the shrillness of doormen's whistles; in the flags billowing from department-store windows; in the trimness of the mounted policemen. All this is there. All the pride and splendor. It has been summed up many times, but never so well as it was in an item that appeared in *The New Yorker* several years ago. In this case, a young man waiting for the uptown bus on the corner of Fifth and 57th Street drifted back from the curb and leaned against Tiffany's. A moment later the jewelry store's doorman approached and tapped him on the shoulder.

"People," he said in a tone of gentle reproof, "don't lean against Tiffany's."

EXOTIC CHINATOWN

HERBERT ASBURY

On the way to Chinatown from mid-town New York, the sight-seeing bus turned into the Bowery, and the guide said: "We are now entering what I have nicknamed the 'Street of Forgotten Men,' the home of the famous Bowery bum. It's late in the day, but if you'll look close you may see a bum sleeping off last night's drunk on the sidewalk. If you spot one call out, so we can all see."

The tourists peered eagerly from the windows, and presently a woman cried, as proud as if she'd found a four-leaf clover: "There's one!"

And sure enough, there he was, asprawl against a lamppost. Everybody stared, and the bus buzzed with such excitement that scarcely any attention was paid to two of the real sights of the Bowery—Olliffe's Drug Store, which has been in business at the same location for 146 years and is probably the only place in New York where leeches and slippery elm may be purchased; and an old-time barbershop and tattoo parlor, with a big eye painted on the window and underneath it the legend, "Black Eyes Treated." Finally, the bus rolled to a stop in Chatham Square and the tourists got out and clustered about the guide.

"Now," he said, "we're going into Chinatown. Keep close together, walk in the middle of the street, and don't speak to anybody."

Having prodded his charges into a properly apprehensive frame of mind—needlessly so, because actually a trip through Chinatown is about as dangerous as a tour of St. Patrick's Cathedral—the guide led them on a forty-five-minute jaunt through the three principal streets of the quarter—Doyers, Pell and Mott. In his haste to get started the guide overlooked a noted landmark—an old building at Chatham Square and Doyers Street where, according to Chinatown legend, a member of the Doyer family buried thirty-five million dollars in gold about the time of the American Revolution. It is now occupied by the Harbor Inn Bar and Grill, where the chief bartender is a lady affectionately known to the derelicts of the Bowery as Miss Mag. When a curious visitor asked Miss Mag how she happened to become a bartender, she replied: "Well, my husband's an alcoholic, and I guess I just drifted into it."

The tourists stopped at No. 5 Doyers Street to inspect the mission of the New York Rescue Society, which once housed a famous Chinese theater; to look at the vacant lot across the street, site of the old Chatham Club, where Eddie Cantor and Jimmy Durante started their careers, and where Irving Berlin appeared when he could get away from his regular job as a singing waiter in Nigger Mike Salter's saloon and cabaret in Pell Street.

From the Rescue Mission the way led around the Bloody Angle of Doyers Street, a sharp turn which has been the scene of more murders than any other place in New York. An arcade, lined with saloons, cabarets and shops, used to run from Doyers Street to Mott Street, but it was closed by the police during the tong wars of the early 1900's. It provided a perfect way of escape for the tong killers who lay in wait for their victims and chopped them down with hatchet and snickersnee as they came around the Bloody Angle. The hatchet man and the highbinder have been extinct for about twenty-five years; nevertheless, some of the tourists cast fearsome glances over their shoulders as they hurried through Doyers Street into Pell Street, and down Pell half a block for a visit to the joss house, or temple, in the building of the Hip Sing Tong. There they sat on hard benches while the voice of an unseen priestess, via loud-speaker, described the joss, the prayer and fortune papers, and the temple dragon, made of cloth and papier mâché, which is brought out to participate in the parades that are a spectacular part of life in the quarter.

The last lap of the tour was up Pell Street into Mott Street—the principal thoroughfare of Chinatown—and down Mott to the bus at Chatham Square. There was a stop at a curio store, and a brief halt in front of Post Office Station No. 233, which may well be, as the guide described it, the smallest post office in the world; the space for customers is about four by seven feet. A room behind the post office is the temple of Chinatown's oldest joss; it has been in existence, at various locations, for more than seventy-five years. A few old men still visit it to learn their fortunes and to worship according to their ancient habit.

In the old days tourists came into the district unescorted, and were shown around by resident guides, called lobbygows, who were always liars and generally thieves or worse. They worked in cahoots with the low saloons and cabarets (all owned by white men) with which Chinatown was liberally sprinkled, and in which tourists were often robbed. The lobbygows also ran fake gambling houses and opium-smoking dens, and the tourist paid from one to five dollars to see three or four Chinese playing checkers at a battered table, or lolling on cots smoking aromatic leaves. At one time Chuck Connors, so-called King of the Lobbygows, had four such resorts in profitable operation. Not an ounce of opium was ever smoked in any of them.

Forty or fifty years ago the use of opium was a great deal more prevalent among the Chinese in New York than it is now, and there were many places where an addict could hit the pipe. But these dives were hidden away in cellars or on the top floors of tenements, and were not open to the tourist. The largest was in the cellar of the Chinese theater, where thirty-odd bunks swung from iron hooks imbedded in the stone walls. It was run for several years by Bridgie Webber, a gambler and gang leader who was a key witness in the famous Becker-Rosenthal murder case in 1912. Today there are no cabarets in Chinatown, and no gambling houses or opium dens—at least as far as the police know.

Because there is nothing to attract them, the bums and homeless men of the Bowery are seldom seen in Chinatown except in Doyers Street, where they seek shelter at the Rescue Mission or, if they have a little money, lodging at the Grand Windsor Hotel for Men Only, which occupies four floors above the Mission. Of its kind, the Grand Windsor is a de luxe establishment. Its floor space is divided by flimsy partitions into some three hundred cubicles, each about four feet by seven feet and containing a cot and a chair. Blankets and sheets are provided, but an occasional lodger prefers to sleep in his clothing, with his shoes tied about his neck or wrapped in his overcoat—if he has one—to form a pillow. The partitions do not extend to the ceiling, and the tops of the cubicles are covered with chicken wire to discourage thievery. These compartments rent at from forty cents to fifty cents a night. The more expensive ones have an electric light.

The building which houses the Mission and the Grand Windsor has a unique place in the history of Chinatown. It's a five-story brick structure; the first floor and cellar were built about 1800, the remaining four floors were added during the Civil War. In 1895, the cellar and the first floor, now occupied by the Rescue Society, were opened as an opium den and a theater, respectively. The theater was the first Chinese playhouse east of San Francisco, and by current standards was sumptuous; a few of the seats were fitted with cushions, and the walls were covered by murals depicting dragon fighting and the trials and tribulations of virtue. These paintings were said to have been stolen from an ancient Chinese temple and smuggled into New York, and were generally regarded, by white men, as masterpieces of Oriental art. Actually, they were the work of the janitor, Chin Yin by name, who did the job for thirty-five dollars.

So popular did the theater become that the management was able to import, from Canton, two of China's most celebrated actors, the tragedian Hom Ling and the comedian Ah Hoon. After a decade of profitable operation the enterprise fell upon evil days during the tong wars. Several men were slaughtered during performances, and Ah Hoon himself, a member of the On Leong Tong, was killed because he interpolated into his act certain biting witticisms ridiculing the Hip Sings and the Four Brothers, both enemies of the On Leongs. The Hip Sings tricked Ah Hoon's guards by lowering a gunman in a boatswain's chair from the roof of the comedian's boardinghouse in Chatham Square. He shot Ah Hoon through a window. There were half a dozen shooting and stabbing affrays on the streets of Chinatown next day, and two Hip Sings were killed. On New Year's night, 1910, while Hom Ling was ranting before a packed house, a string of lighted firecrackers was thrown into the orchestra. Under cover of the explosions, five On Leongs were shot dead in their seats.

The theater was closed within a week, and after several white men had tried unsuccessfully to convert it into a movie house it was taken over in August, 1910, by the Rescue Society, which opened a mission with Tom Noonan, a famous reformed man, as superintendent. Noonan died in 1935, and in 1942 was succeeded by Rev. Howard Wade Kimsey, a well-known revival and radio singer. Mr. Kimsey, an ordained minister of the Disciples of Christ, is also a small-arms expert, and can fan a revolver from the hip in the manner of the old-time Western desperado. The Mission does no work among the Chinese, but takes care of from one hundred to four hundred derelicts from the Bowery every night; they are fed coffee, stew, bread and sometimes pie, at six o'clock, after which they listen to a religious service, revivalist in character, and are permitted to sleep on the benches in the auditorium and in the cellar. In the morning the bums get coffee and two or three slices of raisin bread, and are outfitted with whatever clothing they need —if it is available. Then they are turned out to drag through another day. Since nearly all are alcoholics, they spend their time in a never-ending search for liquor, and will sell or trade anything they possess for a drink. For this reason the Mission doesn't try to keep the moths away from the piles of castoff clothing in the cellar.

"A garment with a few moth holes in it will keep a man warm," said Mr. Kimsey, "but he can't sell it to buy booze."

Despite the inroads of Americanization, symbolized by the ubiquitous cola, hot dogs and hamburgers sold in many Chinese lunch rooms, the quarter has retained its foreign atmosphere to a greater extent than any other racial settlement in New York. The buildings are typical New York tenements, old and dingy, but many have been gaily decorated in the Chinese style and tricked out with pagodas and other architectural doodads which flare out at unexpected angles. When the Chinese build, as in the new national headquarters of the On Leong Tong, constructed at Mott and Canal Streets two years ago at a cost of more than five hundred thousand dollars, they combine Eastern and Western architecture to produce an effect which is always different and sometimes startling. The On Leong building, which is the current pride of Chinatown, was formally opened in mid-November, 1950, with a dragon parade and a grand celebration in which thousands of firecrackers were shot off. It was ready for occupancy a month before, but the omens set forth in the lunar almanac, or Good Luck Calendar, according to which many Chinese conduct their affairs, indicated plainly that an October opening would be disastrous.

The windows of the curio and souvenir shops which flourish by the score in Chinatown are ablaze with gaudy gimcracks and gewgaws, but inside the discriminating buyer can also find jewelry, textiles, fine jades, furniture and ceramics of high quality and, on the whole, reasonably priced. The liquor stores purvey a wide variety of Chinese wines, most of which are about as strong as brandy: Rose Wine, with its delicate suggestion of rose petals; The Five Companies Wine, sometimes called Chinese Dynamite, which is strongly flavored with spices; and Tiger Bone Wine, strong and pungent. Pear Wine and Orange Wine, flavored with those fruits, are milder, more like our cordials.

Many of the staples found in any supermarket are carried in stock by the Chinese groceries, but their principal business is in foodstuffs peculiar to the Chinese—shark fins, dried squid (the Italians buy most of this), hairy melon, winter melon, bean curd, bean sprouts, snow peas (small and tender and to be cooked in the pod), bird's nest, lotus root, canned dragon-eye nuts, sesame seed, lichee nuts, water chestnuts, and bamboo shoots, canned and pickled. Some of the canned goods are imported, but the vegetables are grown by Chinese truck farmers in New Jersey, Long Island and Florida. Most of them are easily adapted to American use; for instance, bean sprouts, chilled, are delicious in salads. The Chinese use very little beef, but they eat large quantities of pork, chicken, duck and fish. They are also large consumers of a famous American delicacy—diamond-back terrapin. This handsome little reptile is not only delicious in soups and stews but is especially recommended as an internal lubricant for the creaky joints of the aged. The old Chinese who can afford to eat terrapin occasionally, and who has in his medicine chest a bit of dried sea horse and a couple of dried lizards, feels that his health problems are well cared for.

There are a number of restaurants in Chinatown; some are very poor, and some are very good. In a few the tourist trade is discouraged, and only Chinese customers receive the best in food and service. In many, notably Tung-Sai, at Park and Mulberry Streets, Hang Far Low, in Pell Street, and the Port Arthur and the Chinese Rathskeller, in Mott Street, the food is superlative. Tung-Sai, which is housed in a building that in prohibition times was occupied by Papa Minetti's famous speakeasy, is a newcomer by Chinatown standards. It was opened in 1942 by Shavey Lee, who runs an insurance agency and other enterprises, and is also the unofficial mayor of Chinatown. The Port Arthur is the oldest restaurant in the quarter; it was opened in 1904 by members of the Ho family which still owns it. Many famous feasts have been held at the Port Arthur; old-timers in Chinatown still like to talk about the great banquet given there in 1906 to celebrate the signing of a truce by the Hip Sing and On Leong tongs. The chefs worked for days to prepare the scores of dishes, and the guests ate steadily for hour after hour. In honor of the occasion Tom Lee, chief of the On Leongs, mayor of Chinatown, deputy sheriff of New York County, and protector of the gambling houses, drank 107 mugs of rice wine —and then walked home, leaning only a little heavier than usual on the shoulders of his two bodyguards. Incidentally, the truce lasted just two days, about as long as Tom Lee's hangover.

The tongs which waged violent warfare in the streets of Chinatown for some twenty-five years were largely responsible for the quarter's reputation as a wicked and dangerous place. In the old days these organizations were little more than rackets, principally concerned with gambling, opium and slave girls. To protect their operations, and to enforce their edicts, they employed "salaried soldiers," or professional killers, and recruited bands of *boo how doy*, or fighting men, from among their own members. Like chop suey, the tong is of American origin; the first was organized about 1860 in the California gold fields near Marysville. They spread rapidly, and within a decade dominated every Chinese settlement in the United States. The On Leongs were the first to gain a foothold in New York, and for almost fifteen years held a virtual monopoly of Chinatown's underworld activities.

The Hip Sings ran a few small fan-tan games, but were not much of a menace to the On Leongs until about 1900, when Mock Duck, a fat, moon-faced little man and a fighter of great courage and resource, ousted one Wong Get from the leadership of the tong. Under the new command, the Hip Sings expanded, and Mock Duck soon felt strong enough to demand an equal share of the gambling privileges. When the On Leongs laughed at his presumptuousness, Mock Duck formed an alliance with a small tong called the Four Brothers and declared war.

With the aid of his *boo how doy*, whom he led in person, and salaried soldiers imported from San Francisco, Mock Duck succeeded in driving the On Leongs from Pell Street. For several years Doyers Street was a neutral area and a favorite battleground; it became Hip Sing territory when the closing of the arcade isolated it from Mott Street. When Mock Duck retired and left Chinatown in 1918, the Hip Sings were at least as powerful as the On Leongs. The Four Brothers, and a few other small tongs which had tried to muscle into Chinatown, had been frozen out.

Nearly all of the tong wars were the result of disputes over the gambling houses, but the most sanguinary of all, the great war of 1909–1910 in which the comedian Ah Hoon was killed, was fought over a slave girl named Bow Kum, or Little Sweet Flower. Bow Kum had been purchased for three thousand dollars in the San Francisco slave market by Low Hee Tong, a high official of the Hip Sings, but he neglected to marry her, and after he had lived with her for four years she was "rescued" by the San Francisco police and placed in a Christian mission. Tchin Len, a member of the On Leong Tong, married her and brought her to New York, whereupon Low Hee Tong made a formal demand for the repayment of the three thousand dollars which the girl had cost him. Tchin Len refused to pay, and was upheld by the supreme council of the On Leongs. The Hip Sings immediately raised the red flag of the highbinder atop their tong house in Pell Street, and the salaried soldiers and the *boo how doy* oiled their pistols and their shirts of chain mail and sharpened their knives and hatchets. On August 15, 1909, Bow Kum was stabbed to death in Tchin Len's house at No. 17 Mott Street, and a few days later a boardinghouse in which several Hip Sing soldiers were lodged was dynamited. The war continued until late in 1910, when a truce was arranged by a committee of forty prominent Chinese appointed by the Chinese Minister in Washington. Fifty men had been killed, several times that number wounded, and much property destroyed by bombs.

The last of the tong flareups occurred in 1924, but only a few men were killed in Chinatown; most of the victims were Chinese who had migrated to Brooklyn and the Bronx. Since then the tongs have lived in peace. They dominate the business and social life of Chinatown, as they did fifty years ago, and the Hip Sings are still supreme in Pell and Doyers Streets and the On Leongs in Mott and Bayard Streets. But the tongs have been transformed into civic and mutual benefit associations akin to Kiwanis and Rotary; they co-operate with each other, and with the American Legion, the churches, the missions, and other groups, in all movements for the welfare of their members and of Chinatown in general. As a result of all this good will, Chinatown has become one of the most orderly and law-abiding communities in New York.

Approximately ten thousand Chinese are crowded into a few blocks on Doyers, Pell, Mott and Bayard Streets, with an overflow in Canal, Park, Worth and Mulberry Streets and the Bowery. About 80 per cent are single men of an average age of fifty-one years, many of whom still have wives and children in China. The population of the quarter is doubled on week ends, when Chinese from New Jersey, Brooklyn, the Bronx, Long Island and Connecticut flock into Chinatown to visit friends and relatives. They spend the long days gossiping, playing fan-tan and mah-jongg, and sipping innumerable cups of tea. Much of the talk has to do with China politics, and of the great day when a new revolution will overturn the regime of Mao Tse-Tung, for Chinatown is 99 per cent anti-Communist.

Few of New York's Chinese go to church, either on week ends or at other times; both Protestants and Catholics have been trying to Christianize Chinatown for many years, but their success has not been overwhelming. The Chinese are not easy to convert. Though most of them have never seen China, they cling tenaciously to a culture that was ancient when the white man was a savage.

WALL STREET:
Men and Money

GENE M. BROWN

A slight, purposeful old lady stands in front of the Roman temple at the corner of Wall and Nassau Streets that formerly housed the United States Sub-Treasury. She wears an ancient bonnet skewered by a massive black hatpin, and laughs to herself as if enjoying some private joke. "Here, read this and make your fortune," she quavers, thrusting a pamphlet into your hand. Its title has intrigued passers-by for years: "How to Get Rich Quick." You open it and read how He, "though He was rich, yet for your sakes became poor."

The old lady is part of the sidewalk show on Wall Street, a narrow, six-block canyon overshadowed by towering buildings. It is the counting-house of the American nation. Today, this makes it the financial heart of the free world. From nightfall to daybreak, Wall Street is deserted, except by policemen and the scrubwomen who clean its offices. From Saturday noon until Monday morning it is mainly left to sightseeing tourists and resident pigeons. But on weekdays, from nine to five, Wall Street collects a population greater than that of many large cities. Bankers, brokers, lawyers, insurance companies, and a vast force of clerical workers crowd its buildings. Evangelists preach on its sidewalks, unheeded by the throngs that scurry by. Taxis, armored trucks, and private cars make the canyon ring with the din of their incessant honking. In the great domain of American business, Wall Street is a separate realm—a society that has its individual history, unwritten laws, and particular language.

Wall Street is the only thoroughfare in New York that emerges from a graveyard to end in a river. It begins at Broadway, opposite Trinity Church. Erected more than a century ago, Trinity is the third church to be built on its site, and it remains a quiet sanctuary in the citadel of high finance. Clerks and office girls flock there during lunch hour. Some attend the daily organ recital, but on warm days many more eat box lunches amidst the crumbling gray tombstones of the churchyard. "Sitting on Gravestones Is Not Allowed," a sign warns. But pigeons can't read, and apparently the pretty girls won't. Many of Trinity's tombstones antedate the Revolution. One marks the grave of William Bradford, who set up New York's first printing press and gave the city its first newspaper. Bradford died in 1752, well past his ninetieth year.

Across Broadway from Trinity, the massive buildings of the First National Bank and the Irving Trust Company form the gateway to Wall Street. A short block to the east, New Street cuts into Wall at a sharp angle. Here is the building of the New York Stock Exchange, which has an ornate, pillared façade on Broad Street. The Stock Exchange is the financial heart of the nation, and it has transformed trading into a science. It is the direct descendant of a group of men who met daily under an old buttonwood tree on Wall Street to trade in securities. On May 17, 1792, twenty-four of these traders formed an association, binding themselves to obey certain rules and to charge a specified commission for executing orders placed by non-members.

Trading on the Exchange today is a highly formalized, complicated activity. To become a member, one has to buy a "seat"—probably the most costly chair in the world, since it has no physical existence. The main trading floor is a huge, domed hall, with a grove of "trading posts" which are a modern equivalent for buttonwood trees. From the visitors' gallery, the floor makes a bewildering impression. Men are running about without apparent direction. Clacking noises issue from two great call boards at the north and south ends of the hall. There is a constant flashing of the ticker tape on large screens, recording the latest transactions. Every company listing its securities on the Exchange receives a coded designation, and to read the ticker you have to master the Exchange's codebook. Stocks are dealt in only in lots of one hundred shares. So, for example, when the mystifying symbol "X38 ¼" is flashed on the screen, brokers on the floor know that one hundred shares of United States Steel common stock has just been sold at a price of $38.25 per share.

There have been times, in a boiling market, when the ticker has failed to keep up with current transactions. This happened on October 29, 1929, when the stock market crashed. The panic of that day spread from the trading floor across the country, and subsequent liquidation plunged the nation into the Great Depression. People still recall the suicides of ruined speculators, the destitution of families formerly prosperous, and haggard men selling apples on street corners.

Wall Street recalls the elder Morgan, who died in 1913, as the most powerful figure in American financial history, the master-mind who formed the nation's first "billion-dollar trust," the United States Steel Corporation. On the second floor of the building on the corner of Broad and Wall Streets occupied by J. P. Morgan & Company, the founder's office is still preserved as it was during his lifetime. His desk is an ornately carved affair of solid mahogany, its leather top so worn and scarred that only a little gold tooling still remains visible. Behind the desk is a grandfather's clock originally owned by Benjamin Franklin. The walls of the office are dotted with framed canceled checks, souvenirs of historic transactions undertaken by the House of Morgan. One of these, for two hundred million dollars, represents the first loan made by the United States to Great Britain in 1917.

Wall Street's most sanguinary episode took place outside the building of J. P. Morgan & Company. September 16, 1920, began like any other work day. When the familiar bell of Trinity Church rang out the noon hour, office workers rose from their desks to pour out into the street. Nobody paid particular attention to a bright-red, horse-drawn wagon parked in front of the Assay Office, opposite the Morgan building. At one minute after noon the wagon exploded. Cast-iron slugs hurtled in all directions. The blast shook the entire district. The final count showed thirty-three people dead and four hundred injured. The act of criminal terrorism was attributed to anarchists or communists. That night, batteries of searchlights kept the financial district brightly illuminated. Infantrymen guarded the Assay Office, where nine hundred million dollars in gold was stored. Fearing a revolutionary plot, the city authorities deployed squads of police at strategic points. The Board of Estimate posted a reward of ten thousand dollars for the apprehension and arrest of the persons who set off the explosion.

The reward has never been collected. The Morgan building still bears the scars of the explosion.

Across Wall Street from the Morgan building, the colonnaded Roman temple that formerly housed the Sub-Treasury is now known as Federal Hall Memorial. It occupies the site of Federal Hall where, on April 30, 1789, George Washington was inaugurated as first President of the United States.

The financial functions performed by the old Sub-Treasury are now carried out by the Federal Reserve Bank of New York. This institution occupies a huge building, resembling an impregnable fortress, located at 33 Liberty Street, a few blocks north of Wall Street. In terms of assets, the Federal Reserve Bank of New York is the largest bank in the world. But it does no business with the general public; it is exclusively a bank for banks, which maintain deposits and checking accounts with it. If the First National Bank of Hohokus requires cash to meet demands by its depositors for Christmas buying, it writes a check on the Federal Reserve Bank and secures the money, which is withdrawn from its account. And when you write a check your bank gets the cash to replace the money it gave you by writing, in turn, a check on the Federal Reserve Bank.

If you take a guided tour of the Federal Reserve Bank, you will notice that the building is, in effect, planned as a fortress. Go down to the "E" level, for example. Once outside the elevator, eighty-five feet below the street and sixty-five feet below sea level, you walk into the "Security Corridor" which leads to a brightly lit vault. Two guards open the vault, and six men escort you into a world of solid gold. More than six hundred million dollars' worth of gold bars are stored here for foreign governments. On the right is a long row of cells, each given to some foreign institution, such as the Bank of England, the Bank of France, the Bank of Belgium. When England, for instance, wants to pay France one million dollars, it instructs the Federal Reserve Bank to move gold bars to that amount from the Bank of England's cell to that of the Bank of France.

Returning to Wall Street, continue eastward through the crowded canyon. Shafts of sunlight now and again penetrate to its floor, making the sidewalks a surrealist chessboard of shadows, light, and motion. The tall and weather-scarred buildings between which you walk in narrow confinement house many of the financial world's most famous institutions. The Bank of the Manhattan Company's stone façade announces that the bank has been located on its present site since 1799, when New York's population totaled sixty thousand. This institution was originally chartered as The Manhattan Company, for the purpose of providing the city with water mains and a central reservoir. Aaron Burr, one of its founders, adroitly had written into the company's charter a provision permitting it to "employ its surplus funds in banking." This provision would have been bitterly contested by Burr's great enemy, Alexander Hamilton, Secretary of the Treasury, had he been aware of it. Some water mains were laid in 1800, and eventually the company distributed water to two thousand homes. But it was the Bank of the Manhattan Company, still doing business at 40 Wall Street, its original location, that fulfilled Aaron Burr's ambitious dream.

In the early years of the young American republic, the wharf at the foot of Wall Street, on the East River, received all the coffee imported into the country. Coffee houses, or taverns, multiplied in this district, the most celebrated being the Tontine Coffee House, erected in 1792 on the northwest corner of Wall and Water Streets, which for two generations was intimately identified with the business and financial history of the city. Descendants of many early coffee importers are still doing business near the Wall Street river front, which is never without the pervasive aroma of roasting coffee.

The history of Wall Street parallels the history of the nation. Its name records the original wood palisade built by Dutch colonists in 1653 to safeguard the town of New Amsterdam from the marauding expeditions of Indians settled on the northern portion of Manhattan Island. Today, Wall Street remains, in a world of economic disorder, the strongest fortification of free enterprise.

LOOK, MA—REAL GRASS!
(*Central Park*)

GEORGE SESSIONS PERRY

The most expensive adornment on earth is not the Hope Diamond, which isn't even in the running, but New York City's gracious, sprightly Central Park. Anything good costs more in New York than anywhere else. This park, which is the queen of the world's finest park system, would, if put under the hammer, bring enough to repay the United

States Treasury many times over what it spent for Louisiana, Nebraska, Iowa, the Dakotas, Montana, most of Minnesota and parts of Colorado and Wyoming. It could also, at the same time, pick up the check for Florida, California, Nevada, Utah, Arizona, New Mexico, the Hawaiian Islands, Puerto Rico, Guam, the Philippines and the Virgin Islands.

After duly scratching its head, the New York City tax office has reached the conclusion that, under present conditions, the Park could be peddled for something like six hundred thousand dollars an acre. In it, there are about 840 acres. If you can make that come out very far from half a billion dollars, your adding machine needs a vacation. Were apartment houses built as thickly and as tall in the Park as elsewhere on Manhattan Island, the Park could handily domicile the populations of Austin, Texas, or Springfield, Illinois, or all the citizens of the State of Nevada.

And yet the people of New York City, whose government, just like any other, sorely needs the money, almost never feel an urge to sell the Park. Indeed, when somebody does, as did one of the Oyster Bay Roosevelts in 1904, they give him all manner of dirty looks and back talk.

Central Park is both an altar and a refuge. It was built, like many others, in the brave hope of compensating an actual aching vacuum in human experience. In this regard, Central Park is the grandiose symbol of the front yard each New York child hasn't got. On this island where people live in the confining interstices of steel and stone columns, the Park serves as a reminder of what the earth is really like before it is paved, pressed into brick or smelted into metal. To hundreds of thousands of New Yorkers, the Park is like an old and fiercely personal love song that was being played at a beautiful and telling moment in their lives. To still other hundreds of thousands of adults, it is a beloved part of their childhood.

Each year twenty million people visit, react to and on the Park. On any fine spring Sunday, one hundred thousand people will visit its altogether charming little Zoo. And, through some sort of benign alchemy, New York's elbows are somewhat blunted as they enter the Park—just as, in the old days in the West, when people entered an amiable household, they left their hats and guns at the front door.

Central Park's southern extremity, hardly a gem's throw from Tiffany's, nestles among the towers of some of the world's finest hotels. Here the Park is visibly a fantasy in which children romp and lovers coo and old folk doze in the sun. Ladies take afternoon spins in victorias driven by coachmen with stove-pipe hats and pulled by horses that have long since learned to read traffic signals. Younger people go cantering along the bridle paths, and their juniors, balloons in hand and high in peanut content, disport themselves on bicycles, skates, in pony carts or on the Carrousel. Other little ones, coming upon the Park's indestructible metal "Keep Off" signs, joyously wrest them from the earth and employ them as tomahawks in chopping down the shrubbery.

At the Reservoir virile health-seekers, whose eyes have seen the glory of Bernarr Macfadden, march around the mile-and-three-quarter cinder path which encompasses this billion-gallon tub. Here boxers, like the tortured dancers in a surrealist ballet, lash out against the imaginary Furies with which they are locked in battle. A portly gentleman, too game simply to grow a beard, comes chuffing along wearing a knitted hood designed to reduce jowls and wattles. Others, less wattle-conscious, address themselves to handsome meals either at the Zoo cafeteria or at the Tavern-on-the-Green.

A little group of keenly interested female citizens is happily reprimanding a Zoo keeper for weaning a baby sea lion, as the latter energetically yawps his own disapprobation. Elsewhere a grammar-school girl is quietly feeding a rubber ball to Sally, the camel, as still another visitor treats Rose, the lady hippo, to an unscheduled snack consisting of an old brief case. In the Zoo kitchen a joint of beef for the bears is simmering merrily away alongside the sweet potatoes being boiled for the monkeys' lunch. If the fleet's in, the Lake is dotted with sailors in rowboats. Artists are busily sketching away, and amateur photographers are taking dead aim and firing. The air is enlivened with kites and model planes. If it's evening, there may be dancing on the Mall, with four thousand couples waltzing by the light of the moon.

Perhaps this scene approximates the vision which editor William Cullen Bryant had back in the 1840's, when he said, in the columns of the Evening Post, that New York's people ought to have somewhere they could go to find solitude. This made sense to the public. After the usual municipal tugging and hauling, the Park's present location, between Fifth and Eighth avenues and running from 59th Street to 110th, was decided upon. The city paid $7,389,727.96 for the land. Next it had to fight a guerrilla war with numerous squatters, who until then had raised pigs on the Park site and engaged in other lucrative callings such as moonshining and counterfeiting.

In 1857 a public competition for a two-thousand-dollar prize was held to try to find a general plan on which the Park could be built. The prize went to Calvert Vaux and Frederick Law Olmsted. With these men in charge, work was begun. Three thousand men, using carloads of explosives, began blasting out rock and grading and filling. Well before General Beauregard paid his respects to Fort Sumter, New Yorkers were already enjoying skating and band concerts in the Park. The Civil War came and went without substantially interfering with the work on the Park, where, in the interval, fourteen imported English sparrows, which were subsequently to populate the entire nation with their pesky offspring, were turned loose.

Then, in 1868, the Tweed political machine took over New York and filled Park jobs with every sort of inefficient pensioner. The Park languished until, in 1934, La Guardia's Fusion ticket won and took over the city. Robert Moses, a Republican, who'd already set the woods afire as State Commissioner of Parks and as Secretary of State in the Democratic administration of Governor Al Smith, became the City Park Commissioner. He came on the stage, like the hero of a children's story, at a time when the city's need for the Park was at its greatest.

At the time Moses took over the city's park system, Central Park's Zoo was both literally and figuratively ratty. Moses' exterminators killed more than two hundred thousand rats in a single week. The cages were so insubstantial that the lion keepers toted shotguns in case their charges should tear the bars down and begin gorging themselves on the taxpayers' kiddies. The Park was overrun with venders selling unsafe food to the children. Then there was the Central Park Casino, which had become a luxury night club where Jimmy Walker had been wont to cavort.

Moses decided the Casino was of no use to any but the privileged, and that it must go. He chased off the venders and replaced them with reputable concessionaires. With a good deal of WPA labor and the expenditure of a couple of million dollars, he rebuilt the Zoo and made it a thing of sanitary and highly useful beauty. Today Central Park is probably the hardest used and, in view of that hard use, the best kept large municipal park in the world.

To protect the Park and the lives of the people who use it, some 136 policemen, working out of the Twenty-second Precinct station house, are assigned to the Park. Inevitably, special situations arise which impose intolerable pressure upon the rules. If, for example, there are not enough places for ball games, when a number of groups of boys are standing around waiting to play, the Park Department is faced with a serious dilemma. If a policeman chases a group of boys off a passive area or out of the Park, he knows he is automatically forming an or-

LOOK, MA—REAL GRASS!

ganized band of anti-cop, anti-Park boys who can do all sorts of mischief without getting caught. The only answer then, when the overflow of ballplayers seriously exceeds the facilities at hand, is more active areas. Reluctantly Moses surrenders another few patches of grass.

During the depression, the going was especially rough for the police, for many homeless people sought refuge in the Park. One man carried all his worldly goods in a large baby buggy. At night he let the dashboard down, lowered the back of the seat, crawled in, covered himself with a rubber sheet and pulled the buggy's hood over his head, thus existing in something less than total discomfort. When one of these homeless people could get a wild duck off one of the ponds or lakes or could catch a nice fish out of one of these bodies of water, he built a fire, cooked it and ate it.

But while the police struggle, on the tactical level, to prevent the destruction of the Park, they would inevitably be defeated except for Commissioner Moses. Moses, working on the strategy level, surrounded Central Park with a veritable Maginot Line of intercepting and diversionary recreation areas and swimming pools. Beginning with the outside limits of narrow Manhattan Island, he lined the banks of the Hudson and East rivers with inviting greensward. By luring those with time on their hands to visit the riverside parks, he prevents tens of thousands of New Yorkers from ever starting in the direction of Central Park. There are also many smaller intervening play and rest areas to entice the parkward-bound into pausing there instead. But even after the most persistent have reached the Park itself, Moses doesn't give up. All around the perimeter, and just inside the Park, are relatively indestructible traps: active areas, floored not with sod, but with such permanent materials as asphalt and concrete, to beckon the young and appallingly energetic into games of volleyball or whatever.

Another menace to the Park is the insistent generosity of some of its well-wishers. There's almost always some group wanting to present the Park with a large, durable and expensive object, usually statuary, which Moses feels he has to decline; some of the proffered statues are monstrosities and all take up valuable space. On the other hand, except for the generosity of "angels," the Zoo would have a considerably sparser animal population.

Most famous of gifts to the Park is the Obelisk, better-known as Cleopatra's Needle. On it are a few hieroglyphs inscribed by the pharaoh whose daughter discovered Moses (the Biblical one) in the bulrushes. It was a present to this country from Ismail, the khedive of

Egypt, though it was William H. Vanderbilt who paid to have it brought over.

Most of the busts and figures in the Park commemorate poets, statesmen, inventors, military heroes or persons important in local politics and affairs. Only one statue honors an animal: Balto, a sled dog, one of those which fetched antitoxin to Nome, Alaska, back in the '20's, and got it there fast enough to circumvent an epidemic.

Halfway up the Park on the east side is the magnificent Metropolitan Museum of Art, the only outside institution, among innumerable ones that have tried, to set up permanently in business on actual Central Park property.

Until World War I, there was considerable elegance displayed in the Park. Members of the Early Risers Club rode in formal attire, followed by liveried grooms, and gave elaborate dinners which, now and then, a horse or two attended. Some of these feasted fillies almost certainly participated in that pleasing custom which so many Northern parks enjoyed as the '90's began to get gay: In Central Park, with the coming of the first snow, the gentry would call for their cutters and race up the East Drive to McGowan's Tavern, at McGowan's Pass, where the first party to arrive would be served a magnum of champagne on the house.

The feeling of a still older New York is yet alive in the Old Arsenal, now used for Park Department offices, where the militia drilled and stored its shooting irons, and which was doing business in the same spot before the Park came into existence. The murals here have the feeling of old prints, and the little iron spindles that support the banisters at the entrance steps were cast in the image of rifles.

There are the remains of two old forts in the north end of the Park, Fort Fish and Fort Clinton, which were built to repel the British in the War of 1812. To the west of them, there is a blockhouse in which you could still put up a pretty good defense against musket balls and arrows. Also in this same end of the Park are the Harlem Meer, a pretty lake, and the Conservatory Gardens, said to be the finest formal gardens in town. The other flower garden, the Shakespeare, was given its name in honor of the three hundredth anniversary of the Bard's death, and it was hoped to try to raise in it every flower mentioned in his work.

Yet for all the splendidly tailored and stage-managed physical properties of the Park—its score of lakes, streams and ponds, its seventy thousand trees, its four hundred thousand man-planted shrubs—it is still primarily people, how they act and what they feel when they come there. The Park changes not only with the seasonal procession, when, in the winter, ice skating replaces roller skating, but with the passing minutes of each day.

In the morning, say around nine thirty, the Park crowd is perhaps at its youngest. Buggy-borne babies, as well as their slightly older preschool brothers and sisters, are taking the sun. A little later, scores of chaperoned groups of children are charging about on this or that official school outing—something that has to do with the huge, glacially exposed and fossil-rich rocks or with plants or animals, or, conceivably, just for fun. The crowd is most numerous from one to three in the afternoon. It is a little weary at five-fifteen, relaxed in half an hour and bold by nightfall, when thousands of lovers make their appearance.

Then, as the evening passes, that nether side which any city has, and which inevitably finds expression in its parks late at night, begins to manifest itself. Because New York's police are extremely efficient, these manifestations are reasonably well controlled, yet the inherent tensions of New York still show their ugly, tortured faces in the huge, night-hidden Park. For perhaps no other city's nerves are as ragged by the time night comes as are those of New York, since no city is more crowded or more overstimulated. Nowhere is the pace so fast or the competition so keen as here where the heavyweight championship is daily fought in thousands of lines of human endeavor. Hundreds of thousands of its people are not, in one or another respect that is important to them, making the grade.

They come to the Park at night to escape from their cubicles and, if possible, from themselves. One miserable soul, driven to desperation by the agony of loneliness and frustration, may explode into a fit of sadism and slash an unknown passer-by. Elsewhere, off in the dark, another kind of defeated person lurks, watching a boy and girl make love, and will, at a propitious moment, grab the girl's purse and dissolve into the darkness. Derelicts, besotted and homeless, crawl into the bushes to live out the night somehow. Carefully avoiding the police, prostitutes ply their dreary trade. A would-be rapist pounces on a passing figure—and if he is unlucky enough to have tackled a policeman on duty in women's clothes, as they sometimes masquerade, gets hauled off to jail. A woman, in despair, goes to the reservoir to jump in, finds it fenced above her reach, walks on—another place. The eyes of muggers watch constantly for victims. The very darkness seems drenched with evil and defeat.

Then with the arrival of the magically cleansing dawn, there comes the first sight of New York's controlled and plausible, freshly washed daytime face. There is the healthy bustle of the early walkers, the invigorating sight of handsome men and women galloping along on spirited horses through the spanking new morning. Then come children with kites, with lunches, with mammas or papas or nurses, with bright eyes and happy, expectant faces. And now the Park comes into fresh and dewy bloom. Everyone feels better than usual, expecting every sort of pleasant adventure to occur, since they're on an outing in the beautiful, big, wonder-filled Park.

EMPIRE STATE BUILDING

The world's tallest building has evoked diverse reactions and utterances, none more remarkable than that of blind and deaf Helen Keller. With her supreme imagination she described what she "saw" on her visit to the greatest manmade peak.

A Romantic Edifice

Standing there 'twixt earth and sky, I saw a romantic edifice wrought by human brains and hands that is to the burning eye of the sun a rival luminary. I saw it stand erect and serene in the midst of storm and tumult of elemental commotion. I heard the hammer of Thor ring when the shaft began to rise upward. I saw the unconquerable steel, the flash of testing flames, the swordlike rivets. I heard the steel drills in pandemonium. I saw countless skilled workers welding together that mighty symmetry. I looked upon the marvel of frail yet indomitable hands that lifted the tower to its dominating height.

—HELEN KELLER

THE OPTICAL CENTER

CHIANG YEE

Here the noted "Silent Traveller," Chiang Yee, a Chinese painter and writer, gives us another fresh perspective on this world-famous structure and symbol.

The statistics about this building make me feel dizzy: 102 storeys; a height of 1,250 feet from the street level to the tip of the mooring mast, which is covered with glass, chrome-nickel-steel and aluminium, and

THE OPTICAL CENTER

illuminated from within; a rentable area of 2,158,000 square feet which can house over 25,000 people. To me, the Empire State Building seemed to stretch out its invisible strings, like a giant maypole, to hold on to me wherever I went on and around Manhattan Island. The further I went the more prominent it became; all the other skyscrapers are subordinate to it, though one other is almost as high. It is the optical center of the skyline: and New York's skyline is its most characteristic feature. It is what you immediately think of when you recall the city.

To climb up a mountain of more than a thousand feet requires determination and energy and brings the satisfaction of achievement. I anticipated a big thrill in the lift of the Empire State Building as it soared from the first to the eighty-sixth floor; but I did not get it. The lift is so well-constructed that there is no vibration or noise, only a necessity to swallow every few seconds to clear one's ears. Apart from that I should not have known we were climbing if the indicator had not moved from one to thirty-four, then to fifty, sixty, seventy, and so on. At the top I was rather concerned at the number of people; I had the sensation that we might make the building top heavy; but I was assured that the floor could accommodate five hundred persons.

From the roof of the Astor Hotel I had thought cars were beetles and people ants: from here they all looked like dust. The surrounding buildings together with the infinitesimal people and things stuck up from the ground like something familiar. What was it? Eventually I got it. Bamboo-shoots in a Chinese grove in early spring.

A large group of visitors, mostly young, were rushing from one corner to the other, to look through the telescopes which a nickle will operate for a specified time. The youngsters shouted out what they had seen and the girls, I noticed, were noiser than the boys. Cameras were clicking on every side. A group of girls were lined up to have their photo taken by a professional cameraman who clung alarmingly high up the wall of the writing room for the purpose. In the high wind, the girls' long hair was blown or tugged in all directions and they tried vainly to control it with their hands. Their varied gestures were charming, and I was delighted at the sight of so many graceful hands and arms, white, pinkish or brown, mingling with golden, red, or dark hair. I am greatly interested in ballet dancing, particularly in the movements of hands and arms. No choreographer could devise a ballet better than that which I then witnessed. The chattering and giggling of the girls provided the music. But the cameraman seemed to find his task troublesome.

Presently I moved on up to the 102nd floor. Here the observation platform is much smaller and can only accommodate one hundred persons at a time. The visibility was so good that everything appeared as clear as from the eighty-sixth floor. More people seemed to want to come up, so I presently descended to the first observatory again. On the way I overheard the elevator man tell a woman that about two million visitors from all parts of the world came up this building each year. "We have no competition," he continued, "we are quite contented." I was interested in his use of the word 'contented.' Do the members of the company who run the building feel contented? Before it was built perhaps the owners of the Flatiron Building felt contented. Surely someone will now try to erect a building even higher than the Empire State? A friend assured me that this is unlikely, as already the offices in the higher floors have been difficult to let, and with the increase in flying, very tall buildings are considered dangerous. Yet I cannot help feeling that someone will try.

In the lounge people were indulging in the immemorial habit of collecting souvenirs. If only half of the yearly two millions of visitors buy a souvenir each, mass production methods are justified! And I saw some visitors buying more than one item. Picture postcards depicting the building, and posted on the spot, seemed to be the favourite form. Outside the refreshment room, in a large space filled with chairs and tables and glassed in all round against wind and rain, was a thick book on a table and a queue of visitors waited to sign their names in it. What a wise provision! How many thousands of defacing penknife scrawls it must prevent! For it is a natural human instinct to leave one's name in a notable place one has visited. The Empire State Building protects its walls by means of this book. How many volumes have already been filled, and what does the company do with them?

I went to lean on the balustrade. The half-oval-shaped crest of the Chrysler Building showed up most distinctively, being the closest. To the south three downtown skyscrapers rose against the sun. Central Park, which I had thought of as a vast and varied area, was revealed to me as a small lacquer tea-tray, inlaid with green and bluish jade, to represent trees and lakes. I took pleasure in the childish fancy that for once I was higher than any winged creature. One or two white seagulls, circling over some lower buildings, did not look like real birds in flight but like ornamental ones of white marble in fixed positions of suspense. Occasional bursts of laughter from the lounge were like unearthly voices near the gate of Heaven. The warm sun in this spot sheltered from the wind 'inclined my eyelids' and the haze in the distance contracted the horizon. The long, slightly twisted, white-silk-like

Hudson River had no end. I murmured to myself how right our T'ang poet Li P'o was when he wrote the line *'Huang Ho Chih Shui T'ien Shan Lai,'* *'The waters of the Yellow River come from Heaven!'* as he gazed at the Huang Ho from a lofty pavilion, or again: *'Wei Chien Ch'ang Chiang T'ien Chi Liu,'* *'I can only see the Yangtse River flowing near the edge of Heaven!'* Both these lines could well describe what I saw of the Hudson River now.

My thoughts drifted to our own ancient pavilions. In a world history of architecture little needs to be said about the ancient buildings of China, for no important ruins of palaces or mansions are extant except the towers along the world-renowned Great Wall, built in the third century B.C. Most of our ancient palaces or mansions were not built of stone, and even the hardest woods do not last much longer than a thousand years. Nevertheless, there are clear and apparently authentic records in our ancient books of a good many lofty pavilions. It is said that in 115 B.C. the Emperor Wu of Han Dynasty felt well satisfied with his peaceful reign and desired to prolong his life. On the advice of his astrologers he ordered a pavilion to be built and sent his ministers up to wait upon the supernatural beings who could deliver to him from Heaven some elixir to prolong his life. The Emperor called his pavilion 'Tung T'ien Lou' or 'Pavilion for Reaching Heaven.' Another tall building, 'Fang Ch'en Lou' or 'Pavilion of Fragrant Dust' is said to have been built about A.D. 335 by the notorious, short-lived and self-titled Emperor Shih Hu. It had a height of four hundred feet, and was decorated with silks, pearls, precious stones and many bells which rang in the wind. The Emperor ordered several hundred men to grind precious gems mixed with scents into minute particles and blow them down from the pavilion so that his subjects should smell the fragrance and be happy in their Capital; hence the name. It was a poetic name and a romantic act. How far would the scented particles have flown had they been blown from the top of the Empire State Building?

SINS AND SECRETS OF TIMES SQUARE

ALLEN CHURCHILL

"Times Square today," a writer said recently, "is like a raddled beauty who has squandered her loveliness and knows it will never come back. She sits on a bar stool in a soiled satin dress, strings of blondined hair brushing the messy make-up on her cheeks, her hand shaking as she gets the drinks to her face. That's about all you can say about her now. She gets the drinks to her face."

Yet she had it once. Until twenty years ago Times Square was practically the Gay White Way. Some of the greatest attractions the theater has ever known played there. The New Amsterdam, on 42nd Street, housed that greatest of all Follies, the 1918 show that starred Marilyn Miller, Will Rogers, W. C. Fields, and Eddie Cantor. A decade later Maurice Chevalier made his American debut on the Amsterdam Roof, and while the Frenchman sang, *Abie's Irish Rose* ticked off another night of its fabulous run at the Republic down the street.

But then the theatrical district began moving uptown from 42nd, and soon it became easy to differentiate between Times Square and Broadway. Today the difference is even sharper. Broadway is the Metropolitan, Sardi's, Lindy's, the legitimate theater, the picture palaces, the better bars. Times Square has what's left, to make a neon wilderness, a hardened artery. As such it has a strange personality. It's a small area and in it probably can be found every known vice. Yet it is not a place into which the average citizen can leap for a night of stimulating dissipation, then leap out again.

Truth is, Times Square lost its last uniqueness for the New Yorker with the departure of burlesque, which Fiorello La Guardia drove out of town in the late 'thirties. La Guardia ended something else, too. The fiery Fiorello hated prostitution with a fierce hatred, and of all the reforms he imposed on the Big Town his ban on this has stuck best. Which is not to say there is no prostitution on Times Square today— for there is. But it is seldom the overt, streetwalking type. Indeed, it is typical of the change in Times Square as well as in the town that the bold, painted girls have been supplanted by a different type of hustler. It's a sad commentary, but the block between Seventh and Eighth, where the girls once wiggled their wares, is now known to the police as Queens County.

One curious thing about Times Square is that there are few bars on it. The sinister stretch of street between Seventh and Eighth has only two, one a chaste Childs. Broadway and Seventh Avenues between 42nd and 47th also have few. Indeed, Times Square's most typical bars are on the side streets branching from it. There are others along Eighth Avenue—but even so, it is hard to find any customary liveliest spot in Times Square on a given night. The reason is the ever-shifting complexion of the area. One week this bar will be the noisy, teeming one.

Next week another will be the place. This state of affairs exists because the true denizens of Times Square—girls, bookies, dope peddlers, grifters—engage in a never-ending struggle to find soft spots in the laws the authorities have arrayed against them.

Getting a bar or cabaret license in New York means agreeing to some of the stiffest regulations known to man. Some are downright ridiculous, but all are enforceable. So the girl who prowls Times Square prowls ceaselessly in search of a place where she can sit alone at the bar. When she finds one, she tells other girls. The place fills with both girls and customers. Then the police take notice, or the Board of Health finds a case of venereal disease that may stem from a pick-up there. The police warn the owner. The owner chases the girls. The girls look for another soft spot.

The shifting atmosphere of Times Square night life, with its uncertainties and changing spots of popularity, makes things hard for the regular prostitute, who, no matter how young, always seems to have a mind like a cash register. "It's ratty around here," one informed a reporter the other day. "New York's the only place I can't make a good living. The cops won't give me a break and the bartenders are scared. There's so few girls hustling that men don't know what to do when you give 'em the eye. When one does stop, people gather around and watch you proposition him, like it was a show or something. I say, shove it. I'm going back to Chi."

Facing such obstacles, Times Square harlots tend to fall into two rough groups. One might be called the semipros, to which belongs the social prostitute who enjoys an evening of drinking, dancing, or necking before taking a man to her room. For this last he must pay at least fifteen dollars, which is enough to keep the girl in nylons, contraceptives, and drug-store meals—all she asks of life.

The real prostitute, her mind beamed on money, usually works the second- and third-rate hotels of the Times Square district and its side streets. Living in one, she has a network of connections with night clerks, elevator operators, and bell boys in the others. Every hour or so she checks with them by phone. If anyone has asked for a girl, she hustles over. For this she, too, asks a minimum of fifteen dollars, from which her pimp in the hotel takes a cut.

In addition to girls, Times Square offers diversion in the way of music, movies, and dancing.

Musically the area has taken the same kind of spin it has taken in the sex department. Forty-second Street, where at the New Amsterdam many of Irving Berlin's finest melodies first caressed the ears, now resounds day and night to the latest novelty tunes played endlessly by loudspeakers outside the record shops along the street.

Police are not enthusiastic about the clientele of 42nd Street movies.

"Maybe you get a few nice people," one cop says, "but you don't get many. These houses stay open until four A.M. You get a lot of girls working them. Queers go in to fraternize and riff-raff goes in to sleep. You don't find many connoisseurs."

Nothing better portrays the paradoxical character of Times Square than the fact that the Avalon dancehall, located at the seamiest corner, Seventh Avenue and Forty-second, is a Fellowship Club. This, in case you haven't heard, means it is open only to those over twenty-eight. A sign outside the Avalon prescribes other Fellowship restrictions: No Jitterbugging, No Liquor, it says.

Up Broadway are dancehalls of another type—the dime-a-dance palaces famed in song and story. Most hallowed of the dime-a-dance halls is the Orpheum, at West Forty-sixth Street. In the 'twenties it was a mecca of young bloods from Harvard, Yale, and Princeton, several of whom married Orpheum girls. It's a shock to old-timers to find the Orpheum still popular with college boys, though there have been no spectacular marriages recently. The fact that it is by way of being an institution gives the Orpheum a dignity not possessed by its rivals. Indeed, visiting Broadway dancehalls is not fun. Business on an average night is none-too-good in any, and the male appearing in one is assailed by seductive cries from an embarrassing number of ordinary-looking girls, all attired in bright, slinky gowns. Any feelings of loneliness banished by this attention are not likely to survive the fact that the girls are far more interested in a man's tickets than in his personality. "Gimme your tickets now," the girl says, melting into your arms. "I'll mind them for you."

It may come as a surprise to Times Square's nighttime inhabitants to learn the district has a day—a time when those who should be hunting jobs fill the Forty-second Street movies, when high-school girls and housewives line up in front of the Paramount, when gravel-voiced auctioneers spiel in the novelty stores, when pimply boys ogle the Atomic Exhibit or the side shows at Hubert's, and when legitimate business goes on from nine to five in the office buildings of the area.

Only when the lights come on at night does Times Square begin to possess a personality—a personality dulled at first by the fact that from six until midnight it is filled by crowds hurrying to and from theaters.

But from midnight until 6 A.M. Times Square is itself—a true neon wilderness in the heart of a huge city. Wide-awake while others sleep, it becomes this: the low-keyed conversation of homosexuals meeting on a corner; the frightened shriek of a girl as two sailors begin fighting over her; the 2 A.M. meeting outside the Diamond Horseshoe of the long-stemmed showgirls with their short-stemmed dates; the pale, shabby man in a doorway who may be just standing there or may be passing dope; the muted music of a one-flight-up dancehall; the shadowy progress of a girl inexperienced enough to solicit along the Main Stem.

Indoors the lonesome majority still drinks at bars. The girls have made their attachments for the night and now, for money or for free, will steer the men to rooms. In dancehalls the girls are saying, "Meet me downstairs at four, but be there."

Out on the sidewalks the restaurant cellars vomit up the remains of a day of serving food. In what Runyon called the tubercular light of dawn, as the hulking Department of Sanitation trucks take over, you pause and look around an area that once was glamorous.

And now, instead of glamour, you see garbage cans. . . .

LINDY'S:

Sturgeon Saga of the Main Stem

MEYER BERGER

Lindy the restaurant man served his four millionth filet of herring last week and, in expanding statistical mood, figured that in his Broadway career he has also served some eight hundred thousand pounds of salmon and over six hundred thousand pounds of sturgeon. He grows ecstatic about the far-away places from which his fish are shipped—the sturgeon from Wapikopa in Ontario and from Winnipeg in Manitoba; the salmon from Newfoundland, Nova Scotia and Gaspé; the herring from Newfoundland, Iceland, Scotland and Holland. He has never visited any of these places, being strictly a Broadway character.

Lindy runs a three-million-dollar business from a cavernous old wooden icebox in the basement of his big establishment at 1655 Broadway at 51st Street. He has a smaller—the original—Lindy's at 1626 on the Main Stem. The icebox is probably the most frigid conference chamber in existence. Originally designed to hold meats, it now does double duty. The icebox door is double-padlocked and marked with a "PRIVATE, KEEP OUT" sign. The box itself stands close to eight feet high, and its crowded interior measures, roughly, eight by fifteen feet. It holds a fair-sized fortune in imported chocolates, rare wines, tinned delicacies and boxes of high-priced cigars. A small green-topped table cluttered with order books, market lists and two telephones stands in dead center, under harsh electric lights.

Every morning from 10:30 o'clock until the place upstairs opens for luncheon, Lindy is on one of the phones—sometimes on both at once, because he is not a patient man—ordering lake sturgeon, butter, sea food, meats, fruits, vegetables and berries. These orders come to around a million and a half dollars a year.

Lindy dictates his elaborate menus in the icebox. Miss L., seldom otherwise identified by Lindy or by his staff of 270 hired hands though she has been with him more than twenty years, writes them out. He holds his conferences in the refrigerator, too, a kind of morning council meeting with his chief pastry man, his chief butcher, and the head chef. If they keep rubbing their hands or grabbing at their upper arms occasionally, a little distressed by the cold, Lindy never seems to notice. The icebox roars back into full operation when Lindy ends his conference each morning. The fan's pace—the cold air is fan-forced—is stepped up again as soon as the padlocks are re-snapped.

Then Lindy goes upstairs to shuffle, quick-eyed, from aisle to aisle, directing luncheon service. He has an extraordinary eye for a faulty table setting, and goes purple if a waiter absentmindedly pats down his own hair-do with a bare hand. The culprit is ordered to the wash room immediately.

Lindy is a little blue-eyed man barely five feet six inches in height, his hair all but gone. His spouse, Clara, to whom he has been married thirty-three years, hardly tops five feet. Damon Runyon dubbed them "Mr. and Mrs. Broadway" and immortalized their first—the smaller—establishment in fiction as "Mindy's," a hangout for quaintly named gamblers, rod men, and for famous band leaders, composers, public officials and theatre folk. Actually, the Lindemanns—that's their real name—do not live up to their literary image. They are still filled with the wonder of their hard-won success and seem always murmuringly grateful for it. They try not to show their pride when the restaurant bobs up in a motion picture, or when Fred Allen, on the air, speaks of Lindy as "The Keeper of the Kipper." These tributes are apt to leave them a little misty-eyed, since, like most Broadway folk, they careen a little toward the sentimental side.

Leo Lindemann's father, Joseph, was an itinerant peddler of linens. He traveled among farm folk outside Berlin and because they seldom had cash, he took whatever cast-off clothing they had to barter. Some of this he sold to get supplies for the meager Lindemann table. Some of it, as necessity dictated, was doled out to Lindy. He had come almost to man's estate before he owned a hat, a pair of shoes, a shirt or suit that actually fit him. The food his poor mother prepared was sternly simple. He never dreamed, in his boyhood, that one day he would serve—and eat—dishes that would attract to his table such people as Alfred G. Vanderbilt, Bernard Gimbel, J. Edgar Hoover, Bernard Baruch, Ingrid Bergman, James Roosevelt, Jack Benny, Jimmy Walker and William O'Dwyer, the Hollywood nabobs, the newspaper columnists, and the top men along Broadway's rialto.

The Lindemanns were still poor when Joseph the peddler died in 1909. Lindy was twenty-one then. He had left school at fourteen to go apprentice in a Berlin delicatessen. Day and night he delivered orders, swept floors, and washed dishes for barely enough money to pay the family rent and to supply a thin larder. "There were days," he concedes now, "when, if we didn't starve, we came close." He shipped to the United States in 1913, leaving his mother with relatives. An aunt took him in. He lived with her in 128th Street between Third and Lexington Avenues. By day he was bus boy in the Hotel Marie Antoinette. By night he struggled with English at night school. It came hard, and there is a Berlin trim to his accent even now. Occasionally he mutilates his terms a little. He refers to the murals on his restaurant walls, for example, as "muriels."

Lindy eventually took his basic waiting course at the Hotel Marie Antoinette. He served the hotel staff there, but not paying customers. When he thought he had a modest idea of English he took on as waiter at a few small hasheries, and at Feltman's in Coney Island. In 1914 he latched onto a waiter's job at Gertner's Restaurant at 1446 Broadway. "I was a hustler," he recalls proudly. "Some weeks I made forty to fifty dollars a week." A substantial part of this was kicked back, according to tradition, to the headwaiter. Lindy's customers included the labor leaders Samuel Gompers and William Green, and stars from the near-by Metropolitan Opera House. Mrs. Lindy was Clara Gertner then. Her brother owned the place. She was perched on a telephone book on a high stool behind the cashier's grille.

The Lindys were married in November, 1915. For six years after that he managed a Gertner restaurant on the East Side. His wife was cashier. They had a little flat at 570 West 160th Street, but the job left them little time to spend in it. Clara Lindy's eyes fill when she remembers how she coveted a coffee percolator that glittered in a soap premium window, and how she hoarded coupons until she could own it. She acquired her first set of dishes the same way.

Eight years after he landed, a bewildered greenhorn, Lindy opened his first restaurant, the one Runyon wrote about, at 1626 Broadway. Only one of the three Lindy partners in that venture remains. He is Joe Kramer, a haberdasher, but he keeps invisible. Patrons never see him, nor know about him.

Lindy labored behind the counter cutting spiced meats and pumpernickel, rye bread and rolls. Clara Lindy helped in the kitchen and took cash. Incidentally, most of the recipes for which the place eventually became a coast-to-coast legend were contributed by Clara Lindy. She got them from her mother, and her grandmother. These ancient recipes, somewhat modified, are still Lindy's mainstays. They include, among other dishes, the gefuelte (stuffed) fish, the borscht (beet soup), pickled and marinated herring, Hungarian goulash, potato pancake, the famous chicken pot of boiled fowl cooked in fresh vegetables, matzoh balls (which are soup dumplings made of unleavened bread reduced to flour), and corned beef.

Lindy gets lyrical when he describes the corned beef dishes he serves. His corned beef brisket, as he tells it, comes from a special breed of aristocratic Angus steer. Instead of undergoing the quick, or needle, curing process—something done with pickling mediums and a special injector—his corned beef spends twenty to twenty-two days in a pickling vat, tenderly nursed by conscientious picklers.

Lindy's, after a few months' hard going, became famous for their sandwiches; for simple sandwiches and for such combinations as lake sturgeon and Nova Scotia salmon; Wiltshire ham and Swiss cheese; ox-tongue, Swiss cheese, tomatoes and Indian relish; Fiddler's Creek smoked turkey and chicken liver; breast of turkey with pastrami and chicken fat.

When the Lindys first started, they got only transient trade. It took a little time before Eddie Cantor, then with the Ziegfeld Follies, and Al Jolson, playing the Winter Garden, found out about the Lindy menus, and became addicts. Before the year closed—the store had opened in August—celebrities were thickly clustered at the tables. Fannie Brice and her spouse, the notorious Nicky Arnstein, were steady customers. So were Sophie Tucker, Jack Haley, Blossom Seeley, Fred Allen, Ed Wynn, Paul Whiteman. Clara Lindy remembers how Jolson, after a benefit show at the Winter Garden one night, announced from the stage: "If you want wonderful sandwiches, folks, follow me after the show. I'll be down at Lindy's."

Mobsters and horse players gave the Lindys a lot of trouble. Arnold Rothstein, the gambler and drug peddler, used the place as a headquarters. His unsavory stooges came to his table to make their reports, or to take orders. When Rothstein got a Lindy cashier to take telephone messages for him in his brief absences, Lindy fired the cashier. Mrs. Lindy used to close early—soon after midnight—in the hope that this would discourage Rothstein. It didn't work. Rothstein was shot and killed one night in 1928, only a few minutes after he had left his table at Lindy's. Runyon came to the Lindys' aid when they were smothered under unfavorable publicity that followed the shooting. "He wrote," Clara Lindy recalls, "that the same thing might have happened to a man after he had left a church. That made people stop and think."

Damon Runyon was Mrs. Lindy's great love. She still worships his memory. She likes to tell how she was flooded with letters when his first "Mindy" stories came out. Young composers and playwrights started sending her manuscripts and scores, because Runyon had named her "Mrs. Broadway." "I got fan mail like an actress," she says self-deprecatingly. "I felt so silly."

Lindy remembers the little well-dressed and cultured old lady who came in one day and timidly asked to see "some of the quaint persons Mr. Runyon writes about." Harry the Horse, Milk Ear Willie, Big Nig, Sorrowful Jones and all the other prototypes from the Runyon books were out at the track at the time, but some of the other regular customers pointed to a serious fellow who was reading a newspaper between courses. "That's Morris the Schnook." He was kind and gentle, but talked tough race track talk. She was delighted. She pressed his hand when she left. When she reached the sidewalk the Lindy habitués roared with laughter. Morris the Schnook was their invention. Their butt was really Abe Lyman, the orchestra leader.

Lindy's prospered. It became famous not only for its sandwiches, but for its amazing list of pastries and cheesecakes—of which there are six delectable kinds—and for its candies and desserts, many of which are sold packed to take home. In 1939 the larger Lindy's was opened. Instead of costing the originally estimated $100,000, the new place came to $170,000. Lindy's competitors rubbed their hands. They said, "That does it. He has lost that certain touch. He will now break his neck."

He thinks he might have, too, if Eugene O'Neill's overtime shows had not opened then, just around the corner. Intermission throngs from the O'Neill shows filled the new place and the news of the wondrous Lindy dishes and desserts was widely spread.

Lindy's waiters are a little unusual. Lindy constantly rides herd on them so that there is no let-down in service, but no one has ever reduced their incorrigibly rugged individualism. There is one Lindy customer, for example, who kicks chronically about the rolls, no matter how fresh they are—and Lindy prides himself that all cakes and rolls are served fresh. The other day the roll-pincher snarled at one of the old waiters. "Take these duds back," he said, mean-edged, "these are yesterday's rolls." The waiter planted a fist on the table. He glared back at the short-tempered customer. "So," he demanded bitterly, "what was wrong with yesterday? It wasn't a nice day?" (A variant on the gag appeared on Milton Berle's TV show a few days later.)

Another waiter, befuddled by customers who threw their orders at him in chorus, left off his hasty scribbling. He put up a traffic-cop hand. "Enough, gentlemen," he said, impressively. "Leave us start over again. Leave us review the bidding."

Lindy seldom takes a vacation from his restaurant. He follows a set routine. He enters his icebox at ten thirty, goes home after the luncheon is served and then walks for a few hours. Even in these walks he mixes business with pleasure. He takes different routes and wherever he sees an interesting cake in a bakery window, goes in, buys it and submits it to Master Baker Landry for analysis. One day when he heard a customer talk glowingly of the cinnamon buns he had enjoyed in a Market Street restaurant in Philadelphia, Lindy took the next train down, tasted the cake and came back with samples for Landry. "I'm a nut on cake," he keeps telling people.

The Lindemanns are childless, but their love for children is extraordinary. At circus time, at Christmas and Easter, Lindy lays in large supplies of toys and gifts for child customers—Disney books, dolls, cowboy hats and stuff like that, and gives them away free. Both he and Mrs. Broadway are prodigally generous. If they like someone, they lavish gifts. Lindy's philosophy about this is, "What good will it do me to be the richest man in the cemetery?" He is a devoted son and lets no morning pass without visiting his aged mother, who lives in the Greystone Hotel. He has no heirs but is training one of his wife's nephews, a boy named Albert, to run the place in the Lindy tradition.

ACTION ON WEST FIFTY-THIRD STREET
(Museum of Modern Art)

DWIGHT MACDONALD

The Metropolitan is, of course, New York's largest art museum, and its collections by far the most extensive. But in singling out the art museum which most typifies the tempo of the city my vote was cast, inevitably, for the nine-ring circus on Fifty-third Street. This account is a portion of a considerably longer, two-part profile of Alfred H. Barr, Jr., Director of Collections of the Museum of Modern Art. The first section, largely reprinted here, documents the fabulously energetic goings on over which Mr. Barr presides.

The world center, institutionally speaking, of the Modern movement in the fine and applied arts is the Museum of Modern Art, which was founded here in 1929, and since 1939 has had its own six-story building on West 53rd Street, a few doors down from the gray Gothic intricacies of St. Thomas Church. Designed in the "international" style of modern architecture, which the Museum has done much to popularize in this country, the structure is predominantly white and flat on the outside and rather more bright, warm, and sumptuous inside—a glass-and-chrome-and-colored-marble surprise package that may contain anything from a Picasso to a Pierce-Arrow, a Matisse to a potato masher, so long as it is in the modern style. Behind the Museum, as a memorial to one of its most loyal and generous supporters, is the Abby Aldrich Rockefeller Sculpture Garden, a spacious area extending to 54th Street and containing a few trees, two square puddles, some statuary, and a great expanse of white marble pavement. "The entire place is a veritable oasis in the drab, gray city," a Tokyo magazine commented recently. "The bright and airy atmosphere does wonders for the tired mind. The works of art are springs of life to those who must live a colorless

Copyright 1953, The New Yorker Magazine, Inc.

routine." Many Americans, it would seem, agree. About half a million admission tickets, at sixty cents each, are bought each year, and in addition there are some sixteen thousand members and perhaps four thousand art students—both groups get in free—who come and go constantly. During the war, the Museum was so popular with soldiers and sailors, who also get in free, that the New York Defense Recreation Center ranked it fourth in a list of the city's ten chief tourist attractions, the first three being at that time the Statue of Liberty, the Empire State Building, and Rockefeller Center. The sixth was the Metropolitan Museum of Art.

The director of the Museum of Modern Art is René d'Harnoncourt, a six-foot-six Austrian nobleman who is one of this country's leading experts on primitive art and on museum exhibition techniques. The chairman of the Museum is John Hay Whitney, who is the son of Payne Whitney, who when he died in 1927 left the biggest estate ($179,000,000) that had up to then been appraised for inheritance taxes. The president of the Museum is William Armistead Moale Burden, who is the great-great-grandson of Commodore Vanderbilt and the grandson of Hamilton McK. Twombly. The director of collections of the Museum is Alfred H. Barr, Jr., who is the son of the late Reverend Alfred H. Barr, a professor of homiletics. Shy, frail, low of voice, and scholarly of mien, the austerity of his beak-nosed, bespectacled face relieved only by the kind of secret smile one sees on archaic Greek statues or on the carefully locked features of a psychoanalyst, Barr, at fifty-one, is at once the spirit and the embodiment of the Museum, much as he was in 1929, when, at twenty-seven, he became its first director—a position he held for fourteen years. . . .

The Museum of Modern Art is dedicated to what Barr has termed "the conscientious, continuous, resolute distinction of quality from mediocrity," and by no means only in the fine arts. Its staff continuously evaluates everything with such conscientious resolution that one of its catalogues praised "a cheese-slicer of rough but noble beauty," another prefaced a show of cash registers, electric toasters, gasoline pumps, and similar artifacts with quotations from Plato and Aquinas. . . . And Barr himself has resolutely discerned in the paintings of Jackson Pollock, Mark Rothko, William Baziotes, and other members of the Abstract-Expressionist school "a high degree of spontaneity, even automatism, and some dependence on accident." If one feels that a certain air of insubstantiality hovers over all these judgments, the impression is not weakened by some rather casual administrative methods. The Museum has not got around to publishing an annual report since 1948, it lacks at the moment both a treasurer and a secretary, and all checks are signed by Allen Porter, the assistant secretary, who also sells postcards and answers questions in the main lobby during the afternoon rush.

Such an impression would, however, be mistaken. Not only has the Museum in its quarter century of almost phrenetic activity exerted a unique influence on public taste, the study and teaching of art, and the practices of other museums, but it is, from a purely business point of view, a most substantial enterprise. It carries its net worth on its books at $7,577,000, chiefly represented by $3,546,000 for its site and building, $2,353,000 for its library and collections, and $1,617,000 for its endowment fund. Its budget runs around a million dollars a year. Two-thirds of this goes to pay its hundred and eighty-five employees, and approximately the same proportion of its income is derived from its own operations. Not the least substantial aspect of the Museum is its board of trustees, which includes, or has included, such great business names as Crane (Mrs. W. Murray), Field (Marshall), Ford (the late Edsel), Guggenheim (Mrs. Simon), Lewisohn (the late Sam A.), Rockefeller (Nelson, David, Mrs. John D., III, and the late Mrs. John D., Jr.), Warburg (Edward M. M.), and Whitney (John Hay). Many an art dealer and museum curator elsewhere has soothed the savage breast of some local magnate, suspicious of "all this modernistic stuff," with a significant reference to names like these, redolent of solid wealth; few Americans care to argue with a hundred million dollars. . . . There has been at least one art dealer on the board, the late Lord Duveen of Milbank, but never a painter, modern or otherwise. On occasion, the trustees have suffered much in the cause of modern art. John D. Rockefeller, Jr., was depicted in a 1934 show crouching behind sandbags and machine-gunning some noble-looking proletarians; the machine-gunner's son Nelson not only uttered no protest but made a personal call on J. P. Morgan to assure him that the proximity of *his* likeness to that of a chorus girl in another mural was merely artistic license. The torments that Lord Duveen, who liked modern art as little as he dealt in it, endured in the service of the Museum may be imagined; he relieved his feelings at board meetings by making elaborate doodles, which his more advanced colleagues insisted were examples of pure Cubism. . . .

In the early years, the trustees financed the Museum of Modern Art almost entirely. Besides making generous annual gifts for running expenses—as late as 1944, the Rockefellers were reportedly giving $100,-000 a year and Stephen Clark $25,000—they raised an initial endowment of $630,000 (mostly out of their own pockets), provided the funds to erect the present building, on a site donated by the Rockefellers, and have given the Museum—either directly or by providing funds for their purchase—by far the greater part of the paintings and sculptures in its permanent collection. . . . In recent years, the Museum has received two large bequests. One, amounting to $40,000, was left to it by Grace Rainey Rogers, a trustee and benefactor of the Museum, and was used to build a six-story annex to the main structure. . . . And in 1950 the Museum was pleasantly surprised when the lawyers for the estate of Jessie Wills Post notified it that Miss Post, who had been a $12.50-a-year member but was known to none of the trustees or staff members (a guard recognized her from a photograph as a frequent visitor, though), had left the Museum $600,000.

The flourishing of the Museum is part of the remarkable success story of modern art, a rags-to-riches drama that Horatio Alger, Jr., himself might have flinched from as implausible. The statistics are familiar and impressive: van Gogh's lifetime earnings of $109 from all his paintings; Renoir's "Mussel Gatherers" selling to a Paris dealer for $100 in 1879 and to Dr. Albert C. Barnes in 1942 for $175,000; the young Degas selling "Danseuse à la Barre" for $100 and the old Degas seeing it bring $100,000; Picasso sending a group of abstract drawings in 1912 to Stieglitz, who succeeded in selling only one of them—for $12, or about one one-hundredth of what a Picasso drawing costs today; the Montross Gallery showing thirty van Goghs in 1920 with no sale; Seurat's "La Grande Jatte" selling at his death, in 1891, for $200 and being bought in 1926 for $25,000 for the Art Institute of Chicago, which five years later refused $450,000 for it. The Museum of Modern Art is related to this inspirational drama as both effect and cause. It couldn't have got the backing it did or attracted the public it has unless it had been launched just as the wave of American interest in modern art was building up; at the same time, its own adroit promotional activities have pushed the wave higher. . . .

Another reason for the Museum's success is that it filled a local vacuum. In 1931, fourteen European cities had museums devoted exclusively to modern art, as compared to one—the Museum—in this country, and sixty-six European museums, half of them in Germany, had special galleries of modern art, as compared to twelve over here. The vacuum was most vacuous in New York—or, rather, in Manhattan. By the end of the twenties, museums in places like Buffalo, Worcester, and even Brooklyn had modern sections, whereas the Metropolitan had almost nothing—a Cézanne, a Redon, and a few prints and drawings by Gauguin, Matisse, and others—and gloried in its poverty. . . .

The operative word in the Museum's name is "Modern." The dictionary defines the adjective as meaning "characteristic of the present and recent times; new-fashioned; not antiquated or obsolete. . . ." "Contemporary," on the other hand, is defined as "living, occurring, or existing at the same period of time." Herein lies the distinction between the Museum of Modern Art and the new neighbor, the Whitney Museum of American Art, whose criterion is simply chronological—anything produced since 1900. To the Museum, then, "modern" is a value term. But what values does it represent? . . . Perhaps the most that can be said is that from the Museum's standpoint "modern" represents a prejudice in favor of the new and against the traditional. In any event, "modern" is a fighting word—a battle cry that has a stirring ring to some, a leaden sound to others. . . .

As of January 30, 1953, the Museum's collection consisted of 829 paintings, 210 sculptures, 310 drawings, 4,000 prints, 2,500 photographs, and 670 pieces of furniture, utensils, and other examples of modern design; it was insured for two and a half million dollars. Occupying the entire second floor and part of the third floor—and even then there is space to show only a small part of it—the collection is the one fairly permanent item, except for its guardian, Barr, to be found on the restless premises of the Museum. . . .

"What is this, a three-ring circus?" a group of artists once asked in a manifesto denouncing the Museum of Modern Art. Their rhetoric was thrice too moderate. The Museum is a nine-ring circus, at least. The traditional function of preserving and displaying its own art works takes up only one ring. In addition, it is a community center, a movie theatre, a library, a publishing house, a school, a provider of shows for other institutions, an arbiter of taste in everything from frying pans to country houses, and, above all, an impresario that every year puts on some twenty all-new productions, with new lighting and scenery and mostly new casts, borrowed from collectors, dealers, artists, and other museums. . . .

As a community center, the Museum is just about the biggest club in town. Its sixteen thousand members are divided almost equally between residents of New York City, who pay dues of fifteen dollars a year, and non-residents, who pay twelve-fifty. In addition to free admission to the Museum, members get from two to four Museum books a year at no cost to them, as well as invitations to openings. They also have the use of a spacious penthouse atop the building, where light refreshments are served at popular prices (sandwiches—small—ten cents) and where there is a sun deck from which an excellent view of the side of Rockefeller Center may be obtained. . . .

As a movie theatre, the Museum runs off two daily showings of movies in its basement auditorium, which accommodates an audience of five hundred in remarkably comfortable seats. The movies come from its Film Library, which collects, preserves, exhibits, and circulates old American and foreign films of aesthetic or historical importance, and which is unique. Without the Library, it is safe to say, a great many film "classics" would now be lost forever. The Library's ten million feet of films include most of D. W. Griffith's work, Erich von Stroheim's "Greed," Sergei Eisenstein's "Potemkin," Carl-Theodor Dreyer's "The Passion of Joan of Arc," and George Seitz's "Love Finds Andy Hardy." Its Circulating Film Programs have to date gone out to some two thousand customers—mainly clubs, colleges, and film societies. . . .

On the Museum's fourth floor, supervised by Bernard Karpel, there is the world's biggest library devoted exclusively to modern art. It contains fourteen thousand books, fifteen thousand slides, twenty thousand photographs, and a hundred files of reference clippings, as well as special sections dealing with the movies, ballet, the theatre, and modern architecture and design.

The Museum is famous for its publications, which are presided over by Monroe Wheeler. . . . In the thirties, Barr developed a style of catalogue that both satisfied the cognoscenti and interested the laity by combining an elegance of format, a scholarly precision, and a richness of data, none of them usual in works on modern art at that time, with a clear, readable style, which was even less usual. The Museum's pioneering catalogues, some of them really books, are still models of how to popularize without vulgarizing. It is said that even French intellectuals were impressed by them. The Museum's varied publications were described a few years ago by *Publishers' Weekly* as "written expressly for simple, democratically-minded people." Together with the circulating exhibitions, they have done much to encourage the teaching of modern art in American colleges. . . .

In the role of an educator, the Museum runs the People's Art Center, which occupies two floors of the Rogers annex and offers classes—both day and evening—in painting, sculpture, woodworking, jewelry making, and ceramics. . . . Victor D'Amico has directed the Center since its founding, in 1937, and in its sixteen years of existence it has instructed around ten thousand pupils, in addition to the large but undetermined number of art teachers who have attended its annual four-day conferences on art education. . . .

Every year, the Museum packs and ships out some fifty of its famous circulating exhibitions, each of which averages eight showings a season. The exhibits range from "Recent American Woodcuts," at seventy-five dollars for three weeks, to "Built in USA: Post-War Architecture," at three hundred and fifty dollars for three weeks. The department is headed by Porter McCray, and in its first twenty years it has dreamed up 518 exhibitions, which have been shown a total of 6,700 times by 3,350 schools, colleges, museums, clubs, and so on. Its scope has become more global since the Rockefeller Brothers' Fund put up $125,000 for a five-year program of exchanging art shows on an international basis. The Museum's first exports were a collection of modern American paintings and sculpture to Paris and one of American water colors to Tokyo, and its first imports were shows of Japanese and Italian architecture.

As an arbiter of taste, the Museum has had something to say—or, rather, to show—about practically every visual aspect of American life. It started off in this field in 1934, with a display of "machine art," and the aspects it has since covered by means of special exhibits include the American snapshot, children's playgrounds, the films of D. W. Griffith, Buckminster Fuller's Dymaxion Development Unit (a bombproof shelter sleeping six), war posters, advertising art, postage stamps, theatre arts, how children paint, and the Thomas Lamb Wedge-Lock Handle (curved to fit the hand, for use on pots, doors, suitcases, and all other objects requiring handles). . . . Behind some of its shows there is an obvious reforming motive, which is sometimes successful, sometimes not. Its subway-art show of 1938, which it put on because it considered the city's subway stations "436 potential underground art galleries" and wanted "to combat an atmosphere which is always lugubrious and occasionally sinister," was a demonstration of experiments in new media for murals "indestructible enough to be suitable for use in subway stations." Nothing came of it. Nor did anything come of the Museum's ingenious "Are Clothes Modern?" show, which made it clear that they are not modern, or beautiful, or rational, or economic, by such devices as a life-size diagram of a man's suit showing how many needless buttons and pockets it has, and models of the female body as it would have looked if it had conformed to the fashions of various periods. On the other hand, the Museum's automobile show of 1951 probably played some part in improving the appearance of our cars from repulsive to so-so. . . .

But the Museum's most effective intervention as an *arbiter elegantiarum* has been in architecture and in home furnishings. Its architecture department has done much to popularize Gropius, Le Corbusier, and Frank Lloyd Wright. And its pre-Christmas exhibitions of utilitarian objects of modern design have influenced the buyers for New York stores. The influence spread in 1950, when the Museum set up a Good Design department, run by Edgar Kaufmann, Jr., to collaborate with the Chicago Merchandise Mart, which is the chief buying center for the country's retailers of home furnishings, in putting on two big shows at the Mart and a smaller one at the Museum—events that have since been repeated yearly.

The ninth ring of the Museum's circus is, like the first, occupied wholly by art, of all things. The Department of Painting and Sculpture is headed by Andrew C. Ritchie, who operates as a theatrical producer rather than as a custodian. Most of the Museum's exhibition space is occupied not by its own collection but by shows of borrowed material, and these are presented in galleries that are specially "set," like a stage—a method that was worked out by the Museum in the thirties and that has had a revolutionary effect on other museums. . . .

By no means all the shows the Museum has offered have been of a pioneering or experimental nature. There are the substantial group shows, like the Cézanne-van Gogh-Seurat-Gauguin one with which it opened; one-man shows of masters like Picasso, Matisse, Braque, and Klee; informative surveys, like those of Cubism and abstract art in 1935 and of the Fauves of 1952; big general retrospectives, like the Museum's fifteenth-anniversary "Art in Progress" show in 1944; and great primitive-art shows, like "African Negro Art" in 1935 and "Arts of the South Seas" in 1946. But there have also been some very odd shows indeed, in which ingenuity sometimes seems mixed with desperation: shows of delphiniums grown by Edward Steichen; of "Large-Scale Modern Painting" (canvases measuring six feet or more in one dimension or the other); of "Objects As Subjects" (still-lifes); of "Mystery in Paint" (mysterious things); of "The Animal Kingdom in Modern Art";

and of "The Most Beautiful Shoe Shine Stand in the World" (a shoeshine stand). There's no business like show business.

Two reasons may be given for the Museum's dramatic, enterprising, multifarious character. One is that Barr planned it that way. His was the flair for showmanship, the conviction and drive, the notion of a "multi-departmental" museum that would rove far beyond the classic confines of the fine arts. The other reason is economic. The Metropolitan has an endowment of $62,000,000 and the city pays part of its operating expenses; the Museum of Modern Art has an endowment of $1,600,000 and it pays for everything itself. The former is thus in the position of a *rentier*, living on income from capital, while the latter is an entrepreneur, dependent on its own exertions. As the word implies, an entrepreneur has to be enterprising, and this fact does a good deal to explain the nine-ring circus and the sideshows. As late as 1940, the Museum of Modern Art's income from endowment funds was less than twenty thousand dollars, and even last year it was only seventy-two thousand dollars, which covered about one-fifteenth of its expenses. Fourteen-fifteenths of its budget, therefore, must be raised either in the form of contributions or by its own operations. The relative importance of these two sources has changed in an interesting way since the Museum was founded. In 1930, it received $107,500 in contributions (almost all from trustees) and less than one fifth of that amount from membership dues, the sale of catalogues, and other sources of operating revenue. Since then, the balance has slowly tilted the other way, until today the Museum is self-supporting to an extent rarely achieved by an art museum. . . . Originally open free to the public, the Museum has charged admission since 1939. It is something of an entrepreneurial triumph to induce people to pay sixty cents to get into an art museum. . . .

GREENWICH VILLAGE:

New Designs in Bohemia

WILLIAM BARRETT

It is not too easy for a native of the Village, let alone a visitor, to know whether he is in Bohemia when he enters the neighborhood. On the surface it is a mile-square jumble on New York's Lower West Side of tenements (still inhabited mainly by first- or second-generation Italians and Irish, the immigrant base of the whole community), relieved here and there by tall new apartment houses, and a sprinkling of small old red-brick houses antedating the Civil War. The latter are generally thought to give the Village its peculiar atmosphere. They are very photogenic and books on the Village usually take advantage of this to create in the outlander the impression that the whole neighborhood looks as elegantly and archaically Georgian as Regent's Park in London.

The inhabitants are a variegated lot and it is easy for the casual visitor to be deceived about them. On a warm spring Saturday or Sunday afternoon you cannot tell, unless you know the people themselves, who are and who are not the real Bohemians sitting around Washington Square. The Village permits, perhaps encourages, an informality of dress not found in other parts of Manhattan. Perfectly "respectable" people who work all week in uptown offices find it pleasant to be able to go around unshaved and carelessly dressed on their day off, if they feel like it.

You have to dig them, as they say, if you want to find the real Bohemians here. To preserve their identity against such interlopers, the young and more extreme Bohemians draw themselves together into intricately knotted groups. They are also on the defensive against a few other Bohemian contenders. Recently, for example, there has been much talk about "The New Bohemia," a strictly midtown affair, an elegant and chi chi world that leads a much faster life than any group in the Village. The New Bohemia is made up of editors and editorial workers, usually of certain large magazines, literary agents, fashion models, a few socialites, and some very successful writers. Now, since the days of Murger's classic *"Vie de Boheme,"* the word Bohemia has always connoted a generous amount of poverty. But this midtown New Bohemia is, on the contrary, very well heeled. Moreover, the poverty of the classic Bohemia was not an accident but resulted from the fact that its artists were engaged in creating a revolutionary, unpopular, and therefore unpaying art. The writers in the New Bohemia, however, are a very salable commodity. The special tastes of this group are marked by an unusual attention to décor, style and elegance—qualities associated with wealth. Its title to the word Bohemia seems to arise only through a certain unorthodoxy in its *mores*. So run the Villagers' arguments against the New Bohemia. The older Villagers look down on this midtown upstart, feeling that they have a tradition of several decades of the real Bohemia behind them.

A legend begins to reach its end when the wreckers start tearing down the props that have supported it. A good deal of relentless chipping away has been going on in Greenwich Village for years. But recently a big piece of the Village legend was set upon: the City of New York decided to rip up the slums of Washington Square Southeast and rebuild them nearer to the middle-class heart's desire. At the same time the old Hotel Brevoort on Eighth Street and Fifth Avenue, once the rendezvous of Theodore Dreiser, Eugene O'Neill, Edna Millay and other famous writers, and the equally fabulous old Hotel Lafayette on Ninth Street and University Place have been pulled down. Most of the spots famous in the Twenties are gone or unfrequented. But the real Bohemia symbolized by such places was dead and buried long before the wrecker's iron ball caught up with the Brevoort and the Lafayette.

One of the great periods of creative ferment in the history of the Village was the decade that came to an end in 1920, but, so far as national publicity was concerned, it was the following decade, the Twenties, that claimed most attention. Bohemia had the luck to have crusades in which it could believe, and so Bohemia itself became a kind of great crusade against the nation. The crusades were chiefly personal freedom (in practice, usually, sexual freedom) and art. Modernism in art was then a new cause and the Philistines of the nation had to be made to swallow the newly discovered giants like Picasso and James Joyce. Vienna and Freud were almost romantic names and psychoanalysis was looked on as a gay adventure in the escape from one's inhibitions. Much of this looks like naïve nonsense now, but naïveté sometimes provides exuberance and some of the exuberance of the Twenties became genuinely creative. Thus the Village of the Twenties did not merely reflect American life at a crucial point of transition, but was, in a way it has never quite been since, an active center that helped form the cultural climate of the period.

Since America was on a spree in the Twenties, it could make use of the Bohemian to let off some of its own steam of revolt and Bohemia, therefore, had a real place in the national life. A painter who came here in 1925 as a stripling fresh from the provinces told me that he has never seen anything since to equal the drinking of those days. Here Bohemia was simply taking part in the national revolt against Prohibition. At the same time the Bohemian was symbolically expressing his defiance of the whole social order. Such was the case, too, my friend told me, with sexual behavior: "When you made love then, you weren't just making love, you were striking a blow for freedom. Promiscuity wasn't promiscuity—it was something else, a kind of social and moral crusade."

In a certain sense, the Village prospered during the long depression of the Thirties: prices had dropped to the bottom, and since nearly all the artists managed to get on W.P.A. projects, they could live fairly comfortably. Certain economic pressures of American life, embarrassing to the Bohemian, were temporarily relaxed. The vast egalitarian feeling that had diffused itself through large sections of American society was concentrated nowhere more densely than in Greenwich Village.

But the depression, leaving Bohemia intact economically, did destroy altogether the intellectual climate of the Twenties. Art gave way to, or was put in the service of, politics. All the politics was on the Left, and the Village and Union Square were never closer in their spiritual geography. Most of the Bohemians moved on the vague utopian fringe of the Left; as they got closer to the Communist party, they learned that politics there was very far from utopian, but a very "practical" business indeed. The phenomenon known as "social consciousness" began to squat like an incubus over the artists. Painters felt compelled to depict workers and strikes. "Literature suffered worse," I was told by one friend, now a journalist, but in that period a budding novelist. "Ideology became more important than experience. The more you believed in the ideology, the harder it became to believe in the value of experience itself—and the novel you were trying to write began to seem unreal."

In comparison with the Twenties and Thirties, which had definite intellectual climates, the Forties seem pretty vague. "What happened during the Forties?" The older Villagers, when asked, return your question. "I don't know. Mostly the war, I guess."

The war did bring some considerable changes to the Village. New York was a boom town for service men on leave and the overflow from Times Square came downtown. The honky-tonk in the Village boomed. Girls came into the neighborhood from all the outlying boroughs to pick up service men. Since the Twenties, the Village has always counted on its "tourist" trade, but during the war the volume became much greater and has held up since, bringing a permanent change of tone to the neighborhood. The visitors also made the housing problem worse after the war. One reason why Bohemia sprouted in the Village in the Twenties was that people could find cheap flats here. Now it is possible to do much better in other sections of the city; there has been a swing of Bohemia toward the lower East Side, where more cold-water flats and lofts are available for artists at lower rents.

Such social and economic encroachments add up, with a few other facts, to the decline of Bohemia. During the Thirties there was a growth of regionalism in American writing and many young writers now feel they can do better by remaining in their own communities close to their material. The painters still seem to find it necessary to cluster together in a metropolitan center. But even here there has been some shift from the Village to Long Island and the Connecticut suburbs.

Thus the Village of the Twenties has vanished altogether: its great crusade for personal and sexual freedom against an older, more puritanical America has been fought and won, while one great lament of the young Bohemia of the Fifties is that it has no crusade left.

Sexual freedom, for example, can hardly be a crusade in a nation that took the Kinsey Report so very much in its stride. Psychoanalysis, which has been installed as a pretty standard fixture in American life, no longer needs its Bohemian prophets. Young people now look upon it as a very serious and even painful task and not as the gay adventure of release it may have seemed to some people in the most light-hearted decade.

Politics is another lost crusade. Ironically enough, this has happened at a time when the Bohemian, like everyone else, knows that his future and the world's, depends upon politics as never before. But the utopian pretenses can no longer be maintained, for this is real politics, a deadly game of power that automatically excludes the Bohemian, the man who exists outside of any power group. And, since politics forgets him, the Bohemian chooses to forget it.

Anyone who wants to measure the past of Bohemia against its present might do well to compare two novels, one about the Village in the Twenties, the other about young Bohemian life in the Fifties. They are "I Thought of Daisy," by Edmund Wilson, which appeared in 1929, and "Go," by Clellon Holmes (1952). The difference between their worlds has the proportions of a geological shift.

Everything is sadder and more tawdry in the Bohemia of the Fifties. Though the older Bohemia had its seamy side, Wilson always managed to see the Village wrapped in an aura of romantic poetry, and at one climactic moment the hero catches up with his vision while walking through Abingdon Square, and the meaning of the Village is revealed to him: "I had turned my back on the world of mediocre aims and prosaic compromises; and at that price—what brave spirit would not pay it?—I had been set free to follow poetry."

This has all the naïve, innocent and exuberant ring of the Twenties, but words like these today would only draw snorts of derision from the more jaded and hard-bitten youths in Bohemia. Wilson sums up this vision of the Village: "Something I had come for, I had found." What he had found in the Village was a home of the spirit where the Bohemian, however cut off from the rest of the nation, had his own place and meaning. By contrast, the hero of Holmes' book in the Fifties is entirely homeless; and his final revelation, which is more a blank wall of interrogation, occurs on a ferry boat while he gazes at the whole island of Manhattan, asking forlornly, "Where is my home?"

Homelessness was the chief characteristic of the generation that came up in Bohemia with World War II. They were the generation of the "hipster," whose contributions to the Village tradition were marijuana and bop music. Homeless, they did not establish exclusive quarters in the Village but spread through other areas of the city, the East Side, up and downtown, and even parts of Brooklyn Heights.

Of the "hipsters" I wrote a few years ago: "Attached to nothing outside themselves, the young Bohemians attempt to fill the vacuum by developing their own codes of behavior. Perhaps this will go down in history as the 'cool' generation. 'Coolness' is that perfect mastery (or numbness) of self that enables the 'hipster,' the cool cat, to listen to the loudest and most throbbing jazz without displaying the least sign of emotion. The hipster (the arch-priest of this new Bohemia) has here made a virtue of necessity, exalting his inability to feel into a positive value. But nature, thrust out, returns by the back door: if you have no feelings, you cease to feel you are alive and require artificial means to restore the sensation of living. Hence the necessity of reefers (marijuana), unknown to the Bohemia of the Twenties.

"In retrospect, the Lost Generation does not now appear to have been so lost, since it possessed all the magnificent and naïve emotions of lament for the world of the past from which it believed it had cut itself off. The present generation has achieved more sophistication, but has also paid a price for this loss of naïveté, since this has also meant a loss of exuberance and therefore a decline in creativity."

The hipsters were the last movement of revolt, and in this respect were distant cousins to the rebels of the Twenties. But generations change very fast in Bohemia, and this one is just about used up. For one thing, some of the ritual antics of the hipster have spread through the whole country, and from being avant-garde have changed into old hat. And now that the hipster generation is on its way out, what has been left in Greenwich Village is something much more domesticated and bourgeois: a popular haven for young marrieds who prefer its informal —they still call it "Bohemian"—atmosphere to the featureless neighborhoods uptown.

The young wife, who may work in publishing, got to know the Village during leaves from Bennington or Vassar, and still finds the place a continuation of the adventures of college. (This collegiate tone has taken over whole bars in the Village that used once to be the haunts of honest-to-God derelicts. The atmosphere of the San Remo on Macdougal Street and Louis' Tavern near Sheridan Square, two favorite hangouts, might best be described as "collegiate-crummy." The collegiate tone is a little smoother in Julius' on Waverly Place and West Tenth and in Lee Chumley's on Bedford Street, but these spots were submerged by the collegiate tide years ago and so have had more time to tidy up.) The young husband is probably a "Bohemian" because he is in publicity rather than advertising, but when the babies come and he wants more security, it will be advertising and our young couple will disappear into a suburb. In the meantime, home may be a whitewashed basement apartment with a couple of African masks on the wall, Swedish glassware and wrought iron lying around, an elaborate hi-fi set ("Bohemian" because its mechanism is unhoused by a cabinet), and the studio couch still a principal article of furniture.

This drive toward domesticity has hit the Village so hard in recent years that more babies and baby carriages have been noticeable than ever before. Real centers of social intrigue are the play pens in Washington Square where the mothers visit with each other while the kids romp.

Naturally, this domestic side of Village life isn't what visitors from Brooklyn, Queens, or Jersey come to goggle at on a Saturday night spree or Sunday afternoon stroll. They come to see the other Village, which without their knowing it has been created just for them: the Village as a gallery of human oddities with its shoddy honky-tonk of cheap night-clubs and homosexual and lesbian bars where exhibitionism runs wild. Actually, sexual vice is no more rampant in the Village than in midtown, but only less well organized and less well concealed.

True, there are plenty of the declassed, the derelict and the spiritually homeless of one kind or another below the domestic and bourgeois layers of the Village, but the life of most Villagers goes on pretty much without turmoil in the neighborhood of these specters from the lower depths. The remaining group of the derelict, if they can be called that, are mainly just maladjusted kids fresh out of or flunked out of college and running away from parental pressures.

These are the fresh recruits of Bohemia year by year, the young blood that should restore its creative juices. Right now, these recruits assemble chiefly at the Rienzi, a coffee shop on Macdougal Street. Here, a new post-hipster generation is already forming, but it is hard to make out its precise spiritual features. The impression in this corner is that they are a much more docile lot than the group that came up right after the war. They read less, and though they talk a lot, they don't say very much about ideas, in which they seem to have no interest at all. If ours is, as critics have already begun to call it, an Age of Conformism, perhaps its supreme paradox may be to produce a conformist Bohemia. This youngest group in Bohemia gives me the heavy impression of something that might be called The Waiting Generation (waiting for what, one can't possibly guess).

Stirrings of new life may lie in the current movement of off-Broadway theatres that are now the hottest thing in the Village. The small art theatre has long been a fixture in the Village, but an extraordinary revolution in its fortunes has been brought about by two recent events: the first was the decline of Broadway and the second was the sudden and sensational success of a small theatre off Sheridan Square, Circle in the Square, in putting on Tennessee Williams' "Summer and Smoke," a play which missed on Broadway but which took fire in its Village production. The fact that a play can succeed in a small theatre, while the economics of Broadway has virtually priced serious drama out of the market, points up the increasingly important role of these smaller off-Broadway theatres in keeping the drama alive.

Parallel with the off-Broadway theatre is the movement toward an off-57th Street art center and there are now a number of smaller galleries—the Tanager, Hansa, Matrix and Gallery A are some of the better-known names—stretching far into the lower East Side, but spiritually a part of the Village, all exhibiting new painters and sculptors.

Most of what the Village once stood for is gone and will never return. What remains is either middle-class or desperate, without charm or prinked up for tourists. Yet, there is an informality, a charm, and an odd human warmth about this neighborhood that makes one prefer it to other parts of Manhattan. True, the charm is thoroughly ambiguous, often shoddy and more often exploited; but, exploitation and all, it is a human thing just the same.

Nothing could be more typical of this ambiguity than the open-air art exhibitions every spring around Washington Square: you know that these are promoted by the local Chamber of Commerce to bring the suckers in; and if you were to take a severely esthetic view, you might wonder whether damage isn't being done to the public's taste by the quality of the pictures exhibited.

Then you relax and think that even in this artistic pathos there is something very human amid the inhuman traffic of the great city, and this is, after all, the only public acknowledgment of art anywhere in the canyoned streets of New York, so that you end by greeting it like the sudden spring blossoming of a bright tired flower on a dusty window ledge. The charm of the Village is something like that.

THE FABULOUS PORT OF NEW YORK

BROOKS ATKINSON

Go down almost any of Manhattan's side streets or avenues and you reach the waterfront. Excepting the inviting park areas, it is a harsh and cluttered neighborhood. For it seems to be a rule all over the world that passengers soothed by unaccustomed luxury and service at sea have to cross a narrow strip of burly hubbub before they can go to their hotels or homes. Although the Port of New York and New Jersey is one of the greatest, if not, the greatest, in the world, it is also infected with crime—occasional murders, organized racketeering and the systematic theft of millions of dollars' worth of goods every year. In the shape-up, which is the method by which longshoremen are chosen for jobs, it preserves one of the few medieval hiring systems that remain in a progressive world. The Port of New York was the haven for pirates in the seventeenth century. It has never shaken off entirely the license of that freebooting inheritance. There is nothing idyllic about the waterfront.

But the passenger tripping down the covered gangway of a liner represents daily business. Every day there are 150 or 175 deep-water vessels using the facilities of our varied waterfront with its 520 miles of frontage on navigable waterways. Only a small portion of this huge fleet of ships is in the passenger trade. Most of them are cargo vessels, many of them flying the American flag but many of them flying the flags of European, South American and Asiatic countries. Last year the port unloaded and dispatched 22,507,586 long tons of imported foreign cargo, or 32.4 per cent of all the foreign cargo that reached the shores of the United States. It exported 5,672,000 long tons.

The waterfront is a working district that moves mountains of cargo every day, clear around the clock. About 250,000 people are directly employed in keeping the port in operation, and about 3,750,000 more are employed in shipyards, assembly plants, oil and metal refineries, or enterprises that are immediately dependent on the business of the port. These people comprise a little civilization of their own, seasoned with salt water. It would be a miracle if a working area of this size and mass power were dainty enough to suit the sensibilities of a passenger debarking from a luxury liner.

Despite the costly cargo installations and the intricate organization of cargo handling, the genius of the port is geographical. Manhattan is situated where it is because nature provided an amazing system of sheltered harbors and waterways. When Giovanni da Verrazano entered the port in 1524, or Henry Hudson in 1609, everything fundamental to the life of the port today was already in existence. For the usefulness of the port lies mainly in its configuration—a huge landlocked area protected from the wildness of the ocean but close to the sea, and offering easy access to the interior.

None of the other great ports of the world has been so generously endowed by nature. Our port is really a combination of ports, with eight large bays, the four straits of the Harlem and East Rivers and the two kills west of Staten Island, and four rivers—the Raritan, the Passaic, the Hackensack and the Hudson. The Hudson, with a 27-foot channel, is navigable by blue-water vessels for 150 miles into the heart of New York and close to the western part of Massachusetts, and it is navigable for tugs and barges through the State Barge Canal to the Great Lakes.

In Hudson's day the harbor was sweeter. When he arrived in September the wild grapes were ripe, and he caught their fragrance when he was in Sandy Hook Bay. In those days Manhattan was heavily forested with oaks, pines and lindens. There were thousands of ducks and herons in the harbor, and the water was full of fish. Until the Revolution, whales liked to lumber through the upper bay, where small fish were plentiful, and until a century ago sturgeon weighing five hundred or six hundred pounds were plentiful. Upriver the sturgeon was dubbed "Albany beef," since it was the basic diet for thousands of people.

In the course of the four centuries since the harbor was discovered by Verrazano some important geographical changes have been made by man—like the enlarging of Governors Island by fill from the subways, the construction of the mammoth naval basin at Bayonne by fill dredged out of the harbor, and the removal of obstructions to navigation in the East and Harlem Rivers. Since the early nineteenth century (there were 661 vessels counted in the port one day in 1802) the waterfront has crept into the rivers by two hundred feet or more to provide more space for ships to work in; and the breakwater around the Erie Basin has been built of ballast dumped there by ships from all over the world. "The international breakwater" it is called in honor of the rocks and rubble discharged there by ships that had crossed the sea in ballast and were taking American cargo for the return voyage.

But the genius of the port still lies in its unique combination of bays, estuaries and rivers, and the short distance a ship has to travel from its pier to the open ocean. It is only seven miles from the Battery to the Narrows. A ship can settle down to the long voyage to Europe, South America or Asia in an hour or two from the time she leaves her pier on the waterfront.

Speed is the driving force in port. For a ship is not earning a profit in port. She is not accomplishing anything, although the overhead of two or three thousand dollars a day for a cargo ship goes on relentlessly. Everything in the Port of New York that speeds up the discharging and loading of a vessel is therefore worth while, for it is a fundamental part of marine economics. The romantic days of the rusty, plodding freighter are over. For shipping cargo is big business now. It deals in equipment that costs huge sums of money. The Liberty ships, with a plodding speed of only ten knots, cost $1,250,000 to build; but the C-3 ships, which are the queens of the American cargo trade, cost three to four million dollars to build, and their service speed of 16 to 18 knots is not a whim of the designer but a basic factor in the ship's capacity to earn money. The clipper ships (which became obsolete in less than twenty years) were built for speed because short passages earned great profits. Today the fast freighters from America, England, Europe and Scandinavian countries are the ones that make good profits.

To the casual ferryboat or tugboat passenger the business of the harbor looks random and lumbering. Big ships slowly pass up and down on their schedules; but car-floats, oil barges, tugboats and ferries are constantly swarming through the turbid city water, sometimes callously bearing down on each other with an apparent indifference that looks alarming to a tourist of the Port. Everything appears to be cheerfully casual.

In point of fact, the Port is organized by the necessities of the daily business, and a number of Government and private agencies keep it operating with a kind of general competence. Every year there are about 10,000 sailings out of New York to all parts of our coast and the rest of the world, partly because New York has the facilities to keep things moving. Ships do not have to hang around for attention ashore. Experienced pilots are always available at the mouth of the dredged channel, and there is a large fleet of tugs with trained docking pilots on call at any hour of the day or night.

The Port includes about two hundred piers equipped for deep-water vessels. Since the local fleet comprises about twenty-five hundred tugs, lighters, barges and floating derricks, ships can discharge and load cargo on the offshore side as well as directly to and from the piers, and this system of double-loading saves time. There are twelve railroads with storage areas and marshaling yards to keep the cargo in transit. The tankers, which come here in great numbers from the Gulf of Mexico and also the Persian Gulf, can discharge their cargo and take on return ballast in less than twenty-four hours and put out to sea again. At the Port Authority's grain elevator pier in the noisy and cluttered little area of Gowanus Bay ships can load four thousand tons of grain in every eight-hour shift, or twelve thousand tons, which would be capacity for the larger ships, in twenty-four hours.

The Port of New York Authority was created by treaty in 1921 between New York and New Jersey to help develop the Port as a unit. During the busy intervening years it has built bridges, tunnels and truck and bus terminals, and it operates the major airfields in the area. Now it operates the grain terminal and an adjacent pier in Gowanus Bay. In 1948 it leased Port Newark from the city of Newark, and after rebuilding piers that had disintegrated, erecting new sheds and undertaking dredging projects, it is building up a trade there in lumber, wood pulp, rubber, copper and pineapples. It has also drawn up long-range plans for modernizing the New York, Jersey City and Hoboken waterfronts.

For the Port is sweeping in size. It includes not only the major waterfronts that are familiar to many people on the Hudson and East Rivers, but Staten Island, where America's first free-trade area is located and goods can be brought in duty-free for inspection; Elizabethport, where cotton, chicle, sugar, flour and cocoa beans are stored and manufactured into finished products; Edgewater, where crude tropical sugar arrives from Cuba, Puerto Rico and the Philippines; Port Raritan, where more than a thousand vessels appear every year with copper ore from Chile and Peru and other cargoes; the Port of Bayonne, with a drydock that can handle the largest ships in the world; Kearny, the home port for many colliers; and even the Bronx, which has docks on the Harlem and East Rivers and Long Island Sound.

EVERYTHING MONEY CAN BUY

ROGER ANGELL

The most informative maps of New York are not in books. They exist instead in the minds of millions of New Yorkers—personal maps drawn up after years of exploration, of patient trial and painful error. They are the maps that every resident must have in his possession to get along for one day in the Big Town. They tell him how and where to change from the B.M.T. Sea Beach local to the I.R.T. Seventh Avenue express; where to go for a $7.00 dinner of *Beef Stroganoff* and a $1.10 lunch of smoked herring; how to drive from Times Square to Darien, Conn., on a crowded Friday afternoon in summer; where to find a $3.00 boy's windbreaker, a $125 Chippendale end table and a Louis Armstrong record made in 1925.

Of all these complex maps, probably the most detailed and most widely differing are the mental guides to New York stores. They vary from the socialite's shopping list ("hat—Mr. John; stop at Bonwit's for fitting; wool sweater—Brooks Bros.; tweed suit—Lord & Taylor; look for gadget-present for Kenneth—Hammacher Schlemmer, Lewis & Conger") to the housewife's careful outline of necessities to be bought at the lowest cost ("saucepan—Macy's basement; winter coat for me—S. Klein's; kitchen curtains—Bloomingdale's"). Only a composite of all these lists would give a complete guide to shopping in New York—a city so big that no one knows exactly the number of retail stores that it contains or even approximately how much money New Yorkers spend annually on mink coats, kitchen hardware, candy, haircuts, imported sidesaddles, or two-bit costume jewelry.

But the absence of a "Compleat Shopper" for New York is not surprising in view of one undeniable fact: It is literally possible to buy *anything* in New York. In a single afternoon a shopper with imagination and a big bankroll could purchase a Chinese ricksha, a $1000 dress for a little girl, a pair of fulminating dueling pistols, and a bucket of live hellgrammites for bass bait, meanwhile leaving directions for a department store to do a $250,000 decorating job on a resort hotel in Syria.

The best-known New York store, in the city and all over the world, is Macy's. The colossus of Herald Square is "The World's Largest Store" not only by claim but by actual size (2,132,000 square feet), and volume of sales (150,000 shoppers daily; 45,000,000 transactions worth $180,000,000 a year). Yet R. H. Macy & Co. is less an example of the importance of size than of the importance of a slogan. The slogan is "6% Less for Cash." This precise statement represents the continuation of the less-for-cash policy in effect ever since Rowland Hussey Macy went into the dry-goods business on 14th Street and Sixth Avenue on October 28, 1858. By contrast, Macy's highly successful competitor, Gimbel's, has succeeded by always changing and always violent promotion and by its efforts to be first in New York to carry a new item of merchandise.

Shopping in Macy's can be as difficult and as rewarding as going in and out of every small store in a twenty-block area. At Christmastime one can be carried along for hours in rib-cracking crowds that run up to 350,000 in a day. Finding the right counter and then a salesgirl (there are normally 4500, about 7000 at Christmas) under such circumstances requires the exploratory instincts of a Stanley and the persistence of a Pasteur. None of this seems to terrify the customers. The fact that most of them are rewarded in the end is a tribute both to Macy's size and its variety. Inside Macy's is the world's biggest bookstore, which carries or promises to find any book, in or out of print; the city's largest pharmacy; a grocery with one of the city's biggest fancy-foods departments; a bank with over 250,000 deposits, placed there against future orders at the store; and a decorating department which does everything from recommending the furnishings for an apartment breakfast nook to carrying out the decoration of the executive mansion in Monrovia, Liberia, or the fitting out of President Truman's yacht.

Macy's also is capable of the fine touch. After the movie *Miracle on 34th Street* had made millions more people conscious of Macy's, the store was plagued with demands as to whether "Mr. Macy" would really send children to other stores to buy toys which Macy's did not carry.

The store promptly set up one of its comparison shoppers in the toy department, named her "Kristine Kringle," and proceeded to do exactly that. Business was terrific. Macy's has always fostered the idea that Santa Claus is its personal property. He arrives annually in Macy's Thanksgiving Day parade, which draws crowds of some two millions with its giant balloons and floats. During the Christmas season five Santa Clauses are on duty, each hidden at the end of a maze so that no kid will be puzzled by seeing two at the same time.

Although Macy's is the best-known New York store, it is not a typical one. It is on the specialty store that New York's reputation as a shopping capital depends. Harry Winston's, for example. Tiffany's and Cartier's are better known and more widely stocked, but they are, after all, still stores; any commoner can walk in and look around. But almost all the customers who enter Harry Winston's chaste establishment do so by appointment. Except for the modest brass plate beside the door, the six-story house on East 51st Street looks just like what it used to be—a private mansion. Inside is one of the world's richest collections of the most special specialty of all—diamonds. Winston's has its own diamonds, its own cutters, polishers, designers, creators and salesmen. They buy their stones in the rough, including such famous specimens as the Jonker, Vargas and Liberator diamonds.

New York also has all the assortment of stores to match its interest in the arts. On 57th Street are the Knoedler and Durand-Ruel Galleries which sell old and new masterpieces. The Rosenbach Company has one of the largest collections anywhere of rare books and manuscripts for sale and also deals in rare autographs. One of its recent purchases was the $151,000 Bay Psalm Book. On 43rd Street, G. Schirmer, Inc., carries every type of musical instrument, from harmonicas to contra-bassoons, and has a stock of some fifty thousand musical scores, most of which are published under its own imprint. It is no exaggeration to say that practically every serious musician—from the unhappy ten-year-old buying *The Happy Farmer* to the Metropolitan Opera orchestra renting the entire score of *Louise*—gets his music at Schirmer's.

Another shrine store is F. A. O. Schwarz. So many New Yorkers were brought up on Schwarz toys that they automatically return there to buy *their* children's electric trains and Teddy bears. Schwarz's does a bigger volume business than it used to, but its heaviest play still comes from the carriage trade. In spite of its prices and posh locale on upper Fifth Avenue, Schwarz's is an informal store where parents are encouraged to try out the toy motorboats (in a long pool), the windup cars and the magic sets.

Schwarz's selection of toys is wide, with prices running from a quarter up to five hundred dollars. Its annual catalogue is considered the bible of the toy world and lists about nine hundred games, costumes, dolls, and gadgets. Schwarz has never hired a Christmastime Santa Claus and doesn't believe in the practice. But the store's proudest story concerns a little boy in Detroit who was taken to visit a department store Santa. When Santa Claus asked what he wanted for Christmas, the erudite tot looked him straight in the eye and replied: "I don't know. I haven't seen Schwarz's catalogue yet."

The nearest thing to a grownup's F. A. O. Schwarz is Hammacher Schlemmer & Co. A fabulously expanded hardware and home-furnishing shop, Hammacher Schlemmer is one of the New York stores that make their customers wish they had an odd five thousand dollars lying around which they could spend foolishly and fancily. The urge here is supplied by a huge line of gadgets—for picnics, kitchen, bar, bathroom, porch, lawn and fireplace. In the basement you can buy penny screws and nuts; upstairs, a three or four-figure check will get you a barbecue pit or a pure lucite table and chair. The firm's line of corkscrews, cocktail shakers and ice buckets is improved and streamlined more often than automobile designs.

Brooks Brothers, although it occupies a solid, ten-story building on 44th Street and Madison Avenue, and has branch outlets in the Wall Street district, in Boston, San Francisco and Los Angeles, is much more than a store; it is an institution. Its reputation as *The* gentlemen's clothiers is based on several rock-solid foundations: its 131-year history; its hardy perennials like the Brooks white button-down shirt and the Brooks Number One sack coat; the quality of its salesmen and the quality of its customers. Hardihood is the Brooks stock in trade. Its ready-to-wear suits are not hung on racks but piled on tables, the way all stores piled suits fifty years ago. The average length of service of its personnel is eighteen years and there are more than one hundred employees who have been there a quarter century. Its steadiest customers are fourth and fifth generation members of families who have maintained charge accounts with Brooks since it was founded. Brooks still carries a slow-moving but regular stock of nightcaps and nightshirts, and has a livery department with large supplies of crested footmen's buttons ready for instant use at the first glimmer of a return of the Good Old Days.

In spite of the number of Morgans and Roosevelts who have grown up, lived and died in Brooks clothes, defining the typical "Brooksy" customer is as hard as describing "Brooksy" clothes. Many young Brooks customers are educated in the north by St. Paul's School and Harvard, and in the south by Princeton and The Hill; but in addition to Teddy and F. D. Roosevelt and Vincent Astor, the Brooks customer also includes Abraham Lincoln, U. S. Grant, Jack Dempsey, Fred Astaire, Gary Cooper and Rudolph Valentino, although the latter was never permitted to open a charge account. The clothes today's customer wears are the unpadded, straight-hanging Number One, the white button-down, a foulard tie, imported Peal shoes and Herbert Johnson hat, but they also may include a bright pink shirt, a polo coat (if not worn to work) and a Tattersall vest (ditto).

Brooks is accustomed to hearing from its regulars when a lighting fixture has been changed, an overexuberant advertisement has been printed, or the tiny button has been dropped from the back of the collar of the white shirt. These complaints are just as apt to come from the salesmen (who *all* wear Brooks clothes) as from customers, and often the store will admit its mistake and quickly rectify it. At the same time, the store tells its customers when *they* are wrong: Brooks will *never* carry the currently popular shirt with widely spread collar points, and blandly says as much to anyone who asks for it. This mutual respect between store and customer leads to unique relationships, such as that between a Brooks customer, the late J. P. Morgan, and a Brooks salesman, the late Frederick Webb, whose customary greetings were: "Good morning, Mr. Webb," and "Good morning, Jack."

Brooks prices are high but not fabulous. Custom suits run from $195 to $215, but the sixth-floor shop carries ready-mades for as little as $70. Much of the merchandise is made by Brooks workmen on the upper floors. Women are as scarce in the store as shoulder padding, except for mothers in the boys' department. However, plenty of twelve- and fourteen-year-old youngsters shop in Brooks alone, by virtue of the family charge account and the family knowledge that Brooks wouldn't sell them anything wrong. The famous Brooks woman's sweater is sold only on the ground floor, so that female shoppers will not get into the habit of snooping around upstairs.

In March, 1946, Brooks Brothers was bought outright by Julius Garfinckel & Co., the Washington specialty store. If old Brooks customers saw their world tottering, they have since been reassured by the fact that Brooks has outwardly changed not at all. Winthrop H. Brooks, the fourth generation of the family, is still chairman and has assured all and sundry that he wouldn't be there if there *had* been any changes. Mr. Brooks is as proud as everyone else of the permanence of the store's styles and institutions. A few years ago he was visited by Tyrone Power, who told him that his forthcoming part in *The Razor's Edge* was that of a rich young scion of the early 1920's. What, Power asked, was the correct gentleman's costume then? Mr. Brooks showed the actor a picture on the wall of his office, of himself and several classmates at Yale. The photograph had obviously been made a good deal before 1920 and obviously all of the young Elis were wearing Brooks suits. "Look at these clothes, young man," said Mr. Brooks. "Do they look so different from what we sell today?" Tyrone Power said no; as a matter of fact, they looked just the same. "Exactly my point!" cried Brooks. "Run downstairs and buy one of our suits; it'll make you the perfect costume for 1920."

One block north of Brooks is a less restrained but, in its own line, equally legendary store—Abercrombie & Fitch. "The Greatest Sporting Goods Store in the World" is highly geared and highly expensive. Its customers shoot more quail than tin cans and bag more marlin than catfish, since Abercrombie's object is to carry absolutely the best in sporting equipment, regardless of price. Their collection of expensive guns is unrivaled, and the good aim of their customers is proved by the vast collection of elephant, lion and antelope heads that festoon their walls—the loan of grateful Abercrombie regulars like Osa Johnson, Lawrence Copley Thaw and Kermit Roosevelt. Although part of the store's annual five million dollars' gross is made up by the sale of two-bit reels and boxes of puppy biscuit, their big effort is reserved for the out-of-doors expert. Thus Abercrombie's carries $1250 embossed Francotte and Purdey shotguns; for an extra fee their privately owned gun smithy, Griffin & Howe, will add a special "cross-eyed" stock for hunters who shoot off the right shoulder and aim with the left eye.

Dapper New York pooches are regularly trotted into A & F's ground-floor pet department, where they are fitted for sterling silver collars while they snarl at a near-by Persian cat who is acquiring a turtle-neck winter sweater. Falconry experts come in for hoods and jesses, and croquet champions for mallets as carefully made and expensive as fine golf clubs. A purchaser of a mah-jongg set (the game was first popularized in this country by an Abercrombie salesman) may find himself standing in line in front of Mrs. Roosevelt, the Duke of Windsor or King Farouk.

In spite of the permanence of Brooks and Abercrombie's and the success of such men's emporiums as Charvet and Countess Mara for neckties, Bronzini for expensive haberdashery, S. J. Feron for rackets and Stoeger for guns, New York belongs, as a shopping center, to the women. Most New York women start their shopping day with a pretty clear idea of what they want and where they can find it. (Third Avenue . . . antique shops; Lexington . . . jewelry shops and small dress stores; Madison . . . every kind of small shop; 57th Street . . . expensive name designers and name stores; Fifth Avenue . . . the best, from department stores to gift shops to beauty salons.) They know that Altman's, Lord & Taylor and Saks Fifth Avenue are the top three department-specialty stores, with Saks the most expensive. They know Best's for its classic dresses and its Lilliputian Bazaar. Those with less money known all the departments of Bloomingdale's or Wanamaker's. The rich ones know the names and addresses of the top-name designers like Mainbocher, Valentina and Charles James, Hattie Carnegie and John-Frederics. For gifts they patronize Georg Jensen and Steuben Glass; Jaeckel, Gunther and Maximilian for furs; Elizabeth Arden and Helena Rubinstein for beauty treatments. They have charge accounts at the top-price, top-quality women's stores: Bergdorf Goodman, Bonwit Teller and Henri Bendel. They know which stores have exclusive rights to the creations of the best American and foreign designers: Dior at Bendel, Don Loper at Lord & Taylor, Howard Greer at Bonwit Teller.

Possessor of the fanciest reputation of any New York women's store is Bergdorf Goodman. Literally, as well as figuratively, it stands at the head of Fifth Avenue, occupying a handsome white building on 58th Street, near Central Park, on the site of the old Cornelius Vanderbilt mansion. Inside, the store still has more the feeling of a grand mansion than of a mart. No customer entering the marble rotunda is left standing until a sales girl feels like waiting on her; chances are she will be greeted by Mr. Jesse, the ground-floor superintendent, who will turn her over to the proper department. Keeping up the personal touch, Bergdorf's encourages any sales girl on the ground floor to accompany a customer through her entire shopping tour of the store. Bergdorf's likes to feel that its customer is a guest and that its personnel are on permanent "company manners."

Obviously a budget shop could not afford these attentions and Bergdorf's is no budget shop. Its prices are unswervingly high. Ready-to-wear dresses, many of which are designed by the store's own Bernard Newman, run roughly from $100 to $235. Custom is the store's biggest business and the price tags on custom street dresses read from $350 to $500, while there is no particular top on the evening clothes, which often reach $1000. They have even made up a $1000 nightgown. At these prices Bergdorf customers are buying not just politeness and service, but the products of the world's best designers, including the store's own ace, Mark Mooring, Hollywood's Irene and many of the best Parisian couturiers.

In addition to its expensive dresses, Bergdorf's carries a large line of custom millinery, some perfumes and antiques, accessories, and a good deal of jewelry which is largely designed by their own craftsmen. Bergdorf's leases a portion of the ground floor to an independent concession, Delman Shoes. The store also sells, without fanfare, a small line of ready-made dresses for as little as $40.

But most of the store's 46,000 active charge accounts represent women who can regularly afford to buy the best in Bergdorf's line and who continue to do so most of their lives. The store has one designer who specializes in clothes for older women, but even these clothes retain as much sophistication and as many new touches as the size and shape of the customer will permit. Bergdorf's is probably right, however, in thinking that its average customer is more apt to be a famously well-dressed woman like Mrs. Byron Foy than a plump and aging dowager. They also know that almost as many of their regular accounts come from fashionable Kansas City, Dallas and Seattle addresses as from Park Avenue and Southhampton. So faithful are these women to Bergdorf's that there are a sizable group who annually spend between $50,000 and $75,000 there; last year the top charge account amounted to $118,000.

Everyone living in a city where one person can blow $118,000 on dresses is bound to be affected by it. Whether or not he can afford to shop at Bergdorf's, Brooks' or Tiffany's, the presence of all these stores on the same streets that he is walking gives every New Yorker and every visitor an occasional feeling of intoxication—the realization that he is part of the big, crazy town where no wild purchase is inconceivable.

PLACES OF WORSHIP

CHIANG YEE

When Henry James revisited New York some half-century ago, he lamented the eclipse of Trinity Church, "so cruelly overtopped" by skyscrapers, and detected an "inexorable law of the growing invisibility of churches." Today Riverside Church is perhaps the only exception to this New York "law." By way of compensation, however, New York probably contains a larger number and greater variety of houses of worship than any other city on earth. The city's two giant cathedrals, St. John the Divine and St. Patrick's, are, of course, internationally famous. But, in a far smaller edifice, the "Little Church Around The Corner," mammoth, flip, possibly fearful, New York has supplied the nation with one of its key symbols of enduring romance. And in the heart of this metropolis of hurry-scurry, inside Grand Central Terminal, a Pullman Porter has arranged to have a railroad car set aside for noonday meditation. Nearby, at a midtown hotel, a meditation room has been permanently endowed by an anonymous, latter-day Medici. Appropriately, the city's largest cathedral, St. John the Divine, built stone-on-stone like the ancient European cathedrals, is a conglomerate of several architectural styles and, like the big town itself, is still a hopeful work in progress.

Among the many notable religious edifices in New York, I visited each of the three big ones on Fifth Avenue: St. Patrick's Cathedral, St. Thomas' Church, and the Temple Emanu-El of the City of New York. There are three other Fifth Avenue churches—the Church of the Ascension, the First Presbyterian Church and the Brick Church—but I got no further with them than reading the names in the porches. How I found the 'Little Church Around the Corner' was purely accidental. I was walking one morning and it suddenly began to rain. I have never minded rain of the English drizzle kind, but here my newly acquired light flannel suit soon began to look limp, so I moved to the shelter of a shop window. The goods displayed attracted me and I sidled along till I found myself taking a turn in East 29th Street. There, in a noticeable gap between the usual tall buildings, stood a little church.

It was named, I was informed, by 'Rip Van Winkle' Joseph Jefferson. When an actor named George Holland died in 1870 and the pastor of a neighbouring church declined to bury him, Jefferson heard that this little church would perform funeral services for strangers and remarked, "God bless the little church around the corner." It is said to have become the church of the theatrical profession from that day, just as St. Paul's, Covent Garden, is the church of the theatrical profession in London. The green grass and the young leaves on the trees in the churchyard, mingled with the sculptural ornaments and statues, appealed to me. The gateway, with its emerald roof and reddish walls, did not look like the churches I had seen in Europe, but the small spire and tower made the building's significance unmistakable. Inside, everything was beautifully polished and clean. There were a number of people in the nave but not a sound could be heard. I was greatly impressed by the stillness so near to the heavy traffic of Fifth Avenue. A young priest came in. He made no enquiry concerning my presence. Then two ladies and a girl in beautiful dresses entered, and one of them asked me where the wedding was to take place. I realised that she mistook me for a guest, and I decided that it was time for me to go. Outside it was now drizzling, and I went up the steps of the house opposite to get a general view of the church. The silver lines of the top of the Empire State Building above some tall darkish masonry behind the church shone in the rain and made a bright and unusual scene only to be found in New York. A passer-by stopped, unasked, to tell me that this was one of the oldest churches in New York, its first services having been held on Mid-Lent Sunday 1850 by the Rev. George Hendric Houghton. I thanked him wholeheartedly. It is rare for anyone in a New York street to be able to spare the time to chat. I wondered how the little church had managed to survive for a hundred years in such an expanding quarter of Fifth Avenue. Its members must have been very full of faith. As Robert W. Service (a poet not well thought of but one who said, I think, many true if not exquisite things) wrote:

> "Yet somehow life's not what I thought it,
> And somehow the gold isn't all."

The two lofty spires of St. Patrick's Cathedral between 50th and 51st Streets, and the spire of St. Thomas' at 53rd Street, stand out unmistakably as replicas of ancient architecture in direct contrast with the modernity of the rest of the great street.

I had a look at the interior of St. Patrick's because I had been told that the Cathedral was Gothic, and similar in style to Cologne Cathedral. I noticed the Italian marble altar and the Altar Tabernacle which are richly decorated and inlaid with sparkling precious stones. Many candles were burning and people were praying or meditating. I moved round as noiselessly as I could. When I came out at the back, on Madison Avenue, I was pleased to find two fine magnolia trees in bloom. Flowers always give me pleasure. These two trees, with their purplish-white blossoms shining in the bright sun like the candles inside the Cathedral, should be a delight to anyone who happens to pass through this neighbourhood where there is otherwise nothing but steel, stone and machines.

One morning I found myself behind a group of photographers in a crowd outside St. Thomas' Church. I thought an important wedding must be about to take place. Two photographers were arguing hotly. One said: "There's a big shot just coming out of the left door. He's got a lot of potatoes. I'll get him." "Never heard of him," said the other, "better wait." "I can show him the picture," replied the first. "You won't get much out of that guy," said the second. The first then squeezed away and was lost to my sight. The exceptional mobility of their faces as they talked fascinated me. I felt I should now understand better the dialogue in stories by O. Henry and Damon Runyon. All kinds of people in their best clothes came streaming out of the church. Most of them paused a moment on the church steps. I hope I was not uncharitable in feeling that they were aware of the photographers. Every one held a long piece of yellowish-green grass, and these went well with the brightly-coloured dresses and fresh faces of the young people. It was Palm Sunday.

Another morning I went to look at the Temple Emanu-El, which I had heard was the third largest religious structure in the City. It is in early Romanesque style showing Byzantine influence. I was particularly impressed by the great recessed arch with the rose window on the Fifth Avenue side, but the whole interior is colourful and interesting. A very amiable fellow-visitor walked towards me and remarked in a manner I did not feel able—even if I had felt inclined—to contradict, that this was the most beautiful building in the world. His chest was nearly double the breadth of mine and his very prominent nose made me conscious of my little flat one. He smiled incessantly, stood by me while I looked my fill, and accompanied me when I left. I was sure he must be the director of some big concern. When he learned that I came from England, he said that he knew London and Paris very well and before the war had visited them nearly every year. "Hyde Park is very good in June," he continued. . . . "Plenty of nice girls!" I was, in Boswell's phrase, 'a good deal stunned' by this remark and did not know what to say. Whereupon he laughed and left me.

❦

OF SCHOLARSHIP AND PEACE
(*Public Library*)
CHIANG YEE

With so many books on sale, it is astounding that there should be four and a half million persons visiting New York's Public Library annually. There are, I was told, about three million books and pamphlets in the Reference Department, more than one million in the Circulation Department, and nearly twelve millions are lent every year for home use. New York should be called 'the most read city in the world.' This Library is as arresting in its solidity as the Empire State Building in its height. Perhaps I am more conventional than progressive as far as architecture is concerned, for I find this white marble building, which is neither highly polished nor over-decorated with carving, very simple, dignified and satisfying. It has only four storeys and is clearly distinguished from the adjoining premises in this busy shopping quarter. Strangely enough, the few skyscrapers near its east wing, with the Empire State Building in the distance, seem to frame the library into a picture. The founders could not have chosen a happier site. The library serves as a reminder of mental refreshment to people otherwise given over, in this part of the city, to the satisfaction of material needs and comforts. I visited it on many occasions, and never walked in with my eyes closed, though I was told that there is a special Department for blind readers, containing more than 20,000 books and 6,000 music scores in Braille, as well as magazines in several foreign languages. I had a look there and was informed that most of the blind readers came unaccompanied. I marvelled how they managed to pass unscratched through the New York traffic. To me, with excellent eyesight, the charging yellow taxis, which look like tigers and hoot like maddened beasts, kept me on the jump.

Inside the Library there were always plenty of people; the revolving doors clinked incessantly. But I noticed once or twice someone dozing on a marble seat at the corner of the hall and even snoring gently. Unlike the British Museum there are many reading rooms, each given over to the study of a particular group of subjects. The Photographic Department was always full of people looking through millions of photographs in search of—what? I should so like to have asked them. I was told that for a very small charge one could get a copy of any picture in a day or two. As the author of a few children's books, I spent a good while in the Children's Department. That there should be such a Department at all in a national library appealed to me.

I was attracted, too, by the great wealth of Americana, one of the Library's most interesting sidelines. The American Indian Department contains all kinds of books and material relating to the American Indians. Once I was taken there to look up some legends and folklore about the dogwood tree and the American robin and was courteously accorded much help by one of the assistants. Had I been able to stay longer in New York I should constantly have been found delving in the books in this Department, for I have a private belief that my honourable race had some connection with the ancient American Indians.

I was fortunate in meeting at a friend's party, Mr. Karl Küp, Curator of the Spencer Collection and the Print Room. He showed me round his Department with its many beautiful sixteenth and seventeenth century illuminated manuscripts in French and English. Though I have never made a study of these illuminated books, I am always interested to see specimens of calligraphy. This meeting with Mr. Küp reminded me of the great joy I had when my good friend, Mr. Strickland Gibson, formerly keeper and sub-librarian of the Bodleian Library at Oxford and author of *Some Oxford Libraries*, showed me many of the most valuable manuscripts there. Mr. Gibson has retired now, but he still goes to the Bodleian every day. He says that he just can't part with the books which have been with him nearly all his life. I think I should be attached to books in the same way if I had been with them for forty years. Books may yet empty my purse and bring me to bankruptcy! Mr. Küp showed me a number of old Chinese books with woodblock illustrations, some in colour. He said that he was proud to have secured so many, but it was I who felt the greater pride.

On the walls of the long corridor outside the Print Room are coloured prints of New York landmarks and scenes. One that particularly interested me was a panorama of the Hudson River from New York to Albany, drawn from nature with words indicating individual places and mountains, and engraved by William Wade in 1845. It reminded me of the famous Sung painting, 'A Thousand Miles of the Yangtse River' by Hsia Kwei, though there was of course no similarity in the artistic rendering. I indulged for a few minutes in fantasies of the romantic mountains up the Hudson River so well described by Washington Irving. Another interesting feature of the Library was the Lenox and Stuart art collections. Here I found works by Reynolds and Turner, but I was more attracted by the exhibits executed by Stuart and Copley, for they were American artists. The other countries of the world that I have seen have a long way to go before they can compete with the United States in the efficiency and enterprise of its public libraries, museums and art galleries.

On the west side of the Library lies the charming Bryant Park. Spacious, without being big, its trees, flower-beds and lawns are a little above the street level. Half of it is surrounded by tall buildings. Many readers come out of the Library to rest or stroll in it. I often spent a little time there before entering the Library. I shared the seats on the steps of the Bryant Statue, watching the pigeons being fed. Sparrows flutter about and enjoy any crumbs left untouched by the pigeons. Here is peace in the midst of the busiest quarter of New York.

MAN'S RIGHT TO KNOWLEDGE

(*Columbia University*)

FROM ''TIME''

New York City plays host to scores of noted colleges and universities. In the College of the City of New York and its related institutions it boasts the largest and most famous municipal system of free higher education in the world. In this sense New York is the most democratic of cities. However, merit and ability are the bases for admission to the free institutions. Hence, it is not surprising that City College, for example, has one of the highest academic ratings in the country. Unquestionably, though, of all Gotham's citadels of learning, Columbia University has the greatest prestige, country-wide and internationally.

To most New Yorkers, the advertisement that appeared in the *Gazette* one day in 1754 was apparently not very exciting. The ad's announcement was that a new College would be opened some time in July, but when the time came for registration, only eight young men signed up. In those days, the institution that was to become Columbia, fourth largest (25,000 students) and fourth richest ($113,589,957.37 in capital endowment) of U.S. universities, had not a single building to call its own. About the only thing it did have was a conviction: that "New York is the Center of English America, and the Proper Place for a Colledge."

In 1954 as Columbia celebrated its two hundredth anniversary, it could summon scholars from all over the world to attend its year-long series of conferences and convocations. But in spite of its international prestige, it has never lost its early sense that the city is its "proper place," nor has it forgotten that its special character is largely a matter of location. It is an Ivy Leaguer minus the ivy, an ivory tower without ivory, a polyglot campus of brick and stone that still draws two-thirds of its undergraduates from a radius of less than one hundred miles. Its bicentennial theme—"Man's right to knowledge and the free use thereof"—is wide as the world; but the university's own official title is still proudly local—Columbia University in the City of New York.

In the course of two centuries, the city itself has not always returned the compliment of such enthusiasm. It was true that George Washington let his stepson go there, and that Alexander Hamilton was an alumnus. But by 1814 the trustees were branding Columbia as "a spectacle, mortifying to its friends, humiliating to the city." In the 1850s, Trustee Samuel Ruggles ruefully pointed out that of two universities that George III chartered, Göttingen had 89 professors and 1,545 students, while Columbia still languished with six professors and 140 students.

It was not until 1865, when bearded President Frederick A. P. Barnard took over, ear trumpet and all, that Columbia began to achieve something like its present stature. The only trouble was that though Dr. Barnard was long on ideas, he was perpetually short of money. An educational statesman, he advocated honors courses, modern languages, the admission of women ("conductive to good order"), uniform entrance requirements for U.S. colleges, and teacher training. He looked forward to the day when Columbia would be a great university, complete with such modern additions as schools of engineering, architecture and commerce. Nevertheless, Columbia stayed put in its former deaf and dumb asylum on East 49th Street. It remained for the Midas touch of millionaire President Seth Low and his autocratic successor Nicholas Murray Butler to put Barnard's ideas into practice on Morningside Heights.

The Butler reign (1902–45) lasted for more than 40 years, and for Columbia it was an age of vast expansion. "It is literally true," Butler once wrote, "that beginning with Gladstone, Prince Bismarck, Cardinal Newman and Pope Leo XIII, it has been my happy fortune to meet, to talk with, and often to know in warm friendship almost every man of light and learning during the past half-century." Along with premiers, princes and pontiffs, Butler also went in for bankers. He had such a way with men of means, in fact, that Muckraker Upton Sinclair finally dubbed Columbia "the University of the House of Morgan."

Today, under able President Grayson Kirk (who succeeded President Eisenhower), Columbia carries on the pursuit of learning on a campus that resembles an oasis in a traffic jam. But it is part of the university's nature that it regards the screeching city not as a distraction but as a stimulus. Students are inclined to treat the Metropolitan Museum of Art as a sort of Columbia annex. There are exchange arrangements with both Union and Jewish Theological Seminaries. Broadway actors, corporation lawyers, Manhattan littérateurs have all given courses, and Columbia professors themselves are as much a part of town as gown.

At the heart of Columbia is Columbia College—one of the smallest (2,255 students) but still one of the most influential in the Ivy League. It was Columbia that first revolutionized its freshman and sophomore years by introducing what has subsequently become known as General Education, and out of the late John Erskine's famed humanities course came the inspiration for the entire Great Books movement.

Meanwhile the university's professional schools and affiliated institutions (including the great fifty-million-dollar Columbia-Presbyterian Medical Center) have exercised an influence of their own. Columbia started the first U.S. School of Mines (1864), awarded the first M.D. in the North American colonies (1770), established the first school of library training, the first professorship of agriculture, the first graduate school of social work. It has turned out three Chief Justices of the U.S. (John Jay, Charles Evans Hughes, Harlan F. Stone), enrolled in its law school the two Presidents Roosevelt ("You will never be able to call yourself an intellectual," huffed Butler after F.D.R. quit school for politics, "until you come back to Columbia and pass your law exams"). For better or worse, Columbia can also claim to have started the most powerful U.S. teachers' college—just across 120th Street, which TC's liberal-arts critics call "the widest street in the world."

Like New York City, Columbia is a melting pot. It is a land of the turban, the fez and the beret, as well as a casual assortment of G.I. shirts, flannel slacks and pin stripes. It bristles with institutes and centers for Russian, Middle East and East Asian studies, has a *Maison Française*, a *Casa Italiana*, a *Deutsches Haus* and a *Casa Hispánica*. Through the portals of Columbia, as through the Port of New York, passes the largest foreign enrollment in the U.S.

If the university has to a large extent assumed the character of the city, the process has also worked in reverse. Among its alumni are 3,000 New York City lawyers, 1,500 physicians, and 1,000 of the city's dentists. Its college and graduate schools have turned out ten New York governors (among them: Thomas E. Dewey, LL.B. '25), and fourteen New York City mayors. Simon and Schuster, Harcourt and Brace, and Alfred Knopf all went there; so did Rodgers and Hart and Hammerstein II. In the newspaper field, Columbia boasts a variety of opinion-makers, from the *Times*'s Arthur Hays Sulzberger to the New York *Post*'s Editor James Wechsler to Hearst Columnist George Sokolsky.

The present faculty, much more than a distinguished cluster of scholars, includes two Nobel Prizewinners (Physicists I. I. Rabi and Hideki Yukawa) and three winners of Pulitzer Prizes (Composer Douglas Moore, Historian Allan Nevins, Poet Mark Van Doren). It is also a reservoir of talent that serves the whole metropolis. Such men as Critic Lionel Trilling and Classicist Gilbert Highet are full-fledged city celebrities. Economist Carl Shoup wrestles with city finances; Historian Harry Carman serves on the Board of Higher Education, and a slew of geologists and planners struggle with the city's water and traffic.

But of all Columbia's contributions to its home town, none is more impressive than the School of General Studies, where anyone from taxi driver to tycoon can get a complete liberal-arts education pretty much on his own schedule. Since 1947 some fifteen hundred students have won their B.A.s there, and of these, 68 per cent have gone on to graduate work. With that school, two-hundred-year-old Columbia has rounded out the promise that President Barnard made nearly a century ago—that "no seeker after knowledge shall fail to find here what he requires, and . . . that no sincere and earnest seeker after knowledge, of whatever age, sex, race or previous condition, shall be denied the privilege of coming here."

HARLEM, KNOWN AND UNKNOWN

FANNIE HURST

The Caleb Smiths live in a six-room apartment on Convent Avenue. There is that about the street which bears out its name. The campus of a university is within sight, trees abound, and on summer evenings the concerts from the nearby Stadium reach the Smiths in their living room.

It is a pleasant living room. Piano, upholstered three-piece suite. Radio. Bookcases of standard works: Charles Dickens, Dumas, Pushkin. On the center table are The Amsterdam News, Reader's Digest, Life and The Saturday Evening Post. A boy's bicycle leans against the wall in the narrow hall off which there are conventional bedrooms.

Dr. Smith is a chiropodist. Harriet, his eighteen-year-old daughter, is studying to become one. Jackie, aged twelve, attends a private school. His room is hung with three-cornered banners, and the ball-and-bat paraphernalia of the average boy are in evidence. The linoleum on the floor is in the design of the map of the United States.

Mrs. Smith replies "Housewife" when she answers the question at the voting booth. She is also active in Y.W.C.A. and church work.

The George Chalmers live in the same apartment house with the Smiths, but in larger quarters. Here there is a grand piano, a considerable spread of good silver on the dining-room buffet. There are three master bedrooms and two baths. Most of the upholstery is fine needlepoint. Mr. Chalmers owns the apartment building, which he maintains adequately, although it is evident that the premises have seen better days. Mrs. Chalmers, who likes to spend hours at her sewing machine, is older than Mrs. Smith, and less modern in her views. She was born in North Carolina. Her daughter and son are married. Roy Chalmers is an insurance agent married to a working school teacher. They have one child. Ellen Chalmers married a Harvard Ph.D. who works for an interracial organization. The Chalmers keep a chauffeur who is also a man-of-all-work in the apartment building.

The Chalmers and the Smiths know each other as neighbors and bridge partners. They also attend the nearby Rock Church. There are blocks and blocks of Smiths, but only a comparative few of the upper-bracket, property-owning Chalmers.

The George K. Washingtons own a prosperous liquor store over on the avenue and occupy a private house in an adjacent side street.

Twenty-five years ago this house was the residence of a Social Register family. Dr. George Johnson, a skin specialist, and his wife maintain a large home and do extensive entertaining. Miss Sarah Splint, an extraordinarily successful spinster lawyer, who ran for the House of Representatives and almost made it, lives next door in an apartment which she shares with a woman doctor and a social worker.

There are stretches of these quiet residential areas. Turn down one of them with me into some factual homes of real people.

Mr. and Mrs. Rupert Griffith live nicely but in a narrow walk-up building so potentially tenement that a cat stalks a garbage can beside the entrance. But their apartment gleams. Beverly, the little girl, is home from private school with tonsilitis. Mrs. Griffith, who wants Beverly to have the education she was denied, is reading aloud to her. Griffith works on intricate machinery and has written a textbook on the subject, entitled, "How to Become an Expeller Operator."

Finally, the Clifford Alexanders, who approach the "intelligentsia group" and whose home of books and music testifies to their common tastes. The Alexanders have had the same housekeeper, who originally served as their son's nurse, for twelve years. Mr. Alexander is head of the Urban Housing Management Association. Recently he was offered the management of a large transient hotel. More lucrative than his present position, he nevertheless declined it because he and Mrs. Alexander did not like the idea of hotel environment for their growing boy.

But in the main, it is the Smith family which represents the middle-of-the-road way of life as it goes on its quiet, unpretentious but comfortable way in this large section of a metropolitan region.

These are Negro homes in Harlem into which we have just peered.

In all probability this sector of American family life does not synchronize with the popular whoop-'em-up, zoot-suited, bear-greased, white man's version of New York's more infamous and famous Harlem. So far as the general white conception is concerned, Harlem is either a forbidden city, a closed, a walled, or a bandit one.

The tree-lined, residential streets which lead off Lenox Avenue, of bygone elegance, to be sure, but where an air of dignity still lingers, figure scarcely at all in the popular version of this Negro city set down within a white one.

What osmosis does take place between the seven million white-skinned New Yorkers and the five hundred thousand brown ones is largely by way of social workers, the Police Department, headlines, courts, slumming parties, domestic help and Negro entertainers.

A certain element of white New York takes its out-of-town guests to the Savoy dance hall and Small's cabaret. The taxi driver points out places of lurid or headline interest, and the visiting fireman, after an evening of comfortable spectator vantage, will return to Duluth or Emporia and describe how your life isn't your own on the streets of Harlem. Still others will make the rounds of the churches or cults— Father Divine's, the Holy Rollers, the Negro Synagogue—never pausing to take note that from 110th Street north and south, from Madison Avenue to Morningside Avenue, there are approximately 150 less spectacular churches of various denominations—Abyssinian Baptist, St. Martin's Episcopal, Church of the Master, Presbyterian; Mount Calvary, Methodist; St. Aloysius, Catholic; Mother Zion, A.M.E.

Harlem, to the millions of whites who close it in on four sides, is a badlands, where the chauffeur or the housemaid goes home to sleep, where the children have rickets, and no man is safe after dark. It is an incubator for vice, a lunatic fringe of savage music, a breeding ground for race riots. All Harlem is musically talented, unreliable, un- or a-moral.

The white mind seldom follows the Negro into his home. He inhabits the New York scene as red-cap, porter, longshoreman, elevator man, waiter, cook, truck driver, soldier. Where he goes, what he does after the hours spent in the white man's world, is of little or no interest.

Statistics of crime, housing, broken homes, delinquency, reach the headlines of the white man's press, but the impact is soft. The white man reasons, if at all: It happens that way in Harlem. The Negro problem we have with us always.

Ask yourself what Harlem means to you. Jazz. Policy numbers. Police cars. Dives. Door-key children. Hazards. Hi-jinks. The Black Belt. The Gin Belt. Vice, dice and lice. The zone of the wench, the policy racket, the trombone.

The pity of it, indeed, the danger of it, is that the large majority of Harlem, who lead ordered, backbone-of-the-nation lives, are seldom heard of. They form little part, if any, of the public's concept of Harlem which, like the foreign section of New York, is a conglomerate; but a conglomerate of native-born Americans from various parts of their own country, with minorities of Virgin Islanders and West Indies groups mixed in.

Set down in the upper reaches of New York City, Harlem is loosely bounded on the south by 110th Street, on the north by 155th Street, on the west by Morningside Avenue, and on the east by the Harlem River.

Most of its boundaries are, of course, somewhat flexible and are rapidly expanding. But, approximately, you could set Harlem down on a Kermanshah rug, three square miles in area.

There are poorly lighted streets, wide as boulevards, that nevertheless glitter with heat lightning as they slash through Harlem. Most notable are Seventh and Lenox Avenues.

By day, the swift flow of the five hundred thousand Negroes who live on this three-square-mile "rug" pour through the wide streets that have seen better days. By night they are merely lurid, but by day the rundown, once-pretentious houses along these main arteries show up for what they are. Derelicts, trussed up. Leftovers from the days when whites occupied them in family groups. Not like rabbits in warrens. Remnants of high-ceiling parlors with fine marble mantelpieces remain. In many there is still evidence of hardwood floors, sound plumbing and expensive chandeliers which are all but obliterated by rooms as crowded as junkshops. These unhappy houses that manage to conceal most of their scrofula behind their façades are literally gorged with human life.

A cross section of many of these Seventh and Lenox Avenue buildings would reveal just what many of you would expect of Harlem. Basement dives of wench, jive and worse, not particularly different from places of similar character on the Great White Way, but italicized in the white mind because they happen to be on the black Great White Way. The cross section of many of these buildings would further reveal underprivileged children crowded into dirty rooms which are packed to capacity with the exploited rent-payers of Harlem. It would reveal an insane conglomerate of trunks, cots, furtive tenants prepared to fly by night, three-shift sleepers who occupy beds that have a new occupant every eight hours. It would further reveal prostitutes, pimps, hallway bathrooms, light housekeeping in rooms of minimum privacy, and the high social hazards that go with lack of privacy.

The unwritten and up to now accepted law is that people living in Harlem simply do not get the same amount for their money in terms of living accommodations as those in other sections of the metropolis—Washington Heights, for instance, which is an adjoining white section of comparable land values.

Negroes, closed in as they are by enforced segregation, are unable to escape and therefore must contend with the limitation of space in which they have learned to live and which makes them so readily vulnerable to exploitation.

But despite the fact that life is more difficult and deprived, injustice, exploitation and discrimination more usual, there is an immense section of unhonored and unsung Harlem which represents decency, family unity and social stability. There are the homes and families of the butchers, the bakers, the candlestick makers, the doctors, the lawyers, the "intelligentsia," the merchants, a certain stratum of wage-earners, and, of course, a large white-collar element.

These are the people who are about as much given to the night life, the dive-life of the great lurid area of Harlem, as the John Owens of West End Avenue, the Feitelbaums of the Bronx, or the Mulaneys of Morningside Heights are given to Broadway's "hot-spots." The majority of Harlem families seldom frequent the night life of Lenox and Seventh Avenues, or go there except to patronize its beauty parlors, chiropodists, dentists or churches. The Smiths do not, nor the Chalmerses nor the Alexanders and their kind. Carefully bred Negro girls are no more permitted by watchful parents to participate in the underworld night life of the black White Way than are their equivalents in white society.

Now all this is not to invite you to dismiss the overpowering statistical story of Harlem's juvenile delinquency, low-health stature, underprivileged children, unsanitary, overcrowded and filthy living conditions, prostitution, destitution and broken homes. All these stack up into statistical narratives that are a blot on a city, a State, a democracy, a world.

Walk its streets and you see men and women flashily attired, racetrack touts, ragged children, light-skinned, dark-skinned, medium-skinned population, disturbers of the peace, streetwalkers wary of plainclothesmen, juvenile delinquents on parole. You will see far too much evidence of the accumulated evils of the long history of injustices that have been heaped upon the American Negro during the generations that he has been among the least alien and the most separate race in America.

To lose sight of this shameful Harlem would be just as invalid as to overlook the prosperous upswinging Harlem, which goes about its serious-minded business of creating and maintaining its homes, educating its children, earning its living and providing all possible security for an insecure people.

No more than this one-world can any longer contain these United States of America in a state of suspended isolation can the City of New York maintain its separateness from this Harlem city within its invisible walls.

One measure of the strength of a democracy is its willingness to examine its own shortcomings. It is in this spirit that I have presented here Fannie Hurst's blunt portrayal of Harlem. But some of the bright gleams on the Harlem horizons need to be further highlighted. In fact, a considerable body of expert Negro opinion believes that Harlem has been making material progress faster than any other community on earth. Today Harlem Negroes own property assessed at nearly three hundred million dollars. One survey reports that the income of the average Harlem family has tripled since 1940, bringing it approximately to the national average. Negro-owned businesses, some of wide scope, have increased substantially, and about a third of them are located outside of Harlem. Many housing projects have been constructed and more are on the way, though, admittedly, the attack on this central difficulty is still only marginal. Ten times as many Harlem youngsters are in college today as in 1940. And there are good reasons to expect the winds of change over Harlem to blow at an even more rapid rate henceforth. In fact, as of 1955, Hulan Edward Jack, a Harlem Negro, is President of the Borough of Manhattan, where Negroes comprise but one fifth of the population.

21:

New York's Most Glamorous Restaurant

LUCIUS BEEBE

To say that the fame of Jack and Charlie's 21 Restaurant is national is a triumph of understatement, for its fame abroad is almost as well established as that of Maxim's, Claridge's, or the Tour d'Argent. It possesses the added distinction of being the hardest restaurant in the world to gain admission to.

Discount, however, its reputation for exclusiveness and as a celebrity trap, strip off its implications of wealth, social position and professional prestige and you still have a restaurant second to none in New York, New Orleans or San Francisco and on a par with the best in Paris. In snob appeal, distinction of clientele and the preparation of Steak Dianne, 21 is tops. It has everything that makes for lush good living.

More or less like Caesar's Gaul, the annals of Jack and Charlie's can be divided into three convenient compartments: its beginnings in the days of prohibition and the torrid 20's, what Scott Fitzgerald called "the years of the great tea dance"; a second period, between repeal and 1941, when New York public life was taken over by café society; and the third period, not yet ended, in which the patronage of such expensive premises has been dominated neither by fashion nor personal wealth, but by the expense-account executive and the expense-account publicist spending corporate funds on entertainment for only vaguely corporate ends.

A great deal of big business has always been transacted at 21, but for years it was almost entirely lunchtime big business, conducted in the crepuscle of the downstairs café and calling for little more than incidental cocktails and highballs. Now big business seems to involve feminine companionship, dinner dress, a five-course dinner and a great deal of sparkling wine. In an age of diminishing personal incomes and confiscatory taxes, luxury life is sharply restricted to what is euphemistically called "business entertainment."

The legend of exclusiveness in the upholstered precincts of 21 is well rooted in the circumstance that the management has never wanted any but upper-case patrons. Jack and Charlie's is a public restaurant and ever since the repeal of prohibition has been open to any persons who can afford its tariff and conform to reasonable standards of propriety in manners and appearance.

"The fact of the matter is that the entire premises of Twenty-one are filled at all times by regular customers," explains Jerry Berns, one of the partners. "We would be glad to welcome anybody of suitable appearance we have never heard of, but with every table reserved and bar space in urgent requisition for old friends, how can we possibly let in people we don't know?"

As has been the case with every other distinguished restaurant in New York history—Delmonico's, Sherry's, the Waldorf, Bustonoby's, the Ritz, Luchow's, the Colony or Pavillon—Jack and Charlie's fame is founded primarily and unequivocally on food. With all of these famed restaurants, other considerations, social distinction or financial implications, came afterward, and the same is true of 21. Robert Sherwood arrived after the fame of the Lobster Thermidor was established, and *couturière* Valentina Schlee put in an appearance when word of the fine service got around. . . .

With the rise, over the years, in facilities for the preservation and transportation of rare, seasonal or uncommon foods, the management of Jack and Charlie's has never yielded to the urge, elsewhere evident, to maintain an enormous repertory of out-of-season delicacies in frozen form with which to embellish the menu.

"We are just old-fashioned enough to think that salmon and green peas belong on the seventeenth of June and that California figs should only appear on the menu when they are naturally ripe and intended by God for human consumption," Bob Kriendler told the author recently. The time for Scotch grouse is right after the twelfth of August when the season opens in England, and we usually manage to have them by the fifteenth but will not produce them for Fourth of July. After all, there are proprieties designed by nature for the service of food as well as for human clothes and manners."

Despite the seasonal restrictions imposed by management policy, the menu by the time it reaches the hands of patrons is studded with enough luxury items to amuse Henry VIII. At various times there are Dungeness crabs, Lynnhaven oysters, Guaymas shrimp, hard-boiled pheasant eggs for the bar trade, grilled black-bear chops, saddle of antelope, Scotch grouse, Norwegian ptarmigan, Mexican quail, Delaware terrapin, and mallard and canvasback duck.

For many years the menus were carefully written by hand in red and blue script as is the Continental custom and patrons cursed the holograph which confused *poissons* and *poussin*, *pamplemousse* and *mousse* of lobster. Now the menus are printed and old-timers curse them as the innovation of a mechanical age.

In the opinion of André Simon, head of the British Wine and Food Society and probably the greatest living advocate and exponent of wine, the cellars that extend underneath 21 and under the adjacent properties contain the finest collections of claret and Burgundy in the United States and some of the most remarkable champagnes and spirits. It is said among those knowing in such matters that only the private collections of Charles and Russell Godman of Boston contain more extraordinary Madeiras in an age when Madeira is no longer a commodity, even though Jack and Charlie's Boals and Sercials are not for sale and are served only in microscopic quantities to old and favored friends.

There is, for example, a Madeira of the vintage of—hold your silk hat—1804, imported by old Peter Goelet of New York aboard the brig *Twins* in January, 1810, and bottled for his use in 1816. There are other Madeiras from the Ogden Goelet collection dating from the 40's, 50's and 60's and bearing the labels of Funchal exporters which would make their descendants in the Madeira trade stand and uncover. In one of his letters to Lady Bradford while he was guest at a great English country house in the eighties, Benjamin Disraeli wrote, "I drink the Grand Chateau Margaux of 1870—by special orders, but it is not given to everyone else. I forget my embarrassment in its exquisite flavor." There are a couple of bottles of Margaux 1870 tucked away somewhere downstairs in 52nd Street.

A wine lover who, some years ago, became trapped in the claret cellar with Jack Kriendler when an electric lock failed, and was offered his choice of the bins until a locksmith could be summoned, was palsied with frustration among such splendors; when, at long last, the doors were unbarred, he hadn't yet made up his mind what to select.

The cellars themselves at 21 date from prohibition times and are one of the sights of the house which visitors unfailingly ask to visit. Concealed behind hinged bulkheads of solid masonry and brickwork which dissolve to the touch, and controlled by electric devices which would be the despair of Jimmy Valentine, they are a perpetual monument to the lengths to which men were forced to go to preserve civilization during the Age of the Great Foolishness.

There are three restaurants in 21 which are daily open to the patrons of the house for luncheon, dinner and supper: the grill, which occupies the same low ceilinged, heavily paneled room a step or so below sidewalk level as the bar, the main formal restaurant on the second floor, which from time immemorial has been known as the Front Room, and the upstairs back restaurant, called the Tapestry Room, off which there opens a very small apartment for diners engaged in close business or personal converse. This last is known as the French Room.

There is a certain contingent of 21 patrons, mostly older persons in the upper social brackets, who advance determinedly to the staircase leading to the upstairs restaurant and proceed directly to their table, squired by Floyd Flom, who announces them to Philip or Pierre at the landing. A much larger contingent heads with equal determination for the bar, pausing only to give the time of day to patrons Joe Cowan and Peter Donald who invariably occupy the bar corner nearest the entrance, and hold their first professional consultation with either Emil Bernasconi, the chief bartender, or Henry Zbikiewicz, his vicar. Emil has a remarkably retentive memory for the drinks preferred by even the most infrequent patron and even if his name should slip, the drink he last ordered, though it was a decade ago, will unfailingly appear before him in its correct proportions.

The cream of the Jack and Charlie regulars, old-timers and social and professional personages to whom appearances are a necessity, are given the super-de-luxe treatment in the Front Room. For one thing, every table and banquette in this gracious apartment is advantageous from the equally urgent standpoints of seeing and being seen. An entry or exit through its doorway with its accompanying courtesies from the service staff cannot possibly go undetected. No new hair-do, beau, or date, no Valentina evening gown or Cartier necklace can go without notice.

Lunch or dinner, it matters not the time of day, is ritual in the Front Room, a ceremonial of elegance presided over by masters of the grand manner and awash with rolling tables of Westphalian ham, flaming desserts, cut flowers, silver wine buckets, foil-topped bottles and the most perfect service of any restaurant in the world. Pierre Pastre, the headwaiter, and Philip Caselli, the maître d'hôtel, are the two men who make the pageant of the Front Room click with a soothing and cheerful precision.

The diplomacy of a Metternich and the courage of a lion tamer are the requisites for administering the Front Room. A preponderance of the regulars demand the same table whenever they put in appearance, a contingency not always announced in advance and one which presents obvious problems of displacement of bodies. Elizabeth Arden, who is so regular as to present no problem at all, must have her accustomed place at the west wall banquette. John Golden and Lee Shubert must be shown to Table 151 on boiled-beef-with-horse-radish day, which is usually Wednesday, but sometimes shifts—with disaster to the seating list. George Vanderbilt, Messmore Kendall, Lawrence Tibbett, Helen Hayes, Niles Trammell, David Sarnoff, Moss Hart, Cole Porter, Greta Garbo, Leland Hayward, Joe Cowan and John Steinbeck each has a whim about seating and each is a whim of iron.

Nor would it be judicious to forget that Mrs. Ogden Reid likes to be seated with the windows to her back, facing the entrance, that Mary Martin must be near the door to make her curtain hours in the show of the moment and that such notables as John Jacob Astor, Joshua Logan, Gen. Jimmy Doolittle and George S. Kaufman don't want to be behind any big hats or potted palms. The management has obviated the potted-palm contingency by simply not having any, but the picture hat is always a menacing possibility. . . .

Until 1935 the establishment occupied but a single brownstone house at the 21 address. In that year the adjacent and closely matching mansion to the east was purchased and the two structures joined, a move which doubled the seating capacity of all public rooms.

The year 1935 also saw the introduction of a monstrous air-conditioning system, the first in any New York restaurant of consequence, and Mr. Jack was inordinately proud of it. The time it was to go into commission, a torrid July noontide, the patrons sat around in humid expectation waiting for the machinery to cool them off. Fans whirred, air currents moved perceptibly. "Refreshing, isn't it?" beamed Mr. Jack. Everyone agreed it was splendid and reached for a handkerchief. Streams of sweat poured down the collars of the best people. The temperature rose alarmingly, but the management remained serene in the assurance of infallibility. Finally, abandoning all pretense, Bert Lahr streaked for the door. "I'm going up to the steam room at the Athletic Club to cool off," he screamed. Someone had unaccountably turned on the hot switch instead of the cold, and for months patrons remarked venomously to the partners: "Refreshing, isn't it?"

Aside from folklore, however, it is its food, its service and its wines and other refreshment that have given 21 its greatest distinction. It imports more game, incidentally, than any other U.S. restaurant.

Two of the classic dishes with which the management at 21 rewards gourmets of sufficient discernment to request them are Steak Dianne and Pheasant Souvaroff, both of which are definitely de-luxe confections and for the carriage trade only. Another luxury which Philip and Pierre serve on state occasions is Pheasant en Plumage. This is simply a roast pheasant which makes its appearance under a shell composed of a cock pheasant's head, body and trailing tail feathers and which is removed when the bird is about to be carved.

Legend gathers thickly about restaurants and in a double murk around those frequented by the great and picturesque of the world. Jack and Charlie's has more than its share. It was at the downstairs bar, for instance, that Bob Benchley arrived one long-ago noontide with an immense man with an even more enormous red bushy beard whom nobody ever recalled having seen before and whom Benchley introduced on all hands as "La barbe qui parle." It was Ernest Hemingway.

Mrs. Jeanne Owen, executive secretary of the Wine and Food Society of New York, is fond of recalling a dinner given for the directors of that august body in the course of which, in an upstairs private dining room, its president, the sage and dignified Henry W. Taft, somehow became seated beneath a painting of a nude who was showing more than her lingerie. When Mr. Taft arose, blissfully unaware of the lady, to deliver a learned paper on the origins of the Pinot grape and its consequences to world viniculture, irreverent members smiled and Alfred Knopf trained a candid camera, then a great novelty, on the scene at the end of the table. The camera broke with a loud whirring of springs and Knopf muttered morosely: "Definitely the luck of the Tafts."

Most festive occasion of the year is an annual dinner given by the management sometime during Christmas week. It is known as the Lonely Hearts. Most of the regulars and old-timers are asked and by late in the evening are of a mood to contribute liberally to the Salvation Army which sends a band and its prettiest young lady vocalists. Some years ago the Army sent a super-duper symphony which included thirty-two cornetists alone. At the instigation of Jack Kriendler, the entire band was bundled into taxis and sent to call on John Perona, at El Morocco. They played *Holy Night* to the interruption of all other activity in the town's poshest night club until Perona bribed them with one thousand dollars, please to go away.

The management of Jack and Charlie's, sentimentalists to the core, celebrated their twenty-fifth anniversary with a dinner where there were songs and speeches, toasts to the departed and the publication of a second edition of the souvenir book of the house, *The Iron Gate*. The Jack and Charlie legend, however, far from having achieved maturity, is still crescent. In 1976, when the rest of the nation will be celebrating its second century of independence, 21 without doubt will put on a celebration of its own which will rival in magnificence the national fireworks. It will be justified.

THE MET

CHIANG YEE

I am not in a position to refer to the history of American music or that of the Metropolitan Opera House; nor can I say anything about New York opera in general. I went to the Metropolitan Opera House as *the thing to see* and I duly saw it. It reminded me of the opera houses in Paris and London, though I think it has more boxes. My friend pointed out various celebrities to me as had my friends in London before the war. Moving my head round in a half circle and then turning back again I got a peculiar angle of vision such as has often been depicted by ultra-modern artists. The auditorium was so brilliantly lit with an indescribable array of lights, that my eyes began to play me tricks, and were still further dazzled by the jewels. After I had gazed round for a while all the audience appeared to me to lose eyes, nose, lips, and ears, so that black jackets seemed to be set off only by a single line of white head and gleaming white shirt front; while alternately there was the long white line of a woman's figure, the neck appearing elongated above white shoulders. When the lights were dimmed, these black and white lines became more distinct. I could see the white lines made by the women in the audience moving slightly from time to time, but curiously enough those which represented the males did not move at all. This experience helped me to understand some modern paintings. I might have had a similar experience in London or Paris, but the Metropolitan Opera House being larger gives the effect more clearly. Also the evening dress rule for theatres and the opera was relaxed in London in wartime and I doubt if even yet the full splendour has reappeared.

During the singing, the house was most appreciatively silent. Not a cough or sneeze broke the spell. I do not mean to imply that a London audience would be less appreciative, but London weather may be responsible for some unavoidable interruptions. However, I did hear a whisper here and there, which was the more perceptible in the otherwise profound silence.

My companion and I moved out with everyone else during the interval, or 'intermission' as it is called in New York. I was taken to look round the lobby and the exterior of the boxes. Then we managed to enter a packed bar for a drink. There were one or two cameramen trying to photograph society people with flash lights; they seemed to have no difficulty in penetrating the throng. I was told that had it been the opening night of the season the jam in this bar would have been much greater and that there would have been many more pressmen and cameramen about. In the bar and the lobby was the best dress parade I ever saw. I may have seen similar dresses in the windows along Fifth Avenue, but here they were on the right figures and enhanced by jewels. There were dresses of every colour, and personally I preferred those of a single colour to the mixed, fussy patterns, though a lot depends on the figure! I must admit that I did not realise there could be so many types of figure nor so many good-looking people in the world. A beautiful dress is a necessity for a beautiful face and figure and vice versa. As a Chinese artist, I have been asked now and then if I did not find Western women beautiful. To this I have found it difficult to give a straightforward reply, as I feel that there is a sort of preconception about Chinese women behind the question. So I have generally replied: "Why not?" The important factor of age is often difficult to discern. In the Metropolitan Opera House I was more than once deceived by a back view, because the wonderful soft voice revealed no hint of age.

I was not only dazzled by the women's dresses and jewels, but also by their talk and gestures, not to mention their manner of smoking and eating. One woman asked her escort to pass along a meat sandwich which disappeared in a flash; another tilted her face to the ceiling after her cigarette had been lit, without realising that her long hair was dipping into someone's glass behind her; several were talking, whispering or joking to each other, apparently unconcerned with the opera. Though the men wore their black and white uniform, they revealed their characters as they talked and laughed. One was doubled up with laughter and just could not straighten out again. Almost every man had a big cigar, while to my surprise I saw one delicately taking snuff. The whole scene seemed typical of New York society yet was at the same time familiar to me, for in many ways it reminded me of Sheridan's play *The School for Scandal*. I had no reason to suppose that this audience's talk was scandalous, but here were characters easily identifiable as Lady Sneerwell, Mrs. Candour, Lady Teazle; Maria too. Lady Teazle said: "My extravagance! I'm sure I'm not more extravagant than a woman of fashion ought to be." What more appropriate comment could there be on the women in the Metropolitan Opera House? The man taking snuff might have been Mr. Snake, who was equally good at spreading scandal and truth, as when he spoke to Lady Sneerwell for the last time: "I beg your ladyship ten thousand pardons: you paid me extremely liberally for the lie in question; but I unfortunately have been offered double to speak the truth." I saw Sheridan's play revived in London, with gorgeous costumes, only a few years ago, and could well imagine that leisurely eighteenth-century life, full of gossip about fashions, drinks and minor grievances, from which present-day London seems so very remote. That sort of life seems to exist today only during the 'intermission' at the Metropolitan Opera House!

NETHER WORLD

RICHARD GEHMAN

The first subway in New York City was opened on February 27, 1870. It ran exactly 312 feet under Broadway from Warren to Murray Streets and carried twenty passengers who each paid a twenty-five cent fare, the price of an excellent meal in those days. They sat nervously on plush-upholstered seats in a cylindrical car made mostly of wood, hoping that the propulsion apparatus, a compressed-air machine called Root's Patent Force Blast Rotary Blower, wouldn't break down and leave them stranded underground. The machine, which had a capacity of 120,000 cubic feet of compressed air per minute, shot the car through the snug-fitting tunnel like some enormous department-store pneumatic-tube system working in reverse.

The subway was operated between 1870 and '73, generally on an irregular schedule. When it wasn't running, tourists were permitted to stroll through the passageway. A healthy man could cover the distance almost as fast as the car, and the subway was no more regarded as a practical means of transportation than a Coney Island roller coaster is today.

If Alfred Ely Beach, the inventor of that primitive underground, were alive, he would observe with satisfaction that the present successor to his little blast tube is perhaps the fastest, most efficient, and safest intra-urban transit system of all time. There is not, and never has been, anything like it anywhere else. London has a subway, the oldest in the world, the first branch of which was doing business as early as 1863; Glasgow, Berlin, Moscow, Tokyo, Hamburg, Boston, Philadelphia, Budapest, Paris, Buenos Aires, Oslo, Stockholm, and Liverpool are all undermined with tunnels of varying lengths. Chicago's subsurface system opened in 1943. In size, these foreign lines are to New York's as the Flatiron Building is to the Empire State, and in complexity of operation, they are as a game of hopscotch to chess.

The Board of Transportation's map of Manhattan. The Bronx, Brooklyn, and Queens, with the crisscrossing subway and elevated lines marked in red, blue, yellow, somewhat resembles an anatomical chart showing veins and arteries. The subways and Els are, as a matter of fact, the chief conductors of the city's lifeblood, at the rate of nearly 6,500,000 pulsebeats, or fares, each day. Passengers jostle each other on a total of 12,959 train trips daily. The trains, made of 6,632 subway and elevated cars, run on tracks extending for 242.06 route miles, or 738.17 track miles.

A passenger interested in long-distance travel can board an IRT train at the 241st Street-White Plains Road station in the Bronx and go all the way to Fulton Street, in Brooklyn, where a free transfer to the BMT Jamaica line will enable him to continue to 168th Street in Jamaica, a distance of 30.69 miles. This is the longest, if perhaps not the quietest, ride in the world for fifteen cents, Japanese rickshaw boys notwithstanding.

There are 43,000-odd employees in the system. Power costs around $26,000,000 a year, and maintenance nearly $25,000,000. The City of New York now owns all rapid transit lines and has since June 12, 1940, but some surface transit lines are operated by private companies on contracts.

As most New Yorkers know, the rapid transit is divided into three main facilities, the IND, or Independent; the BMT, or Brooklyn-Manhattan Transit; and the IRT, or Interborough Rapid Transit. As most New Yorkers do not know, the three divisions are made up of thirty-seven different lines. It's difficult to get clear, explicit information from the average New Yorker on how to travel by subway or El, since he generally uses only the line that goes from his residence to work. It's hard to get clear, definite dope from subway conductors, patrolmen, and cashiers, too—not necessarily because of their don't-bother-me-now-I'm-busy attitude, apparently a job prerequisite, but because any explanation of the interlacing underground system is bound to be confusing. The IRT and the BMT become elevateds for parts of their runs. The IND, the newest and most modern, is almost entirely underground except for a half-mile or so where it crosses a bridge over the Gowanus canal. This is very nearly the highest point in the entire system, or about ninety feet. The deepest point is at 191st Street and Broadway on the IRT; it is 180 feet, or nearly twelve stories, underground.

The IRT, the busiest of the trio, handles two and a half million passengers every twenty-four hours. It is also the oldest: it was opened on October 27, 1904, over and above the protests of Broadway merchants who had staged public protests and torchlight parades, claiming an underground would ruin their businesses. Mayor George B. McClellan drove the first train from City Hall to Broadway and 145th Street, using a silver throttle to apply power. F. B. Shipley, of Philadelphia, was duly recorded as the first man to surrender a seat to a lady. More than three hundred and fifty thousand people rode the trains in the first twenty-four hours. It was quite a day.

The subway system is more than a means of transportation. It is a vast underground city, where people could live almost indefinitely without ever seeing the sunlight or even breathing unfiltered air.

It's not uncommon for Bowery derelicts to catch a few hours of sleep in cars during the lonely night runs, when even the busiest of lines are virtually without traffic, but transit patrolmen are ever on the alert for somnolent passengers. Joe Gould, the acknowledged king of Greenwich Village Bohemians, who for years has been at work on an unpublished book called "An Oral History of the World," used to have a high regard for the subway car as a writing room. Leaving the Minetta Tavern around 2 A.M., he would catch a subway and settle himself with his composition book and pencil stub, riding from one end of the line to the other all night long, recording the conversations he'd heard during the evening's revelry.

"The Subway Sun," published by the Board of Transportation, calls attention to various free municipal attractions. The "Sun" cards also serve as a kind of silent monitor of public conduct and education. "Learn at the Library," the cards advise. "Be Bright—Eat Right. Good Food Every Day Helps Keep You Well for Work or Play." "Prevent Fires." "Courtesy Cools Hot Tempers." The latter sign appears most frequently, possibly because the Board feels that passengers need to mind their manners during rush hours, when courtesy is as rare as comfort and hot tempers as common as trampled toes.

Although the rapid transit is a poor man's system, it certainly is not the exclusive property of the poor. Around 11:30 P.M., when the Broadway shows break, couples in evening dress often board trains at the Times Square entrances, sitting side by side with homing scrubwomen and weary janitors. Riding the subways is not so much a matter of economy as convenience. The most expert hack driver will freely admit that, considering the hysterical condition of New York traffic, he can't hope to compete with the subways and Els in speed. Furthermore, the rapid transit has an unparalleled "on time" record of 94 percent. When the Board of Transportation says this is the safest system in the world, it can back up the claim with figures. In 1949, there were 14 lost-time accidents per 1,000 man-hours worked; the nationwide transit industry rate was 15.6 for the same period. Cloudbursts sometimes flood tunnels in various sections and bring trains to a halt, but when this happens the maintenance crews swing into action with pumps and usually restore ordinary service within a few hours.

For a reason that probably could be partially explained by the Brothers Menninger, the dim-lit, damp, stretching caverns of the subways seem to attract people intent on doing away with themselves. Not all attempted suicides are successful. Several months ago a concert-hall official threw himself under an IND train at the Columbus Circle station of the Eighth Avenue line. The front of the first car passed over him, but the motorman had jammed on the brakes, and the official was unharmed.

The quick reaction of that motorman was supplemented by a system of brakes that is well-nigh perfect. Few other railroads are equipped with so many safety devices. Rapid transit trains have four separate automatic stopping devices: a dead-man's button, which brings the train to a halt if the motorman takes his hand off the power-control handle; an emergency device that shuts off the power if two cars come apart; another that stops the train if it passes a danger signal, and an engineer's brake valve constantly under the motorman's hand. Signaling lights on the lines are virtually foolproof. To ensure passenger safety still further, there is an interlock between the car doors and the motor of the train, so that power will not go on while the doors are open.

As the subways seem to attract people bent on harming themselves, so do they pull people planning to harm others. The deserted platforms and shady mezzanines offer protective coloration for every kind of thug, hoodlum, and pervert. Crime in the subways seems to come in waves, like a virus. Within a period of three hours one chilly morning the following incidents occurred: a young veteran was slugged on the head with a hammer as he sat in a station at Kew Gardens; two women reported stolen purses; two men were arrested for indecent exposure; thieves were reported going through the pockets of sleeping passengers on one line; and a jostler, who was trying to open women's handbags, was seized on the Union Square platform of the IRT.

Weak-wristed young men—or old men, as far as that goes—members of what a modern English poet has called The Homintern, ride the cars constantly, looking for agreeable sailors or other likely-looking youths. Scarcely a young, attractive girl exists whose body has not been inspected, furtively or otherwise, by quiet male hands in the midst of a passenger jam, and there have been instances in which the comely have had intimate garments stolen right off their persons by collectors.

The five-hundred-odd transit patrolmen are kept busy and, as local editorialists are fond of saying, should be supplemented by many more individuals. Their ranks include three women who are professional wolf-baiters; they generally are followed on their rounds by a male who makes sure that they don't run into situations they can't handle.

Late last December, the Board of Transportation outlined plans for constructing bomb shelters and for converting present facilities to accommodate refugees from the streets. If that happens, the rapid transit system, without which the aboveground city could not go on, may actually become the heart of the city. Not a pleasant thought; but, in a curious way, a reassuring one. Today the average New York subway passenger spends ten and one-half twenty-four-hour days underground each year. If total war comes . . . well, as one subway patrolman said recently, "Most people would rather spend three hundred and sixty-five days underground, safe." At the turn of the century, just before the first subway line was opened, the philanthropist Russell Sage remarked, "New Yorkers will never go into a hole in the ground to ride." Before long, New Yorkers may be going into Mr. Sage's holes to live.

URBAN JUNGLE
(Bronx Zoo)

AGNES ROTHERY

People shove and dodge, strain and push. As they dive into subways and clamber into buses they bump into one another and lift defensive arms against unwitting pokes in the ribs. The faces are so many and so close that they make a pattern in dots, and if the dots were observed separately many—perhaps most—would show tension or anxiety.

And yet in this same city, in the borough of the Bronx, there exists another and complete universe whose inhabitants know neither haste nor hunger and are not in the least plagued by anxiety concerning their social or spiritual condition. Furred and feathered, finny and scaled, these birds and beasts and fish are children of nature, and although they are not free as nature intended them to be, they have greater security than most of the human beings who populate the city. Over rolling pastures move, in a dappled mist, delicate deer from China, India,

Ceylon and Japan. Through crystal-clear water step pink flamingoes on fragile legs, and their pink reflections step up to meet them. Black-necked swans float dreamlike on a pool surrounded by flowering shrubs.

To spend an hour or a day in the New York Zoological Park is to be accompanied not only by animals—curious, lovely, ferocious or amusing—but by a happier race of people than those who usually crowd the metropolitan streets. For the time being they have laid aside their broodings and urgencies and are lost in unself-conscious absorption as they follow the walks and paths of another world.

The walks wind past woods and pastures, past flight cages so immense that birds can fly freely and swiftly in them. Past a tree where a lesser panda lies asleep in an uppermost branch, braced by a hind leg and with its head hanging down in a position which would certainly break the neck of anything but a panda. Past an island where the uncaged lions stalk to and fro under the trees or pose majestically.

The largest zoo in the world—largest in extent and in the rarity of its species—has adopted wherever possible moated and barless enclosures. In the four acres of the African plains, the first of the great Continental areas to be opened, half a hundred African animals, from zebras to cranes, roam in virtual liberty behind a moat, their selection the result of long experimentation. In the new Great Apes House, the animals in their five play-yards are separated from one another by walls, and from the spectators by water moats.

Since the Zoo extends over 251 acres, it would take a good deal of walking to cover it. And since it exhibits more than 2500 animals, it would take a pleasantly filled lifetime to become intimately acquainted with them all. To help those visitors whose knees may be weak or whose curiosity is superficial, small tractor buses provide a general tour by trundling from one entrance to the other and making the return trip by a different route. Painted blue with red-topped canopies whose scalloped edges are trimmed with white, their horns tootling strains from "The Sidewalks of New York," they provide cheerful motion and music. But although these toylike trains are always brimming with passengers, the greater number of visitors spend most of their time on foot.

Only on foot can they see, in the Reptile House, the King Cobra uncoiling its length of polished black, and the slender harlequin snake shaking out its rings of scarlet, yellow and black. The twenty feet of the Regal Python are patterned in light and dark browns and yellow, like an oriental rug. The gaboon viper, marked in bold and handsome design, would not tempt anyone to warm it in his bosom, for its head is as broad as a man's hand and its poison fangs are like hypodermic needles.

Other members of the reptile class, alligators, crocodiles—enormous, shell-encased—lie outdoors sluggish as water-soaked logs. The giant tortoises from the Galapagos Islands are quite willing to take children on their backs for a lumbering ride around their big yards.

Only on foot can visitors go through the Large Bird House lined with group cages in which flutter, fly and scream a confusion of strange shapes and colors and cries. Opening out of its main hall there is a room which is semi-darkened, so that the lights in the ten small, specially constructed cages which form its walls are thrown into an emphasized illumination, like the show cases in a jeweler's window. Each cage is furnished to enhance the glittering beauty of its occupant. Plants and flowers enrich the walls. Each has its bath, and its miniature table set forth with little glass dishes holding bits of fresh fruit and seeds as if for an avian St. Agnes' Eve. A slender vial of specially prepared nectar hangs from the ceiling. In these exquisite jewel boxes live the tiny jeweled birds, from whose breasts flash the deep pure hues of ruby, amethyst and emerald, and from whose wings glint the fire of star topaz, and the prismatic rays of the diamond. Their beaks are coral and pearl, jade and silver, gold and ivory. Their crests are garnet and beryl and turquoise. To compare them to precious stones is to minimize their concentrated splendor, for although their plumage vies with raindrops scintillating in the sun, their motions are swift as light and light as air.

In the penguin house the gentlemen birds, in sleek black or pearl-gray coats and gleaming white shirt fronts, stand stiffly around like formally dressed guests at a stag party. This aldermanic gathering struts and waddles, noses in the air, paddle-like fins flat against their sides. But when they take to the water they are as agile as those fat men who puff clumsily when they walk and amaze their partners by being light as a feather on the dance floor.

These drollest of all birds are entirely comfortable on the hottest days in an air-conditioned setting of snow and ice which is on one side of a glass wall, while the onlookers swelter on the other side.

You must walk to visit the Elephant House or the Heads and Horns Museum. But you must bend your head and maybe your knees to enter the children's zoo. And you cannot get in at all unless a child is with you. Here, except during the winter months, live the animals of Mother Goose—the baa-baa black sheep with a ribbon round his neck, the ding-dong bell above the shallow well in which frolic three half-grown kittens. The children may pick up the guinea pigs and rabbits. They can pat the goat and smooth the geese. Children born and reared in a city find a mother hen with her little ones as fascinating as the exotic father emu stalking protectively across the corral behind his scuttling striped chicks. . . .

The tanks of fish in the Lion House hold the few survivors from the old aquarium in Battery Park, and they are being kept here until they can be taken to a new aquarium such as never before has been seen or dreamed of. It will cover 12 acres of shore land along the east end of Coney Island, and visitors will be induced into the proper mood by entering it from the Boardwalk, under a roaring cascade behind a glass curtain. The approach to the world of water will be made still more vivid by an immense moving diorama showing clouds forming, rain falling from them, water flowing from brook to creek, to river, to ocean, and then rising as a vapor to form clouds. Passing beneath this graphic cycle visitors will find themselves among the West Indian and East Indian coral reefs, scintillating with brilliant reef-dwelling fish and studded by living sea anemones. One whole side of this hall will be formed by a mammoth tank for sharks and rays. There will also be a penguin swimming pool in which these amusing birds can be viewed both above and below the water, and a woodland swamp and jungle hall for crocodiles and other amphibians. In two colossal ocean-ariums will sport sea lions, sea elephants, porpoises, walruses and possibly a white whale. . . .

What the public does not see and may not realize is the scientific organization which is unweariedly busy behind the scenes at the Bronx Zoo: the laboratories for the comparative study of animal and human disease; the nursery where some of the most precious newborn are tended as solicitously and affectionately as if they were human infants; the hospital which serves also as a quarantine station for new arrivals. The duties of the Zoo dietitian are staggering, for the otter must have frogs as well as fish, the raccoon demands crabs, the marmoset, tiniest of the monkey tribe, will become paralyzed unless supplied with chininous shells of insects. White grubs, crayfish, earthworms and egg custard are part of the menu of the duck-billed platypus. One 415-pound baby walrus can consume 40 pounds of freshly opened clams daily, requiring the full time service of a special keeper to prepare these tasty snacks. The vampire, of course, must have his heady dram of raw defibrinated blood. . . .

Toward sundown the visitors begin to move in the direction of the Buffalo Gate or the Rainey, Fordham and Crotona Gates toward their waiting cars or toward the subway entrances. For a little while the amusement and wonder which transformed their faces linger in a half smile or in reflective eyes. It is possible, while still under the spell of creatures whose forms and motions are perfectly adapted to their functions and environments, to regard human beings as creatures whose natural grace of movement is merely temporarily obscured.

The men and the women and the children shove and push to find room to sit or to stand before they settle down for the long ride back. The small boys and girls begin to fuss. Parents admonish, hush or scold. Anxious thoughts begin to cast long shadows across faces which, so short a time ago, were free from introspection, foreboding or sadness.

After all, human beings, as we know them, have not inhabited this world very long compared with many of the animals seen here today. Perhaps it is to our credit that although we have not yet been able to create one for ourselves, we are able to offer these lesser inhabitants of our globe the security and the freedom from hunger and fear of a peaceable kingdom.

BROOKLYN BRIDGE

ALFRED KAZIN

At the end of the Civil War, a German-born engineer named John August Roebling, who had grown up in a walled town and amid the Gothic churches where Bach had worked a century before, designed a suspension bridge to connect the cities of New York and Brooklyn. It was to be the most ambitious bridge in the world—sixteen hundred feet across, three hundred feet and more from the center of the bridge to the river below. The cablework was to be strung across two stone towers and anchored at both sides by a unique system of supports embedded in stone. It was to have five lanes, with a central passageway for walkers as well as roadways for carriages and electric railways. "This elevated promenade," Roebling wrote in his prospectus, "will allow people of leisure and old and young to stroll over the bridge on fine days. I need not state that in a crowded commercial city such a promenade will be of incalculable value."

John Roebling was haunted by bridges. He had already built the first suspension aqueducts and the first great suspension bridges in America across the Ohio, and at Niagara Falls. To support bridges he had invented wire rope and made a business of it in the German colony he founded at Saxonburg, in western Pennsylvania. He had emigrated from Germany in 1831, a qualified state engineer, to find an opportunity to build bridges here, and it had taken him a long time to get to build the flying bridges that expressed his inventive, scientific and metaphysical mind. Meanwhile he had invented safety devices for portage railways and taken out many patents on inventions to insure the superior strength and safety of bridges. "The Great East River Bridge," as it was called then, was to be his masterpiece. Suddenly, in 1869, while making a preliminary survey for the Brooklyn tower, he had an accident and died soon after from lockjaw. He never saw his bridge. But when it was finally completed in 1883 by his son, Washington, it was faithful to the original design and to John Roebling's prophecy. When the design was made, he had said, "The Bridge will be beautiful."

Brooklyn Bridge is beautiful—as a complex piece of machinery, as a work of architecture, and as the symbol and connecting tissue of the human history around it. It is a perfect reflection of the mind of its designer and of the world in which he planned it. John Roebling's childhood saturation in Gothic is forever recalled in the port of New York, where two open-stone towers stand in the river like cathedral doors, opening the way to the bay on one side and to the river on the other. It also reflects John Roebling's extraordinary ability to adapt his massive suspension bridge to the esthetic and religious images of his childhood. As a bridge-builder his mind was all on the problems of stresses and strains, masonry and cables. He had to devise that intricate union of materials, from wire and steel ropes to wood and rock, that would give support and provide the tension necessary to a bridge in the railroad age. As an architect he worked on the memory of walled towns, early and massive stone. But architect and bridge-builder could never be separated in the same mind. The problems of support became the problems of form.

Brooklyn Bridge has an iron look, because it was built in an iron age —an age when men could take on the hardness and coldness of the materials in which they worked. John Roebling, who came here not only to build bridges but to establish a new kind of social community, became a man who noted every nickel he gave his sons, and ordered his contributions to be deducted from their portion of the final inheritance. He was indifferent to human relations. When his youngest son was born, he had to be reminded of the fact. He brusquely ordered his son Washington off to the Civil War, and the son, who had been hurt a little too deeply by the father's rigidity, went through it for four years without writing to him once. But John Roebling was also a man who entered daily in his journal not only the details of his business and his unbreaking thoughts on bridges but his metaphysical reflections. He had studied under Hegel at Berlin, and he never lost his German taste for universal ideas. In his spare time—hard as it is to believe that he left himself any—he wrote a thousand-page treatise called "Roebling's Theory of the Universe." He also squeezed any half dollar he could from his laborers' wages. In a nature that seems to have been compounded of commercial hardness, a passion for practical science, and an unspoken feeling for the beauty of his work, the drive of nineteenth-century business and his own creative fury went hand in hand. He was a careful man and an imaginative man—a man who looked on the world as stone and money and wire, but who was forever dreaming of bridges to overleap it. Brooklyn Bridge carries his signature. It is so practical as to be austere, yet its towers suggest the kind of Gothic dear to a man who had grown up amid early churches. It does not have a superfluous line; the towers are two solid walls, cut by arches, and every wire and steel rope is there to insure the maximum safety. John Roebling lived in a prudent age, and he never risked anything. He anchored and re-anchored his bridge, fastened it down and around like a man wrapping a trunk in endless coils of rope. Yet he always found design in the innumerable devices he invented to secure his bridge. So the archaic complexity of cablework on which the bridge is strung, wire within wire, the whole bound by cables, the cables in their turn resting in beds of stone, take on the manifold inner lines of Gothic. The vertical stays from the outlying cables to the floor, the most famous feature of the bridge, were the last knots John Roebling tied to it, and they in their turn make so many checked patterns that they reproduce the cloistral and groined look of a medieval church. Roebling did not merely fix the new supports he needed; he located them with an artist's eye, to provide an inner frame to his bridge.

You cannot see the towers very well from Manhattan, and Manhattan is probably as sure today that the bridge is not needed as it was in the days when John Roebling proposed it. For Manhattan is another walled town, and looks within itself like a tailor squinting at the eye of a needle. It is too flat in its southern half, and always too busy.

But if you cross the bridge from City Hall to Brooklyn Heights and stand on the hills where the Dutch burghers found the limits of Bruekelen just three centuries ago, you can see Brooklyn Bridge in all its massive integrity. And if you go below Fulton Street to the river—where Walt Whitman loved to cross and re-cross on the old ferry that also began here—and look up, the arc Brooklyn Bridge describes as it falls into City Hall Park is a geometer's dream—a line of such precision and lightness in space, and reflecting so nobly that perfection in reasoning which mathematicians call "elegance," that it suddenly colors and transcends the industrial clutter at its feet.

Brooklyn Heights itself is a window on the port. Here, where the perspective is fixed by the towers of Manhattan and the hills of New Jersey and Staten Island, the channels running between seem fingers of the world ocean. Here one can easily embrace the suggestion, which Whitman felt so easily, that the whole American world opens out from here, north and west. It is no accident that the four remarkable men who found here the richest symbols of their lives—Whitman and Hart Crane, the poets, John and Washington Roebling, the bridge-builders—should have been stirred so deeply by it to the epic sense. There is an illusion one gains here, looking down from the hills or up the crooked cobbled streets leading from the wharves, that it was from such a vantage point that men first caught the excitement of the new world.

Brooklyn Heights itself still preserves many qualities of an independent city and a great river port. Here, where some streets are named after fruits (Pineapple, Orange and Cranberry), after old English settlers (Montague, Remsen, Pierrepont, Middagh), where some recall the secluded quaintness of a small nineteenth-century town, there are old frame houses, with blue-gray and russet colors—houses with prim shutters and a proud absence of display, that speak of the time before riches. On the Heights overlooking the bay there are great brownstone houses, bristling like fortresses, that shut out the street and shut in the people who live in them. They speak of wealth and power in the Gilded Age, of families whose children grew up in gardens fenced off by iron railings. Only their solid wooden doors, oak and mahogany that have weathered into a rosy orange look over the years, redeem them from pompousness. But there is a touch about them, too, that reminds you of the merchants' houses of Newburyport and Salem and Provincetown, where everything looks out to sea.

Whitman felt the magic of this spot so intensely that he thought he could breathe the whole world in whenever he crossed on the old Fulton Street Ferry:

The glories strung like beads on my smallest sights and bearings, on the walk in the river and the passage over the river.

And Hart Crane, of Ohio, when he imagined his own epic poem on America, *The Bridge*, from his robin's nest on Columbia Heights. Here he paid his homage like a tortured suppliant before the Madonna of Liberty:

> *O harp and altar of the fury fused,*
> *(How could mere toil align thy choiring strings!)*
> *Terrific threshold of the prophet's pledge,*
> *Prayer of pariah, and the lover's cry.*

For Whitman the ferry was the "passage over the river," and the river itself the boulevard of humanity. For Crane, who came to mourn where Whitman had so idly rhapsodized, America began with the bridge—from which one looked down and back into the national past. In a world of inhumanly "white buildings," in which no institution or person represented home to him; in the atomic world of New York, where he felt himself bombarded, the bridge became the shining base across—the "terrific threshold of the prophet's pledge." Whitman embraced the world from a ferry boat; Crane saw the ambiguity of life in water. He loved Brooklyn Bridge as he loved the novels of Herman Melville: both dealt in the mystery of water. In the end water engulfed his mind. When he could no longer make peace with himself, he jumped from a freighter taking him home from Vera Cruz. But in an earlier period, living near the bridge, he found his anchor. And it is a curious example of the modern poet's life within the industrial culture of our time that when Crane went to live on Columbia Heights (Whitman might have invented the name), he tried to find the exact spot from which Washington Roebling, paralyzed for life from the caisson disease he had caught working under the river, sat in a wheel chair, directing the construction of his father's bridge from a window. Crane had an idea he could fashion a true poem on America from that window. One wonders if he saw the irony of the succession into which he tried to fit himself. Hart Crane saw the structure only as an idea; to the Roeblings the idea was only in the structure. Old Roebling, who never saw his bridge, directed the lives of the two men who came after him. As the paralyzed son lived in the shadow of the father, so the poet came to live in the shadow of the son.

Yet different as they were, all three—like Whitman before them—were involved in the same quest. That quest in one sense is beyond definition. It was only to be experienced, and the completion of Brooklyn Bridge did not end the experience; it projected it on a higher plane. That experience is of America, and the world, from the oceanic capital that is New York.

All bridges, if they are well built, have their own beauty. They recall the passageway that is perhaps the most enduring symbol of life. They speak of the journey across, and they mark the limits within which we must live. At the same time they are something given to us by others, on which we cross. For we never cross entirely naked and alone, and we always rest on some base of human ingenuity provided by others. There is this in Brooklyn Bridge, and something more: the many tangible lives of New York which it projects and unites. For in New York, a series of islands pressing against the mainland, there is always felt that deep inner longing to integrate, to complete the process sundered by the waters, that belongs to an island port. On Brooklyn Bridge that longing is fused with the structure, for the bridge flies in the sight of so many waters and islands that nowhere else does the whole of New York seem so near and full.

Brooklyn Bridge was the first of the great bridges across the East River; the others follow after it, and it alone enjoys the full sweep of the harbor and the cities around it. The bridge, with its central promenade for those who wish to escape the "crowded, commercial city," is a masthead. Brooklyn Bridge may not be convenient to modern traffic—drivers are always cursing it from the narrow roadway—but for walkers, for those who will "look out," as Whitman wrote, it is one of the greatest things in New York. Standing on the raised platform under the arches of the gray-black towers, where birds have their nests in the ledges, one looks south to Governor's Island between the flanks of Brooklyn and New York. Below, in both island cities, are the wharves, piers, markets, iron storage chambers and cars. To the north the river bends under the Manhattan, Williamsburgh and Queensboro bridges, and is lost from sight in the inlets of Manhattan and Queens. Immediately to the north the city opens out briefly from City Hall, and shuts itself up in great stone masses of office buildings. But over the

Municipal Building a stone goddess with bronze wings turns her back to the river, and stands above the pot-bellied, officious governmental buildings that serve for courts, prisons, offices. On the left of the bridge, as you approach Manhattan, is Wall Street and the Battery; on the right the tenements of the East Side and Chinatown, where the last of the elevateds still makes a prison out of the street and where the steerage remains. Wall Street, Bowling Green; the East Side and "the old country," from whose nightmare the children of the poor have not escaped. These are the extremes of New York, as the extremes make up in their bizarre neighborliness the city itself.

The bridge is old, and the world immediately adjoining it is old. Below the bridge, on the Manhattan side, there are tanners' shops and people who deal in skins and hides, perfumes and wines. There are warehouses cut into the belly of the anchorages of the bridge, and the clerks who sit on high stools in them have migrated from prints of old London. Above them is Park Row and Printing House Square, where all the great New York dailies were once published, and where only the statue of Franklin, presented to the printers of New York, and the green dome of the World Building recall journalistic history from Horace Greeley to Joseph Pulitzer.

On both sides of the bridge at the Manhattan end there are factories and warehouses of the 1870's and 1880's. On one of them is preserved a series of ornamental fire escapes, sculptured with the figures of athletes out of the old *Police Gazette*—a living expression of the Oliver Optic period. Above it is the face of a great dead clock, its hands forever resting at three o'clock. An age passed this way. This is where New York first sank its piles in the river, where the age of business began, always in the sight of water; and where now the factory buildings that remain, with their battered fronts and broken windows, the iron storage chambers and warehouses cut into the anchorages, are like the green foam left by the industrial rivers of New York when they wash against the rock.

This is old New York, the bottom deposit of the commercial revolution that began here and then moved away. This is where the clock never goes, over which is lettered the name of a square to which it no longer belongs, and where the tenements and clothes lines of the East Side, like the elevated pillars along the Bowery, have shut in a world from time. And the bridge that rises above it all, itself made of rock and wire, is from one point of view only the great idol to which all these streets are subjected. But from another it transcends them, and speaks not only of warehouses, crooked streets, and the darkness of lower New York, but of the human wish buried so deep in these rejected regions.

IN DEFENSE AND PRAISE OF BROOKLYN
I.

TRUMAN CAPOTE

As a group, Brooklynites form a persecuted minority; the uninventive persistence of not very urbane clowns has made any mention of their homeland a signal for compulsory guffaws; their dialect, appearance and manners have become, by way of such side-splitting propaganda, synonymous with the crudest, most vulgar aspects of contemporary life. All this, which perhaps began good-naturedly enough, has turned the razory road toward malice: an address in Brooklyn is now not altogether respectable. A peculiar irony, to be sure, for in this unfortunate region the average man, being on the edge of an outcast order, guards averageness with morbid intensity; he does, in fact, make of respectability a religion; still, insecurity makes for hypocrisy, and so he greets The Big Joke with the loudest hee-haw of all: "Yaaah, ain't Brooklyn a kick—talk about funny!" Terribly funny, yes, but Brooklyn is also sad brutal provincial lonesome human silent sprawling raucous lost passionate subtle bitter immature innocent perverse tender mysterious, a place where Crane and Whitman found poems, a mythical dominion against whose shores the Coney Island sea laps a wintry lament. Here, scarcely anyone can give directions; nobody knows where anything is, even the oldest taxi-driver seems uncertain; luckily, I've earned my degree in subway travel, though learning to ride these rails, which, buried in the stone, are like the veins found on fossilized fern, requires fiercer application, I'm sure, than working toward a Master's. Rocking through the sunless, starless tunnels is an outward bound feeling: the train, hurtling below unlikely land, seems destined for fog and mist, only the flashby of familiar stations revealing our identities. . . .

II.

LUDWIG BEMELMANS

It was windy, and there were few bums on the Bowery. I drove across the bridge and up to Brooklyn Heights, to a place from which I like to watch the sun set on New York harbor.

Brooklyn has assets other than Murder, Inc. It has a cemetery in which Lola Montez is buried. It has a lovely park. And it has a feeling of being home to people. Its citizens around the Heights section might live in a small town, far removed from New York. They find time to stand and talk in the streets; they wave at each other. Unlike New Yorkers, they smile and go home with quiet, slow steps.

While the most fashionable section of Manhattan looks out on a panorama of insane hospital, prison, railroad bridge, and the various municipal and public service structures across the river, the view from Brooklyn Heights is truly beautiful.

The sky was the color of a sheet of copper reflecting fire. Around where the sun sets it was the red heat of metal. The orange fire of the sunset was reflected in the thousands of Manhattan windows that face south. The east-lying fronts of the buildings were in the deep violet, gray, brown, and purple that play over lava.

A curtain of sleet moved against Manhattan. It looked like rose-colored ashes, and it sailed across the bay in even tempo, and then bashed itself against the skyscrapers. It fled along the streets and out of them up into the sky. It was yellow there, and another gust carried masses of it up the East River against the darkening houses. It was lit up as it passed through the immense bridges, whose wiring is like that of giant harps.

The foghorns doubled their volume. I took my binoculars from the glove compartment and looked at a small tramp steamer coming up the bay. It flew the Greek flag. It was one of the boats that come by way of the Bay of Naples. Perhaps part of its cargo was the opium crop of Istanbul and Iran. By the law of perspective it was now four inches long. It was in a line between the Statue of Liberty and Staten Island. The circular military reservation on Governor's Island, and the old fortress, looked as if a pastry cook had shaken powdered sugar on a chocolate cake. The lights of moving cars blinked on the bridges, and overhead the running lights of planes flashed on and off.

A curtain of snow and of night sank down on the panorama. I drove back over Brooklyn Bridge. On such nights as these I like to wind through the old streets at the end of Manhattan Island, especially the one in which the smell of coffee roasters hangs. We saw some bums pressing their noses against coffeepots, delicatessens, and restaurants with thirty-five-cent dinners. It was all a melancholy Christmas card.

BROOKLYN IS MY NEIGHBORHOOD

CARSON MCCULLERS

Brooklyn, in a dignified way, is a fantastic place. The street where I live has a quietness and sense of permanence that seem to belong to the nineteenth century. The street is very short. At one end, there are comfortable old houses, with gracious façades and pleasant back-yards in the rear. Down on the next block, the street becomes more heterogeneous, for there is a fire station; a convent; and a small candy factory. The street is bordered with maple-trees, and in the autumn the children rake up the leaves and make bonfires in the gutter.

It is strange in New York to find yourself living in a real neighborhood. I buy my coal from the man who lives next-door. And I am very curious about the old lady living on my right. She has a mania for picking up stray, starving dogs. Besides a dozen of these dogs, she keeps a little green, shrewd monkey as her pet and chief companion. She is said to be very rich and very stingy. The druggist on the corner has told me she was once in jail for smashing the windows of a saloon in a temperance riot.

"The square of the hypotenuse of a right triangle is equal to—"

On coming into the corner drug store in the evening, you are apt to hear a desperate voice repeating some such maxim. Mr. Parker, the druggist, sits behind the counter after supper, struggling with his daughter's homework—she can't seem to get on well in school. Mr. Parker has owned his store for thirty years. He has a pale face, with watery grey eyes and a silky little yellow mustache that he wets and combs out frequently. He is rather like a cat. And when I weigh myself, he sidles up quietly beside me and peers over my shoulder as I adjust the scale. When the weights are balanced, he always gives me a quick

Reprinted from *Vogue*. Copyright, 1941, by The Condé Nast Publications, Inc.

little glance, but he has never made any comment, nor indicated in any way whether he thought I weighed too little or too much.

On every other subject, Mr. Parker is very talkative. He has always lived in Brooklyn, and his mind is a rag-bag for odd scraps of information. For instance, in our neighborhood there is a narrow alley called Love Lane. "The alley comes by its name," he told me, "because more than a century ago two bachelors by the name of DeBevoise lived in the corner house with their niece, a girl of such beauty that her suitors mooned in the alley half the night, writing poetry on the fence." These same old uncles, Mr. Parker added, cultivated the first strawberries sold in New York in their back garden. It is pleasant to think of this old household—the parlor with the coloured glass windows glowing in the candlelight, the two old gentlemen brooding quietly over a game of chess, and the young niece, demure on a footstool, eating strawberries and cream.

"The square of the hypotenuse—" As you go out of the drug store, Mr. Parker's voice will carry on where he had left off, and his daughter will sit there, sadly popping her chewing-gum.

Comparing the Brooklyn that I know with Manhattan is like comparing a comfortable and complacent duenna to her more brilliant and neurotic sister. Things move more slowly out here (the street-cars still rattle leisurely down most of the main streets), and there is a feeling for tradition.

The history of Brooklyn is not so exciting as it is respectable. In the middle of the past century, many of the liberal intellectuals lived here, and Brooklyn was a hot-bed of abolitionist activity. Walt Whitman worked on the *Brooklyn Daily Eagle* until his anti-slavery editorials cost him his job. Henry Ward Beecher used to preach at the old Plymouth Church. Talleyrand lived here on Fulton Street during his exile in America, and he used to walk primly every day beneath the elm-trees. Whittier stayed frequently at the old Hooper home.

The first native of Brooklyn I got to know when first I came out here was the electrician who did some work at my house. He is a lively young Italian with a warm, quick face and a pleasant way of whistling operatic arias while on the job. On the third day he was working for me, he brought in a bottle of bright home-made wine, as his first child, a boy, had been born the night before. The wine was sour and clean to the tongue, and when we had drunk some of it the electrician invited me to a little supper to be held a week later at his house on the other side of Brooklyn, near Sheepshead Bay. The party was a fine occasion.

The old grandfather who had come over from Italy sixty years ago was there. At night, the old man fishes for eels out in the Bay, and when the weather is fine he spends most of the day lying in a cart in the back-yard, out in the sun. He had the face of a charming old satyr, and he held the new baby with the casualness of one who has walked the floor with many babies in his day.

"He is very ugly, this little one," he kept saying. "But it is clear that he will be smart. Smart and very ugly."

The food at the party was rich, wholesome Italian fare—*provalone* cheese, salami, pastries, and more of the red wine. A stream of kinsmen and neighbors kept coming in and out of the house all evening. This family had lived in the same house near the Bay for three generations, and the grandfather had not been out of Brooklyn for years.

Here in Brooklyn there is always the feeling of the sea. On the streets near the water-front, the air has a fresh, coarse smell, and there are many seagulls. One of the most gaudy streets I know stretches between Brooklyn Bridge and the Navy Yard. At three o'clock in the morning, when the rest of the city is silent and dark, you can come suddenly on a little area as vivacious as a country fair. It is Sand Street, the place where sailors spend their evenings when they come here to port. At any hour of the night some excitement is going on in Sand Street. The sunburned sailors swagger up and down the sidewalks with their girls. The bars are crowded, and there are dancing, music, and straight liquor at cheap prices.

These Sand Street bars have their own curious traditions also. Some of the women you find there are vivid old dowagers of the street who have such names as The Duchess or Submarine Mary. Every tooth in Submarine Mary's head is made of solid gold—and her smile is rich-looking and satisfied. She and the rest of these old habitués are greatly respected. They have a stable list of sailor pals and are known from Buenos Aires to Zanzibar. They are conscious of their fame and don't bother to dance or flirt like the younger girls, but sit comfortably in the centre of the room with their knitting, keeping a sharp eye on all that goes on. In one bar, there is a little hunchback who struts in proudly every evening, and is petted by every one, given free drinks, and treated as a sort of mascot by the proprietor. There is a saying among sailors that when they die they want to go to Sand Street.

Cutting through the business and financial centre of Brooklyn is Fulton Street. Here are to be found dozens of junk and antique shops that are exciting to people who like old and fabulous things. I came to be quite at home in these places, as I bought most of my furniture there. If you know what you are about, there are good bargains to be found—old carved sideboards, elegant pier-glasses, beautiful Lazy Susans, and other odd pieces can be bought at half the price you would pay anywhere else. These shops have a musty, poky atmosphere, and the people who own them are an incredible crew.

The woman from whom I got most of my things is called Miss Kate. She is lean, dark, and haggard, and she suffers much from cold. When you go into the junk-shop, you will most likely find her hovering over a little coal stove in the back room. She sleeps every night wrapped in a Persian rug and lying on a green velvet Victorian couch. She has one of the handsomest and dirtiest faces I can remember.

Across the street from Miss Kate, there is a competitor with whom she often quarrels violently over prices—but still she always refers to him as an "adela Menchen," and once when he was to be evicted for failure to pay the rent she put up the cash for him.

"Miss Kate is a good woman," this competitor said to me. "But she dislikes washing herself. So she only bathes once a year, when it is summer. I expect she's just about the dirtiest woman in Brooklyn." His voice as he said this was not at all malicious; rather, there was in it a quality of wondering pride. That is one of the things I love best about Brooklyn. Every one is not expected to be exactly like every one else.

BROOKLYN,

The Forty-Ninth State

JACK GAVER and DAVE STANLEY

Interest in whether Alaska or Hawaii will become the forty-ninth state of the union may be feverish in certain quarters, but to a sizable slice of the country's population the question is academic. The three million residents of Brooklyn, no longer even a city in its own right, consider that their community has been the equivalent of a forty-ninth state for years, regardless of statute.

There was evidence of this feeling during a March of Dimes drive in a Florida resort city a few years ago. Each of forty-eight containers set out to catch the contributions of winter visitors bore the name of a state; a forty-ninth was labeled "Brooklyn." On the boardwalk at

Asbury Park, N.J., on a June morning in 1948, workmen were hoisting state flags for a "Salute to the States" ceremony. At the standard reserved for California, they met one Edward Scott, who carried what he said was "the borough flag of Brooklyn" (actually, there is no such thing), and insisted that it be raised "because Brooklyn's as good as California." The flag was not raised.

But because of this sort of spirit, legal statehood would mean little in the way of added distinction to Brooklynites. They are content to know that Brooklyn is the most publicized place in the world and that the City of Greater New York would be a hollow skyscraper shell without this most populous and storied of its five boroughs. They are not professional braggarts, as are Texans, but neither are they inclined to minimize their importance.

And "importance" doesn't mean the notoriety that has accrued to Brooklyn increasingly in the past quarter of a century—the sort of half-sweet, half-sour notoriety resulting from the community's becoming the joke butt of the nation. This sort of thing does help Brooklyn to achieve the headlines, but underneath there is a firm foundation of history and accomplishment that makes the records of some states seem anemic by comparison.

Brooklyn's population of three million is exceeded only by that of Greater New York and Chicago. Only seventeen states have larger populations than Brooklyn, which has five-and-a-half times the combined populations of Alaska and Hawaii. Brooklyn, which makes up all of Kings County, has nine of the twenty-four members of Congress from Greater New York; Manhattan (New York County) has only six. Twenty-nine states have fewer Congressmen than Brooklyn. In national politics the borough is as safely Democratic as any state in the Solid South.

The delightful odor of roasting coffee perfumes much of the Brooklyn air; it is second only to Santos, Brazil, as a coffee-roasting and distribution center. Tootsie Rolls also come from Brooklyn and there is plenty of sugar with which to make them; the borough is the world's largest sugar-refining center. The enormous amount of penicillin it produces comprises merely one of some seven hundred items that give the community the reputation of making more kinds of products than any other. It is the country's fifth-ranking industrial center in total output. Even more important, Brooklyn is the leading foreign trade center of the United States, handling 40 per cent of this vital traffic along its 108.8 miles of commercially developed waterfront. The statistics would surprise even many natives; they include the information that the borough has better than a hundred farmers.

Brooklyn was the master of its own municipal fate until 1898. Those who know Brooklyn only through the jokesmiths will be even more astounded to know that it is one of the most historic spots in North America with a history of organized settlement that goes back to 1646.

Henry Hudson found the New York area for the Dutch in 1609, and his first landing was on what is now Coney Island, then famous as a wampum mint for eastern Indians and later to become renowned as the birthplace of the frankfurter and the site of the world's greatest amusement park.

In 1646 a hamlet named Breuckelen (after a Netherlands village) was started at about the spot where Borough Hall now stands. Breuckelen, which is reputed to have opened the new world's first public school in 1661, was to pass through a score of spellings due to the illiteracy of the time and changes of sovereignty before the present version became permanent late in the eighteenth century.

Almost from the day of its founding, Brooklyn began absorbing other settlements in western Long Island, a process that was to continue until Brooklyn itself was swallowed in 1898 by the colossus across the East River. The New York Legislature first incorporated it as a village in 1816, then as a city in 1834. George Hall, a painting contractor who is remembered for having been opposed to pigs in the street and liquor in the citizens became the first mayor. He made some headway against the pigs.

Two mechanical developments greatly influenced Brooklyn's history. The first came in 1814 when Robert Fulton's steam ferry service was established between Manhattan and Brooklyn. This made Brooklyn considerably more accessible and pointed the way for a gradual change from a predominantly agricultural economy. The second factor was the opening of the famed Brooklyn Bridge in 1893, an event that sealed Brooklyn's doom as an independent city.

The human element in making Brooklyn what it is today was provided by succeeding tides of immigrants during the hundred years following the war of 1812. The Irish were the dominant invading strain for almost a generation and they gained such a foothold that even now their descendants play a major role in the borough's affairs. Germans were the next big contingent. The latter half of the century and the early part of the twentieth century saw a great influx of Italians, Slavs,

Scandinavians, Poles, Syrians, and, most of all, Jews of varied nationalities. Today, possibly a little more than a third of Brooklyn's population is Jewish, making it the largest Jewish community in the world, with half again as many Jews as in all Palestine.

Few of these newcomers had much money and it was cheaper to live in Brooklyn than in Manhattan. That is still true today. Brooklyn became the "bedroom of New York" and the "borough of homes." And because it is the residential district for people of so many different nationalities and faiths, it also became the "city of churches."

Brooklyn became the greatest melting pot in the country. It acquired a color and vitality that are strongly apparent even now, after a generation in which immigrant transfusions have become increasingly small and rare. A recent survey at Nathan Hale Junior High School revealed that 41 nationalities were represented among the parents of the students, but that 98.27 per cent of the students were at least third-generation Americans.

Brooklyn even has that rare thing, a colony of American Indians. These are not the native Canarsie, who apparently became extinct around 1800, but descendants of the upstate Mohawks who used to force tribute from the easy-going Canarsie.

The whole of Brooklyn could be divided into the original six townships—Flatlands, Flatbush, Brooklyn, Bushwick, New Utrecht and Gravesend. It was Gravesend, by the way, that, in 1643, boasted the first woman office-holder in the new world. She was Lady Deborah Moody, an Englishwoman and advanced thinker who received a Dutch charter to colonize.

These six areas could be sub-divided into as many as thirty districts, if desired, a number of them dominated by various foreign blood strains. Red Hook, Coney Island, Williamsburgh, Greenpoint, Canarsie, Park Slope, Bensonhurst and Brownsville are some of the well-known names in this list, but none, perhaps, has the illustrious background of Brooklyn Heights. "The Heights" was once the exclusive home of Brooklyn blue bloods. Mostly of old New England stock, they regarded as upstarts the society people of such places as New York, Boston and Philadelphia. It was there that America's most noted clergyman, Henry Ward Beecher, auctioned off a Negro girl from his Plymouth Church pulpit to further his anti-slavery campaign.

Many of today's elderly Brooklynites are steeped in this atmosphere of sectional pride because they grew up in districts that still had their identities outside the corporate limits of the City of Brooklyn. Those of the younger generations who do not have roots deep into Brooklyn's past still get a diluted version of this regional loyalty through the fact that their schools, clubs and churches bear names derived from the old days.

The champion sectionalist of them all was the late Peter J. McGuinness, Democratic politico extraordinary. His bailiwick was Greenpoint—the "Greenpernt" of the jokes and the home precinct of Mae West. This densely populated, factory-cluttered district was "the garden spot of the world" to Peter. People and not nature were his concern, and Greenpoint has its plentiful share of Brooklyn's millions even if that much-discussed "Brooklyn tree" is hard to find.

Brooklyn pride and loyalty are perennial subjects of editorials in the nation's newspapers. An occasional writer will profess to be fed up with hearing about it, but usually the comment is laudatory and even envious. "What has Brooklyn got that we haven't?" is the common plaint, and the answer comes in as many forms as there are writers. It is significant that your true Brooklynite answers "Brooklyn" when you ask him where he is from, so he is already conditioned to such an individual identity as statehood would entail. The residents of Queens, Manhattan, the Bronx and Staten Island identify themselves only with that colorless generality, "New Yorker."

Although most Brooklynites accept the jokes about the borough in good humor, there is a minority that thinks there is no prestige in being portrayed as ungrammatical, uncouth monsters who have nothing to do but root for the Dodgers and who get lost in their own neighborhoods because the street system is a maze that would defy an educated laboratory rat. Few of the natives understand why Brooklyn has been singled out for its dubious distinction, but the explanation is simple. When vaudeville was the entertainment king years ago, comedians had stocks of humorously slighting remarks about suburbs and sections of the cities in which they played. Brooklyn was the joke butt for more sophisticated New York. A comic would explain, for example, that General Howe captured Brooklyn first so he could have a place to sleep while taking New York. When the movies and radio replaced vaudeville, making necessary entertainment with national appeal, the "local joke" largely lost its meaning. But the formula was too good to abandon altogether, so Brooklyn soon emerged as the joke target of the whole country, thanks to the fact that New York City is headquarters for a majority of those who influence the country through humor—cartoonists, columnists, songwriters, comedians, the radio industry, book and magazine publishers, etc.

World War II also contributed to the Brooklyn gag. Brooklyn had 327,000 of its sons and daughters in uniform, a figure surpassed by only nine states. Wherever the war was, and it was everywhere, there were Brooklynites being kidded by their fellow-Americans and retorting in kind, usually proud of the attention given to their home town. There are foreigners in the byways of the world who will undoubtedly go to their graves believing that Brooklyn is not only the greatest state in the union, but also the national capital.

Much of the humor is based on the so-called Brooklyn accent, dominated by the peculiarity that turns the "oi" sound into "er" and vice versa. Actually, such speech is by no means peculiar to Brooklyn; you can hear it in any part of the New York area and in other large cities, especially in the East. It goes back to certain speech peculiarities of the Irish, Germans and others; and is a product of general speech slovenliness which is by no means confined to Brooklyn. The "Brooklyn dialect" is pretty much the same as the Boweryese so popular in songs, stories and plays fifty years and more ago.

The average Brooklynite may not be too aggrieved personally over being a joke target, but he does have misgivings that this barrage will obscure Brooklyn's real qualities, which, the jokemakers may be surprised to know, actually include culture—culture from all parts of the world.

Brooklyn Heights today is a favorite residential sector for artists, sculptors, composers, writers and musicians, many of whom are not natives but who have found a spirit and quality about Brooklyn that is beneficial to their work. In the past, Walt Whitman was a Brooklyn resident and journalist for years, and it was Brooklyn that gave the world the first printing of his famous *Leaves of Grass*. Ernest Poole made Brooklyn harbor famous in his important novel, *The Harbor*, some thirty years ago. Your Brooklynite is as fond of actor William Bendix as the next one, but he doesn't want the impression to get around that all residents of the borough are cast in Bendix' make-believe mould. Brooklyn, he will remind you, can claim Jane Cowl, the late George Gershwin (a fact which his screen "biography" managed to ignore), Peggy Wood, the late Heywood Broun, Edward Everett Horton, opera star Robert Merrill and the Talmadge sisters, to name only a few accustomed to the limelight.

Brooklyn was the home of one of the first important film studios in the pioneer days of the movies. That was the old Vitagraph plant, as native Paul Kelly can tell you because he started working there as a kid. And it was Brooklyn also that gave the world that film revolution known as the "talkies," for it was in the Warner Brothers studio in the borough that Vitaphone was developed.

The borough has its own public library system, with a five-million-dollar central building. Prospect Park, consisting of 526 acres, ranks with the finest in the world. The nearby Botanic Garden is a center of research and education as well as a thing of beauty, and it is free to any who wants to enter. In the same locality is the Brooklyn Museum, visited by well over a million persons annually. The Museum is not only a repository for arts and crafts from all over the world, but it also is one of the most active educational centers in New York City. There are courses and lectures for both adults and children, concerts, motion pictures, folk festivals and demonstrations of art technique.

Brooklyn is probably the only local community in the country with an official blossom, *Forsythia intermedia*, an offshoot of the olive family and thus symbolic of peace. Some day, Brooklynites hope, the rest of the world will insist on claiming title to it, too. For this is one distinction Brooklyn is willing to share.

CONEY BY THE SEA

JO RANSON

A soaring inflation has hit Coney Island, the aged popcorn peninsula projecting into the salami-strewn Atlantic Ocean. This one-time Nickel Nice is now dubbed the Coney Chambord. Gone is the five-cent Coney chicken (a lofty euphemism for the lowly hot dog), the jitney ride on the BMT subway and Culver Line, and the nickel-for-a-schtickel-knubelwurst.

Coney Island, it is plain to see, isn't what it used to be in the halcyon days and nights when the highly inventive and daringly original outdoor show, game, and ride operators and the purveyors of comestibles captured the imagination and small pocketbooks of the American *moujik* who came in search of fairyland fables.

Antediluvian knights of crumbling Surf Avenue and the depressing alleys that lead to the boardwalk are waiting sadly for such legendary characters as Fred Thompson and Skip Dundy, the unbeatable combination that out-barnumed P. T. Barnum in the building of beautiful Luna Park. Named after Luna Dundy, Skip's sister, the park became an overnight success when it opened in 1903. More than four million people went through its turnstiles into a veritable fairyland the following year. Starting with barely a penny, the team of Thompson and Dundy soon revolutionized the outdoor amusement industry with their extraordinary architectural conceptions and showmanship. The path to riches, however, was road-blocked now and then.

Thompson went to Dundy before Luna Park was completed and displayed his threadbare trousers. "I need a new pair of pants," Fred pleaded. "F-ff-red," said Dundy, who was a stutterer, "did you ever think what a lot of lumber seven dollars will buy?" Fred didn't get the new pants. They had twelve dollars in their pockets the day Luna Park opened, but they knew they had the formula for making money. They had hit upon the successful recipe for drawing crowds into one of the most beautiful parks in the world. To the masses, Luna meant light and the shedding of grubby chores. It was a nickel trolley ride to a lotus land of incredible charm.

Nor were the masses the only ones to be captivated by the Luna Park wonders. The sophisticates and intellectuals dived into the pail of adjectives and came up with glistening words. Maxim Gorki, the Russian writer, looked upon the fabled wonders of Luna Park and was moved to exclaim: "With the advent of night a fantastic city all of fire suddenly rises from the ocean into the sky. Thousands of ruddy sparks glimmer in the darkness, limning in fine, sensitive outline on the black background of the sky shapely towers of miraculous castles, palaces, and temples. Golden gossamer threads tremble in the air. They intertwine in transparent flaming patterns, which flutter and melt away, in love with their own beauty mirrored in the waters. Fabulous beyond conceiving, ineffably beautiful, is this fiery scintillation."

Thompson and Dundy drew record crowds to such memorable attractions as The Streets of Delhi, Fire and Flames, Trip to the Moon, Twenty Thousand Leagues Under the Sea, Shoot the Chutes, The Scenic Railway, The Circle Swing, Whirl the Whirl, The Infant Incubators, Sea on Land, The Fatal Wedding, The Old Mill, The Miniature Railway, and The Laughing Show.

People are just boys and girls grown tall, Thompson pointed out, and elaborated child's play is what they want on a holiday. Sliding down cellar doors and the make-believes of youngsters are the most effective amusements possible for grown-ups, according to him.

"An appreciation of that fact made 'The Trip to the Moon' possible, and 'The Trip to the Moon' made for me and my partner Dundy half a million dollars," Thompson said. " 'The Tickler,' 'Bump the Bumps,' and 'The Virginia Reel' are nothing more than improved cellar doors. 'The Trip to the Moon,' 'Night and Morning,' 'The Witching Waves,' 'The Lost Girl' are only elaborations of the doll-house stunts of childhood, and they are largely successful for that reason. But they must be short and decisive. I would rather have a good show that lasts three minutes than a better one that runs an hour. And I prefer one that is over in a minute, but enables the spectator to become a part of it, to the one that runs three minutes and never permits him to become more than an onlooker. Speed is almost as important a factor in amusing the millions as is the carnival spirit, decency, or a correct recollection of schooldays."

Thompson went to pieces when Dundy died in 1907, and a few years later he was bankrupt and working as a manager at the famous park he had helped to build. A heavy drinker, Thompson died in 1919 and was buried in a Staten Island cemetery. Years later a headstone was placed on his grave. Dr. Martin A. Couney, the colorful baby-incubator expert and exhibitor, and other old friends of the outdoor showman paid for the stone.

Islanders also mourn the loss of George Cornelius Tilyou, master student of crowd psychology and rambunctious founder of Steeplechase Park. It was George C. Tilyou who glorified the early blowhole and the goosing electric stinger. This Coney Island pioneer, at the age of fourteen, sold sand and sea water to the perspiring proletariat for five cents a bottle.

Tilyou always said that "if Paris is France, then Coney Island between June and September is the world." When Steeplechase Park suffered one of its periodic conflagrations, Tilyou rebuilt a portion of the park with the dimes collected from visitors who paid to gaze at the ruins.

Steeplechase boasted the only large pavilion with a roof of glass and steel. When it rained, crowds from other amusement parks made a beeline to Steeplechase, where they could have their pleasures safe from downpours. It was rumored that the Tilyous, faithful church-goers, prayed for rain every afternoon, and were rewarded with a steady deluge from the heavens. The founder of Steeplechase Park died in 1914. His sons, loyal and industrious showmen, took over and are carrying on in the family tradition, but the spark of originality is missing. Innovations are few, the sons evidently working on the theory that what pleased the masses yesteryear will please them again. Steeplechase today has no competition, and inasmuch as the pilgrim to the former nickel empire must find an outlet for his inhibitions, the Tilyous may have a point in refusing to make any changes.

When Dr. Couney, the baby-incubator man, died in 1950 the island lost another of its fabulous personalities. Dr. Couney was a specialist in the care of prematures, a physician first and a brilliant showman after. The baby incubators were unique among Coney Island and other carnival grounds in that over a period of more than forty years they never had a competitor, locally, nationally, or internationally. Showmen who seldom hesitated to imitate any other attraction in the world drew back before the incubators. They were almost as superstitious as the general public about the magic box that developed cyanotic "preemies" into healthy babies of normal size and appearance.

Only a man of rich personality and absolute integrity like Dr. Couney could have made a continuous and significant attraction out of the preemies without drawing down on his head the wrath of the religious and medical authorities. That he died partly of a broken heart is a harsh and carbolic commentary on our society. Dr. Couney's life was an unbelievably rich one in doing good for his fellowmen. In the haunt of thimble-riggers, frenzied carnival ops, bathhouse barons, he stood out as a breath of spring, a scrupulously honest man. He was a combination of wit, culture, and whimsy. He exuded energy at all times, and he was a fervent reformer battling for a cleaner way of life and constantly crusading for the welfare of his all-important preemies.

Dr. Couney never charged a penny for caring for the mites entrusted to him. Rich and poor brought their prematures to his Coney Island station. The nation's top specialists in baby care paid tribute to his medical discoveries, yet he died a poor man, most of his money having been lost at the ill-fated exposition in Flushing Meadows.

It has been said that Coney Island is the summer safety valve for the most explosively packed metropolis in the world. Acutely aware of the crowded city's bathing problems during the stifling summer months is Park Commissioner Robert Moses. This efficient public servant made the observation that bathers at Coney Island had less than the sixteen square feet apiece required for a coffin.

Commissioner Moses' ambition is to eliminate the shoddy amusements and games from the Coney sector and make a park-by-sea for the melting pot of the city. The so-called bingo barons, the feeler-ride federation, and the frozen custard cartelists have fought this highly eccentric notion of Moses'. But Commissioner Moses, who brooks no interference from the local politicos, is a slugger, an infighter who will ultimately knock out the carnival-minded Coney operators. He has done wonders on the beach and boardwalk. What once was a filthy beach and a rotting boardwalk is today a handsome waterfront because of his efforts. In spite of these improvements, Coney Island still remains the most overcrowded waterfront recreation area in the United States, if not in the world.

More than any other community in the world, Coney Island is a powerful, dissolvable agent of racial and religious strains. On its crowded beaches you will find the young Romeos and Juliets of Brownsville and Bensonhurst, Greenpoint and Bay Ridge, Williamsburg, Flatbush, and Manhattan's East Side—an infinite assortment of shipping clerks, bank clerks, messenger boys, clothes cutters, house painters, bookkeepers, file clerks, amateur acrobats, pool-room sharks, and peeping toms, but not one professional lady of rubbery virtue.

Commercial prostitution at Coney Island is virtually unknown today, the amateurs having ruined the highly competitive barter in sex. Hot-blooded swains and full-cheeked damsels check their inhibitions today at the BMT-Stillwell Avenue subway terminal and release their libidinous instincts at the Underwood Hotel, a sentimental synonym for the soft bed of sand beneath the pinewood boardwalk.

CAPITAL OF THE WORLD
(*United Nations*)

AGNES ROTHERY

In considering a permanent site for the United Nations headquarters the British did not favor New York, but neither did they like the idea of San Francisco. The Russians opposed any location on the West Coast. Philadelphia offered a suitable site, but some of the delegates were afraid it was too close to Washington and others were equally afraid it was too far from Broadway. By this time it was evident that the majority of the United Nations did not want to be anywhere but in Manhattan, and in the most costly district of Manhattan. When the Rockefellers donated eight and a half million dollars for the purchase of seventeen acres between the East River and First Avenue, between 42nd and 48th Streets, and the city announced itself willing to contribute street areas, river front rights, and other portions of land to make the site continuous, and the United States Government extended a sixty-five-million-dollar loan interest free, these were joyfully accepted. The intangible glamour which draws hundreds of thousands yearly to New York thus added about five thousand more permanent residents and, through the ideals and activities of the U.N., became the tangible capital of the world.

The most striking unit in the glittering congeries of buildings is composed of two parallel walls thirty-nine stories high, the long eastern and western façades composed of fifty-four hundred windows and fifty-four hundred glass spandrels, and its narrow northern and southern façades of marble, with no windows at all. It is a slim, transparent rectangle, balancing on its thinnest edge and housing the Secretariat. Strikingly geometrical as is this stark airy mass, it is only one of four units of the headquarters, which extend over seventeen acres, with lounges overhanging the Franklin D. Roosevelt Drive, and basements burrowing down three levels below the street.

If you should stand close to the base of the Secretariat Building and look directly up 547 feet of sheer glass wall, you would find it as dizzying as looking down into a steep canyon of the same number of feet. This upside-down effect is further intensified when you step inside, for the glass at the windows, blue-green to reduce the glare, produces a strange under-the-sea light, so you feel you should be swimming or floating instead of walking through the rooms. Neither is there any connection in temperature between the outer world and this transparent segment of it, for not only is the whole building air-conditioned but every separate room has its own air-conditioning unit, so that the occupant from Afghanistan and the one from Finland may each have his accustomed climate at all hours and seasons.

The architectural novelty and the infinite mechanical conveniences of this building which now serves sixty member nations, with facilities for sixty-five and space for an eventual eighty, are the first things which impress the visitor. There are ramps as well as stairways and elevators. Besides the lounges, cafeterias and dining rooms, there is a fully equipped clinic with permanent resident doctors and nurses and X-ray machines. Mail, messages, documents and packages which must pass between floors are handled by a system of electric conveyors, coupled with pneumatic tubes operated from central distributing points.

The visitor's next impression is the realization that he is in the truly international city. There are two working languages, which means that every printed notice is in both English and French: Letter Box is also *Bôite aux Lettres*, the Security Council is *Conseil de Sécurité*, and the delegates' entrance is *Entrée des Délégués*. Not only the printed notices but the faces and speech of the people in the corridors, in the elevators and in the offices are a continual reminder that the personnel of the Secretariat is chosen according to the geographical distribution of the member countries. There are five official languages, English, French, Spanish, Russian and Chinese, but this does not mean that Czechoslovakians and Scandinavians, Syrians and Greeks may not find compatriots to chat with. . . .

The hundreds of visitors who attend a meeting of the General Assembly, or a meeting of the Council, and the hundreds of thousands who hear and see them over radio and television never cease to marvel at the system of interpretation which translates any speech in any of the five official languages, immediately and correctly, into all the others. So instantaneous and so accurate are these interpretations that it seems as if there must be some miraculous mechanism to unscramble and reassemble the flow of words and sentences. There are mechanisms, to be sure, but they are merely aids. The miracle is in those remarkably endowed and specially trained men and women who, while listening to one language, can translate it into another without the hesitation of a split second, catching not only every word but even every nuance, handling every literary allusion or idiom, and in many cases reproducing even the characteristic inflections of the speakers. Each delegate—each visitor, for that matter—can get the translation he wants by pressing a button on the five-place dial on the small selector box attached to each seat.

The other system, which is used by the Security Council only, is called consecutive and, although older and therefore more familiar, is hardly less extraordinary. While a delegate is speaking in any one of the five official languages, the consecutive interpreters listen intently, some of them taking a few notes and others taking no notes at all. When the speaker finishes—he may have taken forty minutes or even an hour—one interpreter rises and repeats what has been said, word for word, in French. When he has finished another interpreter rises and reports the speech with precisely the same verbal accuracy, in English. . . .

If the dizzying glittering walls of the U.N. are conspicuous against the New York sky, its population which throngs council chambers, committee rooms, lounges, dining rooms, offices, corridors and elevators, as soon as it surges out into the street, melts into the general scene. To be sure, one occasionally passes two brown-skinned gentlewomen swathed in the graceful saris of Pakistan, or a pale yellow child with straight black bangs and almond eyes playing in Central Park. But there are so many brown skins, yellow skins, olive, and black skins in the city that one soon ceases to notice them, much less to wonder if their possessors are here because of the U.N. . . .

Even when headquarters were temporarily divided between Lake Success and Flushing Meadow, thousands of visitors found their way thither. Now that permanent headquarters are assembled in one place within walking distance of Grand Central Station, the U.N. is at the top or near the top of the sight-seeing list of most visitors.

This is as it should be. For the "World Parliament" draws its power and influence as well as its financial support from people everywhere.

III
Those Were the Days

EARLY NEW YORK:
Fascinating Little Wench

HENRY COLLINS BROWN

The little hamlet which was turned over to the English conquerors in 1664 was the least important, by far, of the seacoast cities in the New World. It stood at the bottom of the list and was rated as only a tenth-rate Dutch fishing village by its neighbors, if they thought of it at all, which was seldom.

Yet few ports could boast of the colorful life that made New York the fascinating little wench it then was. In front of the Fort, the streets were thronged with gay pageantry; with motley and weird groups. Striking beauties with the olive skins of the Orient in shawls of flaming scarlet, of passionate purple; skirts of soft clinging silks from the Indies; sparkling diamonds, glowing rubies and milk-white pearls glittered on their voluptuous bosoms. These strange exotic women were the consorts of still stranger swarthy, raven-haired men, with long tresses that fell in curling clusters on their broad, powerful shoulders. Shining gold earrings hung from their heavy lobes, and the hilts of jewel-studded sheath knives sparkled in the sun. These swaggering blades, in many-colored coats trimmed with gold lace, mother-of-pearl buttons, white silk knee breeches and embroidered hose with silver buckles on their shoes, gave the town the aspect of an El Dorado. A shower of gold followed their footsteps. No Treasure Island was ever more splendid. The modest clam shell, hitherto used to eke out the meager currency of the little settlement, gave place to shining pieces of eight, the Louis d'Or of France, the dinars of Arabia, and the bysants of Greece. The tinkle of the guitar and the soft murmur of the lute hung on the air. Strange, seductive perfumes imparted a carnival atmosphere to the shore front. It was the Golden Age of Piracy, and New York was a second Madagascar. These strangers were a joyous, free, devil-may-care people; adventure was their handmaiden and danger was their God.

They formed a striking contrast to the stolid Dutch housekeeper and the few comely English women who were gradually becoming more numerous. But that's what New York likes—something unusual—bizarre—and in these revelers of the Sea, she enjoyed an element of relief from the endless psalm-singing of her pious neighbors. She got angry when she heard she was called *"l'enfant terrible."* But when she learned that this meant only "tough baby," she merely grinned. The Cavalier (?) States, Virginia, the Carolinas and Georgia, were so busy raising tobacco and First Families that they knew only in a vague way that such a wicked city as New York even existed. Her growth in population did not keep pace with the rapidly expanding census achieved by the Puritans with their lovely families of from sixteen to twenty-five little olive branches. Had they not passed a law prohibiting the kissing of wives on Sunday, there is no telling to what dizzy heights New England might have attained in the way of population.

But vast changes were now at hand. Piracy was to disappear and maritime commerce was to take its place. Already New York was looming in the distance as a formidable rival to her New England neighbors. Newport, however, was still conceded on all sides to be the natural gateway to the continent. Her natural advantages were unsurpassed. She was everywhere looked upon as the coming Venice of the New World. To a great extent she has realized this ambition, but her wealth comes from New York.

Although to the stranger things looked somewhat semibarbarous, there was, nevertheless, a distinct atmosphere of approaching civilization everywhere. The red man who roamed its roads at will, had largely disappeared; the dock front, moreover, had been shored up and something approaching organized shipping had been attained. The Rattle Watch now patrolled the streets in greater numbers. Every hour you could hear them calling—"Four o'clock a cold and frosty morning. All's well." Fire protection in a limited way had been installed and fire buckets were, by law, part of the equipment of practically every dwelling. There were no engines yet. To quench a blaze water was pumped from the nearest well. Men formed in lines and buckets were passed along as fast as filled. Those at the end of the line threw the water on the flames. Sanitary arrangements were yet extremely crude. Out houses, however, had been removed by decree from direct sight in the public roads and were gradually being relegated to the rear. Sidewalks, slightly elevated, were hard-packed dirt roads, sometimes planked; but the streets were seas of mud, in every degree of consistency. After it rained puddles were frequent, and not at all bashful; they would crawl right up to your knee.

There were no theaters or other public resorts for entertainments. Social diversions, among the Dutch contingent particularly, consisted in little evening gatherings at each other's houses beginning at six o'clock and ending at nine. This select company was probably as bright and cheerful as a "Ladies' Aid" in the Gay '90's, but much more refined than some of the bridge parties of today. The evening was spent in decorous conversation and academic bromides. The younger set were much given to "bundling" parties. Our present necking party is just the good old Colonial bundling custom, with the alcoholic content greatly reduced. Card players were known as "Lost Souls." Cakes and wine were sometimes served, but not always. We would not today vote it a very smart evening.

In summer the long twilight was spent more pleasantly. The walks along the shore were vastly alluring and the view of the harbor by moonlight was never without its charm. Then there were kissing bridges at convenient intervals, and at a kissing bridge you were privileged to kiss your fair companion and it was considered perfectly proper. Two of these pleasant places are officially recorded on old plans and records of the city, but no mention is made of the twenty and two that the young people discovered for themselves and never put on any map.

THE FASHIONABLE LIFE, 1828

JAMES KIRKE PAULDING

James Kirke Paulding (1778–1860) was a well-known New York writer of his day. He collaborated with Washington Irving on the Salmagundi Papers. *In later years he served briefly as Secretary of the Navy.*

The people of New York are very hospitable. They give you a great dinner or evening party, and then "let you run." These dinners seem to be in the nature of a spasmodic effort, which exhausts the purse or the hospitality of the entertainer, and is followed by a collapse of retrenchment. Mr. —— has a fine house, the inside of which looks like an upholsterer's shop, and lives in style. He gave me an invitation to dinner, at a fortnight's notice, where I ate out of a set of China, my lady assured me cost seven hundred dollars, and drank out of glasses that cost a guinea a piece. There can be no doubt these dinners are genteel and splendid, because every body here says so. But between ourselves, I was ennui. The dinner lasted six hours, at the end of which, the company was more silent than at the beginning, a sure sign of something being wanting.

From the dinner party, which broke up at nine, I accompanied the young people to a tea party, being desirous of shaking off the heaviness of that modern merry making. We arrived about a quarter before ten, and found the servant just lighting the lamps. He assured me the lady would be down to receive us in half an hour, being then under the hands of Monsieur Manuel, the hair dresser, who was engaged till nine o'clock with other ladies. You must know this Manuel is the fashionable hair dresser of the city, and it is not uncommon for ladies to get their heads dressed the day before they are wanted, and sit up all night to preserve them in their proper buckram rigidity.

About half past ten the lady entered in all the colours of the rainbow, and all the extravagance of vulgar finery. I took particular notice of her head, which beyond doubt, was the master piece of Monsieur Manuel. It was divested of all its natural features, which I suppose is the perfection of art. There was nothing about it which looked like hair, except it was petrified hair. All the graceful waving lightness of this most beautiful gift of woman, was lost in curls stiff and ungraceful as deformity could make them. . . . Between ten and eleven the company began to drop in; but the real fashionables did not arrive till about half past eleven. It was what they call a conversation party, one at which there was neither cards nor dancing. . . . I venture to affirm, that assemblages of this kind, ought to be called eating, instead of tea drinking, or conversation parties. Their relative excellence and attraction is always estimated among the really fashionable, refined people, by the quality and quantity of the eatables and drinkables. One great requisite, is plenty of oysters; but the *sine qua non*, is oceans of champagne, for there was little conversation, a great deal of eating, and the champagne so plenty, that nine first rate dandies got so merry, that they fell fast asleep on the benches of the supper table up stairs. . . .

It is not to be wondered at, that the indefatigable votaries of fashion should look sleepy at these parties. I am told the major part of them have been at parties five nights in the week, for two or three months past. You will recollect, that owing to the absurd and ridiculous aping of foreign whims and fashions, these evening parties do not commence till the evening is past, nor end till the morning is come. Hence it is impossible to go to one of them, without losing a whole night's rest, which is to be made up, by lying in bed the greater part of the next day. It is no wonder their persons are jaded, their eyes sunk, their chests flattened, their sprightliness repressed by midnight revels, night after night, and that they supply the absence of all these, by artificial allurements of dress, and artificial pulmonic vivacity. . . .

I would not be understood to censure those nations among whom the waltz is, as it were, indigenous—a national dance. Habit, example and practice from their earliest youth, accustom the women of these countries to the exhibition, and excuse it. But for an American woman brought up with certain notions of propriety, to rush at once into a waltz, to brave the just sentiment of the delicate of her own and the other sex, with whom she has been brought up, and continues to associate, is little creditable to her good sense, her delicacy or her morals. Every woman does, or ought to know, that she cannot exhibit herself in the whirling and lascivious windings of a waltz, without calling up in the minds of men, feelings and associations unworthy the dignity and purity of a delicate female. . . .

THE BIG TOWN

Circa 1837

ASA GREENE

Asa Greene (1789–1837) combined many careers during his relatively short life: physician, bookseller, newspaperman and author. The descriptions of several facets of the metropolitan scene of his day are from his book, A Glance At New York, *published anonymously in 1837.*

Traffic, Dirt and Cholera

Not more than a sixth part of the island of Manhattan is compactly covered with houses, stores, and paved streets. The rest is occupied with farms and gardens; though the limits of the city comprise the whole island. . . . The streets of the ancient parts of New York are narrow, crooked, and irregular—running into and crossing each other at all sorts of angles except a right angle. . . . The new parts of the city are more regularly laid out. The streets and avenues are broad and straight; and the squares have generally right angles.

Broadway is a noble street, eighty feet wide and straight as an arrow, extending from the Battery northward nearly two miles, and uniting with the fifth avenue. But broad as Broadway is, it is now quite too narrow for the immense travel, business, and locomotion of various kinds, of which it is the constant scene. This is particularly the case with that part below Canal-street; and more particularly so south of the Park. Here the attempt at crossing is almost as much as your life is worth. To perform the feat with any degree of safety, you must button your coat tight about you, see that your shoes are secure at the heels, settle your hat firmly on your head, look up street and down street, at the self-same moment, to see what carts and carriages are upon you, and then run for your life. We daily see persons waiting at the crossing places, for some minutes, before they can find an opening, and a chance to get over, between the omnibuses, coaches, and other vehicles, that are constantly dashing up and down the street; and, after waiting thus long, deem themselves exceedingly fortunate if they can get over with sound bones and a whole skin. . . .

It must be owned, that, until within a few years, New York was shamefully dirty. Even as late as the year '32, she had not greatly improved. The first thorough cleansing she ever had, was in the summer of that year; and for this cleansing the cholera is to be thanked. While the cholera was on the way from Canada, the fathers of the city began to bethink themselves of abating the fury and shortening the stay of that dread enemy, as much as possible, by divesting the city of that foul aliment on which the pestilence delights to feed.

They resolved to clean the streets; and the streets were cleaned. For the first time, within the memory of living man, the stones of the pavement every where showed their heads. The rain had occasionally washed them bare, but, in the more level streets, the stones, after having once been fixed in the pavior, rarely had shown themselves again to mortal eyes. In 1832, after the arrival of the cholera, they were first scraped and swept clean; and the filth carted away.

Formerly there were no street scavengers. There was a law requiring each householder as often, we believe, as once a week to sweep before his own door; not only the side-walk, but also half way across the street, where his opposite neighbor was to meet him. The dirt, swept in heaps, was to be carried away by the carts. We well remember that the householders swept as often as they pleased; and for the matter of being carried away, the dirt often remained in heaps for several days; or rather the heaps were trodden and scattered about again; and required to be swept and collected anew.

How surprised, then, were the citizens of New York, in the summer of '32, to behold the tidiness of their streets . . . But the cleanliness of New York, during that cholera summer, it must be confessed, was in part ascribable to the want of business and the scarcity of inhabitants: the first having almost entirely disappeared, and the latter in great numbers, by reason of the pestilence. Seventy-five thousand human beings, and several thousand horses, carts, and other vehicles, make a very considerable difference in the generation of street-dirt. Having been once, therefore, thoroughly swept and cleansed, it was comparatively easy to keep streets clean, until the return of the inhabitants and the revival of business. . . . [Still] New York is at least fifty per cent more tidy than she was previous to 1832.

Riots Galore: Doctors, Anti-Abolition, Flour

The first mob of any great notoriety in New York, was called the *"Doctors' Mob"*—not because it was got up *by* the doctors, but *against* them. This happened in the winter of 1787. Some medical students were imprudent enough to let it be known that they were engaged in the offices of dissection—actually dismembering the bodies of men who had not died the death of felons. And as it is ever considered, by the populace, a greater crime to exhume and dissect a dead man, than to kill a live one, so the populace of this city determined to make an example of these sons of Aesculapius. They rushed to the Hospital and destroyed a number of anatomical preparations; and would have done the same by the students, if they had not been rescued by the interference of the mayor, the sheriff, and some of the more intelligent citizens, who lodged them in jail for safe keeping. The mob then attacked the jail but the militia were at length called out; and the mob were finally dispersed by killing five and wounding seven of their number.

The year '34 was famous, in New York, for the *anti-abolition mob*. Commencing on the Fourth of July, at an anti-slavery meeting in

Chatham-street Chapel, it was not completely suppressed for several days. The abolitionists—relying on the Constitution, thought they had a right to express opinions freely on the subject of slavery. But others were not so inclined, and they determined that there was one subject, at least, on which, in a free country, no man should publicly open his mouth. Wherefore, attacking them from the boxes, they hurled down upon their heads, in the pit, the benches, and whatever they could conveniently lay their hands on; and at last succeeded in driving them, with their colored friends, from the house.

The next exploit of the mob was the attack on the house of Lewis Tappan, the leader of the abolitionists. Having broken in the doors and windows, they contented themselves with making a bonfire of all his furniture—valued at about fifteen hundred dollars—and then dispersed, to assemble again the next evening for further mischief. Their next achievement was the demolition of the windows and pews of the churches of the Rev. Dr. Cox and the Rev. Mr. Ludlow; both of which gentlemen were accused of being favorable to immediate abolition. The mob also, attacked the church of the Rev. Peter Williams, a respectable colored clergyman, who happened to be of the opinion that slavery was not the best possible condition for his African brethren.

To do justice to our worthy mayor and corporation, it must be acknowledged that, in almost all cases of outbreaks against the peace, they began to bestir themselves very lustily after the mischief is fairly done. When the city is threatened with a riot, they strenuously keep their own peace, until the mob is completely organized, the work of destruction commenced, and, in general, pretty well finished. It has been so in all the riots that have happened here within our recollection.

The last of these was the *flour-riot*, which happened in the month of February of the present year. In consequence of the high price of bread, growing out of the monopoly of flour by a few speculators in that article, the papers for several weeks had spoken in terms of indignation of the base avarice—the grinding cruelty—of those merchants, who were said to be coining money, as it were, out of the very heart's blood of the people.

At length a great meeting was assembled in the Park, to devise means for the cure of so great a grievance. Warm harangues were pronounced, and spirited resolutions were passed. . . . Immediately after the dismission of the meeting in the Park, a band of rioters proceeded to the store of Eli Hart & Co., the most obnoxious of all the flour monopolists; and demolishing their windows and doors, threw out and destroyed two or three hundred barrels of flour, and nearly the like quantity of wheat. Whether they expected to make the remainder of those articles cheaper by destroying a part, is not specified; but so rapidly did they work for two or three hours, in rolling out and staving in the casks of flour and wheat, that their contents lay mingled together, from one side of the street to the other, to the depth of two or three feet.

The worthy mayor was, by this time, on the ground before the mob had more than half completed the work in hand. The constables were also there, with their long pine sticks. The mayor—like a man of peace, as he is known to be—first began to make a speech. But the rioters, who had just been hearing a much finer oration in the Park, refused to listen; and even proceeded so far as to stop the flow of His Honor's eloquence, with a handful of flour. They treated the constables and their staves of office with quite as little respect; for they broke the staves over the constables' backs.

The mayor and his posse were driven from the ground; but returning, after a while with a larger force, they finally proved victorious.

The Great Fire of 1835

The progress of the GREAT FIRE, of the 16th of December, was owing to several causes, which had never before occurred in combination, and are not likely again to meet for a long time to come. The mischief first commenced in a high building, in a narrow street. But the firemen were on the ground, with their usual alacrity, and before the flames had made any very extensive progress. But their engines were out of order; and this was the first great cause of the succeeding disaster. On the morning previous, they had been employed at a large fire; and the weather being excessively cold, there was much ice collected in the hose, and the pipes: so that very little water could be received or delivered by them; and that little not with sufficient force, to have much effect on a large fire and a high building.

While the flames were fast getting ahead, owing to the condition of the engines, these were continually getting worse and worse, in consequence of the increasing severity of the weather; until they at length became, in a great measure, useless; and nearly all effort to arrest the flames by their means, was abandoned. The firemen, unable to be of service in their proper capacity, were employed in saving goods and merchandize from the stores which were next to be burnt.

But even these efforts in many instances, availed not. The goods, though supposed at first to be removed out of the reach of harm, not being carried, as it turned out, to a sufficient distance, were finally destroyed by the flames; and all the labor of their removal—in some instances twice over—was utterly thrown away.

The first great cause of the progress of the fire, was the unfortunate condition of the engines. But when it had once got the power into its own hands, it seemed to deride the vain efforts of man. Contrary to the course of ordinary fires, it seemed to pay no regard to the winds, but ran as well against them, as along with them. It spread east, west, north, and south at the same time. While one division of its flames, was marching towards the East River, another was proceeding towards Broad-street, another to Wall, and so on.

People on all sides were in the utmost consternation. Terror and dismay sat on every face. Despair was in all men's minds and actions. A species of insanity, in many instances, prevailed. Costly and valuable articles were destroyed, to save them from the flames! One man —a military character, and now a hero in Texas—proposed to blow up the City Hall, standing alone in the Park, to stop the progress of the flames below Wall-street, at a half a mile's distance.

Gunpowder was finally employed, and probably with some advantage. Several stores were blown up, in the neighborhood of the fire, so as to occasion a vacancy in the line of buildings where the flames were progressing. The blowing up of these stores had probably some effect in arresting the progress of the fire; particularly towards Broad street. A bound was put to it in Wall street, by great exertions in keeping constantly wet such of the exposed parts of the buildings, on the upper side of that street, as were combustible. While to the east, it was only arrested by the river itself. The fire in its whole progress destroyed 654 stores, shops, houses, and public buildings— including that expensive edifice, the Merchant's Exchange, in which was the Post Office, and the fine statue of Hamilton by Chantry.

The amount of property, real, and personal, destroyed at this fire, was estimated—after a careful examination by a committee appointed for that purpose—at the round sum of seventeen million dollars. Other fires, during that year, of which the number was large and the result disastrous, are supposed to have raised the whole amount, for the twelve months, to very near *twenty millions of dollars.*

We have hinted at the surprise of strangers at the frequent cries of fire in this city. They are very often alarmed too, as well as surprised; and fancy from the hideous outcry of the boys and the rueful jangling of the bells, that the fire is close to, if not within their very lodgings; and that New York is, every day, on the verge of a general conflagration. To this alarm, the bells very much, perhaps needlessly, contribute. As soon as an alarm of fire is given, they fall to ringing in all quarters, with great zeal and force; and some of them continue their clamor for a considerable time after the danger is past; or after the alarm is ascertained to be a false one.

The number of fire companies in New York, of all kinds, is sixty-four. Each of these consists of twenty-six men. In addition to these, they are permitted to accept of the services of volunteers; who, however, are not entitled to any of the privileges belonging to the regular firemen. All they can claim, is the pleasure of turning out at every cry of fire; and aiding to draw and work the engines.

The regular firemen, as a remuneration for all their toils, dangers, loss of sleep, exposure to heat, cold, and wet, and various expenses in the service of the public, for the space of seven years, are exempted from military, and from jury, duty; not only during those seven years, but for the rest of their lives.

A JAUNDICED VIEW

CHARLES DICKENS

When Charles Dickens was thirty years old he visited America. These observations on New York City, taken from his somewhat jaundiced American Notes, *are typically vigorous and telling, and not without tolerance and humor.*

1842

The beautiful metropolis of America is by no means so clean a city as Boston, but many of its streets have the same characteristics; except that the houses are not quite so fresh-coloured, the sign-boards are not quite so gaudy, the gilded letters not quite so golden, the bricks not quite so red, the stone not quite so white, the blinds and area railings not quite so green, the knobs and plates upon the street doors not quite so bright and twinkling. There are many by-streets, almost as neutral in clean colours, and positive in dirty ones, as by-streets in London; and there is one quarter, commonly called the Five Points, which, in respect of filth and wretchedness, may be safely backed against Seven Dials, or any other part of famed St. Giles's.

The great promenade and thoroughfare, as most people know, is Broadway; a wide and bustling street, which, from the Battery Gardens to its opposite termination in a country road, may be four miles long. Shall we sit down in an upper floor of the Carlton House Hotel (situated in the best part of this main artery of New York), and when we are tired of looking down upon the life below, sally forth arm-in-arm, and mingle with the stream?

Warm weather! The sun strikes upon our heads at this open window, as though its rays were concentrated through a burning-glass; but the day is in its zenith, and the season an unusual one. Was there ever such a sunny street as this Broadway! The pavement stones are polished with the tread of feet until they shine again; the red bricks of the houses might be yet in the dry, hot kilns; and the roofs of those omnibuses look as though, if water were poured on them, they would hiss and smoke, and smell like half-quenched fires. No stint of omnibuses here! Half-a-dozen have gone by within as many minutes. Plenty of hackney cabs and coaches too; gigs, phaetons, large-wheeled tilburies, and private carriages—rather of a clumsy make, and not very different from the public vehicles, but built for the heavy roads beyond the city pavement. Negro coachmen and white; in straw hats, black hats, white hats, glazed caps, fur caps; in coats of drab, black, brown, green, blue, nankeen, striped jean and linen; and there, in that one instance (look while it passes, or it will be too late), in suits of livery. Some southern republican that, who puts his blacks in uniform, and swells with Sultan pomp and power. Yonder, where that phaeton with the well-clipped pair of grays has stopped—standing at their heads now—is a Yorkshire groom, who has not been very long in these parts, and looks sorrowfully round for a companion pair of top-boots, which he may traverse the city half a year without meeting. Heaven save the ladies, how they dress! We have seen more colours in these ten minutes, than we should have seen elsewhere, in as many days. What various parasols! what rainbow silks and satins! what pinking of thin stockings, and pinching of thin shoes, and fluttering of ribbons and silk tassels, and display of rich cloaks with gaudy hoods and linings! The young gentlemen are fond, you see, of turning down their shirt-collars and cultivating their whiskers, especially under the chin; but they cannot approach the ladies in their dress or bearing, being, to say the truth, humanity of quite another sort. Byrons of the desk and counter, pass on, and let us see what kind of men those are behind ye: those two labourers in holiday clothes, of whom one carries in his hand a crumpled scrap of paper from which he tries to spell out a hard name, while the other looks about for it on all the doors and windows.

Irishmen both! You might know them, if they were masked, by their long-tailed blue coats and bright buttons, and their drab trousers, which they wear like men well used to working dresses, who are easy in no others. It would be hard to keep your model republics going, without the countrymen and countrywomen of those two labourers. For who else would dig, and delve, and drudge, and do domestic work, and make canals and roads, and execute great lines of Internal Improvement! Irishmen both, and sorely puzzled too, to find out what they seek. Let us go down, and help them, for the love of home, and that spirit of liberty which admits of honest service to honest men, and honest work for honest bread, no matter what it be.

That's well! We have got at the right address at last, though it is written in strange characters truly, and might have been scrawled with the blunt handle of the spade the writer better knows the use of, than a pen. Their way lies yonder, but what business takes them there? They carry savings: to hoard up? No. They are brothers, those men. One crossed the sea alone, and working very hard for one half year, and living harder, saved funds enough to bring the other out. That done, they worked together side by side, contentedly sharing hard labour and hard living for another term, and then their sisters came, and then another brother, and lastly, their old mother. And what now? Why, the poor old crone is restless in a strange land, and yearns to lay her bones, she says, among her people in the old graveyard at home: and so they go to pay her passage back: and God help her and them, and every simple heart, and all who turn to the Jerusalem of their younger days, and have an altar-fire upon the cold hearth of their fathers.

This narrow thoroughfare, baking and blistering in the sun, is Wall Street: the Stock Exchange and Lombard Street of New York. Many a rapid fortune has been made in this street, and many a no less rapid ruin. Some of these very merchants whom you see hanging about here now, have locked up money in their strong-boxes, like the man in the Arabian Nights, and opening them again, have found but withered leaves. Below, here by the water-side, where the bowsprits of ships stretch across the footway, and almost thrust themselves into the windows, lie the noble American vessels which have made their

Packet Service the finest in the world. They have brought hither the foreigners who abound in all the streets: not, perhaps, that there are more here, than in other commercial cities; but elsewhere, they have particular haunts, and you must find them out; here, they pervade the town.

We must cross Broadway again; gaining some refreshment from the heat, in the sight of the great blocks of clean ice which are being carried into shops and bar-rooms; and the pine-apples and water-melons profusely displayed for sale. Fine streets of spacious houses here, you see!—Wall Street has furnished and dismantled many of them very often—and here a deep green leafy square. Be sure that is a hospitable house with inmates to be affectionately remembered always, where they have the open door and pretty show of plants within, and where the child with laughing eyes is peeping out of window at the little dog below. You wonder what may be the use of this tall flagstaff in the by-street, with something like Liberty's head-dress on its top: so do I. But there is a passion for tall flagstaffs hereabout, and you may see its twin brother in five minutes, if you have a mind.

Again across Broadway, and so—passing from the many-coloured crowd and glittering shops—into another long main street, the Bowery. A railroad yonder, see, where two stout horses trot along, drawing a score or two of people and a great wooden ark, with ease. The stores are poorer here; the passengers less gay. Clothes ready-made, and meat ready-cooked, are to be bought in these parts; and the lively whirl of carriages is exchanged for the deep rumble of carts and waggons. These signs which are so plentiful, in shape like river buoys, or small balloons, hoisted by cords to poles, and dangling there, announce, as you may see by looking up, 'OYSTERS IN EVERY STYLE.' They tempt the hungry most at night, for then dull candles glimmering inside, illuminate these dainty words, and make the mouths of idlers water, as they read and linger.

What is this dismal-fronted pile of bastard Egyptian, like an enchanter's palace in a melodrama!—a famous prison, called The Tombs. Shall we go in?

So. A long, narrow, lofty building, stove-heated as usual, with four galleries, one above the other, going round it, and communicating by stairs. Between the two sides of each gallery, and in its centre, a bridge, for the greater convenience of crossing. On each of these bridges sits a man: dozing or reading, or talking to an idle companion. On each tier, are two opposite rows of small iron doors. They look like furnace-doors, but are cold and black, as though the fires within had all gone out. Some two or three are open, and women, with drooping heads bent down, are talking to the inmates. The whole is lighted by a skylight, but it is fast closed; and from the roof there dangle, limp and drooping, two useless windsails.

A man with keys appears, to show us round. A good-looking fellow, and, in his way, civil and obliging. . . .

'When do the prisoners take exercise?'

'Well, they do without it pretty much.'

'Do they never walk in the yard?'

'Considerable seldom.'

'Sometimes, I suppose?'

'Well, it's rare they do. They keep pretty bright without it.'

'But suppose a man were here for a twelvemonth. I know this is only a prison for criminals who are charged with grave offences, while they are awaiting their trial, or under remand, but the law here affords criminals many means of delay. What with motions for new trials, and in arrest of judgment, and what not, a prisoner might be here for twelve months, I take it, might he not?'

'Well, I guess he might.'

'Do you mean to say that in all that time he would never come out at that little iron door, for exercise?'

'He might walk some, perhaps—not much.'

'Will you open one of the doors?'

'All, if you like.'

The fastenings jar and rattle, and one of the doors turns slowly on its hinges. Let us look in. A small bare cell, into which the light enters through a high chink in the wall. There is a rude means of washing, a table, and a bedstead. Upon the latter, sits a man of sixty; reading. He looks up for a moment; gives an impatient dogged shake; and fixes his eyes upon his book again. As we withdraw our heads, the door closes on him, and is fastened as before. This man has murdered his wife, and will probably be hanged. . . .

'In England, if a man be under sentence of death, even he has air and exercise at certain periods of the day.'

'Possible?'

With what stupendous and untranslatable coolness he says this, and how loungingly he leads on to the women's side: making, as he goes, a kind of iron castanet of the key and the stair-rail!

Each cell door on this side has a square aperture in it. Some of the women peep anxiously through it at the sound of footsteps; others shrink away in shame.—For what offence can that lonely child, of ten or twelve years old, be shut up here? Oh! that boy? He is the son of the prisoner we saw just now; is a witness against his father; and is detained here for safe keeping, until the trial; that's all.

But it is a dreadful place for the child to pass the long days and nights in. This is rather hard treatment for a young witness, is it not? —What says our conductor?

'Well, it an't a very rowdy life, and *that's* a fact!'

Again he clinks his metal castanet, and leads us leisurely away. I have a question to ask him as we go.

'Pray, why do they call this place The Tombs?'

'Well, it's the cant name.'

'I know it is. Why?'

'Some suicides happened here, when it was first built. I expect it come about from that.'

'I saw just now, that that man's clothes were scattered about the floor of his cell. Don't you oblige the prisoners to be orderly, and put such things away?'

'Where should they put 'em?'

'Not on the ground surely. What do you say to hanging them up?'

He stops and looks round to emphasise his answer:

'Why, I say that's just it. When they had hooks they *would* hang themselves, so they're taken out of every cell, and there's only the marks left where they used to be!'

The prison-yard in which he pauses now, has been the scene of terrible performances. Into this narrow, grave-like place, men are brought out to die. The wretched creature stands beneath the gibbet on the ground; the rope about his neck; and when the sign is given, a weight at its other end comes running down, and swings him up into the air—a corpse.

The law requires that there be present at this dismal spectacle, the judge, the jury, and citizens to the amount of twenty-five. From the community it is hidden. To the dissolute and bad, the thing remains a frightful mystery. Between the criminal and them, the prison-wall is interposed as a thick gloomy veil. It is the curtain to his bed of death, his winding-sheet, and grave. From him it shuts out life, and all the motives to unrepenting hardihood in that last hour, which its mere sight and presence is often all-sufficient to sustain. There are no bold eyes to make him bold; no ruffians to uphold a ruffian's name before. All beyond the pitiless stone wall, is unknown space.

Let us go forth again into the cheerful streets.

Once more in Broadway! Here are the same ladies in bright colours, walking to and fro, in pairs and singly; yonder the very same light blue parasol which passed and repassed the hotel-window twenty times while we were sitting there. We are going to cross here. Take care of the pigs. Two portly sows are trotting up behind this carriage, and a select party of half-a-dozen gentlemen hogs have just now turned the corner.

Here is a solitary swine lounging homeward by himself. He has only one ear; having parted with the other to vagrant-dogs in the course of his city rambles. But he gets on very well without it; and leads a roving, gentlemanly, vagabond kind of life, somewhat answering to that of our club-men at home. He leaves his lodgings every morning at a certain hour, throws himself upon the town, gets through his day in some manner quite satisfactory to himself, and regularly appears at the door of his own house again at night, like the mysterious master of Gil Blas. He is a free-and-easy, careless, indifferent kind of pig, having a very large acquaintance among other pigs of the same character, whom he rather knows by sight than conversation, as he seldom troubles himself to stop and exchange civilities, but goes grunting down the kennel, turning up the news and small-talk of the city in the shape of cabbage-stalks and offal, and bearing no tails but his own: which is a very short one, for his old enemies, the dogs, have been at that too, and have left him hardly enough to swear by. He is in every respect a republican pig, going wherever he pleases, and mingling with the best society, on an equal, if not superior footing, for every one makes way when he appears, and the haughtiest give him the wall, if he prefer it. . . .

They are the city scavengers, these pigs. Ugly brutes they are; having, for the most part, scanty brown backs, like the lids of old horsehair trunks: spotted with unwholesome black blotches. They have long, gaunt legs, too, and such peaked snouts, that if one of them could be persuaded to sit for his profile, nobody would recognise it for a pig's likeness. They are never attended upon, or fed, or driven, or caught, but are thrown upon their own resources in early life, and become preternaturally knowing in consequence. Every pig knows where he lives, much better than anybody could tell him. At this hour, just as evening is closing in, you will see them roaming towards bed by scores, eating their way to the last. Occasionally, some youth among them who has over-eaten himself, or has been worried by dogs, trots shrinkingly homeward, like a prodigal son: but this is a rare case: perfect self-possession and self-reliance, and immovable composure, being their foremost attributes. . . .

BOWERY BOY VS. BROADWAY FOP

"A SOUTH CAROLINIAN"

These amusing vignettes appeared in Glimpses of New York *(1852). The unknown author is designated only as a "South Carolinian."*

I would venture the assertion that the searcher for the beautiful would find more to please the eye, gratify the taste, and amuse the mind, in a half hour's stroll in the Bowery on a bright afternoon, than can be met in Broadway in a lunar month.

Here comes the "fashionable" promenader of this street; that's him, in the very last agony of the "ton"—black silk hat, smoothly brushed, sitting precisely upon top of the head, hair well oiled, and lying closely to the skin, long in front, short behind, cravat a-la-sailor, with the shirt collar turned over it, vest of fancy silk, large flowers, black frock coat, no jewelry, except in a few instances, where the insignia of the engine company to which the wearer belongs, as a breastpin, black pants, one or two years behind the fashion, heavy boots, and a cigar about half smoked, in the left corner of the mouth, as nearly perpendicular as it is possible to be got. He has a peculiar swing, not exactly a swagger, to his walk, but a swing, which nobody but a Bowery boy can imitate, and is always upon the *qui vive*—never caught napping.

The Broadway dandy is rigged, as well as I can recollect, somewhat after this manner:—Fine patent-leather boots, rather short, very large striped pants, tight, except round the boot, a flashy vest, very short, watch-chain and seal, with a large bunch of "charms," and a heavy finger-ring suspended on the guard chain, fancy cravat, of the "broad-tie" style, standing shirt collar, coat of some fancy pattern, on the sack order, just covering the hips, sleeves large and loose over the hand, all the beard that can be raised left, to prove that he is not a woman, quizzing-glass over the left eye, hair befrizzled to the utmost, a short walking-stick under the arm, all topped off with one of Leary's white hats, placed on the left side of the head, and you have the real Simon siwassee Broadway fop. He ambles or rather reels when he walks, as if his feet were blistered, and is never seen to speak with any one upon the street.

The Bowery man speaks to every acquaintance he meets, and is hail-fellow-well-met with every body, from the mayor to the beggar.

Another grand difference in these two specimens of humanity. The Bowery boy is a fair politician, a good judge of horse flesh, tragedy, comic acting, music as well as dancing, and renders himself essentially useful as well as ornamental, at all the fires in his ward, and if necessary, in his neighbor's; does a kind, generous act when in his power, pays his board, and splits the Third Avenue wide open occasionally with "Old Pumpkins." The Broadway representative is not only a fop but a ninny, knows about as much of what is going on, out of the very limited circle of his lady friends, as a child ten years old. He ambles up and down Broadway twice or thrice in twenty-four hours, smokes a cigar after dinner, and drives, if he can raise the means for so doing, waits upon a lady friend, if he should be lucky enough to have one, when she will let him, and this is the extent of all his actions and ambition.

The female fops of each, partake of the ingredients of the above representatives in all particulars except in case of rendering assistance at fires in the first instance, but the latter makes it up, by assisting in keeping the sidewalks clean, with the skirts of her dress. You see this street has all the requisites to make it a great business mart; here are several banks, insurance offices, &c. &c. and if the Bowery had a judicial tribunal of her own, it would be a separate kingdom, and as a matter of course, an independent one. Whenever a person who lives upon this street sees an acquaintance getting "large for his size," he is most sure to say, "*You are aping Broadway now*"; and vice versa, the Broadway man says, by way of derision, "That's the Bowery touch," no matter whether it be a bank officer or a street loafer, the same sentiment exists in all.

Take this street, up one side and down the other, and you will find more true, genuine independence, generous hospitality, wit, humor, nobleness of disposition, and liberality than any other portion of the city of New-York. These people feel a sort of "State pride," and where that exists you always find a free, open-hearted, noble, and independent spirit.

THE FIRE RAID ON NEW YORK CITY

HERBERT RAVENEL SASS

Shortly before five o'clock of Thanksgiving afternoon in 1864, Lt. Col. Robert Martin, of the 10th Kentucky Cavalry, C.S.A., strolled slowly up Broadway between Fulton and Vesey streets and turned into the imposing entrance of the Astor House, most famous of New York's numerous hotels.

Even in the conservative dark civilian suit that he was wearing, Bob Martin was a man to attract attention. He was young for a lieutenant colonel, tall, slender but obviously strong, and his somewhat swarthy face had a hawklike look which was exactly right when he was riding at the head of the regiment through some hot-blooded Kentucky town, with sabers clanking, guidons flying and pretty girls waving from the vine-clad porticoes along the street. At such times it was pleasant to know that the eyes of onlookers picked him out and followed him far. But here in New York, when people stared at him hard or followed him with their eyes, it gave him a disagreeable feeling in the region of his neck, as though a noosed rope were already tightening there.

Colonel Martin stopped at the desk, greeted the clerk as one greets a casual but agreeable acquaintance, and inquired, without a trace of Southern accent, whether Mr. W. L. Haines, of Ohio, Room 204, was in the hotel.

"No, sir," the clerk replied at once. "I'm sorry, sir, but you've missed him again. Mr. Haines asked me to tell you, when you came in, that he was going to Barnum's Museum. He said he wanted to have a look at this Indian princess that everybody's talking about. He'd be there till five o'clock, he said, and if you arrived before that hour, he suggested you meet him outside Barnum's at five."

The clerk glanced at the big clock on the wall behind him. "That clock's a little fast," he added. "It's just about fifteen minutes before five now."

Colonel Martin nodded and said whimsically, "My friend Haines is like the Irishman's flea—it's hard to put your finger on him." He paused as though undecided. "I'm glad to see you've got rid of your cold," he added, then listened with evident interest while the clerk recommended at some length Doctor Hyatt's Infallible Life Balsam as the best of all remedies for colds.

Martin looked over the segars arranged on the counter, selected two of a popular French-and-Swartz brand, leafed through the newspapers displayed for sale, and bought a copy of the Tribune, the front page of which was black with headlines about Sheridan in the Shenandoah Valley. A newly arrived couple desirous of registering claimed the clerk's attention, and with a farewell nod, Colonel Martin turned away, retraced his steps across the lobby and walked unhurriedly out through the front door.

Diagonally across Broadway at the corner of Ann Street rose the high façade of Barnum's Museum with its huge posters of impossible animals and its overhanging balcony where a brass band was playing The Union Forever. Colonel Martin moved to the edge of the sidewalk and, before crossing the street to Barnum's, stopped to light his segar and do a little thinking.

There was quite a good deal to think about. This wasn't the first time that Mr. Haines, of Room 204 at the Astor, had sent him a message through the talkative desk clerk. The guest who appeared on the hotel register as W. L. Haines, of Ohio, was really John Headley, of Kentucky—Lt. John Headley, of the Confederate Army, now acting as Colonel Martin's second in command in the campaign to capture New York. At Colonel Martin's direction, Lieutenant Headley had been engaged that afternoon upon a secret and hazardous mission in Washington Place. Colonel Martin knew with complete certainty that Lieutenant Headley hadn't spent the afternoon in Barnum's Museum.

He stepped down from the sidewalk and began to thread his way through the Broadway traffic, denser than usual because it was Thanksgiving afternoon—omnibuses, carriages, barouches, hacks, horseback riders and pedestrians. Nearing the other side of the street, his eyes scanned the throng in front of Barnum's entrance. It was a mixed crowd; the great showman, offering every kind of attraction from the

Feejee Mermaid and Jo-jo, the Dog-Faced Boy, to Doctor Valentine's lectures and the Diorama of the Creation, appealed to every class and taste. Mingled in front of the museum's doors were rich and poor, roughly clad laborers, gentlemen in frock coats with fashionably dressed ladies, much more elaborately dressed women in plumes and silks who obviously weren't exactly ladies, gold-braided officers and blue-clad infantrymen from Gen. Ben Butler's army garrisoning the city.

Colonel Martin reached the sidewalk and turned to pass the main entrance of the museum, his ears almost deafened by the clangor of the brass band on the balcony directly overhead. A moment later he was startled by a touch on his arm, and automatically his hand jumped toward the pistol in his pocket. At once, however, he saw that one of the fancy women was walking beside him. Under her large white hat with its scarlet ostrich plume he couldn't see her face, and she didn't try to speak against the blaring of the brass band, but the pressure of her hand on his arm guided him out of Broadway and around the corner into Ann Street.

Half a block down Ann, she looked up at him, smiling faintly, and even under the paint and rouge of her streetwalker disguise, he recognized her. He had seen her twice at Confederate headquarters in Toronto, and someone had told him then that she was a young widow from Kentucky who was serving as a Confederate secret agent in the Northern states. The second time, Headley had been with him. "Look at that woman, Bob," Headley had whispered, as she passed through the anteroom where they were waiting. "She might be Pocahontas herself." Jet-eyed, dusky-haired, her swarthiness had a golden tint which to Martin's eye seemed more gypsylike than Indian; yet the Indian-princess simile that Headley had pressed into service in his message was apt enough.

Colonel Martin, pleased at having guessed right, leaned toward her, a compliment on his lips, but she spoke first.

"I couldn't find you when I arrived on the morning train from Toronto," she said, "so I got word to Lieutenant Headley at the Astor. He told me to meet you at Barnum's. I bring bad news, Colonel Martin. We've learned that a man we trusted is a Union secret agent. He knows about our plan for New York, and it's likely his dispatch rider is now on the way to Washington. You'll have to strike at once or not at all."

In some such way as this—the record is imperfect here and one has to put two and two together—the Confederate campaign for the capture of New York City began to move swiftly toward its climax. If today the whole grandiose enterprise seems utterly fantastic, there are certain forgotten facts to be recalled.

As early as January, 1861, Mayor Fernando Wood had proposed in his annual message to the Common Council that New York City secede from the Union. Charleston and South Carolina had already seceded, and the lower South would certainly follow them. "California and her sisters of the Pacific," Mayor Wood had told the council in his message, "will no doubt set up an independent republic and husband their own rich mineral resources. The Western states, equally rich in cereals and other agricultural products, will probably do the same." Therefore it was the earnest recommendation of New York's astute and popular mayor that his city get out of the Union and declare itself a free port immediately.

His advice hadn't been adopted, but there were thousands of New Yorkers who believed that Fernando Wood had had the right idea—a sufficient number of thousands to lift him out of the mayor's office, where he had served three terms, into the United States Congress, where he became a favorite of Mrs. Lincoln while continuing to support the propaganda for peace. Meanwhile, in 1862, Horatio Seymour, a scholarly Jeffersonian Democrat with a passionate belief in home rule, had been elected governor of New York State on a platform of opposition to the abolitionists and dissatisfaction with the conduct of the war.

Governor Seymour opposed the Federal enrollment, or draft, act of March, 1863, holding it an invasion of his state's sovereignty, and when, in mid-July, the time for the draft arrived, open rebellion broke out in New York City. Marching columns aggregating at least twenty thousand men surged down the avenues, stormed arsenals and helped themselves to arms and ammunition, wrecked and fired the draft-enrollment offices, withstood and defeated the 11th Regiment in spite of its howitzers and grapeshot, stained the streets with the blood of fifteen hundred slain, including many luckless Negroes hanged to lampposts, sacked stores and homes and held almost undisputed sway for four days, until thirteen regiments from General Meade's army at Gettysburg arrived on hurriedly mobilized express trains and, after stern street fighting, recaptured the city.

If, in that July of 1863, there had been in New York a group of cool and experienced Confederate officers prepared to organize and direct the rebellious forces the South might have won a victory on Manhattan which would have gone far to offset its defeat at Gettysburg. That opportunity had passed. But fifteen months later, with the Lincoln-McClellan contest for the presidency at white heat, with multitudes on Broadway cheering the torch-light processions of the Peace Democrats, and with the threat of a bloody clash on Election Day hanging over the city, the opportunity seemed about to return. And this time the Southerners were ready for it.

They had learned—at least some of them had—that war in the chivalric tradition was outmoded. Across the border in Canada, within striking distance of the great Northern cities, they had established headquarters for the new kind of warfare—a campaign which might be the answer to Sheridan's devastation of the Shenandoah Valley, Sherman's devouring torch in Georgia, and Dahlgren's attempt to raid Richmond, release the Union prisoners, kill President Davis and his cabinet and burn the city. A momentous move was in the making—a mass uprising of the Sons of Liberty and the proclamation of an independent Northwestern Republic, with Chicago as its capital. Arms had already been distributed and Capt. Thomas H. Hines, of the Confederate Army—afterward he would be chief justice of Kentucky—assisted by Col. St. Leger Grenfell and Col. Vincent Marmaduke, had been assigned to direct the revolt. The time had been fixed—the night of November eighth, the day of the presidential election. Simultaneously with the uprising in Chicago, a revolution would be launched in New York.

Therefore, in late October, Colonel Martin led what he called whimsically the Confederate Army of Manhattan secretly into New York City. It was small, consisting of eight men, but it was formidable, for those eight were young Confederate officers, each of whom had been tested and proved in battle. Commissioner Thompson, who had long been in communication with the New York leaders, was confident. On election night, twenty thousand New York Sons of Liberty, already organized and armed, would rise, and Bob Martin and his officers would lead them to the greatest Confederate victory and the most dramatic event of the war—the secession of New York City from the Union.

That was the plan. It seems grotesquely impossible today. But with Fernando Wood's secession proposal on the record, with Governor

Seymour campaigning actively against Lincoln and at bitter odds with the Federal Government, and with the draft riots, which had been incipient rebellion, fresh in memory, it wasn't fantastic at the time. Then, just before the election, disaster struck.

In Chicago, the chiefs of the Sons of Liberty were arrested by the Federal military authorities. Colonels Grenfell and Marmaduke were captured. Simultaneously, a Federal army under Gen. Benjamin F. Butler arrived in New York and took up strategic positions throughout the city. This rendered the projected rising impossible. There was nothing to do, the New York leaders had informed Colonel Martin, but wait until Butler's army was withdrawn. So, ever since then, Martin and his officers had been waiting; and now, with Butler's army still on guard, this message had come from headquarters at Toronto that either the blow must be struck at once or the whole enterprise be abandoned.

Martin and the woman had stopped, one supposes, half a block from Barnum's and were standing close to the curb of the crowded street. Except to glance at the girl's painted face, set off by the large imitation rubies in her ears, the passers-by probably paid no attention to them. More than ever since the coming of Butler's army, Broadway and its side streets swarmed with fancy women; here simply was a pretty Jezebel engaged in hooking a young man. As the significance of her message came home to him, Bob Martin felt utterly tired. So this was the end of his great adventure—an ignominious retreat or a desperate stroke against almost hopeless odds.

The woman's gypsylike face, with its painted cheeks and streetwalker's crimson mouth, was still turned up to him, framed in the wide white hat with its scarlet plume. He said, "Very well, my dear, we'll strike tomorrow and be hanged the day after."

Lieutenant Headley's mission to Washington Place was completed that evening about dusk.

In a basement on the west side of Washington Place, Headley had found a burly old man with, as he described it afterward, "a long beard all over his face." Following instructions, Headley said simply, "I've come for Captain Longmire's baggage," whereupon the bearded one, without a word, but with remarkable strength for a man of his age, lifted a large leather valise over the counter.

The thing was so heavy that Headley could scarcely carry it, but he reached City Hall Park with it, and finally he got it on a horse car which took him up the Bowery. In the upper Bowery he got off with his precious and dangerous burden. A small cottage uptown which had been provided apparently by one of the New York Sons of Liberty, served the Confederates as headquarters where they met from time to time, and it was to this rendezvous that Lieutenant Headley brought the valise containing—Greek fire.

The next morning, Friday, November twenty-fifth, the Confederate Army of Manhattan deployed for action. Only Lieutenant Headley's movements can be given in complete detail, but they were typical of all the others'. He awoke early in his room at the Astor and after a quick breakfast, went to a luggage shop and bought a black leather valise. Placing his overcoat in his valise, he went to the United States Hotel, on Fulton Street, registered there under the name of W. B. Brown and was assigned to Room 172. After a short while, he went out, leaving his valise in his room, but wearing the overcoat, walked to another luggage shop, bought another valise, put the overcoat in it, walked to the City Hotel and registered there under a third name. Again, after a brief stay in this room, he went through the same routine, this time registering at the Everett House. Thus, when he had completed his round, Lieutenant Headley had rooms in four hotels, with a valise in each room.

Meanwhile his comrades, with two exceptions, had been carrying out a similar maneuver.

This deployment was completed by midafternoon. About dark, six of the eight men gathered at the cottage headquarters uptown, two failing to report. All six wore overcoats—the November air was chill—and in the pockets of his coat each man now placed ten of the bottles of Greek fire wrapped in paper. Then they stood up, glanced briefly and a little awkwardly at one another.

"Well, gentlemen," Colonel Martin said in the soft voice he sometimes had, "we'd better start. Good luck to you one and all, and no shooting unless you have to. Those of you that aren't hanging from lampposts rally here tomorrow night."

Again we must follow Headley, because he alone left a record of his movements. It was seven twenty when he reached the Astor House. He got his key—his friend, the talkative day clerk, wasn't on duty—and went to his room, a corner room facing both Broadway and Vesey Street. The plan was to start the fires early in the evening, "so that," as

Headley said afterward, "the guests of hotels might all escape, as we did not want to destroy any lives." He lit the gas jet, hung the bed clothes loosely on the headboard, piled chairs, bureau drawers and washstand on the bed, and stuffed newspapers in the gaps of this pile. He opened the door, fixed the key on the outside, then uncorked a bottle of the Greek fire and flung the liquid on the pile.

It blazed up instantly and silently—he was barely out of the door before the whole interior of the room was in flames. He slammed the door shut, locked it, walked down the hall and stairway to the lobby, which was crowded, and left his key at the desk.

He went at once to the City Hotel, and repeated the process there without a hitch. Going down to the Everett House, he looked up at his room in the Astor; there was a bright light in it, but he saw no sign of alarm. Finishing quickly at the Everett, he started for the United States Hotel, at Fulton and Pearl streets, when he heard the first fire bells uptown. *That would be Bob Martin,* he said to himself. At the United States he got through without trouble, though, in leaving his key, he thought the clerk looked at him strangely.

Coming back up Fulton to Broadway, it seemed to him that now one hundred fire bells were ringing. Evidently the work was going well; already the enormous city heaved and throbbed in a vast and nameless excitement. It was now a quarter past nine by the City Hall clock. Strangely, he could see neither flame nor smoke at the Astor, but across the street at Barnum's Museum there was panic. People were coming down ladders from the second- and third-story windows, fire engines were arriving with clanging bells and screaming whistles, an immense crowd surged in the street.

Headley walked down Broadway and then across to the North River piers. Standing in a dark, deserted spot where ships and barges lay close to the street, he hurled his remaining bottles of Greek fire with all his strength. Here and there, red fountains leaped upward. In their glare he saw for an instant a big barge, its deck piled with baled hay; the next moment it erupted in a huge volcano of flame. He remembered suddenly that a squadron of the new ironclads—he didn't know how many —were lying in the harbor; he wondered whether the burning shipping might not drift down among them and destroy them.

With the sky red behind him, he hurried back to City Hall Park and plunged into the multitude milling in Broadway.

"What's up?" he yelled in the ear of a gray-faced man beside him.

"The rebels!" the man gasped. "They're burning New York in revenge for Atlanta! The Copperheads—the Sons of Liberty—are rising!"

If you will go to one of the libraries where files of old newspapers are available and will get down the New York Herald of Sunday, November twenty-seventh, 1864, you will find the whole front page devoted to the story under headlines huge for those days: ATTEMPT TO BURN THE CITY the top deck reads. DISCOVERY OF A VAST REBEL CONSPIRACY is the second deck, and under these are fourteen other black-letter decks extending halfway to the bottom of the page.

"The city of New York," said the Sunday Herald in its lead, "has undoubtedly had a most wonderful escape"—an escape which was "an unmistakable interposition" of Providence. Had the plan been executed as skillfully as it was conceived, said the Times, "no human power could have saved this city from utter destruction. It was evidently the intention of the conspirators to fire the city at a given moment, at a great many different points, each as remote from the others as possible, except through Broadway, and this thoroughfare they wished to see in a complete blaze from end to end. . . . Had all these hotels, hay barges, theaters, etc., been set on fire at the same moment, and each fire well kindled, the Fire Department would not have been strong enough to extinguish them all and . . . the best portion of the city would have been laid in ashes."

What saved the city? A partial explanation may be found in the Greek fire supplied by the mysterious bearded chemist—unquestionably, it was defective. Though it blazed up mightily upon exposure to the air, it had little power to ignite the surfaces upon which it was thrown, so that in most cases the flames were extinguished quickly—of the nineteen hotels set ablaze, only the St. Nicholas was badly damaged.

There was no rising of the Sons of Liberty. When Butler's army moved in, that possibility vanished and Fernando Wood's plan for the secession of New York became a fantasy. As for the Confederate Army of Manhattan, it rallied the following night at its cottage headquarters with all six men accounted for, and Colonel Martin, like a skillful, cool commander, took it safely out of the city and back across the Canadian border to Toronto.

HIGH, WIDE AND HANDSOME

LLOYD MORRIS

"The papers are full of the underworld; and the people must see it everywhere, whether they seek for it or not," a widely circulated book told the nation. "The New York underworld is a very passable imitation of its Parisian original. Perhaps in some respects it has surpassed its model."

Brooding on the iniquities of the metropolis in January, 1866, Bishop Simpson of the Methodist Episcopal Church was moved to protest. He made no invidious comparisons with Paris, for he was more startled by a purely domestic equation. There were as many public prostitutes in New York as there were Methodists, he told an audience at Cooper Union, and in a sermon at St. Paul's Church he set their number at twenty thousand.

These "monstrous statements" saddened John A. Kennedy, Superintendent of Police. Was it not his duty to correct the misguided impressions of such well-meaning men as Bishop Simpson? Superintendent Kennedy ordered a census taken by the police, and issued some reassuring statistics. New York had only six hundred and twenty-one houses of prostitution, ninety-nine houses of assignation, and seventy-five concert saloons of ill repute. The number of public prostitutes was a mere thirty-three hundred, and these included seven hundred and forty-seven "waiter girls in concert and drinking saloons." There were, of course, "other women," Superintendent Kennedy acknowledged, but he had no means of determining their number, presumably large. Yet, on the whole, he felt relieved. Conditions in New York were far better than might have been expected.

But statistics were actually irrelevant. Variety, not number, was the distinctive feature of New York's life of pleasure. Its available satisfactions, as the whole nation knew, catered to every form of taste. In no other American city was temptation as perfectly adapted to the versatility of which the single-minded male is capable. The metropolitan underworld never slept; it did business round the clock in every quarter of the town; there was almost no idiosyncrasy which it failed to gratify. Day and night, at all seasons of the year, women of the town paraded Broadway from Canal Street to Madison Square. Formerly, they were never seen before dusk. But now, tripping along in the promenade of the fashionable afternoon shopping hours, they were called "streetwalkers" or "cruisers." You could distinguish them by a saucy stare, a quick backward glance of invitation cast over a trim shoulder. They loitered at the show windows of the finest shops, and before the entrances of the luxury hotels: the St. Nicholas, Metropolitan and Fifth Avenue. On sun-drenched spring days they flirted their parasols; in the early winter twilight, when Broadway was deep in snow and rang with sleigh bells, they swung their muffs with a jaunty air. You saw them in the evening, after the dinner hour, and again as the theaters were closing, moving slowly under the flare of the gaslamps; at midnight, at one, two, three or even four o'clock in the morning. On summer nights, the benches of the pleasant midtown parks—Washington Square, Union Square and Madison Square—were occupied by young women demurely but explicitly accessible.

For the hurried businessman, during his crowded working hours, New York had developed a peculiar institution of pleasure: the "cigar-store battery." These batteries flourished in abundance far downtown. To uninitiated passers-by, they had the appearance of bona-fide cigar stores. Their display windows were filled with cigar boxes, and inside a few cigars were actually exposed for sale. These, as misguided customers were always perplexed by discovering, were reluctantly parted with at from twenty-five to fifty cents apiece. The batteries were presided over by young women of keen discrimination, invariably able to recognize a knowing male when they saw one. To potential clients, they suggested that behind the shop, or upstairs, there were private rooms desirably occupied and that liquid refreshment was to be had at a price. . . .

All visitors to New York wanted to see Greene Street by night, for it was the most notorious thoroughfare in the United States. Two blocks west of Broadway, extending from Canal Street northward to Clinton Place, later Eighth Street, by daylight it had the look of a decaying residential quarter lined with red-brick, low-stooped houses now grown shabby—a quiet, deserted street. Greene Street only came alive after dark. Along its whole length, on both sides, nearly every house was a brothel. Over the front doors, gaslamps blazed in bowls of tinted glass, usually red but of other colors also. On these lamps the names of the proprietor, or of the establishment, were etched in clear white: "Flora," "Lizzie," "The Gem," "The Forget-Me-Not," "Sinbad the Sailor," "The Black Crook.". . .

There were far more luxurious establishments—called "parlor houses"—in better quarters of the city. Two of these achieved nationwide celebrity. "The Seven Sisters" took its name from a musical revue produced by Laura Keene in 1860, which achieved an unbroken run of more than two hundred and fifty performances. Appropriately, "The Seven Sisters" occupied seven adjoining brownstone residences on West Twenty-fifth Street near Seventh Avenue, which made it the largest establishment of its kind in the city. It was one of the most expensive brothels in New York, and was conducted with an almost intimidating elegance. No lamp or sign identified it, but it was known to every cab-driver and hotel clerk, and patrons of the great hotels whose arrival in the city had been noted in the newspapers usually found, in their morning mail, a chaste engraved invitation to visit "The Seven Sisters." Their reception was likely to be more cordial if they arrived in formal evening attire. The girls in this establishment—so it was promised—were cultivated, conversationally resourceful, versed in the etiquette of the best society, proficient pianists, guitarists and singers.

The establishment of Josephine Woods on Clinton Place between University Place and Broadway was smaller, less ostentatious, but professedly more select. Josie Woods, though no longer young, was a dark-haired, graceful woman of arresting beauty whose costly dresses, magnificent diamonds and fine carriage and horses were the talk of the city. Ladies who saw her at the theater, or driving in Central Park, or at Long Branch and Saratoga Springs in the summer, found it hard to believe that she actually cultivated so unspeakable a profession. She had the air of belonging in superior social circles. And in a sense she did. Her establishment received no strangers. Its clientele was drawn from New York's aristocracy, and aspirants to admission required preliminary certification. A butler answered the doorbell, but did not open the door until he had inspected the visitor through a grille. The parlors of the house were as sumptuously appointed as those of a Fifth Avenue mansion, with chairs and sofas upholstered in satin and brocade, velvet carpets, crystal chandeliers, with gilt-framed mirrors and fine paintings on the walls, with pianos and harps and marble statues on pedestals, and little tables displaying the latest books and magazines among a clutter of decorative objects in silver and enamel. In these rooms the visitor waited before being joined by Josie's girls. The establishment offered only twenty. They entered, two or three at a time, wearing evening dresses. All were beautiful, and as a collection they were remarkable for the variety of their attractions. Nothing but champagne was served in Josie's parlors; the cheapest brand sold at eight dollars a bottle. All prices in this house were extremely high. They had to be. The girls were charged from fifty to one hundred dollars a week for their rooms and board, but it was said that on a busy night any of them might earn as much as two hundred dollars. Josie Woods, a cultivated woman, disliked any allusion to the financial aspect of her hospitality. She was a gracious hostess, and was seen at her best on New Year's Day. Then, with her girls, she kept open house in the traditional manner of New York ladies, remaining at home to dispense refreshment to the gentlemen who, from noon until midnight, were engaged in paying rounds of ceremonious calls.

THE SEX IN NEW YORK

MARK TWAIN

New York,
May 26th, 1867.

EDITORS ALTA: They do not treat women with as much deference in New York as we of the provinces think they ought. This is painfully apparent in the street-cars. Authority winks at the overloading of the cars—authority being paid for so winking, in political influence, possibly, for I cannot bring myself to think that any other species of bribery would be entertained for a moment—authority, I say, winks at this outrage, and permits one car to do the work of at least two, instead of compelling the companies to double the number of their cars, and permits them, also, to cruelly over-work their horses, too, of course, in the face of the Society for the Prevention of Cruelty to Animals. The result of this over-crowding is to set the people back a long stride toward semi-civilization. What I mean by that dreadful assertion is, that the over-crowding of the cars has impelled men to adopt the rule of hanging on to a seat when they get it, though twenty beautiful women came in and stood in their midst. That is going back toward original barbarism, I take it. A car's proper cargo should be twenty-two inside and three upon each platform—twenty-eight—and no crowding. I have seen fifty-six persons on a car, here, but a large portion of them were hanging on by the teeth. Some of the men inside had to go four or five miles, and naturally enough did not like to give up their seats and stand in a packed mass of humanity all that distance. So, when a lady got in, no man offered her a seat—no man dreamt of doing such a thing. No citizen, I mean. Occasionally I have seen a man, under such circumstances, get up and give his place to a lady, but the act betrayed, like spoken words, that he was from the provinces. . . .

When I am with the Romans I try to do as the Romans do. I generally succeed reasonably well. I have got so that I can sit still and let a homely old maid stand up and nurse her poodle till she is ready to drop, but the young and the blooming, alas! are too many for me. I have to get up and vacate the premises when they come. Some day, though, may be, I shall acquire a New York fortitude and be as shameless as any.

The other day an ill-bred boy in a street-car refused to give up his seat to a lady. The conductor very properly snatched him out and seated the lady. Consequence: Justice Dowling fined that *conductor* a month's wages—sixty dollars—and read him a lecture worth sixty dollars more.

BOSS TWEED:
What Are You Going to Do About It?

LLOYD MORRIS

On the night of October 27, 1870, it was raining hard and steadily. The bad weather kept some New Yorkers indoors. This was a pity, because they would miss a magnificent parade. Very early in the evening thousands of loyal Democrats had assembled outside their district political clubs. Every one was handed a torch. You might have noticed that all these storm-defying citizens were wearing red shirts. This was a compliment to William Marcy Tweed, State Senator, Grand Sachem of Tammany and boss of the city. The illustrious tribune of the people had begun his political career, twenty-two years earlier, by helping to organize the celebrated "Big Six" brigade of volunteer firemen whose engine, at his suggestion, was adorned with the emblem of a ferocious tiger. The tiger seemed to be his favorite creature. It was the emblem of Tammany Hall, to which, under the driving rain, fifty thousand red-shirted citizens carrying flaring torches were marching in the largest political parade that New York had yet witnessed. The marchers had been instructed to go to the polls on Election Day, November 8th, and immediately return to their homes. No disturbances of any kind must occur at the polls or in the streets.

To older men who remembered when quite contrary instructions were the order of the day, this seemed very odd. But there were a number of reasons both for this spectacular demonstration and for the unusual instructions. Two days earlier President Grant had ordered several regiments of the army to the city, and they were quartered in the harbor forts. He had stationed two warships in the East and Hudson Rivers. He had directed the commander of the New York National Guard to have his men aid the United States Marshal and the regular troops in enforcing the election laws, should the Marshal so request. Did President Grant presume to think that he could deal with New York as if it formed part of the conquered South? Undoubtedly he remembered the acclaim that had greeted ex-Mayor Wood's proposal for secession, the Strong Copperhead movement, the insurrectionary draft riot. But these did not account for his peculiar orders. He had taken military and naval precautions in response to an appeal by certain Republican leaders.

The Republican leaders had urged the President to protect the polls, if necessary, on Election Day. They asserted that Boss Tweed controlled the metropolitan police force, that probably a majority of all Republican election inspectors were his hirelings. Under these conditions only the presence of Federal troops could assure a fair election should Tweed find the tide running against him at the polls. And there was reason to believe that this might be the case. For two years, in nearly every issue of *Harper's Weekly*, the great cartoonist Thomas Nast had been attacking Tweed as the head of a ring that was systematically looting the city. But now the effect of Nast's powerful cartoons was being immensely reinforced. George Jones, publisher of *The Times*, had joined the attack. Every day his brilliant managing editor, Louis John Jennings, was assailing Tweed and his Ring. Tweed, Jennings declared, was supported by corrupt Republican politicians whom he had put on his payroll. Without their aid, he could neither perpetuate his power nor perpetrate his thefts. Would the merciless daily bombardment of Tweed in *The Times* have any influence on the approaching election? If so, Tweed would not hesitate to steal the election. Such was the conviction of the Republican leaders who had appealed to President Grant.

But Tweed could have told them that they were wrong. There would be no need for him to steal the election. He already had it in his pocket. A careful survey had showed that the Democrats would carry the city by a perfectly safe majority. That was why orders had gone out to the red-shirted, torch-bearing marchers forbidding any violence, any destruction of ballot boxes in Republican districts on Election Day. There would be no opportunity for the President's military forces to come into the city. While the great torchlight parade was in progress, Tweed faced an enthusiastic audience in Tammany Hall. He was forty-seven years old, tall, heavily bearded, growing bald, a man of enormous bulk. His eyes glittered as coldly as the huge diamond adorning his shirt front, but his ruddy face wore a jovial expression. Tweed sat between dapper, sallow, enigmatic August Belmont and hulking, flamboyant James Fisk. In the realm of finance, Fisk and Belmont were irreconcilable enemies. Fisk, the "Prince of Erie," had appointed Tweed to the executive committee of that much plundered railroad; their relations were cordial as well as mutually profitable. Fisk had always been known as a Republican. But he cherished a deep grudge against President Grant. On Black Friday in 1869, the President had ruined the plan of Jay Gould and Fisk to effect a corner in gold. Now, from the platform of Tammany Hall, Fisk would soon announce his adherence to the Democratic Party, and his intention to have all Erie employees vote the Democratic ticket.

There were other hostilities plainly in view on the platform, no less inveterate than that of Belmont and Fisk, who merely ignored one another's presence. Ex-Governor Horatio Seymour had come to make a speech. He was the close friend and political associate of Samuel J. Tilden, Tweed's greatest enemy in the Democratic Party. Tweed had recently made it a point to humiliate Tilden publicly, and nobody doubted that Tilden would revenge himself should he ever have an opportunity. Ex-Mayor Fernando Wood was likewise present to speak. Having disbanded his Mozart Hall Democracy after a crushing defeat by Tweed, Wood was back in the Tammany fold. He was a member of Congress, now. But everyone knew that there was no love lost between Wood and Tweed. On the platform, also, were Tweed's three associates in the Ring, all Sachems of Tammany. Mayor A. Oakey Hall, known as "the Elegant Oakey," was a fashion plate, clubman and notorious playboy. He had been a journalist, had written plays, had achieved local fame as a wit and after-dinner speaker; he was also an astute lawyer. Richard B. Connolly, City Comptroller, and Peter B. Sweeny, Commissioner of Public Parks and former Chamberlain, were the other two members of the Ring.

Tweed received a frenzied ovation when he arose to speak, and his brief address was constantly interrupted by outbursts of cheers and applause. "We know and feel," he said in closing, "that although an aggressive hand is upon us, yet we must, by a judicious exercise of law and order, which is our only protection, show that it is a law-abiding and, as all the world knows, a well-governed city." Tweed intended no irony in asserting that New York was well governed. Notwithstanding the scandalous accusations made by Thomas Nast and *The Times*, the truth of his claim was being attested by many of the city's most prominent citizens, irrespective of their party affiliation. Only five months earlier there had been a municipal election to choose a Board of Aldermen. Tweed's candidates received the endorsement of the Citizens' Association, a nonpartisan organization dedicated to civic reform and purity in politics. The president of this group was old Peter Cooper, a man venerated for his philanthropies, whose personal honor was unimpeachable. "The Democratic leaders are pledged to good government and progress, and the Association has full confidence that these pledges will be kept," Cooper's group declared. Many of its members were sincerely convinced that Tweed and his Ring, all men of wealth, had "become conservative" and would therefore give up their corrupt practices. Was it not better to continue them in power than to replace them by new men who, ambitious for riches, would inevitably rob the taxpayers? This was the policy recommended by Nathaniel B. Sands, secretary of the Association and its political adviser. Sands was a Republican. He was also, by Tweed's appointment, a Tax Commissioner, receiving an annual salary of fifteen thousand dollars.

Even before the great meeting at Tammany Hall, Tweed had found a way to cope with *The Times's* allegations of wholesale theft. The newspaper constantly challenged him to have Comptroller Connolly authorize a thorough public investigation of the city's finances. Undaunted, Tweed chose six eminent citizens to undertake this inquiry and report to the public. The committee was headed by John Jacob Astor III, and among its members were Moses Taylor and Marshall O. Roberts. These gentlemen commanded vast wealth and enjoyed high repute; their colleagues were no less distinguished, though certainly less abundantly rich. Could there be any doubt of their absolute integrity? It was ridiculous to suppose any of them capable of collusion with corrupt politicians. None of them, obviously, would condone flagrant looting of the city. Whatever their findings, their report could be taken as authoritative and final, and all New York awaited it in a fever of impatience. The report was published on November 7th, 1870, just before Election Day. "We have come to the conclusion and certify," its eminent signers declared, "that the financial affairs of the city under the charge of the Comptroller are administered in a correct and faithful manner." The report was a complete vindication of Tweed and his associates. Only the most disreputable of cynics would have suggested that the honorable members of the committee were among the city's largest taxpayers, that the Tweed Ring could greatly increase their taxes should it have any good reason to do so, that it could inflict other forms of punishment scarcely more agreeable.

But moral cynicism was profoundly repugnant to New Yorkers. Conscience and conviction enlightened their verdict at the polls. They re-elected Tweed's governor, John T. Hoffman, and his mayor, "the Elegant Oakey." They didn't have to do anything about the State Legislature, where Tweed for a year had commanded a majority. He owned a large number of the Republican minority at Albany, and in New York County he actually owned the Republican machine. Naturally, the cost of "good government and progress" was not cheap. Later estimates placed it as between forty-five and seventy-five millions of dollars during the Tweed Ring's thirty months of democratic dictatorship. For the new County Court House alone taxpayers had spent more than twelve million dollars. It was the most costly public building in the United States, though far less ostentatious than the Capitol at Washington, or many another. And what could be more gratifying to Tweed than the knowledge that this monument to his glory had likewise contributed to his material welfare? Of its total cost, about nine million dollars had been siphoned into the perquisites that rewarded the Ring for their unselfish devotion to the public interest.

It was not surprising that millionaires and other prominent citizens praised Tweed, even eulogized him as a reformer. Was not innovation synonymous with progress? Was not progress the only genuine reform? Tweed, too, was a millionaire: a director of many important corporations, the president of a bank, the principal stockholder of a printing establishment which—deservedly, no doubt—received the business of public utilities, banks and many large industries, in addition to that of the city. Tweed maintained a fine home on Fifth Avenue and Forty-third Street, a yacht, an excellent stable; he had invested a large fortune in real estate. Did he not exemplify progress as well as foster it? That he was an innovator in politics nobody could deny. He applied, to public business, methods no less modern than those which had enabled such magnates as Vanderbilt, Gould and Fisk to realize their grandiose projects. In fact, they had profited by Tweed's superb efficiency, his admirably co-operative nature. If legislation was required to effect their purposes, Tweed's celebrated "Black Horse Cavalry" at the Capitol in Albany stood ready to pass it—at a price. If there was any quibbling about the price, they were equally ready to block and defeat the hoped-for measures. If the legality of any legislation had to be judicially determined, or if quick injunctions were needed to forestall hostile action from any quarter, or if important lawsuits were coming up for decision—well, the required dispensation of justice would be forthcoming from one of Tweed's eminent contributions to the State judiciary: Justices George G. Barnard and Albert Cardozo of the Supreme Court, and Justice John H. McCunn of the Superior Court.

Justice Barnard, especially, was almost as outstandingly progressive as Tweed himself. In an emergency, for example, he would hold court in the home of Josie Mansfield, Jim Fisk's mistress, where he happened to be visiting when told of the sudden need for justice. He would also, if the need was desperate, issue his judicial orders by telegraph; they could be served, within an hour or two, at any remote point in the state. And at Tweed's instigation, he simplified and perfected a political formula devised by ex-Mayor Fernando Wood. Before doubtful elections, Wood had often secured the rapid naturalization of immigrants; several hundred additional voters were sufficient for his purposes. But this was a new industrial and financial era, dedicated to quantity production—of stock-certificates, capital and, sometimes, tangible goods. Why not citizens also? Justice Barnard saw the point, and he helped Tweed, on one occasion, to make sixty thousand new citizens in twenty days.

Efficiency was the gospel of this postwar era of industrial expansion. Nobody understood this better than Boss Tweed, aware as he was of the wastefulness, the needless delays, the absurd uncertainty of traditional processes of making law and administering it. He brought the whole machinery of government up to date, adapted it to the imperative, unforeseen necessities of the time. And the Ring operated this machinery on a sound, modern business basis. Take the case of contractors, manufacturers and others who sold goods and services to New York City. The Ring told them precisely what they must charge. It also told them how much of the money they received must be returned to the Ring. The city was an insatiable purchaser, and this helped general prosperity. Keenly aware of its economic duty, the Ring deplored the infrequent periods when buying by the city slackened, and bills payable diminished. So, at such times, the Ring ordered vouchers made out to fictitious creditors. This expedient kept municipal funds in circulation. Surely it was only a financial paradox that, the faster money moved, the more it stuck to Tweed, Hall, Connolly and Sweeny.

Everybody who really counted in New York understood this process, and the fortunes of many of the best people prospered because of it. Why interfere with a mechanism so patently efficient, so generally advantageous? Even its supposed extravagance ought to be a point of pride. Did not the costliness of the Tweed Ring proclaim to the world the incalculable wealth of New York? Did it not declare that, unique among cities, New York could afford any expense to promote the welfare of its most enterprising citizens?

Many prominent New Yorkers, therefore, had reason to regret the consequences of a quarrel between Tweed and one of his subordinates. Sheriff James O'Brien presented claims against the city amounting to three hundred and fifty thousand dollars, a mere pittance. Boss Tweed disallowed them. O'Brien led a revolt against Tweed in Tammany Hall, seeking to oust the Boss. The attempt failed ignominiously, and this made O'Brien even keener for vengeance. One night in July, 1871, he delivered to *The Times* a mass of documents. They were exact transcripts from the books of Comptroller Connolly. O'Brien asserted that they would substantiate all the charges which the newspaper had been making, for nearly a year, against Tweed and the Ring. They would absolutely contradict the report made by Astor and his committee. On July 8th, 1871, *The Times* began publishing O'Brien's transcripts in daily installments; they ran for three weeks. They roused the city to a high pitch of excitement. Interviewed by a newspaper reporter, Boss Tweed angrily demanded, "Well, what are you going to do about it?"

The answer came at a citizens' mass meeting at Cooper Institute early in September. Distinguished speakers analyzed the criminal financial operations disclosed by *The Times*. Resolutions calling for the prosecution of Tweed and the Ring had been prepared in advance, and were presented to the audience by an eminent lawyer, Joseph H. Choate. "This," said Choate defiantly, "is what we are going to do about it." A Committee of Seventy was formed to carry out the program adopted at the meeting. Samuel J. Tilden and Charles O'Conor undertook its legal direction. Justice Barnard was the first of Tweed's minions to desert him, capitulating to Tilden and the Committee. He was quickly followed by Comptroller Connolly, who appointed Andrew H. Green, a member of the Committee, as Acting Comptroller, thereby giving the prosecution access to the Ring's financial records. In the election of 1871, Tweed was returned to the State Senate, but nearly all his other candidates for public office were voted down. Thereafter, a Grand Jury began turning out criminal indictments of Tweed, his associates in the Ring and many of their beneficiaries. Tweed retained his seat in the State Senate, but resigned every other position, public and private, even being replaced as Grand Sachem of Tammany. Connolly and Sweeny fled to Europe. Justice Cardozo resigned from the Supreme Court to escape impeachment; Justices Barnard and McCunn were impeached, and removed from their judicial posts. Mayor Hall remained in office, though he, too, was under indictment. His first trial was halted by the death of a juror; his second resulted in a disagreement by the jury. Tried a third time, "the Elegant Oakey" was acquitted. Defeated for re-election as Mayor, this debonair mountebank returned to journalism and playwriting, and in 1878 himself played a role in *The Crucible*, his most successful contribution to the stage. He was the first, though not the most conspicuous, exemplar of New York's predilection for the luxury of installing a wisecracking playboy in City Hall, and thereafter rewarding him generously for the diversion he furnished.

But Tweed fell a victim to civic virtue. Conscience required a scapegoat because the incompatibility of high principle and wanton conduct—discreetly managed by many enterprising citizens—had led to scandal. A scandal of this magnitude could not be ignored. Tweed's practices had been acceptable to the righteous; it was his carelessness that they could not condone. At Tweed's first trial, the jury disagreed. At a second, he was convicted; a cumulative sentence of twelve years in prison and a fine was imposed. But a year later this verdict was overruled. Set free, he was immediately rearrested in a suit brought by the State to recover six million dollars, a share of his personal plunder for which there existed abundant evidence. By this time, Samuel J. Tilden had been elected Governor of New York and inaugurated. Tweed was confined in the Ludlow Street Jail, the debtors' prison, where he was accorded all the privileges to which so distinguished a citizen was entitled. That was how, on a visit to his home accompanied by a warden and a keeper, he managed to make his escape. After remaining in hiding near New York, he made his way to Florida in disguise, thence to Cuba, finally to Spain, where the lack of an extradition treaty promised him permanent immunity. On landing in Vigo, Tweed was recognized; a cartoon by Thomas Nast revealed his identity. The Spanish authorities delivered him to an American warship sent to bring him back to the United States. In the suit to recover six million dollars, judgment had been taken against him, but he still faced trial on many additional indictments.

Back in jail, Tweed offered a full surrender of his remaining property, and expressed a willingness to become a witness against all his former associates, in return for assurances of mercy. Five years had passed since *The Times* had begun its exposure of the Tweed Ring. Connolly was still at liberty in Europe. Sweeny was to return and escape punishment by paying over somewhat less than four hundred thousand dollars of his personal loot. Hall, acquitted, had resigned from one of his clubs but remained a member in good standing of the others. Tilden, the great reformer, had never published the promised list of citizens revealed, by Connolly's books, to have acted in collusion with the Ring. Perhaps too many distinguished and honorable New Yorkers were implicated in the profitable avocation of looting public funds. But for Tweed, his personal enemy, Governor Tilden had no mercy.

Tweed died in jail in the Spring of 1878. Two years earlier, Tilden had been Democratic candidate for President of the United States. Many Americans believed that he had been elected and then defrauded of the high honor to which his prosecution of Tweed was a steppingstone. Of the estimated forty-five to seventy-five million dollars which the Ring had plundered, New York City recovered approximately one million, one hundred and twenty-one thousand dollars. And it could be surmised that John Jacob Astor III's acquaintance with accounting had merely suffered a temporary lapse when, with his distinguished associates, he certified to the sound condition of the city's finances. The death of his father, William Backhouse Astor, in 1875, left him the wealthiest man in the United States. He often rewrote telegrams to save one word, and in many other ways was known to keep his vast fortune in excellent repair.

※

PLEASURES GONE BY

HENRY COLLINS BROWN

All the Perfumes of Arabia

There were no safety razors in those days and the general custom was to patronize the local barber twice a week. If you were a permanent customer, the barber provided you with a special mug with your name in shiny gilt letters on the outside. Some went so far as to add a symbolic sign indicating the nature of your business or profession. Thus, if you were a plumber, you were shown mending a gas leak, with *all* your tools in front of you—not one forgotten! If you were a butcher, they would picture you with your hands on the counter gazing ecstatically at a large piece of meat on the scales. It was considered bad form to depict the butcher weighing his hands in with the meat. If you kept a saloon—we had four on every corner in those days—a foaming bucket of suds would be on the reverse of your cup. This friendly atmosphere did much to create a spirit of camaraderie within our charmed circle. One brush, one towel and the same soap did for all. A great sensation was created when one Knight of the Razor advertised "A Clean Towel for Every Customer," which was declared financial suicide by his envious rivals. While waiting your turn, you perused such unrighteous literature as the *Police Gazette* and the *Day's Doings*. *Puck* and *Judge* were also carried as a camouflage for the unregenerate pink sheets. A shave cost 10 cents and a hair cut 15 cents. No tips, and journeyman barbers worked seven days a week.

The shop was usually run by a German, who invariably kept a canary, and was a sort of social center. Scented oils, heavy pomades, bear's grease and brilliantine were highly popular, and when you left that barber shop you not only had the latest neighborhood scandal but all the perfumes of Arabia as well. . . .

Red Flannels to the Rescue

Among our more intimate attire, the most significant article that I recall was "medicated" red flannel underwear. Promptly upon the approach of cold weather all we normal men were immediately encased in this health-possessing garment by our solicitous helpmates. In some peculiar manner, a strange and unreasoning faith prevailed in the efficiency of this peculiar garment to prevent colds, asthma, fallen arches, dandruff and nearly all the other ails to which human flesh is heir. I cannot account for it. Nobody could.

THAT WAS NEW YORK: JIM FISK

RUSSEL CROUSE

In 1928 when Russel Crouse penned this portrait, Fisk apparently was largely forgotten. It is typical of the fluctuations in the composition of the city's legend that today, thanks to a generation of gifted social historians, Fisk is probably far better known than he was a decade or two after his death.

William Marcy Tweed bequeathed a great and horrible name, Jay Gould handed down a vast fortune and heirs enough to fight over it eventually, but poor old Jim Fisk, who was both better and worse than these two, his colleagues, left only a memory that scarcely outlasted his grave-clothes.

His was, I think, the most dramatic career in all the vivid pages of New York's history. He lived and died as someone a playwright might have created. He was clown and caitiff, as honest, and kindly as he was dishonest and ruthless. And when, on a January afternoon in 1872, he was shot down, one could almost have expected a curtain to fall and an orchestra to strike up something for the exit of a nationwide audience. But it was, after all, a real Jim Fisk who died.

Everyone knew Jim Fisk then. Just why he should have been forgotten so completely in these intervening years is inexplicable. Perhaps "Jubilee Jim," a fine, discursive, full-flavored biography by the late Robert H. Fuller, which has just come posthumously from the presses, will revive his picturesque memory. He may not merit all of Mr. Fuller's whitewash but certainly he deserves more than a fraying monument in a little Vermont cemetery.

James Fisk, Jr., was born in Bennington, Vermont, in 1834. His father was a peddler, and occasionally a hotelkeeper. The turning point

Copyright, 1928, by The New Yorker Magazine, Inc.

in young Fisk's life came when he was no more than seventeen and Van Amberg's circus came to town. When it left he followed its gaudy banners down the country road and almost round the world, as tent-hoister and as ticket-taker. When he shook its sawdust from his shoes his fate was sealed. He was forever to be a mountebank. He was often more than that, but he was always that.

He went back to Vermont and into the only pursuit he knew—peddling. But he was no ordinary higgler. He had a gilt-covered wagon, four white horses, and shining harness. Soon he was known all over New England. Jordan Marsh, the great Boston dry goods firm, bid for him and he abandoned the road. Counter-jumping, however, was too small a field for him, and he was about to desert it when the Civil War broke out.

War clouds provided just the right sort of shadows for his chicanery. Within a few weeks he had unloaded on the government, at a fancy price, a storeroom full of blankets that his Boston employers had been unable to sell to the retail trade at bargain rates. In a hotel room in Washington, by the free use of whiskey and cigars, he made other profitable supply contracts. Before long he had an extensive organization smuggling cotton up from the South to Northern mills. Lee's surrender left him with a comfortable fortune.

He first came to New York, shortly after the war ended, to buy the Stonington line of steamboats for a Boston syndicate. He negotiated this deal with Daniel Drew, then the city's shrewdest capitalist, with such flair that Drew sensed his genius. Fisk immediately recognized New York as the great circus tent. He came back to have a fling at the stock market and lost his last cent. But Drew knew a thimble-rigger when he saw one and soon had him here again—trading in a firm he established, and doing very well.

It was shortly afterward that Fisk formed his alliance with that amazing financial metaphysician, Jay Gould, who saw, with his burning black eyes, money in everything. They were an astounding combination—Fisk the bland, ostentatious showman who could carry off any sort of situation; Gould the dark wizard who could devise, with the cunning of an alchemist, the ways and means of making gold out of thin air.

They joined with the hypocritical Drew at the start of their joint career, but when he double-crossed them later they crushed him to the bankruptcy in which he died. They fought every dragon that showed its head, including old Commodore Vanderbilt, before whom all had trembled. And Fisk it was who conceived the plan of drawing "Boss" Tweed into their schemes. He was always a circus man and knew that to run a shell game one must see the sheriff first.

The story of how they gained control of the Erie Railroad, held it and milked it while sitting on the three-legged stool of court protection, is too long and too involved for these pages. Their audacity made them millions. Their high-handed attempt to carry off the Albany & Susquehanna is another incredible tale of high finance.

Nothing, apparently, was to stop them. They were the first to perfect the use of that legal blunt instrument, the injunction, which Henry VIII had had created for his own use. Judges who were under their thumb issued these in bunches and even by telegraph. Once, when they were almost trapped, they slipped quietly over to New Jersey where, as legal exiles, they started over again.

Their attempt to corner gold in 1869 was the height of impudence. This was Gould's scheme, but he finally had to lure Fisk into it to make a go of it. By involving President Grant's kin, thus bringing about rumors that the President himself was in their pool and therefore would not let the Government sell its supply of gold to beat down the price, they drove it to 162 and had the nation in a frenzy.

Then, on a day that is chronicled as Black Friday because of the ruin and suicides it brought in financial circles, the President broke the bubble with a flood of Government gold. In spite of this, however, Fisk and Gould were ready with their unending supply of injunctions and managed to make millions out of defeat.

These, however, are the stories of the great financial ogre. There was the other Jim Fisk, too, the man who kept hundreds of families alive with charity disbursed by a left hand that evidently did not know what the right was doing. Out of nothing more than friendship he saved one of the largest banks in the city from ruin by an overnight loan. An hour before he was shot he advanced, out of his own pocket, money to pay the city's police, whose payroll had been legally tied up in the Tweed scandal.

And there was, too, Jim Fisk the showman, a side of him that made him a winning figure in spite of everything. In cold records his career in the Erie was hardly beautiful. But he made it garish and attractive. He purchased the old Grand Opera House, where movies now flicker, at Twenty-third Street and Eighth Avenue, fitted it up for the railroad's offices with marble and gold and cherubs and nymphs, and ruled there so lavishly that he was known as Prince Erie.

He bought the Narragansett fleet of steamers; and, on the theory that "if Vanderbilt can be a commodore I can be an admiral," decked himself out in full brass-buttoned naval attire and sent each ship off from its pier with mock naval ceremony. It was on one of these vessels that he escorted President Grant to the Boston Jubilee celebration and won himself the name which Mr. Fuller used for the title of his book.

When the Ninth Regiment fell upon less than prosperous days he became its colonel, staged a moonlight parade up Fifth Avenue, gave resplendent balls, and flaunted its uniform. He came to military grief, however, when his outfit was attacked in the parade of the Orangemen in 1871. Colonel Fisk fled over back fences and finally wound up in Long Branch, a bruised and weary pacifist.

He brought French opéra bouffe to the Grand Opera House and made a great show place of it. Here he was in his element. He imported companies from France. It was his idea that on one night the ballet should be blonde, on the next brunette. And he liked nothing better than to drive through the streets, his coach filled with chattering actresses and drawn by six horses, one white and one black in each pair.

And then there was his heart. As a boy he had married Lucy Moore. When he came to New York and made his fortune he installed her in a great mansion in Boston, which he still considered home. Here, however, he met Helen Josephine Mansfield, a divorcée of obscure past. She was a beauty of the ample proportions of the day. Buxom, perhaps, is the word.

It was not long until she was established in a fine house of her own just down the street from his Opera House offices. Here she reigned, the Cleopatra of Twenty-third Street. It was clandestine at first, but Fisk was too frank to keep it so long. He was madly and passionately in love with her, but by some twist in his makeup he remained sentimentally faithful to his wife by writing her an endearing letter every day of his life.

Josie Mansfield was Jim Fisk's pride. One night he introduced her to Edward S. Stokes, a handsome and none too scrupulous young man he had befriended in a business way. It was all over at that moment. Stokes satisfied his inferiority complex by taking the powerful Fisk's girl away from him. Jim won her back with money, but not for long. Josie joined Stokes in a scheme to live by Fisk's wits, or lack of them. There were love-letters which would seem pathetic in the cold light of uninterested eyes.

It all led to the courts, where Fisk took everything in those days. There were suits and counter-suits. Tweed's power had crumbled before an awakened civic righteousness, but this time Fisk felt that he needed no controlled judges, that he was in the right. On the morning of January 6, 1872, there had been a hearing on a libel suit that had been brought by Stokes against Fisk. Things had not gone well for Ned and Josie. When they left the court they learned they had been indicted for attempted blackmail.

At four o'clock Jim Fisk set out from his offices in his stylish clarence to call upon the widow of a late friend at the Broadway Central Hotel, which still stands on Broadway, below Union Square. He started to climb its red-plush stairs. At the first landing a man waited with a nervous hand in the pocket of a cream-colored overcoat. As Fisk neared the top of the flight the man stepped out and fired twice. It was Stokes.

Fisk fell. He was carried to a near-by room and died next morning. His wife was at his bedside and Josie Mansfield was trying to raise bail for the man who had shot him. "Boss" Tweed got out of jail in time to drop what may have been an honest tear on Fisk's bier. His body lay in state at his great opera house and thousands viewed it. A special train, greeted everywhere by crowds, took him to the soil that bore him.

The first jury that tried Stokes disagreed, the second decreed he should be hanged, and the third convicted him of manslaughter. He was sentenced to six years at Sing Sing, served four, and eventually returned to become embroiled in several suits over business matters. He became something of a figure to be pointed out, but little more. He died in 1901, and in that same year Josie Mansfield asked to be admitted to a Catholic home in South Dakota. Meanwhile the circus which Jim Fisk had enlivened with his showmanship had all but forgotten him.

PRIVATE JOYS THROUGH PUBLIC NOTICES

JAMES D. MCCABE, JR.

During the 1870's the "Personals" columns of New York City newspapers flourished on the front pages each day. This amusing contemporary exposé also reveals the official moral tone of the day.

Personals

The first column of one of the most prominent daily newspapers, which is taken in many respectable families of the city, bears the above heading, and there is also a personal column in a prominent Sunday paper. Very many persons are inclined to smile at these communications, and are far from supposing that these journals are making themselves the mediums through which assignations and burglaries, and almost every disreputable enterprise are arranged and carried on. Yet such is the fact. Many of these advertisements are inserted by notorious roués, and others are from women of the town. Women wishing to meet their lovers, or men their mistresses, use these personal columns.

Respectable women have much to annoy them in the street conveyances, and at the places of amusement. If a lady allows her face to wear a pleasant expression while glancing by the merest chance at a man, she is very apt to find some such personal as the following addressed to her in the next morning's issue of the paper referred to:

Third avenue car, down town yesterday morning; young lady in black, who noticed gent opposite, who endeavored to draw her attention to Personal column of ———— in his hand, will oblige admirer by sending address to B., Box 102, ———— office.

If she is a vile woman, undoubtedly she will do so, and that establishment will deliver her letter, and do its part in helping on the assignation.

A gentleman will bow to a lady, and she, thinking it may be a friend, returns the bow. The next day appears the following:

Tall lady dressed in black, who acknowledged gentleman's salute, Broadway and Tenth street, please address D., box 119, ———— office, if she wishes to form his acquaintance.

Sometimes a man will whisper the word "personal" to the lady whom he dares not insult further, and the next day the following appears:

Tuesday, December 7, 4 P. M.—"can you answer a personal?" Fifth avenue stage from Grand to Twenty-third street. Please address Ben. Van Dyke, _____ office, appointing interview. To prevent mistake, mention some particulars.

Others more modest:

Will the lady that was left waiting by her companion on Monday evening, near the door of an up-town theatre, grant an interview to the gentleman that would have spoken if he had thought the place appropriate? Address Romano, _____ office.

It is really dangerous to notice a patron of the paper mentioned, for he immediately considers it ground for a personal:

Lady in Grand street car, Saturday evening 7.30.—Had on plaid shawl, black silk dress; noticed gentleman in front; both got out at Bowery; will oblige by sending her address to C. L., box 199, _____ office.

Young ladies with attendants are not more free from this public insult, as shown by the following:

Will the young lady that got out of a Fifth avenue stage, with a gentleman with a cap on, at 10 yesterday, at Forty-sixth street, address E. Roberts, New York Post-office.

This public notice must be pleasing to the young lady and to "the gentleman with the cap on." It is a notice that the gentleman believes the lady to be willing to have an intrigue with him. If it goes as far as that, this newspaper will lend its columns to the assignation as follows:

Louise K.—dear. I have received your letter, last Saturday, but not in time to meet you. Next Tuesday, Dec. 7, I will meet you at the same time and place. East. Write to me again, and give your address. Your old acquaintance.

The personal column is also used to publicly advertise the residences of women of the town. The following are specimens:

Miss Gertie Davis, formerly of Lexington avenue, will be pleased to see her friends at 106 Clinton place.

Erastus—Call on Jennie Howard at 123 West Twenty-seventh street. I have left Heath's.

The *World* very justly remarks: "The cards of courtesans and the advertisements of houses of ill-fame might as well be put up in the panels of the street cars. If the public permits a newspaper to do it for the consideration of a few dollars, why make the pretence that there is anything wrong in the thing itself? If the advertisement is legitimate, then the business must be."

FLORAL TRIBUTES AND MIDNIGHT SUPPERS

HENRY COLLINS BROWN

1890's

A peculiarity of the theater in those days was the adoration of the matinee girl for her favorite on the stage. During the run of *The Little Minister*, the stage entrance of the Empire was thronged with violet-laden devotees who stood patiently waiting for Maude Adams to come out to her hansom, hoping that, as she hurried by, she might accept one of the bouquets held out to her or perhaps by some lucky chance drop a glove or a handkerchief. These would be snatched up and carried off to some schoolgirl sanctum. Ethel Barrymore's admirers were about evenly divided between the young bloods of the day who wanted to marry her and the matinee girls who tried to copy her delightful, seductive, throaty voice and mobbed her after performances in the hope that the haughty Ethel would glance their way, which she rarely did. Mary Mannering likewise had her quota of stage-door followers who imitated the Janice Meredith curl which the actress made famous during the run of that play. Unlike the shy Ethel and the mystery-enshrouded Maude Adams, Mary Mannering rewarded her devotees with a dazzling smile and always some warm-hearted expression of appreciation of their devotion, so that when she married Hackett, it seemed a right and fitting climax to the many romantic love scenes they had seen these two enact.

In those days we said it with flowers to our stage favorites right out in front of everybody, usually at the end of the first act when the hurried tramp of the ushers' feet, as they rushed the huge floral offerings to the stage and handed them over the footlights to riotous applause, was as much a part of the *entr'acte* as the selections by the orchestra. Nor did the audience wait until the end of an act, either, to show its appreciation of some particularly thrilling or charming bit of acting. A heroic speech, a rescue of the leading lady in the nick of time, and bouquets which a moment before had ornamented the bosoms of the well-dressed feminine theater-goers, were torn loose from their moorings and hurled at the stage, sometimes with disastrous results. It must also be confessed that the behavior of the audience was frequently embarrassing to the players, since they often insisted that the dead or fainting Thespian arise, take the flowers and bow, before the action was allowed to proceed.

Out in the lobby, before the performance, these floral tributes were on display so that all who looked might see which members of the cast received the greatest number; but alas for this most charming custom, it was whispered by some old meanies that many of the five-foot floral offerings were purchased by the actors themselves and sent to the theater with fictitious names attached. Of course, there was no truth in this, but the rush of the flower-laden ushers down the aisles was found to be a serious interference with the carefully selected *entr'acte* program. Some hard-boiled conductors were even said to have objected strenuously to being hit on the head with the flying bouquets. Followed a managerial pronouncement and one more prerogative of the audience passed into history along with the wearing of hats by the ladies.

Another and more celebrated feature of New York after-theater life was the bird and bottle supper with the musical comedy stars. The witching hour at these parties was eleven-thirty, when the show girls began to drift in from the various Broadway successes. It was a sight for the gods to watch their majestic progress down the room. The famous beauties, whose pictures were in the lobbies and whose names were in the feature stories, knew just the right moment for their entrance into the crowded restaurants. The wise orchestra leader knew his cue and, as a headliner appeared at the door with her escort, he gave the signal to his men and the strains of her song hit greeted her. She was always just so surprised; fluttered nervously with the great bouquets of violets or orchids which her well-repaid admirer carried for her and finally, with every eye upon her, walked slowly to their reserved table. Her costly pearl dog-collar was well displayed upon her shapely neck; her beautiful arms bare to the shoulder, her tightly laced waist throwing into bold relief the rounded bosom and the swelling hips, swathed in the most clinging of satin skirts that swept the floor in a long, billowing train.

Each talked-about beauty, whether show girl, high-priced star or member of the chorus, had her similar entrance, drew her own little crowd of devotees and provided ample thrills and excitement for the crowd without the slightest effort. True, these abandoned creatures did not smoke in those days—for well they knew that an outraged proprietor would have had them unceremoniously escorted to the door, at such an open affront to public decency. However, there were compensations. Hundred dollar bills and diamond necklaces were frequently tucked into the bunches of flowers that the flower girls sold from high-heaped trays; champagne flowed like water; it did not need Texas Guinan in those rosy days to plead: "Give this little girl a hand." The little girl of the '90s didn't need a bit of help.

IN THE BROADWAY CARS

STEPHEN CRANE

1890's

The cable cars come down Broadway as the waters come down at Lodore. Years ago Father Knickerbocker had convulsions when it was proposed to lay impious rails on his sacred thoroughfare. At the present day the cars, by force of column and numbers, almost dominate the great street, and the eye of even an old New Yorker is held by these long yellow monsters which prowl intently up and down, up and down, in a mystic search.

In the grey of the morning they come out of the up-town, bearing janitors, porters, all that class which carries the keys to set alive the great down-town. Later, they shower clerks. Later still, they shower more clerks. And the thermometer which is attached to a conductor's temper is steadily rising, rising, and the blissful time arrives when everybody hangs to a strap and stands on his neighbour's toes. Ten o'clock comes, and the Broadway cars, as well as elevated cars, horse cars, and ferryboats innumerable, heave sighs of relief. . . .

The cable car's pulse drops to normal. But the conductor's pulse begins now to beat in split seconds. He has come to the crisis in his day's agony. He is now to be overwhelmed with feminine shoppers. They all are going to give him two-dollar bills to change. They all are going to threaten to report him. He passes his hand across his brow and curses his beard from black to grey and from grey to black.

Men and women have different ways of hailing a car. A man—if he is not an old choleric gentleman, who owns not this road but some other road—throws up a timid finger, and appears to believe that the King of Abyssinia is careering past on his war-chariot, and only his opinion of other people's Americanism keeps him from deep salaams. The gripman usually jerks his thumb over his shoulder and indicates the next car, which is three miles away. Then the man catches the last platform, goes into the car, climbs upon some one's toes, opens his morning paper, and is happy.

When a woman hails a car there is no question of its being the King of Abyssinia's war-chariot. She has bought the car for three dollars and ninety-eight cents. The conductor owes his position to her, and the gripman's mother does her laundry. No captain in the Royal Horse Artillery ever stops his battery from going through a stone house in a way to equal her manner of bringing that car back on its haunches. Then she walks leisurely forward, and after scanning the step to see if there is any mud upon it, and opening her pocket-book to make sure of a two-dollar bill, she says: "Do you give transfers down Twenty-eighth Street?"

Some time the conductor breaks the bell strap when he pulls it under these conditions. Then, as the car goes on, he goes and bullies some person who had nothing to do with the affair.

The car sweeps on its diagonal path through the Tenderloin with its hotels, its theatres, its flower shops, its ten million actors who played with Booth and Barret. It passes Madison Square and enters the gorge made by the towering walls of great shops. It sweeps around the double curve at Union Square and Fourteenth Street, and a life insurance agent falls in a fit as the car dashes over the crossing, narrowly missing three old ladies, two old gentlemen, a newly-married couple, a sandwich man, a newsboy, and a dog. . . . Meanwhile, the gripman has become involved with countless truck drivers, and inch by inch, foot by foot, he fights his way to City Hall Park. On past the Post Office the car goes, with the gripman getting advice, admonition, personal comment, an invitation to fight from the drivers, until Battery Park appears at the foot of the slope, and as the car goes sedately around the curve the burnished shield of the bay shines through the trees. . . .

The combination of wide-brimmed hats and crowded cable cars is tremendous in its power to cause misery to the patient New York public. Suppose you are in a cable car, clutching for life and family a creaking strap from overhead. At your shoulder is a little dude in a very wide-brimmed straw hat with a red band. If you were in your senses you would recognise this flaming band as an omen of blood. But you are not in your senses; you are in a Broadway cable car. You are not supposed to have any senses. From the forward end you hear the gripman uttering shrill whoops and running over citizens. Suddenly the car comes to a curve. Making a swift running start, it turns three hand-springs, throws a cart wheel for luck, bounds into the air, hurls six passengers over the nearest building, and comes down a-straddle of the track. That is the way in which we turn curves in New York.

Meanwhile, during the car's gamboling, the corrugated rim of the dude's hat has swept naturally across your neck, and has left nothing for your head to do but to quit your shoulders. As the car roars your head falls into the waiting arms of the proper authorities. The dude is dead; everything is dead.

There was once a person possessing a fund of uncanny humour who greatly desired to import from past ages a corps of knights in full armour. He then purposed to pack the warriors into a cable car and send them around a curve. He thought that he could gain much pleasure by standing near and listening to the wild clash of steel upon steel—the tumult of mailed heads striking together, the bitter grind of armoured legs bending the wrong way. He thought that this would teach them that war is grim. . . .

In the Tenderloin, the place of theatres, and of the restaurant where gayer New York does her dining, the cable cars in the evening carry a stratum of society which looks like a new one, but it is of the familiar strata in other clothes. It is just as good as a new stratum, however, for in evening dress the average man feels that he has gone up three pegs in the social scale, and there is considerable evening dress about a Broadway car in the evening. A car with its electric lamp resembles a brilliantly-lighted salon, and the atmosphere grows just a trifle strained. People sit more rigidly, and glance sidewise, perhaps, as if each was positive of possessing social value, but was doubtful of all others. The conductor stands on the platform and beams in a modest and polite manner into the car. He notes a lifted finger and grabs swiftly for the bell strap. He reaches down to help a woman aboard. Perhaps his demeanour is a reflection of the manner of the people in the car. No one is in a mad New York hurry; no one is fretting and muttering; no one is perched upon his neighbour's toes. . . .

Late at night, after the diners and theatre-goers have been lost in Harlem, various inebriate persons may perchance emerge from the darker regions of Sixth Avenue and swing their arms solemnly at the gripman. If the Broadway cars run for the next seven thousand years this will be the only time when one New Yorker will address another in public without an excuse sent direct from heaven. In these cars late at night it is not impossible that some fearless drunkard will attempt to inaugurate a general conversation. He tells of the fun he thinks he has had; describes his feelings; recounts stories of his dim past. None reply, although all listen with every ear.

In the meantime the figures on the street grow fewer and fewer. Strolling policemen test the locks of the great dark-fronted stores. Nighthawk cabs whirl by the cars on their mysterious errands. Finally the cars themselves depart in the way of the citizen, and for the few hours before dawn a new sound comes into the still thoroughfare—the cable whirring in its channel underground.

DR. PARKHURST INVESTIGATES

LLOYD MORRIS

Early in 1892 Dr. Charles R. Parkhurst, one of New York's leading clergymen, denounced the city as a den of iniquity and dubbed the Tammany municipal authorities "a lying, perjured, rum-soaked and libidinous lot," who shielded and patronized the town's vice-purveyors. But, when Dr. Parkhurst was summoned before a Grand Jury and asked, in effect, to put up or shut up, he had no concrete evidence to offer and was scored publicly by the court. So, as Lloyd Morris narrates here, Dr. Parkhurst hitched up his clerical suspenders and really went to work.

Realizing that in future he would have to speak from personal knowledge, Dr. Parkhurst undertook to journey into the hell of New York's nocturnal depravity. A zealous young parishioner, John Langdon Erving, volunteered to accompany him. But since neither of them knew the ropes, Dr. Parkhurst engaged Charles W. Gardner, a detective, to serve them as guide, at a fee of six dollars a night and expenses. Gardner studied his clients and declared that they would have to be disguised. They agreed, but Dr. Parkhurst wished to preserve his whiskers, and the detective remarked that, if due caution were taken, it would not "be necessary to harvest your lilacs at present." On the evening fixed for their first rendezvous, Gardner called for his clients and found that their disguises did not disguise them. Dr. Parkhurst was unmistakably a clergyman; Erving looked like an outmoded fashion plate. He took them to his room and proceeded to improve their makeup. Gardner began with Dr. Parkhurst. He attired the clergyman in a dirty shirt, a pair of loudly checked black-and-white trousers, a worn double-breasted reefer jacket, a tie made from the sleeve of an old red-flannel shirt. Still, Dr. Parkhurst appeared more representative of the ecclesiastical than of the sinful world, and the addition of a battered slouch hat failed to make him look sufficiently disreputable. Only when Gardner had smeared the clergyman's long, luxuriant, curly hair with laundry soap was his air of clerical austerity finally effaced. Erving was given rubber boots and a red necktie; his blond hair, parted in the middle, was suitably mussed up. Piloted by Gardner, the self-sacrificing reformers, in their undignified garb, set out on a tour of New York's "dens of vice" that continued for three weeks.

Gardner soon learned that he would have to work strenuously for his fees. Dr. Parkhurst was a very hard man to satisfy. " 'Show me something worse,' was his constant cry. He really went at his slumming work as if his heart was in his tour." In the Cherry Street saloon of Tom Summers, a notorious "fence," he downed a drink of Cherry Hill whiskey, acting, so Gardner noted, "as if he had swallowed a whole political parade—torchlights and all." He watched a stream of ten-year-old children buying pint bottles of whiskey, for ten cents, presumably to take home to their parents. In front of a sailors' dive on Water Street, three prostitutes grabbed the reformers and hauled them indoors; Dr. Parkhurst, resisting their blandishments, chatted with them amiably. The party visited a five-cent lodging house on Park Row, where the clergyman remarked—quite correctly—that the naked men lying on cots became, on Election Day, Tammany voters. Gardner took his clients to Chinese opium dens, to ordinary houses of prostitution, to houses where the prostitutes gave indecent performances, to others known as "tight houses" because all the inmates wore tights.

One incident of the tour later became celebrated because Tammany, after it had been aired in a courtroom, sought to persuade reputable citizens that Dr. Parkhurst was an evil-minded hypocrite. In the brothel run by Hattie Adams, Gardner arranged to have a "dance of nature" performed by five girls who, for furnishing this diversion, were to be paid three dollars each. When the party arrived, the girls were dressed in their usual garb and a broken-down musician, called "the Professor," sat at a piano in the parlor. Gardner blindfolded the Professor because the girls refused either to disrobe, or dance, before him. The five girls then stripped, and to a lively jig performed a dance which Gardner incorrectly described as "the can-can." Because Gardner could not dance, and Dr. Parkhurst would not if he could, Erving was compelled to represent the visitors as a dancer. As Gardner later recorded, the "dance of nature" was followed by "the celebrated 'leapfrog' episode, in which I was the frog and the others jumped over me. The Doctor sat in the corner with an unmoved face through it all, watching us and slowly sipping at a glass of beer. Hattie Adams was quite anxious to find out who Dr. Parkhurst was. I told her he was 'from the West' and was 'a gay boy.' Then Hattie tried to pull Dr. Parkhurst's whiskers, but the Doctor straightened out with such an air of dignity that she did not attempt any further familiarities."

Dr. Parkhurst's constant demand for "something worse" was apparently satisfied, according to Gardner, by a visit to the Golden Rule Pleasure Club on West Third Street. The proprietress of this establishment, a woman known as "Scotch Ann," received the party cordially and ushered them into the basement. The basement was subdivided, by flimsy partitions, into cubicles each of which contained a table and two chairs. "In each room sat a youth," Gardner later reported, "whose face was painted, eyebrows blackened, and whose airs were those of a young girl. Each person talked in a high falsetto voice, and called the others by women's names." Mystified by what he saw, Dr. Parkhurst questioned Gardner in a whisper. The detective explained. The clergyman "instantly turned on his heel and fled from the house at top speed. 'Why, I wouldn't stay in that house,' he gasped, 'for all the money in the world.'" As later investigations showed, this establishment was not unique. Similar resorts were being operated in other quarters of the city: Manila Hall, The Black Rabbit, The Palm; and Paresis Hall on Fourth Avenue between Twelfth and Thirteenth Streets. The name of this resort was grimly reminiscent of advertisements plastered on the walls of public toilets, offering the services of "Old Dr. Gray" and "Old Dr. Grindle." At Paresis Hall investigators observed, among the visitors, the captain of the precinct police station. "We saw Captain Chapman come in there," one of them testified, "and look around about two or three minutes, and then speak to the proprietor four or five minutes, and then walk out." The inference of police protection seemed not to be impossibly far-fetched.

One month after delivering his first sermon, Dr. Parkhurst carried to his pulpit a massive bundle of sworn affidavits. To his appalled congregation, he rendered an account of his journey into the Inferno. "Anyone who, with all the easily ascertainable facts in view, denies that drunkenness, gambling and licentiousness in this town are municipally protected, is either a knave or a fool," he declared. He denounced Tammany Hall as "a commercial corporation, organized in the interest of making the most possible out of its official opportunities." Tammany, he charged, had efficiently organized crime and vice for the financial profit of its hierarchy. And it embodied the tyranny of crime. He had received an immense correspondence from citizens who, abominating the whole system, assured him of their approval of his course. Many of these citizens had also stated that they did not dare sign their letters with their real names—such was their fear of the power of Tammany Hall. This astonished Dr. Parkhurst. But, during the next two years, he became inured to facts that were equally surprising. Much of the information upon which he proceeded came to him from a man who, although intimately connected with Tammany Hall, was willing to enter into a secret, silent working alliance with the clergyman and his militant organization. On the other hand, many reputable New Yorkers, of high social and financial standing, condemned his efforts to overthrow Tammany rule, actively opposed his crusade and supported, with their own prestige, the men directly responsible for the prevailing state of affairs. There was no apparent link between these gentlemen and the criminal underworld, yet they were bitterly averse to "reform." Reform, they said, "hurt business." . . .

> Dr. Parkhurst continued his clean-up efforts for some years. Local and state committees carried out repeated investigations. There were sporadic police crackdowns in the Tenderloin. In 1894 Tammany Boss Croker resigned and sailed for an indefinite stay in Europe. But by 1897 moral fervor had waned. Boss Croker resumed business at the old stand. The Tenderloin and the Bowery were more "wide open" than ever. And the winning slogan of the 1897 municipal campaign was: "To Hell with Reform."

MEET ME AT THE WALDORF

LLOYD MORRIS

To the nation and the world, as the nineteenth century waned, the Waldorf-Astoria Hotel interpreted the spirit of New York. It symbolized the city of titanic power and inexhaustible wealth. It made credible the metropolis that had vaulted the barriers of its girdling rivers, and had begun to lift its towers into the skies. It represented the city which, driven by a gluttonous craving for beauty, was pillaging Europe and the Orient. Most of all, the Waldorf-Astoria spoke eloquently for New York's prodigal extravagance, its delight in costly pleasures, its determination to achieve a scale of luxury and splendor such as men had never before conceived. Like New York itself, the Waldorf-Astoria crystallized the improbable and fabulous. It was more than a mere hotel. It was a vast, glittering, iridescent fantasy that had been conjured up to infect millions of plain Americans with a new ideal—the aspiration to lead an expensive, gregarious life as publicly as possible.

Dedicated to creating desires which it had anticipated, and to inculcating the etiquette of their satisfaction, the Waldorf-Astoria became, in effect, a national university. Teaching the amenities of the highest social life, it wrought profound changes in the tastes, manners and customs of Americans. To citizens of Keokuk and Kokomo and Kansas City it made available, for a few weeks or days, a palace of more stupefying grandeur than any Vanderbilt chateau. To residents of New York's brownstone East Side, to Harlemites and Brooklynites and the cliff dwellers of Central Park West, it afforded an opportunity to duplicate the repast being served to members of the Four Hundred at a nearby table or—far more cheaply—to sit and watch their entrance and exit. All New York knew that, in their Fifth Avenue chateaux, Elbridge T. Gerry and Ogden Mills could entertain one hundred guests at dinner on an hour's notice. At the Waldorf-Astoria any American able to pay the price could do the same. Indeed, the anonymous citizen had at his command services, a cuisine and a décor equaled only by those of multimillionaires. As the wit Oliver Herford remarked, it was the mission of the Waldorf-Astoria to bring exclusiveness to the masses. It existed to fulfill a universal American daydream that had never before become articulate.

As a cultural institution, the influence of the Waldorf-Astoria far exceeded that of the Astor Library, established by a bequest of John Jacob Astor, founder of the dynasty. The great hotel was not, however, conceived as an Astor philanthropy. It merely commemorated the outbreak of a family feud between the founder's descendants. Before repudiating his native land and taking up permanent residence in England, William Waldorf Astor wished to revenge himself on his august aunt, Mrs. Astor. Having failed to displace her as the supreme ruler of New York society, he proposed to evict her from the home which she had made its major shrine. Her mansion occupied the southwest corner of Fifth Avenue and 34th Street. A spacious garden separated it from the residence, on the northwest corner of Fifth Avenue and 33rd Street, which William Waldorf Astor had inherited from his father, John Jacob Astor III. To accomplish his vindictive purpose, William Waldorf Astor razed his father's home and, on its site, built the Waldorf Hotel.

In 1894, one year after the new hotel opened, Mrs. Astor capitulated to its dishonoring presence. She engaged Richard Morris Hunt to provide her with a new palace far uptown, remote from all plebeian caravanseries. Diplomatic negotiations followed between representatives of her son, John Jacob Astor IV, and agents of his expatriated cousin. The cousins were implacable enemies, but they shared an ancestral trait: neither disdained an accretion to his enormous wealth. The prospect of mutual advantage therefore prevailed over the fact of mutual hatred. John Jacob Astor IV agreed to build, on the site of his mother's home, another hotel—taller, more imposing, in every way more magnificent than the adjoining thirteen-story Waldorf. Designed to form an architectural unit with the Waldorf, the seventeen-story Astoria was built to be operated in conjunction with it as a single hotel. But John Jacob Astor IV protected his spleen by a monitory clause. A bond was required that, on his demand, every interior passage uniting the two buildings would be permanently walled up. Thus his mother's whim, or his own, could immediately terminate a mercenary, provisional alliance with their despised relative.

The alliance between hostile capitalists was inspired by George C. Boldt, a Philadelphia hotel keeper who had leased the Waldorf and there began his apostleship of "marvelous ways of living and luxuries hitherto unattainable." Even before revealing the marvels of the combined Waldorf-Astoria, Boldt managed to impress upon New Yorkers certain fastidious prerequisites of the higher life. If they wished to dine in the Palm Room of the Waldorf—the most exclusive of its restaurants —they would have to appear in full formal attire; white tie and tails were mandatory for gentlemen, evening gowns for ladies. This produced a flutter among the rich and well born, but the decree made a table in the Palm Room almost as desirable as a box at the Metropolitan Opera—and, presently, almost as difficult to secure. Another edict, drastically curtailing the democratic right of American freemen to look as they pleased, became a political issue in New York and the subject of a controversy in the nation's press. Waiters and other functionaries in the Waldorf's restaurants were required to have a fluent command of French and German as well as English; this was considered a legitimate demand, however capricious. But in insisting that all members of his service staff be clean-shaven, and in extending this provision to the cabmen who awaited fares at the entrance to the Waldorf, was not Boldt invading the sacred area of civil liberties guaranteed by the Constitution? Labor unions representing waiters and hack-drivers carried the issue to Governor Roswell P. Flower, himself impressively whiskered. A gubernatorial election was imminent. Warned that thirty-six thousand waiters and cabmen in the state of New York were voters, Governor Flower issued a formal statement sustaining their right to cultivate any kind of facial foliage they wished. But the prestige of connection with the Waldorf outweighed the Governor's spirited defense of personal liberty, and the ban on beards was eventually accepted. Nobody, during the long, bitter battle, drew public attention to the fact that Boldt affected a flowing mustache and trimly pointed beard.

For the unveiling of his hyphenated hostelry in the autumn of 1897, Boldt organized a function to benefit various philanthropic institutions favored by New York's élite. The appeal of sweet charity permitted the sophisticated world of fashion to gratify a curiosity scarcely avowable, because so intensely shared by millions of their undistinguished fellow-citizens. Popular curiosity was abundantly justified. Everybody had heard that the monster structure contained one thousand bedrooms and seven hundred and sixty-five private baths; that three floors were given over to public rooms and state apartments; that the chief chef, Xavier Kuesmeier, received an annual salary of ten thousand dollars—a sum so startling "for merely running a kitchen" that it evoked passionate editorials in both the American and foreign press.

The Waldorf-Astoria was not only the largest hotel in the world, but the costliest in point of investment; nearly ten millions, rumor alleged, had been poured into it. Its opening, therefore, became an event of national importance, and this was officially recognized. Unable to attend the affair himself, President McKinley deputed Vice-President Garret A. Hobart to act as his personal representative.

As New Yorkers quickly realized, as Americans from every region of the country and visitors from every country of the world soon learned, there was always something going on at the Waldorf-Astoria. The vast ground floor, with its multiple restaurants and myriad public rooms, was in effect a theater offering a continuous performance in which the actors and actresses also constituted the audience. From noon until the early hours of the morning the greatest show in the city proceeded without intermission, so you went there both to see and be seen. A wide, amber-marble corridor, furnished with luxurious chairs and sofas, stretched for three hundred feet along the 34th Street side of the hotel and became famous, the world over, as "Peacock Alley"—although it was the plumage of the female bird rather than the male that made this promenade New York's most impressive fashion show.

CARRY NATION VS. JOHN L. SULLIVAN

HERBERT ASBURY

In August 1901, when Carry Nation's spectacular efforts to hasten the advent of the dry millennium by wrecking mid-Western saloons and speakeasies with a hatchet formed the principal topic of conversation in New York bar-rooms, John L. Sullivan made a mistake. With his magnificent mustache quivering indignantly, the celebrated pugilist smote the bar of his saloon in West 42nd Street with a ham-like fist and boastingly told reporters that "if that old woman ever comes to New York and tries to poke her nose into my business, I'll push her down the sewer." While the reporters doubted that Mr. Sullivan would be so ungallant, they nevertheless obligingly published his ultimatum.

Copyright, 1933, The New Yorker Magazine, Inc.
Copyright, 1933, 1934 by Alfred A. Knopf, Inc.

A week or so later, on August 28, 1901, Carry Nation *did* come to New York. A horde of eager newspaper men met her at the railroad station, and the first thing she said was:

"Boys, I'd like to see this Mr. Sullivan. He thinks he's mighty smart, but I won't allow any man to push me down a sewer. Not while I've got my senses."

The reporters gleefully clambered into carriages, and with Carry Nation leading in an open barouche, they set out to call upon the famous John L. For this, her first visit to the metropolis, the smasher had characteristically arrayed herself in a black poke-bonnet with long white ribbons tied under her chin, a black alpaca dress over innumerable petticoats and whatnots, and a linen duster, belted at the waist. From her shoulder hung a satchel bulging with miniature hatchets, photographs, souvenir buttons, and sample copies of her newspaper, *The Smasher's Mail*. An enormous hatchet, almost as large as a small broad-ax, was stuck in her belt, but when she started on the ride across town, she shouldered the fearsome weapon, rifle-fashion, the better to protect herself against attack by the liquor interests.

Naturally, the cavalcade attracted considerable attention, and an enormous crowd quickly gathered when Carry Nation's coachman drew up before Sullivan's saloon with a flourish and a crack of his long whip. Standing erect in her carriage, the crusader loudly invited Mr. Sullivan to come out and take his medicine. Instead, a bar-tender presently appeared and said that Mr. Sullivan was asleep and could not be disturbed.

"Is that so?" said Carry Nation. "Then I'll come in and wake him up!"

Escorted by the reporters and as much of the crowd as could push through the swinging doors, the crusader rushed into the saloon. A newspaper man pointed out the noted pugilist, who cowered at one end of the bar with his face half-buried in a mug of beer.

"Mr. Sullivan," said Carry Nation, sternly, "put down that hell-brew and come here. I want to talk to you."

Slowly wiping the beer off his mustache, John L. stared for a moment at her embattled figure, then turned and fled. Carry Nation brandished her hatchet and started in pursuit, but Sullivan ran down the cellar stairs and bolted the door behind him. The crusader hammered upon the thick panels for a moment, but at length she became discouraged and shouted through the keyhole:

"All right, Mr. Sullivan! You wait! I'll be back, and we'll see if you'll push me down the sewer!"

A muffled grunt was John L.'s only response, and Carry Nation swept grandly from the saloon. Half an hour later the pugilist emerged sheepishly from his hiding-place and sought to cover his discomfiture with blustering talk, but he never quite succeeded in living down the incident.

Carry Nation invited the reporters to lunch, and the entire party clattered over to a Sixth Avenue restaurant, where the crusader was effusively greeted by a flashily dressed woman who said she wanted publicly to thank God that New York would now be rescued from the evil clutches of the Demon Rum.

"I believe in temperance myself," she gushed. "I really do!"

"If that is the case," said Carry Nation, coldly, "go home and put about four inches more of solid cloth on top of your corset cover!"

After lunch the terror of the prairies went to the Hotel Victoria, at Fifth Avenue and 27th Street, where she registered as "Carry Nation, Your Loving Home Defender, Kansas." Turning from the desk, she espied a marble Diana in a fountain in the center of the lobby, and promptly covered her face with her hands.

"Look!" she shrieked. "She ain't got a thing on!"

She made such a commotion that the hotel manager hastily procured a large piece of cheesecloth and threw it over the statue, promising to keep it covered so long as Carry Nation remained a guest of the house. Thus pacified, the indignant crusader repaired to her rooms, where she gave each of the reporters a small hatchet inscribed "Carry Nation, Joint Smasher," and sang them a song which she had herself composed:

> *Sing a song of six joints,*
> *With bottles full of rye;*
> *Four and twenty beer kegs,*
> *Stacked up on the sly.*
> *When the kegs were opened,*
> *The beer began to sing,*
> *"Hurrah for Carry Nation!*
> *"Her work beats anything!"*

Neither on this nor subsequent visits to New York was Carry Nation officially greeted by the religious and temperance organizations which in recent years have practically canonized her; and the Prohibition agents who later imitated her destructive antics were then only a wild dream of the future. The rowdier element, however, had made great preparations for her coming. Most of the Times Square and Tenderloin saloons and beer-gardens offered special drinks named in her honor, and bar-room windows and mirrors were decorated with gayly beribboned hatchets and bore signs saying: "All Nations Welcome But Carry." Several saloon-keepers publicly offered to provide beer-kegs and whisky-bottles for her to smash, and employed press-agents to see that they received proper journalistic credit for their generosity.

COSMOPOLIS UNDER THE EL

LLOYD MORRIS

At Rector's temple of pleasure and perdition any patron willing to spend twenty dollars on a supper party for five was able to include in his hospitality two bottles of champagne and a round of cigars. The lower end of Orchard Street, near East Broadway, was less than three miles distant from Longacre Square. Down there were two restaurants scarcely less popular than Rector's, though very unlike it. One of these establishments served a dinner of soup, meat stew, bread, pickles, pie and a "schooner" of beer for thirteen cents. Its neighboring competitor charged fifteen cents for a similar dinner, and offered two schooners of beer and a cigar, or cigarette, as an extra inducement. But the thirteen-cent restaurant had an edge on its rival. To many customers, two cents made a vital difference. Most of them were Polish Jews, fugitives from pogroms in their native land. In New York, they labored long hours in "sweatshops" and herded in squalid, overcrowded tenements. Tenement families often had to take in lodgers to make ends meet. A lodger, as some of them said, could "live like a lord" for twenty-five cents a day.

Prosperous New Yorkers couldn't tell whether this statement was ironical, or merely grotesque. To them, existence in the slums had the look of social misery. Dire mass poverty was all too visible. Men, women and many children worked for eighteen hours a day at low wages. Ceaseless privation, widespread disease and helpless ignorance were obvious to anyone who cared to investigate. Sociologists asserted that no other city in the world had so many dark, windowless rooms, so many persons crowded on the acre, so many families deprived of light and air. . . .

Although the slums had spread over the city, many New Yorkers maintained that they were confined to the area south of Fourteenth Street. Journalists named this region the "melting pot," for there a vast immigrant population was supposedly being made American. Yet the fusion of nationalities was less obvious than their persistently maintained identity, their continuing separateness. The slums below 14th Street were, in fact, Cosmopolis. They harbored swarming colonies, all foreign in language, customs, institutions; some, even in costume. Between the Bowery and the East River was the congested "ghetto" inhabited by Russian, Polish and Rumanian Jews. There you saw venerable, scholarly-looking men, patriarchally bearded, wearing skullcaps and long-skirted kaftans; elderly women who shaved their heads and wore the traditional wig. The signs on the shops were in Hebrew characters, and you heard Yiddish spoken more frequently than English on the noisy, thronged streets. In two small rooms of a six-story tenement it would not be unusual to find a "family" of father, mother, twelve children and six lodgers.

West of the Bowery, you passed into Italy. The colorful Italian quarter had spread uptown from the rookeries of Mulberry Bend as far as the decrepit buildings on Thompson and Sullivan Streets, south of Washington Square. The Negroes who had formerly occupied these buildings had been driven northward by the Italian incursion. They had migrated to Seventh Avenue in the Thirties; to Ninth Avenue in the Fifties, a district soon to become known as San Juan Hill, because of the bravery of Negro troops in the Spanish-American War. In the sprawling Italian quarter, as in southern Italy, life was lived on the street in mild weather. Whenever the sun shone, everybody turned out on the sidewalks to carry on their household work, their bargaining, love-making or mere idling. Hucksters' and peddlers' carts made two rows of booths in the roadways; on the sidewalks, ash barrels served for counters.

Below the Italian quarter, opening off Chatham Square, Chinatown was squeezed between Pell and Mott Streets, bisected by twisting, narrow Doyers Street. Here you saw no women. The older men wore Chinese costume and pigtails. The walls of buildings were plastered with red-and-white posters bearing Chinese characters in orange and black. Silence, a sullen stare, an air of distrust greeted the too curious visitor. Southeast of Chinatown was the district inhabited by the Greek colony. Down near the Battery, on Greenwich and Washington Streets, where Turks, Syrians and Arabs had settled, you found coffee houses and bazaars like those of the Levant. North of the Bowery and east of Third Avenue lay Little Germany. Along Second Avenue, near St. Mark's Place, a stone's throw from the grave of Peter Stuyvesant, was Little Hungary, with its brightly lighted cafés where gypsy musicians played, where, on summer nights, the sidewalk terraces were crowded. Further up Second Avenue, clustering about the huge cigar factories in which they earned their livelihood, were colonies of Bohemians. Many of them carried on their trade in their tenement homes. By working from dawn to midnight a man and wife might produce three thousand cigars a week, and be paid at the most fifteen dollars.

To explore these quarters of the city was an adventure on foreign soil. Only the façades of the buildings persuaded you that you were actually on Manhattan Island, reminded you that nowhere else could you become an alien so abruptly and diversely. It gave you an odd feeling to learn that many dwellers in the area below 14th Street passed their lives without ever once crossing that barrier, or seeing the wonderful modern city that lay north of it. New York had become a metropolis virtually invisible, if not unknown, to millions of its own residents. Yet the segregation of the downtown slums from the life of uptown Manhattan was more apparent than real. The two regions, however insulated from one another socially, were vitally connected.

Nothing seemed more remote from the world of the tenements than that of the palaces on Fifth Avenue. But Mrs. Astor's annual ball was nourished by the income derived from immense tracts of slum property. Her world included many members of Trinity Church, which drew huge revenues from ownership of houses unfit for human habitation. An intricate network connected the slums with the office of Boss Richard Croker in Tammany Hall. This network crossed the lines which linked the slums to the society of the Gay White Way. The underworld celebrities who frequented Rector's, the vice-rings whose operations were so ably safeguarded by "Little Abe" Hummel, were native to the blighted area south of 14th Street. Hardworking residents of the Jewish quarter formed no part of the audiences at Broadway theaters. But many of them took pride in the legendary fame of Weber and Fields. They knew that short, explosive Joe Weber and lank, deadpan Lew Fields were children of the tenements, had begun their careers as little boys playing a "Dutch act" in Bowery dime museums. They had heard, too, about bearded, silk-hatted Oscar Hammerstein, builder of theaters, producer of operas, eccentric genius and shrewd businessman who was said to be reaping a fortune from an *Amerikaner* amusement called vaudeville in a new theater named the Victoria. They knew that Hammerstein had got his start as a cigar-maker. Weber, Fields, Hammerstein—they had risen to fame, to fabulous financial success, from dire poverty, and now they were accepted, honored, by the great ones of this strange new world. The knowledge was like a beacon of hope. It proved that the gateway of opportunity had not closed. . . .

Still the fact remained that three-quarters of the city's population lived in tenements. Wasn't the misery that darkened their lives a threat to democracy, and a challenge to conscience? Nobody felt this more deeply, more aggrievedly, than Jacob A. Riis, a talented writer on the staff of *The Sun*, assigned by that newspaper to cover Police Headquarters. Himself an immigrant from Denmark, Riis had experienced many of the hardships familiar to the foreign-born poor. Writing stories of crime for his newspaper, he made it his business tirelessly to investigate conditions in the slums. Appalled by what he saw and learned, his indignation boiled up in a book, *How The Other Half Lives*. This blistering exposure shocked the city and the nation; with his new prestige, Riis became a powerful, insistent crusader for reform. A similar sense of personal, moral responsibility afflicted a young graduate trained nurse. Called one day on an errand of mercy to a squalid rear tenement on Ludlow Street, Miss Lillian D. Wald was aghast at the unsuspected horrors suddenly revealed to her. All the maladjustments of social and economic relations seemed epitomized by what she saw during a brief walk, and what she found at the end of it. She was convinced that the conditions she had discovered were tolerated only because, like herself, uptown New Yorkers did not know about them; she felt challenged to learn about them, and to tell. Presently, with her friend Miss Mary M. Brewster, she went to live in the heart of the "ghetto." Identifying themselves with the neighborhood, socially and as citizens, they established a volunteer district-nursing service, then opened the Henry Street Settlement. By virtue of her experience in all forms of social welfare—gained by the experimental, trial-and-error method of meeting problems as they arose—Miss Wald soon achieved national celebrity. Insisting on group co-operation within the neighborhood, she overcame the apathy and helpless acquiescence of its residents. The "house on Henry Street" developed social services that later became municipal functions. It initiated progressive social legislation. It provided a forum where representatives of labor, management and government met to discuss and solve controversial problems. . . .

Undaunted by the stubborn resistance of their employers, the workers were organizing trade unions. In the cafés, you heard much talk about two young women residents of the neighborhood. Miss Rose Schneiderman, working ten hours a day as a capmaker, had organized a women's union in her trade. Women workers, she preached, must stand together, not only for their own rights, but in behalf of those who would come after them. Miss Fannia M. Cohn, a garment worker, was eloquently demanding a crusade against the sweatshop. This was admirable, everybody agreed. But what about another project that seemed to be an obsession with her? She was forever discussing a program of adult education—nothing less than a workers' university would do!—to be conducted by the unions for the benefit of their members. It seemed fantastically visionary, and even the most optimistic unionists could not foresee that Miss Cohn would eventually carry it through on a scale that far exceeded her early ambitions.

Meanwhile, nobody could deny that the intellectual and literary life of the "ghetto" was running at full tide. Even "uptowners" who understood no Yiddish made the long journey downtown to see the great actor, Jacob Adler, play Shylock. And the same thing occurred when Adler performed the powerful dramas written by Jacob Gordin: *The Jewish King Lear, God, Man and the Devil, The Wild Man.* Gordin's plays dealt with such problems of "ghetto" life as the conflict of ideals between the older, immigrant generation and their children, born in the new land and thoroughly Americanized. Among younger writers, Mary Antin was presently to write in English *The Promised Land*, a memorable study of the hardships suffered by immigrants, and Abraham Cahan would soon afterward use English to tell, in a notable novel, *The Rise of David Levinsky*, the story of progress from hardship to material success. In the Jewish quarter a love of art was so obstinate that even extreme poverty could not quench it.

PAINT, PROTEST AND PARTIES

LLOYD MORRIS

The streets of Greenwich Village had been laid out on a diagonal to the north-south axis of Manhattan before the checkerboard street plan of the island was mapped early in the nineteenth century. It was a maze where even native New Yorkers lost their way in confusion, a labyrinth of narrow, twisting streets that seemed to cross and recross one another without ever arriving anywhere. In the Village, West Twelfth and West Fourth Streets improbably met. Most of the streets had names rather than numbers, and were lined by old, low, dormered red-brick houses slowly crumbling to decay; houses innocent of modern conveniences, with large, stately rooms. There were quaint cul-de-sacs like Milligan Place and Patchin Place, and odd byways like Minetta Lane. In its picturesque decrepitude, part slum, part shabby-genteel, the Village was curiously isolated from the roaring modern city that surrounded it. Presently, artists and writers, social radicals of all kinds, young people from all over the country who hoped to make careers in New York, found congenial refuge there. Life in the Village was simple and cheap. It was a place where people were free to "be themselves."

It was the painters who first proclaimed a revolution in the arts. In his little gallery on the top floor of a brownstone building at 291 Fifth Avenue, the photographer Alfred Stieglitz showed the work of some American artists whose canvases looked like nothing that anybody had ever seen before and of some Europeans whose pictures were even more queerly incomprehensible. A shy, fragile little man, Stieglitz hectored the visitors who came to his tiny gallery to gape or laugh at "the craziest painters in America." He had an evangelical fire and fervor when he preached about Modern Art, about the Spirit of Life, about the Wonder of Things—somehow, you knew that he capitalized the initial letters—and his eloquence brought about conversions. When a Washington millionaire, Duncan Phillips, began collecting the paintings of John Marin, Stieglitz scored a public victory. Meanwhile, he kept his other protégés from starving, buying their work himself when nobody else would and laying the foundations of a collection which, forty years later, was to enrich a number of American museums, notably, New York's Metropolitan. In the studio on West Eighth Street where she practiced sculpture, Gertrude Vanderbilt Whitney held exhibitions of the work of unknown young artists. She had already determined to establish there a museum of American art chiefly devoted to living painters and sculptors. But the most ominous portent of revolution was a collective show put on by eight painters whose pictures, derided by the critics and scandalizing the public, won them the name of "the Ash Can School."

They gloried in the name. They despised all academic conventions. They detested the slick, "pretty-pretty" pictures exhibited by fashionable dealers, liked by a public which wanted to avoid all "unpleasant" aspects of life. Robert Henri, leader of the eight rebels, invented their battle cry: "Don't imitate; be yourself!" Of the others, John Sloan, William J. Glackens, George Luks and Everett Shinn had been newspaper illustrators, pictorial reporters of city life in the raw. They lived near Washington Square, or in the Village. They wanted to record the look and feeling of New York's workaday existence; the humor and squalor of streets and back alleys by day and by night; the drinkers in neighborhood bars, the crowded gallery of a vaudeville theater, frowsy women reeling out their wash on tenement clotheslines, shopgirls hurrying home from work. They weren't squeamish, and several of them had a talent for ribaldry which got expressed on their canvases....

The rebellious eight soon attracted adherents. Among these were Jerome Myers, who found a romantic aspect of New York in the streets, cafés and theaters of the lower East Side; Walt Kuhn, who painted the backstage life of theater and circus; George W. Bellows, whose favorite subject was prize fights. They joined Arthur B. Davies, one of the derided eight, in organizing an art exhibition which soon had New York in an uproar that spread over the country. The International Exhibition of Modern Art opened, early in the winter of 1913, at the armory of the Sixty-ninth Regiment on Park Avenue and Thirty-fourth Street. This "Armory Show" put on view sixteen hundred paintings and sculptures by American and European artists. Its emblem, significantly, was the pine tree symbolic of the American Revolution. Yet it was not the work of American rebels, but that of European experimenters, which made the show sensational. Outrage and protest flared up in newspaper headlines. Cubism, futurism, post-impressionism became issues in a battle that engaged the general public. Critics blasted at the baffling "Nude Descending a Staircase," by Marcel Duchamp; Constantin Brancusi's roughly hewn block, "The Kiss"; the distorted, crudely colored nudes of Henri Matisse; the incomprehensible vagaries of Pablo Picasso and Francis Picabia. Obviously these were the work of degenerates or imposters. Conservative New Yorkers spluttered and raged. Some demanded that the show be closed by the police, on the ground of obscenity....

The revolutionary pine tree, emblem of the Armory Show, also symbolized the new spirit abroad in Greenwich Village. To the horror of patrician residents, people now included in the Village the quarter around Washington Square. For the Village wasn't merely a neighborhood. It was also a state of mind. It was hell-bent for change; "the old ways must go, and with them their priests." It wanted to precipitate another American revolution. Not only in art and literature. In morals—in social institutions and economics and politics. Even sex, presumably the oldest thing in the world, was taking on seriously revolutionary implications. A current story illustrated the difference between the Village and the rest of America. At the Ferrer School, a center of light and learning conducted by anarchists, where Robert Henri and George Bellows taught art and many distinguished writers gave lectures, one speaker had given a lecture on the new theories about sex. At the end of his address, an earnest little cloakmaker rose from her chair and indignantly announced, "Comrade Speaker, you talk about revolution, but I been in this here sexual movement for over twelve years, and I ain't seen no progress yet." . . .

Freedom, experiment, change—these were the keynotes struck by Mabel Dodge's celebrated "Evenings." Pretty, plump Mrs. Dodge was a personage. Other people were intense—it was a quality highly approved—but she carried intensity to a pitch that astonished everyone. There seemed never to be enough "causes" to satisfy her ardor. She acquired and fostered them with impartial affection: the new art, the new poetry, birth control, free speech, the unemployed, the I. W. W., psychoanalysis. A woman of wealth, Mrs. Dodge came to Washington Square from long residence in Europe, cherishing a notion but seeking a mission. She believed that one must just let life express itself in whatever form it will. Her mission suddenly became clear; she would persuade life to express itself faster. Perhaps she could upset America, dynamite New York, bring ruin to the old order of things. The first step was "to get people together so that they can tell each other that they think." Of course, they must be people who "believe in life." Mrs. Dodge installed herself on one floor of a decaying mansion on the corner of Fifth Avenue and Ninth Street. She set out to dynamite New York from a beautiful white drawing room filled with delicate French furniture, illuminated by an ornate Venetian chandelier, and adorned with modern paintings, Persian miniatures and a collection of antique colored glass.

In Mrs. Dodge's drawing room daring projects were incubated. The Armory Show was developed there. So was the great pageant held in Madison Square Garden to dramatize the bitter strike of workers in the silk mills of Paterson, New Jersey, a strike organized by the militant, hated I.W.W. Handsome young John Reed wrote the pageant enacted by two thousand strikers. His Harvard classmate, Robert Edmond Jones, designed the scenery for it and staged it. Fifteen thousand New Yorkers turned out to see it, and high up on the Garden Tower the letters I. W. W. blazed in red electric lights which the police failed to extinguish. At Mrs. Dodge's gatherings, the air was always "vibrant with intellectual excitement, and electrical with the appearance of new ideas and dawning changes." You could listen to Emma Goldman preaching anarchism. Or hear "Big Bill" Haywood, leader of the I.W.W., and Elizabeth Gurley Flynn, the fiery "Wobbly Joan of Arc," expound the doctrine of syndicalism. When an "Evening" was devoted to the new art, modernist painters like Marsden Hartley or John Marin made it sound quite as explosive as the doctrines of the political radicals. Naturally, the queer theories of Dr. Sigmund Freud came up for discussion. Gnomelike Dr. A. A. Brill, the master's disciple and translator, was asked to elucidate them. Several guests got up and left, because they were either disturbed or incensed by his assertions about the subconscious, and the startling elements of one's personality that behavior revealed to the initiated. You might hear Mrs. Margaret Sanger also. She had been imprisoned for her birth-control crusade. She spoke as an ardent propagandist for the joys of the flesh, ridiculing the traditional sense of sin, explaining the physical possibilities of "sex-expression." Gentle Hutchins Hapgood asserted that many brave young American women were conscientiously practicing free love, "adapting themselves in this way of life, and thus doing their share towards a final disintegration of the community." At Mrs. Dodge's "Evenings" you couldn't help believing that "the old ways were about over, and the new ways all to create." . . .

George Cram Cook and his wife, Susan Glaspell rented a ramshackle stable on MacDougal Street, adjoining the Liberal Club, converted it into The Playwrights' Theater, assembled a company of actors in the Village as The Provincetown Players, and launched a venture that soon achieved celebrity. The Provincetown Playhouse, as it came to be called, produced the works of many young playwrights, but it was chiefly to see the early plays of O'Neill that audiences came from all over New York to sit on hard benches in a dim, narrow stable and watch a company of gifted amateurs perform on a stage little larger than a handkerchief.

An early recruit to the company of amateurs was a young girl who came to the Village from Vassar College, and settled in a bleak room on Waverly Place to write poetry while seeking to earn her living as an actress. Slender, red-haired, undeniably pretty, Edna St. Vincent Millay captivated the Villagers with her frivolous ways, her gaiety, her delight in life. She wanted to live fearlessly and fully, at whatever cost, and it was this attitude, expressed in her verse, that made her the idol of youth all over the land. She invoked the lovely light of a candle burned at both ends, all too quickly consumed. She wrote bitter-sweet, skeptical love songs which made her the accredited spokesman of a generation that seemed resolved to purchase its wisdom at "the booth where folly holds her fair."

Presently, the claim of some residents that the Village had become "the cradle of modern American culture" seemed beyond dispute. Willa Cather, whose novels everybody was reading, lived there. Theodore Dreiser, who had been living uptown, moved into a studio on West Tenth Street. A large, awkward, friendly man, he had a great zest for serious conversation, and at his parties Kirah Markham, a dark, statuesque beauty, presided over the punch bowl in a setting lit by flickering candles and dull lamps. At Dreiser's you might hear Edgar Lee Masters read his *Spoon River* poems, or you might find a crowd gathered around ouija boards to receive communications from the supernatural realm. Sherwood Anderson made long visits from Chicago, a stout, florid man who seemed permanently perplexed but was nevertheless persistently oracular. The poet Edwin Arlington Robinson spent much of his time in the Village. Tall, thin, slightly stooped, Robinson had a storklike, scholarly look. Incurably shy, he was a legendary recluse, and you needed long acquaintance to break down his habitual reserve. Sometimes you saw him dining at Regnaneschi's table d'hôte, near Jefferson Market Court, with one or two friends. But he had a curious prejudice against sitting at a table with more than three people; he thought it "uncivilized." . . .

Some of the battles that convulsed the Village rang out over the nation. Censorship, in one or another guise, initiated many of them, lifting into high relief the conflict between conservatives and radicals. Even before the United States entered the First World War, *The Masses* was constantly in trouble with the authorities. With the advent of war, it was suppressed by the Department of Justice; its editors were indicted, and twice brought to trial, under the Espionage Act. Meanwhile, the Society for the Suppression of Vice had banned the sale of Theodore Dreiser's novel *The "Genius*," and under the leadership of H. L. Mencken American liberals launched a crusade to establish the freedom of writers. In courtrooms where pacifists were standing trial you would have seen Miss Millay who, hating war as bitterly as they did, came to comfort them by reciting her poems while juries decided on their cases.

By the end of the war, the Village had become nationally famous as New York's "Latin Quarter." The best advertised of American Bohemias, it was a lure to sightseers and a destination for all types of eccentrics. . . . It was a bitter thing, Floyd Dell said, to look at the new generation of "professional Villagers," playing their antics in public for pay, and realize that this was the kind of person one was supposed, by the public, to be. . . .

The younger writers and painters who had settled in the Village with intentions of serious work soon learned to avoid the more publicized gathering places. Many of them rallied around *The Little Review*, which handsome Margaret Anderson and stout, forthright Jane Heap had transferred from Chicago to New York. This eclectic publication, dedicated to the work of the literary advance guard, was the most influential of a series of little magazines which had sprung up in the Village, had briefly flourished there but had usually died for want of support. Unlike its predecessors, *The Little Review* found readers throughout the United States, and even in Europe. In part this was due to the fact that every issue carried an installment of James Joyce's *Ulysses*, the publication of which kept its intrepid editors under constant attack by the Society for the Suppression of Vice. But Miss Anderson and Miss Heap were dauntless, and you would not have surmised that they never had a week when their morning coffee was assured, or that it was not unusual for them to live for three days at a time on biscuits because they had no money for other food.

In their apartment, in an old house on Sixteenth Street just west of Fifth Avenue, you heard the best talk to be had in New York, and sometimes the most exciting music also, for Miss Anderson was a talented pianist, and the *Little Review* circle included advance-guard musicians as well as writers and painters. The large living room in Sixteenth Street, with its gold-papered walls and old mahogany furniture and blue divan swung from the ceiling on heavy black chains, was an oasis for creative minds, and there you were likely to meet young writers whose work was blazing new trails for their contemporaries: the brilliant, unhappy poet Hart Crane; tall, slim, auburn-haired Djuna Barnes, an innovator in both verse and prose; the poet Lola Ridge. Presently, however, *The Little Review* was suppressed, and Miss Anderson and Miss Heap transferred it to the more favorable climate of

Paris. Another magazine thereafter maintained the Village's repute as a citadel of culture. Generously subsidized, and domiciled on West Thirteenth Street, *The Dial* became the accredited champion of the advance guard. Its roster of contributors included many eminent European writers and artists. But it also published the early work of some Americans identified with the Village either by residence or affiliation; among them, Marianne Moore, Glenway Wescott and William Carlos Williams.

THE VICIOUS CIRCLE

MARGARET CASE HARRIMAN

One day in 1919, just after World War I ended, two rotund young men entered the Algonquin Hotel on West 44th Street in quest of angel cake. The tall, serene gentleman was a theatrical press agent named John Peter Toohey; the short, explosive one was Alexander Woollcott, then drama critic of *The New York Times*. Toohey had earlier discovered the wares of Sarah Victor, the Algonquin's pastry cook, and knowing his friend Woollcott's sweet tooth, had brought him there for lunch.

The cozy combination of critic lunching with press agent was to become a familiar one around the Algonquin, and was to lead to some lively accusations of "log-rolling" from certain jaundiced observers; but all that came later. On this particular day, it is safe to say that Woollcott and Toohey had nothing on their minds more sinister than cake.

Seated at a table for two, Woollcott focused his revolving stare upon the room. He was then thirty-two years old and already a striking combination of hero-worshipper and Madame De Farge. On this, his first visit to the Algonquin, his roving appraisal found food for speculation as rich as Sarah's cake. As on most days at the luncheon hour, there was Ethel Barrymore sitting at a corner table, perhaps with her brother Jack or her uncle, John Drew. At other tables were Laurette Taylor, Jane Cowl, Elsie Janis, Rex Beach, Commander Evangeline Booth of the Salvation Army, Irvin S. Cobb, Ann Pennington, Constance Collier . . . all the stimulating array of people that had already made the hotel famous. Woollcott's starry-eyed gaze sharpened into the knitting-needles of Madame De Farge only when it encountered the two columnists in the room, O. O. McIntyre and S. Jay Kaufman. McIntyre was gently dismissed as a kindly old corn-fed writing slob by Woollcott's generation of newspaper men, but they really hated S. Jay Kaufman, a more debonair type who ran a column in the *Telegram* called "Around the Town." No one now knows the exact reason for this dislike. Some say that the boys considered Kaufman's city-slicker airs a little too grand and glossy, a touch pretentious; others trace the distaste to the fact that S. Jay once referred in his column to their pal, Marc Connelly, as "poor Marc" after a play of his had failed, and they found this sympathy patronizing. At any rate, their disinclination for Mr. Kaufman is notable because it was a feature of the first gag to be pulled off by the Algonquin Round Table as a group, at what might be called its first luncheon.

It is hard to say just when the first luncheon of the Round Table took place, or just which *was* its first luncheon. Like any other group which meets mainly for companionship, with no formal organization, no by-laws, and no dues, it came into being gradually. Many of its members—Bob Benchley, Brock and Murdock Pemberton, Toohey, Heywood Broun—had lunched at the Algonquin singly or together for some years before there was a Round Table. Franklin P. Adams, one of its oldest patrons, had originally gone there to call on his friend Samuel Merwin, the novelist. Adams, Woollcott, and Harold Ross had known one another during the war in France where they were all attached to the A.E.F. and to the staff of *The Stars and Stripes;* as F.P.A., a former captain, wrote in his "Diary of Our Own Samuel Pepys" in 1926, "To my office, and remembered that nine years ago this day we had declared war against Germany, and if it had not been for that, methought, Private Harold Ross never would have carried my gripsacks through the streets of Paris, and called me 'Sir.'"

None of these men ever said to another, "Hey! Let's start a regular lunch-group at the Algonquin and call it the Round Table." Nobody ever said anything like that. The whole thing just bloomed as slowly and pleasantly as any June moon, so it's difficult to pin down its moment of inception. Perhaps it was Toohey's introduction of Alex Woollcott to the angel cake. But more probably it was the occasion of Toohey's next lunch with Woollcott a few weeks later, in company with Heywood Broun, the Pembertons, Laurence Stallings (who was yet to write *What Price Glory?*), Deems Taylor, Art Samuels (then editor of *Harper's Bazaar*), Adams, and Bill Murray, a music critic on the *Brooklyn Eagle* who was later to become an ex-husband of Ilka Chase and one of the heads of the William Morris Agency.

This luncheon was a Welcome-Home to Woollcott from the Wars, tendered by the above long-suffering friends who had been listening to him tell about his experiences ever since his return from France some months earlier. "From my seat in the theater of War . . ." he would begin, taking a long breath, this introduction once goading Bill Murray into muttering, "Seat 13, Row Q, no doubt?" Fresh from a Woollcott recital at lunch one day, Murdock Pemberton and Murray repaired to the Hippodrome across the street, where Murdock, the Hippodrome's press agent, had his office. There they set a covey of stenographers to typing out announcements of a great rally at the Algonquin in honor of Woollcott the Warrior, hopefully designed to shut him up for a while. Knowing Woollcott's extreme touchiness about the correct spelling of his name (three o's, two l's, two t's, *if* you please), they laboriously spelled it wrong in all possible ways throughout the announcement—Wolcot, Woolcot, Wolcott, and Woolcoot. Having mailed this document to all their friends, and Woollcott's, they got the Hippodrome's wardrobe department to make a huge red felt flag, lettered in gold as follows:

A W O L
cot

and, conscious of his aversion to S. Jay Kaufman, the man-about-town columnist, they thoughtfully added:

S. Jay Kaufman Post No. 1

This banner, on the appointed day, they hung over the luncheon table in the Algonquin. It was a table in the dining room now called the Oak Room, but then known as the Pergola and economically decorated with murals of the Bay of Naples along one wall and mirrors along the other, so that you saw the Bay of Naples twice for the cost of one mural. All the invited guests turned up, and the luncheon was such a success—although it never achieved its aim of stifling Woollcott—that somebody said, "Why don't we do this every day?" According to most people's recollection, it was Toohey who said it. As far as anyone knows, the Round Table was born then and there.

At first the group had no name, and it didn't meet at a round table. After some months at a long table in the Pergola, it moved to another long table in the Rose Room, up front near the door. As more people kept coming, they overflowed into the aisles and upon adjoining tables; so my father, Frank Case (who operated but did not yet own the hotel), had Georges, the headwaiter, move them for greater comfort to a large round table in the center of the room, toward the rear. This was the table they made famous. Father, who liked them individually and loved faithfulness in anyone, gave them one or two extra little attentions—free olives and celery and popovers, and their own pet waiter named Luigi. The nearest the group had come to a name was when certain members referred to it lightly as The Board, and to the luncheons as Board-Meetings. With the regular appearance of Luigi it was no time at all, of course, before they took to calling the table the Luigi-Board.

Their own favorite name for themselves soon became The Vicious Circle; but as the members grew in prominence and achievement, and began entertaining even more famous people at lunch, other guests in the Rose Room fell to pointing them out to their own guests: "There's Mrs. Fiske over there, between Woollcott and Benchley at that round table," or, "That's Arnold Bennett sitting over there next to Heywood Broun, at the round table." Columnists and out-of-towners would drop in to ask Georges, "Who's at the round table today?" About 1920, a cartoonist named Duffy on the *Brooklyn Eagle* published what was probably the first caricature of the group, seated at a luncheon table which he called the Algonquin Round Table. Soon newspaper columns began featuring quips and other items that originated at the Algonquin Round Table. Although other tables in the Rose Room still had their own smaller groups of celebrities, these were altered from day to day, so that the unchanging circle in the center became the focal point.

The Round Table became a focal point, too, to the people who lunched at it. They were hard-working young men and women who led busy and scattered lives; but they were a group close-knit by common tastes, common standards, and the same kind of humor, and they enjoyed one another's company better than anybody else's in the world. At the Round Table they were sure to find it, at least once a day, and they gravitated to it like skiers to a fireside.

The charter members of the Round Table were Franklin P. Adams, Deems Taylor, George S. Kaufman, Marc Connelly, Robert Benchley, Harold Ross, Heywood Broun, Art Samuels, Alexander Woollcott, John Peter Toohey, the Pembertons, Bill Murray, Robert E. Sherwood, John V. A. Weaver, Laurence Stallings, and a couple of theatrical press agents named David Wallace and Herman J. Mankiewicz; and, on the distaff side, Dorothy Parker, Jane Grant, Ruth Hale, Beatrice Kaufman, Peggy Wood, Peggy Leech, Margalo Gillmore, Edna Ferber, and Neysa McMein. F.P.A. was generally considered the dean of the group since he was, in 1920, one of its few solvent members, with a steady job and a large reading public. His column, "The Conning Tower," ran in the New York *Tribune,* and a good part of his fellow-lunchers' waking thoughts were devoted to trying to write something good enough to "land" in it. Once a year Adams gave a dinner and a gold watch to the contributor who had landed the greatest number of verses or bits of prose in the column during the year, and one year the proud winner of this award was Deems Taylor, then music critic of the New York *World,* who contributed under the name of "Smeed." When somebody once asked Adams why he gave a prize for the *most* contributions, and not for the best single one, he threw back his head and closed his eyes in his familiar gesture of thought, and intoned, "There is no such thing as the 'best' contribution. The fact that any contribution is accepted by me means that it is peerless."

Another constant, and fairly peerless, contributor to the "Conning Tower" in the days when the Round Table started was "G.S.K.," or George S. Kaufman. Kaufman was drama editor of *The New York Times*—a job he held onto long after his plays were successful—but in 1920 he was known as a playwright only as co-author, with two men named Evans and Percival, of a majestic failure called *Someone in the House*. The only thing that anyone now remembers about *Someone in the House* (aside from the inevitable cracks about there being no one in the house where it was playing) is that Kaufman, during the influenza epidemic in New York when the health authorities urged people to stay away from crowds, sent out an urgent behest to all New Yorkers to hurry to the theater where *Someone in the House* was on view. "Only place in town you can be absolutely safe from a crowd," he pointed out.

Marc Connelly, with whom Kaufman was to write *Dulcy, Merton of the Movies,* and many other hits, was a newspaper reporter from Pittsburgh who also had written a play. It was *The Amber Empress;* and if anybody asks Marc about it now, he just says, "Oh, God. But, you know—I kind of *liked* that show."

None of the charter members of the Round Table was much more of a celebrity than Kaufman and Connelly, in fact, when Duffy published his cartoon in 1920. Broun was a sportswriter on the *Tribune,* Laurence Stallings a reporter from the *Atlanta Journal* who had lost a leg in the war, but was a long way from writing *What Price Glory?* or even from Maxwell Anderson, who was then an editorial writer for the *World*. Harold Ross was editor of the *American Legion Weekly*, and known mainly for his crew-cut, which, measured one day by a friend in a statistical mood, proved to be an inch and a half high. Johnny Weaver had not yet written *In American*, the poems that were to make him famous, and Brock Pemberton was an assistant producer to Arthur Hopkins.

The girls at the Round Table were doing a little better than the men, in 1920. Edna Ferber had already written *Dawn O'Hara* and the Emma McChesney stories, Peggy Wood was making a hit in musical comedies like *Pomander Walk* and *Sweethearts*. Jane Grant, a *Times* reporter who later married Harold Ross, and Ruth Hale, a Selwyn press agent who married Heywood Broun, had made good in jobs that were not usually open to women in 1920; and they had, besides, made so much noise about Votes for Women that they were instrumental in getting the Woman Suffrage Act passed in that year. In contrast to these militant gals there was Neysa McMein, the ultra-feminine, the siren, who painted magazine covers and illustrations and had begun to be successful, in a softer way, in 1920. There were Peggy ("Peaches-and-Cream") Leech, who wanted to be a writer, Margalo ("The Baby of the Round Table") Gillmore, who wanted to be an actress, and Beatrice Kaufman, who just wanted to lunch with her husband, George. In order to be eligible to the Round Table as a professional worker, Bea took a job as reader for Horace Liveright, the publisher, a man so generally disliked that the Round Table hated him even ahead of S. Jay Kaufman. For some time Liveright, a daily luncher at the Algonquin, had to watch his employee, Mrs. Kaufman, slip into her accustomed seat at the Round Table—which he was never asked to join. One day he spoke to Mrs. Kaufman about it in his office.

"Look here," he said, "those kids at what you call the Round Table are starving to death. I could *publish* them."

Bea looked at him. "Do you think so?" she said.

The three glossiest members of the group were Bob Benchley, Bob Sherwood, and Dorothy Parker—not because they were any more prosperous than the others, but because they all worked on *Vanity Fair*, as managing editor, drama editor, and drama critic respectively. There was great prestige in working for *Vanity Fair* in those days, if not much money. What presently happened to these three proved that the Round Table friends, although they could—and later did—bicker and even quarrel violently among themselves—had an unswerving loyalty to one another in time of trouble.

In 1920 Dorothy Parker reviewed in *Vanity Fair* a Maugham play called *Caesar's Wife*, starring Billie Burke. "Miss Burke," wrote Mrs. Parker, "is at her best in her more serious moments; in her desire to convey the girlishness of the character, she plays her lighter scenes rather as if she were giving an impersonation of Eva Tanguay." When this tribute appeared on the newsstands, Florenz Ziegfeld threatened to tear the offices of *Vanity Fair* apart, and what was more drastic, to remove his advertising from all Condé Nast publications unless Mrs. Parker were fired. Mrs. Parker was fired. Without a moment's hesitation her friends Benchley and Sherwood quit, too, in sympathy and protest, and all three repaired to lunch at the Round Table, where they calmly announced their unemployment. Everyone at the table applauded the Benchley-Sherwood gesture, but took it, as they themselves did, as a matter of course; injustice had been done and a pal roughly treated—what else could anyone do but string along with her?

Such loyalty meant a real sacrifice to Benchley and Sherwood at that time. They had no money to speak of, and no other jobs, and neither had yet had much success in selling his own stuff. Sherwood, before long, got a job as an associate editor on the old *Life;* but Benchley and Mrs. Parker, disdaining the career of wage-slaves, rented an "office" in the loft building over the Metropolitan Opera House and set up joint shop as free-lance writers. Little work got done in this *atelier*, mainly because of their habit of subscribing to undertakers' trade journals and other hilarious publications, and whiling away the mornings reading them until it was time to go up to the Algonquin for lunch. They nearly always found the money for a taxi, especially for open cabs in fine weather, and on at least one Spring day enlivened the journey by Dottie's leaping to her feet and shrieking wildly to passers-by, "Help! Help! This man is abducting me!" while Benchley whipped off his scarf and proceeded to gag her with it.

After some months of free-lancing, Benchley gave in to financial pressure and took a job as drama editor on *Life*, but Mrs. Parker announced that she would stay on alone in the office over the "Met" and get some real work done.

Dottie Parker was then—and is still—a little dark-haired woman with bangs and an almost overpowering air of dulcet femininity. She was married to Edwin Parker, a young insurance man generally liked but seldom seen. She wore bows on her shoes, spoke in muted tones, and had a way of resting a hand confidingly on yours when she talked to you. From this honeyed exterior, like the bee-sting from the rose-petal, regularly issued, of course, a gunfire of devastating cracks. One day another lady writer, pausing at the Round Table (although not invited to sit down), was congratulating herself at some length on the success of her marriage and the virtues of her husband, whom the Round Table privately considered a rather dull fellow.

"I've kept him these seven years!" crowed this happy matron complacently.

"Don't worry," cooed Dottie, "if you keep him long enough he'll come back in style."

Dottie's barbs were never pointedly directed toward outsiders in those days, however; she was as happy in making herself ridiculous as in making the next one. Toward the end of lunch that same day she said, "Excuse me, everybody, I have to go to the bathroom." Halfway out of her chair, she added, "I really have to telephone, but I'm too embarrassed to say so."

A wave of easy laughter followed her as she left. The Round Table wasn't trying to impress anybody in those days, and the members had no thought of treasuring remarks for the anthologies.

Talk at the Round Table was mostly like that in 1920—easy, unrehearsed, and full of unexpected pleasures. It took Herman J. Mankiewicz, the press agent (now a gold-plated Hollywood producer), to put his finger on the bitter fact that none of this fun was bringing in any money. Mank watched his friends leaving the Algonquin one day after lunch: Benchley, Sherwood, Parker, Ross, Kaufman, Connelly, Broun, Stallings, and so on. Mank shook his head sadly.

"There," he said to Murdock Pemberton, "goes the greatest collection of unsaleable wit in America."

The question that most people of this generation ask about the Round Table is, "Why was it important?" That's a hard question to answer. Almost anybody can explain the Golden Age in Elizabethan England or the Renaissance in Italy; they are far away and history has sharpened the perspective. People can also explain the 1929 stock market crash and the 1930s' depression. These are closer to home, and besides, disasters are always easier to analyze than blessings; everybody has an explanation for a disaster, but nobody can explain a miracle . . . or a renaissance that has taken place under his own eyes.

The Round Table symbolized an American Renaissance, I think

(although any member of it would probably have pulled a knife on me for suggesting anything so highfalutin'). Its influence on American literature, drama, and humor was acute, untiring, and permanent for two reasons. First, the people who sat at the Round Table were interesting people whose doings and sayings caught and held public attention; second, they were as brave mentally as any dashing medieval cavalier was physically brave. They not only encouraged everything that was shining good; they were ready, at the risk of losing jobs, money, or friends, to fight to the death against anything that was, according to their standards, bad.

They had a good deal to fight against, in the early 1920's. The postwar intellectual level was low. People were reading *The Sheik* and crowding in by the thousands to see Miss Ann Nichols' masterpiece, the play called *Abie's Irish Rose*. The Round Tablers shrugged at *The Sheik*, but the theater was in their hearts and they winced away from *Abie's Irish Rose* in loud bursts of print throughout the play's six-year run. Benchley in particular doggedly ran his own little wailing-wall of comment about it every week in *Life's* play directory. But not all of Benchley's crusades were so light-hearted. During the famous Sacco-Vanzetti case he had been one of the witnesses who came forth hotly to testify that he had heard the trial judge, Webster Thayer, speak improperly of the defendants outside of court. "I'll get the bastards good and proper," Judge Thayer declared one day in a Worcester, Mass., golf club, according to Benchley.

The entire Round Table rose up in arms to protest the arrest and conviction of Sacco and Vanzetti, as indeed did thousands of other people in Europe and America. The case was a *cause célèbre* of the 'twenties. As many of us remember, Sacco and Vanzetti were a Boston shoemaker and fishmonger who were tried, sentenced, and—after seven years in jail—finally electrocuted for the killing of a paymaster in a holdup. The two men were members of the Anarchist party, and their defenders felt a deep conviction that not only were they innocent and the charge a frame-up, but they had been convicted for their political beliefs.

The nearest thing to an anarchist at the Round Table was Heywood Broun, who was a socialist, and what fired the group with a burning sense of injustice was not sympathy with the politics of Sacco and Vanzetti, but an unshakable belief in the sacred right of any man to embrace whatever politics he desired. (It was simpler in those days, before the atom and hydrogen bombs.) With one accord the Round

Tablers—notably Benchley, Dorothy Parker, Heywood Broun, and his wife, Ruth Hale—shouldered their banners and marched off to Boston to help organize the Sacco-Vanzetti Defense Committee.

When all appeals failed and Sacco and Vanzetti were executed, in 1927, Broun wrote: "They are too bright, we shield our eyes and kill them. We are the dead, and in us there is no feeling nor imagination nor the terrible torment of lust for justice. And in the city where we sleep smug gardeners walk to keep the grass above our little houses sleek and cut whatever blade thrusts up a head above its fellows." The *World* (to which Broun had gone in 1921) printed this column, and a second one the following day—it then proceeded to omit the next four, explaining in a box on Page Op. Ed. that Broun had ignored instructions to select other topics than Sacco and Vanzetti and that the editors maintained their right of final decision as to what would be published in their columns. Broun sent a telegram from Connecticut saying he was on strike. He stayed away for four-and-a-half months until Herbert Bayard Swope, returning from Europe, patched up a kind of peace and wooed Heywood back onto Page Op. Ed. All might have been well had not Broun, another four months later, written a piece in *The Nation* proclaiming the need for a great liberal newspaper—one that could venture into "the vast territory which lies between the radical press and the New York *World*." He accused the *World* of lacking courage, tenacity, and guts, and of being—along with the rest of the press—terrified of the Catholic Church. "There is not a single New York editor," he wrote, "who does not live in mortal terror of the power of this group. Of course, if anybody dared, nothing in the world would happen. If the church can bluff its way into a preferred position, the fault lies not with the Catholic Church but with the editors. . . . Perhaps the first thing needed for a liberal paper is capital, but even more important is courage."

That did it. Next day, in place of Broun's column on Page Op. Ed., this notice appeared: "The *World* has decided to dispense with the services of Heywood Broun. His disloyalty to this paper makes any further association impossible." As usual with Broun, the knight had tangled with the dragon and got slightly scorched. Broun didn't know he was fired until he saw the announcement.

Broun never worked on one crusade at a time—he always had half a dozen going. In his years on the *Tribune*, the *World*, and later the *Telegram* and *World-Telegram*, he was consistently and passionately against censorship, bad manners on the dance floor (to the extent of getting in fist fights on the dance floor with anyone who practiced them), John Roach Straton, Nicholas Murray Butler, badly written books, badly written plays, and using dirty words in the presence of ladies. He was *for* a free press, courteous behavior at all times, Eugene V. Debs, Sacco and Vanzetti, good books, good plays, and the use of four-letter words in literature if they improved the quality of the work. Like the rest of the Round Tablers, he would go to bat instantly for anything he thought was good, and he once wrote a review of John Dos Passos' *Three Soldiers* and twisted the arm of the Sunday *Times* Book Supplement (which had already published one review) until they published it on Page One, because the first review had been unfavorable and Broun thought the book deserved better.

Nobody at the Round Table was ever alone in any crusade, the sympathies being too close and infectious, and Broun was never alone in his. He and Aleck Woollcott, for example, joined up to demand—in their columns and, later, in their radio broadcasts—an audience for Ernest Hemingway, Floyd Dell, John V. A. Weaver, F. Scott Fitzgerald, and many other new writers. Publishers will tell you now that Broun and Woollcott, individually or together, could sell more books than any critics and commentators had ever sold before, or—with the possible exception of Walter Winchell—have ever been able to sell since.

Woollcott, too, was a passionate crusader, although not built for it. (It was a fellow critic, G. J. Nathan, who likened him, during his intense moments, to a butterfly in heat.) Besides, nobody could even be sure just what Woollcott would be crusading for *next*. He could, and did, shout as loud in praise of *Good-Bye, Mr. Chips* as in acknowledgment of *The Sun Also Rises*. Often, becoming nostalgic, he wrote so fulsomely in favor of *Little Women* that the Round Table declared, to a man, that by God, he was likely to put that book over sooner or later. Howard Dietz, a frequent member of the group, even took to calling him "Louisa M. Woollcott." But Woollcott's voice was powerful and his intentions honest, and that was true of many other members of the Round Table as well.

F.P.A., for example—whenever he wasn't fussing away at imperfect prose wherever he met it—waged a campaign in his column against illegible or obscure house numbers in New York. Pity the poor delivery man, he wrote again and again. He also inveighed in print against householders who swept their sidewalks with a dry broom, wafting germs to the nose of the passerby. He pointed out that city ordinances already forbade these evils, and that the city ordinances were ignored. When his frequent reproaches in "The Conning Tower" brought no results from the authorities, Adams started a department in his column headed "Nothing Will Ever Happen." This section was concerned with civic annoyances such as illegible house numbers and dry sweeping, and it also carried a repeated plea which strikes even more poignantly now at the hearts of 1950 New Yorkers . . . that theater managers and ticket brokers get together and stop gouging the public on the price of theater tickets. The fact that theater tickets, in the 'twenties, cost a fast $3.30 top for most shows, with a broker's fee of 50 cents, was not the point; a principle was involved, and Adams' gauntlet was ready.

Adams, today, says that his campaigns got nowhere. "I said nothing would happen, and nothing *did* happen," he reminds you, with the mournful ferocity that is his usual tone. But failure never discouraged a Round Tabler for long.

When the members of the Vicious Circle were not crusading about something outside their particular fields, their own work amounted to a crusade against everything that was phony, pretentious, or untrue, and moreover it established a standard of excellence that turned out to be enduring. Benchley was probably the first satirist to proclaim, with a kind of comic despair, the fallibility of 20th Century Man; and Donald Ogden Stewart, who often lunched with the group, was among the first to debunk social climbers, in *Mr. and Mrs. Haddock Abroad*. Frank Sullivan, another frequent luncher, loved to prick the balloons of pretentiousness, as he still does in his "Cliché Expert" pieces. Dorothy Parker's poems crisply put love and infatuation where they separately belonged (a thing Mrs. Parker seemed personally unable to do). And Edna Ferber, although no satirist, was also a pioneer; with the able assistance of Jerome Kern and others, *Showboat*, the musical adapted from her novel, surely helped create the modern operetta, or *good* play with music, which was to banish forever the old-fashioned, loosely-strung True Story Romance interspersed with songs and dances.

Perhaps those boys and girls accomplished no more than any gifted and active individual accomplishes in these days. The point is that those gifted and active individuals were all members of the same group, and that this group was merely a casual, unorganized gathering of friends who met at the Round Table for no more serious purpose than their enjoyment of one another.

One thing is certain: nothing like the Round Table—for color, interest, and lasting influence—had ever been seen before; and nothing like it has been known since.

DON JUAN IN NEW YORK

BEN HECHT

1920'S

There were many curiosities in New York. Nearly all the "Radicals" I met were extremely rich. Its poets were ambitious and worldly fellows. Its finest ladies, including happily married ones, engaged in promiscuous sex as if they were college boys on a spree. Conversation consisted mostly of offering clever insults to your fellow guests. Every other celebrity was being either psychoanalyzed or having his glands tinkered with. You never had to pick up a check in the expensive restaurants. There was always a millionaire in the group waiting to assert himself by seizing the bill.

But these were minor oddities, along with the strange odor of streets and the Turkish-bath smells of the subway, to which I became quickly accustomed. There were other strange matters, however, which continued to keep me wondering. One of these was a new type of male fornicator whom I had met nowhere before. They were men who made seduction their chief activity.

I had known lusty fellows in Chicago, including our local Charlemagne—the immortal Harry C.—who had futtered twenty-five whores in a single night in Minnie Shima's House of All Nations. Reliable newspapermen had kept the score. Bawdiness, in fact, had been a natural atmosphere since boyhood. But in Chicago I had come on no Don Juans. In New York they appeared to be blocking traffic.

As a psychologist I was pleased, for these were the first men I had known who were eager to relate the ins and outs of amour to me. I was introduced conversationally into dozens of interesting bedrooms and given play-by-play accounts of sexual maneuvers. I was privileged, also, to watch the Don Juan at his preliminary chores, for he was a fellow who craved publicity with his courtships. I wondered which was more the object of his desires—the woman he cooed to bed or the men before whom he performed most of his amorous rites.

I needed no help from Freud to understand this Eastern fornicator.

He wooed his quarry with a sort of female silliness. He talked as women did, giggled like them, was ruthless and snippy as are flirtatious girls. He was full of a feminine talent for dancing, gossiping, cooking, giving parties, overdressing and idling. He was able to flit from one pair of thighs to another with no sense of proprietorship and a minimum of romance.

Listening to the Don Juan's bedroom anecdotes, I sometimes thought my informants were lying their heads off. How was it possible for a man to meet a famous actress at lunch and have her undressed in his bed by four o'clock? And how could you cohabit with a ballerina in a taxicab, or seduce your hostess with her husband playing backgammon in the next room? Such speed and hazards would have nipped romance for me. But I learned that, for the most part, the Don Juans did not lie. They told all the truth they knew.

The fact that I had never discussed a woman I knew with any man made this spate of confession doubly surprising. I became aware that my appeal to the Don Juan was a fatherly one. Despite my youth (I was usually a good ten years younger than my confidant), I appeared to offer a sort of fatherhood to lean on. I hesitate to say motherhood. If it was "mama" rather than "papa" to whom they brought their problems, the shoe was on their foot, not mine.

I discussed this "new" gentry with Liveright, who was one of them. He pursued women as openly as a small boy running down the street after a fire engine—and this, despite the fact that he was greatly devoted to his wife. In fact, most of the Don Juans I met were doting husbands, and a half of their confessions was concerned with how terrified they were of bringing pain to their spouses.

"I'd die if she ever found me out," Horace used to say a little sadly of his mate. "She's the most wonderful and sensitive woman in the world."

He had a long-nosed, eighteenth-century face. It was a masklike face that became alive only when a smile lit it or drunkenness elated it.

"What fun is there in laying a woman you hardly know?" I asked.

"You use crude words," said Horace. "One doesn't lay a woman. One loves her."

"A stranger?"

"No woman is a stranger," said Horace. "I mean that a beautiful woman is somebody you know with one look. You know she's meant to be loved—and expects it. Not to make love to a beautiful woman is to insult her. And yourself, too. It's like refusing a challenge."

One night in Long Island we were guests at Otto Kahn's country estate. I had retired at one A.M., leaving Horace in deep talk with a young woman he had met that afternoon. I was unable to sleep, for the deep talk continued in a grotto under my window. At four A.M., irritated by the Liveright phrases that kept floating into the magnificent guest room, I walked into the night. It was raining.

Soaked to the skin, Horace was still bombinating in the grotto. As I approached, I heard him saying, "God, it's wonderful to be real! I'm glad we stayed out, because I can see you now, as you really are."

I interrupted. Pulling Horace around a Kahn castle buttress, I pointed out he would get pneumonia if he stayed out in the rain all night, particularly since he was not an outdoor type.

"The girl is obviously mad about you," I said, "so why the hell don't you bring her in the house?"

"I can't," said Horace. "If I go in the house I'll have to take her to bed. And I'm impotent."

"How do you know you're impotent?"

"I always know when one of these impotent spells hits me," said Horace. "Always the same symptoms. An apprehension, a fluttering in the lower bowel region and a dryness of the mouth. She'll be sleepy in an hour or so. So kindly beat it and let a lack of nature take its course."

Though he seemed to do nothing but pursue women and drink himself into nightly comas, Liveright was actually a hard worker and a brilliant one. He published scores of fine books and produced a number of successful plays. He loaned courage and money to many fumbling talents. He fought ably against censorship and was one of the chief forces that freed the literature of the Republic from the strangle hold of its old maids. He launched the Modern Library—the first introduction to the larger public of the world's fine writing. There was in New York no more popular and exciting figure than Liveright. Beauty, success and admiration attended him like a faithful retinue, and hundreds of hangers-on were proud to boast of his friendship.

I was in Hollywood some ten years later when Beatrice Kaufman, who had once worked as a reader in the Liveright firm, telephoned with the news that Horace was dead. He had died broke and full of debts.

"I wonder if you could come to his funeral," Beatrice said. "I've been on the phone all day. So far I've only gotten six people to agree to come."

I was unable to leave Hollywood. On a drizzly day, Beatrice Kaufman and five other New Yorkers accompanied the forgotten pauper, Horace Liveright, to his grave.

WHEN THE NEGRO WAS IN VOGUE

LANGSTON HUGHES

The 1920's were the years of Manhattan's black Renaissance. It began with *Shuffle Along*, *Running Wild*, and the Charleston. Perhaps some people would say even with *The Emperor Jones*, Charles Gilpin, and the tom-toms at the Provincetown. But certainly it was the musical revue, *Shuffle Along*, that gave a scintillating send-off to that Negro vogue in Manhattan, which reached its peak just before the crash of 1929, the crash that sent Negroes, white folks, and all rolling down the hill toward the Works Progress Administration.

Shuffle Along was a honey of a show. Swift, bright, funny, rollicking, and gay, with a dozen danceable, singable tunes. Besides, look who were in it: The now famous choir director, Hall Johnson, and the composer, William Grant Still, were a part of the orchestra. Eubie Blake and Noble Sissle wrote the music and played and acted in the show. Miller and Lyles were the comics. Florence Mills skyrocketed to fame in the second act. Trixie Smith sang "He May Be Your Man But He Comes to See Me Sometimes." And Caterina Jarboro, now a European prima donna, and the internationally celebrated Josephine Baker were merely in the chorus. Everybody was in the audience—including me. People came back to see it innumerable times. It was always packed.

To see *Shuffle Along* was the main reason I wanted to go to Columbia. When I saw it, I was thrilled and delighted. From then on I was in the gallery of the Cort Theatre every time I got a chance. That year, too, I saw Katharine Cornell in *A Bill of Divorcement*, Margaret Wycherly in *The Verge*, Maugham's *The Circle* with Mrs. Leslie Carter, and the Theatre Guild production of Kaiser's *From Morn Till Midnight*. But I remember *Shuffle Along* best of all. It gave just the proper push—a pre-Charleston kick—to that Negro vogue of the 20's, that spread to books, African sculpture, music, and dancing.

Put down the 1920's for the rise of Roland Hayes, who packed

Copyright, 1940, by Alfred A. Knopf, Inc.

Carnegie Hall, the rise of Paul Robeson in New York and London, of Florence Mills over two continents, of Rose McClendon in Broadway parts that never measured up to her, the booming voice of Bessie Smith and the low moan of Clara on thousands of records, and the rise of that grand comedienne of song, Ethel Waters, singing: "Charlie's elected now! He's in right for sure!" Put down the 1920's for Louis Armstrong and Gladys Bentley and Josephine Baker.

White people began to come to Harlem in droves. For several years they packed the expensive Cotton Club on Lenox Avenue. But I was never there, because the Cotton Club was a Jim Crow club for gangsters and monied whites. They were not cordial to Negro patronage, unless you were a celebrity like Bojangles. So Harlem Negroes did not like the Cotton Club and never appreciated its Jim Crow policy in the very heart of their dark community. Nor did ordinary Negroes like the growing influx of whites toward Harlem after sundown, flooding the little cabarets and bars where formerly only colored people laughed and sang, and where now the strangers were given the best ringside tables to sit and stare at the Negro customers—like amusing animals in a zoo.

The Negroes said: "We can't go downtown and sit and stare at you in your clubs. You won't even let us in your clubs." But they didn't say it out loud—for Negroes are practically never rude to white people. So thousands of whites came to Harlem night after night, thinking the Negroes loved to have them there, and firmly believing that all Harlemites left their houses at sundown to sing and dance in cabarets, because most of the whites saw nothing but the cabarets, not the houses.

Some of the owners of Harlem clubs, delighted at the flood of white patronage, made the grievous error of barring their own race, after the manner of the famous Cotton Club. But most of these quickly lost business and folded up, because they failed to realize that a large part of the Harlem attraction for downtown New Yorkers lay in simply watching the colored customers amuse themselves. And the smaller clubs, of course, had no big floor shows or a name band like the Cotton Club, where Duke Ellington usually held forth, so, without black patronage, they were not amusing at all.

Some of the small clubs, however, had people like Gladys Bentley, who was something worth discovering in those days, before she got famous, acquired an accompanist, specially written material, and conscious vulgarity. But for two or three amazing years, Miss Bentley sat, and played a big piano all night long, literally all night, without stopping—singing songs like "The St. James Infirmary," from ten in the evening until dawn, with scarcely a break between the notes, sliding from one song to another, with a powerful and continuous underbeat of jungle rhythm. Miss Bentley was an amazing exhibition of musical energy—a large, dark, masculine lady, whose feet pounded the floor while her fingers pounded the keyboard—a perfect piece of African sculpture, animated by her own rhythm.

But when the place where she played became too well known, she began to sing with an accompanist, became a star, moved to a larger place, then downtown, and is now in Hollywood. The old magic of the woman and the piano and the night and the rhythm being one is gone. But everything goes, one way or another. The '20's are gone and lots of fine things in Harlem night life have disappeared like snow in the sun—since it became utterly commercial, planned for the downtown tourist trade, and therefore dull.

The lindy-hoppers at the Savoy even began to practise acrobatic routines, and to do absurd things for the entertainment of the whites, that probably never would have entered their heads to attempt merely for their own effortless amusement. Some of the lindy-hoppers had cards printed with their names on them and became dance professors teaching the tourists. Then Harlem nights became show nights for the Nordics.

Some critics say that is what happened to certain Negro writers, too —that they ceased to write to amuse themselves and began to write to amuse and entertain white people, and in so doing distorted and over-colored their material, and left out a great many things they thought would offend their American brothers of a lighter complexion. Maybe —since Negroes have writer-racketeers, as has any other race. But I have known almost all of them, and most of the good ones have tried to be honest, write honestly, and express their world as they saw it.

All of us know that the gay and sparkling life of the so-called Negro Renaissance of the '20's was not so gay and sparkling beneath the surface as it looked. Carl Van Vechten, in the character of Byron in *Nigger Heaven*, captured some of the bitterness and frustration of literary Harlem that Wallace Thurman later so effectively poured into his *Infants of the Spring*—the only novel by a Negro about that fantastic period when Harlem was in vogue.

It was a period when, at almost every Harlem upper-crust dance or party, one would be introduced to various distinguished white celebrities there as guests. It was a period when almost any Harlem Negro of any social importance at all would be likely to say casually: "As I was remarking the other day to Heywood—," meaning Heywood Broun. Or: "As I said to George—," referring to George Gershwin. It was a period when local and visiting royalty were not at all uncommon in Harlem. And when the parties of A'Lelia Walker, the Negro heiress, were filled with guests whose names would turn any Nordic social climber green with envy. It was a period when Harold Jackman, a handsome young Harlem school teacher of modest means, calmly announced one day that he was sailing for the Riviera for a fortnight, to attend Princess Murat's yachting party. It was a period when Charleston preachers opened up shouting churches as sideshows for white tourists. It was a period when at least one charming colored chorus girl, amber enough to pass for a Latin American, was living in a pent house, with all her bills paid by a gentleman whose name was banker's magic on Wall Street. It was a period when every season there was at least one hit play on Broadway acted by a Negro cast. And when books by Negro authors were being published with much greater frequency and much more publicity than ever before or since in history. It was a period when white writers wrote about Negroes more successfully (commercially speaking) than Negroes did about themselves. It was the period (God help us!) when Ethel Barrymore appeared in blackface in *Scarlet Sister Mary!* It was the period when the Negro was in vogue.

I was there. I had a swell time while it lasted. But I thought it wouldn't last long. (I remember the vogue for things Russian, the season the Chauve-Souris first came to town.) For how could a large and enthusiastic number of people be crazy about Negroes forever? But some Harlemites thought the millennium had come. They thought the race problem had at last been solved through Art plus Gladys Bentley. They were sure the New Negro would lead a new life from then on in green pastures of tolerance created by Countee Cullen, Ethel Waters, Claude McKay, Duke Ellington, Bojangles, and Alain Locke.

I don't know what made any Negroes think that—except that they were mostly intellectuals doing the thinking. The ordinary Negroes hadn't heard of the Negro Renaissance. And if they had, it hadn't raised their wages any. As for all those white folks in the speakeasies and night clubs of Harlem—well, maybe a colored man could find *some* place to have a drink that the tourists hadn't yet discovered.

Then it was that house-rent parties began to flourish—and not always to raise the rent either. But, as often as not, to have a get-together of one's own, where you could do the black-bottom with no stranger behind you trying to do it, too. Non-theatrical, non-intellectual Harlem was an unwilling victim of its own vogue. It didn't like to be stared at by white folks. But perhaps the downtowners never knew this—for the cabaret owners, the entertainers, and the speakeasy proprietors treated them fine—as long as they paid.

The Saturday night rent parties that I attended were often more amusing than any night club, in small apartments where God knows who lived—because the guests seldom did—but where the piano would often be augmented by a guitar, or an odd cornet, or somebody with a pair of drums walking in off the street. And where awful bootleg whiskey and good fried fish or steaming chitterling were sold at very low prices. And the dancing and singing and impromptu entertaining went on until dawn came in at the windows....

Almost every Saturday night when I was in Harlem I went to a house-rent party. I wrote lots of poems about house-rent parties, and ate thereat many a fried fish and pig's foot—with liquid refreshments on the side. I met ladies' maids and truck drivers, laundry workers and shoe shine boys, seamstresses and porters. I can still hear their laughter in my ears, hear the soft slow music, and feel the floor shaking as the dancers danced.

JIMMY WALKER, THE DREAM PRINCE

STANLEY WALKER

"A reformer is a guy who rides through a sewer in a glass-bottomed boat."—From the sayings of former Mayor James J. Walker of New York.

The great James was the paradox of American politics. He was esteemed as a wit; his favorite humorist was Arthur (Bugs) Baer. He was called the best-dressed man in public life; actually his clothes were ultra-Broadwayish, in highly questionable taste according to Racquet and Tennis Club standards, and designed principally to keep him from looking as skinny as he was. He was accounted a public speaker with a gift for clear statement; a transcript of any of his extemporaneous speeches will show that many of his sentences don't parse (this is a curious weakness possessed also by that overrated orator, William Jennings Bryan, whose sentences, as spoken, sometimes trailed off into nothingness).

He could, on occasion, put on a solemn face and be as dignified as Buddha; on other occasions he could, in high glee, get down on the floor and roll the dice with the boys, for he loved African golf with a Beale Street fervor. His favorite tear-jerker, in his speeches, was a declaration of his great affection for New York City, the magnificent metropolis where he was born; when hard times were pressing, he raised salaries, and plunged his beloved city into a financial mess from which it may not be extricated for a generation.

He was supposed to be glib, and quick-witted, as on the famous day when, in the Legislature, he killed the so-called Clean Books Bill with the observation, "I never heard of a man or a woman who was ruined by a book"; summoned before Governor Roosevelt to answer charges, he didn't make sense, among his answers being, "If it is wrong, it is unethical." He always insisted that he was open, forthright, aboveboard and all that sort of thing; he used the phrase "off the record" to handcuff his newspaper questioners more than any man who ever held public office.

He spoke at Holy Name breakfasts, and always had a good word for his Church, which was the Catholic; at the funeral of Marty McCue at St. Patrick's, Monsignor John P. Chidwick's praise of the dead man was interpreted as an almost cruelly pointed criticism of the private life of James J. Walker. Alfred E. Smith made him Mayor in the campaign of 1925 to succeed Hearst's marionette, John F. Hylan, and Walker fought for Smith for President at the Chicago convention in 1932 that nominated Roosevelt; actually Smith and Walker hated each other, for their whole patterns of life and thought were different.

Walker, as the old prizefight managers say of goofy and unmanageable geniuses of the ring, could have been as good as he wanted to be. When he was attending to business, and his attention held for a time to serious matters, he won the admiration of the most hard-headed of New York's bankers and business men by the clarity of his thought and the apparent honesty of his approach. He could see through a tangled situation instantly. If he had wanted to study, he could have led the class.

Sometimes he drank too much, and felt bad the next day. There were days when he wouldn't go to City Hall. At other times he was deathly ill, for he was a frail fellow, and his nerves were pitched in a high key. Always he was boxing with buzz-saws and phantoms, and thinking he could smile off the hurts. He held what probably is the most difficult and complicated administrative job on earth, and if that was not enough to worry him, he had plenty of other things—his own carefree inclinations, his deadly inability to say "no," his bills and his friends, his lack of sleep and rest, and the suspicion, which must have come to him, that the harpies of Tammany would be with him just so long and then they would turn and tear the flesh from his little bones.

Jimmy was a symbol of release to millions of strap-hangers, and they loved him. Even after he had been out of office almost a year, and was sunning himself in the south of France, little groups of New Yorkers would get together and tell each other that Jimmy could come back and sweep the city. Napoleon, back from Elba, would have seemed as nothing. Wrong? Perhaps, but that's the way many persons felt about him.

Was he seen with Betty Compton at prizefights on nights when his wife was either at their home in St. Luke's place or in Florida? Very well. Good for Jimmy. Many a man would rather be at a prizefight with a woman other than his wife.

Did he quit the Mayor's office under fire, in the face of almost certain removal by Governor Roosevelt? Certainly he did. But he was charming anyway, and a poll of the streets of New York a week after his resignation showed that all sorts of people would vote for him again.

Did he trample the tenets of his faith and strike at the foundations, by his flagrant personal conduct, of the sacred American home? Yes, yes. But most of the women of New York, even though they may only have seen his pictures, loved him and thought that this saucy-faced, boyish-looking little man should be allowed to do as he pleased.

Did he take too many long vacations, and let the business of the city drift along, or be attended to by incompetents and worse? Of course, but he seemed, for a long time, able to stop all rising criticism by one serious speech or by some spectacular move or crisp aphorism.

He was, for many dizzy, splendiferous years, immune to the more serious forms of criticism which, in other times, would have ruined any man in public life. Father Knickerbocker, his pockets full of new money and his innards full of night club champagne, was more than tolerant to Jimmy. At dinners, parades, luncheons and rallies the band played his old song, "Will You Love Me in December as You Do in May?" which Jimmy had written as a young man, and then Jimmy, the Spirit of New York, would appear to charm the crowd.

Jimmy was of New York, and to the country he typified its gaudiness, smartness and insouciance to perfection.

WAITING FOR LEPKE

WALTER WINCHELL

Chicago can probably claim first place as the world symbol of crime. But New York has had its Dutch Schultz, its Arnold Rothstein, its "Lucky" Luciano; and in Louis "Lepke" Buchalter and his incredible Murder, Inc., New York provided the world with probably the ultimate example of American-style, efficiency-engineered racketeering and homicide. For some fifteen years Lepke, though frequently arrested, repeatedly avoided imprisonment by systematically having all potential witnesses against him exterminated. In 1936 Lepke was arrested once more. Freed on bail, Lepke disappeared. District Attorney Thomas E. Dewey offered a reward of twenty-five thousand dollars for Lepke; so did the F.B.I. Police were assigned to guard all witnesses day and night, and both local police and F.B.I. agents combed the city for the killer. After more than two years in hiding, Lepke decided to give himself up to the F.B.I. to stand trial on a narcotics-smuggling charge, hoping thus to by-pass an indictment for murder by Dewey. Fearing that the G-Men might shoot him on sight, Lepke contacted Walter Winchell to arrange the actual surrender. Winchell waived the monetary reward, asking instead, and getting, a one-edition scoop. Lepke was convicted on several counts. Eventually, after long legal maneuvers, he was executed, on March 15, 1944. This account of Lepke's surrender, as Winchell wrote it an hour or so after it occurred, appeared in the New York Daily Mirror *of August 26, 1939.*

NEW YORK, August 25 (INS)—The surrender of public enemy "Lepke" Buchalter to the government last night took place while scores of pedestrians ambled by, and two police radio cars waited for the lights to change, near Twenty-eighth Street and Fifth Avenue.

The time was precisely 10:17 P.M., and the search for the most wanted fugitive in the nation was over. The surrender was negotiated by this reporter, whom G-man John Edgar Hoover authorized to guarantee "safe delivery."

After a series of telephone talks with persons unknown, and with the head of the FBI, Lepke appeared to drop out of the sky, without even a parachute. The time was 10:15. The scene was Madison Square between Twenty-third and Twenty-fourth Streets, where we had halted our car as per instructions.

The following two minutes were consumed traveling slowly north on Fourth Avenue and west on Twenty-seventh Street to Fifth Avenue, where the traffic lights were red—and to the next corner at Twenty-eighth Street where Mr. Hoover waited alone, unarmed and without handcuffs, in a government limousine. Hoover was disguised in dark sunglasses to keep him from being recognized by passersby.

The presence of two New York police cruisers, attached to the Fourteenth Precinct, so near the surrender scene startled Hoover as well as Lepke. The G-man later admitted he feared "a leak."

Lepke, who was calmer than this chauffeur, was on the verge of rushing out of our machine into Hoover's arms. The police cruisers, ironically, were the first observed by this reporter in two hours of motoring to complete the surrender.

Not until the final seconds was there a sign of uniformed law. But it was too late. The long arm of the government had reached out and claimed another enemy. The Federal Bureau of Investigation and the city of New York had saved $50,000—the reward offered.

While pausing alongside one police car at the Twenty-seventh Street intersection for the lights, Lepke, who was wearing spectacles as part of his disguise, threw them to the corner pavement. They crashed noisily. Two passers-by, middle-aged men with graying temples, stopped and looked up at a building.

Apparently they thought a window had broken above. They never realized that the man for whom every cop in the land was searching was within touching distance.

After parking our car behind a machine which was parked behind Hoover's, we shut off the ignition and escorted Lepke into Hoover's car.

"Mr. Hoover," we said, "this is Lepke."

"How do you do?" said Mr. Hoover affably.

"Glad to meet you," replied Lepke. "Let's go."

"To the Federal Building at Foley Square," commanded Hoover. His colored pilot turned swiftly south.

Lepke was a little excited. He seemed anxious to talk—to talk to anybody new—after being in the shadows for over two years with so many hunted men.

"You did the smart thing by coming in, Lepke," comforted Hoover.

"I'm beginning to wonder if I did," Lepke answered. "I would like to see my wife and kids, please?"

Mr. Hoover arranged for them to visit him shortly after Lepke was booked, fingerprinted, and Kodaked. He had $1700 on him. He gave $1100 to the boy and $600 to the jailer—for "expenses."

When the government car reached Fourteenth Street, we got out and went to the first phone to notify our editor who groaned:

"A fine thing! With a World War starting!"

The negotiations which led to Lepke's surrender began in this manner. On Saturday night, August 5 last, a voice on the phone said:

"Don't ask me who I am. I have something important to tell you. Lepke wants to come in. But he's heard so many different stories about what will happen to him. He can't trust anybody, he says. If he could find someone he can trust, he will give himself up to that person. The talk around town is that Lepke would be shot while supposedly escaping."

"Does he trust me?" we inquired.

"Do you really mean that?" said the voice anxiously.

"Sure," we assured. "I'll tell John Edgar Hoover about it and I'm sure he will see to it that Lepke receives his constitutional rights and nobody will cross him."

"O.K., put it on the air tomorrow night if you can get that promise," and then he disconnected.

We wrote a brief radio paragraph which was addressed to Lepke, "if you are listening now," which said we would try to get him assurance of a safe delivery. The next afternoon, Sunday, we phoned Mr. Hoover and read him the paragraph.

"You are authorized to state," said Hoover, "that the FBI will guarantee it!"

Hoover and his assistant director, Clyde Tolson, came to the studio and witnessed our microphoning. They remained for the repeat broadcast to the coast an hour later—in case another phone call came in.

For two nights, voices contacted us by phone and said:

"You're doing very well. You'll hear more later. If he agrees to come in, he will do it through you. But he may change his mind. Good-by."

And then all the dickering abruptly stopped—until last Tuesday night. Then a person we had never seen before, or since, approached us at Fifty-third Street and Fifth Avenue and said: "Where can you be reached on a pay-station phone in an hour?"

We went to the nearest phone booth, where the stranger marked down the number and instructed: "This is about Lepke. This time it's important. Please be here in an hour."

He hastened away, hailed a passing cab, and taxied north.

When we so reported to Mr. Hoover, after what seemed to him like too much stalling, he was exasperated. For the first time in our seven years of knowing him, he barked at us:

"This is a lot of bunk, Walter. You are being made a fool of and so are we. If you contact those people again, tell them the time limit is up! I will instruct my agents to shoot Lepke on sight."

Promptly an hour later, right on the button, that pay-station phone tinkled. We didn't give the voice a chance to talk. "I just spoke to Hoover," we said breathlessly. "He's fed up. If Lepke doesn't surrender by four P.M. tomorrow, Hoover says no consideration of any kind will ever be given him. For every day he stays away it may mean an extra two years added to his sentence."

The voice interrupted: "He's coming in, but you simply have to wait until he can arrange things. He's willing to come in, but it can't be tomorrow. Maybe the next night. Where can you be reached tomorrow night at six?"

We gave him another phone number. He said he'd call—and the call came. But it didn't seem to be the same voice. This time the instructions included: "Drive up to Proctor's Theater in Yonkers."

How sure could we be that the "meet" was for the surrender of Lepke? We weren't sure at all. But we hoped to convince the G-men that we weren't being made any "goat-between"! And so we motored up to Yonkers, and before we reached Proctor's Theater a car loaded with strangers—faces we don't recall ever seeing before—slowly drew alongside. We heard a voice say, "That's him."

One of the men got out, holding his handkerchief to his face as though he intended to blow into it. He got into our car, sat alongside, and kept the kerchief to his face throughout the brief conversation.

"Go to the drugstore on the corner of Nineteenth Street and Eighth Avenue," he instructed. "There are some phone booths there. Get in one and appear busy. About nine P.M. somebody will come up to you and tell you where to notify the G-men to meet you."

At 8:55 P.M. we were in that drugstore. We ordered a coke. The boy behind the counter looked at us as though we seemed familiar. Perhaps we imagined it. At any rate, we didn't get a chance to appear busy in the phone booth. A face met ours as we turned to look through the open door. The stranger jerked his head as though to telegraph "Come here." We joined him outside and walked to our car slowly.

"Go back in there and tell Hoover to be at Twenty-eighth Street on Fifth Avenue between 10:10 and 10:20," he instructed.

We did so. When we returned to the car, the man was at the wheel. He drove slowly, to kill time, for more than an hour. Up and down Eighth Avenue, Ninth, Tenth, in and out of side streets, down to Fourteenth, back to Twenty-third, and east to Madison Square, where he stopped the car and said:

"Just wait here—and good luck."

And so saying he left hurriedly. We took the wheel, turned our eyes left, and noticed many people across the street lounging around. It was very humid. Our clothes were dripping. The butterflies started to romp inside of us.

Suddenly a figure approached our car in haste. Out of the nowhere, it seems. He opened the door, got in, and said: "Hello. Thanks very much."

We released the brake and stepped on the gas. "We'll be with Mr. Hoover in a minute or two," we said. "He's waiting in his car at Twenty-eighth Street."

"Yes, I know," said Lepke. "I just passed him."

THE EMPIRE THEATRE: SHRINE AND SYMBOL

RICHARD MANEY

1953

Within the year the Empire Theatre will be rubble. Once Shirley Booth has had her final word in "The Time of the Cuckoo," its hallowed walls will be battered down that a skyscraper, trumpeting the triumph of commerce, may be reared on its site. Outraged at this blasphemy, Broadway's romantics are already crying into their beer or, if profitably employed, their vintage cups. A classic wake is brewing. For the Empire is both a shrine and a symbol to those who recall the golden age of our theatre, an age which reckoned not of movies, talkies, radio, television and other mechanical intruders.

The Fabulous Invalid has survived many sinking spells but the razing of the Empire will have implications darker than those born of any of its prior comas. For of all the theatres on Manhattan Island, it is the only survivor of the nineteenth century still devoted to the spoken word. On its opening more than sixty years ago, only the Broadway at 41st Street was farther north, on its destruction the National will be the only theatre south of 43rd Street. It is ironic that with the passing of the Empire, Broadway, the thoroughfare as distinguished from the synonym, will boast of but one odeon, the Winter Garden.

Gone are the Empire's neighbors of the Nineteen Twenties—the Knickerbocker, the Casino, the Thirty-ninth Street, the Comedy, the Princess, the Garrick and a dozen others, all hit-and-run victims of industry and the uptown trend. True, Maxine Elliott's still stands in 39th Street, but mocking a glorious era in its devotion to the upstart TV.

Most of the immortals of our stage have trod the Empire's boards as have such laureled aliens as Ellen Terry, Nazimova, Marie Tempest, Sybil Thorndike, John Gielgud and Sir C. Aubrey Smith. There John Drew reigned for twenty years in thirty plays, in one of which, "The Bauble Shop" (1894), his 15-year-old niece, Ethel Barrymore, faced her first audience.

Thrice the Empire's proscenium framed John and Ethel Barrymore simultaneously, in "His Excellency, the Governor," in Barrie's "Slice of Life," in "Clair de Lune." Lionel of this regal clan scorned such collusions, but with Uncle John Drew he played there in "The Second in Command" and "The Mummy and the Humming Bird," and with rebellious Richard Bennett in "The Other Girl."

Over the Empire's first twenty years Maude Adams, ethereal and aloof, was a constant communicant, chiefly in the plays of that fanciful Scot, James Barrie. When she renounced the New York stage forever in 1917 following her engagement in "A Kiss for Cinderella," she had twenty-one assignments at the Empire to her credit. It was there that she reached stardom in "The Little Minister" (1897), there that she first played Peter Pan in 1905.

Loyal, too, were Henry Miller, Viola Allen and William Faversham. In his ten years as leading man of the Empire Stock Company, Miller answered seventeen opening night curtain calls, Miss Allen twenty-four, Faversham twenty-seven.

It was at the Empire that William Gillette flourished in plays of his own coinage—"Sherlock Holmes," "Too Much Johnson," "Secret Service," "The Private Secretary," in Sardou's "Diplomacy," in Barrie's "Dear Brutus." In the last named one of his aides was a young actress named Helen Hayes (1918) who first graced the Empire's stage in "The Prodigal Husband" when but 14. It was a Gillette run that destroyed a concession management made to the times in 1915 by installing a soda fountain in the rear of the auditorium. This oasis flourished until its operator turned on the seltzer spigot while Mr. Gillette was engaged in some badinage with Dr. Watson in "Sherlock Holmes." Gillette interpreted the hiss as critical comment, went up in his lines, hence into an extravagant dudgeon. End of soda fountain.

It was at this historic theatre that "Life with Father" played without interruption for eight years, longest run ever enjoyed by any play anywhere, and it was from the Empire's stagedoor that the cast of "The Captive" rode to the Forty-seventh Street police station in 1927, when its theme, the unnatural affection of two women for each other, outraged local puritans and politicos. Here our flower and chivalry shelled out $22.50 each on opening night to hear Señorita Raquel Meller sing "El Pelegro de las Rosas" and "Ay! Cipriano," here Gertrude Stein's "Four Saints in Three Acts" all but unhinged the minds of music lovers in April of '34.

Miss Stein's anagram was not the only oddity to find haven at the Empire. Of an afternoon in 1900, Mrs. Langtry, the Jersey Lily, beloved of Bernard Shaw, could be heard reciting Kipling's "Absent-Minded Beggar." On still another afternoon Polish Helena Modjeska addressed the congregation; on still another the great Frenchman, Coquelin, let fly with a monologue as a preface to "A Pair of Lunatics."

The Empire opened on Wednesday night, Jan. 25, 1893. Benjamin Harrison was in the White House, Victoria sat on England's throne, and Leo XIII was in the Vatican. Five months earlier James J. Corbett had liquidated John L. Sullivan at New Orleans, and before the year was out Cole Porter, Harold Lloyd, Mary Pickford, Harpo Marx, Alfred Lunt and Sir Cedric Hardwicke would be born. Bernard Shaw's first play, "Widower's Houses," had just opened in London, and a bill was before the Assembly at Albany "to provide for the construction of an underground railroad from the Battery to the northern limits of the city." This was the year that Thomas A. Edison announced the invention of the motion picture, the year that the Duryea brothers demonstrated a gasoline buggy at their bicycle shop in Springfield, Mass.

Facing the Metropolitan Opera House, ten years its senior, the Empire was built for Charles Frohman by Al Hyman, Frank Sanger and William Harris. Frohman, who had learned the fundamentals of his craft in theatres of his elder brothers, Gustave and Daniel, had hit the jackpot in 1888 with "Shenandoah," a traveling melodrama which made him a fortune. Flushed with this success he sought a New York theatre from which to radiate. His old friend, William Harris, recommended the purchase of the Union Square, but Hyman argued that the amusement sector was edging northward. He had empty lots at Broadway and Fortieth Street. So great was his confidence in Frohman he built him a theatre and turned it over to him without the formality of a contract.

Assured of a new theatre, Frohman's next concern was a suitable play with which to dedicate it. To ease the odds against so devout a consummation, he turned to David Belasco, playwright, director, playdoctor. Still under the spell of "Shenandoah," Frohman was partial to bluecoats, brass buttons and bugle calls, while Belasco was deep in his Indian phase, with white-tie overtones. A fusion of their preferences agreed upon, Franklin Fyles, dramatic critic of The New York *Sun*, was drafted as a collaborator. Daniel Frohman, credited with magical skill as a play-christener, named the Belasco-Fyles fracas "The Girl I Left Behind Me."

Following a week's scuffle in Washington, "The Girl I Left Behind Me" opened on schedule, even though the seats still dripped paint and the electrical fixtures suffered from an attack of hiccoughs.

The anonymous reviewer on *The New York Times* avoided judgment on the play, but wrote the next day that the theatre was well constructed, fireproof, its architectural lines perfect, the decorations handsome and tasteful. His opposite on the New York *Tribune* was more enthusiastic. Said he: "'The Girl I Left Behind Me' is an excellent piece of romantic melodrama."

Whatever the artistic merit of "The Girl I Left Behind Me," it enjoyed a run of 181 consecutive performances. By current standards box-office trade was absurd. In its most opulent week the play grossed $8,800. In its final week the figure had shrunk to $1,299.50. Top price for tickets was $1.50; stage hands received $12 a week, as against a present minimum of $84.

Charles Frohman's multiple enterprises prospered at the Empire until his death on the Lusitania in 1915. For the next six years the Frohman interests and the Empire were operated by Alf Hyman, brother of the Al Hyman who built the theatre. Thereafter the Empire had several operators, including Famous Players-Lasky and its corporate extension, Paramount Pictures, for twenty years. In 1946 the Hyman estate sold the property to Jacob Freidus who, two years later, resold it to the William Waldorf Astor estate.

When the Empire is leveled not only will Miss Booth and her confederates be dispossessed but some twenty other tenants as well. Among them are the theatrical producing firms of Aldrich and Myers, Lindsay and Crouse, Bonfils and Somnes, such practitioners in allied crafts as Theron Bamberger, Jean Rosenfeld, lighting expert and caterer to stock and community theatres, and the author of this threnody. Four floors of offices about the Empire's auditorium, serviced by one of the smallest and certainly the most erratic elevators ever to outrage the memory of Elisha Graves Otis. Each of these floors has four rooms, distinguished for their nonconformity. In them Jed Harris, Orson Welles, E. Ray Goetz and kindred yogis have given way to lofty reveries, such time as they were not distracted by the clouds of pigeons who find the Empire's broad window ledges an ideal parade ground.

Other casualties with a more personal grief at the Empire's passing include Clara Borback, head usher for twenty-six years; Anne Morris, for more than a quarter of a century head cleaning woman, and Alberta Ryland, still sane though she has been matron of the ladies' rest room for almost thirty years. The husband of the last named, John Ryland, a giant extrovert, beaming and boisterous, on his death in 1939 had served the Empire for forty years and was its most vocal advertisement.

Long the theatre's superintendent, Mr. Ryland added to his income by giving trick bicycle exhibitions in front of the theatre, passing the hat at the finish of his act. Ryland was famed in theatrical circles as an omen of good luck, was always the guest of Florenz Ziegfeld at openings of his "Follies," was occasionally drafted by William Hammerstein, father of Oscar, to roll the dice for him in high-stake crap games at the Victoria.

In design, as well as in its appointments, the Empire reflects a more spacious, a more leisurely and comfortable age. Its wide foyer measures fifty feet from entrance to ticket-taker, a miraculous arena for between-act speculations and ostentations. Because of its roomy dimensions and the cushioned benches which flank its walls, it has more than once been mistaken for a bus terminal. Once past the ticket-taker, the visitor enters an expansive inner lobby, from whose walls hang oil paintings of Ethel Barrymore, Ina Claire, Katharine Cornell, Otis Skinner, Margaret Anglin, Dorothy Stickney and Leslie Howard, eloquent reminders of fabulous first nights.

Will the destruction of the Empire initiate the New York theatre's final phase? Moist-eyed alarmists point out that the symptoms of the patient have worsened progressively in the last twenty years. In 1932, at the pit of the depression, sixty-eight theatres were available. Today there are but twenty-eight. These statistics suggest a toboggan ride rather than a trend. Production costs of plays have trebled over that span; the profitable touring companies of an earlier day have been reduced to a scant dozen. Radio, the screen and, now, television have raided the theatre's personnel, made vast inroads on its revenues. No new theatre has been built in New York in twenty-four years, thanks, in part, to our archaic building regulations which outlaw offices over an auditorium.

Black as are the auguries, the incurable romantics who function haphazardly in the profession point out that the theatre has always been resident on the brink of doom. By all available economic standards it's the meeting place of speculative lunatics. Its destiny is to live dangerously. At its best it dwarfs all its mechanical rivals. Its advocates flout the evidence establishing the *corpus delicti*. It may shiver, it may shrink, it may suffer from chronic fantods, say these optimists, but it will never perish. The death of the Empire may bring heartbreak to these fanatics, but it cannot blast from them the conviction that the theatre is immortal.

IV

It Takes All Kinds: People, Places, Things

NEW YORK WOMEN:
A French View

JULES ROMAINS

We were strolling south along the west side of Fifth Avenue and had reached Rockefeller Center. It was late afternoon. Moving at a steady pace, and accompanying the change in the traffic lights from red to green and back again, the crossing of the lateral streets was easily accomplished. The crowd was gay, the day warm but bearable. We had certainly no feeling of struggling against a hostile world.

"Will you look at those two pretty girls walking in front of us!" Salsette exclaimed in a tenderly lyrical tone.

Assuming that their faces were not unworthy of their figures, the young women might certainly have been called pretty.

"Those legs, in particular," he went on. "Those long, straight legs. Slender but not skinny, and rising in a single fine line to the point where they disappear; where they cease to be a pleasure to the eye in order to become a pleasure to the imagination."

"Psst!"

"What is it? Am I talking too loud?"

"No."

"Are you afraid that people round us understand French?"

"It isn't that, either. For if they do, then either they are French themselves, or they are accustomed to French ways. No, it is simply that they can guess too easily what you are talking about."

"The legs of those young women? But are they not legs made to be looked at?"

Copyright, 1942, by Alfred A. Knopf, Inc.

"Perhaps. But you mustn't seem to notice them too much."

Salsette stared at me. "Look here. Haven't you let yourself be influenced a bit by American notions of propriety?"

"Maybe so. Who knows? There's a lot to be said on the subject. It is full of pros and cons."

"I've noticed that myself."

"But it isn't so much that. I do not ask you, my dear chap, to change the subject. I merely invite you to talk about those legs a little less—demonstratively."

"You mean that I am free to give you my opinion—confidentially of course—of the legs of these young creatures? Thank you. Let me say, then that they are not, evidently, the legs of professional dancers, nor even of girls who walk very much. The muscles are scarcely discernible. They are legs, I repeat, made to be looked at; and for my part I shall not complain of the fact. It is particularly for legs like those, and for strollers like me who have an eye for legs like those, that silk stockings and short skirts were invented."

Salsette was now caught between the desire to remain a well-behaved stroller for whom Fifth Avenue need not blush, and the need to give full expression to the notions born of his impression. He sent forth a sigh and took off his glasses, seemingly to wipe them, but more (I suspect) because a man who takes off his glasses and wipes them cannot be accused of staring too indiscreetly at the animate and inanimate objects within his field of vision.

"I want you to notice something else," he muttered in the tone of a detective slipping a remark to his pal as they trail a suspect together. "Look at the way they set their feet down on the sidewalk. That almost insolent freedom of spirit. Less brisk than the gait of a Parisian woman; more the assurance of a lovely colt, a deer. A kind of serenely confident ostentation, as if they were on parade."

A shuffle in the crowd separated us from the amiable objects by whom Salsette had been so candidly fascinated, and I must say that he made no attempt to catch up with them. He put his glasses back on his nose. Other objects of the same order offered themselves to our inspection, presumably no less amiable in Salsette's eyes.

"The number of pretty women is really extraordinary," Salsette murmured into my ear.

"That, my dear fellow, is something you are permitted to say aloud. Nobody will be in the least shocked."

"You say you are struck by their number?" I went on encouragingly. It amused me that he should have the same impression as I had had on first walking about New York. And I added, to test the strength of his conviction: "You must not forget that we are on Fifth Avenue, skirting Rockefeller Center. This is, for New York, the equivalent of the Champs-Elysées and the rue de la Paix combined. If you were now walking on Ninth Avenue, or Third Avenue, not to speak of many other streets, you would have a quite different impression, I'm afraid. You would discover that dumpy little brunettes with broad cheeks and short necks, thickset peasant-like blondes, square-built redheads covered with freckles, and even what we call at home 'fat mammas' of the most voluminous and sagging figures, were to be found in New York as elsewhere. . . ."

"I don't doubt it," said Salsette, "and I have even had a look at them in the back streets. But you must admit, nevertheless, that here we walk among an extraordinary proportion of very pretty women, even beautiful women, and girls who, while not really pretty, have wonderful figures and are a delight to the eye. But there is another impression I want your opinion about. Those dumpy brunettes, those pudgy blondes, those voluminous and sagging ladies—seeing them here and there I have had no difficulty in relating them to one or other of our European races or types. . . . Compare that with what I see here. These pretty girls and women seem to me to belong to a single breed, to bear a very distinct family resemblance to one another; and yet I see in them no resemblance whatever to any specific European race or type. For example, the English are thought to be fairly close to the Americans. Do you see in these American women any resemblance to Englishwomen, even pretty Englishwomen? I don't. They seem to me totally different. Don't you agree?"

"Fully!"

"Yet would you say they were any more German for that? Or Italian? Perhaps Scandinavian; I don't know the Scandinavian countries."

"There are pretty women among the Scandinavians; but you are right. The effect is quite different. . . ."

"Really rather mysterious, isn't it?" Salsette said dreamily.

But he did not fall into the error of letting his musing turn him from the passing show. He continued to check everything we said by a ceaseless scrutiny of the surrounding passers-by. Yet he was still under the influence of the little admonition I had ventured a moment earlier. The way in which he put an uneasy brake upon his glance, the expression of respectable detachment with which he would suddenly extinguish a too lively gleam in his eye, was amusing to see. I felt a little sorry that I had been so severe.

"In any case," I said to restore his self-confidence, "your last observation would certainly not displease the Americans."

This seemed to cheer him up considerably. His eyes began to sparkle with more freedom.

"My dear fellow, what shall I say?" he exclaimed. "I am in love with all these women . . . literally. And since I can't say so to them, I say it to you. It is a state of mind at once delightful and irritating. If I were a poet, I should write little pieces for them in the manner of the Greek Anthology. . . . Look, now, at those two coming toward us."

I felt that once again he was about to violate the limits of perfect decorum; but I had not the heart to clip his wings.

"I can't decide what it is in the lines of these women," he went on, "that seems so special to them and excites my interest to such a point. Certainly, the way they dress has something to do with it—though I must say I do not entirely approve. Look, for instance, at that woman in the short jacket. See the exaggeratedly square shoulders and chest it gives her. I can't bear it: it is detestable. The other day, when we had a sudden cold snap, and the women brought out their furs, it was even more marked. Some of them, seen from behind, looked really frightful in those things—like great sacks of coal balanced on short skirts and long legs. Today, when they are out 'in their figures' as we say at home, they are delicious. . . .

"And let no one tell me," he went on, "that the question is a frivolous one, unworthy of the attention of a serious mind. Are not painting and sculpture serious subjects? And what are they except the product of natures particularly sensitive to sights like these?"

We walked on, and I smiled to myself affectionately over my friend's enthusiasm. . . .

After a bit I said, "You put me in mind of a conversation I overheard last winter between a number of fashionable Parisian women here in New York. They were being extremely critical of American dressmaking, in particular of the most expensive dressmaking houses, as concerns both the quality of the materials and the finish of the sewing. . . . But they acknowledged that even the cheap clothes, the ready-to-wear clothes, were most ingeniously and incisively cut and somehow fit these women most remarkably. . . . Finally, they added one consideration of a very special sort."

"Which was—?"

"Nobody is listening to us. Nobody, therefore, will be scandalized at hearing two presumably respectable old codgers solemnly discussing a subject of this kind. I freely contribute this to your notes on America. Our ladies from Paris, I must tell you, maintained that the sheaths, the girdles, the—what one might call plastic nether-garments in general—you see what I mean?"

"Perfectly. Go on."

". . . are almost without exception the object of infinitely greater concern here than anywhere else—as much so on the part of those who make them as of those who wear them. At home, these ladies affirmed, it was only the makers of luxury articles who took the trouble to study the subject. And only rich Frenchwomen could be properly served in this matter. The poorer Frenchwoman had to take whatever trumpery stuff was handed her. Here, on the other hand, even a little shop girl can afford to buy plastic nether-garments whose cut has been studied with care and sufficiently diversified to adapt itself as closely as possible to the variety of individual forms. . . ."

"What you say is passionately interesting," Salsette exclaimed; and then he burst into a laugh at the earnestness with which he had spoken. "I should like to obtain confirmation of it, consult authority on the subject."

He went on, again in a discreet voice:

"Look here. If by chance I were invited into an American home and there were ladies present, do you believe I could bring the conversation round to those garments?"

"The effect might be amusing; though it is possible that the raising of such a subject by a male would be considered peculiarly French."

"Peculiarly French?" Salsette repeated in bewilderment.

"Why, yes. Since it is related to the matter of sex, and sex is still considered the peculiar preoccupation of the French mind."

"But, but . . ." Salsette was spluttering with indignation. "What has it to do with sex? My inquiry is in the domain of sociology, my question is intellectual!" . . .

He thought a moment. "Suppose, then," he suggested, "that, purely out of anthropological interest, I were to raise the subject in the smoking-room—nobody present but men."

"I say that once again you embarrass me, my friend, for once again I am not sure. My impression is that the subject would go down less well with American men than with their wives. . . . American men have a curious—and in a way admirable and touching—sense of modesty about their own women. You may talk to them freely about other women—French, Chinese, Tahitian—it doesn't matter. But their own women! . . . It is as if suddenly all the women of America became the virtuous spouse or the virgin daughter of the man you were addressing."

The interest, the sympathetic concern with which Salsette stood stock still in Fifth Avenue listening to my little speech testified to the dear fellow's candid and open-minded nature.

"That," he breathed, "is something I should never have guessed. And it is, as you say, both admirable and touching." He went on with vigorous emphasis: "But in that case they are a wonderful race, these men! They have other gods besides their money and their work. They too dwell in a temple and observe its rites. In that case their civilization is not all veneer. Their civilization too is dense, substantial."

"Yes," I said, "their civilization too is dense. And by no means all their gods are visible to the European at the first glance."

"I must think about this," my friend said.

TRANSLATED BY LEWIS GALANTIÈRE

SIDEWALK FISHERMAN

MEYER BERGER

Sam Schultz has always been hydrophobic. Even as a kid, in a Central Park rowboat he would go white with fear of the water. When he grew up and friends invited him on fishing parties he'd always refuse, saying he had a tendency to seasickness. It took a vast economic disturbance, the depression, to throw him into grate fishing when all his natural instincts were against it, but today he is probably the world's champion grate fisherman, the man who can haul up coins from subway gratings with more efficiency than anybody else in the business. Grate fishing was a primitive art when Sam became identified with it after losing his job as a truckman's helper seven years ago. It was just something that bums worked at for beer money. Sam has made it an exact science, and he earns a living by it.

Copyright, 1942, by Meyer Berger.
Originally published in *The New Yorker*.

Sam works with a few feet of light twine and a plummet of his own design—a piece of steel five inches long, an eighth of an inch thick, and about an inch and three quarters wide, just right to lower through the grate slot. He lets it down endways until it gets to the bottom, and then lets it fall broadside on the coin. Sam will point out that his five-inch plummet thus covers a potential working area of almost ten inches. The flat side of the plummet is greased so that the coin sticks to it; all Sam has to do then is to haul away and he's got the money. The bums of the grate-fishing industry use tiny weights for plummets and have to maneuver their lines a long time before they hit. "My way," Sam will tell you, "is pure headwoik."

Sam's second and equally important contribution toward uplift of the industry was an all-weather stickum to take the place of the chewing gum or taxicab-wheel grease which the bums use on their casting plummets. Chewing gum was all right in summer but it hardened at the first frost. Taxi grease worked into your pores, got under your fingernails, and made your hands untidy. It took months of experiment before Sam found the right thing—white petroleum jelly, or vaseline. A thin coat of this on the plummet will pull pennies, dimes, nickels, and even big money out of any subway grate, come frost or heat wave.

Sam buys the vaseline in the Liggett's drugstore on Times Square. The clerks there know him now and they plop the jar on the counter the minute he walks in. A single jar will last a month in winter and about three weeks in summer, if you husband it and don't oversmear, which is the general fault of amateurs. Runoff, because of heat, accounts for the extra summer waste, and so far Sam hasn't found a way around that. When you're after big money (quarters and halves), it is better to thicken the vaseline coating on your plummet, but not too much. Sam figures, for example, that proper bait for a silver dollar would be around a sixteenth of an inch. That's pure theory, because cartwheels are practically extinct in New York and he has never had a chance to work on one.

Sam may not look it now, but he was a machine gunner in the World War. Hunching over grates has rounded his shoulders and has taken something from his five feet, seven inches. He keeps his hat brim far down over his face, which is red from exposure. He got into that habit when he first took up grate fishing. He was ashamed of his work and always afraid he might be recognized by the Brooklyn crowd who used to invite him around to pinochle and poker games when he was a truckman's helper. Incidentally, he thinks that stuff about Times Square being the crossroads of the world is just a myth. He's fished the Square almost every night for seven years and hasn't seen one of his old acquaintances.

Sam's people were German-American. They died before he got through 6B in Public School 25 on First Avenue at Fifth Street. He wasn't much at school except in history and arithmetic, and most of that is gone now. He doesn't think, though, that he will ever forget the stuff about George Washington, Abraham Lincoln, and Captain John Smitz. The sturdy Captain sticks in his mind. "Captain Smitz," he will say, "was so tough a tommyhawk bounced off his neck and the Indians had to turn him loose."

Sam always liked horses, and when he got out of school in the middle of the sixth year he drove a wagon for a neighborhood fruit-and-vegetable man. That's how he came to get his first job as a truckman's helper when he lived in Harlem. He had to give that up when he was drafted into the Thirty-second Machine Gun Battalion and sent to Camp Meade. He liked machine gunning. He recalls that it made a man feel like somebody to have a Lewis gun kicking against his shoulder. Sadness overtakes him now when he remembers how Spanish flu swept the camp in October of 1918, forty-eight hours before his outfit was scheduled to go to France. The quarantine held until the war ended.

When he got back to New York from Camp Meade, Sam looked around for another helper's job and finally landed one over in Brooklyn. He started at twelve dollars a week and worked up to twenty-six. That had been cut to twenty-one dollars when the job was swept out from under him altogether by the depression. With that he lost all his Brooklyn interests, even his (up to then) unshaken faith in the Dodgers. He doesn't get to the ball games on Sunday as he used to, but if he could raise the price of a bleacher seat he supposes he might root for the Yanks. Sam thinks a man ought to be loyal to some team and he never liked the Giants anyway.

Grate angling prickles with fine points that you'd never dream of if you hadn't put your mind to it as Sam has. He knows all the midtown gratings by heart and can tell you, within a few cents, what his yield has been in each one. He watches waste cans for discarded newspapers, and scans the lists of goings-on in town to figure out the night's working schedule. If there is nothing happening at Madison Square Garden, for example, he will stick to Times Square, which is to the grate angler what the Grand Banks are to a Gloucesterman. Sometimes he'll just play a hunch and go over to the East Side, now that the Kingfish has disappeared. The Kingfish was a giant Negro who would pound your ears right down to your ankles if you poached on his Lexington and Madison Avenue grates. No one seems to know what has happened to him, but he hasn't been around. Rival fishermen hope it's nothing slight; Sam, in any case, is uneasy every time he works on the East Side. He figures that the Kingfish, who used to spend all his haul for gin, may merely be doing a short bit on the Island for assault or something and may get back any day. Sam, by the way, isn't a drinking man at all, though he will take a glass of beer on hot days.

The Garden is the best spot in town on fight nights, or when there's wrestling or hockey. Patrons of those sports are A-1 droppers. If you're a fast worker, like Sam, you can fish from fifty or sixty cents all the way up to a dollar on the Garden side of Eighth Avenue, from 47th Street north, on any night when there's a good fight card. Sam keeps away, though, during the Horse Show or when there is a Communist rally. He has come to learn that the Horse Show crowd either use their own cars or, when they pay off a taxi, simply don't drop any change. Communists, he'll advise you bitterly, are the lousiest droppers in the world. You can't count much on special events, either. Sam figures from what he'd read in the newspapers, for example, that the American Legion Convention would bring a big week of fishing. He worked like hell all through the thing, and at the end, what had he? Less than if those apple-knocking wise guys with their electric shockers had stayed home on the farm. The whole thing still puzzles him. Sam hates to see his carefully worked-up theories go to pieces. Things like the flop of the American Legion Convention make him lose confidence in his judgment.

Newspaper stands set up on subway gratings are highly favored spots, for obvious reasons. When Sam first figured that out, he had wild ideas about canvassing the stand people all along Broadway and Seventh and Eighth Avenues to move their positions from building fronts to the curb. He toyed with the project for a while, but could never quite bring himself to making the proposition. Some of the paper sellers looked sour, and then, too, maybe it wouldn't have been honest. Sam is a stickler for honesty. He turned down an idea advanced by a Broadway chiseler who thought Sam might induce some kid to bump into people counting out change near the gratings. Sam just walked away from the fellow.

He has a working arrangement, however, with several of the busier newsstand owners. The man who operates the big stand on the northwest corner of 42nd Street and Seventh Avenue drops on an average of $1.80 or $2 a month. Every time Sam comes by, the stand man indicates where coins have been dropped and Sam does his stuff. If the haul is small money he keeps all of it. On quarters, though, he gets only ten cents and on half dollars only thirty cents. He thinks that's fair enough, and even if he didn't what could he do? Let some other fisherman get the business? He had a trade argument one time with another stand owner, a woman, and before he knew it she had her own kid fishing for the drops.

Movie-house barkers will tip Sam off when people drop money, as they often do while fighting to buy tickets in a crowd. Some barkers, though, are apt to be snooty, especially the ones with fancy uniforms. Sometimes they snarl at Sam and tell him to scram. That always makes him curl up inside. Whenever it happens he tries to think of Camp Meade and the machine gun kicking away at his shoulder. One night a man dropped a twenty-dollar bill, wrapped around a half dollar, through the grating in front of the Rialto. Sam got the flash from the barker but a subway porter beat him to the money—lifted one of the grates and got two dollars' reward for the job. Whenever Sam thinks of the incident he grows wistful. Even without the reward it was a swell chance to set a world record for grate fishing.

Sam walks from ten to fifteen miles every night covering the grates, but never has foot trouble. The only time he ever had sore feet was a few years ago when he took a laborer's job up in Narrowsburg, New York, clearing out underbrush on the site of a Boy Scout camp. The ground was so soft and so alien to his feet that they slid all over the place and finally burst out in big blisters. He quit the sylvan quiet and was glad to get back to Times Square.

Sam usually works twelve hours a day, from five o'clock at night until daybreak. In addition to the general avenue runs he visits certain selected spots, in the manner of a trapper looking over his traps. After the early-evening rush the bus stop on the east side of the Times Building in the Square is nearly always good for twenty to thirty cents. The yield might be even better if some busybody hadn't wired boards under part of that grating. Sam doesn't know who's responsible, the *Times* people or the I.R.T. Another favored spot is the Lexington Avenue side of Grand Central Terminal in the morning and evening rush hours. Commuters use that entrance and they're very good droppers, especially on quarters; Sam can't say why. Loew's Lexington, between

50th and 51st, isn't bad either. At both places, of course, you've got to watch out for the Kingfish. The Waldorf is a continual disappointment —not nearly as good as Bickford's Restaurant at 582 Lexington Avenue or Foltis-Fischer's, next door to Bickford's. They're on the same side of the street as the Waldorf, one block farther north.

No part of the garment center is worth working, and that goes, generally, for everything below 42nd Street except the Hotel New Yorker. At that, the best bit of fishing Sam ever did was in front of the Hotel York, on Seventh at 36th, but it was just one of those freak things. He fished up a fountain pen with a lot of people watching and someone thought it might be a good idea to hold a sidewalk auction. The bid went to $1.10, the highest single sum Sam has ever earned at grate angling. He fished another pen—a two-minute job in front of the United Cigar Store at 42nd and Seventh—but that was a flat-rate assignment from the owner and paid only fifty cents. The pen was a gift, with initials on it, and the fellow was very grateful; couldn't get over Sam's skill.

Sam tried Brooklyn once, on a sudden inspiration, but came back disgusted. He didn't so much as make carfare and bait money there, although he surveyed every grate in the neighborhood of the Fulton Street department stores. The same goes for the Manhattan shopping district around Macy's, Saks, and Gimbels. Women drop less than men because their handbags are so big-jawed that change usually falls right back into them. He's never tried Queens, but feels instinctively it would be no better than Brooklyn.

Sam figures his fishing nets him an average of a dollar a day, or a little more. Some days, he says, you're lucky, and you may get as much as $1.65 or even $1.85. Lots of days, though, it's like going out for trout; you just don't have any luck at all. Once Sam hauled out only six cents in fourteen hours on the grates—a nickel in front of the Rialto and one cent from the Times island bus stop. He knew the recession was coming even before the papers began to notice it. Almost overnight Times Square was overrun with outsiders (any newcomer is an outsider to Sam) working the grates with disgustingly primitive equipment.

When the day's yield is a dollar or over, Sam feels justified in spending fifty cents for a room in the Seventh Avenue Mills Hotel. If it happens to be a little less, he puts up at the Vigilant, on Eighth Avenue near 28th, where they charge only forty cents. He prefers the Mills because the guests are more genteel—not so apt to get boisterous. You don't get soap or towels with the rooms, so Sam carries his own, neatly wrapped in newspapers. He carries two suits of underwear, too; an extra pair of socks, a Gillette, and a stick of shaving soap. He bathes once a week in the Municipal Baths on Forty-first Street, at Ninth, when it's cold, but will go two or three times in hot weather. He feels a man loses his grip altogether if he doesn't clean up at least once a week.

Sam has no fancy tastes in food, although his work in the open air sharpens his appetite. When he finishes the early-morning run of the grates he has breakfast at the Manhattan, on Seventh Avenue near 41st. It's pretty nearly always the same—wheatcakes and coffee, for a dime. On good days he tries to get down to Beefsteak John's, at Third Avenue and 21st, where they serve a stew, coffee, and bread for fifteen cents. If the day's haul warrants it, Sam may have a cut of coconut pie, the only dessert that ever tempts him. Sometimes, but not unless he has room money reserved, there's a late snack at the Manhattan and, because Sam's imagination doesn't seem to work where food's concerned, it's very likely to be wheats and java again. He has a good stomach—always did have—and never gets sick.

It's a mistake, unless you're out to bait Sam, to bring up the subject of stinkers. You wouldn't know about them, but stinkers are the parasites of the grate-fishing industry. When they sense that Sam is having a lucky night, they run on ahead and cut in on his grates. There's nothing you can do about it, either. Gratings are more or less public domain and anybody can fish them. What stirs Sam's gall, though, is the utter lack of ethics (he says "ettics") in the business—something he's tried to correct, but without much luck. "By me," he's apt to tell you with astonishing violence, "a stinker is rat poison—in spades."

Most grate fishermen are antisocial. They don't so much as ask one another's names. Oh, once in a while one of them may look up from a grate and say, "Hya, fisherman!" but you can't count on it. On chatty occasions they may ask about your luck, but that's more or less perfunctory, too. No old-timer in the business will tell another fisherman how much he's made; certainly not *where* he made it. Sam does have a working arrangement with a young grate angler who has been in and around the Square the past four years. He's a shy, shabby fellow who has an expression of constant bewilderment. Cab drivers make him the butt of their unsubtle jokes (Shellshock is their name for him, because of that rabbity look), but he's rather handy with the plummet. Once a week he or Sam will ride down to Barclay Street on the B.M.T. and buy a dozen flashlight batteries at a cut-rate hardware store. All grate anglers use flashlights to show up what's at the grating bottoms. At the cut-rate stores the batteries are three cents apiece, against five cents for the same thing at Woolworth's, so Sam and Shellshock save a total of fourteen cents on the deal, even when you count in the carfare. There's always a chance, too, to fish carfare out of the downtown grates, but outside of William Street and maybe Church, financial-district fishing is lousy.

Three batteries make one fill for the flashlight and will last about three days. Sam always has three extra ones bulging his pockets, along with his portable toilet kit. Most grate anglers are rather sloppy—carry their plummets in their pockets, grease and all. Sam is a neat fellow and packs his equipment in a Prince Albert Tin. It took him quite a while to convince Shellshock that it wasn't nice to get his pockets all smeary, but he never has sold Shellshock the vaseline idea. Shellshock just wipes off his plummet after each performance and gets new grease from the wheels of the nearest cab.

People keep asking Sam if it's true that grating fishermen find valuable diamonds and things like that. He knows of but two cases. One time a traffic cop lost a diamond ring near Penn Station. This cop went home at the end of the day, rigged up a childish fishing outfit, and came back to fish. By that time, of course, the ring was gone. Sam doesn't know who got it. In the other case (Sam won't vouch for this, because it's only hearsay), the Kingfish was supposed to have done a job for a woman who lost a five-thousand-dollar bracelet on Lexington Avenue. The woman gave him a quarter, so the story goes, and the Kingfish would have busted her crumpet if she had been a man.

Sam is doing some research on a pocket-battery outfit—something on the automobile-lighter principle—that will melt thin ice at the bottom of the grating. If he perfects this invention, he feels he can practically control the industry. He hasn't thought the whole thing through yet, but he's the dogged type and will probably work it out all right.

THE CAPUCHINS

MEYER BERGER

The heavy oak doors closed. They shut out street cries, the shrill voices of East Side children, the discolored and untidy rookeries of Pitt and Stanton Streets. At once you stood in another world, in another age. Dim halls, religious statues faintly touched by late-afternoon light, the sound of sandals on black and white marble squares. This was the Monastery of the Capuchin Friars.

When it was built, seventy-two years ago, the lower East Side was *Kleines Deutschland*. Everything has changed. The East Side *Saengerhalle* are gone. Gone, too, are the *Studentenhalle* and Becker's Hall.

A tall friar came down the shadowed corridor. His sandals slapped gently on the marble. He wore the Capuchins' brown habit and the pyramidal hood of this austere order. His cassock was caught up at the waist with thick white cord. Sun, diffused by the mellow stained-glass window, softly gilded the tall monk's grave features. It struck a tiny glitter from his silver spectacles, made faint halos in his hair and in his beard. When he spoke his voice was rich in timbre. He said, "I am Father Edwin."

Father Edwin spoke of the great change in the parish, how it flourished threescore and ten years ago and how it waned as the neighborhood changed. Now it has some six hundred families.

The monk said: "But the old ones return. They come in August to the *Gemeindefest*, the Yard Festival. They come at Christmas. They do not forget the old parish."

The hooded friars still move through the streets on brief errands. They visit the sick or go out at night on emergency calls. On longer journeys they put aside the habit.

"It is more convenient so," Father Edwin said, "but in the old country Capuchins never put aside the habit."

Ten Capuchins tend the spiritual needs of the parish of Our Lady of Sorrows. Seven are friars. Three are lay brothers. All are bearded, as St. Francis was. Father Benedict is their superior. Father Edwin opened a great oaken door. He said, "We enter the enclosure here."

The way was down another marble corridor. The sandals started whispering echoes. An ancient hall clock gave the hour in tuneful melancholy that sounded like bass notes on the harp. They padded at the old oak walls, sighed into sad silence. Father Edwin opened another door. He said, "We go into the church."

The church was hushed. In the dome the light of waning day lay on seven warmly painted panels—"The Seven Dolors." Here and there, the paint seemed to be flaking away.

"It is peeled," Father Edwin said. "The old Penzarozi, the painter who touched up these panels when we had our golden jubilee, he comes here. He stands here and he weeps, this Penzarozi."

In this church the monks chant their offices in Latin.

Father Edwin said, "We are up at dawn, at five o'clock, and at our divine offices. Seven times a day."

He looked about him, a shadowy figure in the shadowy edifice. The altar was gray in twilight. In the brass sanctuary lamp steady flame burned in the ruby bowl. The refectory had the look of some medieval hall. Brother Accursius, the porter, gray-bearded and rosy-cheeked, thumped the thick oak table and the thick oaken benches.

"In your house," he said, "you do not have such a table, hey?"

He brought out the wooden plates on which the monks have their meat. These are pale with age and much washing. Many are cracked but it is difficult to replace them.

Father Edwin said: "It is so with sandals, too. We had a brother cobbler, but he died. We had a parishioner who was a cobbler, but he is gone, too."

In the old kitchen, Brother Louis fussed with meats and vegetables for dinner. He barely looked up. Brother Accursius set out the beer flagons.

The step from the Hall of the Capuchins to the old stone stoop outdoors was a step from a distant yesterday. The shrill voices of East Side children, after the monastic calm and stillness, seemed curiously vitreous.

You felt, somehow, that you had achieved, awake, a spanning of vast time, something that ordinarily happens only in a dream.

EVERY DAY A JUBILEE

CHIANG YEE

Watching people moving about in the streets and houses from the windows of a train on the elevated gave me a new slant on them. I also saw many interesting things inside the subway trains. In certain parts of the City, most people got into the train chewing gum. They reminded me of the inhabitants of Singapore, Penang, Malaya, and some southern parts of China who chew pingnan, areca nut or betel nut, which gives a reddish stain to the mouth and lips which is considered attractive. I remember that a Chinese writer of the eighteenth century wrote that he often shut his eyes so as to try to imagine the taste of the fruit inside the eater's mouth rather than to watch the facial movement, though he could not help hearing the little sucking noise produced from time to time.

I very seldom tried to sit down in a train in case I had then to practise the courtesy of letting-the-lady-have-the-seat which I learned in England. Actually there was hardly a vacant seat in the subway. In every coach there is a detailed map of the line about three feet square but the words on it are in very small print because the name of nearly every station is given. I seldom dared to look closely at it lest I should fall. I would not have minded falling on a man, who could at most have given me a punch on the nose. But suppose I fell on a lady? 'One can't be too careful' was my motto in New York. And anyway the subway map is generally in a corner or near the door and I could not often get near it. I was much struck by one notice on the windows warning the passengers in big letters not to do 'unlawful things' in the train, otherwise they would be heavily fined or sent to prison. I could not guess what the 'unlawful things' might be. The notice reminded me of a similar warning appearing beside the communication cord in the London Underground, saying, but in very small letters, 'Penalty for improper use £5.' Five pounds seems to be practically a standard sum for a fine in London.

In the Underground, there are different compartments for smokers and non-smokers. In New York Subways smoking is absolutely forbidden. I often wondered how heavy smokers could endure this prohibition, for they have to stop smoking as soon as they enter a subway station. Surely not all can afford to travel by taxi all the time!

Most passengers on the Underground smoke either a pipe or a cigarette or do one of the crossword puzzles in the daily papers. They generally look very calm and sit at ease. I found that subway passengers, being forbidden to smoke, did not so entertain themselves. In the morning some of them were still rubbing their eyes and yawning. At midday they were busy wiping the sweat from their foreheads or exclaiming: "Hot." In the evening and late at night I enjoyed studying the different positions of drooping heads and relaxed bodies. But no matter how late it might be, all came to life again as soon as the train stopped at 42nd Street, preferably at the side of Times Square. Times Square has a magic power of revitalisation.

Sometimes the passengers inside a subway train were entertained by one of their number. Once, in a train not as full as usual, a big man with a bushy beard like Robinson Crusoe got in. He stared dead ahead and was obviously blind. He walked slowly and steadily and his wide-apart feet were wrapped in some sort of red bindings. He did not utter a word. Some of the passengers dropped a nickel or a dime into the hat he held out. I thought he must be collecting for a religious charity, so one of my nickels went into his hat too. But then I was informed by my neighbour that he was a beggar. Another time someone in the middle of the train suddenly shouted details of the goods he had for sale. He even displayed a few of them and asked the passengers to pass them round. So one way or another the travellers are prevented from becoming lethargic.

I am well acquainted with the rush hours in London. I had anticipated that every hour would be a rush hour in New York, but I found that there are specially busy periods there too. The first seems to begin about three o'clock in the afternoon and to reach its climax at half-past five. Then between seven and eight in the evening there is another big rush for Times Square. I may be wrong, of course, but that was my impression. I wanted to sample a New York rush hour, so one day I purposely went down a subway in Times Square just after five o'clock. Once en route I dared not hesitate or I should have hindered the people behind me, who were either squeezing me aside or pushing me on. At one point I tried to stop but in vain. Fortunately I could not understand what one or two people said to me! I suppose I should have been as annoyed as they if I had had to count the time minute by minute. I moved on non-stop in a single file until I reached a gap, presumably opposite the train's doors. Except for a small space round this gap the whole platform was full of people. The other platforms were equally crowded. I was shoved aside by a dark-faced porter and made to line up, unlike London queues. Soon there were crowds of people behind me. There were iron chains on either side of the gap to keep back the waiting crowds. A soon as the train doors opened, a flock of people poured out like the huge volume of water down Niagara Falls. At the same time, I was involuntarily moved forward. If the railings and chains had not been made of steel we should have broken through them. I say 'we' because I could not have avoided taking part. While the train was emptying, the porter had to hold on to the railings, with his back strained against the crowd, from which he was protected by the chain. He looked like Joe Louis posing before a fight for the world title. When he eventually undid the chain, he at once vanished from sight, and I did not see him again until he relocked the chain. For the train moved off without me. But I was now near the chain and stood a good chance of getting on the next train. It soon arrived, but I was pushed aside by the crowd who streamed into the train as if they were being chased. Once again, I was left standing in the same gap as before close to the chain. The third time I was carried into the train, with my feet suspended a few inches above the ground, which made me feel like an ancient Prince or a modern hero returning in triumph from the war! It was better than any Circus show. I held my breath at first and when I did venture to breathe out and then try to breathe in again, there was no room for my lungs to expand. My arms had to be kept folded in front of my chest and my shoulders were bent. Despite the great noise produced by the friction between the wheels of the train and the track, I could hear the faint music of chewing gum quite close to one of my ears!

At last I reached my destination and had a meal to calm my excitement. I have had three similar experiences in London, once on the Jubilee night of the late King of England, George V, again on the Coronation night of George VI, and the last on VE day at Piccadilly Circus Station. I think I could have had one in New York every day if I had wished.

TUMMLER

A. J. LIEBLING

This portion from a somewhat longer profile, originally published in The New Yorker, *chronicles some of the fascinating and devious maneuvers of that hardy New York genus, "the promoter." The I. & Y. referred to in the opening paragraph is a Broadway cigar store whose folklore Mr. Liebling explored in detail in a series of articles.*

To the boys of the I. & Y. Hymie Katz is a hero. He is a short, broad-shouldered, olive-complexioned man who looks about forty-two and is really somewhat older. In his time he has owned twenty-five night clubs.

"Hymie is a tummler," the boys at the I. & Y. say. "Hymie is a man what knows to get a dollar."

Hymie at present is running a horserace tipping service in an office building on Longacre Square. "What is a night club made of?" he sometimes asks contemptuously. "Spit and toilet paper. An upholstered

Copyright, 1938, by A. J. Liebling. Originally published in *The New Yorker*.

joint. The attractions get the money and the boss gets a kick in the pants." His admirers understand that this is only a peevish interlude. Soon he will open another night club.

The tipping service requires no capital. Hymie reads out-of-town telephone books for the names of doctors and ministers fifty or a hundred miles from New York. Then he calls them, one by one, asking the operator to reverse the charges. Hymie tells the operator, let us say, that he is Mr. Miller whom Dr. Blank or the Rev. Mr. Doe met at Belmont Park last summer. If the man accepts the call, Hymie knows he has a prospect. The man probably hasn't been at Belmont, and certainly hasn't met a Mr. Miller there, but thinks he is the beneficiary of a case of mistaken identity. Hymie tells him about a horse that is sure to win. All the doctor or minister has to do, Hymie says, is to send him the winnings on a ten-dollar bet. Sometimes the horse does win, and the small-town man always remits Hymie's share of the profits. He wants to be in on the next sure thing. Doctors, Hymie believes, are the most credulous of mortals. Ministers never squawk.

Hymie picks his horses very carefully from the past-performance charts of the Morning Telegraph. He usually tips three or four entries in each race. Naturally, the physicians and clergymen who get bad tips send him no money, but the supply of small-town professional men is practically unlimited. Hymie says it is an ideal business for a man satisfied with a modest, steady income. Personally, he is resigned to opening another night club. "If I wasn't ashamed," he says, "I would put a couple of hundred dollars in it myself." The investment of his own money, according to Hymie's code, would be unethical.

All Hymie needs to open a night club is an idea and a loan of fifty dollars. There are fifteen or twenty basements and one-flight-up places between 45th and 55th Streets that cannot economically be used as anything but night clubs. They have raised dance floors, ramps, numerous light outlets, kitchens, and men's and women's washrooms. Because they are dark during the day, or can be reached only by staircases, they are not adapted to ordinary restaurant use. Such a place may be worth six hundred dollars a month as a night club. Dismantled, it would bring only a hundred or so as a store. The owner of a night-club site makes out pretty well if his space is tenanted for six months of the year.

Hymie has been around Broadway since 1924. He is a good talker. In the past, some of his clubs actually have made money, although none of it has stuck to him. As a matter of ritual he always tells the owner of the spot he proposes to rent that he is going to spend forty thousand dollars to fix it up. The owner does not believe this, but the sound of the words reassures him. If Hymie said more than forty thousand dollars, the landlord would sense a certain lack of enthusiasm. It is customary to mention forty thousand dollars when talking about redecorating a night club. If the owner appears to be hooked, Hymie goes out and spends the borrowed fifty dollars. He pays it to a lawyer to draw up a lease. The lawyer Hymie patronizes is the only man in the world whom Hymie has never been able to put on the cuff. But he draws a fine lease. It contains all sorts of alluring clauses, like "party of the first part and party of the second part agree to share equally in all profits above ten thousand dollars a week, after reimbursement of party of the second part for outlays made in equipping the Dopey Club (said outlays for this purpose not to exceed forty thousand dollars)." It makes provision for profits of Aluminum Trust magnitude.

Hymie takes the lease to a hat-check concessionaire. This is the really critical phase of the enterprise. He must convince the concessionaire that the place has a chance to do business ("Look at the figures in the lease, you can see what we're expecting"). He must fill the concessionaire with enthusiasm for the entertainers, who have not yet been engaged. For it is up to the concessionaire to provide the cash that will make the enterprise go—three thousand dollars in advance, in return for the hat-check and cigarette concession for six months. Hymie is a great salesman. He does impersonations of his hypothetical acts. He tells about the Broadway columnists who eat out of his hand and will give yards of free publicity. While Hymie talks, the concessionaire distills drops of probability from his gallons of conversation. In his mind he turns Hymie's thousands of anticipated revenue into fifties and hundreds. If the club runs three months, the concessionaire knows, he will get his money back. If by some fluke it runs six months, he will double his money. If nobody financed night clubs, there would be no concession business. So the concessionaire lets Hymie have the three thousand.

Hymie goes back to the landlord, signs the lease, and pays him a month's rent in advance—say six hundred dollars. That leaves twenty-four hundred dollars for the other expenses. If possible, he saves himself from headaches by renting out the kitchen. The kitchen concessionaire provides the food, cooks up a stew on which all the night-club help feed every night, and even pays half of the cost of the table linen. (Linen is rented, not bought.) The proprietor of the club gets from twelve to twenty per cent of the gross receipts for food. Since night-club food is absurdly high, the food concessionaire, like the hat-check man, is bound to make a good profit if the place lasts a few months.

The club may contain tables, chairs, and any amount of miscellaneous equipment abandoned by a former tenant in lieu of rent. If it doesn't, Hymie goes to a man named I. Arthur Ganger, who runs a Cain's warehouse of the night club business on West 45th Street. Ganger can provide out of used stock anything from a pink-and-onyx Joseph Urban bar to a wicker smörgasbord table. Some of his silverware has been in and out of ten previous clubs. Usually Ganger will accept a twenty-five-per-cent down payment, which for one of Hymie's clubs amounts to a few hundred dollars. He takes notes payable weekly for the rest. Ganger is amenable to reason when the notes fall due. He has a favorite joke for customers like Hymie. "Your mother carried you only nine months," he says, "but I been carrying you all your life." The supply man retains title to his things until they are entirely paid for, and if the club folds he carts them back to his warehouse. Ganger decorates some clubs, but Hymie would not think of hiring him for such a job. Hymie gets a girlish young man to perform a maquillage for a hundred and fifty dollars, including paint.

Of the three thousand dollars received from the concessionaire, Hymie has now disbursed at most twelve hundred. He pays another six hundred dollars for a liquor licence good for six months, and puts the rest of the money in the bank as profit in case the club flops. The remaining preparations are on the cuff. Hymie hires acts for his new club on the understanding that he will pay off a week after the place opens. He engages a band on the same terms. If there is to be a line of girls in the show, the girls rehearse free. But Hymie is not a bad fellow. He sends out for coffee and sandwiches for the girls during rehearsals. Once or twice he has been known to lend a girl five dollars for room rent before a club opened.

Liquor is harder to buy on credit these days than before repeal. Mob credit was flexible, and if you bought from a bootlegger independent of the gangs, Hymie says, you never paid him at all. Wholesalers now are allowed to extend only twenty-one days' credit, according to the regulations of the State Liquor Authority. But matters sometimes may be arranged by paying a bill on the twenty-first day and then borrowing most of the money back from the wholesaler on the twenty-second.

A few days before the opening Hymie effects a deal that always puts him in especially good humor. He sells twenty waiters their jobs. The headwaiter pays four hundred dollars, two captains pay two hundred dollars each, and ordinary waiters fifty dollars. Waiters like to work for Hymie because he lets them take what they can get. He wastes no time watching his employees. "Most of the stealing they do is from the customers, so what do I care?" says Hymie.

Despite all his forethought, exigencies sometimes arise which demand fresh capital. Perhaps an unusually stubborn landlord demands three months' security, or a police official must be heavily greased before he will let the club stay open after hours. In some places, especially black-and-tan or crudely bawdy spots, all the money comes in during the illegal early hours of the morning, after the bigger clubs have closed. In such emergencies Hymie sometimes has to take in partners. He usually bilks his partners for the principle of the thing. He is not avaricious. Dollars, Hymie thinks, are markers in a game of wits as well as a medium of exchange. He refuses to let his partners keep any markers.

Once he had to take a partner in a roadhouse he was running near Babylon. He sold the fellow fifty per cent of the place for one season. It happened to be a very good season, so Hymie built a sliding metal roof over a garden one hundred feet square, installed a swimming pool, and presented all his employees with a large bonus out of the receipts.

"I thought I would make some improvements and build up good will for next year, when Milton would be out," he says.

Some persons may wonder why even a concessionaire would trust Hymie with his money. But concessionaires know that he will not skip before the club opens, for he is under a compulsion as strong as the drive of a spawning salmon to swim upstream. His clubs satisfy his craving for distinction.

A week before an opening Hymie gets out a mailing list of exhibitionists which he has accumulated through a decade of night-club operation, and sends out his announcements. Then he makes the entertainers write letters to their friends inviting them to buy ringside tables. He insists on the attendance of every salesman who has ever sold him anything for the club, even if it all was on credit. The costumer who has dressed the show is expected to take part of his pay in trade. Since this may be the only part of it he will ever collect, the costumer usually brings a large party. It is a nice arrangement for Hymie, because he pays off on the costume bill with Scotch at about six cents on the dollar. The band leader, if he has any considerable reputation in the trade, forces music publishers' pluggers to reserve tables. If the pluggers don't spend money, the leader slights their tunes.

A week after the opening, if it was profitable, Hymie gives his entertainers three days' pay. He tells them he is holding something back so they won't run out on him. Of course they never get it. If the opening has been bad, the entertainers and the concessionaire are likely to find the door locked the next night. In the event of a sour opening, Hymie takes the thousand or fifteen hundred dollars of concession money remaining to him out of the bank and lays it on a ten-to-one shot at some obscure race track. He shares the weakness for betting common to most night-club people, but he has it in an exaggerated form. He has never played a horse at less than eight-to-one in his life, because he is sure that every race is fixed. When a favorite wins he attributes it to a double-cross. Hymie almost always loses.

Occasionally the personality of one of Hymie's entertainers catches on, or the décor hits the fancy of the Broadway high-life crowd, and the club begins to make money legitimately. Under these circumstances Hymie sells it to a corporation called Hymie-club, Inc. As manager for the corporation he kicks out the hat-check concessionaire and sells the concession over again for a higher price. The entertainer who draws the crowd gets a manager and demands more money. Hymie pays blackmail in the form of weekly raises. He spends a great part of his receipts in competitors' clubs to show how prosperous he is. He stalls off all creditors on general principles.

"Sometimes you can hold them off for six months," he says. "Meanwhile everything that comes in is profit."

Finally the creditors close in, or the entertainer either loses his brief vogue or goes on to a larger club. Hymie returns to the horse-tipping business. He has written one more chapter in his saga; he has been in the money again.

Hymie admits readily that it was vanity that drew him into the night-club business in the first place, and that keeps him at it.

"Take a fellow who is born in Brooklyn," he says, "and he is a cloak-and-suiter or a shoe clerk, which he would feel honored even to talk to a trumpet player in a famous orchestra. He goes into this business and in two years celebrities like Rudy Vallée and Harry Thaw are calling him Hymie. It makes him feel wonderful. But it don't mean nothing."

NEW YORK'S BROWNSTONE GIRL

ROBERT LOWRY

Like that green, distant lady who stands out there in the water at Manhattan's gates, Carol Reed (twenty-five, five-foot-six, single, very attractive) also carries a torch for liberty—for a kind of feminine freedom, that is, which Carol came to New York four years ago to find, and found.

It amounts to this: one two-and-a-half-room elevator apartment on East 53rd Street; a telephone ringing with more invitations to drinks and dinners and parties than Carol can keep up with; an address book full of Grade A and Grade B contacts in the New York women's magazine world, the right to see whom she likes and go where she likes and get home when she likes—three conditions which wore a rosy, faraway aura a decade ago when Carol was a high school girl in Pittsburgh, or even a few years ago when she was going to Bennington.

For Carol, you see, is a full-fledged, five-star, success-scintillating member of Manhattan's Uptown Bohemia. Her spiritual arena is an area bounded on the north by smooth-running taxicabs and smart bars; on the east by young and not-so-young—but all very "interesting"—men; on the west by boats and planes and trains that can whisk a girl off to Westport for a weekend or to Paris for the standard Left Bank tour; on the south by Greenwich Village, where the tradition which Carol lives by has its roots.

Carol glides about like a long, flashing fish in this metropolitan goldfish bowl, looking, to those who gawk longingly at her in restaurants or on the street, like life's golden girl. But Carol cried last night. She cries at least once a week, and Hubert is usually there when she does.

Hubert is Carol's soul confidant, a pudgy, pink-faced young man who publishes poems in *The New Yorker* (as well as in *The Kenyon Review*) and who treasures his admitted, but seldom practised, homosexuality as "a precious link with the ancient Greeks" (we're quoting *him*). Every real Uptown Bohemian girl has her Hubert to confide in on slow evenings; he's as much a part of her surroundings as the framed Toulouse-Lautrec poster on the wall, the Billie Holiday albums under the phonograph, the shelf of books that always includes Joyce's *Ulysses*, with its two-year-old bobby-pin bookmark about a third of the way through, and the Modern Library *Sanctuary*, a holdover from her college days when it was all the rage among the freshman girls. Hubert, who has a cozy reputation in Carol's set for his caustic volubility and his *double-entendres*, adds just the right amount of sugar and spice to one of Carol's blue evenings.

Carol cried last night because she can't love Paul, the well-heeled young advertising executive who wants to marry her. Like a lot of sharp, eager Gotham men who've paddled in and out of Carol's life in the past few years, Paul was attracted there as much by the amused detachment with which she appeared to regard life, love and sex, as by her shining, cleanly scrubbed good looks. She was not the usual clotheshorse zombie, the flesh-and-blood manikin that many American women, aping Hollywood and the fashion magazines, tried so hard to be. She had a mind, and seemed more interested in showing it than either her profile or her chest. What also intrigued him was her independence: he thought an affair with her would lack the deadening weight of responsibility that girls with families and family futures presented. Just how wrong he could be soon became apparent to him when he found out what Carol's "problem" really was—but by that time he'd already left his heart on Carol's pillow and his mind in Carol's care.

She had a defiant way of arranging to be out with someone else at the very moment a man in love wanted to talk to her most. And she took a cool delight in shattering all moments of passion by bringing up her "lack of affinity for men." Though she could do these things with a detached air that precluded cruelty, Paul's predecessors had, one by one, left her as they found her, and drifted on to newer Carols with similar problems. But Paul, poor poodle, made the mistake of discovering that he owned a conscience and a heart—even though Carol seemed to want no part of them. What rocked him most, however, was Carol's preference for that mincing little scribbler in whom she confided.

"I know I *ought* to love Paul," Carol told Hubert, the scribbler, over their fourth Scotch-and-soda last night. "I know it would be the best thing in the world for me if I could love Paul and even marry him, God help me. Don't you think Dr. Pollock would tell me to—if he ever consented to tell me *anything?*"

Dr. Pollock is Carol's analyst. Almost everyone Carol knows (including Hubert) is going, has gone, or is planning to go to one kind of mental healer or another: like the five-thirty cocktail, he's a standard prop in the Uptown Bohemian world. Carol goes twice a week, at fifteen dollars per hour-session—the kind of price that is bound to keep a girl at her typewriter, tapping out that overdue article on "Parties— With and Without Couples" for *Glamour* and wading drearily into that pat newlyweds-meet-a-problem short story for *McCall's*.

"My dear," Hubert answered, making the ice in his glass tinkle, "I don't think Dr. Pollock would be likely to tell you any such thing. I think he'd be much more tempted to suggest that you snap on your bow tie, do your hair in a boyish bob, and *be* what you're afraid you are."

"Oh God, Hubert—*no*," Carol moaned, pretending to be engulfed by the idea but actually shivering deliciously in secret over it. "Do I *have* to be one? It's so *complicated*."

For Carol, it all started at Bennington during the war. There, pretty nearly all the really bright, really artistic girls—the girls who wrote stories or poems, painted pictures, or at least *wanted* to do something of the sort—decided they had some vague, but terribly smart peculiarity called "lesbian tendencies," and that the only men worth talking to were homosexual. It gave them a rich, goose-pimpling feeling of liberation—the same one that the First World War female generation had gotten out of the thought of rolling its stockings, and petting, and drinking bathtub gin.

Within the hothouse fastnesses of Bennington and Vassar and Mills and Sarah Lawrence, this queer tingle of liberation seemed an original answer to a young lady's most paralyzing problem: how to be "truly" oneself and "truly" creative in the face of such perils as husbands, babies and general domesticity on the one hand, and the depersonalizing threat of mass-market glamor on the other. If you could decide that you were a lesbian, of course, the domestic problem disappeared by itself. And you were challenging men with something a lot more unique and much more personal than a fashion frock or a frozen pose. You had really managed to crawl under the barbed wire that surrounded their camp and challenge them on their own ground at last.

Not that Carol's friends at college—or Carol herself—ever did much more about their thrilling "inclinations" than chatter, shudder, whisper three or four celebrated names they'd heard gossip about, and raise a few eyebrows. But even such meager titillations really did give them some relief from the overpowering ogre of the faceless, mindless futures which society, one way or the other, seemed to be pushing them into.

It is true that after graduation the great majority of Carol's classmates accepted society's values concerning their maturity and drifted into marriage, or went back to their home towns where they lost themselves in mediocre jobs a thousand miles removed from the special college world they had created. But the daring few, Carol among them, made the break and came to Manhattan, where they found two versions of a new, feminine bohemia in the making. In spite of the Dylan Thomas-like poems she had been writing for the past few years, Carol sensed immediately in which version she belonged: the uptown set.

For a year she worked as a *Life* researcher, a job she hated, and quit the day she sold an article to a fashion magazine. Now her free-lance income has about it a bohemian uncertainty, and her life has taken on a bohemian irregularity. The only difference is that the checks which the men who buy her drinks and dinners pick up have very unbohemian-like totals on them, and the clothes she wears, the apartment she lives in, the weekends she goes off on are hardly the kind of thing an old-style bohemian can afford. For something has happened to Bohemia since the war: part of it has moved uptown and become *chic*. Aging society matrons mix happily with it at ballet theater openings.

The chief membership requirement is a jumbo-sized contempt for all the mediocre, machine-made aspects of modern life—from the vacant-eyed glamor girl who stares out from every magazine cover and movie poster, to the stuffy, stodgy, predictable world of business and family. Carol conforms and agrees to the membership requirements, and yet now and then she vaguely hears, in a life that on the surface seems to be a high-powered, lucre-lubricated world of fun and freedom, a certain hollow ring.

Strange that Jill Jamison, who was a member of Carol's snobbish little clique of poetry-writing young females at Bennington, should have scorned this new world of Uptown Bohemia, and settled for the old, Downtown one. Strange because while Carol, who aimed at the moneyed bohemia, comes from a mere haberdasher's family in a middle-class Pittsburgh neighborhood, Jill Jamison was born in Manhasset, Long Island, and her father, though never what you could call "rich," did very well in real estate and belongs to a country club. Jill could belong to a country club too, or live on East 53rd Street like Carol, if she chose. But she prefers her coldwater place on Vandam Street, below Greenwich Village.

Jill is only five-foot-two, an energetic towhead with big blue eyes and a determined mouth. She rented this warehouse loft as casually as if it were a furnished apartment on Sutton Place, and with the help of one or two friends, plunged in and painted it, installed a spaceheater, suspended a couple of bamboo shades from the ceiling to divide the room's one-hundred-foot sweep of space, and settled down to living the life of the *Downtown* Bohemian—a term which designates more a spiritual than a geographic difference in a city where, as the housing shortage continues, a true-blue Greenwich Villager like Jill may have to settle for Yorkville, the Upper West Side, or even the Lower East Side, while an "uptown" girl like Carol may find herself living as far downtown as Brooklyn Heights. Jill has a telephone in her loft, but it seldom rings. Like her friends (two extremely serious abstract painters with beards, a girl who fashions lamps out of old beer bottles and new tin, the arty owner of an arty bookshop on Christopher Street, and a Negro poet who used to be an office boy at PM), Jill cultivates the casual quality of her life. She scorns a regular job, refuses an allowance from her father—although he does come through now and then in a pinch—and earns money sporadically by working part-time in her friend's bookshop, or typing for a novelist she knows, or baby sitting. She keeps her vision pure, and occasionally even finds time in her casual life to write a casual story or poem, which she sends to the nonpaying literary quarterlies, and usually gets back.

Those "lesbian tendencies" that bother Carol so much no longer bother Jill Jamison at all. She got over them by having an affair with the girl who makes lamps out of bottles and not liking it very much (they're still good friends, however), so that now, although she buys half her clothing at an Army & Navy Store, and has her silky hair chopped short, she accepts her womanhood with resignation. She doesn't really like men very much either, in spite of the half-dozen half-hearted affairs she's had since the war. What she's after is a way of life: the chance to feel that she's in the avant-garde of the avant-garde, which is very avant-garde indeed, and a long way ahead of Carol.

Jill knows that most of the things Carol lives by are already old hat and really quite "bourgeois" in their acceptability. Kafka is boring rather than profound, Calder's mobiles and Henry Moore's sculpture are tiresome monstrosities, Freudian analysis is passé (even Reich's orgone boxes are beginning to show signs of wear), and anyone who would frame a Toulouse-Lautrec poster and hang it on her wall—!

Jill feels there's nothing in America worth staying around for; that the place in which to be is Rome. She'll probably go there to live this year or next, if she can muzzle her pride long enough to ask her father for the money. Or maybe something else will happen to her: maybe she'll tire of her drab surroundings and her erratic, poorly-paid jobs, and move uptown, next door to Carol, where she'll find work as a publisher's reader or a copy writer, or free-lance like Carol by turning out machine-made short stories and pieces for the big magazines.

Taken together, Jill and Carol provide the two slightly-contrasting profiles of New York's new woman. What the Gibson Girl was to the turn-of-the-century, the flapper to the twenties, the sallow, serious, horn-rimmed intellectual girl to the thirties, Jill and Carol, bohemians, are to the fifties. They may be a minority when weighed against the thousands of young women who merely pound typewriters in offices or wheel baby carriages in Central Park, but their revolt influences every female in America under thirty, makes such costumes as dirndls and ballet slippers and jeans fashionable in spite of what Paris tells American women to wear, coaxes thousands of college girls into thinking, not that a man or a family or even an ordinary career is important, but that only a new way of life, like Carol's or Jill's, is worth having.

Is it? Carol and Jill can't answer, for they haven't taken time out to question it. Their attitude forbids consideration of such a state of mind as "happiness," that outmoded word which has had to give way in their vocabulary to "fulfillment." Yet their search for "fulfillment" has led them into an arid no-man's land where love can't flourish. They once thought that the trap of their futures gave them a choice of two poisoned baits: the pose-deadened "dream girl" and the domesticity-dulled work horse. But their flight from one trap led them into another.

The story sometimes has a happy ending—one so corny that a few years ago Jill and Carol would have trembled at the thought. But at twenty-eight or thirty or thirty-five, they will probably be swept up by an anxiety that was hovering just beneath the surface of their lives all the time. They'll suddenly want, after all, to get married and take a well-traveled road that less imaginative girls took in the beginning. With luck they *will* marry, and have children, and disappear, bless them, into the very world of pots and pans and predictables which they took such pains to avoid—never really to solve the problems that their longing to be "themselves" once made so obsessively urgent.

MANHATTAN'S WONDERFUL CAB DRIVERS

GEORGE WEINSTEIN

Despite legends to the contrary, not every one of New York's 33,000 cab drivers is a Damon Runyon-esque oracle, pundit, or wit. Nor is he necessarily an expert on love, foreign affairs, or baseball. He may not even be able to quote Shakespeare, the Bible, or Ogden Nash. But he is generally a smart cookie who knows how to buck for tips, and if what his customer wants is a little entertainment, or some extra service, he is usually not averse to providing it.

He knows that people expect him to be the newspaper, movie, radio, and TV stereotype of the hackie—the gabby extrovert whose fares are a succession of screwy characters whom he has to jolly along, advise, deliver of babies, and accompany on all sorts of wild adventures. And so, he's ready to talk at the drop of a meter flag.

Let's tune in on one of my favorites.

"There's the time I take this guy out to one of the local race tracks. As we pull up in front of the horse factory, he says, 'Driver, how would you like to see the races—as my guest?'

" 'This would be fine, mister, but I gotta make a living. A wife and two kids need a lotta groceries."

"So the guy counters with, 'How much could you make this afternoon?'

"I raise the ante a little and tell him, 'Maybe ten bucks.'

" 'Well, supposing I take care of that—and set you up for each race, besides. How would that be?'

"Nothin' could be fairer, so I park the cab in a hurry and in we go. As soon as we get by the ticket-choppers, he says, 'Before we do a thing, let's get something down on the daily double.'

"And so help me, it wins and I walk out of the joint with twelve hundred and ninety bucks, plus the sawbuck for my time, plus the five-twenty on the meter. I ain't seen a race since. And I ain't gonna until this guy comes around again.

"And then there's the night I pick up a well-dressed feller around Times Square who looks like he had a couple under his belt. He tells me to drive him to an office building downtown.

"When we get there, he asks me to wait. I do, but in about fifteen minutes, I'm beginning to get the idea he's taking a powder on me. Just then he comes out and says, 'Driver, I need your help. Come upstairs with me.'

"The night man takes us up, no questions asked. We walk into an office and he leads me to a safe.

" 'Now, driver, here's my problem. I've got to open this safe and I can't seem to do it. I guess that last drink made my hands a little shaky. And I'm not sure of all the numbers now, either. I want you to see what you can do.'

"This nearly floors me and I tell him, 'So what am I, a safecracker? Pay me my fare, mister, please, and lemme outa here in a hurry. I want no part of this.'

" 'You don't understand, driver. I own this place and the safe belongs to me. Would the elevator operator take us up here if he didn't know me? I'll call him in.'

"Well, this convinces me. And so the pair of us kneel down in front of this big sardine can and go to work. I try to make like all those Jimmy Valentines I see in the movies. The guy is calling numbers and I'm twirling the knob. An hour of this and I'm going blind. Finally, we hear a click and that's it. The guy yanks open the door, shuffles around inside a minute or so and then pulls out a cash box. He opens it, peels a fifty off a pile of bills, hands it to me and says, 'You don't know how much I appreciate this, driver.'

"I nearly fall into the safe.

" 'Now,' he says, 'let's lock it up and you take me home.'

"When we arrive in front of his place I ask, 'Mister, excuse me for being so nosy, but could you tell me why you wanted that safe opened?'

"He scratches his noggin. 'I really don't know. I just had an urge to see if everything was OK. Now I feel better. I really appreciate what you did for me. Good night.' "

Every driver has a million of them.

Some individualists try another pitch. There's Abe Heller, for example, a rapid-fire punster who claims he can click them off for the duration of any ride from the Battery to Hell Gate, and can also out-wisecrack any professional comedian in the business. Or "Psychology" Goldstein, the "greatest psychologist who ever pushed a hack," whose technique is flattery, no matter how much of a schnook his fare appears to be—and believe him, plenty are. And there's David Gould, the self-styled "cabbie philosopher," who says he is sincerely interested in helping people solve their problems. Gould has made a recording of one of his best lectures. "How to Relax and Gain Peace of Mind," which is available to the general public at five dollars.

Other drivers offer their passengers little appurtenances like free cigarettes, tickets to radio and TV shows, aspirin, newspapers, magazines, Scotch tape, smelling salts, lighter fluid, cleansing tissues, lollipops for the kiddies, hot coffee in the winter, ice water in the summer.

And some evening you may find yourself riding with August Menzies, who feels that flowers make people happy, and so presents one to each of his passengers. Thus far, he has handed out close to twenty thousand fresh-cut roses, tulips, carnations, chrysanthemums, and even orchids.

Also working the hearts-and-flowers vein are the numerous musical drivers, many of them surprisingly good, some even real pros. Paul Insetta, for example, regales customers with his own compositions. One day Vic Damone heard one and asked its name. It was something Insetta called "Sitting by the Window." Damone thought it sounded like a hit and immediately got in touch with the song publishing house of Shapiro, Bernstein and Company. They felt the same way. Vic appointed himself the song's chief plugger and helped swing it into the hit parade.

If you're an opera-goer, you may enjoy a ride with Arturo, a former singer in European opera companies. Arturo was supposedly on the way to stardom when his teeth began to give him trouble. Before long he was wearing a complete set of store dentures which, because of some defect in his gums, refused to stay put. He had to cut his career short, and eventually drifted into cab driving. During the season he snares passengers leaving the Met so that he can discuss things operatic with them. When his teeth feel especially secure, he may illustrate some point with a snatch from an aria.

There are dozens of instrumentalists around, ranging from an ocarina player to a glockenspieler. But about the only one who ever entertains his fares is a young guitarist who is ready to strum away whenever there's a wait for traffic.

Even without these extras, the city's taxi service is rated by many world travelers as the best anywhere. All drivers are under the supervision of a special hack bureau of the Police Department. Every applicant for a license is thoroughly investigated and fingerprinted. More than a hundred rules and regulations governing the operation of taxis are strictly enforced by inspectors who patrol twenty-four hours a day. Their work is supplemented by a Motor Inspection Corps maintained by the cab companies.

New York's taxi drivers have done much on their own to clean up the business. The old stunt of taking you to Madison Square Garden by way of Yonkers hasn't been pulled in years—even on the sappiest-looking hayseed. And meticulously fair treatment is now the usual.

Anything forgotten in a cab is immediately turned over to the police, as it must be by law. Among the fabulous items found by drivers in the last few years were a $10,000 bill which a press agent really didn't mean to lose; a bag containing $30,000 worth of jewelry; a $27,200 wad, which slid out of Frank Costello's pocket; and a briefcase carrying a king's ransom, $250,000 in cash.

A member of Phil Spitalny's all-girl band forgot a tuba, over which she probably had to stumble to get out of the cab. Tennis star Alice Marble dropped a five-hundred-dollar cigarette case on the seat. There have been mink capes, false teeth, stuffed alligators, trunks, wigs, and even babies.

There are several authors among New York's hack drivers who gather material as they ride. One of them is Reuben Hecht, a condensation of whose book, *Human Nature Through the Rearview Mirror*, appeared in *Reader's Digest* not long ago. Everything happens to Hecht. He patches up lovers' quarrels, rescues damsels in distress, foils holdup men —and then dashes home to record his adventures.

James Maresca also hit the jackpot with *My Flag Is Down*, which reputedly was selling up to one hundred thousand copies a month in a quarter edition. Four or five more drivers are reported to be working on books or plays. So there's always the possibility that you may eventually find yourself delineated as some cab driver's problem child.

Especially if you insist on having your baby in his cab, as so many women seem to be doing these days. "If this trend continues," complained an obstetrician recently, "we'll soon be out of business."

For most get-me-there-in-a-hurry passengers, the cabbie uses the standard routine—screaming at other drivers, giving pedestrians dirty looks, muttering at cops, weaving in and out of traffic—all of which cons the customers, but gets him nowhere—and slowly.

The next time you step into a cab, look at the driver's hack license directly in front of you. If it displays a gold bar and the words, "Commended for Public Service," you've picked up a hero. And if you should spot the name of Paolino di Marco, you've picked a super-hero, a man who seems to make a hobby of being in the right place at the right time.

There was the time he was cruising down Eighth Avenue one morning about three o'clock. As he approached 50th Street, he noticed four men in a scuffle on the sidewalk. It looked like an even match until one of them suddenly pulled a knife and buried it in his nearest opponent. As Di Marco swung his cab over to the curb and jammed on his brakes, the knife flashed again and a second man went down. The cab driver jumped at the thug, and the pair hit the sidewalk. Di Marco then found he had another adversary on his hands—the thug's partner. How he did it he's not sure, but he managed to hold the pair down until the arrival of a squad car.

Di Marco's other citations were for chasing a hit-run driver and eventually cornering him on foot; capturing a burglar who had slipped out of a policeman's hands; rescuing several people trapped in a banquet-hall fire. In this last one he was badly burned on face, hands, and feet.

All told, close to eleven hundred such awards have been made since 1925, so your chances for catching a hero are not too remote. You might also enjoy the story of Anthony De Lillo, a winner last year.

De Lillo was returning from a trip uptown about four-thirty one morning last spring. At 31st Street and East River Drive he saw a crowd—unusual for that hour. He stopped and found out that a car had just skidded into the river with two passengers, a man and a woman. Just then, a man came to the surface, and as De Lillo was about to dive in, he began to paddle toward shore. He proved to be the driver of the car, who, in his dazed condition, had no idea where his companion was.

As the crowd milled around the shivering young man, De Lillo kept searching the river. Then, far out, he noticed what looked like a body floating downstream. He stripped to his shorts and jumped in. After a hard swim he reached the apparently lifeless form of the girl and brought her ashore, where she was eventually revived and taken to a hospital.

De Lillo climbed back into his clothes—and then discovered that a five-dollar bill was missing. The story of the rescue made the papers—with special emphasis on the lost money and the fact that De Lillo was studying interior decorating in his spare time. Several days later the girl, a waitress, was released from the hospital. She had read all about her rescuer, and was eager to make some financial reward. Having no money of her own, she decided that an appearance on a radio quiz show might be the answer. With her story she did get on a show—and came away with $665, which she presented to De Lillo to further his education.

Yes, a cab ride in New York can be fun.

JOE DOCKS

BUDD SCHULBERG

There is a forgotten man on the waterfront. His voice is lost among the gravel-throated alibis of high-bracket hoodlums, the oily explanations of labor politicians and the suavely martyred inflections of the shippers.

JOE DOCKS

You whiz by him on the West Side Highway but you don't see him. You hurry past him as you board ship for Europe or a winter cruise through the Caribbean, and never notice his face. But his muscles move your groceries and your steel; he carries your baggage on his back. From his pocket comes the notorious kickback you've read about. He's the one who has to show up every morning for the "shapeup" you've been hearing about. He is the human material with which racketeers, masquerading as union officials, pull flash strikes to shake down shipping companies and force the employment of such key personnel as boss loader and hiring boss. He is the man who performs the most dangerous work in America, according to the statistics on labor injury and death.

He's the longshoreman, the dock walloper, the little man who isn't there at investigations; the forgotten man in the great city of New York, the forgotten man of American labor. Miners, railroad men, even sailors were fighting fifty years ago against the kind of medievalism that passes for work conditions on the docks this very morning. In a day when social security and old age pensions are accepted as economic facts of life by both major parties, the longshoreman hasn't got job security from one day to the next.

If he's the forgotten man here's the forgotten fact: it is this basic insecurity—breeding fear, dependence, shiftlessness, demoralization—that feeds the power of the mob. The weaker, more frightened and divided are the dock workers; the stronger and more brazen are the Anastasias, Bowers, Florios and Clementes who manipulate them.

I went down to the waterfront for what I thought would be a few days' research for a film about the docks. Long after I had enough material for a dozen waterfront pictures I kept going back, drawn by these forgotten men performing a rugged, thankless job in a jungle of vice and violence where law and constitutional safeguards have never existed.

About thirty-five thousand men are paid longshoremen's wages in the course of a year. Of these, about half are regular longshoremen, men who depend on this work for their livelihood. The rest are what you might call casuals, now-and-theners who drift in to pick up an occasional extra check. Many of these are city employes, policemen and firemen who like to grab off the overtime money on nights and weekends. Some 50 per cent, for instance, earn less than $1,000 a year. Another 10 per cent earn less than $2,000. About a third of all the longshoremen, fifteen thousand at most, earn from $2,000 to $4,000 a year. These are the regulars, the ones who have to hustle every day to keep meat and potatoes on the table for the wife and kids. An upper crust of favored workers averages more than $75 a week on a yearly basis. The base pay of $2.27 per hour sounds all right. It's the irregularity and mob intimidation that make longshoremen the most harassed workmen in America.

Nine out of ten are Catholic—if not Irish Catholic, then Italian or Austrian. This accounts for the influence of certain waterfront priests who have championed the dock workers, in a few dramatic cases going so far as to challenge known hoodlums face to face on the piers. You'll find the Irish on the West Side and in Brooklyn, some six thousand of them, but they are now outnumbered by the Italians, which explains the growing influence of the Italian underworld that controls the Brooklyn waterfront, as well as the Jersey, Staten Island and East River docks. Irish longshoremen are devout. Before the 7:55 A. M. shape, you will see them going to Mass at St. Bernard's, St. Veronica's or St. Joseph's. Italians follow the Latin tradition of letting the wife handle the church responsibilities.

The Irish longshoremen, while kept in line by strong-arm boys and plagued by an inhuman hiring system, have a better deal than their fellow Italians, who in turn are a niche above the Negroes, who work in traveling gangs picking up the extra work when they can get it and are often relegated to the hold, the job nobody wants. The Irish are hardly ever asked to kick back any more. In other words, when the hiring boss picks his four or five gangs of twenty men each from the 200–250 men who shape themselves into an informal horseshoe around him, the Irish no longer return part of their day's pay to him in order to assure themselves of a job. But the Italians and Negroes systematically kick back as much as five dollars per man per day. With seven or eight thousand men kicking back, this quickly becomes big business, some $30,000 or $40,000 a day in illegal fees being passed up from the hiring boss to his superiors as part of the $350,000,000 illegal take from the New York harbor each year.

"It's a stinkin' feelin' standin' there in the shape every mornin' while some thievin' hirin' boss looks you over like you were so much meat," one of the Irish dockers was telling me the other day. "But once in a while an Italian gang is brought in to work with us and that really looks like something you've heard about in Europe, not America. They work in a short gang—sixteen instead of twenty—so the cowboys c'n pick up the extra checks for themselves. But they've got to do the work of twenty—or else. If they squawk, the boys work 'em over—or they don't get no more work. I've actually seen 'em beaten like cattle for a question.

"So the rules take a beatin'," my Irish friend went on. "In the first place, 90 per cent never read the contract. In the second place, it's just a piece of paper if the shop steward and the delegate are part of the mob. Jerry Anastasia, for instance, he's a delegate. A lotta help you get from a stiff like that. Half them I-talians are ship-jumpers, which leaves 'em at the mercy of the trigger boys. They ain't citizens and they can't even apply for unemployment insurance. The way I see it we got it lousy and they got it double lousy."

Today most of the Irish workers are picked up by gangs—in this case a legitimate work group, not the Mickey Bowers type. Each gang has its own leader and when the hiring boss points to him it means his whole crew works that day. But the Italians, Austrians and Negroes are still hired on an individual basis by gang carriers, exactly as Henry Mayhew described it in his book, "London Labor and London's Poor" a century ago:

"He who wishes to behold one of the most extraordinary and least-known scenes of his metropolis should wend his way to the docks at half past seven in the morning. * * * [When] the "calling foremen" have made their appearance, there begins the scuffling and scrambling forth of countless hands high in the air, to catch the eye of him whose voice may give them work. * * * It is a sight to sadden the most callous to see thousands of men struggling for only one day's work, the scuffle made fiercer by the knowledge that hundreds out of the number must be left to idle the day out in want."

Not a word need be changed in this description to apply it to hiring methods in New York Harbor a hundred years later. Now, as then, two or three times as many men as will be needed loiter near the dock entrance waiting for the hiring boss to blow his whistle when a ship is ready to be loaded or unloaded. Now, as then, he will pick them out according to his own whim and preference. But on too many docks in the great harbor of New York, the nod is given to the man who plays ball, kicks back, buys the ticket for the benefit he will not be expected to attend or signs up for haircuts in a barber shop where all the seats are filled by labor racketeers. Too often the numbered metal tag which a dockworker gets from the hiring boss, his admission card to a four- or eight-hour shift on the pier, is a badge of compliance, an acceptance of inferior status on the waterfront. Thousands of longshoremen are wondering why a modern metropolis insists on maintaining a practice so barbarous that it was outlawed in England sixty years ago and is now abandoned in nearly all American coastal cities but not in the great Port of New York. . . .

The men passed over in the shape must have eating money and they get it from the loan sharks who are part of the mob. If you "borry" four dollars you pay back five and the interest keeps mounting each week. A rap of 30 per cent isn't unusual. Nor is it unusual for a longshoreman getting the nod in a shape to turn over his work tab to the loan shark who collects the debtor's check directly from the pay office. So our longshoreman winds up a day's work by borrowing again.

"I was born in hock and I'll die in hock," a longshoreman told me in a Chelsea saloon. In some locals a longshoreman who wants to be hired has to go the route—come up with a bill for spurious "relief" drives and play the numbers and the horses with books belonging to the syndicate. In Brooklyn Albert Anastasia had everything for six blocks in from the river. Longshoremen have to buy their wine from the mob liquor store, and their groceries and their meat.

Unquestionably their incomes are supplemented by regular filching of meat and liquor from the supplies flowing through the piers. Even the insurgents who are doing their best to buck the graft and large-scale pilferage are no different in this respect. Their ethics may be questionable but they stem from a deeply ingrained cynicism that is easy to understand. For years they have watched the fantastic loading racket make off with whole shipments of valuables. The pilferage of ten tons of steel reported to the Crime Commission by a shipping executive may have been front-page headlines to the general public but it was hardly news to the dock workers. "If five per cent of everything moving in and out is systematically siphoned off by the mob, why shouldn't I take a few steaks home for the wife and kids," a longshoreman figures.

"Takin' what you need for your own table is never considered pilferage," it was explained to me rather solemnly. Shortly before Thanksgiving a longshoreman who could double for Jackie Gleason noticed barrels of turkeys being unloaded from a truck. He was not working that day but he simply got in line and waited for a barrel to be lowered onto his back. Everybody in his tenement got a free turkey.

Another longshoreman, known for his moxie in standing up to the goons of a pistol local ("one of them locals where you vote every four years with a gun in your back"), told me he was starved out on the docks for sixty straight days. "I stand there lookin' the crummy hirin' boss right in the eye but he never sees me." In a whole year he made less than $1,500 and he had kids to feed. "We couldn't 've made out if I hadn't scrounged the groceries on the dock," he said.

What are their politics? Traditionally Democratic, as befits good New York Irish and Italians, but you might say their universal party is cynicism. Because so many mobsters were aligned with the Democratic city machine, some longshoremen took to wearing Ike buttons on the docks as a sign of defiance.

But longshoremen have a feeling of being political orphans inevitably betrayed by the people for whom they vote. They'll tell you their cause has been ignored by the politicians, the police and even the press. Still, they aren't fooled by communism. Despite periodic outcries against subversive influences on the docks—unfortunately used as a cover-up for various forms of racketeering, communism is as unpopular among longshoremen as among stock brokers, farmers or railroad workers.

Men in the Chelsea area are still bitter at the editorials calling their strike Communist-inspired. The local involved, 791, is made up of staunch Irish Catholics, many of them under the influence of the waterfront priest Father John Corridan. It is safer to call these men Communists in print than to deliver that opinion face to face.

"I belt guys for less 'n that," said an embattled member of 791, identified with opposition to Joe Ryan, to strong-arm methods, and to chronic insecurity on the docks.

Father Corridan, of the Xavier Labor School on the Lower West Side, who has become a kind of one-man brain trust of the rank-and-file, sums up the Communist angle this way:

"In '45 the Communists did move in and try to take credit for the leaderless, rank-and-file strike. But right now their influence is nil, no matter what the I.L.A. brass says. The men down here—almost without exception—are loyal, God-fearing Americans. The way to fight Communism in the labor movement is to accentuate the positive—in other words find out what the men really need in order to live healthy, happy, dignified lives and then fight for it."

What longshoremen want has nothing to do with ideologies and millenniums. Their aims are so modest as to be taken for granted by some sixty million American wage earners. What they want most is an assurance that the job they're lucky enough to have today is the same one they'll have tomorrow—and next week—and next month. They don't want to keep wandering from pier to pier like a lot of miserable strays begging for work.

An old man with forty years on the docks compared his status—or lack of it—with a railroad engineer's. "Look at him, he goes to work every morning knowing he's got a place in the world. The more time he's got behind him the more secure he feels. That's seniority. He knows if he does his job well his pay'll increase, his position improves and he'll finally retire with a good pension. He's got dignity, that's what he's got. Now take me. All my life on the dock. And I know my job. I know how to handle copper in the rain and how to get my fingers into a bag of flour. I c'n work fast. I like to take pride in my work. But what kind of pride can I feel when some punk comes out of the can and starts makin' five times as much as I am for doin' nothin' except pushin' us around?"

The old man insisted on buying me another drink. It may have been loan-shark money, but longshoremen are proud and open-handed and fine drinking companions when they feel they can trust you.

"After forty years I get up t'morra mornin' an' stan' over there on the dock like an orphan. I'll be lucky if I bring home twenty-five bucks this week."

The other morning a little fellow who sounded enough like Barry Fitzgerald to make the Ed Sullivan TV show was left standing on the dock by an ex-Sing Sing hiring boss for the fourth consecutive jobless day. "In Liverpool back in 1912 they knocked out this kinda hiring," he was saying. "I could tell them judges on the Crime Commission a thing or two about this stinkin' setup." Even now, early in the morning with another jobless day ahead and the Good Lord only knew what tomorrow, there was a twinkle in his eye. These are indestructible men (until a strong-arm man, a St. John or an Ackalitis, has the last word) and laughter comes easy to them for all their grief and frustration. "When those high mucky-mucks get all through and there's a zillion words of testimony all nicely bound, they'll know what we knew in the first place—down here it's really time for a change."

He gave his cap a jaunty poke, stuck his hands into his battered windbreaker, pushed his chest out in a gesture of general defiance and crossed Forty-fourth Street to McGinty's Bar and Grill.

ROSS AND *THE NEW YORKER*

ALLEN CHURCHILL

New York is the only city currently producing a local magazine which exerts wide national and even international influence. The New Yorker's *circulation—the major portion of which now goes out of town—is relatively small, only a fraction of the readership of such mass magazines as* Reader's Digest, Life, Saturday Evening Post *or the giant women's periodicals. Yet,* Advertising Age *points out that, as far back as 1934* Fortune Magazine *published articles analyzing "the little* New Yorker *as exhaustively as if it were Big Steel." In this sense,* The New Yorker *is significantly different from so many other Gotham phenomena which make their impact through quantity, through sheer mass.*

Indirectly, of course, The New Yorker's *success has been dependent on the great city's capacity to attract and support the best and largest pool of editorial, art and writing talent, from which Harold Ross could select a staff and contributors. The magazine's influence, however, has been achieved not by quantity but by quality. This quality is an amalgam of many elements, including wit, brashness, sophistication (originally, though today the term has really lost its meaning), urbanity, a leavening of intellect, a willingness to play David to varied Goliaths (e.g.,* Reader's Digest, Henry Luce, Walter Winchell*), a fairly catholic editorial taste and a particularly high estimate of itself which, in the main, has been justified.*

Perhaps The New Yorker's *central original function was to help a barbarous, uncouth city, suddenly grown to self-conscious and immature adulthood to achieve a measure of self-acceptance, without getting too pompous about its top-dog status. And, culturally, as New York goes, so goes the nation—eventually.* The New Yorker's *efforts to avoid smugness and yet maintain its uniqueness have, inevitably, resulted in certain poses and rituals. But, by and large, the magazine has avoided any serious congealing of the arteries; its sacred taboos and shibboleths—while undoubtedly excluding much fine material, even by some of the best writers of our age—are far fewer than one would expect from such a successful institution.*

Here, Allen Churchill recounts some of the legends and

facts about both the magazine and its founder and long-time editor, the late Harold Ross. As is often the case with a richly embroidered legend, hardly a man is now alive who will say for sure where fact leaves off and legend begins. But all of it is definitely part of the unique metropolitan phenomenon, The New Yorker.

Harold Ross, who has been editor of the *New Yorker* ever since he originated it in 1925, is one of the most incongruous figures ever to walk on the American literary scene. The *New Yorker*, as everybody knows, is the sophisticated magazine designed for smart New Yorkers and read by smart people everywhere. Ross, however, is a walnut-faced, gap-toothed, frontier roughneck who might have been expected to land in almost any berth but the one he chose. The contrasts between him and his magazine are as glaring as those between New York City and Aspen, Colorado, where Ross was born in 1892.

In appearance a man whose leathery features combine the cowboy look of Will Rogers with the moon-mad expression of Harpo Marx, and whose manners are rough, Ross seems many layers of civilization removed from the elegant, top-hatted Eustace Tilley, whose aloof scrutiny of a butterfly has become the trademark of *New Yorker* urbanity. In action Ross, who is tireless, cantankerous and probably happy, is equally far removed from the unruffled calm of his magazine, and over the years his uninhibited doings have practically assumed the proportions of a Manhattan legend.

According to legend, Ross, a garrulous man, spends most of his day uttering a lament on his troubles. In moments of greatest anguish he lifts his eyes to heaven and yells, "God, how I pity me!" Asked how he feels, his standard reply is a thundering *"Terrible."* "If Ross ever answered *'fine,'* " Dorothy Parker cracked once, "I'd know the *New Yorker* was finished." Ross particularly enjoys complaining about being needlessly consulted on petty office matters. One day as he discoursed on this theme before a new employee, an office boy burst in. "I hate to bother you, Mr. Ross," the boy panted, "but what shall I do? A gentleman is trying to commit suicide in the men's room." Ross cast a triumphant look at the new employee. "See what I mean?" he asked.

In the company of men no sentence Ross speaks is without its chunk of unadorned, top-sergeant profanity. Asked if he had been a happy man, he answered, "It's been a son of a bitch of a life, I guess." Bidding farewell to a writer, he threw an affectionate arm around the departing one. "God bless you, McNulty, God damn it," he said. In the presence of women Ross heroically confines his swearing to the word Buckwheat, a term of scorn. Moreover, he has labored to stem profanity among others in the *New Yor* office. "If you put swear words in memos to me," he warned males on the staff, "put the memos in envelopes and seal. There are women around."

On occasions when Ross undertakes to be charming the results are usually strange. Once James Thurber introduced him to his eye doctor. "I have no use for professional men," Ross stated loudly. Then he began a happy cross-examination of the doctor. At the end of the evening he declared himself an authority on the human eye. Inviting a writer to lunch to offer him a job, Ross announced, "I'm late, God damn it," when they met. Learning the writer was from the South he expounded for two hours on patent medicines and Coca-Cola. Stopping abruptly he demanded, "Want to work up here?" After the writer joined the staff, Ross did not speak to him for three years. Now when the two meet, they talk about eels.

How Ross, the rough Colorado diamond, has been able to produce the *New Yorker*, a magazine unerring in its excellent taste, is a major mystery. He has, for one thing, displayed a steady lack of interest in popular taste. Where other editors devote themselves to studying reader-interest charts, Ross maintains, "An editor prints only what pleases him—if enough people like what he likes, he is a success." There can be no doubt that Ross, whose magazine is now worth five million dollars, has been a success, though a maddening and inexplicable one. "Without question he is the most brilliant magazine editor of our time," Bennett Cerf (whose wedding Ross attended carrying an antique shotgun) once wrote. "No man," says Russell Maloney, who spent eleven years working for Ross, "has been the subject of so much analysis, interpretation and explanation—with so little result." His staff, when asked to explain him, falls back on the simple statement that Ross is a genius; but the answer may be that Ross, who teems with notions and prejudices, knows best what he does not like and, being a genius, what he does like is exactly right.

Ross himself, who once said to Robert Benchley, "I don't want you to think I'm not incoherent," is seldom coherent about what guides him as an editor. Only about morals in his magazine does he appear to have a definite standard. "I don't know," he will mutter over a realistic piece, "some pregnant woman might read it and have a miscarriage." Office legend has it that such a woman once wrote him about being shocked by a story in the *New Yorker*, with such results. This frightened Ross for life, though if the lady suffered it was probably from laughter rather than realism. Over the years an aggressive prudishness, coupled with instinctive good taste, has kept questionable material from Ross' tightly-edited magazine. One of James Thurber's first jobs on the staff was to search for innuendo the copy of such worldly writers as Dorothy Parker and Robert Benchley. Knowing Ross' prudishness they delighted in devising subtle *double entendres*.

Personally editing everything that goes into the *New Yorker*, Ross, who does not look his age and has about him the quality of a grown-up Tom Sawyer, reads all material in galley form. He hauls his typewriter to him, leans over it and begins to read the galley, concentrating so intensely that his tongue hangs from his mouth like that of an overworked horse. Tearing into each sentence before him for accuracy, complete information and straightforward style, he is driven by a passion for perfection, a furious determination to make each issue better than the one before. In this he is assisted by an ignorance fantastic in a grown man—an ignorance which enables him to approach material as an editor ideally should, without prejudice or previous information. No one knows when Ross left school. He himself is vague on the subject, admitting only that he was a part-time newspaper reporter at thirteen and full-time shortly after. Quitting school so young, Ross had little time to learn. After he had proceeded to immerse himself completely in day-to-day newspaper work, he never found time to make himself an educated man. Behind his ignorance, however, lies a vast though oddly negative curiosity. Only when a galley is placed before him does he burn to know every detail of the subject it covers. Often Ross' queries, which he types and numbers to correspond with numbers he puts on the galley, run longer than the original piece. Once he spent a happily profane afternoon exposing the inadequacies of a Reporter-at-Large article, only to discover it was the second half of two parts.

New Yorker writers insist that their magazine has no definite style, though there is a widespread belief that they are trained to write a certain way. Rather, they say, it is the checking, re-writing and re-checking, spearheaded by Ross and followed by every editor down the line—the constant, meticulous insistence on perfection—that creates the *New Yorker* style.

Ross, who was among the first to use one-line captions and to link cartoons with contemporary events, goes through the same inspired fussing over the cartoons and covers, which are perhaps more famous than *New Yorker* prose. His memory for art is phenomenal. At one drawing, re-submitted after nearly a year, he barked, "He's darkened the sky." "No, he hasn't," the art editor assured him. "Find out," Ross ordered. The sky had been darkened. Ross' determination on excellence inevitably carries over to captions. Seldom is the artist's own caption used; often the caption is first perfected in the office, then farmed out to an artist. But no matter how short, captions are re-written numberless times. To date the office record is held by a Peter Arno caption, which passed through every typewriter in the office and was three years in the perfecting.

Ross was born on November 6, 1892, the son of a militant anti-Mormon who, when Harold was seven, moved his family from Colorado to Salt Lake City, in order to be nearer the fray. Another anti-Mormon of the period was the publisher of the Salt Lake City *Tribune*. This man shortly became a friend of Ross' father, and Ross started part-time work in the city room of the *Tribune* while still in grammar school, becoming a full-time reporter a little later. Soon the *Tribune* began to confine the juvenile journalist and, still under eighteen, he set out for California, beginning a career as journeyman reporter which took him to newspapers up and down the West Coast, to Atlanta, Washington, and finally, during the first world war, to editorship of the Army paper, *Stars and Stripes*.

Exactly when the idea of the *New Yorker* first exploded in Ross' teeming brain is not known. Today he says he developed ideas for six different magazines in the years between 1919 and the start of the *New Yorker*. He was an editor of the humor magazine, *Judge*, when one day early in 1924 he invited Raoul Fleischmann, of the baking family, to lunch. Addicted to poker and masculine companionship, the pair had met at the celebrated Thanatopsis Literary and Inside Straight Club, whose members included such New York literary wits as Alexander Woollcott, Franklin P. Adams and George S. Kaufman. An urbane and ingratiating man, Fleischmann was one of the few men of wealth allowed in the Thanatopsis. At their luncheon, Ross informed Fleischmann that he wanted to start his own magazine and needed financial backing. A veteran of seventeen years in the baking business, Fleischmann was looking for a more colorful career, and showed interest until Ross began outlining one of his six ideas, Fleischmann did not like it and, after a moment of confusion, Ross spoke about a smart local magazine which would have the light, sophisticated approach to life of the Thanatopsis wits. Fleischmann liked this idea better. At later luncheons he agreed to put up the necessary capital and become the publisher, which he is today. The name *New Yorker* was supplied by the late John Peter Toohey, a Broadway press agent.

Ballyhooed by posters of Eustace Tilley, the Rea Irvin dandy who has decorated every anniversary issue since, the magazine first appeared on New York newsstands on February 21, 1925. Through its first spring and summer the magazine did badly. Its circulation dwindled so alarmingly that Fleischmann considered withdrawing his investment, and called a luncheon at the Princeton Club for the purpose of doing this. He, Eugene Spaulding, the business manager, Ross, and John Hanrahan, a publishers' counsellor, sat down to a gloomy meal. Only Hanrahan, whose connection with the magazine had been slight, radiated hope. He was a brisk, voluble Irishman who talked in a husky whisper and who used words in such peculiar combinations that his associates collected Hanrahan phrases, as Hollywood wags collect the utterances of Sam Goldwyn. In picturing a bright future, Hanrahan's talk rose to intoxicating heights, and it is possible that listening to his dizzying verbiage weakened Fleischmann. At any rate, as the four parted after luncheon Fleischmann made up his mind to stay with the *New Yorker*.

By January 1926 the magazine was catching on and Ross, who for the first months had practically worked alone, in the offices at 25 West 45th Street, began accumulating a staff. For an editor with his high standards, this was comparable to assembling a symphony orchestra, yet Ross operated largely on the theory that by hiring enough people he would eventually find the perfect ones. Quickly the *New Yorker* became populated with men he liked as drinking companions, others who merely drifted in the door, and strays from all quarters of the literary world. Among the writers Ross hired was one who developed the shakes if he touched paper: an office boy had to stand at his side, feeding the paper into his typewriter. One female writer usually behaved normally except that at intervals each day she carefully removed her rings, wristwatch and other jewelry. Leaving these on her desk, she walked to another office where she telephoned her husband, to whom she delivered an unmerciful tongue-lashing. Then, returning to her desk, she put on her jewelry and again applied herself to work.

Fanatically determined that each issue of his magazine be perfect, Ross demanded endless re-writes, queried all facts and howled endlessly for improvement. This drove his frantic and constantly shifting staff to sanitariums, to fits on the floor and to threatening him with violence. Ross further added to the general discomfiture by a magnificent impatience with office design. Seeking to achieve the perfect office, as well as the perfect magazine and staff, he ordered walls smashed, built up, and smashed again, while partitions and furniture were switched almost daily. Returning from lunch to find a pneumatic drill busy outside his office, James Thurber, Ross' most celebrated writer and cartoonist, gathered all the available metal wastebaskets and bowled them down the hall in noisy protest. Finally the drill retired, leaving Thurber free to write. At another time the confusion became so complete that Thurber posted a sign, *Alterations Going On as Usual During Business*.

Ross' fond dream during this period was to sit at a central desk with push buttons and supervise each issue by remote control, like a general directing a campaign. Temperamentally unsuited to organizing such a utopian system, he hoped for a managing editor who would. With colossal naïveté he believed that most of the men he hired for his editorial department were just the ones he wanted for this position. These men—who were referred to as the Jesuses to Ross' God—would be told, immediately on being hired, to start organizing the office. Wandering off, they quickly discovered that Ross ran everything himself and that no one, Jesus or otherwise, had been able to get the slightest organizing authority away from him. Some time later the Jesus would pass Ross in the hall. Ross would not speak—he had either forgotten the new man or had hired another managing editor. After that the Jesus would sit collecting his pay until Ross summoned the nerve to fire him, which sometimes took years.

While driving his staff Ross also drove himself. Considering the *New Yorker* a twenty-four-hour job, he seldom thought or talked of anything else. The image of Ross concentrating on his magazine became so impressed on this staff that, learning the man was to become the father of a child, one editor murmured, "Conceived in an absent-minded moment, no doubt."

At this time Ross, in manner and appearance, was the roughest of rough diamonds, a sloppy dresser who permitted his hair to grow straight up from his scalp so that he would not have to use a comb. "He is essentially a desert rat," wrote a friend at the time, "unequal to the amenities that well-mannered people, even well-mannered plumbers, consider necessary to living." Ross could not, for example, summon up the geniality required to say Good Morning to anyone on arriving at the office. Office boys at the *New Yorker* were instructed never to speak to Mr. Ross. The men working for him admired his ability and integrity to such an extent that they were willing to overlook anything, while outside friends often found his lack of manners appealing. "Ross is the only man I know," said Charles MacArthur, "who has charm in his roughness." Ross early went on record as objecting to women in offices, believing that association between the sexes inevitably led to trouble. Often he announced at the top of his voice, "I will keep sex out of this office if it's the last thing I do." After the inter-office marriages of Katherine Angell and E. B. White, and Lois Long and Peter Arno, Ross was forced to abandon these efforts, confining himself to announcing on occasion, "Sex is an incident."

From the very first days of his magazine, Ross has insisted that no representative of the advertising or business departments ever set foot in the editorial office. Unlike others which began with this noble resolve, the *New Yorker* has hewed to it. In the days when the magazine occupied a single floor Ross ordered a partition erected between editorial and business departments. Members of those departments christened this partition the Chastity Belt, but there is no record of anyone violating it. When a member of the advertising department won the Irish sweepstakes, the halls of the business office rang with celebration, while reporters and photographers tore in to interview the lucky girl. Despite the sounds from across the partition, however, no member of the editorial department joined, or even investigated, the fun. Even Raoul Fleischmann, the publisher, is subject to Ross' iron non-fraternization decree. Encountering him in the editorial office, one writer was taken aback. "What are you doing here?" he asked. "I have permission to come," Fleischmann answered humbly.

"I have been laid up with duodenal ulcers, half the staff has gone to war, and I'm sorely pressed," Ross wrote to a friend in 1944. The war as well as his ulcers had a sobering, even a mellowing, effect on the rambunctious Ross. Always believing that, with the exception of men like Thurber, White and Wolcott Gibbs, he could easily staff his magazine, Ross was suddenly faced with a frightening shortage of editors and writers. This caused him to appreciate those he had, and the selfless way they served him through the war brought more appreciation. Today Ross, always the man of extremes, values his staff mightily and speaks to everyone, including office boys, in the halls.

Ross' ulcers have forced him to tame his actions, but he remains a highly active man, proud that 24 intense, dedicated years have kept him young. They have also kept him refreshingly folksy and unspoiled. Some years ago he heard that Henry Luce, the publisher of *Life*, *Time* and *Fortune*, objected to a Profile of himself which was to be published in the *New Yorker*. Ross decided to call Luce. When his secretary said, "Mr. Luce is on the phone," Ross casually lit a cigarette, sauntered over to the phone and said, "Hi, Luce." The two men decided to get together to discuss the Profile. "There isn't a single nice thing about me in the whole piece," Luce sputtered when they met. "That," said Ross, "is what you get for trying to be a baby tycoon."

Actual issues of the *New Yorker* have changed even less than Ross. While most other publications have been re-designed his remains the same size, with practically the same departments, and even the same type. (The type was designed by Rea Irvin, the magazine's first art director and called Irvin type.) An unabashed luxury magazine, the *New Yorker* by fast editorial footwork has survived a depression and a world conflict—in the latter case surprising everyone by producing superb war reporting.

Today the magazine is more serious than ever before; indeed, in a supposedly humorous magazine, the cartoons are the only feature which consistently strive to be funny. The magazine has run important stories on the bombing of Hiroshima (by John Hersey) and the Greenville lynching (by Rebecca West). Like most fruits of Ross' editorial judgment, these two articles were highly successful and easily justified the more serious turn the magazine has taken.

Still a relentless perfectionist in the office, Ross even now makes efforts toward supreme office efficiency. As part of his new policy of catering to the staff, he recently decided a lounge would make his writers more contented. By shifting partitions and reducing office space, a lounge was created. The lounge was windowless; it derived light from the halls through heavy glass which gave it an air of elegance different from other offices on the floor. This much accomplished, Ross found another interest and no one bothered to provide furniture for the room.

Ross still appears to labor 24 hours a day, working at home in the morning—either in his apartment on Park Avenue or at his country home in Stamford, Connecticut—then going to the office after lunch at the Algonquin to work until anywhere from 6 P.M. to midnight. His closest friends outside the office are a private detective, a wholesale grocery dealer and a photographer. For his vacation trips he usually meets Dave Chasen, the comedian turned Hollywood restaurateur. With Ray Schindler, his detective friend, Ross has played innumerable practical jokes over the years. Once he stole a small metal sign from a bookstore which said, "This property is under the protection of the Schindler Detective Agency." After seeing this in Ross' office, Schindler repaired to the Hotel New Yorker, where he lifted a bath mat which said "The New Yorker." When Ross in turn had seen this in Schindler's bathroom he got some New Yorker Hotel stationery and wrote a letter demanding the mat, signing the letter "House Detective." There this gag seems to have died, but as a result of his practical jokes Ross' office for years was a museum of oddities which has boasted such collectors' items as the opera hat Rudolph Valentino wore on the night of his fatal collapse. Another collector around town had secured this choice item and enshrined it in a glass case. Seeing it there, the redoubtable Charles MacArthur smashed the case with his fist and ran with the trophy to the *New Yorker* office. There, with fitting ceremonies, he presented the hat to Ross.

One of the most fascinating games in literary Manhattan is speculation about what will happen to the *New Yorker* when Ross no longer edits it. More than any other magazine editor, it is pointed out, Ross *is* his magazine. Many observers believe that William Shawn, Ross' number-one managing editor who though unlike Ross personally reflects him as an editor, will be the successor who will continue the course of the magazine. Others predict its speedy collapse after Ross leaves.

Ross himself is aware of this speculation and will have none of it. A man who seldom looks beyond next week's issue of his magazine, he has settled for himself the question of what will happen to the *New Yorker* when he retires or dies. "It will go its Goddamn way, I guess," he says.*

BILLION-DOLLAR BABY

FROM "TIME"

In a dazzling bright room high above the late summer landscape of Manhattan's Central Park stood an exquisite blonde in a regal white

---

* Shawn has been appointed editor and all seems to be going well, substantiating Ross' own statement that the magazine has long been a team effort.

dress. She rustled her billowing petticoats and smiled a smile of quiet rapture. Above her *décolletage*, as bare as a lie and as bold as fashion, sparkled a small cascade of diamonds—or what looked like diamonds. Her slender, black-gloved hand gripped a black cigarette holder from which, now and again, she flicked a trace of ash with gracious disdain. A man's voice cooed to her.

"Just enjoy the whole thing," said the man. . . . Let the action transfer to the whole body . . . Relax the shoulders . . . Hollow the chest . . . That's wonderful, wonderful! . . . Now just gently . . . close your mouth please . . . Go on now, really moving . . . Yes, *yes*, YES! . . . That's *so* beautiful . . ."

This passionate effusion was punctuated by the constant, brittle click of a camera. The ecstatic monologuist was *Vogue's* talented photographer Irving Penn and the woman in white was his model. Well might Penn be ecstatic. In that strange, flood-lit world whose heaven is Paris and whose economic life force is the American woman's checkbook, his model was a reigning queen. She was Lisa Fonssagrives, the highest-paid, highest-praised high-fashion model in the business, considered by many of her colleagues the greatest fashion model of all time. Says Photographer Horst Paul Horst, who helped her get started: "She has one of the most beautiful bodies I have ever seen." . . . Historically, the model was the descendant of the come-on girl posted in front of a Midway show tent; socially, she ranked high above the chorus girl and not far below the movie star. In the bright parade, with the assurance of a duchess and the accomplished posturing of an actress, floated Lisa Fonssagrives. Thin, slightly bony, gowned and groomed with superhuman perfection, she was undeniably beautiful, but in her pictures a bit distant and ethereal, and not altogether real. Lisa Fonssagrives was, in fact, an artfully posed, painstakingly lighted, lavishly printed image which bore about as much resemblance to an ordinary woman as Plato's "forms" to their imperfect earthly copies. But the model is an illusion that can sell everything from diapers to cemetery plots, aspirin to Zonite. She is a billion-dollar baby with a billion-dollar smile and a billion-dollar salesbook in her billion-dollar hand. She is the new goddess of plenty.

In the past century, America underwent a great economic revolution. Americans made more things, and created more power to create still more things, than all past ages put together. The force chiefly charged with selling this breathless, and sometimes choking, proliferation of wealth is advertising.

At the Victorian era's high noon, most businessmen were warmed by the belief that the biggest rewards would automatically go, by economic law, to the producer of the best and cheapest product. It was mainly patent medicinemen who "took advertising" regularly. In 1888, there were only two men in New York who admitted to being professional writers of advertising; one of them resided in a Bowery hotel, at twenty-five cents a night.

But the living standard of the ad-smiths improved rapidly. Other manufacturers, led by the makers of such simple consumer items as soap and baking powder, began to learn the lessons of trademarks, contact with the customer, expanding demand. In church one Sunday morning in 1879, Harley T. Procter, of Procter & Gamble, listened to a passage from the forty-fifth psalm (". . . all thy garments smell of myrrh, and aloes, and cassia, out of the ivory palaces, whereby they made thee glad . . .") and coined the label "Ivory Soap." In 1890, Kodak launched one of the first relentlessly successful slogans: "You press the button—we do the rest." As other manufacturers ventured into advertising's strange new land, a blaze of new slogans followed: "Pink Pills for Pale People," "Do You Wear Pants?" Slogans temporarily gave way to jingles, alarming forerunners of the singing commercial. Then destiny struck in Chicago; a photographer named Beatrice Tonneson used pictures of live girls in ads for the first time.

By the end of World War I, the rush to put women in ads was on. Coca-Cola used a black-haired beauty and a kitten. Hole-proof Hosiery pioneered cheesecake by lifting skirts and showing legs. Chesterfield made shocking history by subtly inciting women to smoke: a flapper cuddled up to her smoke-puffing boy friend and whispered, "Blow some my way."

With the motorcar had come the Fisher Body Girl. In Paris, Harvard-educated, Poet E. E. Cummings sneered:

> . . . Spearmint
> Girl With The Wrigley Eyes . . .
> of you i
> sing . . .
> from every B.V.D.
> let freedom ring . . .

Admen, in league with psychology, following charts marshaled by armies of researchers, plotted a never-ceasing campaign to capture the public's attention, and stab to the psychological soft spots of men and women. They appealed to fear, to snobbery, to romance. They spoke in euphemisms, wrapped like cotton around the harsh facts of life, and invented dread new diseases. They found that endorsements by real people, from tobacco auctioneers to movie stars, were astoundingly successful sales plugs. They sponsored contests, told jokes, wrote essays, and often told a straight story about the things they had to sell. They appealed to all men's desire for better things by dazzling them with glowing pictures of the new and better things American industry was making. But always present was advertising's simplest and most potent symbol, the female figure.

At least one-third of all advertisements today use models. The proportion is nearer half in beer, cigarettes, cosmetics, the biggest users of models outside the fashion field. The figures add up to the simple conviction that there is nothing like a girl to catch the public's eye.

To supply the huge demand made by the advertisers on America's vast reservoir of beauty, the highly specialized and erratic model business has materialized. An appendage of advertising, model agencies combine the ethics of theatrical agents with the esthetics of bathing beauty judges. Modeling is concentrated in a few crowded Manhattan blocks between Fifth and Third Avenues, brightened by the parade of breathless, breath-taking young women dressed at fashion's extreme, hatboxes in their hands, their feet fleet and flat-heeled, their pancaked faces as blank as a baby's conscience. There are about one thousand professional photographic models active in New York (including twenty-five men, twenty-five children and several dogs).

Thousands more knock on agency doors every year, driven by their own ambitions, by unscrupulous "modeling schools" which promise to turn them into cover girls in six easy lessons, or by relentless mothers. But disillusion awaits them. Even if a girl is accepted by one of New York's twenty-three agencies it is still a long road to a magazine cover or a four-color ad. Most agencies register far more models than they can possibly place, are little more than clearinghouses which keep the models' bookings, relay telephone messages, give them a place to sit around and wait between jobs, and collect 10 per cent of their fees. It is usually the model who has to sell herself, tramping in and out of photographers' studios, showing her scrapbook, trying to look like the advertisers' cryptic specifications ("We need the soap and motherhood type"). By great good fortune she may land a movie contract. But in most cases, she will achieve a glamourous life only in the ads she poses for.

Nor will her income be glamourous. Virtually all statistics in the modeling business are the figment of someone's creative imagination.

Best estimates are that only about fifty or sixty of New York's 1,000 photographic models make between $10,000 and $20,000 a year. Most models charge from $5 to $15 an hour and often do not find enough work to make ends meet. Lisa Fonssagrives is alone in charging $40 an hour. What makes a face and a figure worth $40 an hour? The answer to that lies in the way Lisa Fonssagrives works.

Recently one of Lisa's typical days began at 7 A.M., when she arose at her converted gardener's cottage in Muttontown, Long Island. She breakfasted in bed, listened to her eight-year-old daughter Mia read her lessons. She drove thirty-five miles to Manhattan in her red-upholstered convertible. On the road, she was something of a hazard. An amateur plane pilot, she considers any speed under 70 m.p.h. dull. . . .

Her first Manhattan stop was her office, where she picked up gloves, shoes and a list of bookings which her secretary had prepared for her. Then she went to Seventh Avenue for a fitting of a dress she would model later in the week. From Seventh she taxied two blocks east to Fifth. After a session with the hairdresser (Lisa's hair, which used to be black and then red, is now ash blonde), she rushed to a sitting with old friend Horst at the *Vogue* studios. Two hours later, she raced on (without stopping for lunch) to another sitting with Photographer Henry Gravneek. She retouched her make-up in the taxi. As she entered the studio, Designer Taylor was on hand to introduce Lisa to the black cocktail dress she was to model. While the designer pulled and pinned the dress into place, she patted Lisa Fonssagrives' modest bosom and said: "Darling, you'll simply have to fill that out. You know what I want—the Maxime look."

"Well," said Lisa with resignation, "it's a leettle difficult when one has never been chez Maxime, but I think the feeling will come." The feeling came with the addition of some falsies (worn by almost all models when the occasion requires). There were crises over shoes (wrong ankle straps) and gloves (too shiny) and the necklace (too large). But presently the massed lights went on, all shadows withering in the merciless crossplay. Then Photographer Gravneek quietly started shooting, only now and then asking Lisa to turn a bit this way or that. Thirty minutes and sixteen camera clicks later, it was all over.

Working with a less accomplished model, the photographer might spend hours trying to prod and push her into the proper pose. But not with Lisa. With a dancer's discipline and grace, she responds instantly to the photographer's every direction, almost before it is spoken. Her body (bust and hips thirty-four inches) is so supple that she can pull in her normally twenty-three-inch waist to eighteen inches. She has the gift of mimicry every good model needs, and a keen fashion sense. Once, she appeared 103 times in a single issue of a magazine, scarcely looked like the same girl in two pictures. Says she: "The photographer says, 'Look sexy,' and I look sexy. He says, 'Look like a kitten,' and I look like a kitten. It is always the dress, it is never, never the girl." As one satisfied customer put it: "A lot of models will not move a muscle for a cheap dress. Lisa makes a ten-dollar cotton dress look like a Schiaparelli." Mockingly, Lisa Fonssagrives puts it another way: "I'm just a good clothes hanger."

The life dedicated to the task of being a paragon of fashion for American women began thirty-eight years ago, far from the U.S. and far from fashion. Lisa was born in the small Swedish town of Uddevalla, the daughter of Dr. Samuel Bernstone, a dentist. Although her parents sent her to cooking school ("with the idea that I should be a good housewife"), Lisa had her heart and her nimble feet set on dancing. The town still remembers how, in a school play, she stole the show dancing the role of an Oriental slave.

She went to Paris where she got engagements with minor ballet companies (her 5 foot seven inches made her too tall for the Paris Corps de Ballet). In 1935, she married her fellow dancer, handsome Fernand Fonssagrives. Both soon gave up dancing, he to be a photographer, she to be a model. A young photographer asked her to pose for him. The results were sensational. *Vogue* and *Harper's Bazaar* fought to get her services as a mannequin; she has worked for both. Horst, one of the first photographers for whom she posed, recalls that she trembled with fear during her early sittings, but soon lost her stage fright, and became a top Paris model. When war broke out, Lisa and Fernand came to the U.S. Soon after her first pictures appeared in U.S. magazines, smitten strangers sent her presents, including a bottle of champagne from Stork Club Impresario Sherman Billingsley, whom she has never met. She recalls, "I thought: what a strange country this is. Maybe I'd better go home *now*. . . ."

Lisa has been a top model for fourteen years while younger and prettier ones have come and gone, but no one was yet ready to name her successor when and if she stops modeling. In one sense, of course, Lisa Fonssagrives would never stop. If her face should disappear from the magazines tomorrow, other faces would crowd to take its place and the American public would scarcely know the difference. For the model is more than an individual; she has become a type and an inevitable part of the American scene. She is everywhere; she smiles down from mountains and from steely skyscraper façades, from billboards and from the most exclusive bars.

As, in her ads, she moves along in constant and successful pursuit of happiness, from high school prom to church wedding to a mortgage-free white frame house, she becomes a nearly epic figure: America's Everywoman. Her great and simple message is: life can be happy and Everywoman can be beautiful.

In an important sense she exercises an unsettling influence by making men and women dissatisfied with reality. She proclaims that homeliness is a sin and unnecessary. Her every image assures men that women look like goddesses, while their experience tells them that women only look like women. She assures the women, in their turn, that they can clean a two-story house, take the children to school, make a dress at home, cook a four-course meal, wash the dishes, and then slip into an opera gown, make brilliant conversation and look as ravishing as an ad.

But it was precisely the desire for a bigger and richer life, for more and better things (constantly stimulated by advertising), that created the demand for the goods which made American men and women better housed, better clothed, better groomed than any on earth. American business civilization—leaving aside the poets and the painters—has not put its cult of beauty and its belief in progress into formal philosophies. Yet in a sense, it is writing a statement to posterity into the glossy pages and towering lights of its advertising. It was somewhat sobering to imagine that just about all of this message that might remain for the contemplation of future ages might be the image of a pretty girl blowing smoke rings through a seductive smile. But it would certainly give posterity a sight to see.

THE TYPICAL NEW YORKER

ROBERT BENCHLEY

One of the most persistent convictions reported by foreign commentators on the United States (a group which evidently embraces all unoccupied literates of England and the more meditative sections of the Continent) is that the real America is represented by the Middle West.

Aside from the not entirely adventitious question of who is to decide just what "the real America" is, there arises a fascinating speculation for breeders and students of climatic influence as to why a man living in Muncie, Indiana, should partake of a more essential integrity in being what he is than a man living in New York City. Why is the Middle Westerner the real American, and the New Yorker the product of some complicated inbreeding which renders him a sport (in the biological sense) and a man without a country?

Of course, at the bottom of it all is the generally accepted theory (not limited by any means to visiting scribes but a well-founded article in our national credo) that there is something about the Great Open Spaces which makes for inherent honesty and general nobility of character. Hence the firmly rooted superstition that a boy who has been raised on a farm is somehow finer and more genuine than a boy who has been raised in the city.

I remember once a mother whose three children were being brought up in the country (and very disagreeable and dishonest children they were, too) saying, with infinite pity of the children of a city acquaintance: "Just think, those kiddies have probably never seen a cow!" Just what sanctity or earnest of nobility was supposed to attach itself to the presence of a cow in a child's life I never could figure out, but there was an answer which might have been made that her own kiddies had never seen the Woolworth Building or the East River bridges at night. Among the major inquiries which will one day have to be made is one into the foundation for this belief that intimacy with cows, horses, and hens or the contemplation, day in and day out, of great stretches of crops exerts a purifying influence on the souls of those lucky enough to be subjected to it. Perhaps when the answer is found, it may help solve another of the pressing social problems of the day—that of Rural Delinquency. . . .

For most visitors to Manhattan, both foreign and domestic, New York is the Shrine of the Good Time. This is only natural, for outsiders come to New York for the sole purpose of having a good time, and it is for their New York hosts to provide it. The visiting Englishman, or the visiting Californian, is convinced that New York City is made up of millions of gay pixies, flitting about constantly in a sophisticated manner in search of a new thrill. "I don't see how you stand it," they often say to the native New Yorker who has been sitting up past his bedtime for a week in an attempt to tire his guest out. "It's all right for a week or so, but give me the little old home town when it comes to *living.*" And, under his breath, the New Yorker endorses the transfer and wonders himself how he stands it.

The New York pixie element is seen by visitors because the visitors go where the pixie element is to be found, having become, for the nonce, pixies themselves. If they happen to be authors in search of copy, they perhaps go slumming to those places where they have heard the Other Half lives. They don't want to be narrow about the thing. There are the East Side push-carts, which they must see and write a chapter about under the title of "The Melting Pot." Greenwich Village they have heard about, but that only fortifies their main thesis that New York is a gay, irresponsible nest of hedonists. Wall Street comes next, with its turmoil and tall buildings—rush-rush-rush-money-money-money! These ingredients, together with material gathered at the Coffee House Club and private dinners, and perhaps a short summary of the gang situation, all go into a word picture called "New York," and the author sails for home, giving out an interview at the pier in which he says that the city is pleasure-mad and its women are cold and beautiful. . . .

Our visitors are confronted with so much gaiety in New York, especially where the lights are brightest, that they fall into the literary error of ascribing any metropolitan utilization of voltage to the pursuit of pleasure. And it *is* difficult to look at the lighted windows at the end of the island and not idealize them into some sort of manifestation of joy and exuberance. But if the writers who thrill so at the sight and translate it into terms of New York's light-heartedness could, by some sardonic and unkind force, be projected along any one of those million beams of fairy light, they would find that it came directly from an office peopled by tired Middle Westerners, New Englanders, and Southerners, each watching the clock as lighting-up time comes, not to start out on a round of merrymaking but to embark on a long subway ride up town. And this ride will take them on past the haunts that the visitors and their hosts know, past the clubs and theatres and squash-courts, to an enormous city above 125th Street, where life is, with the exception of a certain congestion in living-quarters, exactly the same as life in Muncie, Indiana, or Quincy, Illinois. For the inhabitants of this city have come direct from Muncie and Quincy and have never become assimilated into the New York of the commentators. It is not even picturesque, as the East Side is picturesque. It is a melting pot where the ingredients refuse to melt. The people are just as much New Yorkers as those in the Forties, and they outnumber the "typical" New Yorkers to so great an extent that an intramural battle between the two elements could not possibly last for more than twenty minutes, even if the pixies had machine guns.

I am not speaking of Harlem or the Bronx, where the standard of living is radically different from that of the much-advertised denizens of pleasure. Up in the Heights and beyond, as well as in the side streets farther down town, there are hundreds of thousands of men and women who go to bed at ten o'clock for the same reason that residents of Dodge City, Kansas, go to bed at ten o'clock—because they can't think of anything else to do, and because they have to be up at seven. There are streets north of Central Park through which a cooler breeze blows in summer than many a Mid-Western hamlet can boast, where life is quiet and its pace even. These streets are peopled by the very types who are supposed to make the Middle West the "real America," as alien to the New York of the magazine articles as their kinsfolk back home. They are in New York for many reasons, chiefly to make more money or because the head office in South Bend sent them there, and many of them wish that they had never come. But there they are, just as much New Yorkers as the patrons of Webster Hall or the Embassy Club, and a great deal more numerous. . . .

My first dissipation in New York was a church supper, so identical with the church suppers I had known in New England that it was impossible to imagine that farther down on this same island was the gay Gomorrah I had heard and been warned so much about. The people at this bacchanalia of chicken salad and escalloped oysters matched to a man the people I had eaten chicken salad and escalloped oysters with in my home town. There was the same aroma of coffee and hot rolls as one entered the vestry, and the same satyristic little boys were chasing the same coy little girls around the Sunday School room with as much vigor and obnoxiousness as if they had all been raised on a farm. Practically all of those present were small-town people, with small-town outlooks, and I venture to say that not one of them would have been recognized by a specialist in New Yorkese as a New Yorker. And yet there they were, they and their kind, a million strong. . . .

Whatever mysterious qualities the Middle Westerner has which fit him for the role of "real American," his brother in New York possesses to an equal degree, although with perhaps not quite so much volubility. Just what the real America is supposed to be is a bit hard to define, for each commentator has a different idea. But almost all agree that the America of the Middle West is made up of bustling Babbitts, children of energy, forward-looking perhaps in politics but incurably chauvinistic and provincial in their world outlook. All of which might be a word picture of the rank and file of New York's great Region of Respectability. . . .

On a scale such as statisticians draw showing the comparative sizes of the standing armies of Europe, this man would tower over the small figures of the night-club rounder, the sophisticated *literatus*, the wage slave of the East Side, and the other popular conceptions of the New Yorker as the S.S. *Majestic* standing on end towers above a soldier in a Swiss uniform. He cannot be called a "typical New Yorker" because there is no such thing, but, if the man seen in the Middle West by the visiting writers is a "typical American," then this man is one too. Furthermore, he is the product of no one section of the country but of all sections.

All of which would seem to give New York a right to claim that within its boundaries alone can be found the real, composite America. But New York does not apparently care enough to make such a claim, which lack of civic pride and booster-spirit is perhaps the most un-American thing about New York.

HOTHOUSE FLOWER ON THE BIG DRAG

MEL HEIMER

There are, of course, a thousand happy marriages along the main stem, and more than a thousand happy affairs being carried on. But in the main, Broadway is a tough spot for a girl.

The women who come to Broadway are usually of two kinds—either they are fresh out of high school in Jackson, Michigan or Fall River, Massachusetts and have seen too many movies in which the undeniable glamour of the Big Drag has been polished a hundredfold, or they are those who come along because only in Broadway can they find the opportunity for the kind of life they want. Maybe they are would-be actresses. For them, only among the magic caverns of the Forties can producers' offices be found. Maybe they are potential nightclub performers. Batting in any other nightclub league but the big one that is Broadway's is a sad state of affairs. Maybe they are sexed wrongly. Nowhere else can a lesbian bury herself in anonymity and avoid the outraged looks and snide mutterings of the populace. Or maybe they are cut and dried in their approach to life; they are going to trade sex for achievement, and have found that the Big Drag, which asks not of your morals but only of your bank roll, is the place to shop for customers.

There never is room, of course, for them all—even the ones who stay. You see the actresses ushering or cashiering, and the nightclub singers waiting on table in Child's. Some of the lesbians cut out places for themselves in the world of the theater, but the others ultimately melt away to the Village and after that, God knows what. The amateur whores, if they have looks and legs, are usually more successful than the rest, because Broadway *is* a bit short in its complement of ladies of easy virtue. And sooner or later, you will find many of them in the big apartment houses or the better hotels with mink on their backs and charge accounts at Bonwit's and Saks. If they don't make that grade, they turn professional, and furnish us with the party girl, who will do anything within reason and a number of things out of it, for a price.

The facts really are that Broadway girls' morals are no better or worse than Boston girls' morals or New Orleans girls' morals—*except* that they are given more rein. The most high-minded girl, when cut loose in a place where nobody gives a damn whether you sleep with no men or with two or twenty, is hard put not to relax just a little. Let us say it this way: Broadway women are rarely chaste, which of itself is a technical and unimportant thing—but so, too, are they rarely promiscuous, which is a most important thing.

The Big Drag is the one place where a woman can earn a salary commensurate with her ability. But on Broadway, money runs a poor second always in importance to fame and glory; indeed, sometimes it is tossed around so lavishly, that it takes on the aspects of racetrack money, as contrasted with "real" money. If a girl can sing or dance or shake her hips, Broadway will hire her and pay her well.

No matter what kind of girl you were, nor in what kind of business you are, if you have been in Broadway for, say, five years, you are of a type.

You dress well, and as expensively as your purse allows. You have poise and you wear high heels, and you spend more time on your hair than on any other of your attributes. You smile easily and you tip well, and more often than not your dress is black—although you haven't a worry in the world about dressing strikingly and very frequently do. You don't have any stomach, unless you are over forty, and then it's only a little one. Your hands are white and carefully kept, and it's been some time since you turned around at a corner whistle.

You drink a bit, but not too much, and you smoke at least a pack of cigarettes a day. Your apartment is comfortable and you pay more for it than you can afford, unless you are married, in which case your husband pays more than you both can afford.

Most of your out-of-town friends bore you, and you not only hate to put up with them for a night, but you candidly duck them and don't answer your letters or your doorbell. Once upon a time, you had great dreams about Broadway and what you would do to it when you got it by the scruff of the neck, but somehow things seem to have gotten a little out of hand and passed you by, but what the hell, it's a good life. You get drunk once a year and mutter about leaving the main stem for a place out on Long Island, but you never do, you never do.

The men—ah, the men. They're the moths around the flame, the flies to the honey, the bees at the rose. To some, the flame is money and to the others the rose is power and fame, but, whatever the lure it hauls in the starry-eyed ones like a giant magnet. The East Side kid who can imitate Jackie Miles or Bing Crosby—he's going to be a big one some day, you can bet your bottom dollar, and you know where he has to go to be big. The Pennsylvania pool shark, with the fast hands and the talented eye for the horses—you know where he's going to end up, following the floating crap game from one hotel to another. The serious-minded youth from Raleigh, North Carolina, who is grimly determined to make a success in the restaurant business—there's only one place for a really serious restaurateur, and that's the big time, where the tips are bigger, the prices higher and the profits bigger. All of them—all of them who want to make the world sit up and notice, they come to the greatest arena of them all, to try it.

So when they tell you that Broadway is only a big little town at heart, and that all of its assorted men are only townies in their soul—laugh at them. The ordinary kids don't come to Broadway. The ordinary kids stay home and follow Pop in the insurance business, or farm the land in the good old-fashioned way, or sell autos to the kids with whom they went to school.

Broadway gets the ones who are out of line. The ones who were twisted under the desk during schooldays, paying no heed to teacher; the ones who sang and danced and cut up so worthlessly that everyone predicted a dark end for them; the extremists; the great phonies and the greatly talented. These are the boys who grow up to be Broadwayites, fast with a dollar and bright with a tie, and if one of the other kind gets caught in the wheels occasionally, he is a pitiful, bewildered, baffled sight.

If you want to spot the Broadwayite in embryo, a good idea is to take a spin down through the lower East Side some Sunday afternoon. For it is there, in the welter of dirt and noise and curses, that the opportunist is born. Maybe he's the kid you see running along lower Houston Street at one o'clock in the morning, dirty and ragged, with a big stack of morning papers under his arm. He grows up to run theaters, or manage actors, or do something along the White Way that pays his rent and keeps forever from his door the wolf that walked side by side with him as a boy.

Maybe he's the kid who sings or dances, desperately, frantically. He becomes the mournful nightclub star, whose tired face brightens into an unbelievable white smile the minute the spotlight's hard finger touches it. These, in large part, are those aggressive ones who later in life will take over the Big Drag. For that fairyland is not, like the earth, to be inherited by the meek.

Maybe *you* don't have to be a crook to make the grade in Broadway, but you certainly have to be on the watch for the other crooks twenty-four hours a day. To midtown Mannie, the greatest sin in life is to be a sucker. How your stature drops, how you descend the scale in the eyes of the Lindy's crowd, when you're "taken"!

Once he has become part and parcel of Broadway, the citizen is easily recognized. He dresses the part. Broadwayites don't wear bright horseblankets of coats, or racetrack trousers on which you can play checkers. More often than not, you will find them in blue or gray suits—the sharp touch being the Harlem cut of the suits. The drape is a little more pronounced, the shoulders a little wider, the lapels more flared. Tweeds are out; tweeds are for the East Side or for butlers on their day off. Besides, you can't get a razor crease in tweeds, and a gentleman of the main stem would sooner be found at 48th Street and Seventh Avenue in his underwear than in a pair of unpressed pants. There is a reason for the plain blue and gray suits, incidentally, they serve as beautiful backgrounds for the major item of dress, the tie.

The Broadwayite, from learned Doc Mischel, the big street's favorite physician, down to Broadway Sam Roth, probably has a wider variety of neckties and undoubtedly spends more time on research and investigation of necktie counters than any other character in the book. Riotous colors, weird designs, lush batik prints, paintings of horses or ducks or geese—the Broadway boy goes for them all.

Most of Broadway lives in hotels—the Park Central, the Victoria, the Abbey, the Waldorf, the Essex House, the Astor, and the like— the two-buck flophouses in the Forties and the ten-buck joints along Central Park South. Whatever its price or its reputation, it remains simply a place in which to sleep. For when the Big Drag character leaves the reservation in the afternoon, he doesn't return until early or late the next morning, and then only to peel off his sharp costume and crawl under the covers for four or five hours' sleep.

His home life is an existence made up of equal parts of lobbies, cigar stands, bellhops, the maid who cleans up, floor clerks and elevator girls. He claims that he has never washed or dried a dish in his life and if anyone so much as suggested the pipe-and-slippers-routine after dinner for him, he'd become apoplectic and scream "for God's sake just how old do you think I am, anyway?" He read a book once, but it was long ago and it bored him; and besides, man, the only dough in those things is movie rights, so why not concentrate right on the film people themselves.

He has eaten in restaurants all his life, and when he is trapped into a homecooked meal, doesn't think too much of it. His food is steak and pie, and green vegetables were meant to be shoved to one side of the plate and ignored. He should drink milk, because he has an ulcer, of course, but instead he drinks countless cups of coffee. He has a dry martini in the afternoon and Scotch with a water chaser is his regular drink, but he doesn't get drunk.

He might have a regular occupation, he might be a song plugger or a prize fighter or a band leader or a ticket broker. But it's six, two and even, as the bookies put it, that he does a couple of other things on the side to keep body and soul together. Maybe he has a piece of a concern that manufactures juke boxes, or he knows how to get you a new car at discount, or he does a Broadway column by night and writes songs by day.

He knows everybody, of course; the last time Bing Crosby was in town, he and good old Bingo got drunk together and had a hilarious time. Because he reads *Variety* religiously, he knows a week ahead of time, from the out-of-town reviews, whether Max Gordon's new show will be a flop or not, and if it won't be, it just so happens he has a couple for opening night, sixth row center.

He's good for a touch, if you're down and out, but for God's sake, take the money and beat it, because it don't do nobody no good to be seen talking to a has-been.

He'd rather be dead than out of the know. If Errol Flynn slugged Tommy Dorsey in El Morocco last night, he just *has* to know about it no less than three hours later, and by noon of the next day he *has* to know the real why behind the fight. Nothing gives him a more vicarious thrill than to be able to say, "Yeah, yeah, a' course I heard. Who di'n't? You know why Flynn did it, a' course? No? Oh, my country cousin. Well, you see this Flynn has been . . . ."

He never gets into fights himself. Fights are for suckers. He might be getting a pot belly and probably is, but would no more go near a gymnasium or a tennis court than he would take poison. A Turkish bath; that's the ticket. Every now and then he cuts down on cigarettes, but that only lasts for a day. He might use benzedrine to stay awake or sleeping tablets to go to sleep, but he tries not to; those are for suckers, too, like trumpet players or Park Avenue debutramps.

In a way, there is something poignant, God forgive us, about all this, because it isn't as if there never had been any other kind of world for our hero. Long ago he—how was it Rupert Brooke put it?— . . . *felt, breathed, came aware* . . .

But if he was sensitive once, he is not now; he can't afford to be. Broadway is a rowdy place and a tough one. Skulls are cracked and crosses doubled with frightening regularity, and there is no niche in the place for the squeamish. . . .

But a man can grow to love a rattlesnake in time, especially when the rattlesnake has a beauty of movement and a shiny skin. So it is with the Big Drag; Lord only knows why or how many of its citizens get there in the first place, but after a few years there is no other place on the face of the earth that can keep them content. There is the sound of a lullaby in its subway rumble and its harsh rattle of taxicabs, and its incessant din, washing back and forth like tinny breakers. There is the soothing prick of the dope needle in its violence and its startling happenings of the gaudy night. We each of us must have our anchor, and to the Broadwayite, a weird hothouse flower, the Big Drag is home.

THE FINEST

MEYER BERGER

In midafternoon of March 30, 1948, a dark little man worked the tumbler out of a patent lock in a one-room third-floor apartment in a converted brownstone on East 55th Street in midtown Manhattan. He used a screw driver. He stuck a practiced finger into the opening and sprang the lock. He was looting the place of trinkets and clothing when the tenant, Mrs. Vera Lotito, who owned the Gotham Travel Bureau down-street, came in with a bag of groceries.

The dark little man killed her with screw-driver thrusts and by strangulation. He stripped off her wrist watch, wedding band and engagement ring, bundled several men's suits and her fur coat into an improvised bag. He was positive he had left no telltale clues—and he was right. He had used gloves to prevent fingerprints. No one heard the thrusts that pierced her. No one saw the little man come or go. He figured he could never be traced in a city of some eight million persons.

He was wrong. He had touched the quivering center of a hypersensitive and complex human machine that reacts to crime as a wispy web shudders to the infinitesimal impact of a gnat. The little thief had stirred the New York City Police Department with its eighteen thousand "finest."

The dead woman's husband, Robert Lotito, service manager for an insurance company, found the body at 5:35 P.M., about two hours after the murderer vanished. He called "Spring 7-3100." His call showed as a light on Patrolman Rudolph Blaum's position—one of twelve—at the Police Headquarters switchboard on the top floor at 240 Center Street, three miles downtown. The departmental web trembled over every foot of the 323 square miles it covers.

Patrolman Blaum walked a few feet from his board to the radio room where six policemen sat with eyes fixed on a city map dotted with 450 movable numbered disks. Each disk marked the location of a radio patrol car.

Patrolman James Harrigan, acting as message recorder in a car two blocks from the Lotito house, heard his number called and with it the crisp order: "Proceed at once to 144 East Fifty-fifth Street, third floor. Thirty." "Thirty" is the code for any crime of violence. With siren open, the car cut through evening rush-hour traffic. Within seconds, three other radio cars pushed into the block. Harrigan sat by his radio receiver—the first recorder at a crime scene always does that—to await further messages from headquarters. The other policemen pounded up the stairs. They met Robert Lotito outside his door, shaken and miserable.

At 5:37 P.M. Patrolman Blaum notified the Chief Inspector of the murder. Blaum called Police Commissioner Arthur W. Wallander thirty seconds later. He also flashed word to George Mitchell, chief of the city's fifteen hundred detectives, at 5:39; to the deputy commissioner's office at 5:40; to the East 51st Street Detective Squad at 5:45; to the Homicide Squad at 5:47; to department photographers at 5:48; to the Technical Research Laboratory at 5:49; to the ballistics man at 5:51; to the medical examiner at 5:52; to Policewoman Gertrude Gruin (to search the body) at 5:54—and the web kept shaking. Police experts of one kind or another, and the District Attorney, followed to East 55th Street.

There was grim conclave over the dead woman who lay face down on the floor, as the experts worked silently, each at his task—the fingerprint men, the ballistics man and the medical examiner trying to figure what kind of weapon had been used, the photographer shooting pictures of the body and of the room for the detectives' and for courtroom use; Technical Research gathering a lock of the dead woman's hair, scrapings from under her nails, cigarette stubs and cigarette ash, bits of lint from the couch and from her gray suit. They took the dead woman's fingerprints, her papers, her books, her bills, her checks, letters and her memorandum pads. From the husband they got a list of what had been stolen.

Before seven o'clock the teletype in Center Street had a copy of this list in each of the city's eighty-six station houses. The department's teletype network, incidentally, covers twelve neighboring States. Combined with the police radio it can spread an alarm from the Gulf of Mexico into Canada, or to the West Coast, in a matter of minutes. Four department planes—two of them amphibian—and twelve fast patrol boats are in on this communication system too.

The morning after the Lotito murder, a squad of detectives sorted through pledge cards turned in overnight by city pawnshops. One showed that a few hours after the killing, Mrs. Lotito's wrist watch and some of her husband's clothing had turned up in a Seventh Avenue pawnbroker's. Chief of Detectives Mitchell, meanwhile, had discreetly withheld from newspapermen the fact that the Lotito apartment had been looted. The cruel nature of Mrs. Lotito's wounds, he had suggested instead, showed she must have been killed for vengeance rather than robbery. The Department misleads the newspapers in this way to give a hunted criminal a false sense of security. This time it worked. The little man kept pledging Lotito items all over town.

In one Ninth Avenue shop the murderer bought a cheap ring with the proceeds of his pledges. The pawnbroker recalled, after the pledged items had been identified through cleaner's markings, that the man's ring finger was badly scratched. He described the customer in detail. One more move, and the murderer would be fast in the web. He turned up blandly at noon on April 2 in another Ninth Avenue pawnshop, carrying Mrs. Lotito's fur coat. As he left the shop, the manager signalled to a detective waiting at the curb.

The dark little man was arrested for murder. He confessed, was convicted, and sentenced to die. The New York Police Department had snatched him from among eight millions.

New York City's Police Department is, roughly, three hundred years old. It started as a Burgher Guard in the Dutch settlement of New Netherland in November, 1643. Today the force is larger than the individual standing armies of Denmark, Ecuador, Ireland, New Zealand, Norway, Venezuela. It is the most mechanized police unit in the world, geared to function as an army to suppress widespread riot, or to give its arm to the little old lady who is afraid to cross the street. It has its own fleet and its own air force, and more and more its personnel is made up of polite and literate young men, instead of beefy, untutored larrikins as in Tammany's romping heyday. A recent class of close to two thousand rookies fresh out of the Police Academy, for example, included 607 high-school graduates, and 391 college men and women holding—among other degress—thirty-seven B.A.'s, seventeen B.S.'s and two M.A.'s.

No other police force in the world has anywhere near as complicated a problem. It stands against not only indigenous criminal species but must know and circumvent the tricks and skulduggery of virtually every race and creed on earth. Because the city leaps skyward, the department's traffic burden is without parallel and 2000 men are assigned to it. A single cloud-brusher will hold a greater population than fair-sized cities elsewhere. Within the city's corporate limits range 11,507 taxicabs. Some 2,000,000 motorcars and trucks are on its streets every day, 400,000 of them in the midtown area, and 2,500,000 pedestrians contend with them for *lebensraum*.

The police force guards some 4,000,000 Gothamites who spend part of their day under the pavement in subways and sub-street corridors and runways. Its patrol does not end with the watch on 650 miles of water front where the earth's riches pile up as ocean-borne freight; the Harbor Squad's boats and the two Grumman amphibians do rescue work, stop water-borne thieves and smugglers, and guard not only the harbor proper but the ocean around it to the three-mile limit. Some of the Harbor Squad's tasks are on the macabre side. It takes 350 to 370 suicides and other dead from harbor waters each year.

The Lotito murder case was comparatively simple. None of the experts who responded to it on routine call was needed. Frequently, though, their skill is the only hope. On April 10, 1936, Nancy Evans Titterton, wife of a scholarly book reviewer, was found dead in her bathtub in Beekman Place. The only clue was a strand of cord found under her body. The Department's Technical Research Laboratory traced it to the manufacturer in Hanover, Pa., then back to a little upholsterer's shop in New York's Third Avenue. The upholsterer's apprentice had used the cord to bind his victim. He confessed the killing and went to the electric chair.

In another case, the Technical Research Laboratory, with chemicals and photomicrography, reconstructed stolen bonds burned in an empty lot and subjected to weeks of weather. They jailed the bond thief. Scientific miracles are their specialty. In 95 per cent of the intricate puzzles put up to them last year, they got the right answers. Their testimony in court was conclusive. They roll to murder scenes in a portable laboratory, work out problems in bloodstains, latent fingerprints, shoeprints, burglar-tool marks, bomb fragments—among other things. They keep files on the latest of dyes, lipsticks, auto paints and a wide range of poisons, use modified mine detectors to locate hidden metallic articles.

Perhaps the weirdest assignments in the department go to the Emergency Squads. Twenty of these are spread around the city. One night, some months ago, a girl hurled her five-thousand-dollar engagement ring at her fiancé in a street quarrel. It went down the sewer. The local Emergency Squad patiently retrieved it. This arm of the force releases oversized matrons caught fast in their bathtubs, little boys jammed in picket fences or in turnstiles, cats imprisoned in walls. It lassoes runaway beef, catches swarming bees, rescues and revives drowning persons and would-be gas suicides. Four Emergency men brought a frightened boy down from the topmost girder of George Washington Bridge, 375 feet above the Hudson River, where he had wedged himself, heaven knows how. Wherever the situation looks impossible the cry is for "Emergency."

The Missing Persons Bureau traces, each year, more vanished men, women and children than make up the population of a city of 28,000. Twenty-three detectives, including one woman, are assigned to the Bureau. The last printed report showed 27,158 cases reported, 26,795 solved in a single year.

Included in the solved cases were 1013 unidentified dead. This outfit, incidentally, is apt to find some of its cases not merely "missing," but murdered. A woman lawyer on its list had been cut to fragments with razor blades, had been reduced further with acids and let down a bathtub drain. The murderer was traced to Czechoslovakia, and caught.

Not all the department's assignments are so grim. The Bureau of Special Service and Investigation, for example, guards visiting royalty and diplomats and is busiest when the United Nations is in session in New York. The men and women in this unit guard the suites of such dignitaries as Prince ibn-Saud of Arabia. They were with the British king and queen every moment of their visit in 1939. They guarded Russian bigwigs, too, but the Russians resented it and asked they be withdrawn. The men of Special Service take their orders from the State Department. This unit was originally called the Criminal Alien Squad. The name was changed because it horrified visiting nobility.

When they are not in fancy clothes mixing with diplomats, the men of Special Service and Investigation work quietly among subversive elements, teamed up with the State Department and the FBI. They keep up-to-date lists on their subjects, just as the Public Morals Bureau —the old Vice Squad—keeps complete lists of gamblers.

The 156 women on the force, like latter-day men cops, are somewhat more streamlined than the old. Only a few are detectives. Their principal work is rounding up abortionists, prostitutes, fortunetellers, runaway girls, and psychopaths who annoy women in theaters, subways and in crowds. Sometimes they get tougher assignments. Several months ago, after a number of women had been attacked by a psychopath in McComb's Dam Park, uptown, in the Bronx, Miss Catherine Barry, a policewoman, was used as a decoy to trap the offender. She sat demurely on a bench, night after night, until he showed up. Then she pulled her service revolver out of her handbag and turned him over to the detectives. Occasionally, policewomen mix with the girl friends of wanted criminals to get information. They do well at this.

The department's air fleet—two Grumman amphibians, a Stinson land plane and a newly acquired Bell D-47 helicopter—is kept at Floyd Bennett Field on the city's Brooklyn rim, but is in constant radio communication with Headquarters. It is an Emergency Service adjunct manned by licensed pilots and engineers. It enforces CAA regulations against low flying and stunting over the city, patrols the beaches, and has flown to sea to capture criminals fleeing on tugs and liners. It helps the Traffic Division by sighting arterial bottlenecks from the air. It makes aerial photographs for the Board of Estimate, and brings fugitives and witnesses back from distant points. The amphibians have figured in a number of sea rescues.

Mechanized as it is, though, the force still uses 311 police horses, on the ancient theory that one horse is worth ten men when it comes to handling riotous—or orderly—crowds. Something about a man on horseback cows a mob, especially in New York City, where horses are rare.

The force effected a wedding recently between its horses and motorized units. A special twenty-nine-foot motor van with its own water tank, forage locker and forge can now run six horses at a time—and their riders—to any given spot in the city.

The paper work that piles up in running the New York City Police Department would shame the armed forces. Nothing is left to memory. Licenses for taxicabs, parades, street meetings, cabarets, block parties, pistol toting, masquerades, pile it up.

The Bureau of Planning and Operations works every police assignment out in fine detail, laying out orders for handling mass demonstrations, strikes, disasters, elections, special orders to precincts, general orders and heaven knows what else. It keeps an assistant chief inspector, an acting captain, ten lieutenants, ten sergeants and thirty-five patrolmen busy. Ten stenographer-typists grind the stuff out in its final form.

The Property Clerk, custodian of lost, abandoned, unclaimed articles, of cash and of material evidence and the possessions of the kinless dead, runs a major-sized warehouse in Broome Street opposite the old French-baroque Headquarters building. The stuff turned in may be anything from a lost freight car to a package of canary seed.

The department maintains a Legal Bureau which answers any questions that puzzle a cop—and there are many—prepares briefs and law memoranda. It studies codes and has broken down some that stem from music, foreign languages, hieroglyphics and ancient Hebraic and Phoenician. A police Juvenile Aid Bureau helps poor children and directs their play.

The Building and Repair Bureau has a staff of artificers of its own, and lets by public contract what it cannot handle itself. The Engineering Bureau does a prodigious job maintaining automatic signals at some 7000 street intersections, and 7000 No Parking signs. It has care of the 23,000 wooden barriers used to hold crowds at the curbs during parades.

Though the department as a whole is highly mechanized, the bluecoats in it are not robots. Beat pounders maintain the warm human touch. East Side, West Side, all around the town, the foot-slogging cop gets to know the neighbors and the shopkeepers.

Each precinct assigns a certain number of its men to PAL, the Police Athletic League activity. These men know how to handle kids. They help them at local recreation centers and work with co-ordinating councils on social activities and for elimination of racial differences. When neighborhood small fry seem to lean toward the wayward, the PAL men warn the parents. Juvenile delinquents are taken before a Court only after every other move has failed. PAL has done a lot to wipe out potential gang menace in the grub, or larval, stage.

Cops on beat still deliver from thirty-five to fifty babies a year and assist in hundreds of other births. They are trained for this service in the first-aid phase of their education in Police Academy. A Bronx cop who delivered twins for a mother on his beat outstrutted the father in his pride. Other cops say of him, with a certain amount of reverence, "He's the guy came up with a two-bagger."

BLUE BLOOD AND PRINTER'S INK

CHARLES J. ROLO

A short time back, word spread through the smart sector of Manhattan Bohemia that a certain dowager—a lady field marshal of the American aristocracy—was going to attend a red-wine-and-cheese *klatsch* in the surrealistic lodgings of one of Bohemia's most indefatigable impresarios. Telephones hummed with anticipatory gossip; the uninvited schemed busily for invitations or nursed a bleeding ego; desirable guests were busily reminded they simply must not fail to be on hand. As it happened, the great lady herself failed to put in an appearance—but she might well have. There are relatively few strongholds of the New York aristocracy which have not succumbed to the attractions of today's de luxe Bohemia: an altogether different company from the threadbare disciples of art portrayed in Balzac's *A Distinguished Provincial in Paris*. Out of the intermingling of today's *ersatz* Bohemia and patrician society there has burgeoned a fashionable metropolitan coterie which, its pace setters claim, has made Café Society if not obsolete rather old hat.

Of course, members of Café Society and members of the international set, and people who are neither noticeably blue-blooded nor remotely Bohemian belong to this sizable new coterie. In addition to the socialites, writers, artists, actors and actresses, it includes dress designers; decorators; fashionable photographers; editors (senior and junior) of the fashion magazines; a sprinkling of fashion models; a few literary agents and literary journalists; recherché craftsmen who have made a name for themselves with avant-garde ceramics or avant-garde cinema; rentiers with artistic leanings; and a somewhat incongruous company of officially accredited camp followers—the *petits amis* and *petites amies* of the members in good standing.

If there exists an apprentice Yankee Balzac, secretly preparing a fictional fresco of the new smart set, his notebook must contain such scenes as the following: In the dining room of the Hotel El Fahar, perched on a cliff outside Tangiers, a group of young American writers are listening to a be-bop man or hipster celebrating the virtues of hashish. . . . In a Fifth Avenue drawing room, one of the doyennes of American Society is pouring tea while four or five of yesteryear's Bohemians, now graying *maîtres*, evaluate the arts in the ringing tones of the academy. . . . In four rooms on upper Lexington Avenue, three hundred people are jammed together in a steamy communal embrace, which brings together Park Avenue and Harlem; Broadway, Hollywood and Greenwich Village; Mayfair and Chelsea; and both banks of the Seine. . . . Each of these tableaux, despite their divergent moods and colors, forms part of a contemporary canvas which has a bizarre unity of its own.

In this canvas you find a picturesque fusion of blue blood and printer's ink; silver teapots and dime-store highball glasses; gowns by Jacques Fath and turtle-neck sweaters; interiors by Sloane or Robsjohn-Gibbings and junk shoppe classicism or Third Avenue dada; Groton accents and Southern accents and staccato, tough-guy accents which have had their d's softened and their a's broadened but which sound, when they refer to Kafka and Gide, as though the talk were about two hot tips in the fifth at Hialeah. You find a coalescence of eminent matrons and talented juveniles; of steelmen with investments in art, and art men with investments in steel; of art-consciousness and snob-consciousness.

The group which has sprung out of Society and Bohemia forms a distinctly cohesive entity, but one that is decidedly hard to categorize. Its inner circle might be defined, impressionistically, as that sector of metropolitan society in which, when people say "Truman," they refer not to the President of the United States but to the young novelist, Truman Capote; when they say "Tennessee," they refer not to the state, but to the playwright Tennessee Williams.

This new smart set turns out in full force at important museum previews; opening nights at the ballet; first nights of plays written by its members or in which its members are featured; and parties given by certain favored salonniers. It has its own chosen resorts and rendezvous; its literary fads; even its favorite physician, a practitioner of psychosomatic medicine, who is more often called on to minister to psyche than to soma. Its special playgrounds are not the French Riviera or Capri or Palm Beach. They are Capri's neighbor, Ischia; Portofino, a minute resort, cut off from the motor road, on the Italian Riviera; Taormina in Sicily; North Africa; and Fire Island, N.Y. In winter, you are certain to find some of the group's artist members at the Hotel Chelsea in downtown Manhattan; during the Paris season, the Bohemian element makes the Hôtel de l'Université on the Left Bank its headquarters.

Sartorial extravagance, once the badge of self-respecting Bohemians, is the exception in this bohemianized society. A good many of its younger male members, with their rumpled tweeds, moccasins and short haircuts, are indistinguishable from the conventional undergraduate. Insofar as there are any noticeable fashions, they run to such items, among the men, as turtle-neck sweaters, Bronzini ties, fancy waistcoats and, for the outdoor life, form-fitting, ankle-length blue jeans. In the feminine department, there is still a penchant for Phelps belts, hair done up in buns, and ballet slippers.

In this not-so-tight little world, the heirs to large fortunes do their damndest to look like struggling writers and usually succeed. The writers usually go on looking like struggling writers, though their only economic struggle may be with income tax. The patrician hostesses give dinner parties at which black ties are not worn, and they cheerfully go to Bohemian parties where, if they sit down at all, they will probably be sitting on the floor. The patrician element is inclined to talk art; the Bohemian element is inclined to talk gossip. All in all, it is Bohemia rather than Society which sets the prevailing tone. But then neither Society nor Bohemia is anything like what it used to be.

Mrs. Winthrop Chanler once said that in her youth the Four Hundred would have fled in a body from a poet, a painter, a musician (or a clever Frenchman). A member of the Vanderbilt clan was once severely censured for inviting the great prima donna Geraldine Farrar to tea. But in the twenties, Society's more daring individualists went a-hunting for thrills in Bohemia—for sex and their soul and a share in forging the classless utopia. And when "social consciousness" became epidemic during the Depression, Socialites joined hands in earnest endeavor with proletarian-minded writers and artists. Then, in the early forties, there came a sweeping change in the economic status of the arts that set the stage for the emergence of a different kind of de luxe Bohemia, with a strong accent on youth. The change (which had been taking shape for several decades) was that the arts had reacquired a patron, the public, a public large enough and prosperous enough to make the arts a paying proposition on a widespread scale. Mass education multiplied the potential market for culture and *kitsch;* and the boom of the forties made the potential consumer a cash customer. The arts and their lowbrow derivatives promptly became a biggish business. The movies, radio, magazines, lecture bureaus, purveyors of "popular art," book clubs—even book publishers—were ready to pay generously for creative talent or anything which resembled it. The artist was, after a fashion, back in court.

The gifted young writer who turned up in New York in search of fame and fortune did not have to serve a grueling apprenticeship in Grub Street. Literary agents got wind of his talent, seemingly by telepathy, and offered to "sell" him; magazine editors were eager to buy him. When he had published a promising short story or two, he found himself lunching at the Ritz with an expansive publisher prepared to subsidize his novel-in-progress. Literary fellowships by the score paved the path to fame with an adequate supply of dollars. The more fortunate newcomers—with money in their pockets, a reputation in the making and what might be termed "scribophilia" rampant on the

Social circuit—had an unprecedented opportunity to effect an entry into Society, in one jump. Some were too serious or too devotedly bourgeois to want to; a good many did. It was a parachute invasion, and the invaders were received with open arms and dry Martinis.

The fashion magazines had played a considerable part in the staff work behind this operation. They brought to Society's attention the work of promising young writers; and, at the same time, they brought to the young writer's attention (as he reread his story in print) a glamour-coated picture of the good life in Society.

In Café Society, the lions were what the columnists (themselves among the lions) referred to as celebrities: a novelist such as Steinbeck; a critic such as George Jean Nathan; a foreign correspondent such as John Gunther. In the new smart set, the excitement centers not on big-name writers but on débutants—not really on lions but on pets. According to some prophets of the social weather, the young man from the provinces who wants to make a splash in Society would be well advised, nowadays, to go slow about earning a public reputation: the tendency, they say, is for his social éclat to diminish as his reputation grows.

The adoption of very young writers by American Society marks the completion of a social revolution. Society began by accepting, hesitantly, great artists of impeccable respectability. Then it accepted great artists who were not altogether respectable but who were unquestionably great. Then, without asking any questions, it extended its hospitality to the large regiment of artists and journalists in the public eye. And now it is giving the accolade to gifted tyros and is even going out to meet the new arrivals in Bohemia.

In the past, when Society and Bohemia coalesced, each party performed a strictly logical function. Bohemia provided Society with food for the intellect and wine for the spirit. Society provided Bohemia with food and wine. Today's de luxe Bohemians, however, have enough money to feed themselves—often at "21"—and not very many of them have enough culture to nourish others. Most of those who do are alumni of the old Bohemia: intellectuals such as Glenway Wescott or W. H. Auden. The younger literary folk in this set— the Southern contingent have been described as "hillbilly Rimbauds" —certainly make no pretense to being well lettered. One of the most talented among them recently summed up his knowledge of ancient Greece and Rome with touching candor: "Well, I've read some of Homer, but not the other chap."

In the past, Bohemia has also provided Society with causes, and

Society has backed them with cash. But the new Bohemia isn't spearheading anything; it is not, as Mr. Sartre would say, "engaged" in contemporary reality.

The nearest approach to a cause in this society is its interest in advance-guard art. But while a number of individuals are champions of revolutionary work, the group as a whole is a sympathetic patron rather than an embattled ally seeking (as in the past) to educate the Philistine and force new works upon him. A good many of its members, it's sad to report, can't find time to force the new works upon themselves. Never have so many people spent so much time in the company of so many writers—and read so few of their books. Everyone, however, is in the know. Kafka, Sartre, James—the correct name has been uttered at the fashionable moment; the appropriate comment registered; and the subject decorously dropped.

With politics, there is not, in many cases, even a platonic liaison. The story that a well-known poet asked a well-known novelist, "What is Latvia?" is possibly a libel; the novelist himself, however, confessed that he had never voted and that few of his friends had—"We find politics a joke." There are, to be sure, nuclei within the new Bohemia which have political interests, coupled with something of the crusading spirit. One of the several meeting places of the "engaged" minority is the salon of Mrs. Dorothy Norman, who for a decade ran a publishing enterprise devoted to "art and action." Her circle forms part of a larger group that is active in support of racial tolerance, civil liberties and liberal democracy in general. To Mrs. Norman's there also come the political illiterates of the new Bohemia, some of them in search of understanding; and they go home fortified by exposure to such visitors as Arthur Koestler and Prime Minister Nehru.

A more typical salon is that of Mr. Leo Lerman, a bearded magazine writer who looks rather like a benevolent edition of Lenin and into whose orbit newcomers gravitate in the same way that conspirators gravitated into Lenin's. Mr. Lerman, a professional athlete of the telephone, is a key figure in the G-2 of the new Bohemia as well as in its entertainment corps. His parties, which usually mobilize a large cross-section of this society, are purely social in character. The host's pleasure is to assemble as impressive a company as possible; the guest's pleasure is to form part of the impressive company.

There being no program to promote, the chief promotional activity in the new Bohemia is the cultivation of social prestige and of the ego. The Bohemian gains face and bolsters an insecure ego by fraternizing with the oldest families; the Socialite adds to his luster and gratifies an acquisitive ego by collecting the newest artists—a shining example of reciprocal aid at its fullest. For those with enough to work on, the cultivation of their personal legend is also a serious business in the new Bohemia. The most richly embroidered legend, of course, is that of Mr. Truman Capote. It has been reported that on one of his trips across the Atlantic, Mr. Capote hired the bridal suite on the *Queen Mary;* that in Italy he was taken for the President's son and, stepping into the role of good-will ambassador, did a power of damage to the Communist party; that after traveling through Spain, he landed in North Africa partially accoutered as a bullfighter (and so on in this vein). The legend contains one ounce of fact to every pound of fancy.

With its accent on youth, play, talk and the ego, the communal life of this coterie smacks, slightly, of a return to the nursery—with father and mother banished from the household. In this, it is not unrepresentative of a society in which the theme song of psychologists and sages is that infantilism is epidemic. In a good many respects, in fact, the new Bohemia mirrors—in a magnifying glass and through a highly colored lens—the spirit of an age traversing the vacuum between a revolt that is played out and an affirmation that has not yet taken shape.

The chronicle of the new Bohemia contains a piquant footnote to social history. For the time being—no doubt a very short time—the entering wedge into Society is no spectacular achievement or a vast accumulation of dollars, but a small accumulation of words in print. The success story of the young provincial in New York represents a great epic reduced to the dimensions of a sonnet. It is a diminutive, with a hint of parody, of the American dream.

THE WILDNESS OF NEW YORK:

How Nature Persists in a Metropolis

LEWIS S. GANNETT

Perhaps this optimistic report really belongs under the heading of "Those Were the Days," for admittedly, the facts of urban nature which Lewis Gannett noted several decades ago, no longer hold true in every detail. But I like to believe that the persistence of many New Yorkers in cultivating plants and flowers despite every urban discouragement has not abated. And nature's persistence assuredly has remained constant.

To those of us who grew up in the fresh-water country, where daisy-strewn vacant lots reach into the hearts of the cities, where shade-trees carry bird song well "down-town," and the woods and open fields are within easy reach of the two hours between school-end and supper, New York was at first an appalling prospect. The endless death of the brownstone blocks, the sterile bricks of the perpendicular office buildings, the grimy piers that separate river from city, even the stunted, sawed-off trees in the tiny parks, seemed to make the city a prison. There was no escape from it. Miles away, perhaps, there were green fields and butterflies, but in between were only treeless streets and the subway.

But New York is not birdless or flowerless or even without butterflies. How birds flying high overhead discover the patches of green deep down among the stones and cement I do not know, but every spring and every fall flocks of migrants find that miserable triangle which is gifted with the name of City Hall Park. The city gardeners have to replace its earth almost every year, but the birds seem not to mind. Juncos always find it, warblers often, occasionally a catbird, a woodpecker, or a thrush; once or twice I have caught the gleam of a scarlet tanager's fiery coat on the grass among the English sparrows, as oblivious to the passing throngs as the multitudes were of it. And I shall never forget the thrill of stepping out upon the roof of one of the Hudson Terminal buildings, twenty-two floors above the city, one crystal spring day, and hearing the whistle of a white-throated sparrow singing the same song which would rejoice the Adirondacks a month later. There they were, a whole happy flock of them, flitting about three miserable window-boxes filled with winter-killed privet. A white-throat by a woodland brook could never pipe so gratefully as there.

I have a little garden, literally within a stone's-throw of Brooklyn Bridge. It is a very little garden, and the only garden in the block. But every year, spring and fall, the shy hermit thrushes find it, although I have never seen there one of the familiar robins of less metropolitan backyards. Kinglets and brown creepers and warblers come too, usually a dozen or fifteen species every year. Once a big flicker landed in our single tree, but he plainly felt uncomfortable; hardly as perplexed however, as a disillusioned sapsucker which I found flitting miserably from cable to cable on the Brooklyn Bridge, now and again tapping at the stout iron cables as if in hope that one at least of that forest of upright trunks would turn out to be nourishing.

The birds that once sang on Murray Hill and along Minetta Brook are gone, but there are probably as many individual birds on Manhattan Island today as when Peter Stuyvesant was stumping about. There are, of course, fewer kinds. Migration-time still brings its swarms of warblers to Central Park; one hundred and sixty-eight species of birds have been noted in its three square miles. The number of birds that make it their home, however, is declining; it is outside the park that the census registers growth. In 1912 cardinals and goldfinches and wrens and wood thrushes still nested there, and twenty years ago the scarlet tanager found space enough to hide in. To-day these all depart in June or do not come at all; only the robin, the flicker, and the grackle, the Baltimore oriole, the yellow warbler, and the red-eyed vireo remain, and most of these will be gone in a few years. The English sparrow and the pigeon are of course blissfully at home in the midst of roaring traffic, although since the automobile drove out the horses their food supply has notably declined. A few native birds, too, have learned to adapt themselves to urban life. The night-hawk finds the city roof a safer nesting-place than the bare hillsides and rocky pastures where it used to lay its moss-speckled eggs; the chimney swift has forgotten hollow trees and delights in forests of chimneys; and the little screech-owl, too, finds warm shelter among the chimney-pots.

And the gulls! The great bridges which reach skyward out of the tenement regions like city mountains provide ideal observatories from which to watch the gulls. Except for the breeding months, gulls are almost always visible high above any downtown yard. From the Brooklyn Bridge the harbor sometimes seems fairly snowy with them, lazily circling or ploddingly flapping, diving, soaring, eternally graceful; and no Indian ever sighted such flocks as the rich provender cast overboard by the ocean liners brings to New York to-day....

The fauna and flora of my back-yard garden are a perennial mystery. Butterflies one can understand. I have met errant butterflies—mourning cloaks and fritillaries—in Wall Street; and to my garden sulphur-wings come by scores in the summer, laying their eggs on the shrubs to hatch new creatures on the spot. One is so accustomed to miracles from ants that one hardly stops to wonder how they find their way to build their sand-hills in that crevice of the city. Bees, too, have wings good for long flights. But how did a grasshopper ever find my fifteen-foot square of grass?

Bats too persist and thrive, and the abundance of mosquitoes in September leaves no doubt of the adequacy of nutriment. Insects, somehow, manage to do very well in the city. Beetles and lady-bugs and nasturtium-aphids have no difficulty in discovering any plant I set out, and the caterpillars are a pest. I have on a single day plucked two hundred fat caterpillars from a spiraea-bush no higher than my head. . . .

Downtown New York has its wild flowers, too. They are few and wee, but they exist. Where they can find no back yards, they take to roofs. Swept roofs, of course, support no vegetation, but look out from a high window in the dirty East Side, and you will see bits of grass in almost any gutter. Where tall buildings make a protected corner and the dust lies, in wet weather you may spy a dandelion managing to get as far as blossom, and the tiny daisy-like bloom of the galinsoga. . . . Not so many years ago there were other back yards in the block, and near-by corner lots had never been planted. Here are shepherd's purse and peppergrass, yarrow and dandelion, two kinds of cinquefoil, and half a dozen tiny flowerlets like the veronica and the galinsoga. We are all immigrants within a fraction more than three centuries at most, and so are these weeds. Neither the omnipresent dandelion nor the daisy, not the common buttercup or yarrow, the wild carrot or wild mustard, the tansy, chicory, plantain, burdock, "cheese" mallow, or red clover is native American. Most of our common roadside weeds came with the white men from Europe. By some curious accident, too, Chinese trees seem best able to endure New York's burden of smoke and soot. The ailanthus, the Chinese tree of heaven, has so naturalized itself that it is often identified to-day as "the back-yard tree." Short-lived as it is and despised by the foresters, it furnishes shade and rich, plumy foliage where any other tree would wither. My own back yard supports a less familiar, but no less thriving, Chinese tree, the paper mulberry, which seems to enjoy the daily deposit of soot from the neighboring chocolate-factory, and each year starts new, quick-growing seedlings in other parts of my tiny domain. The horse-chestnut is also an importation from the Orient, and so is that strange fern-like tree with the outline of a spruce, the gingko, which is proving itself the ideal tree for city sidewalk-planting. . . .

One sometimes hears returning travelers bewail America's lack of interest in flowers. "Why," they ask, "cannot we have window boxes as people do in Europe?" They should turn their steps from the desert brownstone streets of the fifties and sixties and come down to New York's East Side. A ride on the Second Avenue "L" in September is a journey between gardens. Hardly a building is without the glow of marigold or calendula; some of them contrive golden glow and sunflower and even windowbox Indian corn.

Marigold and sweet alyssum and chrysanthemum seem not to mind summer droughts and inattention. And there are petunias. The first year we sowed petunia seed in our yard without result. The second year we accepted defeat and planted no more. But something had happened to the disappointing seed of the previous year. It came up, and in multitudes. It crowded out the lettuce, and escaped to remote corners of the yard. It grew between the paving-stones of the area, and in the midst of the tiny grass-plot. We have never had to sow petunia seed again; and last year I proudly supplied young plants, in lots of one hundred each, to our friends for their country estates. . . .

And there are wild flowers. Nothing is more exquisite than the carved leaves of the yarrow, and no garden flower lovelier than a dandelion in full bloom. I have two majestic dandelion plants which have been fertilized and watered with loving care. They yield each a score of magnificent tall balls of gold at a time of year when other plants are struggling with their early leaves. At the other end of the season come asters and goldenrod, both indifferent to clouds of dust and soot. . . .

Smoke and an acid atmosphere, however, work night and day to ruin soil when you have it. There are moments when it seems unnatural to expect anything to bloom in any part of my garden, for the house was a medicine factory two decades ago, and the yard is full of small glass bottles and ashes. Yet, on the whole, the more baskets I fill with broken bottles and bits of brick removed from the inadequate soil, the more I understand the reverence with which European peasants regard the earth that yields their crops. They look upon the creative dirt with a kind of superstitious awe, marvelling that a black speck set an inch underground should develop into a branching plant radiant with blossom. I too regard my garden as a miracle. That flowers and fruit should come out of such an ash-dump is always marvelous. . . .

THE GIANTS AND ME

TALLULAH BANKHEAD

Attending a Giant game with me, say my cronies, is an experience comparable to shooting the Snake River rapids in a canoe. When they lose I taste wormwood. When they win I want to do a tarantella on top of the dugout. A Giant rally brings out the Roman candle in me. The garments of adjoining box-holders start to smolder.

I once lured the young Viennese actor, Helmut Dantine, to a set-to between the Giants and the Pirates. Mr. Dantine had never seen a game before. My airy explanations confused the *émigré*. Rapt in his attention to my free translation of the sacrifice hit, Helmut was almost decapitated by a foul ball. Mr. Dantine looked upon the *faux pas* as a hostile act. He felt I had tricked him into a false sense of security that the hitter might have an unsuspecting target. He left before the ninth, a grayer if not a wiser man.

It's true I run a temperature when watching the Giants trying to come from behind in the late innings, either at the Polo Grounds or on my TV screen. I was hysterical for hours after Bobby Thomson belted Ralph Branca for that ninth inning homer in the final game of the Dodger-Giant playoff in '51. The Giants had to score four runs in the ninth to win. Remember? There was blood on the moon that night in Bedford Village. But I don't know nearly as much about baseball as Ethel Barrymore. Ethel is a real fan, can give you batting averages, the text of the infield fly rule, and comment on an umpire's vision.

Someone has said that Ethel Barrymore has the reticence born of assurance whereas my monologues indicate my insecurity. The point is moot. It's unlikely I'll ever submit to a psychiatrist's couch. I don't want some stranger prowling around through my psyche, monkeying with my id. I don't need an analyst to tell me that I have never had any sense of security. Who has?

My devotion to the Giants, dating back to 1939, has drawn the fire of renegades, eager to deflate me. One of these wrote that on my first visit to Ebbets Field in Brooklyn I rooted all afternoon for Dolph Camilli, the Dodger first baseman. I had been tricked into this treason, swore my enemy, because I wasn't aware that the Giants wore gray uniforms when traveling, the residents white. Though I invaded Flatbush to cheer Mel Ott, Giant right fielder, I wound up in hysterics over Camilli because both had the numeral "4" on the back of their uniform. Stuff, balderdash and rot, not to use a few other words too hot to handle in a memoir.

A daughter of the deep South, I have little time for the "Yankees." They're bleak perfectionists, insolent in their confidence, the snobs of the diamond. The Yankees are all technique, no color or juice. But they keep on winning pennants year after year. Not the Giants! They've won one flag in the last fourteen years.

I blew my first fuse over the Giants in the summer of '39, when introduced to Harry Danning and Mel Ott. Ott was so good-looking, so shy, so gentlemanly—and from Louisiana. For two weeks I got up in the middle of the night—around noon by the actor's clock—to charge up to the Polo Grounds.

I worked myself up into such a fever that I invited the team to see a performance of *The Little Foxes*. After the play I served them a buffet supper, and drinks compatible with their training rules, on the promenade which fringed the rear of the balcony. The Giants, following this soiree, dropped eight games in a row. Had I hexed them? The suspicion chilled me. I denied myself the Polo Grounds and they started to win again.

FABULOUS YANKEES THROUGH FIFTY YEARS

ARTHUR DALEY

It was the rarest of rare bargains. For the trifling sum of eighteen thousand dollars Frank Farrell and Big Bill Devery, a couple of ex-bartenders, bought the New York Yankee franchise in the American League. Strictly speaking, it was the Baltimore franchise they purchased for transfer to New York.

The deal was consummated on a winter's night in 1903 at the old Fifth Avenue Hotel. The official Yankee historians have set the date as March 12, 1903, although there are some experts who believe it happened two months earlier. It doesn't matter particularly.

It almost seems ridiculous now that a franchise worth many million dollars should be bought for a paltry eighteen thousand dollars. But back in 1903 Ban Johnson was dubious about the entire transaction. Johnson, a reformed baseball writer who had started the American League, had struggled for two years against the powerful and established National League, knowing in his heart that he couldn't succeed unless he placed a club in New York.

Desperate as he was for help, he still was skeptical of Farrell when the latter was introduced to him by Joe Vila, a sportswriting friend. All that Ban knew about Farrell was that he was an ex-bartender who became saloonkeeper, gambling house proprietor and race track plunger, none ranking as the heartiest of recommendations.

But Farrell shattered all qualms when he tossed a certified check for twenty-five thousand dollars on the table in front of the American League president.

"Hold this as a guarantee of good faith, Mr. Johnson," said Farrell. "If I don't put the ball club across, you can keep it."

Devery, Farrell's partner in the deal, had veered from bartending to the police force, risen to chief of the department, and then retired to the real estate business. He was rolling with wealth. More important at the moment, however, were the powerful political connections of the two, for John T. Brush, owner of the Giants, had successfully denied the American League a foothold in New York either by outbidding Johnson for options on potential ball park sites or threatening to use his Tammany Hall connections to have a street cut through whatever property Johnson might obtain.

Farrell and Devery, however, already had the site for a ball park at 168th Street and Broadway, where the Medical Center now stands. "That's pretty far uptown," said the dubious Johnson. But Farrell and Devery insisted that the new subway, soon to be opened, would provide the necessary transportation.

They worked frantically to get the park ready for the opening of the season. It was a rickety layout, with wooden stands, wooden fences and a ravine in right field. Because the park was on one of the highest points in Manhattan the team was called the Highlanders.

The proud and haughty Giants snickered at their new neighbors. So did the fans, for the new owners soon discovered New York was a Giant town. John McGraw then was beginning his fabulous career at the Polo Grounds, and would win pennant after pennant or always be in close contention.

In 1913 the Highlanders moved to the Polo Grounds as tenants of the Giants. They also changed their name to Yankees. They were still insignificant, so much so that the Giants felt they could safely house them without fear of building up a rival attraction at the Polo Grounds. For two years the Highlanders stumbled along. Then, on Jan. 11, 1915, Farrell and Devery sold them for $460,000 to Col. Jacob Ruppert and Col. Tillinghast L'Hommedieu Huston.

A new era was dawning for the Yankees although at that time it was only a flicker on the horizon. The colonels strengthened their team slowly but steadily. But the shape of the Yankee history actually was being made in Boston.

There, Ed Barrow, a powerfully built man with an iron fist and a steel-trap mind, was the manager of the Boston Red Sox. In 1918 he had steered them to a pennant, placing most of his reliance on an extraordinary left-handed pitcher named Babe Ruth. Ruth not only was the league's best left-handed pitcher, he was so gifted as a hitter that Barrow had used him in the outfield whenever he wasn't pitching. In the spring of 1919 Barrow converted Ruth into a full-time outfielder. He was an instant sensation, setting a new home-run record of twenty-nine and making the turnstiles spin all over the league.

Ruppert coveted Ruth and didn't have to wait long to buy him. The Red Sox owner, Harry Frazee, also was a theatrical producer. A series of "turkeys" had left him broke. When Ruppert offered him one hundred thousand dollars for Ruth plus the extension of a personal loan of three hundred and fifty thousand dollars (with Fenway Park as collateral) Frazee couldn't say no.

New York fans, who never dreamed of going to the Polo Grounds except when the Giants were in town, stormed the gates to see Ruth set an even greater home run record of fifty-four in 1920. Ruppert, satisfied with Ruth, got himself a prime minister. He hired Barrow away from the Red Sox as his general manager and nothing could stop the Yankees henceforth.

Barrow knew there were other good Red Sox available. The Yankees raided Boston so heavily that embittered baseball writers there referred to the deals as "The Rape of the Red Sox," and the willing Frazee was denounced throughout the league.

The Yankees won the first pennant in their history in 1921.

As they rose in prestige, it soon became a case of the tenants at the Polo Grounds overshadowing—and outdrawing—their landlords. McGraw couldn't take it. "Get 'em out of here. Make 'em build their own ball park. They'll have to move so far away, maybe to Long Island City, that everyone will forget them," McGraw ordered Charlie Stoneham. Although Stoneham owned the Giants, McGraw was the boss and he got his way. The Yankees were tossed out, but they didn't move to Long Island City. Ruppert found a perfect plot of ground just on the other side of the Harlem River and built the Yankee Stadium.

The personnel was to change but the success pattern would remain. Miller Huggins gave way to Joe McCarthy and Casey Stengel. Barrow was succeeded by George Weiss. Ruppert's heirs handed ownership over to Larry MacPhail, Dan Topping and Del Webb. But the winning tradition remained, in fact grew, until Yankee became the label of invincibility.

This label didn't come by accident. It was put there by design and Barrow was the man who put it there. He gave the ball club an organization and a purpose. He knew only three words, "Do it now." His talent scouts invariably got there "fustest with the mostest" to corral promising young ball players.

The Yankees were lucky, too, of course. They had to be. There was once a Coast League sensation every major league team wanted. But when he wrenched a knee, all other teams shied away. The Yankees didn't, though. They bought him from San Francisco for a trifling $25,000. He was Joe DiMaggio.

Barrow didn't approve of the farm system for the sport but when Colonel Ruppert got himself talked into buying Newark in the International League, Barrow reacted typically.

"One team is no good," he barked. "As long as we're stuck with Newark, we better do the job right."

So he bought lesser teams to feed players to Newark and still lesser teams to feed them. To run the chain, Barrow brought in Weiss, a man for whom he had no personal fondness but who was the best minor league man in the business. Again it was a typical Barrow gesture. Weiss was a perfect cog in a perfect machine.

The Yankees kept winning with such monotonous regularity that the cry arose around the league, "Break up the Yankees!"

The irreverent Jimmy Dykes, then manager of the White Sox, was merely trying to be flippant when he mischievously tossed off a crack which still causes Marse Joe McCarthy great pain.

"McCarthy?" said Dykes. "He's just a push-button manager."

Then he went on to explain how McCarthy merely had to push a button whenever he needed a new regular and one would pop up out of the Newark incubator.

Yankee greatness made it the most feared team in baseball. When Waite Hoyt, a typical Yankee of the Ruthian day, was in the twilight of his career, he pitched in the National League and one day faced the Chicago Cubs. The Cubs were riding him unmercifully from the dugout. Hoyt strode over to the Chicago dugout. "If you guys don't shut up," he snapped, "I'll put on my old Yankee uniform—and scare you to death."

In 1927, the greatest of all Yankee teams—the team of Murderers' Row—won the world series during batting practice before the first game. They had set an American League record by winning 110 games and losing only 44. Their first-place margin was an astounding seventeen games. Ruth broke his own 54-home-run record with 60. Lou Gehrig batted .373 and made 47 homers. Hoyt was the league's leading pitcher.

The Pittsburgh Pirates, who barely won the National League flag, were so curious about the Yankee supermen that they violated the unwritten law to watch them in their final workout the day before the opener.

"Gee, but they're big guys," whistled Paul Waner, a little guy himself.

Ruth hit one over the wall. Gehrig did the same. As the Yanks took turns in the batting cage, everything they hit either went over the fence or against it. It was an eye-opening performance and no eyes opened wider than those belonging to the Pirates. The Yankees beat them in four straight games.

The Yanks of that era achieved greatness in spite of themselves. Miller Huggins managed them with a loose rein. Every time he made ready to fine and suspend Ruth for breaking training rules, the Babe would hit a couple of home runs. Once, when the Yanks were involved in an overtime game in Chicago, Mark Roth, the traveling secretary, was worried for fear the team would miss its train, even then being held, back to New York.

"Relax," growled the Babe. "I'll get us outa here."

He hit a home run and the Yanks caught the train.

Ruth and Gehrig and other members of Murderers' Row gave the Yankees their reputation as sluggers. But few realized that this also was a team of expert fielders and expert pitchers. Their biggest contribution, however, was to establish their tradition of victory.

In Joe McCarthy the Yankees had a far more exacting taskmaster than Miller Huggins ever had dreamed of being. The bubbling color and effervescence of the Ruthian era was gone. In its place came "the Yankee type," the cool, precise craftsman.

To McCarthy just being a Yankee was a mark of distinction, a privilege. They were champions, the aristocrats of baseball, and they had to behave like aristocrats. No Yankee ever dared go into a dining car or a dining room without wearing a jacket and a tie. They were gentlemen always.

One night a group of young ball players sat over in a corner of the hotel lobby, quietly singing. They weren't disturbing a soul. McCarthy walked in and his blazing glance burned them to a crisp.

"Have you forgotten?" he snarled. "You're Yankees now. Start acting like them."

On the bench, however, McCarthy demanded no funereal silence. Once the Yanks in the dugout were whooping it up during a batting rally—all except one, Charlie Devens, a pitcher from Harvard and a blue blood from Back Bay. He sat austerely quiet and motionless until McCarthy's roving eye spotted him at one end of the bench.

"What's the matter with you, Devens?" he barked. "Stand up and shout. Wave your arms. Where do you think you are—in a canoe?"

When McCarthy's successor, Casey Stengel, who had failed miserably as manager in talent-poor Brooklyn and Boston, arrived at his first Yankee training camp, he repeated over and over again, "I never had so many good ball players to work with before."

And the future? A new generation of Yankees is taking over, the Mickey Mantles, the Gil MacDougals and others who will succeed the era of DiMaggio and Henrich as they succeeded the era of Ruth. The earliest years of the Yanks were truly lean, but their story, for the most part, is not one of rags to riches. Rather it would appear to be from riches to riches.

THOSE DAFFY DODGERS

HY TURKIN

Sports historians try to sum it up with "Everything happens in Brooklyn." Specifically, the slogan refers to that ungodly green acre deep in the heart of Flatbush, known as Ebbets Field. Here the Dodgers cavort daily and gaily. After each day's total of hits, runs and errors, their fans are mad with joy or mad with grief—but always mad.

Typical of how their rooters have come to expect only the unexpected is this true story of a cruising cab. Stopped by a red light on Bedford Avenue, the cabby yelled to a patron in the last row of the upper bleachers, "Hey, buddy, how are Dem Bums doing?"

"Pretty good," came the report. "Last of the sixth inning, tie score, and we have three men on base."

"Which base?" cried the cynical cabby, driving off.

Such sarcasm stems from the ignoble afternoon when Babe Herman doubled into a double play. Three Dodger runners wound up jointly occupying third base. Sure, that happened way back in 1926, but the malady lingers on, to wit:

In 1950 a couple of All-Star nominees from Brooklyn, Jackie Robinson and Gil Hodges, became ensnarled in a traffic jam that landed both runners on third base. The enemy catcher yelled for the ball, tagged Robinson, tagged Hodges, tagged the bag, tagged the umpire, then screamed in glee, "I know *somebody* is out!"

If the handwriting on the wall could be deciphered, it probably would say, "Once a Dodger, always a Dodger." Babe Herman helped to prove it. Returning to Brooklyn in 1945, the fabulous Babe immediately bridged the gap of his fourteen-year absence. On his first try, he pinch-hitted a line drive against the right field wall—but tripped over first base in rounding the bag and fell flat on his face.

When Herman was in his heyday, he batted well but fielded each pop fly as if it were an adventure. "Hoiman, don't get hoited!" was the war cry of bleacher regulars. In spite of their warnings, a fly ball once actually hit him on the head. Yet Herman was only one of many bizarre Brooklyn outfielders. Casey Stengel once responded to the fans' jeers by lifting his cap—and a sparrow flew out!

Frenchy Bordagaray, a likable zany who was rather gilding the lily by growing a Van Dyke beard to keep him company in the outfield in 1936, was chasing a long drive one day when his hat suddenly blew off. Frenchy ran back to pick up his cap, then resumed pursuit of the extra-base hit.

Umpires regard Ebbets Field as an open-air Dante's Inferno. Arguments are a dime à dozen, and often a dozen an inning.

One balmy day in 1940, umpire George Magerkurth started to walk off the field after rendering a last-inning decision that cost Brooklyn the game. A five-foot-seven fan rushed out of the stands, barged into the six-foot-four Magerkurth, tripped him, sat on his chest and flailed away with both fists, shrieking "You blind bum! You crook!"

Police peeled him off and rushed him to the station house, where the irate fan turned out to be a convicted thief out on parole!

Brooklyn fans loathe umpires, and grade them barely one notch above the most hated human beings of all—the Giants.

Dodger rooters can also let off steam in subtler ways. One day, just before game time, a grandstand regular lugged a heavy sack into the manager's dressing room and explained: "We read in the papers that the League president fined you twenty-five dollars for arguing with the umpire. So we took up a collection in the stands. Here's your twenty-five bucks—all in pennies. When that meat-head of an umpire asks you to pay your fine today, just bring up this sack and dump the twenty-five hundred pennies all over home plate . . . and let him collect!"

Somehow, the League president got wind of the stunt. He frantically phoned Ebbets Field and threatened suspension if the manager went through with it.

Flatbush fantasia pervades top-level management. Stengel gets a chuckle every time he tells of the board of directors' meeting he attended. To give his bosses a complete picture of the Dodger playing personnel, he started discussing the best prospects out on the club's "farms"—meaning their minor league affiliates. Exasperated, one of the Brooklyn bankers finally snapped: "Why all this talk about farm hands? We want ball-players not somebody to thresh wheat!"

One September afternoon of 1941 in Boston, Leo Durocher managed the Dodgers to their first pennant in twenty-one years. Yet he was fired that night! His crime? Leo ordered the home-coming Victory Special to by-pass 125th Street Station. Unbeknownst to Leo, Club President Larry MacPhail was waiting on the platform to board the train, so he could share in the triumphal plaudits of fifty-thousand fans waiting around Grand Central Terminal. Cooling off in the morning-after, MacPhail rehired Durocher.

No one is immune to the daffy Dodger spirit. Clubhouse aide Babe Hamberger, since promoted to ticket supervisor, announced over the ball park's loudspeaker system one day: "A small boy has been found lost in the grandstand."

Another employee who has become a fixture at Ebbets Field is Benny Weinrig. Master of the malapropism, he is an attendant for the literati of the press. In his unadulterated Brooklynese, Babe Herman was "Hoiman," and Waite Hoyt, "Hert." One summer, he added to the press-box memorabilia with a comment on Music Appreciation Night. This was at the game where all fans were admitted to the park free, when accompanied by a legitimate musical instrument. As the discord sounded between innings from every sector of the grandstand, Benny murmured: "I hope they have this Music Depreciation Night again. This is the best music I ever *saw!*"

Even scribes somehow become infected. Brooklyn baseball writers were given final blueprints for Ebbets Field in 1912. They checked, rechecked, and gave their hearty approval. Only after the park was built did they learn that no provision had been made for a press box!

Not the least in the cast of characters of Brooklyn's baseball burlesque is the rooter himself. You can always tell a Dodger fan, but you can't tell him much. No genus of sports spectator is louder or more loyal, none more bizarre.

Hilda Chester and her cowbell, making more noise than six fire engines, has been a long-time landmark in the bleachers. Multiply her by several thousand, and you can understand why a soldier who survived a Banzai attack on Leyte in World War II said: "The Japs made the weirdest sounds as they rushed at you. It sounded like Ladies Day at Ebbets Field."

On Ladies Day, the (don't-you-believe-it) weaker sex is admitted for only twenty-five cents. However, attendants at the turnstiles have to keep on the alert for men who masquerade as women, just to beat the regular $1.25 tariff.

Old-timers proudly recall Abie the Iceman. A raucous character, he used to buy a box seat daily so he could blare "Youse Bums!" at the Dodgers. This rattled the players so severely that the frustrated management presented him with a season pass, on condition that he keep quiet. At the end of one week, Abie returned the pass, crying: "The deal is off. I can't choke it down any more. Dey *are* bums!"

Center fielder Duke Snider has cause to remember critical customers, too. One afternoon he threw to the wrong base and cost the Dodgers a run. Half an hour after the game, he stopped at a soft-drink stand across the street from Ebbets Field. Two fans were arguing heatedly over the wrong throw. Not recognizing Duke, one of them turned to him to prove a point, asking, "Don't you think that Snider is a bum?"

Duke downed the rest of his drink, shrugged and replied, "Who am I to judge?"

Though it doesn't cost a cent to become a Dodger fan, the strain on heart and soul is extremely costly. That's because, win-lose-or-draw, the Dodgers never do things the easy way.

For three years running the Dodgers were still in a first-place tie after having played the ninth inning of the last regularly scheduled game of the season! It's so nerve-wracking that the Brooklyn chapter of the American Red Cross issues special disaster leaflets: "Care and Protection of Dodger Fans—Emergency Treatment at Ebbets Field."

Brooklyn's battiest era came during the 1914–31 managerial reign of Wilbert Robinson. The team was often called the Robins in his honor. And the Falstaffian mentor himself was affectionately called Uncle Robbie by the fans. One day Robinson decided to start rookie Oscar Roettger in right field. While penciling the line-up that had to be handed to the umpire, he sputtered, "R-o-t-t, R-e-t-g . . . aw, heck, let Cox stay in right field!"

Uncle Robbie always had a fondness for pitchers, but even he lost patience with an eccentric known as Clyde "Pea Ridge" Day, a hog-calling champion from Arkansas. Pea Ridge would stop a game, strike a pose on the mound and let out a bellow that shook the park.

Day boasted to teammates that his pastime of hog-calling developed his chest to superman strength. When Del Bisonnette asked him to prove it, Pea Ridge exhaled, tied a leather belt around his chest and said he would break the belt by expanding his chest. Pea Ridge inhaled till he almost got blue in the face, then—pop!—broke three ribs, putting him out of action for a month.

BIG DRAG VIGNETTES

MEL HEIMER

The Ham What Am: At Sardi's and Environs

I think the best description of an actor on the Big Drag is to call him a wonderfully insane peacock. His ego is boundless, and unless the conversation revolves around him and his activities, he is utterly bored; but at the same time his charm is so lush and his personality so overpowering that pretty soon you find yourself talking about him and liking it. . . .

Any time from the afternoon on until eight, and then from, say, eleven on for a couple of hours, you can meet almost any working actor in town by sitting at the tiny bar in Sardi's, up 44th Street on the West Side, across from Shubert Alley. Started a couple of decades ago by Vincent Sardi and now carried on by his enterprising son, young Vincent, this establishment is the Stork Club of the theatrical world.

The food is excellent and the drinks are good, but on the whole it must be said that Sardi's charm springs from the fact that most actors and actresses have played in at least one English drawing-room comedy and know which fork to use and how low to keep their voices pitched. Good manners are something of a novelty in any joint along Broadway, but they are gaudily on display in Sardi's.

Sardi's has several coincidental features. Chief among them is Renee Carroll, likely the world's most famous hatcheck girl. Stories have been written and movies filmed around the life of Renee, who has the shrewd knack of remembering customers' names and who also has achieved some prominence in the past as a backer of shows herself. It is customary, on entering Sardi's, to rouse Miss Carroll from the reading of a play manuscript, and it would not be too startling to find her rehearsing some matinee idol in his lines. Another interesting item at Sardi's are the caricatures by Alex Gard of stage celebrities which line the walls.

It is in Sardi's that the noted exhibitionism and affectation of the children of the theater are on display. Gloria LaSwitch, mink-coated and mascaraed to the hilt, will stride into the place at high noon or in the early evening, and spot Valerie Flipbottom, whose guts she hates because she ousted her from the leading feminine role in last season's smash hit. "*Valerie!*" Gloria will screech. "Gloria, *darling!*" Valerie will fire back, and will get up from her table and trip halfway across the room for the inevitable clinch and wet, lipsticky kiss on the cheek.

Men actors also will use this approach at luncheon in Sardi's; indeed, if you see a male actor and female actor approach each other rather conservatively and shake hands or bow, you can assume that they are carrying on a fierce, tempestuous love affair in private. Displays of affection are taken for granted, of course, but sometimes it does seem as if a ravenous leading man is taking advantage of tradition and holding his chance acquaintance a bit overlong.

The nadir of an actor's life is to be caught in Sardi's at night between the hours of eight-thirty and eleven. Unless he is big enough—a Lunt or a Fontanne—so that people will know he is idle at the moment because he chooses to be, an appearance at the gilded watering-place during those hours is a blunt admission that he is down on his luck. He is in that distressing fog known as At Liberty. If the actor is a smart one, he steers clear of Sardi's during theater-going hours. He buries himself in his hotel room or takes in a movie, or swills coffee at some Eighth Avenue joint until the witching hours are past. Then, gloves in hand and shoulders squared bravely, he sallies forth among the living once more.

Like all Broadwayites actors are inveterate horse players. The casual intruder backstage at intermission would be startled to find, say, Macbeth, his royal robes dragging on the floor, intently studying the fifth at Belmont between acts of the matinee performance. There is always an electrician or property man somewhere in the building whose real vocation is booking bets, and to him in a never-ending stream come the Ophelias, the Amandas, the King Lears and the Elizabeth Brownings of our day. Actors have a tremendous capacity for talking shop (mostly in withering criticisms of contemporaries), but they will abandon that tack occasionally to talk of the horses.

Besides Sardi's, there are several other gathering spots for the theatrical set in town. One is Louie Bergen's Theater Tavern on West 45th Street, a little joint with the cuisine of a Village spaghetti joint and an Actors' Equity clientele. The big shots and the little shots of the stage mix freely in the Theater Tavern, although most of its customers are second leads and bit players, walk-ons and chorus boys or girls who some day, by God, are going to become Bernhardts and Booths.

Along Broadway and just down 44th Street from Sardi's is the real hotbed of the theater—Walgreen's drugstore. Here is the breeding-place of tomorrow's performers; here the star-kissed speeches of Juliet are tossed off earnestly between lettuce and tomato sandwiches. For Walgreen's is the poor man's Sardi's. There was a time when its famous basement lunchroom contained so much budding talent per square inch that they even spilled over to the upstairs luncheonette, where they occasionally baffled the more sedate customers by going through scenes from *Winterset* or *Elizabeth the Queen*. Since those happy days in the Thirties, however, Walgreen's management has cracked down a trifle on its complement of would-be geniuses and today the ranks are fewer. But the place still has its full share of young actors and actresses; indeed, in the last five or ten years, nearly all of those who have come upon sudden fame in films or on the stage—girls like Bacall or Lizabeth Scott, for example—spent their customary apprenticeship in Walgreen's, mulling over Leo Shull's *Actors' Cues*.

The Night-Life Blues

John Perona's El Morocco, though more social than Broadway, still attracts a great many of the Big Drag crowd. El Morocco—or as *The New Yorker* once labeled it so brilliantly, the "splendid old goldfish bowl, full of some very ornate specimens"—is the place to spend the last part of your evening. By midnight or 1 A.M., the suburbanites and college children have usually cleared out, and Broadway and Park Avenue gather in equal parts to sit and stare.

The exceedingly respectable atmosphere of this East Side nightclub makes even the transaction of business seem a cardinal sin, and Broadwayites usually carry on their affairs in normal voices, which for them amounts to whispering. But the average socialite is unawed by this splendor, and very frequently goes in for fist-swinging and nosebloodying. There have been some good, lusty battles in El Morocco, but the number of Broadwayites involved have been comparatively few, which might prove that on the whole their behavior is somewhat better than that of their brothers from Groton and Andover.

Newspapermen on the prowl for stories are wont to pay an occasional visit to El Morocco—it was the favorite stamping-ground of the late Maury H. B. Paul when that rotund eccentric was setting the nation on its ear in his capacity as "Cholly Knickerbocker." However, if it is columnists you are after, Sherman Billingsley's Stork Club, on 53rd off Fifth Avenue, is the place to which to carry your old bones. For Mr. Billingsley, perhaps more than any other café owner in New York, has a gift for and an appreciation of publicity.

It is in the Stork, sandwiched between giggling and over-mellow debutantes and all the motley characters who make up the Broadway night-life crowd, that you will find Winchell, telephone in hand and determined look of eagles on his face; or amiable Earl Wilson, the celebrated saloon editor; or bluff, good-looking Ed Sullivan; or small, intense Leonard Lyons, searching, ever searching for his O. Henry-formula anecdotes.

The Versailles is another spot to which Broadway occasionally foots it across town. Its habit of presenting an elaborate floor show and its policy of aiming at the suburban trade, in town for a night, have made it one of the goldmines of the Broadway gold coast. Here, incidentally, is one of the few bars in town where an authentic, Grade-A French .75, the drink of the devil, can be procured, if anyone cares.

There are dozens of others where you will find the Broadway mob scattered at night—the Carnival at Eighth Avenue and 51st Street, where a slight, quiet man named Nicky Blair, an old hand at the night-club profession, runs the works; the Zanzibar, a glittering, hoopla joint on Broadway at 49th that is a showcase for the best of the Negro show talent; the Copacabana, the East 60th Street café operated by one-time press-agent Monte Proser, that is an authentic gathering spot for the Big Drag mob; and Billy Rose's Diamond Horseshoe in 48th Street, generally fitted out with stenographers and their boy friends from Weehawken and Union City who are in town for a big time, but occasionally studded with Broadwayites who feel nostalgic and want to listen to some hit songs of yesteryear.

In visiting a majority of these establishments, one oddity may strike you. Generally speaking, the manners on exhibition are those of pigs at the trough, with the screaming and yelling, the table-hopping, the brawling and the incomparable rudeness, but there usually is one man around who is dressed immaculately, mannered exquisitely and who is soft-spoken and courteous. You decide that he makes a grotesque addition to the goings on and you wonder how he ever became involved with this crowd—until you discover that he *has* to be there. He owns the joint.

THE CRACK-UP CITY

HELEN LAWRENSON

Last summer I went to a party where, in the due course of events, the men wound up huddled together in the kitchen, laughing fit to kill at their own jokes, and the women were left in the front room with nothing to do but talk about men—their own and everybody else's. As an old China hand at these sessions, I soon detected a strange undertone, a note of baffled but genuine worry. The usual classic complaints were there all right—the male misdeeds from malingering to mutiny—but something new had been added.

Every man they mentioned had the jitters in one form or another. This one couldn't sleep nights. That one had a nervous breakdown, had to quit his job. Poor Mary X's husband just up and left town without a word to her or anyone else! "Harry's much happier since he changed analysts" . . . "I wish Sylvia could get Joe to go to someone. He needs help . . ."

Alcoholics, it seemed, presented a major problem, because you had to wrap them in cotton wool and treat them like pregnant women, cater to them and never cross them. But the chief basis for uneasiness was that men are becoming so depressed they're losing interest in sex. One red-haired girl with appetizing contours claimed that half the men she met turned out to be fairies, and the rest were neurotics of one brand or another.

"What's happening to men, anyway?" she cried. "Are they all going crazy?"

This is taking an overly dim view, perhaps, but it must be admitted that the question is more than purely rhetorical. *The urban American male is increasingly neurotic.* He suffers from melancholia, acute anxiety, high tension, frantic uneasiness, inexplicable fears. He takes sleeping pills to make him sleep nights and Benzedrine to keep him awake days. Between times he swallows phenobarbital to quiet his jitters. He is frequently impotent, or alcoholic or both. Sometimes he takes refuge in homosexuality; sometimes in narcotics. He is racked with diseases caused by mental and emotional disorder: premature heart attacks, nervous headaches, asthma, stomach ulcers and other gastric and intestinal afflictions.

Surveys show that the average urban rate of first admissions to mental hospitals is nearly twice as high as the rural; and that the rate is twenty-seven per cent higher among males than among females. It looks as if there is something about city life which has a peculiarly corroding influence on the male nervous system.

There are two important factors on which the psychiatrists do agree. One is the destructive effect of the dog-eat-dog competition of life in the city, where everyone is seething with determination to forge ahead at top speed, and frequently can do it only at the expense of someone else. In contrast, farmers pool resources, lend a hand to help each other and live as neighbors. In addition, the average farmer knows the soothing dignity of being his own boss. He is not involved in cut-throat office politics, or a nerve-wracking maneuvering for advancement, or a pathological race for success. . . .

The second point of agreement is that to maintain mental health a man must feel that he is doing work which serves a useful purpose. In many varieties of city occupations there is room for doubt that the work is any help at all to mankind; the farmer on the other hand, gets from his labors a deep and honorable satisfaction. A book salesman could starve to death trying to sell him a copy of *How To Sleep*. Nor does he feel the need to rush out and buy *Peace of Mind* or *You Must Relax* or any other of the dozens of books which, in their desperate, panicky search for serenity, our city dwellers have put on the best-seller lists. . . .

In addition, the city male is bombarded daily with various small reminders of the perilous state of his health. "Can't sleep nights?" shrills his radio. "Lie awake and toss?" "Stomach tied in knots?" . . . A world conference of dentists notes "a marked increase in bruxism, due to the stress of modern life." Bruxism is the habit of unconsciously gnashing and grinding the teeth) . . . Department stores boost sales of special beds to induce slumber, while magazines feature articles telling what position you should get into in order to fall asleep . . .

What can be done to save this pale, teeth-gnashing, sleepless city fellow before he peters out on us? Well, we can't move *all* of them to the country. Besides, it shouldn't be necessary. Residents of Paris and Rome, for example, do not battle wildly in subways, or race to "get ahead." The basic difference in values is illustrated by the custom in many large Latin-American cities of closing all stores and offices for two hours at noon so that employees and employers alike can go home for a leisurely lunch or even a nap. The London practice of taking time off for tea during business hours has long been a topic for derisive comment from our own hard headed efficiency experts.

For their part, foreign observers of the American scene retaliate by commenting that with all our famed know-how we don't know how to relax. Too many American businessmen rush off to country or beach, vacation-bound, only to find themselves so helplessly bored that the only recreation they can think of is getting drunk.

The wisest of our men take steps to relieve the tension long before they reach the breaking point. Thus you find more and more doctors and lawyers who paint pictures or sculpt statues or climb mountains. Then there are all the mighty tycoons who work at fancy lathes—Philip Wrigley, who repairs machinery; or Roger Hackney, treasurer of Johns-Manville Corporation, who putters around his Larchmont home with power tools.

Here are men who have, in many instances, worked their way up from mechanics and simple craftsmen to places as multimillionaire captains of industry—and then their doctors put them to work carving furniture (right back where they started from, so to speak) to slacken the strain of their high-pressure lives. Most men, apparently, need to satisfy a basic urge to work with their hands, to make something of their own. For many of them, this need is denied expression in city life.

"People who are essentially intellectuals and verbalizers, who have no major manual outlets, tend to feel the stresses of life more acutely," says Theodore S. Weiss, M.D., Senior Psychiatrist for the New York City Department of Hospitals. "We often find serious emotional disorders among the business and professional classes, especially the tense professions of the big city, where they work in terms of deadlines and lose their positions in the field if they don't keep up the pace. In rural districts men work with the earth and with animals, with daily concrete problems they can solve with their hands, and they feel a basic satisfaction. Also, they don't as readily lose sight of their essential relation to the natural universe. In the cities some business and professional men tend to subordinate everything else to their job—family, fellow men, relations with nature and with God. In the country their job is more apt to be an integrated part of the whole. There's a more balanced set of values involved. . . ."

Women seem to hold together better than men. The average housewife, in the city as well as in the country, is kept busy straightening bureau drawers, putting blankets in moth balls, sewing on buttons, feeding and bathing the children, and so forth. Like the farmer, she has no doubt in her mind as to the importance of her job—she knows that without her the whole household would immediately fall apart. Moreover, she bears and rears children, which gives her a sense of fulfilling her natural role. . . .

But it isn't going to do women much good if the men all collapse. Here, in the greatest country in the world, we have built fabulous cities of soaring steel and glittering lights. But while these dazzling citadels of power grow ever larger and more resplendent, the men who live and work in them are rattling apart.

CONTEST

FRANCIS STEEGMULLER

My fourteen-year-old nephew Jack, whose parents live in the suburbs, spent a few days of his Christmas vacation from his Connecticut school with my wife and me in our apartment on 58th Street, between Sixth and Seventh Avenues. That is, he slept with us. Most of the time he was out on his own business, about which he was highly uncommunicative. We saw very little of him. When he said goodbye, though, he thanked us with an enthusiasm which was certainly unfeigned and which surprised us a little, coming from one usually so blasé. "I've had a wonderful time," he said. "This is sure a swell neighborhood."

"Is it?" I asked. "Swell in what way?" It had never seemed particularly swell to me.

"Well, I think I stand a chance of winning the contest that some of us set up before leaving school," Jack said. "And if I do win, it will be due entirely to you. I'd never have got to know this particular neighborhood if you didn't live here."

Copyright, 1945, by Francis Steegmuller. Originally published in *The New Yorker*.

This aroused our curiosity and we pressed him to explain what he meant. He seemed only too glad to.

"You know how you can wander around from block to block in the Grand Central zone without ever coming onto the street, don't you?" he said. "You know—the way you can get from the Commodore to the Biltmore to the Roosevelt and so on, just by walking through passages or buildings. And you can do the same thing in Times Square, only it's mostly in the subway station, and of course you can do it some in Radio City without crossing streets. Well, we set up a contest to see how many blocks it's possible to cover by walking through buildings in other sections of New York. We ruled out Grand Central, Times Square, and Radio City because everybody knows about them. Of course, in the parts of town allowed by our contest there aren't many underground passages, so you have to cross streets between buildings. But whoever gets the furthest without walking along avenues wins, and I think that may be me.

"I began on Central Park South," Jack continued, consulting a slip of paper he took from his pocket, "and walked right through Essex House to Fifty-eighth Street. And then I crossed Fifty-eighth Street to Number One-twenty-four and walked through to Fifty-seventh—you come out at Number One-nineteen. And then I crossed Fifty-seventh Street and walked through the Great Northern Hotel to Fifty-sixth, and crossed Fifty-sixth and went in the back door of the City Center and came out the front door on Fifty-fifth."

"Didn't anybody challenge you in the City Center?" I asked.

"Nope, there wasn't anybody around at all," Jack said. "I just walked right through. And nobody challenged me in Public School Sixty-nine, either. That's just across Fifty-fifth Street from the City Center. I walked right through that, too, and came out on Fifty-fourth. And in the Adelphi Theatre, right across the street—you know, the theatre where 'On the Town' is playing—everybody was swell to me. They didn't want to let me in at first, but when I told them about the contest they seemed awfully interested, and showed me right through the theatre and out the stage door onto Fifty-third Street. Gee, it was great, going right through a theatre like that.

"Across Fifty-third Street some trucks were coming out of the garage entrance of the Manhattan Storage and Warehouse Company, and I slipped in and walked through the place and came out what they call the receiving-office door, on Fifty-second Street.

"That makes seven blocks," Jack went on, "all covered by walking through buildings. I did go two more blocks without walking along an avenue, but I'm not sure they'll count, because I had to go through parking lots. After coming out of the Manhattan Storage and Warehouse Company, I crossed Fifty-second Street and walked through the Kim parking lot to Fifty-first Street, and then from Fifty-first to Fiftieth I went across what they call the Victory Square parking lot. Of course you *should* be able to get from Fifty-first to Fiftieth by going through the Roxy—I'm sure there's a perfectly good way of walking through it, because it has doors on both streets. But the man wouldn't let me in, even when I told him why. He was pretty mean, that guy at the Roxy. Not interested in the contest at all.

"Anyway," Jack went on, more cheerfully, "when I got to Fiftieth Street and happened to look north, there just happened to be a swell view of Essex House, where I began. It made me feel pretty good, thinking I'd come all that way, even if the last two blocks maybe won't count. Fiftieth Street is as far as you can go," he added. "There's no way of getting from Fiftieth to Forty-ninth in that block that I could find."

We congratulated Jack on his accomplishment. He laughed. "Bill Wright was talking to me yesterday," he explained, "and he asked me —you know, with a kind of a leer—if I realized that the hotel his family lives in, the New Weston, goes right through from Fiftieth Street to Forty-ninth between Madison and Park and that the Chatham goes through from Forty-ninth to Forty-eighth. I just laughed at him. That's only two blocks to my seven or nine, and then you run right into the Grand Central zone, out of bounds. There's not much possibility of going *north* from the New Weston through buildings. I know, because I went over to check up on it and see if he was holding anything back. There's that big brownstone house behind St. Patrick's, but I couldn't get through it, and if I couldn't, Bill couldn't— I know that. I'm not worried about Bill Wright.

"The only other fellow I've heard from is Frank Miller," Jack ended, his face clouding a little. "He lives up near Columbia—his father's a professor there, you know, and Frank's pretty clever. He said something mysterious to me over the phone the other day about a Columbia tunnel, some kind of a tunnel connecting all the buildings on the campus, or something like that. I must say that has me a little worried. Do you suppose there is a tunnel at Columbia longer than seven or nine blocks?" Jack didn't even wait for us to answer. "Why, that would turn the place into a regular Grand Central or Times Square," he said incredulously. "They wouldn't want the university to be that kind of a place, would they, even at Columbia?"

I told him certainly not, Dr. Butler would never want that, and we urged him to let us know how the contest came out. But my nephew isn't much of a correspondent. We haven't had a letter since he went back to school.

THE SPIRIT HAS MANY MANSIONS

IRWIN EDMAN

Someone, I think it was H. L. Mencken, said that trying to be a philosopher in New York is like trying to sing in a boiler factory. There are many people in other parts of the country who feel that, for all its cultural resources, its theatres, concerts, art galleries, colleges, universities, museums, adult education centers, New York is the last place for a man or woman happily to live the life of the mind and imagination. Thoreau long ago told us that most men lead lives of quiet desperation, but people outside New York feel that New Yorkers lead lives of noisy distraction. Yet the fact remains that it is not only New Yorkers who say they could not and would not live anywhere else—largely for reasons summed up in the word "culture."

Every year there come to New York from small towns and villages in Arkansas or South Carolina, from large cities in the Southwest or the Northeast, even from Boston (once generally assumed to be the Athens of America), young men and women, some of them, undoubtedly, in the hope of making their fame and fortune. But many arrive here, especially young men and women graduates of the state universities, because they find our town full of intellectual opportunities and advantages which they cannot find or believe they cannot find as well in the America that is not New York.

These young people often stay when the interests of fame and fortune would perhaps encourage them to go back to their native grounds in the South or the Northwest, in Kansas, or in Maine. They stay for what are generally called the cultural resources of New York, many of which are free. Sometimes when professional or business opportunities force them away from New York, young men and women, often not more than three years domiciled in New York, feel they are being sentenced to spiritual Siberia.

It is curious that this should be so. There are fine symphony orchestras in Minneapolis, in Cincinnati, in Dallas, in Detroit. There is a first class art museum in Toledo. There are little theatres in Texas where exciting new ventures in drama and stage technique are constantly appearing. There are books available everywhere, and lively intellectual communities all over the country, not least in the state universities of the Middle West. Yet, much as the French people (and with more reason) think all French culture is concentrated in Paris, so do many Americans (not all of them native New Yorkers) feel that New York and the cultural life are one. Why do they feel this? The answer is simple. New York *is* the cultural center of America.

For reasons often rehearsed, the theatre, however inadequately, is concentrated in New York. New York is the music capital of the nation; there is not a day in New York that there is not some concert that would be the highlight of a season in many large cities in this country and certainly of any small town. Though books and magazines are available everywhere, New York is the capital of the book world and writers as well as publishers congregate here. There are museums of high quality in two dozen cities in the United States. Yet not simply by virtue of the Metropolitan Museum of Art and the Frick Collection and the Museum of Modern Art and the Whitney Museum, but because of the constant procession of distinguished contemporary shows in the 57th Street area, one feels, perhaps, as nowhere except in Paris, that one is in the center of the living art world.

Even for radio and television (which are in many quarters considered the enemies of the cultural life of this country), in so far as they *are* cultural media, they are more so in New York than in any other place in this country. There is hardly a place in the United States of America except New York where at almost any hour of the day, thanks to WQXR and WNYC, one has available at the turn of a dial the finest music available in our time.

The American Museum of Natural History has a deserved world reputation. It is a wonderful place to see everything in nature, from pre-historic reptiles to the movements of the stars. In New York one lives right around the corner from everything, including, by means of the Planetarium, outer space and, by means of the lifelike exhibits just down the street, Neolithic Man and the fauna of Equatorial Africa.

The living fauna of many regions may be seen at their outdoor leisure at the Bronx Zoo.

Yet a catalogue of the theatres, the concert halls, the museums, do not, I think, account for the sense that people living in New York have of inhabiting a cultural center. Nor is the above catalogue complete. One must add the universities—Columbia, Fordham, New York University, the city colleges with their vast student populations. One must add, further, half a dozen leading theological seminaries and the large centers of adult education, the courses in the School of General Studies at Columbia and New York Universities, the evening sessions of the city colleges. One would have to list the semi-professional theatres and the series of Poetry Readings, usually a sell-out, at the Y.M.H.A., in which such eminent poets as the Sitwells, Yeats, Dylan Thomas and T. S. Eliot have appeared. One would have to include the Asia Institute and the Brooklyn Institute of Arts and Sciences, and the famous series of lectures given Tuesday and Sunday evenings, free, in the auditorium at Cooper Union where Lincoln once spoke.

But even a complete catalogue of official cultural resources would not quite explain the very vivid sense which most native and naturalized citizens of New York have about the city, a sense of being a vital part of a culture that is extraordinarily alive. This conviction is shared even by those who cannot pretend to turn up regularly at the Metropolitan Museum of Art and who appear at the Museum of Modern Art only to attend some antique movie. It is the conviction, even of those who are seldom seen at first nights (or, with the prices of tickets being what they are, at thirty-third nights), who miss many exhibitions that they meant to visit, and lectures they had planned to attend, and read only the reviews of books they had intended to read. It is a persuasion shared and an excitement felt by many thousands who do not write or paint or compose.

First; there is the sense, communicated even by the announcements in the Sunday newspapers, of all that is going on in a given week, the awareness of the liveliness and variety of the cultural life of the city. There is (abetted by the presence of the United Nations and its indubitably original modernistic building) the awareness of New York as the focus not only of American culture but of the world culture. Where else but in New York does a Greek company come from Athens to play Euripides or a French group to play Molière? In five minutes' walk or ten minutes' ride one hears a variety of languages and has the choice of a whole United Nations of cuisine.

Culture in the genteel sense means a modest cultivation. But culture in the anthropologist's meaning of a pattern of culture is also a multiform experience to New York. A generation ago some citizens of Italian descent in New York gave to Columbia University the Casa Italiana, and one can participate there in many activities representing Italian civilization, its art, its literature, its thought. But one can hear Italian and have a sense of Italy in many places outside the Casa Italiana, in a thousand shops and restaurants and over more than one radio station. Nor does one need to wait, pleasant as it was to have them, for the Barrault players to arrive in New York to hear beautiful French spoken and to have a glimpse of French civilization. One is as likely to overhear French or Italian or Spanish or German in New York as English, as outsiders sometimes—not altogether with enthusiasm—point out.

There is something else than variety of culture. There is the discovery that in this large city are people who share one's interest, however specialized. One hears of individuals who became acquainted and subsequently good friends because they met in a course in creative writing at the New School, or a class in chair caning at the Riverside Church. On East 94th Street a great many Americans have learned at the Ramakrishna-Vivekananda Center to nourish their own knowledge of Indian thought and religion and to find those who share their interests. Long ago, when Sinclair Lewis wrote "Main Street" he gave a picture of the loneliness someone with intellectual and spiritual interests feels in a small place where those concerns are not current or highly regarded.

In New York the very diversity of people and interests makes it possible that even a person most esoteric in his dedications will find companions. I encountered once, after I had addressed a small group that met monthly to discuss philosophy, a retiring, youngish man, highly informed and enlightened, who turned out to be a subway motorman. Amateur Egyptologists, part-time ethnologists, devotees of small religious cults can find their friends in New York. Nor in the tolerant anonymity of a large city will those of specialized intellectual or spiritual interests be regarded as eccentric, nor will the intellectual life itself be looked upon as freakish.

One of the qualities of a cultural capital is that it communicates, like London or Paris, a sense of the past. At the Comédie Française a member of the audience is deeply conscious that he is viewing a performance in a long tradition. Attending a lecture at the Sorbonne, one is sensible that lectures have been given in this university since the Middle Ages. Almost every street in old Paris, or in central London, is filled with associations of an ancient past.

Such a sense of history is perhaps unattainable to the same extent in New York. But there are still landmarks that go back to the Revolution and even before. And New York is filled with echoes of the nineteenth century; Washington Square and Gramercy Park, and the now shabby brownstone houses on the side streets of the Upper West Side that are reminders of the solid bourgeois life that inhabited them in the Eighties and Nineties of the last century, as the still surviving mansions on Fifth Avenue are links with the fabulous ways of living of the vanished society of the very rich of fifty years ago. St. Paul's Church and graveyard are eloquent of the eighteenth century, present still in the shadow of modern skyscrapers.

"I am a citizen of no mean city," Saint Paul announced, proud of his citizenship in Imperial Rome. New Yorkers are often proud of the heights, the towering splendors of their metropolis. Seeing these from a ship coming up the harbor, from a sight-seeing boat making a tour of Manhattan Island or from a plane soaring over their light-sparkled magnificence, one's breath catches. Even residents who have learned to take New York for granted are, on occasion, awed still by a sudden glimpse of the immensity, of the massiveness, of the citadel of riches and power that is New York. But in a subtler sense, New York is no mean city. Here the spirit has many mansions and there are many incitements to the spirit. For all its distractions, its rush, its brashness, there is hardly a place in the world where there are so many nourishments for the life of the imagination and the mind.

SAVAGE SUNSETS

BROOKS ATKINSON

If New York were not celebrated for more materialistic wonders, people would travel here to admire the splendor of the sunsets over New Jersey. They are regular events of transcendent splendor. A savage might be frightened by them, for they have the flaming grandeur of primordial catastrophe. They fill our western sky with tongues of fire. Since we understand the science of sunset colors we can admire them with equanimity. There is a commonplace practical reason for their barbaric magnificence. The industrial plants, railroad locomotives and steamships of New Jersey send up a thick cloud of sullen smoke that rolls across the Palisades, showers us with specks of grit and soot, and breaks up the light. The blue rays, which have a short wave length, are widely scattered. But the red rays, which have long wave lengths, pierce the barrier of smoke and come through to us. When the sun gets low in the western sky, the light of the sun comes to us at a long angle through the whole width of the New Jersey smoke bank, and all the color except red is diffused. Our sunsets are, therefore, abnormally red. Our days end violently—the great western arch of the sky incarnadined as if the day had taken fire.

This afternoon the sun is transmuted into an enormous orange sphere when it slips behind the smoke above the Jersey shore. I can look at it with unprotected eyes as it sinks out of sight through the smoke, gas and fumes of a huge industrial bastion. For another quarter of an hour the clouds in the west are banks of crimson. South and north of the sunset pit the clouds are washed with blue, and blue swims on the placid surface of the river. Between the celestial blue of the river and the crimson of the sky the long crag of the Palisades wall is like a deep blue band dividing the firmament from the waters. Presently the Weehawken Boulevard lights come on, the jewels on the crown of the imperial Palisades.

Tomorrow's sunset will be quite different, for the sunset pattern is infinitely varied. The western sky never repeats a design. From day to day it retains nothing but its immutable magnificence.

V
Perspectives: The City and the Dream

WALT WHITMAN
1856–1885

Crossing Brooklyn Ferry

1

Flood-tide below me! I see you face to face!
Clouds of the west—sun there half an hour high—I see you also face to face.

Crowds of men and women attired in the usual costumes, how curious you are to me!
On the ferry-boats the hundreds and hundreds that cross, returning home, are more curious to me than you suppose,
And you that shall cross from shore to shore years hence are more to me, and more in my meditations, than you might suppose.

. . .

3

It avails not, time nor place—distance avails not,
I am with you, you men and women of a generation, or ever so many generations hence,
Just as you feel when you look on the river and sky, so I felt,
Just as any of you is one of a living crowd, I was one of a crowd,
Just as you are refresh'd by the gladness of the river and the bright flow, I was refresh'd,
Just as you stand and lean on the rail, yet hurry with the swift current, I stood yet was hurried,

Just as you look on the numberless masts of ships and the thick-stemm'd pipes of steamboats, I look'd.

I too many and many a time cross'd the river of old,
Watched the Twelfth-month sea-gulls, saw them high in the air floating with motionless wings, oscillating their bodies,
Saw how the glistening yellow lit up parts of their bodies and left the rest in strong shadow,
Saw the slow-wheeling circles and the gradual edging toward the south,
Saw the reflection of the summer sky in the water,
Had my eyes dazzled by the shimmering track of beams,
Look'd at the fine centrifugal spokes of light round the shape of my head in the sunlit water,
Look'd on the haze on the hills southward and south-westward,
Look'd on the vapor as it flew in fleeces tinged with violet,
Look'd toward the lower bay to notice the vessels arriving,
Saw their approach, saw aboard those that were near me,
Saw the white sails of schooners and sloops, saw the ships at anchor,
Fifty years hence, others will see them as they cross, the sun half an hour high,
A hundred years hence, or ever so many hundred years hence, others will see them,
Will enjoy the sunset, the pouring-in of the flood-tide, the falling-back to the sea of the ebb-tide.

. . .

8

Ah, what can ever be more stately and admirable to me than mast-hemm'd Manhattan?
River and sunset and scallop-edg'd waves of flood-tide?
The sea-gulls oscillating their bodies, the hay-boat in the twilight, and the belated lighter?

What gods can exceed these that clasp me by the hand, and with voices I love call me promptly and loudly by my nighest name as I approach?

What is more subtle than this which ties me to the woman or man that looks in my face?
Which fuses me into you now, and pours my meaning into you?

We understand then do we not?
What I promis'd without mentioning it, have you not accepted?
What the study could not teach—what the preaching could not accomplish is accomplish'd, is it not?

9

Flow on, river! flow with the flood-tide, and ebb with the ebb-tide!
Frolic on, crested and scallop-edg'd waves!
Gorgeous clouds of the sunset! drench with your splendor me, or the men and women generations after me!
Cross from shore to shore, countless crowds of passengers!
Stand up, tall masts of Mannahatta! stand up, beautiful hills of Brooklyn!
Throb, baffled and curious brain! throw out questions and answers!
Suspend here and everywhere, eternal float of solution!
Gaze, loving and thirsting eyes, in the house or street or public assembly!
Sound out, voices of young men! loudly and musically call me by my nighest name!
Live, old life! play the part that looks back on the actor or actress!
Play the old role, the role that is great or small according as one makes it!
Consider, you who peruse me, whether I may not in unknown ways be looking upon you;
Be firm, rail over the river, to support those who lean idly, yet haste with the hasting current;
Fly on, sea-birds! fly sideways, or wheel in large circles high in the air;
Receive the summer sky, you water, and faithfully hold it till all downcast eyes have time to take it from you!

Diverge, fine spokes of light, from the shape of my head, or any one's head, in the sunlit water!
Come on, ships from the lower bay! pass up or down, white-sail'd schooners, sloops, lighters!
Flaunt away, flags of all nations! be duly lower'd at sunset!
Burn high your fires, foundry chimneys! cast black shadows at nightfall! cast red and yellow light over the tops of the houses!
Appearances, now or henceforth, indicate what you are,
You necessary film, continue to envelop the soul,
About my body for me, and your body for you, be hung our divinest aromas,
Thrive, cities—bring your freight, bring your shows, ample and sufficient rivers,
Expand, being than which none else is perhaps more spiritual,
Keep your places, objects than which none else is more lasting.

You have waited, you always wait, you dumb, beautiful ministers,
We receive you with free sense at last, and are insatiate henceforward,
Not you any more shall be able to foil us, or withhold yourselves from us,
We use you, and do not cast you aside—we plant you permanently within us,
We fathom you not—we love you—there is perfection in you also,
You furnish your parts toward eternity,
Great or small, you furnish your parts toward the soul.

Mannahatta

I was asking for something specific and perfect for my city,
Whereupon lo! upsprang the aboriginal name.

Now I see what there is in a name, a word, liquid, sane, unruly, musical, self-sufficient,
I see that the word of my city is that word from of old,

Because I see that word nested in nests of water-bays, superb,
Rich, hemm'd thick all around with sailships and steamships, an island sixteen miles long, solid-founded,
Numberless crowded streets, high growths of iron, slender, strong, light, splendidly uprising toward clear skies,
Tides swift and ample, well-loved by me, toward sundown,
The flowing sea-currents, the little islands, larger adjoining islands, the heights, the villas,
The countless masts, the white shore-steamers, the lighters, the ferry-boats, the black sea-steamers, well model'd,
The down-town streets, the jobbers' houses of business, the houses of business of the ship-merchants and money-brokers, the river-streets,
Immigrants arriving, fifteen or twenty thousand in a week,
The carts hauling goods, the manly race of drivers of horses, the brown-faced sailors,
The summer air, the bright sun shining, and the sailing clouds aloft,
The winter snows, the sleigh-bells, the broken ice in the river, passing along up or down with the flood-tide or ebb-tide,
The mechanics of the city, the masters, well-form'd, beautiful-faced, looking you straight in the eyes,
Trottoirs throng'd, vehicles, Broadway, the women, the shops and shows,
A million people—manners free and superb—open voices—hospitality—the most courageous and friendly young men,
City of hurried and sparkling waters! city of spires and masts!
City nested in bays! my city!

SINCLAIR LEWIS

That Was New York—and That Was Me

1903

David Copperfield terrified by hackney coaches in London? That was nothing, nothing at all. A third of a century ago, in September of 1903, I first came to New York, on my way to college. The Pacific cable had just been opened, Whistler had just died, the Wright brothers were

Copyright, 1937, by The New Yorker Magazine, Inc.

three months later to make the first airplane flight, and, in August (to crib from Mr. Mark Sullivan), for the first time an automobile had crossed the continent under its own power. It was the beginning, then, of the new world of gasoline, and I should have found New York, which, except for trolleys and the elevated, was as horsified as it had been in 1700, a serene and provincial old town, to be remembered with nostalgia in these days of taxis.

I didn't find it anything of the kind. Decidedly no.

Born in Minnesota, I had never been east of Chicago except for a couple of months at Oberlin College, Ohio, an institution which singularly failed to resemble Columbia or the Sorbonne. Smoking was forbidden there, and class parties were opened with a powerful prayer by some student who was in training as a Y.M.C.A. secretary.

From Minnesota to Albany, New York, there was nothing sensational about my journey, though later I found that the high-nosed youth to whom I had confided, on a station platform, that, proudly, I was a "Yale Man" was also going East to enter the business of being a "Yale Man." Having attended a prep school instead of a Western high school, he knew that there was nothing more boorish, nothing that, in the cant of the day, would so thoroughly "queer" you, as to call yourself a "Yale Man." He let me know all about it afterward, in New Haven, with the beneficent result that to this day, if anyone (usually it's in a Pullman) demands, "Aren't you the author?" I protest, "Certainly not. The fellow who you prob'ly saw his picture, he's my cousin, they say he looks like me, on account of because we're both skinny. But me, thank God, I'm in the wholesale-grocery racket, and say, have I got fun. Why, say, brother, my territory takes in—" By that time, he has usually fled. Try it.

With my trunk sent on to New Haven, I debarked from the train at Albany and came down to Manhattan by a Hudson River Day boat. That's the sort of thing one has the sense to do at eighteen and never in the duller years thereafter: to swim into New York on a tide of history. There were my first mountains, the Catskills; there were Ichabod Crane and Rip Van Winkle, visible on the blue uplands or in the mountain gorges; George Washington rode all over the place; and there were stone houses that, compared with the frame cottages of a prairie village, seemed to me coeval with the Acropolis—and in considerably better repair. This, I decided, this was *good;* I was simply going to love the East, particularly New York; love it, yes, and dominate it. Give me twenty years and I would be a literary fellow there, with an income of eighteen hundred dollars a year—prob'ly two thousand, by the time I was fifty—and a fine four-room flat, decorated with Japanese prints and Della Robbia plaques, in which I would entertain all the great artists of the day: Richard LeGallienne and Maxfield Parrish and James Huneker—the last of whom I prized, I imagine, not because he was a sound appraiser but because he furnished to the young yearner so many lovely names of Czech etchers and Finnish trioletists. (In the preciosity of college preparation, I had only nibbled at the really enduring craftsmen of the day: Hamlin Garland, Booth Tarkington, George Ade, Finley Peter Dunne, William Gillette, while William Dean Howells wasn't romantic enough for me. LeGallienne's "Quest of the Golden Girl" and Tennyson's "Idylls of the King" were my meat; chicken à la king was tastier than mutton chops. That is as it should be: Freshmen should be romantics, sophomores should be Socialists, juniors should be bums, and after that it doesn't matter.)

Yes, I came into New York an emperor on a barge. It wasn't the skipper who was taking the boat in, but my will to conquer, and I was almost sorry for the New York that would have to yield so completely to my demands.

The boat docked at early dusk. I don't know whether the same pier served ferries also or whether there were ferryhouses hard by, but from the safe deck of the river boat I was cast out into a riot of fiends.

I know now that they were only Jersey commuters, with their little hearts as white as snow, scampering home with Italian sausage and shin guards for Junior and copies of *The Century*, thinking of nothing more alarming than an evening of Five Hundred or crokinole, and if they looked agitated, it was because they were afraid they would miss the 6:17. But to me, then, they were by Doré out of the Inferno. In that smoky darkness, on the rough floor of the pier and the rougher pavement outside, pushed, elbowed, jabbed by umbrellas, my suitcase banging my legs, I saw them as the charging troops of Satan himself, their eyes hateful, their mouths distorted with fury, their skinny hands clutching at me. From provincial embarrassment I turned to utter panic fear. I gabbled at a policeman, asking what trolley I should take for the Grand Central. Another dozen hussars of hell had shouldered me, bumped me, and turned me about before the policeman took time to indicate a trolley with a jerked thumb.

God knows where the streetcars took me in Manhattan that night —from the Harlem River to the Battery and back again, I should think. I know I changed cars several times, and each time desired to weep upon the shoulder of some exceedingly unsympathetic conductor or cop. The golden streets of the dream city were not merely tarnished; they were greasy. Everywhere, people bumped along the shadow-spotted sidewalks as viciously, as threateningly, as they had at the ferry-house. Their eyes seemed full of malice and every manner of crime, and in their deft dodging at street corners, amid traffic, they showed a surly, defiant, urban competence which the young man from Minnesota could surely never emulate. (Yes, and he never has; it is only moral cowardice that keeps him from taking a taxi to cross Madison Avenue or Times Square.) He dominate the city? He was beaten before he started, by this dirty-gray, hoarse, rearing dinosaur of a city; he would never drive it. (Nor ever has!)

On that erratic trolley journey I saw, but was too overpowered to enjoy seeing, real live Italians and Chinamen and Negroes. I think—possibly I imagined it afterward—but I think I gawked up from the trolley window at the fabulous Flatiron Building, the most famous and fourth highest business structure in the world—seven or eight times as high as the building in Sauk Center which housed the *Weekly Avalanche* (sic), the Masonic lodge, and the town photographer. But I know that miraculously, without merit, I did come to the red-brick barn that then was the Grand Central Station, and to a dirty day coach for New Haven.

Even had it not been dark, I doubt if, in my exhausted disillusion, I could really have seen the Connecticut apple orchards and the hilly fields, accented with stone walls, to which I had been looking forward these five years. I was simply hiding in that day coach, which brought me, rather surprisingly, to New Haven.

It was quiet enough in New Haven, near the station, as with my suitcase I diffidently looked for an inexpensive hotel. I remember that the hotel I found wasn't much of a hotel. In fact, it was a thundering bad hotel. My room lacked air, running water, and a rug. But its stillness, the gentility of its walls in not falling in and crushing me to death, as that New York crowd had so resolutely tried to do, were heavenly.

So I started thirty-three years—so far—of New York and the East.

Seven years later I went to New York to stay. I was twenty-five then—not so young and promising—and I had a job in a publishing house at fifteen a week, with a pretty fair chance that if I stayed on the job ten years, I might possibly rise to twenty-five a week. Yes, and that wasn't so enticing a New York, either, that fifteen-a-week New York where, pay day being Saturday noon, neither my closest associate in the publishing house—George Soule, now of the *New Republic*—nor I ever had anything left for Saturday-morning breakfast. Little we saw in Nature that was ours, but getting and spending we didn't lay waste our powers.

London, Paris, Berlin, Rome, Vienna, San Francisco—I have found them to be comfortable and easily familiar cities. If no cit talks to you in London, the bobbies do give you directions. If in Paris on a wet day the taxis skid three times to the block, no one is ever hurt save in the vocabulary. But New York is still to me very much what it was on that September evening in 1903. O. O. McIntyre can have it. As for me, I would not take taxi from, say, Ninetieth Street to the Village even to go to a party at which the presence was guaranteed, under penalty, of Gandhi, Stephen S. Wise, Dr. Harvey Cushing, General Göring, Bernarr Macfadden, Evangeline Booth, and J. Edgar Hoover complete with sawed-off shotgun. My first day in New York has never quite ended. And eighty cents still seems too much to pay for orange juice.

HENRY ADAMS

No Constantine in Sight

1904

Nearly forty years had passed since the ex-private secretary landed at New York with the ex-Ministers Adams and Motley, when they saw American society as a long caravan stretching out towards the plains. As he came up the bay again, November 5, 1904, an older man than either his father or Motley in 1868, he found the approach more striking than ever—wonderful—unlike anything man had ever seen —and like nothing he had ever much cared to see. The outline of the city became frantic in its effort to explain something that defied meaning. Power seemed to have outgrown its servitude and to have asserted its freedom. The cylinder had exploded, and thrown great masses of stone and steam against the sky. The city had the air and movement of hysteria, and the citizens were crying, in every accent of anger and alarm, that the new forces must at any cost be brought under control. Prosperity never before imagined, power never yet wielded by man, speed never reached by anything but a meteor, had made the world irritable, nervous, querulous, unreasonable and afraid. All New York was demanding new men, and all the new forces, condensed into corporations, were demanding a new type of man—a man with ten times the endurance, energy, will and mind of the old type—for whom they were ready to pay millions at sight. As one jolted over the pavements or read the last week's newspapers, the new man seemed close at hand, for the old one had plainly reached the end of his strength, and his failure had become catastrophic. Every one saw it, and every municipal election shrieked chaos. A traveller in the highways of history looked out of the club window on the turmoil of Fifth Avenue, and felt himself in Rome, under Diocletian, witnessing the anarchy, conscious of the compulsion, eager for the solution, but unable to conceive whence the next impulse was to come or how it was to act. The two-thousand-years' failure of Christianity roared upward from Broadway, and no Constantine the Great was in sight.

O. HENRY

The Voice of the City

1905

Twenty-five years ago the school children used to chant their lessons. The manner of their delivery was a singsong recitative between the utterance of an Episcopal minister and the drone of a tired sawmill. I mean no disrespect. We must have lumber and sawdust.

I remember one beautiful and instructive little lyric that emanated from the physiology class. The most striking line of it was this:

"The shin-bone is the long-est bone in the human bod-y."

What an inestimable boon it would have been if all the corporeal and spiritual facts pertaining to man had thus been tunefully and logically inculcated in our youthful minds! But what we gained in anatomy, music, and philosophy was meagre.

The other day I became confused. I needed a ray of light. I turned back to those school days for aid. But in all the nasal harmonies we whined forth from those hard benches I could not recall one that treated of the voice of agglomerated mankind.

In other words, of the composite vocal message of massed humanity.

In other words, of the Voice of a Big City.

Now, the individual voice is not lacking. We can understand the song of the poet, the ripple of the brook, the meaning of the man who wants $5 until next Monday, the inscriptions on the tombs of the Pharaohs, the language of flowers, the "step lively" of the conductor, and the prelude of the milk cans at 4 A.M. Certain large-eared ones even assert that they are wise to the vibrations of the tympanum produced by concussion of the air emanating from Mr. H. James. But who can comprehend the meaning of the voice of the city?

I went out for to see.

First, I asked Aurelia. She wore white Swiss and a hat with flowers on it, and ribbons and ends of things fluttered here and there.

"Tell me," I said, stammeringly, for I have no voice of my own, "what does this big—er—enormous—er—whopping city say? It must have a voice of some kind. Does it ever speak to you? How do you interpret its meaning? It is a tremendous mass, but it must have a key."

"Like a Saratoga trunk?" asked Aurelia.

"No," said I. "Please do not refer to the lid. I have a fancy that every city has a voice. Each one has something to say to the one who can hear it. What does the big one say to you?"

"All cities," said Aurelia, judicially, "say the same thing. When they get through saying it there is an echo from Philadelphia. So, they are unanimous."

"Here are 4,000,000 people," said I, scholastically, "compressed upon an island, which is mostly lamb surrounded by Wall Street water. The conjunction of so many units into so small a space must result in an identity—or, or rather a homogeneity—that finds its oral expression through a common channel. It is, as you might say, a consensus of translation, concentrating in a crystallized, general idea which reveals itself in what may be termed the Voice of the City. Can you tell me what it is?"

Aurelia smiled wonderfully. She sat on the high stoop. A spray of insolent ivy bobbed against her right ear. A ray of impudent moonlight flickered upon her nose. But I was adamant, nickel-plated.

"I must go and find out," I said, "what is the Voice of this City. Other cities have voices. It is an assignment. I must have it. New York," I continued, in a rising tone, "had better not hand me a cigar and say: 'Old man. I can't talk for publication.' No other city acts in that way. Chicago says, unhesitatingly, 'I will'; Philadelphia says, 'I should'; New Orleans says, 'I used to'; Louisville says, 'Don't care if I do'; St. Louis says, 'Excuse me'; Pittsburgh says, 'Smoke up.' Now, New York—"

Aurelia smiled.

"Very well," said I, " I must go elsewhere and find out."

I went into a palace, tile-floored, cherub-ceilinged, and square with the cop. I put my foot on the brass rail and said to Billy Magnus, the best bartender in the diocese:

"Billy, you've lived in New York a long time—what kind of a song-and-dance does this old town give you? What I mean is, doesn't the gab of it seem to kind of bunch up and slide over the bar to you in a sort of amalgamated tip that hits off the burg in a kind of an epigram with a dash of bitters and a slice of—"

"Excuse me a minute," said Billy, "somebody's punching the button at the side door."

He went away; came back with an empty tin bucket; again vanished with it full; returned and said to me:

"That was Mame. She rings twice. She likes a glass of beer for supper. Her and the kid. If you ever saw that little skeesicks of mine brace up in his high chair and take his beer and— But, say, what was yours? I get kind of excited when I hear them two rings—was it the baseball score or gin fizz you asked for?"

"Ginger ale," I answered.

I walked up to Broadway. I saw a cop on the corner. The cops take kids up, women across, and men in. I went up to him.

"If I'm not exceeding the spiel limit," I said, "let me ask you. You see New York during its vocative hours. It is the function of you and your brother cops to preserve the acoustics of the city. There must be a civic voice that is intelligible to you. At night during your lonely rounds you must have heard it. What is the epitome of its turmoil and shouting? What does the city say to you?"

"Friend," said the policeman, spinning his club, "it don't say nothing. I get my orders from the man higher up. Say, I guess you're all right. Stand here for a few minutes and keep an eye open for the roundsman."

The cop melted into the darkness of the side street. In ten minutes he had returned.

"Married last Tuesday," he said, half gruffly. "You know how they are. She comes to that corner at nine every night for a—comes to say 'hello!' I generally manage to be there. Say, what was it you asked me a bit ago—what's doing in the city? Oh, there's a roof-garden or two just opened, twelve blocks up."

I crossed a crow's-foot of street-car tracks, and skirted the edge of an umbrageous park. An artificial Diana, gilded, heroic, poised, wind-ruled, on the tower, shimmered in the clear light of her namesake in the sky. Along came my poet, hurrying, hatted, haired, emitting dactyls, spondees and dactylis. I seized him.

"Bill," said I (in the magazine he is Cleon), "give me a lift. I am on an assignment to find out the Voice of the City. You see, it's a special order. Ordinarily a symposium comprising the views of Henry Clews, John L. Sullivan, Edwin Markham, May Irwin and Charles Schwab would be about all. But this is a different matter. We want a broad, poetic, mystic vocalization of the city's soul and meaning. You are the very chap to give me a hint. Some years ago a man got at the Niagara Falls and gave us its pitch. The note was about two feet below the lowest G on the piano. Now, you can't put New York into a note unless it's better indorsed than that. But give me an idea of what it would say if it should speak. It is bound to be a mighty and far-reaching utterance. To arrive at it we must take the tremendous crash of the chords of the day's traffic, the laughter and music of the night, the solemn tones of Dr. Parkhurst, the rag-time, the weeping, the stealthy hum of cab-wheels, the shout of the press agent, the tinkle of fountains on the roof-gardens, the hullabaloo of the strawberry vender and the covers of *Everybody's Magazine*, the whispers of the lovers in the parks—all these sounds must go into your Voice—not combined, but mixed, and of the mixture an essence made; and of the essence an extract—an audible extract, of which one drop shall form the thing we seek."

"Do you remember," asked the poet, with a chuckle, "that California girl we met at Stiver's studio last week? Well, I'm on my way to see her. She repeated that poem of mine, 'The Tribute of Spring,' word for word. She's the smartest proposition in this town just at present. Say, how does this confounded tie look? I spoiled four before I got one to set right."

"And the Voice that I asked you about?" I inquired.

"Oh, she doesn't sing," said Cleon. "But you ought to hear her recite my 'Angel of the Inshore Wind.'"

I passed on. I cornered a newsboy and he flashed at me prophetic pink papers that outstripped the news by two revolutions of the clock's longest hand.

"Son," I said, while I pretended to chase coins in my penny pocket, "doesn't it sometimes seem to you as if the city ought to be able to talk? All these ups and downs and funny business and queer things happening every day—what would it say, do you think, if it could speak?"

"Quit yer kiddin'," said the boy. "Wot paper yer want? I got no time to waste. It Mag's birthday, and I want thirty cents to git her a present."

Here was no interpreter of the city's mouth-piece. I bought a paper, and consigned its undeclared treaties, its premeditated murders and unfought battles to an ash can.

Again I repaired to the park and sat in the moon shade. I thought and thought, and wondered why none could tell me what I asked for.

And then, as swift as light from a fixed star, the answer came to me. I arose and hurried—hurried as so many reasoners must, back around my circle. I knew the answer and I hugged it in my breast as I flew, fearing lest someone would stop me and demand my secret.

Aurelia was still on the stoop. The moon was higher and the ivy shadows were deeper. I sat at her side and we watched a little cloud tilt at the drifting moon and go asunder quite pale and discomfited.

And then, wonder of wonders and delight of delights! our hands somehow touched, and our fingers closed together and did not part.

After half an hour Aurelia said, with that smile of hers:

"Do you know, you haven't spoken a word since you came back!"

"That," said I, nodding wisely, "is the Voice of the City."

HENRY JAMES

New York Revisited

1907

The single impression or particular vision most answering to the greatness of the subject would have been, I think, a certain hour of large circumnavigation that I found prescribed, in the fulness of the spring, as the almost immediate crown of a return from the Far West. I had arrived at one of the transpontine stations of the Pennsylvania Railroad; the question was of proceeding to Boston, for the occasion, without pushing through the terrible town—why "terrible," to my sense, in many ways, I shall presently explain—and the easy and agreeable attainment of this great advantage was to embark on one of the mightiest (as appeared to me) of train-bearing barges and, descending the western waters, pass round the bottom of the city and remount the other current to Harlem; all without "losing touch" of the Pullman that had brought me from Washington. This absence of the need of losing touch, this breadth of effect, as to the whole process, involved in the prompt floating of the huge concatenated cars not only without arrest or confusion, but as for positive prodigal beguilement of the artless traveller, had doubtless much to say to the ensuing state of mind, the happily-excited and amused view of the great face of New York. The extent, the ease, the energy, the quantity and number, all notes scattered about as if, in the whole business and in the splendid light, nature and science were joyously romping together, might have been taking on again, for their symbol, some collective presence of great circling and plunging, hovering and perching sea-birds, white-winged images of the spirit, of the restless freedom of the Bay. The Bay had always, on other opportunities, seemed to blow its immense character straight into one's face—coming "at" you, so to speak, bearing down on you, with the full force of a thousand prows of steamers seen exactly on the line of their longitudinal axis; but I had never before been so conscious of its boundless cool assurance or seemed to see its genius so grandly at play. This was presumably indeed because I had never before enjoyed the remarkable adventure of taking in so much of the vast bristling promontory from the water, of ascending the East River, in especial, to its upper diminishing expanses.

Something of the air of the occasion and of the mood of the moment caused the whole picture to speak with its largest suggestion; which suggestion is irresistible when once it is sounded clear. It is all, absolutely, an expression of things lately and currently *done*, done on a large impersonal stage and on the basis of inordinate gain—it is not an expression of any other matters whatever; and yet the sense of the scene (which had at several previous junctures, as well, put forth to my imagination its power) was commanding and thrilling, was in certain lights almost charming. . . . There is the beauty of light and air, the great scale of space, and, seen far away to the west, the open gates of the Hudson, majestic in their degree, even at a distance, and announcing still nobler things. But the real appeal, unmistakably, is in that note of vehemence in the local life of which I have spoken, for it is the appeal of a particular type of dauntless power.

The aspect the power wears then is indescribable; it is the power of the most extravagant of cities, rejoicing, as with the voice of the morning, in its might, its fortune, its unsurpassable conditions, and imparting to every object and element, to the motion and expression of every floating, hurrying, panting thing, to the throb of ferries and tugs, to the plash of waves and the play of winds and the glint of lights and the shrill of whistles and the quality and authority of breeze-borne cries—all, practically, a diffused, wasted clamour of *detonations*—something of its sharp free accent and, above all, of its sovereign sense of being "backed" and able to back. The universal *applied* passion struck me as shining unprecedentedly out of the composition; in the bigness and bravery and insolence, especially, of everything that rushed and shrieked; in the air as of a great intricate frenzied dance, half merry, half desperate, or at least half defiant, performed on the huge watery floor. This appearance of the bold lacing-together, across the waters, of the scattered members of the monstrous organism—lacing as by the ceaseless play of an enormous system of steam-shuttles or electric bobbins (I scarce know what to call them), commensurate in form with their infinite work—does perhaps more than anything else to give the pitch of the vision of energy. One has the sense that the monster grows and grows, flinging abroad its loose limbs even as some unmannered young giant at his "larks," and that the binding stitches must for ever fly further and faster and draw harder; the future complexity of the web, all under the sky and over the sea, becoming thus that of some colossal set of clockworks, some steel-souled machine-room of brandished arms and hammering fists and opening and closing jaws. The immeasurable bridges are but as the horizontal sheaths of pistons working at high pressure, day and night, and subject, one apprehends with perhaps inconsistent gloom, to certain, to fantastic, to merciless multiplication. In the light of this apprehension indeed the breezy brightness of the Bay puts on the semblance of the vast white page that awaits beyond any other perhaps the black overscoring of science.

Let me hasten to add that its present whiteness is precisely its charming note, the frankest of the signs you recognize and remember it by. That is the distinction I was just feeling my way to name as the main ground of its doing so well, for effect, without technical scenery. There are great imposing ports—Glasgow and Liverpool and London—that have already their page blackened almost beyond redemption from any such light of the picturesque as can hope to irradiate fog and grime, and there are others, Marseilles and Constantinople say, or, for all I know to the contrary, New Orleans, that contrive to abound before everything else in colour, and so to make a rich and instant and obvious show. But memory and the actual impression keep investing New York with the tone, predominantly, of summer dawns and winter frosts, of sea-foam, of bleached sails and stretched awnings, of blanched hulls, of scoured decks, of new ropes, of polished brasses, of streamers clear in the blue air; and it is by this harmony, doubtless, that the projection of the individual character of the place, of the candour of its avidity and the freshness of its audacity, is most conveyed. The "tall buildings," which have so promptly usurped a glory that affects you as rather surprised, as yet, at itself, the multitudinous sky-scrapers standing up to the view, from the water, like extravagant pins in a cushion already overplanted, and stuck in as in the dark, anywhere and anyhow, have at least the felicity of carrying out the fairness of tone, of taking the sun and the shade in the manner of towers of marble. . . . Crowned not only with no history, but with no credible possibility of time for history, and consecrated by no uses save the commercial at any cost, they are simply the most piercing notes in that concert of the expensively provisional into which your supreme sense of New York resolves itself. They never begin to speak to you, in the manner of the builded majesties of the world as we have heretofore known such—towers or temples or fortresses or palaces—with the authority of things of permanence or even of things of long duration. One story is good only till another is told, and sky-scrapers are the last word of economic ingenuity only till another word be written. This shall be possibly a word of still uglier meaning, but the vocabulary of thrift at any price shows boundless resources, and the consciousness of that truth, the consciousness of the finite, the menaced, the essentially *invented* state, twinkles ever, to my perception, in the thousand glassy eyes of these giants of the mere market. . . .

If it had been the final function of the Bay to make one feel one's age, so, assuredly, the mouth of Wall Street proclaimed it, for one's private ear, distinctly enough; the breath of existence being taken, wherever one turned, as that of youth on the run and with the prize of the race in sight, and the new landmarks crushing the old quite as violent children stamp on snails and caterpillars.

The hour I first recall was a morning of winter drizzle and mist, of dense fog in the Bay, one of the strangest sights of which I was on my way to enjoy; and I had stopped in the heart of the business quarter to pick up a friend who was to be my companion. The weather, such as it was, worked wonders for the upper reaches of the buildings, round which it drifted and hung very much as about the flanks and summits of emergent mountain-masses—for, to be just all round, there *was* some evidence of their having a message for the eyes. Let me parenthesize, once for all, that there are other glimpses of this message, up and down the city, frequently to be caught; lights and shades of winter and summer air, of the literally "finishing" afternoon in particular, when refinement of modelling descends from the skies and lends the white towers, all new and crude and commercial and over-windowed as they are, a fleeting distinction. . . .

In the Bay, the rest of the morning, the dense raw fog that delayed the big boat, allowing sight but of the immediate ice-masses through which it thumped its way, was not less of the essence. Anything blander, as a medium, would have seemed a mockery of the facts of the terrible little Ellis Island, the first harbor of refuge and stage of patience for the million or so of immigrants annually knocking at our official door. Before this door, which opens to them there only with a hundred forms and ceremonies, grindings and grumblings of the key, they stand appealing and waiting, marshalled, herded, divided, subdivided, sorted, sifted, searched, fumigated, for longer or shorter periods—the effect of all which prodigious process, an intendedly "scientific" feeding of the mill, is again to give the earnest observer a thousand more things to think of than he can pretend to retail. The impression of Ellis Island, in fine, would be—as I was to find throughout that so many of my impressions would be—a chapter by itself; and with a particular page for recognition of the degree in which the liberal hospitality of the eminent Commissioner of this wonderful service, to whom I had been introduced, helped to make the interest of the whole watched drama poignant and unforgettable. It is a drama that goes on, without a pause, day by day and year by year, this visible act of ingurgitation on the part of our body politic and social, and constituting really an appeal to amazement beyond that of any sword-swallowing or fire-swallowing of the circus. The wonder that one couldn't keep down was the thought that these two or three hours of one's own chance vision of the business were but as a tick or two of the mighty clock, the clock that never, never stops—least of all when it strikes, for a sign of so much winding-up, some louder hour of our national fate than usual. I think indeed that the simplest account of the action of Ellis Island on the spirit of any sensitive citizen who may have happened to "look in" is that he comes back from his visit not at all the same person that he went. He has eaten of the tree of knowledge, and the taste will be forever in his mouth. He had thought he knew before, thought he had the sense of the degree in which it is his American fate to share the sanctity of his American consciousness, the intimacy of his American patriotism, with the inconceivable alien; but the truth had never come home to him with any such force. In the lurid light projected upon it by those courts of dismay it shakes him—or I like at least to imagine it shakes him—to the depths of his being; I like to think of him, I positively *have* to think of him, as going about ever afterwards with a new look, for those who can see it, in his face, the outward sign of the new chill in his heart. So is stamped, for detection, the questionably privileged person who has had an apparition, seen a ghost in his supposedly safe old house. Let not the unwary, therefore, visit Ellis Island. . . .

There was no escape from the ubiquitous alien into the future, or even into the present; there was an escape but into the past. I count as quite a triumph in this interest an unbroken case of frequentation of that ancient end of Fifth Avenue to the whole neighborhood of which one's earlier vibrations, a very far-away matter now, were attuned. The precious stretch of space between Washington Square and Fourteenth Street had a value, had even a charm, for the revisiting spirit—a mild and melancholy glamour which I am conscious of the difficulty of "rendering" for new and heedless generations. Here again the assault of suggestion is too great; too large, I mean, the number of hares started, before the pursuing imagination, the quickened memory, by this fact of the felt moral and social value of this comparatively unimpaired morsel of the Fifth Avenue heritage. Its reference to a pleasanter, easier, hazier past is absolutely comparative, just as the past in question itself enjoys as such the merest courtesy-title. It is all recent history enough, by the measure of the whole, and there are flaws and defacements enough, surely, even in its appearance of decency of duration. The tall building, grossly tall and grossly ugly, has failed of an admirable chance of distinguished consideration for it, and the dignity of many of its peaceful fronts has succumbed to the presence of those industries whose foremost need is to make "a good thing" of them. The good thing is doubtless being made, and yet this lower end of the once agreeable street still just escapes being a wholly bad thing. What held the fancy in thrall, however, as I say, was the admonition, proceeding from all the facts, that values of this romantic order are at best, anywhere, strangely relative. It was an extraordinary statement on the subject of New York that the space between Fourteenth Street and Washington Square *should* count for "tone," figure as the old ivory of an overscored tablet. . . .

There are new cities enough about the world, goodness knows, and there are new parts enough of old cities—for examples of which we need go no farther than London, Paris and Rome, all of late so mercilessly renovated. But the newness of New York—unlike even that of Boston, I seemed to discern—had this mark of its very own, that it affects one, in every case, as having treated itself as still more provisional, if possible, than any poor dear little interest of antiquity it may have annihilated. The very sign of its energy is that it doesn't believe in itself; it fails to succeed, even at a cost of millions, in persuading you that it does. Its mission would appear to be, exactly, to gild the temporary, with its gold, as many inches thick as may be, and then, with a fresh shrug, a shrug of its splendid cynicism for its freshly detected inability to convince, give up its actual work, however exorbitant, as the merest stop-gaps. The difficulty with the compromised charmer is just this constant inability to convince; to convince ever, I mean, that she is serious, serious about any form whatever, or about anything but that perpetual passionate pecuniary purpose which plays with all forms, which derides and devours them, though it may pile up the cost of them in order to rest awhile, spent and haggard, in the illusion of their finality. . . .

G. K. CHESTERTON
A Meditation in Broadway

1921

When I had looked at the lights of Broadway by night, I made to my American friends an innocent remark that seemed for some reason to amuse them. I had looked, not without joy, at that long kaleidoscope of coloured lights arranged in large letters and sprawling trade-marks, advertising everything, from pork to pianos, through the agency of the two most vivid and most mystical of the gifts of God; colour and fire. I said to them, in my simplicity, 'What a glorious garden of wonders this would be, to any one who was lucky enough to be unable to read.'

Here it is but a text for a further suggestion. But let us suppose that there does walk down this flaming avenue a peasant, of the sort called scornfully an illiterate peasant; by those who think that insisting on people reading and writing is the best way to keep out the spies who read in all languages and the forgers who write in all hands. On this principle indeed, a peasant merely acquainted with things of little practical use to mankind, such as ploughing, cutting wood, or growing vegetables, would very probably be excluded; and it is not for us to criticise from the outside the philosophy of those who would keep out the farmer and let in the forger. But let us suppose, if only for the sake of argument, that the peasant is walking under the artificial suns and stars of this tremendous thoroughfare; that he has escaped to the land of liberty upon some general rumour and romance of the story of its liberation, but without being yet able to understand the arbitrary signs of its alphabet. The soul of such a man would surely soar higher than the sky-scrapers, and embrace a brotherhood broader than Broadway. Realising that he had arrived on an evening of exceptional festivity, worthy to be blazoned with all this burning heraldry, he would please himself by guessing what great proclamation or principle of the Republic hung in the sky like a constellation or rippled across the street like a comet. He would be shrewd enough to guess that the three festoons fringed with fiery words of somewhat similar pattern stood for 'Government of the People, For the People, By the People'; for it must obviously be that, unless it were 'Liberty, Equality, Fraternity.' His shrewdness would perhaps be a little shaken if he knew that the triad stood for 'Tang Tonic To-day; Tang Tonic To-morrow; Tang Tonic All the Time.' He will soon identify a restless ribbon of red lettering, red hot and rebellious, as the saying, 'Give me liberty or give me death.' He will fail to identify it as the equally famous saying, 'Skyoline Has Gout Beaten to a Frazzle.' Therefore it was that I desired the peasant to walk down that grove of fiery trees, under all that golden foliage and fruits like monstrous jewels, as innocent as Adam before the Fall. He would see sights almost as fine as the flaming sword or the purple and peacock plumage of the seraphim; so long as he did not go near the Tree of Knowledge.

In other words, if once he went to school it would be all up; and indeed I fear in any case he would soon discover his error. If he stood wildly waving his hat for liberty in the middle of the road as Chunk Chutney picked itself out in ruby stars upon the sky, he would impede the excellent but extremely rigid traffic system of New York. If he fell on his knees before a sapphire splendour, and began saying an Ave Maria under a mistaken association, he would be conducted, kindly but firmly by an Irish policeman to a more authentic shrine. But though the foreign simplicity might not long survive in New York, it is quite a mistake to suppose that such foreign simplicity cannot enter New York. He may be excluded for being illiterate, but he cannot be excluded for being ignorant, nor for being innocent. Least of all can he be excluded for being wiser in his innocence than the world in its knowledge. There is here indeed more than one distinction to be made. New York is a cosmopolitan city; but it is not a city of cosmopolitans. Most of the masses in New York have a nation, whether or no it be the nation to which New York belongs. Those who are Americanised are American, and very patriotically American. Those who are not thus nationalised are not in the least internationalised. They simply continue to be themselves; the Irish are Irish; the Jews are Jewish; and all sorts of other tribes carry on the traditions of remote European valleys almost untouched. In short, there is a sort of slender bridge between their old country and their new, which they either cross or do not cross, but which they seldom simply occupy. They are exiles or they are citizens; there is no moment when they are cosmopolitans. But very often the exiles bring with them not only rooted traditions, but rooted truths. Indeed it is to a great extent the thought of these strange souls in crude American garb that gives a meaning to the masquerade of New York.

THEODORE DREISER
The Color of a Great City

THE CITY OF MY DREAMS

1903–1923

It was silent, the city of my dreams, marble and serene, due perhaps to the fact that in reality I knew nothing of crowds, poverty, the winds and storms of the inadequate that blow like dust along the paths of life. It was an amazing city, so far-flung, so beautiful, so dead. There were tracks of iron stalking through the air, and streets that were as cañons, and stairways that mounted in vast flights to noble plazas, and steps that led down into deep places where were, strangely enough, underworld silences. And there were parks and flowers and rivers. And then, after twenty years, here it stood, as amazing almost as my dream, save that in the waking the flush of life was over it. It possessed the tang of contests and dreams and enthusiasms and delights and terrors and despairs. Through its ways and cañons and open spaces and underground passages were running, seething, sparkling, darkling, a mass of beings such as my dream-city never knew.

The thing that interested me then as now about New York . . . was the sharp, and at the same time immense, contrast it showed between the dull and the shrewd, the strong and the weak, the rich and the poor, the wise and the ignorant. This, perhaps, was more by reason of numbers and opportunity than anything else, for of course humanity is much the same everywhere. But the number from which to choose was so great here that the strong, or those who ultimately dominated, were so very strong, and the weak so very, very weak—and so very, very many.

I once knew a poor, half-demented, and very much shriveled little seamstress who occupied a tiny hall-bedroom in a side-street rooming-house, cooked her meals on a small alcohol stove set on a bureau, and who had about space enough outside of this to take three good steps either way.

"I would rather live in my hall-bedroom in New York than in any fifteen-room house in the country that I ever saw," she commented once, and her poor little colorless eyes held more of sparkle and snap in them than I ever saw there, before or after. She was wont to add to her sewing income by reading fortunes in cards and tea-leaves and coffee-grounds, telling of love and prosperity to scores as lowly as herself, who would never see either. The color and noise and splendor of the city as a spectacle was sufficient to pay her for all her ills.

And have I not felt the glamour of it myself? And do I not still? Broadway, at Forty-second Street, on those selfsame spring evenings when the city is crowded with an idle, sightseeing cloud of Westerners; when the doors of all shops are open, the windows of nearly all restaurants wide to the gaze of the idlest passer-by. Here is the great city, and it is lush and dreamy. A May or June moon will be hanging like a burnished silver disc between the high walls aloft. A hundred, a thousand electric signs will blink and wink. And the floods of citizens and visitors in summer clothes and with gay hats; the street cars jouncing their endless carloads on indifferent errands; the taxis and private cars fluttering about like jeweled flies. The very gasoline contributes a distinct perfume. Life bubbles, sparkles; chatters gay, incoherent stuff. . . .

I often think of the vast mass of underlings, boys and girls, who, with nothing but their youth and their ambitions to commend them, are daily and hourly setting their faces New Yorkward, reconnoitering the city for what it may hold in the shape of wealth or fame, or, if not that, position and comfort in the future; and what, if anything, they will reap. Ah, their young eyes drinking in its promise! And then, again, I think of all the powerful or semi-powerful men and women throughout the world, toiling at one task or another—a store, a mine, a bank, a profession—somewhere outside of New York, whose one ambition is to reach the place where their wealth will permit them to enter and remain in New York, dominant above the mass, luxuriating in what they consider luxury.

The illusion of it, the hypnosis deep and moving that it is! How the strong and the weak, the wise and the fools, the greedy of heart and of eye, seek the nepenthe, the Lethe, of its something hugeness. I always marvel at those who are willing, seemingly, to pay any price —*the* price, whatever it may be—for one sip of this poison cup. What a stinging, quivering zest they display. How beauty is willing to sell its bloom, virtue its last rag, strength an almost usurious portion of that which it controls, youth its very best years, its hope or dream of fame, fame and power their dignity and presence, age its weary hours, to secure but a minor part of all this, a taste of its vibrating presence and the picture that it makes. Can you not hear them almost, singing its praises?

THE CITY AWAKES

Have you ever arisen at dawn or earlier in New York and watched the outpouring in the meaner side-streets or avenues? It is a wondrous thing. It seems to have so little to do with the later, showier, brisker life of the day, and yet it has so very much. It is in the main so drab or shabby-smart at best, poor copies of what you see done more efficiently later in the day. Typewriter girls in almost stage or society costumes entering shabby offices; boys and men made up to look like actors and millionaires turning into the humblest institutions, where they are clerks or managers. These might be called the machinery of the city, after the elevators and street cars and wagons are excluded, the implements by which things are made to go.

Take your place on Williamsburg Bridge some morning, for instance, at say three or four o'clock, and watch the long, the quite unbroken line of Jews trundling pushcarts eastward to the great Wallabout Market over the bridge. A procession out of Assyria or Egypt or Chaldea, you might suppose, Biblical in quality; or, better yet, a huge chorus in some operatic dawn scene laid in Paris or Petrograd or here. A vast, silent mass it is, marching to the music of necessity. They are so grimy, so mechanistic, so elemental in their movements and needs. And later on you will find them seated or standing, with their little charcoal buckets or braziers to warm their hands and feet, in those gusty, icy streets of the East Side in winter, or coatless and almost shirtless in hot weather, open-mouthed for want of air. And they are New York, too—Bucharest and Lemberg and Odessa come to the Bowery, and adding rich, dark, colorful threads to the rug or tapestry which is New York.

Since these are but a portion, think of those other masses that come from the surrounding territory, north, south, east and west. The ferries—have you ever observed them in the morning? Or the bridges, railway terminals, and every elevated and subway exit?

Already at six and six-thirty in the morning they have begun to trickle small streams of human beings Manhattan or cityward, and by seven and seven-fifteen these streams have become sizable affairs. By seven-thirty and eight they have changed into heavy, turbulent rivers, and by eight-fifteen and eight-thirty and nine they are raging torrents, no less. They overflow all the streets and avenues and every available means of conveyance. They are pouring into all available doorways, shops, factories, office-buildings—those huge affairs towering so significantly above them. Here they stay all day long, causing those great hives and their adjacent streets to flush with a softness of color not indigenous to them, and then at night, between five and six, they are going again, pouring forth over the bridges and through the subways and across the ferries and out on the trains, until the last drop of them appears to have been exuded, and they are pocketed in some outlying side-street or village or metropolitan hall-room—and the great, turbulent night of the city is on once more.

And yet they continue to stream cityward—this cityward. From all parts of the world they are pouring into New York: Greeks from Athens and the realms of Sparta and Macedonia, living six, seven, eight, nine, ten, eleven, twelve, in one room, sleeping on the floors and dressing and eating and entertaining themselves God knows how; Jews from Russia, Poland, Hungary, the Balkans, crowding the East Side and the inlying sections of Brooklyn, and huddling together in thick, gummy streets, singing in street crowds around ballad-mongers of the woes of their native land, seeking with a kind of divine, poetic flare a modicum of that material comfort which their natures so greatly crave, which their previous condition for at least fifteen hundred years has scarcely warranted; Italians from Sicily and the warmer vales of the South, crowding into great sections of their own, all hungry for a taste of New York; Germans, Hungarians, French, Polish, Swedish, Armenians, all with sections of their own and all alive to the joys of the city, and how eager to live—great gold and scarlet streets throbbing with the thoughts of them!

And last but not least, the illusioned American from the Middle West and the South and the Northwest and the Far West, crowding in and eyeing it all so eagerly, so yearningly, like the others. Ah, the little, shabby, blue-light restaurants! The boarding houses in silent streets! The moral, hungry "homes"—how full they are of them and how hopeless! How the city sings and sings for them, and in spite of them, flaunting ever afresh its lures and beauties—a city as wonderful and fateful and ironic as life itself.

H. L. MENCKEN

There Are Parts for All in the "Totentanz"

1927

It is astonishing how little New York figures in current American literature. Think of the best dozen American novels of the last ten years. No matter which way your taste and prejudice carry you, you will find, I believe, that Manhattan Island is completely missing from at least ten of them, and that in the other two it is little more than a passing scene, unimportant to the main action. Perhaps the explanation is to be sought in the fact that very few authors of any capacity live in the town. It attracts all the young aspirants powerfully, and hundreds of them, lingering on, develop into very proficient hacks and quacks, and so eventually adorn the Authors' League, the Poetry Society, and the National Institute of Arts and Letters. But not many remain who have anything worth hearing to say. They may

Copyright, 1927, by Alfred A. Knopf, Inc.

keep quarters on the island, but they do their writing somewhere else.

Primarily, I suppose, it is too expensive for them: in order to live decently they must grind through so much hack work for the cheap magazines, the movies and the Broadway theaters that there is no time left for their serious concerns. But there is also something else. The town is too full of distractions to be comfortable to artists; it is comfortable only to performers. Its machinery of dissipation is so vastly developed that no man can escape it—not even an author laboring in his lonely room, the blinds down and chewing-gum plugging his ears. He hears the swish of skirts through the key-hole; down the areaway comes the clink of ice in tall glasses; some one sends him a pair of tickets to a show which whisper promises will be the dirtiest seen since the time of the Twelve Apostles. It is a sheer impossibility in New York to escape such appeals to the ductless glands. They are in the very air. The town is no longer a place of work; it is a place of pleasure. . . .

Such is the effect of organized badness, operating upon imperfect man. But what is bad is also commonly amusing, and so I continue to marvel that the authors of the Republic, and especially the novelists, do not more often reduce it to words. . . .

New York is not all bricks and steel. There are hearts there, too, and if they do not break, then they at least know how to leap. It is the place where all the aspirations of the Western World meet to form one vast master aspiration, as powerful as the suction of a steam dredge. It is the icing on the pie called Christian civilization. That it may have buildings higher than any ever heard of, and gin enough to keep it gay, and bawdy shows enough, and door-openers enough, and noise and confusion enough—that these imperial ends may be achieved, uncounted millions sweat and slave on all the forlorn farms of the earth, and in all the miserable slums, including its own. It pays more for a meal than an Italian or a Pole pays for a wife, and the meal is better than the wife. It gets the best of everything, and especially of what, by all reputable ethical systems, is the worst. It has passed beyond all fear of Hell or hope of Heaven. The primary postulates of all the rest of the world are its familiar jokes. A city apart, it is breeding a race apart. Is that race American? Then so is a bashi-bazouk American. Is it decent? Then so is a street-walker decent. But I don't think that it may be reasonably denounced as dull. . . .

If only as spectacle, the city is superb. It has a glitter like that of the Constantinople of the Comneni. It roars with life like the Bagdad of the Sassanians. These great capitals of antiquity, in fact, were squalid villages compared to it, as Rome was after their kind, and Paris, Berlin and London are to-day. There is little in New York that does not issue out of money. It is not a town of ideas; it is not even a town of causes. But what issues out of money is often extremely brilliant, and I believe that it is more brilliant in New York than it has ever been anywhere else. A truly overwhelming opulence envelops the whole place, even the slums. The slaves who keep it going may dwell in vile cubicles, but they are hauled to and from their work by machinery that costs hundreds of millions, and when they fare forth to recreate themselves for to-morrow's tasks they are felled and made dumb by a gaudiness that would have floored John Paleologus himself. Has any one ever figured out, in hard cash, the value of the objects of art stored upon Manhattan Island? I narrow it to paintings, and bar out all the good ones. What would it cost to replace even the bad ones? Or all the statuary, bronzes, hangings, pottery, and bogus antiques? Or the tons of bangles, chains of pearls, stomachers, necklaces, and other baubles? Assemble all the diamonds into one colossal stone, and you will have a weapon to slay Behemoth. . . .

What I contend is that this spectacle, lush and barbaric in its every detail, offers the material for a great imaginative literature. There is not only gaudiness in it; there is also a hint of strangeness; it has overtones of the fabulous and even of the diabolical. The thing simply cannot last. If it does not end by catastrophe, then it will end by becoming stale, which is to say, dull. But while it is in full blast it certainly holds out every sort of stimulation that the gifted literatus may plausibly demand. The shocking imbecility of Main Street is there and the macabre touch of Spoon River. But though Main Street and Spoon River have both found their poets, Manhattan is still to be adequately sung. How will the historian of the future get at it, imagining a future and assuming that it will have historians? The story is not written anywhere in official records. It is not in the files of the newspapers, which reflect only the surface, and not even all of that. It will not go into memoirs, for the actors in the melodramatic comedy have no taste for prose, and moreover they are all afraid to tell what they know. What it needs, obviously, is an imaginative artist. We have them in this bursting, stall-fed land—not many of them, perhaps—not as many as our supply of quacks—but nevertheless we have them. The trouble is that they either hate Manhattan too much to do its portrait, or are so bedazzled by it that their hands are palsied and their parts of speech demoralized. Thus we have dithyrambs of Manhattan—but no prose.

I hymn the town without loving it. It is immensely amusing, but I see nothing in it to inspire the fragile and shy thing called affection. I can imagine an Iowan loving the black, fecund stretches of his native State, or a New Englander loving the wreck of Boston, or even a Chicagoan loving Chicago, poets, Loop, stockyards and all, but it is hard for me to fancy any rational human being loving New York. Does one love bartenders? Or interior decorators? Or elevator starters? Or the head-waiters of night clubs? No, one delights in such functionaries, and perhaps one respects them and even reveres them, but one does not love them. They are as palpably cold and artificial as the Cathedral of St. John the Divine. Like it, they are mere functions of solvency. When the sheriff comes in they flutter away. One invests affection in places where it will be safe when the winds blow.

But I am speaking now of spectacles, not of love affairs. The spectacle of New York remains—infinitely grand and gorgeous, stimulating like the best that comes out of goblets, and none the worse for its sinister smack. The town seizes upon all the more facile and agreeable emotions like band music. It is immensely trashy—but it remains immense. Is it a mere Utopia of rogues, a vast and complicated machine for rooking honest men? I don't think so. The honest man, going to its market, gets sound value for his money. It offers him luxury of a kind never dreamed of in the world before—the luxury of being served by perfect and unobtrusive slaves, human and mechanical. It permits him to wallow regally—nay, almost celestially. The Heaven of the Moslems is open to any one who can pay the *couvert* charge and honorarium of the hat-check girl—and there is a door, too, leading into the Heaven of the Christians, or, at all events, into every part of it save that devoted to praise and prayer. Nor is all this luxury purely physiological. There is entertainment also for the spirit, or for what passes for the spirit when men are happy. There were more orchestral concerts in New York last Winter than there were in Berlin. The town has more theaters, and far better ones, than a dozen Londons. It is, as I have said, loaded with art to the gunwales, and steadily piling more on deck. Is it unfecund of ideas? Perhaps. But surely it is not hostile to them. There is far more to the show it offers than watching a pretty gal oscillate her hips; one may also hear some other gal, only a shade less sightly, babble the latest discoveries in antinomianism. All kinds, in briefs, come in. There are parts for all in the *Totentanz*, even for moralists to call the figures. But there is, as yet, no recorder to put it on paper.

ALEXANDER WOOLLCOTT
No Yesterdays

1928

Since God lifted this continent above the waters and so clad its plains and valleys that it could be a homestead for a numberless multitude, it must fill Him at times with mingled surprise, amusement and exasperation to note how many of us are perversely scrouged together in a monstrous determination to live crowded on Manhattan Island and there only—there or not at all.

It is to be sure an enchanted isle. When one of us makes a home on it, that home is just around the corner from the Metropolitan when they are singing "Coq d'Or." We can see a harlequinade when the *coryphées* are still young and we can go to "What Price Glory?" before its lusty laughter is forbidden because America has gone to war again. In all the land there is no ball like the Beaux Arts ball and in no other town can one run down to Mr. Morgan's library and look at the manuscript of "The Christmas Carol" whenever one happens to feel like it.

But notes are missing from Manhattan's symphony. We whose homes are on it can go from spring to spring without once hearing the neighborly, communal music of a lawnmower. We never have a chance to stand at sundown, hose in hand, and water the brave beds of nasturtiums and phlox and blue delphinium which we ourselves have planted. We don't even know the names of the nice-looking people next door and it does not matter much, because before long the moving vans will back up callously for their furniture—or ours. For above all we have no yesterdays, no reminders from one day's dawn to the next that ever folk have walked before in the streets where now we walk. Here we are today, indeed. But in our cramped and hurried habitations there is no murmur of a year gone by to suggest a little hopefully that here we may also be tomorrow.

In the fly-by-night flats where we hang our hats and try to sleep, there is no space for the chance memorabilia of a family. Among the other dwellers in this city whom I happen to know, I can think now of only two families or three who are living this spring where they lived four springs ago. And none of us mounts a dubious ladder to hang a picture in October without a gray foreboding that it will have to come down again in May. For, as like as not, we shall be on the move again in May, perhaps because the rent has leaped beyond our reach, perhaps because the house itself is to make meek room for a new steel thrust at the amused stars.

So we become tentative in our living and take to thinking of the little odds and ends of possession as so much afflicting impedimenta. We grow expert in the reduction of all our portable property to the severe dimensions of a suitcase and the very copies of *Punch* and the *American Mercury* that might be fun to look over again some day go hastily out the backdoor not many days after they come in the front. For this is true of our Manhattan—it is a town without any attics. Wherefore it has no more orientation in time than an airedale has. And the man who dwells within its gates is like the luckless fellow who must improvise the concerto of his life on a violin of which the strings are fastened only at one end.

HELEN KELLER

I Go Adventuring

1929

Cut off as I am, it is inevitable that I should sometimes feel like a shadow walking in a shadowy world. When this happens I ask to be taken to New York City. Always I return home weary but I have the comforting certainty that mankind is real flesh and I myself am not a dream.

In order to get to New York from my home it is necessary to cross one of the great bridges that separate Manhattan from Long Island. The oldest and most interesting of them is the Brooklyn Bridge, built by my friend, Colonel Roebling, but the one I cross oftenest is the Queensborough Bridge at 59th Street. How often I have had Manhattan described to me from these bridges! They tell me the view is loveliest in the morning and at sunset when one sees the skyscrapers rising like fairy palaces, their million windows gleaming in the rosy-tinted atmosphere.

I like to feel that all poetry is not between the covers of poetry books, that much of it is written in great enterprises of engineering and flying, that into mighty utility man has poured and is pouring his dreams, his emotions, his philosophy. This materializing of his genius is sometimes inchoate and monstrous, but even then sublime in its extravagance and courage. Who can deny that the Queensborough Bridge is the work of a creative artist? It never fails to give me a poignant desire to capture the noble cadence of its music. To my friends I say:

> *Behold its liberal loveliness of length—*
> *A flowing span from shore to shore,*
> *A brimming reach of beauty matched with strength,*
> *It shines and climbs like some miraculous dream,*
> *Like some vision multitudinous and agleam,*
> *A passion of desire held captive in the clasp of vast utility.*

New York has a special interest for me when it is wrapped in fog. Then it behaves very much like a blind person. I once crossed from Jersey City to Manhattan in a dense fog. The ferry-boat felt its way cautiously through the river traffic. More timid than a blind man, its horn brayed incessantly. Fog-bound, surrounded by menacing, unseen craft and dangers, it halted every now and then as a blind man halts at a crowded thoroughfare crossing, tapping his cane, tense and anxious. . . .

I usually know what part of the city I am in by the odours. There are as many smells as there are philosophies. I have never had time to gather and classify my olfactory impressions of different cities, but it would be an interesting subject. I find it quite natural to think of places by their characteristic smells.

Fifth Avenue, for example, has a different odour from any other part of New York or elsewhere. Indeed, it is a very odorous street. It may sound like a joke to say that it has an aristocratic smell; but it has, nevertheless. As I walk along its even pavements, I recognize expensive perfumes, powders, creams, choice flowers, and pleasant exhalations from the houses. In the residential section I smell delicate food, silken draperies, and rich tapestries. Sometimes, when a door opens as I pass, I know what kind of cosmetics the occupants of the house use. I know if there is an open fire, if they burn wood or soft coal, if they roast their coffee, if they use candles, if the house has been shut up for a long time, if it has been painted or newly decorated, and if the cleaners are at work in it. . . .

I know when I pass a church and whether it is Protestant or Catholic. I know when I am in the Italian quarter of a city by the smells of salami, garlic, and spaghetti. . . .

One of my never-to-be-forgotten experiences was circumnavigating New York in a boat. The trip took all day. I had with me four people who could use the hand alphabet—my teacher, my sister, my niece, and Mr. Holmes. One who has not seen New York in this way would be amazed at the number of people who live on the water. Someone has called them "harbour gypsies." Their homes are on boats —whole fleets of them, decorated with flower boxes and bright-coloured awnings. It is amusing to note how many of these stumbling, awkward harbour gypsies have pretty feminine names—*Bella, Floradora, Rosalind, Pearl of the Deep, Minnehaha, Sister Nell*. The occupants can be seen going about their household tasks—cooking, washing, sewing, gossiping from one barge to another, and there is a flood of smells which gives eyes to the mind. The children and dogs play on the tiny deck, and chase each other into the water, where they are perfectly at home. These water-babies are familiar with all manner of craft, they know what countries they come from, and what cargoes they carry. There are brick barges from Holland and fruitboats coming in from Havana, and craft loaded with meat, cobblestones, and sand push their way up bays and canals. There are old ships which have been stripped of their majesty and doomed to follow tow ropes up and down the harbour. These ships make me think of old blind people led up and down the city streets. There are aristocratic craft from Albany, Nyack, Newburg. There are also boats from New London and Boston, from the Potomac and Baltimore and Virginia, from Portland, Maine, bringing terra cotta to Manhattan. Here comes the fishing fleet from Gloucester hurrying past the barge houses, and crawling, coal-laden tramps. Tracking the turmoil in every direction are the saucy ferry boats, bellowing rudely to everyone to get out of the way.

It is a sail of vivid contrast—up the Hudson between green hills, past the stately mansions of Riverside Drive, through the narrow straits that separate Manhattan from the mainland, into Harlem and the East River, past Welfare Island, where a great modern city shelters its human derelicts, on to the welter of downtown docks, where longshoremen heave the barge cargoes ashore, and the crash of traffic is deafening, and back to your pier in the moonlight when the harbour gypsies sleep and the sense of peace is balm to the tired nerves.

As I walk up Broadway, the people that brush past me seem always hastening toward a destination they never reach. Their motions are eager, as if they said, "We are on our way, we shall arrive in a moment." They keep up the pace—they almost run. Each on his quest intent, in endless procession they pass, tragic, grotesque, gay, they all sweep onward like rain falling upon leaves. I wonder where they are going. I puzzle my brain; but the mystery is never solved. Will they at last come somewhere? Will anybody be waiting for them? The march never ceases. Their feet have worn the pavements unevenly. I wish I knew where they are going. Some are nonchalant, some walk with their eyes on the ground, others step lightly, as if they might fly if their wings were not bound by the multitude. A pale little woman is guiding the steps of a blind man. His great hand drags on her arm. Awkwardly he shortens his stride to her gait. He trips when the curb is uneven; his grip tightens on the arm of the woman. Where are they going?

Like figures in a meaningless pageant, they pass. There are young girls laughing, loitering. They have beauty, youth, lovers. They look in the shop windows, they look at the huge winking signs; they jostle the crowds, their feet keep time to the music of their hearts. They must be going to a pleasant place. I think I should like to go where they are going.

Tremulously I stand in the subways, absorbed into the terrible reverberations of exploding energy. Fearful, I touch the forest of steel girders loud with the thunder of oncoming trains that shoot past me like projectiles. Inert I stand, riveted in my place. My limbs, paralyzed, refuse to obey the will insistent on haste to board the train while the lightning steed is leashed and its reeling speed checked for a moment. Before my mind flashes in clairvoyant vision what all this speed portends—the lightning crashing into life, the accidents, railroad wrecks, steam bursting free like geysers from bands of steel, thousands of racing motors and children caught at play, flying heroes diving into the sea, dying for speed—all this because of strange, unsatisfied ambitions. Another train bursts into the station like a volcano, the people crowd me on, on into the chasm—into the dark depths of awful forces and fates. In a few minutes, still trembling, I am spilled into the streets.

F. SCOTT FITZGERALD
My Lost City

July, 1932

There was first the ferry boat moving softly from the Jersey shore at dawn—the moment crystallized into my first symbol of New York. Five years later when I was fifteen I went into the city from school to see Ina Claire in *The Quaker Girl* and Gertrude Bryan in *Little Boy Blue*. Confused by my hopeless and melancholy love for them both, I was unable to choose between them—so they blurred into one lovely entity, the girl. She was my second symbol of New York. The ferry boat stood for triumph, the girl for romance. In time I was to achieve some of both, but there was a third symbol that I have lost somewhere, and lost forever.

I found it on a dark April afternoon after five more years.

"Oh, Bunny," I yelled. *"Bunny!"*

He did not hear me—my taxi lost him, picked him up again half a block down the street. There were black spots of rain on the sidewalk and I saw him walking briskly through the crowd wearing a tan raincoat over his inevitable brown get-up; I noted with a shock that he was carrying a light cane.

"Bunny!" I called again, and stopped. I was still an undergraduate at Princeton while he had become a New Yorker. This was his afternoon walk, this hurry along with his stick through the gathering rain, and as I was not to meet him for an hour it seemed an intrusion to happen upon him engrossed in his private life. But the taxi kept pace with him and as I continued to watch I was impressed: he was no longer the shy little scholar of Holder Court—he walked with confidence, wrapped in his thoughts and looking straight ahead, and it was obvious that his new background was entirely sufficient to him. I knew that he had an apartment where he lived with three other men, released now from all undergraduate taboos, but there was something else that was nourishing him and I got my first impression of that new thing—the Metropolitan spirit.

Up to this time I had seen only the New York that offered itself for inspection—I was Dick Whittington up from the country gaping at the trained bears, or a youth of the Midi dazzled by the boulevards of Paris. I had come only to stare at the show, though the designers of the Woolworth Building and the Chariot Race Sign, the producers of musical comedies and problem plays, could ask for no more appreciative spectator, for I took the style and glitter of New York even above its own valuation. But I had never accepted any of the practically anonymous invitations to debutante balls that turned up in an undergraduate's mail, perhaps because I felt that no actuality could live up to my conception of New York's splendor. Moreover, she to whom I fatuously referred as "my girl" was a Middle Westerner, a fact which kept the warm center of the world out there, so I thought of New York as essentially cynical and heartless—save for one night when she made luminous the Ritz Roof on a brief passage through.

Lately, however, I had definitely lost her and I wanted a man's world, and this sight of Bunny made me see New York as just that. A week before, Monsignor Fay had taken me to the Lafayette where there was spread before us a brilliant flag of food, called an *hors d'oeuvre*, and with it we drank claret that was as brave as Bunny's confident cane—but after all it was a restaurant and afterwards we would drive back over a bridge into the hinterland. The New York of undergraduate dissipation, of Bustanoby's, Shanley's, Jack's, had become a horror and though I returned to it, alas, through many an alcoholic mist, I felt each time a betrayal of a persistent idealism. My participance was prurient rather than licentious and scarcely one pleasant memory of it remains from those days; as Ernest Hemingway once remarked, the sole purpose of the cabaret is for unattached men to find complaisant women. All the rest is a wasting of time in bad air.

But that night, in Bunny's apartment, life was mellow and safe, a finer distillation of all that I had come to love at Princeton. The gentle playing of an oboe mingled with city noises from the street outside, which penetrated into the room with difficulty through great barricades of books; only the crisp tearing open of invitations by one man was a discordant note. I had found a third symbol of New York and I began wondering about the rent of such apartments and casting about for the appropriate friends to share one with me.

Fat chance—for the next two years I had as much control over my own destiny as a convict over the cut of his clothes. When I got back to New York in 1919 I was so entangled in life that a period of mellow monasticism in Washington Square was not to be dreamed of. The thing was to make enough money in the advertising business to rent a stuffy apartment for two in the Bronx. The girl concerned had never seen New York but she was wise enough to be rather reluctant. And in a haze of anxiety and unhappiness I passed the four most impressionable months of my life.

New York had all the iridescence of the beginning of the world. The returning troops marched up Fifth Avenue and girls were instinctively drawn East and North toward them—this was the greatest nation and there was gala in the air. As I hovered ghost-like in the Plaza Red Room of a Saturday afternoon, or went to lush and liquid garden parties in the East Sixties or tippled with Princetonians in the Biltmore Bar I was haunted always by my other life—my drab room in the Bronx, my square foot of the subway, my fixation upon the day's letter from Alabama—would it come and what would it say? —my shabby suits, my poverty, and love. While my friends were launching decently into life I had muscled my inadequate bark into midstream. The gilded youth circling around young Constance Bennett in the Club de Vingt, the classmates in the Yale-Princeton Club whooping up our first after-the-war reunion, the atmosphere of the millionaires' houses that I sometimes frequented—these things were empty for me, though I recognized them as impressive scenery and regretted that I was committed to other romance. The most hilarious luncheon table or the most moony cabaret—it was all the same; from them I returned eagerly to my home on Claremont Avenue—home because there might be a letter waiting outside the door. One by one my great dreams of New York became tainted. The remembered charm of Bunny's apartment faded with the rest when I interviewed a blowsy landlady in Greenwich Village. She told me I could bring girls to the room, and the idea filled me with dismay—why should I want to bring girls to my room?—I had a girl. I wandered through the town of 127th Street, resenting its vibrant life; or else I bought cheap theatre seats at Gray's drugstore and tried to lose myself for a few hours in my old passion for Broadway. I was a failure—mediocre at advertising work and unable to get started as a writer. Hating the city, I got roaring, weeping drunk on my last penny and went home. . . .

. . . Incalculable city. What ensued was only one of a thousand success stories of those gaudy days, but it plays a part in my own movie of New York. When I returned six months later the offices of editors and publishers were open to me, impresarios begged plays, the movies panted for screen material. To my bewilderment, I was adopted, not as a Middle Westerner, not even as a detached observer, but as the arch type of what New York wanted. This statement requires some account of the metropolis in 1920.

There was already the tall white city of today, already the feverish activity of the boom, but there was a general inarticulateness. As much as anyone the columnist F.P.A. guessed the pulse of the individual and the crowd, but shyly, as one watching from a window. Society and the native arts had not mingled—Ellen Mackay was not yet married to Irving Berlin. Many of Peter Arno's people would have been meaningless to the citizen of 1920, and save for F.P.A.'s column there was no forum for metropolitan urbanity.

Then, for just a moment, the "younger generation" idea became a fusion of many elements in New York life. People of fifty might pretend there was still a four hundred or Maxwell Bodenheim might pretend there was a Bohemia worth its paint and pencils—but the blending of the bright, gay, vigorous elements began then and for the first time there appeared a society a little livelier than the solid mahogany dinner parties of Emily Price Post. If this society produced the cocktail party, it also evolved Park Avenue wit and for the first time an educated European could envisage a trip to New York as something more amusing than a gold-trek into a formalized Australian Bush.

For just a moment, before it was demonstrated that I was unable to play the role, I, who knew less of New York than any reporter of six months' standing and less of its society than any hall-room boy in a Ritz stag line, was pushed into the position not only of spokesman for the time but of the typical product of that same moment. I, or rather it was "we" now, did not know exactly what New York expected of us and found it rather confusing. Within a few months after our embarkation on the Metropolitan venture we scarcely knew any more who we were and we hadn't a notion what we were. A dive into a civic fountain, a casual brush with the law, was enough to get us into the gossip columns, and we were quoted on a variety of subjects we knew nothing about. Actually our "contacts" included half a dozen unmarried college friends and a few new literary acquaintances—I remember a lonesome Christmas when we had not one friend in the city, nor one house we could go to. Finding no nucleus to which we could cling, we became a small nucleus ourselves and gradually we fitted our disruptive personalities into the contemporary scene of New York. Or rather New York forgot us and let us stay.

This is not an account of the city's changes but of the changes in this writer's feeling for the city. From the confusion of the year 1920 I remember riding on top of a taxicab along deserted Fifth Avenue on a hot Sunday night, and a luncheon in the cool Japanese gardens at the Ritz with the wistful Kay Laurel and George Jean Nathan, and writing all night again and again, and paying too much for minute apartments, and buying magnificent but broken-down cars. The first speakeasies had arrived, the toddle was *passé*, the Montmartre was the smart place to dance and Lillian Tashman's fair hair weaved around the floor among the enliquored college boys. The plays were *Declassée* and *Sacred and Profane Love*, and at the Midnight Frolic you danced elbow to elbow with Marion Davies and perhaps picked out the vivacious Mary Hay in the pony chorus. We thought we were apart from all that; perhaps everyone thinks they are apart from their milieu. We felt like small children in a great bright unexplored barn. Summoned out to Griffith's studio on Long Island, we trembled in the presence of the familiar faces of the *Birth of a Nation;* later I realized that behind much of the entertainment that the city poured forth into the nation there were only a lot of rather lost and lonely people. The world of the picture actors was like our own in that it was in New York and not of it. It had little sense of itself and no center: when I first met Dorothy Gish I had the feeling that we were both standing on the North Pole and it was snowing. Since then they have found a home but it was not destined to be New York.

When bored we took our city with a Huysmans-like perversity. An afternoon alone in our "apartment" eating olive sandwiches and drinking a quart of Bushmill's whiskey presented by Zoë Atkins, then out into the freshly bewitched city, through strange doors into strange apartments with intermittent swings along in taxis through the soft nights. At last we were one with New York, pulling it after us through every portal. Even now I go into many flats with the sense that I have been there before or in the one above or below—was it the night I tried to disrobe in the *Scandals*, or the night when (as I read with astonishment in the paper next morning) "Fitzgerald Knocks Officer This Side of Paradise"? Successful scrapping not being among my accomplishments, I tried in vain to reconstruct the sequence of events which led up to this dénouement in Webster Hall. And lastly from that period I remember riding in a taxi one afternoon between very tall buildings under a mauve and rosy sky; I began to bawl because I had everything I wanted and knew I would never be so happy again.

It was typical of our precarious position in New York that when our child was to be born we played safe and went home to St. Paul— it seemed inappropriate to bring a baby into all that glamor and loneliness. But in a year we were back and we began doing the same things over again and not liking them so much. We had run through a lot, though we had retained an almost theatrical innocence by preferring the role of the observed to that of the observer. But innocence is no end in itself and as our minds unwillingly matured we began to see New York whole and try to save some of it for the selves we would inevitably become.

It was too late—or too soon. For us the city was inevitably linked up with Bacchic diversions, mild or fantastic. We could organize ourselves only on our return to Long Island and not always there. We had no incentive to meet the city half way. My first symbol was now a memory, for I knew that triumph is in oneself; my second one had grown commonplace—two of the actresses whom I had worshipped from afar in 1913 had dined in our house. But it filled me with a certain fear that even the third symbol had grown dim—the tranquillity of Bunny's apartment was not to be found in the ever-quickening city. Bunny himself was married, and about to become a father, other friends had gone to Europe, and the bachelors had become cadets of houses larger and more social than ours. By this time we "knew everybody" —which is to say most of those whom Ralph Barton would draw as in the orchestra on an opening night.

But we were no longer important. The flapper, upon whose activities the popularity of my first books was based, had become *passé* by 1923—anyhow in the East. I decided to crash Broadway with a play, but Broadway sent its scouts to Atlantic City and quashed the idea in advance, so I felt that, for the moment, the city and I had little to offer each other. I would take the Long Island atmosphere that I had familiarly breathed and materialize it beneath unfamiliar skies.

It was three years before we saw New York again. As the ship glided up the river, the city burst thunderously upon us in the early dusk—the white glacier of lower New York swooping down like a strand of a bridge to rise into uptown New York, a miracle of foamy light suspended by the stars. A band started to play on deck, but the majesty of the city made the march trivial and tinkling. From that moment I knew that New York, however often I might leave it, was home.

The tempo of the city had changed sharply. The uncertainties of 1920 were drowned in a steady golden roar and many of our friends had grown wealthy. But the restlessness of New York in 1927 approached hysteria. The parties were bigger—those of Condé Nast, for example, rivaled in their way the fabled balls of the nineties; the pace was faster—the catering to dissipation set an example to Paris; the shows were broader, the buildings were higher, the morals were looser and the liquor was cheaper; but all these benefits did not really minister to much delight. Young people wore out early—they were hard and languid at twenty-one and save for Peter Arno none of them contributed anything new; perhaps Peter Arno and his collaborators said everything there was to say about the boom days in New York that couldn't be said by a jazz band. Many people who were not alcoholics were lit up four days out of seven, and frayed nerves were strewn everywhere; groups were held together by a generic nervousness and the hangover became a part of the day as well allowed-for as the Spanish siesta. Most of my friends drank too much—the more they were in tune to the times the more they drank. And as effort *per se* had no dignity against the mere bounty of those days in New York, a depreciatory word was found for it: a successful programme became a racket—I was in the literary racket.

We settled a few hours from New York and I found that every time I came to the city I was caught up into a complication of events that deposited me a few days later in a somewhat exhausted state on the train for Delaware. Whole sections of the city had grown rather poisonous, but invariably I found a moment of utter peace in riding south through Central Park at dark toward where the façade of 59th Street thrusts its lights through the trees. There again was my lost city, wrapped cool in its mystery and promise. But that detachment never lasted long—as the toiler must live in the city's belly, so I was compelled to live in its disordered mind.

Instead there were the speakeasies—the moving from luxurious bars, which advertised in the campus publications of Yale and Princeton, to the beer gardens where the snarling face of the underworld peered through the German good nature of the entertainment, then on to strange and even more sinister localities where one was eyed by granite-faced boys and there was nothing left of joviality but only a brutishness that corrupted the new day into which one presently went out. Back in 1920 I shocked a rising young business man by suggesting a cocktail before lunch. In 1929 there was liquor in half the downtown offices, and a speakeasy in half the large buildings.

One was increasingly conscious of the speakeasy and of Park Avenue. In the past decade Greenwich Village, Washington Square, Murray Hill, the châteaux of Fifth Avenue had somehow disappeared, or become unexpressive of anything. The city was bloated, glutted, stupid with cake and circuses, and a new expression "Oh yeah?" summed up all the enthusiasm evoked by the announcement of the last super-skyscrapers. My barber retired on a half million bet in the market and I was conscious that the head waiters who bowed me, or failed to bow me, to my table were far, far wealthier than I. This was no fun—once again I had enough of New York and it was good to be safe on shipboard where the ceaseless revelry remained in the bar in transport to the fleecing rooms of France.

"What news from New York?"

"Stocks go up. A baby murdered a gangster."

"Nothing more?"

"Nothing. Radios blare in the street."

I once thought that there were no second acts in American lives, but there was certainly to be a second act to New York's boom days. We were somewhere in North Africa when we heard a dull distant crash which echoed to the farthest wastes of the desert.

"What was that?"

"Did you hear it?"

"It was nothing."

"Do you think we ought to go home and see?"

"No—it was nothing."

In the dark autumn of two years later we saw New York again. We passed through curiously polite customs agents, and then with bowed head and hat in hand I walked reverently through the echoing tomb. Among the ruins a few childish wraiths still played to keep up the pretense that they were alive, betraying by their feverish voices and hectic cheeks the thinness of the masquerade. Cocktail parties, a last hollow survival from the days of carnival, echoed to the plaints of the wounded: "Shoot me, for the love of God, someone shoot me!", and the groans and wails of the dying: "Did you see that United States Steel is down three more points?" My barber was back at work in his shop; again the head waiters bowed people to their tables, if there were people to be bowed. From the ruins, lonely and inexplicable as the sphinx, rose the Empire State Building and, just as it had been a tradition of mine to climb to the Plaza Roof to take leave of the beautiful city, extending as far as eyes could reach, so now I went to the roof of the last and most magnificent of towers. Then I understood—everything was explained: I had discovered the crowning error of the city, its Pandora's box. Full of vaunting pride the New Yorker had climbed here and seen with dismay what he had never suspected, that the city was not the endless succession of canyons that he had supposed but that *it had limits*—from the tallest structure he saw for the first time that it faded out into the country on all sides, into an expanse of green and blue that alone was limitless. And with the awful realization that New York was a city after all and not a universe, the whole shining edifice that he had reared in his imagination came crashing to the ground. That was the rash gift of Alfred E. Smith to the citizens of New York.

Thus I take leave of my lost city. Seen from the ferry boat in the early morning, it no longer whispers of fantastic success and eternal youth. The whoopee mamas who prance before its empty parquets do not suggest to me the ineffable beauty of my dream girls of 1914. . . .

All is lost save memory, yet sometimes I imagine myself reading, with curious interest, a *Daily News* of the issue of 1945:

MAN OF FIFTY RUNS AMUCK IN NEW YORK
*Fitzgerald Feathered Many Love Nests Cutie Avers
Bumped Off By Outraged Gunman*

So perhaps I am destined to return some day and find in the city new experiences that so far I have only read about. For the moment I can only cry out that I have lost my splendid mirage. Come back, come back, O glittering and white!

FRANK LLOYD WRIGHT

The Disappearing City

1932

Let us say that before the advent of universal and standardized mechanization, the city was more human. Its life as well as its proportion was more humane.

In planning the city, spacing was based, fairly enough, on the human being on his feet or sitting in some trap behind a horse, or two. Machinery had yet brought no swifter alternative. And a festival of wit, a show of pomp and a revel of circumstance rewarded life there in the original circumstances for which the city was planned. So, originally the city was a group life of powerful individualities true to life, conveniently enough spaced. This better life has already left the modern city, as it may, either for travel or the country estate. And such genius as the city has known for many a day is recruited from the country: the foolish celebrant of his "success," as such, seeking the city as a market, only to find an insatiable maw devouring quantity instead of protecting quality—eventually devouring himself as it is now devouring itself. "Fish for sale in the marketplace" but none in the streams. Frequent escape is already essential to any life at all in the overgrown city which offers nothing to the individual in bondage he cannot better find on terms of freedom in the country.

What, then, is the overgrown city for? The necessity that chained the individual to city life is dead or dying away. It is only as life has been taken from him and he has accepted substitutes offered to him that the "citizen" now remains.

The fundamental unit of space-measurement has so radically changed that the man now bulks ten to one and in speed a thousand to one as he is seated in his motor car. This circumstance would render the city obsolete. Like some old building the city is inhabited only because we have it, feel we must use it and cannot yet afford to throw it away to build the new one we know we need. We will soon be willing to give all we have, to get this new freedom that is ours for our posterity, if not for ourselves.

Devouring human individuality invariably ends in desertion. Eventually, as history records, it invariably ends in the destruction of the devourer.

Instead of being modern in any phase the devourer is senile in every phase.

The overgrown city of the United States stands, thus, enforced upon our undergrown social life as a false economy.

Like some tumor grown malignant, the city, like some cancerous growth, is become a menace to the future of humanity. Not only is the city already grown so far out of human scale by way of commercial exploitation of the herd instinct that the human being as a unit is utterly lost, but the soul, properly citified, is so far gone as to mistake exaggeration for greatness, mistake a vicarious power for his own power, finding in the uproar and verticality of the great city a proof of his own great quality. The properly citified citizen, reduced to a pleasing inferiority in the roar of congestion and terrific collision of forces, sees in this whirling exaggeration, his own greatness. He is satisfied to have greatness, too, vicarious.

But who, coming into New York, say, for the first time, could feel otherwise than that we were a "great" people to have raised the frame of such a relentless commercial engine so cruelly high, and hung so much book-architecture upon it regardless, at such cost?

Such energy, too, as has poured into a common center here to pile up material resources by way of riches in labor and materials and wasted attempts at "decoration," cramming the picturesque outlines of haphazard masses upon the bewildered eye peering from the black shadows down below? We see similar effects wherever irresistible force has broken and tilted up the earth's crust. Here is a volcanic crater of blind, confused, human forces pushing together and grinding upon each other, moved by greed in common exploitation, forcing anxiety upon all life. No noble expression of life, this. But, heedless of the meaning of it all, seen at night, the monster aggregation has myriad, haphazard beauties of silhouette and reflected or refracted light. The monster becomes rhythmical and does appeal to the love of romance and beauty. It is, then, mysterious and suggestive to the imaginative, inspiring to the ignorant. Fascinating entertainment this mysterious gloom upon which hang necklaces of light, through which shine clouds of substitutes for stars. The streets become rhythmical perspectives of glowing dotted lines, reflections hung upon them in the streets as the wisteria hangs its violet racemes on its trellis. The buildings are a shimmering verticality, a gossamer veil, a festive scene-drop hanging there against the black sky to dazzle, entertain and amaze.

The lighted interiors come through it all with a sense of life and well being. At night the city not only seems to live. It does live—as illusion lives.

And then comes the light of day. Reality. Streams of beings again pouring into the ground, "holing in" to find their way to this or that part of it, densely packed into some roar and rush of speed to pour out somewhere else. The sordid reiteration of space for rent. The overpowering sense of the cell. The dreary emphasis of narrowness, slicing, edging, niching and crowding. Tier above tier the soulless shelf, the empty crevice, the winding ways of the windy, unhealthy canyon. The heartless grip of the selfish, grasping universal stricture. Box on box beside box. Black shadows below with artificial lights burning all day in the little caverns and squared cells. Prison cubicles. Above it all a false, cruel, ambition is painting haphazard, jagged, pretentious, feudal skylines trying to relieve it and make it more humane by lying about its purpose. Congestion, confusion and the anxious spasmodic to and fro —stop and go. At best the all too narrow lanes, were they available, are only fifty per cent effective owing to the gridiron. In them roars a bedlam of harsh sound and a dangerous, wasteful, spasmodic movement runs in these narrow village lanes in the deep shadows. Distortion.

This man-trap of gigantic dimensions, devouring manhood, denies in its affected riot of personality any individuality whatsoever. This Moloch knows no god but "More." Nowhere is there a clear thought or a sane feeling for good life manifest. In all, even in the libraries, museums and institutes is parasitic make-believe or fantastic abortion. But, if the citizenry is parasitic, the overgrown city itself is barbaric in the true meaning of the word. As good an example of barbarism as exists.

How could it be otherwise?

Some thriving little village port driven insane by excess: excess of such success as current business ideals or principles knows as such. And it is nothing more than much more of much too much already.

The finer human sensibilities become numb.

And even the whole callous, commercial enterprise, pretentious as such, stalls its own engine! . . .

Let us turn, now, to these forces that are thrusting at the city to see how they will, eventually, return such human nature as survives this festering acceleration, body and soul to the soil, and, in course of time, repair the damage cancerous overgrowth has wrought upon the life of the United States.

As one force working toward the destruction that is really emancipation, we have the reawakening of the slumbering primitive-instinct of the wandering tribe that has come down the ages and intermingled with the instincts of the cave dweller.

The active physical forces that are now trained inevitably against the city are now on the side of this space loving primitive because modern force, by way of electrical, mechanical and chemical invention are volatilizing voice, vision and movement-in-distance in all its human forms until spaciousness is scientific. So the city is already become unscientific in its congested verticality and to the space loving human being, intolerable. The unnatural stricture of verticality can not stand against natural horizontality.

As another force—a moving spiritual force—the fresh interpretation to which we have referred as a superb ideal of human freedom—Democracy comes to our aid. Our own new spiritual concept of life will find its natural consequences in the life we are about to live. We are going to move with that new spiritual concept the nation has been calling Democracy only half comprehending either ideal or form. This ideal is becoming the greatest subconscious spiritual moving force now moving against the city with new factual resources.

THOMAS WOLFE
Enchanted City

1925–1935

There is no truer legend in the world than the one about the country boy, the provincial innocent, in his first contact with the city. Hackneyed by repetition, parodied and burlesqued by the devices of cheap fiction and the slap-stick of vaudeville humor, it is nevertheless one of the most tremendous and vital experiences in the life of a man, and in the life of the nation. It has found inspired and glorious tongues in Tolstoy and in Goethe, in Balzac and in Dickens, in Fielding and Mark Twain. It has found splendid examples in every artery of life, as well in Shakespeare as in the young Napoleon. And day after day the great cities of the world are being fed, enriched, and replenished ceaselessly with the life-blood of the nation, with all the passion, aspiration, eagerness, faith, and high imagining that youth can know, or that the tenement of life can hold.

For one born to the obscure village and brought up within the narrow geography of provincial ways, the city experience is such as no city man himself can ever know. It is conceived in absence and in silence and in youth; it is built up to the cloud-capped pinnacles of a boy's imagining; it is written like a golden legend in the heart of youth with a plume plucked out of an angel's wing; it lives and flames there in his heart and spirit with all the timeless faery of the magic land.

When such a man, therefore, comes first to the great city—but how can we speak of such a man coming first to the great city, when really the great city is within him, encysted in his heart, built up in all the flaming images of his brain: a symbol of his hope, the image of his high desire, the final crown, the citadel of all that he has ever dreamed of or longed for or imagined that life could bring to him? For such a man as this, there really is no coming to the city. He brings the city with him everywhere he goes, and when that final moment comes when he at last breathes in the city's air, feels his foot upon the city street, looks around him at the city's pinnacles, into the dark, unceasing tide of city faces, grips his sinews, feels his flesh, pinches himself to make sure he is really there—for such a man as this, and for such a moment, it will always be a question to be considered in its bewildering ramifications by the subtle soul psychologists to know which city is the real one, which city he has found and seen, which city for this man is really there.

For the city has a million faces, and just as it is said that no two men can really know what each is thinking of, what either sees when he speaks of "red" or "blue," so can no man ever know just what another means when he tells about the city that he sees. For the city that he sees is just the city that he brings with him, that he has within his heart; and even at that immeasurable moment of first perception, when for the first time he sees the city with his naked eye, at that tremendous moment of final apprehension when the great city smites at last upon his living sense, still no man can be certain he has seen the city as it is, because in the hairbreadth of that instant recognition a whole new city is composed, made out of sense but shaped and colored and unalterable from all that he has felt and thought and dreamed about before.

And more than this! There are so many other instant, swift, and accidental things that happen in a moment, that are gone forever, and that shape the city in the heart of youth. It may be a light that comes and goes, a grey day, or a leaf upon a bough; it may be the first image of a city face, a woman's smile, an oath, a half-heard word; it may be sunset, morning, or the crowded traffics of the street, the furious pinnacle of dusty noon; or it may be April, April, and the songs they sang that year. No one can say, except it may be something chance and swift and fleeting, as are all of these, together with the accidents of pine and clay, the weather of one's youth, the place, the structure, and the life from which one came, and all conditioned so, so memoried, built up into the vision of the city that a man first brings there in his heart.

. . .

Perhaps it is just here, in the iron-breasted city, that one comes closest to the enigma that haunts and curses the whole land. The city is the place where men are constantly seeking to find their door and where they are doomed to wandering forever. Of no place is this more true than of New York. Hideously ugly for the most part, one yet remembers it as a place of proud and passionate beauty; the place of everlasting hunger, it is also the place where men feel their lives will gloriously be fulfilled and their hunger fed.

In no place in the world can the life of the lonely boy, the countryman who has been drawn northwards to the flame of his lust, be more barren, more drab, more hungry and comfortless. His life is the life of subways, of rebreathed air, of the smell of burned steel, weariness and the exhausted fetidity of a cheap rented room in the apartment of "a nice couple" on 113th Street, or perhaps the triumph of an eighty-dollar apartment in Brooklyn, upper Manhattan, or the Bronx which he rents with three or four other youths. Here they "can do as they please," a romantic aspiration which leads to Saturday night parties, to cheap gin, cheap girls, to a feverish and impotent fumbling, and perhaps to an occasional distressed, drunken, and half-public fornication.

If the youth is of a serious bent, if he has thoughts of "improving" himself, there is the gigantic desolation of the Public Library, a cut-rate ticket at Gray's and a seat in the balcony of an art-theatre play that has been highly praised and that all intellectual people will be seeing, or the grey depression of a musical Sunday afternoon at Carnegie Hall, filled with arrogant-looking little musicians with silky mustaches who hiss like vipers in the dark when the works of a hated composer are played; or there is always the Metropolitan Museum.

Again, there is something spurious and unreal in almost all attempts at established life in the city. When one enters the neat little apartment of a young man or a young married couple, and sees there on neat, gaily-painted shelves neat rows of books—the solid little squares of the Everyman, and the Modern Library, the D. H. Lawrence, the *Buddenbrooks*, the Cabell, the art edition of *Penguin Island*, then a few of the paper-backed French books, the Proust and the Gide, and so on—one feels a sense of embarrassment and shame: there is something fraudulent about it. One feels this also in the homes of wealthy people, whether they live in a "charming little house" on Ninth Street which they have rented, or in the massive rooms of a Park Avenue apartment.

No matter what atmosphere of usage, servants, habitude, ease, and solid establishment there may be, one always has this same feeling that the thing is fraudulent, that the effort to achieve permanence in this impermanent and constantly changing life is no more real than the suggested permanence in a theatrical setting: one would not be surprised to return the next morning and find the scene dismantled, the stage bare, and the actors departed. Sometimes even the simplest social acts—the act of visiting one's friends, of talking to them in a room, of sitting around a hearth-fire with them—oh, above all else, of sitting around a hearth-fire in an apartment in the city!—seem naked and pitiful. There is an enormous sadness and wistfulness about these attempts to simulate an established life in a place where the one permanent thing is change itself.

In recent years many people have felt this insistent and constant movement. Some have blamed it on the war, some on the tempo of the time, some have called it "a jazz age" and suggested that men should meet the rhythm of the age and move and live by it; but although this notion has been fashionable, it can hardly recommend itself to men who have been driven by their hunger, who have known loneliness and exile, who have wandered upon the face of the earth and found no doors that they could enter, and who would to God now that they might make an end to all their wandering and loneliness, that they might find one home and heart of all their hunger where they could live abundantly forever. Such men, and they are numbered not by thousands but by millions, are hardly prepared to understand that the agony and loneliness of the human spirit may be assuaged by the jerky automata of jazz.

Perhaps this sense of restlessness, loneliness, and hunger is intensified in the city, but if anyone remembers his own childhood and youth in America he is certain to remember these desires and movements, too. Everywhere people were driven by them. Everyone had a rocking chair, and in the months of good weather everyone was out on his front porch rocking away. People were always eager to "go somewheres," and when the automobile came in, the roads, particularly on Sunday, were choked with cars going into the country, going to another town, going anywhere, no matter how ugly or barren the excursion might be, so long as this terrible restlessness might in some measure be appeased.

In the city, it is appalling to think how much pain and hunger people—and particularly young men—have suffered, because there is no goal whatever for these feverish extravasations. They return, after their day's work to a room which, despite all efforts to trick it out with a neat bed, bright colors, a few painted bookshelves, a few pictures, is obviously only a masked cell. It becomes impossible to use the room for any purpose at all save for sleeping; the act of reading a book in it, of sitting in a chair in it, of staying in it for any period of time whatever when one is in a state of wakefulness, becomes intolerable.

Yet, what are these wretched people to do? Every instant, every deep conviction a man has for a reasonable human comfort is outraged. He knows that every man on earth should have the decency of space—of space enough to extend his limbs and draw in the air without fear or labor; and he knows that his life here in this miserable closet is base, barren, mean, and naked. He knows that men should not defile themselves in this way, so he keeps out of his room as much as possible. But what can he do? Where can he go? In the terrible streets of the city there is neither pause nor repose, there are no turnings and no place where he can detach himself from the incessant tide of the crowd, and sink unto himself in tranquil meditation. He flees from one desolation to another, he escapes by buying a seat "at some show," or snatching at food in a cafeteria, he lashes about the huge streets of the night, and he returns to his cell having found no doors that he could open, no place that he could call his own.

It is therefore astonishing that nowhere in the world can a young man feel greater hope and expectancy than here. The promise of glorious fulfillment, of love, wealth, fame—or unimaginable joy—is always impending in the air. He is torn with a thousand desires and he is unable to articulate one of them, but he is sure that he will grasp joy to his heart, that he will hold love and glory in his arms, that the intangible will be touched, the inarticulate spoken, the inapprehensible apprehended; and that this may happen at any moment.

Perhaps there is some chemistry of air that causes this exuberance and joy, but it also belongs to the enigma of the whole country, which is so rich, and yet where people starve, which is so abundant, exultant, savage, full-blooded, humorous, liquid, and magnificent, and yet where so many people are poor, meager, dry, and baffled. But the richness and depth of the place is visible, it is not an illusion; there is always the feeling that the earth is full of gold, and that who will seek and strive can mine it.

In New York there are certain wonderful seasons in which this feeling grows to a lyrical intensity. One of these are those first tender days of Spring when lovely girls and women seem suddenly to burst out of the pavements like flowers: all at once the street is peopled with them, walking along with a proud, undulant rhythm of breasts and buttocks and a look of passionate tenderness on their faces. Another season is early Autumn, in October, when the city begins to take on a magnificent flash and sparkle: there are swift whippings of bright wind, a flare of bitter leaves, the smell of frost and harvest in the air; after the enervation of Summer, the place awakens to an electric vitality, the beautiful women have come back from Europe or from the summer resorts, and the air is charged with exultancy and joy.

Finally, there is a wonderful, secret thrill of some impending ecstasy on a frozen Winter's night. On one of these nights of frozen silence when the cold is so intense that it numbs one's flesh, and the sky above the city flashes with one deep jewelry of cold stars, the whole city, no matter how ugly its parts may be, becomes a proud, passionate, Northern place: everything about it seems to soar up with an aspirant, vertical, glittering magnificence to meet the stars. One hears the hoarse notes of the great ships in the river, and one remembers suddenly the princely girdle of proud, potent tides that bind the city, and suddenly New York blazes like a magnificent jewel in its fit setting of sea, and earth, and stars.

There is no place like it, no place with an atom of its glory, pride, and exultancy. It lays its hand upon a man's bowels; he grows drunk with ecstasy; he grows young and full of glory, he feels that he can never die.

LE CORBUSIER
The Fairy Catastrophe

SAVAGE AND MYSTIC

1936

A hundred years have been enough to make cities inhuman.

Monday morning, when my ship stopped at Quarantine, I saw a fantastic, almost mystic city rising up in the mist. But the ship moves forward and the apparition is transformed into an image of incredible brutality and savagery. Here is certainly the most prominent manifestation of the power of modern times. This brutality and this savagery do not displease me. It is thus that great enterprises begin: by strength.

In the evening, on the avenues of the city, I began to appreciate the people who, by a law of life which is their own, have been able to create a race: handsome men, very beautiful women.

The world is undergoing one of the great metamorphoses of history. The collective and the individual collide instead of combining. Is a synthesis possible? Yes, in a program on a *human scale* and guided by *human wisdom*.

This is architecture's hour. There can be no new architecture without a new city planning. New cities have always replaced old cities, by periods. But today it is possible for the city of modern times, the happy city, the radiant city, to be born. . . .

VERTICAL CITY

New York is a vertical city, under the sign of the new times. It is a catastrophe with which a too hasty destiny has overwhelmed courageous and confident people, though a beautiful and worthy catastrophe. Nothing is lost. Faced with difficulties, New York falters. Still streaming with sweat from its exertions, wiping off its forehead, it sees what it has done and suddenly realizes: "Well, we didn't get it done properly. Let's start over again!" New York has such courage and enthusiasm that everything can be begun again, sent back to the building yard and made into something still greater, something mastered! These people are not on the point of going to sleep. In reality, the city is hardly more than twenty years old, that is the city which I am talking about, the city which is vertical and on the scale of the new times. . . .

I am not able to bear the thought of millions of people undergoing the diminution of life imposed by devouring distances, the subways filled with uproar, the wastelands on the edges of the city, in the blackened brick streets, hard, implacably soulless streets—tenement streets, streets of hovels that make up the cities of the century of money—the slums of New York or Chicago.

I am offended by this blow at legitimate human hopes. Nevertheless, if I am observant, I discover that my despair is not always shared by the victims themselves. In New York, the people who have come in order to "make money" shake off black thoughts and, looking at the sparkle of the great avenues, the entrances of apartment houses and fine homes, think: "O.K., it will be my turn tomorrow!"

Seven million people are bound in the chains of New York, and that turn will never come unless they learn to adopt drastic measures.

Knowing quite well that the turn cannot come quickly enough for seven million beings, there are moments when I hate the city of today; clearly and coolly I know that a proper plan can make New York the city par excellence of modern times, can actively spread daily happiness for these oppressed families—children, women, men stupefied by work, stunned by the noise of the rails of the subways or elevateds—who sink down each evening, at the end of their appointed tasks, in the impasse of an inhuman hovel.

In sober offices, on the fifty-sixth floor of the newest skyscraper, men carry on business. Big business probably. I do not have a sense of figures and I know from experience that it is often more difficult to make small matters come out right than big ones. In the domain of money, the law is like that of the swing at the fair: at the beginning the effort is normal; everyone can take off and make a start. But at a certain point in the swing, when the acrobat is on the horizontal, it becomes precarious; he is too far away from the gravitational norm, and gravity acts on him. Then it takes an effort of a very particular kind to achieve a vertical position, with head down, and having passed the "meridian" of the swing, to come on around effortlessly from that point. Brute strength is not enough. The repeated attempts require a regular and harmonious progression. Harmonious, that's the word. Harmony is the cause of the success. The most difficult thing—the real difficulty—comes when you are a hair's-breadth from success: at the moment of swinging over. If you manage it, you are thenceforth launched! Many will not succeed in managing it. Those who have passed over this financial hazard owe it to their merits just as they owe it to the combination of circumstances: the things necessary to make the effort profitable, to stimulate it, to support it, were present. It was a happy conjuncture. And now the financial swing moves easily, with no further effort required except a scrupulous supervision.

That is why the skyscrapers were not constructed with a wise and serious intention. They were applauded acrobatic feats. The *skyscraper as proclamation* won. Here the skyscraper is not an element in city planning, but a banner in the sky, a fireworks rocket, an aigrette in the coiffure of a name henceforth listed in the financial Almanach de Gotha.

Beneath the immaculate office on the fifty-sixth floor the vast nocturnal festival of New York spreads out. No one can imagine it who has not seen it. It is a titanic mineral display, a prismatic stratification shot through with an infinite number of lights, from top to bottom, in depth, in a violent silhouette like a fever chart beside a sick bed. A diamond, incalculable diamonds.

The great masters of economic destiny are up there, like eagles, in the silence of their eminences. Seated in their chairs, framed by two plate glass windows which fuse their rooms with the surrounding space, they appear to us made out of the substance of this event which is as strong and violent as a cosmic mutation: New York standing up above Manhattan is like a rose-colored stone in the blue of a maritime sky; New York at night is like a limitless cluster of jewels. . . .

THE SKYSCRAPERS ARE TOO SMALL

The cardinal question asked of every traveler on his arrival is: "What do you think of New York?" Coolly I replied: "The skyscrapers are too small."

And I explained what I meant.

For a moment my questioners were speechless! So much the worse for them! The reasoning is clear and the supporting proofs abundant, streets full of them, a complete urban disaster.

The skyscraper is not a plume rising from the face of the city. It has been made that, and wrongly. The plume was a poison to the city. The skyscraper is an instrument. A magnificent instrument for the concentration of population, for getting rid of land congestion, for classification, for internal efficiency. A prodigious means of improving the conditions of work, a creator of economies and, through that, a dispenser of wealth. But the skyscraper as plume, multiplied over the area of Manhattan, has disregarded experience. The New York skyscrapers are out of line with the rational skyscraper which I have called: *the Cartesian skyscraper*. . . .

Now we are ready to state the fundamental principle: the skyscraper *is a function of capacity* (the offices) *and of the area of free ground at its base*. A skyscraper which does not fulfill this function harmoniously is a disease. That is the disease of New York.

The Cartesian skyscraper is a miracle in the urbanization of the cities of machine civilization. It makes possible extraordinary concentrations, from three to four thousand persons on each two and one-half acres. It does so while taking up only 8 to 12 per cent of the ground, 92 to 88 per cent being restored, usable, available for the circulation of pedestrians and cars! These immense free areas, this whole ward in the business section, will become a park. The glass skyscrapers will rise up like crystals, clean and transparent in the midst of the foliage of the trees. . . .

The skyscrapers of New York are too small and there are too many of them. They are proof of the new dimensions and the new tools; the proof also that henceforth everything can be carried out on a new general plan, a symphonic plan—extent and height. . . .

A PLACE OF RADIANT GRACE

The George Washington Bridge over the Hudson is the most beautiful bridge in the world. Made of cables and steel beams, it gleams in the sky like a reversed arch. It is blessed. It is the only seat of grace in the disordered city. It is painted an aluminum color and, between water and sky, you see nothing but the bent cord supported by two steel towers. When your car moves up the ramp the two towers rise so high that it brings you happiness; their structure is so pure, so resolute, so regular that here, finally, steel architecture seems to laugh. The car reaches an unexpectedly wide apron; the second tower is very far away; innumerable vertical cables, gleaming against the sky, are suspended from the magisterial curve which swings down and then up. The rose-colored towers of New York appear, a vision whose harshness is mitigated by distance.

The bridge has a story which almost turned out ridiculously. Mr. Cullman, president of the Port of New York, told me about it. The bridge was constructed under his supervision. The problem required the utmost engineering boldness. Calculation aided by a fortunate hypothesis gave the work the severity of things which are exact. The bridge leaps over the Hudson in a single bound. Two steel-topped concrete piers between the banks and the apron hold the suspension chains. I have mentioned the extraordinary dimensions of the two towers. Constructed of riveted steel they stand up in the sky with a striking nobility. Now the towers were to have been faced with stone molded and sculptured in "Beaux-Arts" style (New York term for the aesthetic ideas current on the quai Voltaire in Paris)..

Someone acted before it was too late. Then the whole committee of the Port of New York Authority. Little by little the spirit of modern times makes itself felt: these men said, "Stop! no stone or decoration here. The two towers and the mathematical play of the cables make a splendid unity. It is one. That is the new beauty." They made some calculations; the maintenance of the towers by proper painting would cost an amount equal to the interest on the capital which would have been invested in stone-faced towers. Thus the two proposals were financially equivalent. They were not looking for a means of saving expense. But "in the name of beauty and of the spirit" they dismissed the architect with his decorations. Those men are citizens!

LESSON FOR TOMORROW

I could never have imagined such a violent, such a decisive, such a simple and also such a diversified arrangement of the ground of a city. The eight or nine longitudinal avenues mark off the character of areas in a quickly changing gamut which runs from the hideous to the luxurious. Manhattan—a kind of sole stretched out on a rock—has value only along its spinal column; the borders are slums. On foot, you can walk across town in twenty minutes and see that spectacle of contrasts. But what satisfaction can rationality find in it? The borders—the East River and the Hudson are inaccessible! The sea is inaccessible, invisible. Looking at the plan of New York or an airplane view, you think: "It is certainly the best organized city in the world." Well, the sea and the vast rivers are invisible and no one gets the benefit of their beauty, their spaciousness, their movement, the splendid play of light on the water! New York, an immense seaport, is as landlocked for its inhabitants as Moscow! And the admirable terrain, seemingly destined to be taken up by immense apartments with windows opening on space, that terrain is desolating: it is filled with slums! A well-managed municipal operation could easily restore the value of those sections and the profit would make it possible to do something about the rest of the city, which is in violent disorder. It astounds a visitor to learn that Manhattan, bristling with skyscrapers, has an average building height of four and one-half stories. Do you realize that: *four and one-half stories?* But it is the imperative and revealing statistical fact which brings hope for the success of a transforming plan capable of establishing order in the city.

Here the skyscraper is negative: it kills the street and the city, it has destroyed circulation. More than that, it is a man-eating monster: it sucks the life out of the neighboring areas; it empties them and ruins them. Once again, saving solutions of the urban problem come to mind. The skyscraper is too small and it destroys everything. Make it larger, true and useful: it will restore an immense area of ground, it will pay for the ruined properties, it will give the city verdure and excellent circulation: all the ground in parks for pedestrians and cars up in the air, on elevated roads, *a few roads* (one-way), permitting a speed of ninety miles an hour and going . . . simply from one skyscraper to another. Collaborative measures are needed to achieve that goal; without them, no salvation is possible! We shall have to think about that someday, through the organization of co-operatives or real-estate syndicates, or through strong and paternal governmental measures (with all the energy of the father who knows what the children should do).

Between the present skyscrapers there are masses of large and small buildings. Most of them small. What are these small houses doing in dramatic Manhattan? I haven't the slightest idea. It is incomprehensible. It is a fact, nothing more, as the debris after an earthquake or bombardment is a fact.

Central Park has a different lesson. Notice how normal and spontaneous it is for the great hotels and large apartment houses to come there and open their windows on the clear space. But Central Park is too large and it is a hole in the midst of buildings. It is a lesson. You go through Central Park as if you were in a no man's land. The verdure, and especially the space, of Central Park should be distributed and multiplied throughout Manhattan. . . .

THE FAIRY CATASTROPHE

A hundred times I have thought: New York is a catastrophe, and fifty times: it is a beautiful catastrophe.

One evening about six o'clock I had cocktails with James Johnson Sweeney—a friend who lives in an apartment house east of Central Park, over toward the East River; he is on the top floor, one hundred and sixty feet above the street; after having looked out the windows, we went outside on the balcony, and finally we climbed up on the roof.

The night was dark, the air dry and cold. The whole city was lighted up. If you have not seen it, you cannot know or imagine what it is like. You must have had it sweep over you. Then you begin to understand why Americans have become proud of themselves in the last twenty years and why they raise their voices in the world and why they are impatient when they come to our country. The sky is decked out. It is a Milky Way come down to earth; you are in it. Each window, each person, is a light in the sky. At the same time a perspective is established by the arrangement of the thousand lights of each skyscraper; it forms itself more in your mind than in the darkness perforated by illimitable fires. The stars are part of it also—the real stars—but sparkling quietly in the distance. Splendor, scintillation, promise, proof, act of faith, etc. Feeling comes into play; the action of the heart is released; crescendo, allegro, fortissimo. We are charged with feeling, we are intoxicated; legs strengthened, chests expanded, eager for action, we are filled with confidence.

That is the Manhattan of vehement silhouettes. Those are the verities of technique, which is the springboard of lyricism. The fields of water, the railroads, the planes, the stars, and the vertical city with its unimaginable diamonds. Everything is there, and it is real.

The nineteenth century covered the earth with ugly and soulless works. Bestiality of money. The twentieth century aspires to grace, suppleness. The catastrophe is before us in the darkness, a spectacle young and new. The night effaces a thousand objects of debate and mental reservation. What is here then is true! Then everything is possible. Let the human be written into this by conscious intention, let joy be brought into the city by means of wisely conceived urban machinery and by generous thinking, aware of human misery. Let order reign.

The Fairy Catastrophy! That is the phrase that expresses my emotion and rings within me in the stormy debate which has not stopped tormenting me for fifty days: hate and love.

For me the fairy catastrophe is the lever of hope!

Translated by Francis E. Hyslop, Jr.

HEYWOOD BROUN

The Place of Sacrifice

1938

I have a letter from Miss L. K. G., who lives in Great Falls, Montana, and the burden of her letter is that Great Falls is dull and humdrum and that she would like to be in and of New York. "How can it be accomplished?" Miss G. would like to know. And she adds, "I am a competent stenographer and I think that I am more metropolitan-minded than most of the girls out here because I read Walter Winchell and the *New Republic* religiously. Tell me something about New York."

That is a large order, Miss G., and may I make a guess and call you by your first name? Is it the world of Broadway, Lucinda, or the intellectual approach of this particular sanctum which enlists your curiosity? To be sure, these are not always mutually exclusive. Mr. Winchell begins to emerge from political isolation, while the *New Republic* runs a paragraph column and serves Scotch or rye to favored contributors on Friday.

The chances are all against your getting a job here, Lucinda, for the town is filled with stenographers who assert that they are competent. I will not be presumptuous enough to say that you are better off in Great Falls (where you can vote for O'Connell instead of O'Connor) but New York is not the ideal place for the perpetuation of the comfortable life. If you plan no more than a visit of forty or fifty years, that is all right, but I would advise no man or woman to take up permanent residence in Manhattan. As soon as parole is possible I would suggest Stamford, Connecticut.

The late O. O. McIntyre used to tell his country customers that in their own Main Street all the joys and treasures of the metropolis could be found. But that just isn't true, save for the materially minded. I have no doubt that in either Great Falls or Ashtabula one may find love, loyalty, T-bone steaks and iced beverages. But the esthetic and spiritual values of New York are not to be had in the smaller cities.

In all the United States man has made with his own hands no such beauty as exists in New York City. The name Great Falls suggests to me that in your immediate neighborhood, Lucinda, there is some kind of mill race and that the tumbling water may be pretty under the moonlight. But I have found that a week with a waterfall, even a large one, is plenty for any man. Twice I have looked upon Niagara and it is not graven upon my heart. The song it sings is repetitious and I shall not return until I hear that the wall of water has begun to hesitate upon the brink, adding some element of dramatic suspense like the famed choice of Candida. The river does fall quite a distance, but what else can it do? What else has it ever done?

And if other natural wonders are to be brought forward for contemplation, I must admit that I would much rather crane my neck to look up at the Empire State Building than stoop to survey the bottom of the Grand Canyon. The making of towers is a more noble endeavor than the digging of ditches.

Works of nature often leave one chilled because they offer no vicarious satisfaction to the tourist by enabling him to say, "I might have a shot at that myself some rainy afternoon."

It is true that the odds are all against my ever painting a Rembrandt or your capturing the flight of a skylark in some spare poetic moment. Still these are achievements of the race and not the fortuitous product of a slow geologic cataclysm. And so I would turn off the moon and toss aside even a successful sunset as being nothing more than a chance hit. Beauty without plan is also beauty without meaning.

Your Great Falls, Lucinda, is near some one of the National Parks, if I remember, and I assume you have a vast expanse of forest, hot springs which smoke and roar and mountains lumbering toward the sky. But believe no one who tells you that any one of these set pieces can produce the same wonder as the spidery span of a bridge across the Hudson. That leap of steel broad-jumping into space makes even the rapids of a troubled stream seem slow-paced and indecisive.

If you can keep body and soul apart, come rushing to the magical city, Lucinda, whether a job waits or not. But remember that Manhattan is also the place of sacrifice. It is only for those who can subsist on locusts and wild honey. In many respects it is an American equivalent of Ceylon's Isle and there be those who have been borne down by too much beauty and who walk through the canyons of the city as impervious to visual excitement as any pack mule. The plain fact of the matter is that New York is much too good for New Yorkers. Complete appreciation will come only when some Vesuvius has laid it low and posterity is forced to dig down into the dust to bring to light the buried treasure. If you have patience, Lucinda, it might not be a bad idea to postpone your trip to some such time when the guide, pausing in his patter to speak with deep emotion, may say, "And now beneath your foot, lady, is a crumbled stone which is all that is left to remind us that here the *New Republic* once functioned in offices which were considered very modern."

But, Miss L. K. G., you have every right to ask why I have put beauty behind me and fled to the drab landscape of the Connecticut countryside. It is not so much from a fear of impending doom but rather because the wine of loveliness comes to be too heady a draught after protracted maturity. I shall not look much again upon the George Washington Memorial Bridge at dawn or Brooklyn Bridge in twilight. My arteries grow too precarious to watch the Chrysler needle grow dim and lost in fog as if it had been thrust into a specter haystack.

We have tame flowers and wild ones, too, here on Hunting Ridge and a bit of greenery. But everything is under control. A local stock company is going to do *The Jest*, but I shall see no Barrymores nor watch the rain sweep down the street of hits. I have begun to taper.

And you, young lady, I think you said Lucinda, may come from Great Falls to Manhattan if that is your pleasure. But as you value your return-trip ticket, bring a mirror and never dare to look Medusa in the eye.

JEAN-PAUL SARTRE

Manhattan: the Great American Desert

1946

I knew very well that I would like New York. But I thought that I would be able to like it immediately, as I had immediately liked the red bricks of Venice and the sombre, massive houses of London. I did not know that for the newly arrived European there is a "New York sickness," just as there are seasickness, airsickness, and mountain sickness.

An official car took me from La Guardia Field at midnight to the Plaza Hotel. I pressed my forehead against the window but could see only red and green lights and dark buildings. The next day I found myself, without any transition, at the corner of 58th Street and Fifth Avenue. I walked a long time under the icy sky. It was a Sunday in January, 1945—a deserted Sunday. I looked for New York and I could not find it. It seemed to retreat before me, like a phantom city, as I walked down an avenue that appeared coldly formal and without distinction. I was undoubtedly looking for a European city.

We Europeans live on the myth of the large city we constructed during the nineteenth century. The myths of the Americans are not the same, and the American city is not the same. It has neither the same nature nor the same functions. In Spain, Italy, Germany, France, we find *round* cities, formerly encircled by ramparts which served not only to protect the inhabitants from enemy invasion but also to hide from them the inexorable presence of Nature. The cities in turn are divided into districts equally round and closed upon themselves, where buildings piled up and tightly clustered weigh heavily upon the earth. They seem to have a natural tendency to draw close together—to such an extent that from time to time we must hack out new paths with the ax as we do in a virgin forest. Streets bump into other streets; sealed at both ends, they give no sign of leading out of the city. They are more than just thoroughfares, they are social milieus; you pause there, meet others, drink, eat, and live there. Sunday you dress up and go for a walk for the pleasure of greeting friends, to see and be seen. These are the streets that inspired Jules Romains with his "unanimism." They are infused with a collective spirit which varies with each hour of the day.

Thus my European, my myopic glance, advancing slowly and prying into everything, tried in vain to find something in New York to arrest it—anything, no matter what—a row of houses suddenly barring the way, the turning of a street, some house weathered and tanned by time. For New York is a city for the farsighted: there is nothing to focus upon except the vanishing point. My glance encountered only space. It slid over blocks of houses, all alike, and passed unchecked to the misty horizon.

Céline said New York was a "standing" city. True; but it seemed to me from the very first a *lengthwise* city. All priorities are given to length. Traffic stands still in the side streets but rolls tirelessly on the avenues. How often do cab drivers, who willingly take passengers north and south, refuse flatly to drive them east and west! The side streets are hardly more than the outlines of the buildings between the avenues. The avenues pierce them, tear them apart, and speed toward the north. It was because of this that, a naïve tourist, I sought for *quartiers*, a long time and in vain. In France these neighborhoods encircle and protect us: the rich neighborhood protects us from the envy of the poor; the poor neighborhood protects us from the disdain of the rich, just as the entire city protects us from Nature.

In New York, where the great axes are the parallel avenues, I could not find these neighborhoods, but only atmospheres—gaseous masses extending longitudinally without well-defined beginnings or endings. Gradually I learned to recognize the atmosphere of Third Avenue, where people meet, smile, talk together in the shadow of the noisy elevated without ever knowing each other, or where a German, passing near my table in an Irish bar, stopped a moment to ask, "Are you French? As for me, I am a Boche"; the reassuring comfort of the stores on Lexington; the sad elegance of Park Avenue; the cold luxury and stucco impassibility of Fifth; the gay frivolity of Sixth and Seventh; the food fairs of Ninth; the no-man's-land of Tenth. Each avenue draws the neighboring streets into its atmosphere but a block further away you are suddenly plunged into another world. Not far from the palpitating silence of Park Avenue, where private cars pass, I am on First, where the earth trembles perpetually as the trucks go by. How can I feel secure on one of those endless north-south trajectories when a few steps away, to east or west, other longitudinal worlds await me? Behind the Waldorf-Astoria and the white-and-blue awnings of fashionable buildings I see the elevated, still reeking of the Bowery.

All New York is thus striped with parallel, uncommunicable meanings. The long lines, drawn as if with a ruler, gave me suddenly the feeling of space. Our cities in Europe are built as a protection *against* space; the houses huddle like sheep. But space traverses New York, animates it, stretches it. Space, the great empty space of the Russian steppes and the pampas, flows through the streets like a cold draught, separating the inhabitants of one side from those of the other. An American friend who went for a walk with me in Boston on one of the fashionable streets said, pointing to the left side, "The best people live there"; and he added ironically, indicating the right, "No one has ever known who lives on this side." Similarly in New York, no one knows who lives across the street. All space is between them. When I flew above the great American desert of Texas, New Mexico, and Arizona, I was not astonished, for I had already seen the whole American desert in New York, where space, the great factor of separation between people and between things, has crept in. While I was in Los Angeles an acquaintance said, "Come see me tomorrow. I live very near you—only ten miles away." And when I went for a walk along the Cienega, beside a road lined with autos, I was the only pedestrian to be seen for miles. I don't mean to imply that New York is like that; it is halfway between the city for pedestrians and the city for autos. You do not go for a walk in New York; you either loiter at a drugstore or travel by express subway.

Your streets and avenues have not the same meaning as ours. You go *through* them. New York is a city of movement. If I walk rapidly I feel at ease, but if I stop for a moment I am troubled, and I wonder: Why am I in this street rather than in one of the hundred other streets that resemble it, why near this particular drugstore, Schrafft's, or Woolworth's, rather than any other drugstore, Schrafft's, or Woolworth's from among the thousands just like it? Pure space suddenly appears. I imagine that if a triangle were to become aware of its position in space it would be frightened at seeing how accurately it was defined and yet how, at the same time, it was simply *any* triangle. In New York you never get lost; a glance suffices to show you that you are on the East Side, at the corner of Fifty-second Street and Lexington. But this spatial precision is not accompanied by any sentimental precision. In the numerical anonymity of the streets and avenues I am simply *anyone*—as defined and as indefinite as the triangle—I am anyone who is lost and conscious of being unjustifiable, without valid reason for being in one place rather than another, because one place and another look so much alike.

Am I lost in a city, or in Nature? New York is no protection from the violence of Nature. It is a city of open sky. The storms overflow its streets, which are so wide and long to cross when it rains. Blizzards shake the brick houses and sway the skyscrapers. In summer the air trembles between the houses, in winter the city is flooded, so that you might think you were in the suburbs of Paris when the Seine had overflowed, though it is only the snow melting. Nature's weight is so heavy on it that this most modern of cities is also the dirtiest. From my window I watch the wind playing with thick, muddy papers that flutter over the pavement. When I go out I walk in blackish snow, a sort of crusted swelling the same color as the sidewalk, as if the sidewalk itself were warped. Even in the depths of my apartment a hostile, deaf, mysterious nature assails me. I seem to be camping in the heart of a jungle swarming with insects. There is the moaning of the wind, there are the electric shocks I receive when I touch the doorknob or shake hands with a friend; there are the roaches that run through my kitchen, the elevators that make my heart contract, the unquenchable thirst that burns me from morning till night.

New York is a colonial city, a camping ground. All the hostility, all the cruelty of the world are present in this most prodigious monument man has ever raised to himself. It is a *light* city; its apparent lack of weight amazes most Europeans. In this immense, malevolent space, in this desert of rock that supports no vegetation, they have constructed thousands of houses in brick, wood, or reinforced concrete which give the appearance of being on the point of flying away.

I like New York. I have learned to like it. I have accustomed myself to looking at it in massive ensembles and great perspectives. My glance no longer lingers on façades seeking a house which, impossibly, would not be like every other house. It goes at once to the horizon and looks for the buildings which, hidden in mist, are nothing but volumes, nothing but the austere framework of the sky. If you know how to look at the two uneven rows of buildings that line the thoroughfare like cliffs, you are rewarded: they achieve their fulfillment below, at the end of the avenue, in simple harmonious lines, and a patch of sky flows between them. New York is revealed only from a certain height, from a certain distance, from a certain speed; they are not the height, distance, and speed of the pedestrian. The city very closely resembles the great Andalusian plains: it is monotonous if you pass through on foot, superb and ever-changing if you motor.

I learned to love its sky. In European cities, with their low roofs, the sky drags to the earth's level and seems tame. The New York sky is beautiful because the skyscrapers push it high above our heads. Solitary and pure, like a wild animal, it keeps watch over the city. It is not only the local covering; you feel that it reaches far out over all America. It is the sky of all the world.

I learned to love the avenues of Manhattan. They are not staid little promenades enclosed between houses; they are national highways. As soon as you set foot on one of them, you can see that it must run to Boston or Chicago. It vanishes outside the city, and the eye can almost follow it into the country. A savage sky above parallel highways: that is what New York is, first of all. In the heart of the city you are in the heart of Nature.

I had to become accustomed to this, and now that I am acclimated I can say that nowhere have I felt more free than in the midst of its crowds. This light, temporary city, which the sun's glancing rays reduce morning and evening to an arrangement of rectangular parallelepipeds, never stifles or depresses. Here you may suffer the anguish of loneliness, but not that of crushing defeat. In Europe we love a particular neighborhood in a city, become attached to a cluster of houses, are captivated by a little corner of a street; and we are no longer free. But hardly have you plunged into New York than you are living completely in the dimensions of New York. It is possible to admire it in the evening from the Queensborough Bridge, in the morning from New Jersey, at noon from the fifty-seventh floor of Rockefeller Center; but you will never be held by any of its streets, for none of them is distinguished by beauty peculiar to itself. The beauty is present in all of them, just as all Nature and the sky of all America are present. Nowhere more than here can you feel the simultaneity of human lives.

In spite of its austerity, New York moves Europeans. Certainly we have learned to love our own ancient cities; but what touches us in them is a Roman wall forming part of the façade of an inn, or a house that Cervantes has lived in, or the Place des Vosges, or the Hôtel de Ville in Rouen. We love our museum-cities—and all our cities are a little like museums, where we wander casually around among the dwellings of our forefathers. New York is not a museum-city; nevertheless, for Frenchmen of my generation, it has already acquired the melancholy of the past. When we were twenty, back in 1925, we were hearing about skyscrapers. They symbolized for us the fabulous American prosperity. We beheld them with stupefaction in the moving pictures. They were the architecture of the future, just as the movie was the art of the future and jazz the music of the future. Today we know about jazz. We know there is more past than future in it. It is a music of popular Negro inspiration, capable of but limited development; it carries on by slowly degenerating. Perhaps it has outlived its time. The talking films also have not fulfilled the promise of the silent films. Hollywood walks in the old ruts. Undoubtedly, during the war, America established herself as the mightiest power in the world. But the era of easy living has passed. She was profoundly shaken by the war, and many economists fear another crisis. So, they are no longer building skyscrapers; it seems they are "too difficult to rent." The man walking in New York before 1930 saw in the tall buildings that dominated the city the first signs of an architecture that would spread over the entire country. In their thrust toward the sky he saw a living symbol of the American urge toward a peaceful conquest of the world. The skyscrapers were alive. But today, for a Frenchman just come from Europe, they are no longer alive. They are already historical monuments, witnesses of a past epoch. They still rise toward the sky but my spirit no longer follows them, and New Yorkers pass at their feet without looking at them. I cannot view them without sadness: they speak of a time when we thought the last war had been fought, when we believed in peace. Already they are slightly neglected; tomorrow, perhaps, they will be demolished. In any event, to build them in the first place required a faith we no longer feel.

I walk among the small brick houses, the color of dried blood. They are younger than European houses, but because of their fragility they seem much older. I see in the distance the Empire State Building or the Chrysler Building pointing vainly toward the sky, and it occurs to me that New York is about to acquire a history, that it already has its ruins. This is enough to adorn with a little softness the harshest city in the world.

CECIL BEATON

The Unreal City

1938–1948

On Thursday, the 24th June, in 1497, John and Sebastian Cabot arrived at New York, but decided not to land, saying, "This is a fine place to visit, but we wouldn't live here for the world." Visitors from Europe, the Orient, Chicago, Kansas City, Houston, Minneapolis and Boston have not been ashamed to plagiarize this remark. Yet, rightly, New Yorkers are proud of their city, so proud of it that they can be tolerant of criticism. As a topic New York is constantly on the lips of its citizens, many of whom have seen it largely constructed before their very eyes. New York is an entire world in itself. Every nationality and every kind of interest is to be found there. It is the great world market of to-day, a centre to which artists, writers and musicians necessarily migrate. It contains the greatest banks, railways, stores, shipping-lines and entertainment. It is the one great world city.

Goethe said:

> "Amerika, Du hast es besser
> Als unser Kontinent, der alte,
> Hast keine verfallenen Schlösser
> Und keine Basalte."

In a manner, New York may be said to be the essential America: acutely conscious of itself as an entity and yet composed, as no other city in the world is composed, of a thousand alien elements. But the capital of every country in the world is something quite apart from the country itself, and this may be said even more of America and New York than of England and London, France and Paris, Italy and Rome. In the United States, each State has its capital and its own tradition, while New York represents the cosmopolitan world which is growing up on the western shores of the Atlantic.

New York contains more people than the other eight great cities of America combined. It is only possible for a percentage of the population to be out of doors at the same time. The idle leave it, the *élite* escape from it.

The cultural civilization of a people is judged by its art. Clemenceau (was it?) said that "the Americans had passed from a state of barbarism to decadence without the customary interim of civilization." Oscar Wilde said that "the Americans are not uncivilized, as they are often said to be, they are decivilized." But, judging by its art, civilization here has reached as far as the appreciation of music and painting, the most primitive of the arts. . . .

The beauty of London lies hidden in lonely squares, in unexpected corners of the City, in the Temple, in Chelsea, or Westminster. But New York is seen at its best in the distance, as from the approaching liner, when the clusters of shining, metallic buildings, as tall as and taller than the Eiffel Tower, seem to rise like ascending fountains of beauty.

The liner moves slowly up the broad Hudson River, accompanied by a plaintive choir of gulls floating on motionless wings, until mournful sirens startle them. The Statue of Liberty slips slowly by, that *demodé* but magnificent matron, coppery green, like the doorknobs of ancient country greenhouses. The smooth water, cut by the ship's bows, and the impersonal pageant of passing ships, seem to belong as much to eternity as to a desolate region where mountains lie still for centuries.

Two groups of skyscrapers—the Downtown business section and the Midtown residential section of Gotham—appear unrelated to utility. On a misty day, the towers will gradually fade and vanish before your eyes, giving further testimony to their aspect of unreality. They seem to be some romantic fantasy, specifically calculated to create an emotional effect. They are like mythical Baghdad, and, indeed, Mr. O. Henry has referred to New York City as "Baghdad-on-the-subway." A more realistic Chicago architect described Manhattan as an "asparagus bed" with its sword-like shoots springing from the dense population and the fertile manure of wealth. . . .

The expected seldom happens in New York. The cataclysm, the stock market crash or the hurricane is always sudden. Events forestalled seldom occur.

Life is never free and easy in New York. One has too little to do or too much. In no other city must existence be planned so carefully. Not to go out is to be forgotten, but one invitation accepted leads to a dozen more. Rich people go to hospital in order to rest from their usual existence. In winter the poor freeze, in summer they suffer from the heat. In winter the rich asphyxiate in heated rooms and in summer they are frozen by air conditioning.

One has the impression of being in much closer contact with everyday events in New York. The daily routine is more easily dispensed with. Everyone is more available and on hand. Everybody seems to know where and how the other person is spending his day, and without instructions having been left, you are successfully tracked down by the telephone, even in the obscure restaurant that has been chosen for lunch. In Paris, to make a telephone call is an event. Here, telephoning is as easy as breathing. Only for a minute has the man in the straw boater abandoned his Coke, as he drops in the coin, dials, speaks in monosyllabic undertones and is back at the counter while the coin tinkles to its resting-place, and a dying flutter of metal denotes that another telephone call has been made.

In no other country are there so many fans, autograph-hunters, beggars and anonymous letter-writers. In a city made up of such variety of nationalities and men, dangers lurk in everyday activities. It is difficult not to offend someone present when expressing an opinion in public. . . .

New York is a city of perspectives. They are as clearly visualized as is the miniature Palladian theatre at Vicenza. In the clear atmosphere and brilliant light the distances are as sharp as the foreground.

The streets in the business sections, and even in some residential areas, are straight tunnels beneath mountainous buildings. With their metal kerbs and tarmac or concrete surfaces, they reverberate with a noise that is unlike that of any other city. The sidewalk on Park

Avenue at any point within several blocks of Grand Central Station is constantly vibrating sympathetically with the trains moving underground from the railroad station. The whole city quivers with a universal vibration, and it has been said that "even inanimate objects of art, in hushed museums, move slowly across their shelves in the course of the year." The apartment blocks are often made of Manitoba marble or Portland cement, though, functionally, with the Bessemer steel process, these walls are superfluous. Wood is forbidden, even for decoration.

Throughout the day, the same group of buildings are transformed by the varied effects of light. The shadow thrown from one skyscraper on to another has the sharp quality of the steel hidden beneath the marble casing. It is startlingly dramatic. Some of the East Side streets resemble paintings of the early Di Chirico period, with the long line of tenements in perspective and the strange shapes and colour of the buildings themselves producing a curious melancholy.

In winter there is so much static electricity charging the air that sudden contact with the door-handle or telephone creates a flash. As you stoop to smell a lily a spark will emanate from its pistil. . . .

New York is, as Baudelaire spoke of Paris, an "unreal city." Humanity runs the spectrum from infra-poor to ultra-rich. Beneath the line of skyscrapers is an American pattern of jumbled paradoxes. Americans are materialistic and idealistic at the same time: F. Scott Fitzgerald understood this, and saw it as the cross on which the American dream was crucified. His novel, *The Great Gatsby*, beneath its deceptively superficial style, touched upon the main undercurrents of American life. Though his novel was of the 'twenties, it seems timeless and fresh to-day. The New Yorkers have big hearts and small souls, they are cruel, yet sentimental; they are superficial, yet often profound; they are children, but they can be adults as well. The European has a background of hundreds of years, a solid tradition. The American tradition is young, and yet the swift rise of American capitalism has polevaulted the people over whole areas of mind and spirit which there was no time to explore. If they are intimate they are intimate with all and sundry, if they are shy they are universally shy, with their wife, friends and strangers alike. They have no relative qualities of behaviour. The result is a bizarre *collage* of a people. Money is their standard of success, and the soul gets lost in the shuffle. Yet the "brave new world" ideality of their forefathers is inherent in the lifeblood of America, and their ambiguous symbol is a dollar-bill in one hand and a dream in the other. New Yorkers use the dream to obtain the dollar-bill, and the dollar-bill to buy the dream, but at the cross-roads of the dream and the dollar stands Radio City as the temple to Apollo. The skyscraper is the concrete fusion of the American ideal which would pierce the rainbow, and the materialistic capitalism which immured that ideal forever within the atoms of steel and stone. It is inevitable that this country produces devils and saints from the same crucible: the ideal is a two-way catalytic agent.

Hart Crane, the tragic American poet, and last of the Faustian Romantics, selected the Brooklyn Bridge as a symbol for his long poem on America. The bridge was to be the symbol of modern man's continuum, spanning time and space. It was "the harp and altar of the fury fused." The subway was a vast umbilical cord, shuttling him through the historical womb of America. That his poem was ultimately a failure indicates that the Brooklyn Bridge could not stand the strain of holding both dream and reality, for the reality has corrupted the dream, and the dream has undermined the reality. The American, passionately involved in his attempts to make this double meaning single, is acutely aware of his failure.

TRUMAN CAPOTE

The Diamond Iceberg

1950

It is a myth, the city, the rooms and windows, the steam-spitting streets; for anyone, everyone, a different myth, an idol-head with traffic-light eyes winking a tender green, a cynical red. This island, floating in river water like a diamond iceberg, call it New York, name it whatever you like; the name hardly matters because, entering from the greater reality of elsewhere, one is only in search of a city, a place to hide, to lose or discover oneself, to make a dream wherein you prove that perhaps after all you are not an ugly duckling, but wonderful, and worthy of love, as you thought sitting on the stoop where the Fords went by; as you thought planning your search for a city. . . .

Lunch today with M. Whatever is one to do about her? She says the money is gone finally and, unless she goes home, her family refuse absolutely to help. Cruel, I suppose, but I told her I did not see the alternative. On one level, to be sure, I do not think going home possible for her. She belongs to that sect most swiftly, irrevocably trapped by New York, the talented untalented; too acute to accept a more provincial climate, yet not quite acute enough to breathe freely within the one so desired, they go along neurotically feeding upon the fringes of the New York scene.

Only success, and that at a perilous peak, can give relief, but, for artists without an art, it is always tension without release, irritation with no resulting pearl. Possibly there would be if the pressure to succeed were not so tremendous. They feel compelled to prove something, because middle-class America, from which they mostly spring, has withering words for its men of feeling, for its young of experimental intelligence, who do not show immediately that these endeavors pay off on a cash basis. But if a civilization falls, is it cash the inheritors find among the ruins? Or is it a statue, a poem, a play?

Which is not to say that the world owes M., or anyone, a living; alas, the way things are with her, she most likely could not make a poem, a good one, that is; still she is important, her values are balanced by more than the usual measure of truth, she deserves a finer destiny than to pass from belated adolescence to premature middle age with no intervening period, and nothing to show. . . .

At night, hot weather opens the skull of a city, exposing its white brain and its central nerves, which sizzle like the inside of an electric-light bulb. . . . I should probably get a good deal more work done if I left New York. However, more than likely that is not true either. Until one is a certain age, the country seems a bore; and anyway, I like nature not in general, but in particular. Nevertheless, unless one is in love, or satisfied, or ambition-driven, or without curiosity, or reconciled (which appears to be the modern synonym for happiness), the city is like a monumental machine restlessly devised for wasting time, devouring illusions. After a little, the search, the exploration, can become sinisterly hurried, sweatingly anxious, a race over hurdles of Benzedrine and nembutal. Where is what you were looking for? And by the way, what *are* you looking for? It is misery to refuse an invitation; one is always declining them, only to put in a surprise appearance; after all, it is difficult to stay away when whispers eerily persist to suggest that, in keeping to yourself, you've let love fly out the window, denied your answer, forever lost what you were looking for: oh to think! all this awaits a mere ten blocks away: hurry, put on your hat, don't bother with the bus, grab a taxi, there now, hurry, ring the doorbell: hello sucker, April fool.

Today is my birthday and, as always, Selma remembered: her customary offering, a dime carefully wadded in a sheet of john paper, arrived with the morning mail. In both time and age, Selma is my oldest friend; for eighty-three years she has lived in the same small Alabama town; a hooked little woman with parched cinder-dark skin and spicy, hooded eyes, she was for forty-seven years a cook in the house of my three aunts; but now that they are dead, she has moved to her daughter's farm, just, as she says, to sit quiet and take her ease. But accompanying her gift there was a sort of note, and in it she said to make ready, for any day now she was going to take a Greyhound bus for that "grandus city." It does not mean anything; she will never come; but she has been threatening to for as long as memory. The summer before I first saw New York, and that was fourteen years ago, we used to sit talking in the kitchen, our voices strumming away the whole lazy day; and what we talked about mostly was the city where I was soon to go. It was her understanding that there were no trees there, nor flowers, and she'd heard it said that most of the people lived underground or, if not underground, in the sky. Furthermore, there were "no nourishin' vittles," no good butterbeans, blackeyes, okra, yams, sausage—like we had at home. And it's cold, she said, yessireebobtail, go on up in that cold country, time we see you again your nose will have freeze and fall off.

But then Mrs. Bobby Lee Kettle brought over some picture slides of New York, and after that Selma began telling her friends that when I went north she was going with me. The town seemed to her suddenly shriveled and mean. And so my aunts bought her a round-trip ticket, the idea being that she should ride up with me, turn around, and go back. Everything was fine until we reached the depot; and there Selma began to cry, and say that she couldn't go, that she would die so far from home.

For a child the city is a joyless place; it was a sad winter, inside and out. Later on, when one is older and in love, it is the double vision of sharing with your beloved which gives experience texture, shape, significance. To travel alone is to journey through a wasteland. But if you love enough, sometimes you can see for yourself, and for another, too. That is the way it was with Selma. I saw twice over everything: the first snow, and skaters skimming in the park, the fine fur coats of the funny cold country children, the Chute-the-Chute at Coney, subway chewing-gum machines, the magical Automat, the islands in the river and the glitter upon the twilight bridge, the blue upward floating of a Paramount band, the men who came in the courtyard day after day and sang the same ragged, hoarse songs, the magnificent fairytale of a ten-cent store where one went after school to steal things; I watched, listened, storing up for the quiet kitchen-hours when Selma would say, as she did, "Tell stories about that place, true stories now, none of them lies." But mostly they were lies I told; it wasn't my fault, I couldn't remember, because it was as though I'd been to one of those supernatural castles visited by characters in legends: once away, you do not remember, all that is left is the ghostly echo of haunting wonder.

CYRIL CONNOLLY

Notes on Today's Supreme Metropolis

1953

Friday. Up at six to see New York in the darkness—sunrise, the Narrows, the first houses, the ferries, *l'aurore rose et verte*, the Statue of Liberty, skyscrapers in fog, general impression much more European than I had expected. . . . Tony and Wystan are there and we go off to lunch. Auden warns us of the perils of the big city, he seems obsessed with hold-ups, the proper use of the subway system, and with jumping to it at the traffic lights; his welcome is like that of the town mouse to the country mouse in the Disney film. I discover only later that his battle with the traffic lights is a kind of personal obsession with the machine age, a challenge to his desire to pass efficiently in the crowd. Hugging our wallets tightly and plunging over the crossings we proceed in short rushes to the Holliday bookshop, an oasis where carefully chosen books are sold like handmade cushions; here Wystan introduces the two new mice and leaves us, with instructions on how to take the subway back. . . .

The new mice compare notes. Peter says the U.S.A. is a place where only the very rich can be the least different from anyone else, but where the poor are not crushed and stunted (as in England, where the upper class is twice as tall as the lower). Here, he said, the poor are picturesque and often beautiful—the true creators of the American dream—and that there was also a great poetry about the country when one travelled over it. On the other hand it was awful seeing nothing but copies—of buildings, houses, furniture, pictures, and where the originals were in private hands they gave no intimacy. I found the skyscrapers depressing, a huge black ferro-concrete architecture of necessity shutting out the light from the treeless streets

> *Whose constant care is not to please*
> *But to remind of our, and Adam's curse*
> *And that, to be restored, our sickness must*
>   *grow worse.*

Saturday. To the Lafayette after strolling round delicious Washington Square which in the morning sun considerably revives me from the gloomy thoughts of the night before, sleepless beside the sizzling radiator. Greenwich Village, which reminds me more and more of Soho, is still cheap, and apparently not quite spoilt, 'the one place in New York where different income groups are still mixed up, and where the queers and misfits from the Middle West can all find sanctuary.' 'There is an immense cleavage here,' says Tony at lunch, 'between the intellectuals and everyone else, who are really quite uninterested in books, though they like to keep up with the best-sellers. Intellectuals thus have to join political movements or attach themselves to causes or become dons for they cannot otherwise survive. They become over-serious, "culture" requires one hundred per cent efficiency and is a whole-time business, everyone becomes extremely bellicose and erudite; publishers work so hard that even they have no time for pleasure, and without pleasures the intellectual becomes uncivilized, a pedantic variation of the business man.'

After lunch to the top of Rockefeller Center. Asked the bald elevator boy on the last lap why we were told to face outwards. He made no reply at first, then broke down into helpless laughter; the only words to come from him were, 'It's all so silly'—mountain sickness, perhaps. The view was the first beautiful thing I had seen in New York, where one can go for weeks without the knowledge of being surrounded by water. If one need never descend below the fortieth floor New York would seem the most beautiful city in the world, its skies and cloudscapes are tremendous, its southern latitude is revealed only in its light (for vegetation and architecture are strictly northern); here one can take in the Hudson, the East river, the midtown and down-town colonies of skyscrapers, Central Park and the magnificent new bridges and curving arterial highways and here watch the evening miracle, the lights going on over all these frowning termitaries against a sky of royal-blue velvet only to be paralleled in Lisbon or Palermo. A southern city, with a southern pullulation of life, yet with a northern winter imposing a control; the whole nordic energy and sanity of living crisply enforcing its authority for three of the four seasons on the violet-airy babel of tongues and races; this tension gives New York its unique concentration and makes it the supreme metropolis of the present. Dinner with Auden's friend Chester. At last the luxury of poverty; stairs, no lift, leaking armchairs, a bed-sitting-room with bath-kitchenette curtained off, guests with European teeth (who was it said that Americans have no faces?), a gramophone library, untidy books not preserved in cardboard coffins, an incompetent gas stove—and an exquisite dinner cooked and served by C. . . . Much conversation about the U.S.W. reverts always to the same argument, that a writer needs complete anonymity, he must break away from the European literary 'happy family' with its family love and jokes and jealousies and he must reconsider all the family values. Possibly he could do this in any large impersonal society, but only in America is it so easy for the anonymous immigrant to make money. He is, of course, extremely lonely, but then so is every American; 'you have no idea,' he says, 'how lonely even the married are.' I make the inevitable point that surely it is important to live in attractive surroundings, and in New York (where all want to live) only the rich can afford them. Why live an exile in a black slum, looking out on a fire-escape, in a city which is intolerable in winter and summer, when for the same money one might flourish in Regent's Park or on the Île Saint Louis? But then, I imagine Auden replying, you would at once have the family all about you, and he concentrates on planning my return journey to Washington Square. Walking back from the subway station at two in the morning I find a second-hand bookstore open all night in West Eighth Street, I go in and buy more Cummings. To purchase early works of Cummings in the small hours, in the heart of

> the little barbarous Greenwich perfumed fake

and march home with them in the frosty night, while the tugs hoot and central heating plants under the long black street puff away through its many manholes like geysers on the moon, that is to enjoy that anonymous urban civilization that Auden has chosen, and of which Baudelaire dreamed and despaired!

At a time when the American way, backed by American resources, has made the country into the greatest power the world has known, there has never been more doubting and questioning of the purpose of the American process; the higher up one goes the more searching becomes this self-criticism, the deeper the thirst for a valid mystique of humanity. Those who rule America, who formulate its foreign policy and form its opinion, are enormously conscious of their responsibility and of the total inadequacy of the crude material philosophy of life in which they grew up. The bloody-minded, the smug, the imperialist, the fascist, are in a minority. Seldom, in fact, has an unwilling world been forced to tolerate, through its own folly, a more unwilling master.

The New York scene reveals many traces of this unrest. Insecurity reigns. Almost everyone hates his job. Psychiatrists of all schools are as common as monks in the Thebaid. 'Who is your analyst?' will disarm any interviewer; books on how to be happy, how to attain peace of mind, how to win friends and influence people, how to breathe, how to achieve a cheap sentimental humanism at other people's expense, how to become a Chinaman like Lin Yutang and make a lot of money, how to be a Bahai or breed chickens (*The Egg and I*) all sell in millions. Religious houses of retreat merge imperceptibly into disintoxication clinics and private mental homes for the victims of traffic lights and nervous breakdowns. 'Alcoholics Anonymous' slink like house detectives around the literary cocktail parties. A most interesting phenomenon is the state of mind apparent in *Time, Life, The New Yorker*, and similar magazines. Thus *Life*, with its enormous circulation, comes out with excellently written leading articles on the dearth of tragedy in American literature or the meaning of suffering, and a closer acquaintance reveals them to be staffed by some of the most interesting and sensitive minds in that insensitive city.

It is easy to make fun of these three papers, but in fact they are not funny. Although they have very large circulations indeed, they only just miss being completely honourable and serious journals, in fact 'highbrow.' Hence the particular nemesis, ordeal by shiny paper, of those who manage them; they work very hard, and deliver *almost* the best work of which they are capable. But the gap is never quite closed between the public and the highbrow writer, because the American organism is not quite healthy. I mention this at some length because it indicates how very nearly New York has achieved the ideal of a humanist society, where the best of which an artist is capable is desired by the greatest number. Thurber's drawings, Hersey's *Hiroshima*, the essays of Edmund Wilson or Mary MacCarthy, *Time*'s anonymous reviews, show that occasionally the gap *is* closed; when it is closed permanently the dream of Santayana will be near fulfilment.

But these anxiety-forming predicaments (*Time*-stomach is a common trouble) are for those who live in New York and have to earn their living. To the visiting non-competitive European all is unending delight. The shops, the bars, the women, the faces in the street, the excellent and innumerable restaurants, the glitter of Twenty-one, the old-world lethargy of the Lafayette, the hazy view of the East River or Central Park over tea in some apartment at the magic hour when the concrete icebergs suddenly flare up; the impressionist pictures in one house, the exotic trees or bamboo furniture in another, the chink of 'old-fashioneds' with their little glass pestles, the divine glories—Egyptian, Etruscan, French—of the Metropolitan Museum, the felicitous contemporary assertion of the Museum of Modern Art, the snow, the sea-breezes, the late suppers with the Partisans, the reelings-home down the black steam-spitting canyons, the Christmas trees lit up beside the liquorice ribbon of cars on Park Avenue, the Gotham Book Mart, the shabby cosiness of the Village, all go to form an unforgettable picture of what a city ought to be: that is, continuously insolent and alive, a place where one can buy a book or meet a friend at any hour of the day or night, where every language is spoken and xenophobia almost unknown, where every purse and appetite is catered for, where every street with every quarter and the people who inhabit them are fulfilling their function, not slipping back into apathy, indifference, decay. If Paris is the setting for a romance, New York is the perfect city in which to get over one, to get over anything. Here the lost *douceur de vivre* is forgotten and the intoxication of living takes its place. . . .

One thing only seems to me impossible in New York—to write well. Not because the whirl and pleasurable bustle of the gregarious life built around writing is so irresistible, not because it is almost impossible to find a quiet room near a tree, or to stay in of an evening, not because intelligent conversation with a kindred spirit is hard to come by (it is not), but because this glowing, blooming and stimulating material perfection over-excites the mind, causing it to precipitate into wit and conversation those ideas which might have set into literature. Wit and wisecrack, not art, are the thorny flowers on this rocky island, this concrete Capri; they call the tune for which our proud new bass is lent us. 'Yah,' one may say instead of 'yes,' but when 'fabulous,' 'for Chris' sakes,' 'it stinks,' 'way off the beam' and 'Bourbon over ice' roar off our lips, and when we begin to notice with distaste the Europeanism of others—it's time for flight, for dripping plane-trees, misty mornings, the grizzling circle of hypercritical friends, the fecund London inertia where nothing stirs but the soul.

JOHN STEINBECK
The Making of a New Yorker

1953

New York is the only city I have ever lived in. I have lived in the country, in the small town, and in New York. It is true I have had apartments in San Francisco, Mexico City, Los Angeles, Paris, and sometimes have stayed for months, but that is a very different thing. As far as homes go, there is only a small California town and New York. This is a matter of feeling.

The transition from small town to New York is a slow and rough process. I am writing it not because I think my experience was unique; quite the contrary. I suspect that the millions of New Yorkers who were not born here have had much the same experience—at least parallel experiences. . . .

When I came the first time to New York in 1925 I had never been to a city in my life. I arrived on a boat, tourist, one hundred dollars. It was November. . . .

From a porthole, then, I saw the city, and it horrified me. There was something monstrous about it—the tall buildings looming to the sky and the lights shining through the falling snow. I crept ashore—frightened and cold and with a touch of panic in my stomach. This Dick Whittington didn't even have a cat.

I wasn't really bad off. I had a sister in New York and she had a good job. She had a husband and he had a good job. My brother-in-law got me a job as a laborer and I found a room three flights up in Fort Greene Place in Brooklyn. That is about as alone as you can get.

Copyright, 1953, by John Steinbeck. Appeared originally in *The New York Times* magazine.

The job was on Madison Square Garden which was being finished in a hurry. There was time and a half and there was double time. I was big and strong. My job was wheeling cement—one of a long line—one barrow behind another, hour after hour. I wasn't that big and strong. It nearly killed me and it probably saved my life. I was too tired to see what went on around me. . . .

My knowledge of the city was blurred—aching, lights and the roar of the subway, climbing three flights to a room with dirty green walls, falling into bed half-washed, beef stew, coffee and sinkers in a coffee-pot, a sidewalk that pitched a little as I walked, then the line of barrows again. It's all mixed up like a fever dream. There would be big salamanders of glowing coke to warm our hands and I would warm mine just for the rest, long after I couldn't feel my hands at all. . . .

I don't even remember how long the job went on. It seems interminable and was maybe a month or six weeks. Anyway, the Garden got finished for the six-day bicycle races and Tex Rickard congratulated us all, without respect to race or color. I still get a shiver from the place sometimes.

About that time, my rich and successful uncle came to town from Chicago. He was an advertising man with connections everywhere. He was fabulous. He stayed in a suite at the Commodore, ordered drinks or coffee and sandwiches sent up any time he wanted, sent telegrams even if they weren't important. This last still strikes me as Lucullan. My uncle got me a job on a newspaper—The New York *American* down on William Street. I didn't know the first thing about being a reporter. I think now that the twenty-five dollars a week that they paid me was a total loss. They gave me stories to cover in Queens and Brooklyn and I would get lost and spend hours trying to find my way back. I couldn't learn to steal a picture from a desk when a family refused to be photographed and I invariably got emotionally involved and tried to kill the whole story to save the subject.

But for my uncle, I think they would have fired me the first week. Instead, they gave me Federal courts in the old Park Row Post Office. Why, I will never know. It was a specialist's job. Some of the men there had been on that beat for many years and I knew nothing about courts and didn't learn easily. I wonder if I could ever be as kind to a young punk as those men in the reporters' room at the Park Row Post Office were to me. They pretended that I knew what I was doing, and they did their best to teach me in a roundabout way. I learned to play bridge and where to look for suits and scandals. They informed me which judges were pushovers for publicity and several times they covered for me when I didn't show up. You can't repay that kind of thing. I never got to know them. Didn't know where they lived, what they did, or how they lived when they left the room.

I had a reason for that, a girl. I had known her slightly in California and she was most beautiful. I don't think this was only my memory. For she got a job in the Greenwich Village Follies just walking around —and she got it with no trouble whatever. . . .

Now New York changed for me. My girl lived on Gramercy Park and naturally I moved there. The old Parkwood Hotel had some tiny rooms—six walk-up flights above the street—for seven dollars a week. I had nothing to do with New York. It was a stage set in which this golden romance was taking place. The girl was very kind. Since she made four times as much money as I did, she paid for many little dinners. Every night I waited for her outside the stage door.

We would sit in Italian restaurants—she paid—and drink red wine. I wanted to write fiction—novels. She approved of that in theory, but said I should go into advertising—first, that is. I refused. I was being the poor artist, shielding his integrity.

During all this time, I never once knew or saw one New Yorker as a person. They were all minor characters in this intense personal drama. Then everything happened at once. The girl had more sense than I thought. She married a banker from the Middle West and moved there. And she didn't argue. She simply left a note, and two days later I was fired from *The American*.

And now at last the city moved in on me and scared me to death. I looked for jobs—but good jobs, pleasant jobs. I didn't get them. I wrote short stories and tried to sell them. I applied for work on other papers, which was ridiculous on the face of it. And the city crept in—cold and heartless, I thought. I began to fall behind in my room rent. I always had that one ace in the hole. I could go back to laboring. I had a friend who occasionally loaned me a little money. And, finally, I was shocked enough to go for a job as a laborer. But by that time short feeding had taken hold. I could hardly lift a pick. I had trouble climbing the six flights back to my room. My friend loaned me a dollar and I bought two loaves of rye bread and a bag of dried herrings and never left my room for a week. I was afraid to go out on the street—actually afraid of traffic—the noise. Afraid of the landlord and afraid of people. Afraid even of acquaintances.

Then a man who had been in college with me got me a job as a workaway on a ship to San Francisco. And he didn't have to urge me, either. The city had beaten the pants off me. Whatever it required to get ahead, I didn't have. I didn't leave the city in disgust—I left it with the respect plain unadulterated fear gives.

My second assault on New York was different but just as ridiculous as the first. I had had a kind of a success with a novel after many tries. Three of my preceding novels did not make their advance and the advance was four hundred dollars. The largest amount I had ever got for a short story was ninety dollars, for "The Red Pony." When royalties for "Tortilla Flat" went over a thousand dollars, and when Paramount bought the book for $3,000—$2,700 net, I should have been filled with joy but instead I was frightened. During the preceding years I had learned to live comfortably, and contentedly, on an absolute minimum of money—thirty-five to fifty dollars a month. When gigantic sums like $2,700 came over the horizon I was afraid I could not go back to the old simplicity.

Whereas on my first try New York was a dark, hulking frustration, the second time it became the Temptation and I a whistle-stop St. Anthony. As with most St. Anthonys, if I had not been drawn toward luxury and sin, and to me they were the same thing, there would have been no temptation. I reacted without originality: today I see people coming to success doing the same things I did, so I guess I didn't invent it. I pretended and believed my pretense, that I hated the city and all its miles and traps. I longed for the quiet and contemplation of the West Coast. I preferred twenty-nine-cent wine and red beans. And again I didn't even see New York. It had scared me again but this time in another way. So I shut my eyes and drew virtue over my head. I insulted everyone who tried to be kind to me and I fled the Whore of Babylon with relief and virtuous satisfaction, for I had convinced myself that the city was a great snare set in the path of my artistic simplicity and integrity.

Back to the West I plunged, built a new house, bought a Chevrolet and imperceptibly moved from twenty-nine-cent wine to fifty-nine-cent wine. Now I made a number of business trips to New York and I was so completely in my role of country boy that I didn't look at it because I must have been enjoying my triumph over the snares and pitfalls. I had a successful play but never saw it. I believed I wasn't interested but it is probable that I was afraid to see it. I even built up a pleasant fiction that I hated the theatre. And the various trips to New York were very like the visits of the Salvation Army to a brothel—necessary and fascinating but distasteful.

The very first time I came to the city and settled was engineered by a girl. Looking back from the cool position of middle age I can see that most of my heroic decisions somehow stemmed from a girl. I got an apartment on East 51st Street between First and Second Avenues, but even then I kept contact with my prejudices. My new home consisted of the first and second floors of a three-story house and the living room looked out on a small soot field called a garden. Two triumphant Brooklyn trees called ailanthus not only survived but thumbed their noses at the soft coal dust and nitric acid which passed for air in New York.

I was going to live in New York but I was going to avoid it. I planted a lawn in the garden, bought huge pots and planted tomatoes, pollinating the blossoms with a water-color brush. But I can see now that a conspiracy was going on, of which I was not even aware. I walked miles through the streets for the exercise, and began to know the butcher and the newsdealer and the liquor man, not as props or as enemies but as people.

I have talked to many people about this and it seems to be a kind of mystical experience. The preparation is unconscious, the realization happens in a flaming second. It was on Third Avenue. The trains were grinding over my head. The snow was nearly waist-high in the gutters and uncollected garbage was scattered in the dirty mess. The wind was cold, and frozen pieces of paper went scraping along the pavement. I stopped to look in a drug-store window where a latex cooch dancer was undulated by a concealed motor—and something burst in my head, a kind of light and a kind of feeling blended into an emotion which if it had spoken would have said, "My God! I belong here. Isn't this wonderful?"

Everything fell into place. I saw every face I passed. I noticed every doorway and the stairways to apartments. I looked across the street at the windows, lace curtains and potted geraniums through sooty glass. It was beautiful—but most important, I was part of it. I was no longer a stranger. I had become a New Yorker.

Now there may be people who move easily into New York without travail, but most I have talked to about it have had some kind of trial by torture before acceptance. And the acceptance is a double thing. It seems to me that the city finally accepts you just as you finally accept the city.

A young man in a small town, a frog in a small puddle, if he kicks his feet is able to make waves, get mud in his neighbor's eyes—make some impression. He is known. His family is known. People watch him with some interest, whether kindly or maliciously. He comes to New York and no matter what he does, no one is impressed. He challenges the city to fight and it licks him without being aware of him. This is a dreadful blow to a small-town ego. He hates the organism that ignores him. He hates the people who look through him.

And then one day he falls into place, accepts the city and does not fight it any more. It is too huge to notice him and suddenly the fact that it doesn't notice him becomes the most delightful thing in the world. His self-consciousness evaporates. If he is dressed superbly well—there are half a million people dressed equally well. If he is in rags—there are a million ragged people. If he is tall, it is a city of tall people. If he is short the streets are full of dwarfs; if ugly, ten perfect horrors pass him in one block; if beautiful, the competition is overwhelming. If he is talented, talent is a dime a dozen. If he tries to make an impression by wearing a toga—there's a man down the street in a leopard skin. Whatever he does or says or wears or thinks he is not unique. Once accepted this gives him perfect freedom to be himself, but unaccepted it horrifies him.

I don't think New York City is like other cities. It does not have character like Los Angeles or New Orleans. It is all characters—in fact, it is everything. It can destroy a man, but if his eyes are open it cannot bore him.

New York is an ugly city, a dirty city. Its climate is a scandal, its politics are used to frighten children, its traffic is madness, its competition is murderous. But there is one thing about it—once you have lived in New York and it has become your home, no place else is good enough. All of everything is concentrated here, population, theatre, art, writing, publishing, importing, business, murder, mugging, luxury, poverty. It is all of everything. It goes all right. It is tireless and its air is charged with energy. I can work longer and harder without weariness in New York than any place else. . . .

I live in a small house on the East Side in the Seventies. It has a pretty little south garden. My neighborhood is my village. I know all of the storekeepers and some of the neighbors. Sometimes I don't go out of my village for weeks at a time. It has every quality of a village except nosiness. No one interferes in our business—no one by any chance visits us without first telephoning, certainly a most civilized practice. When we close the front door, the city and the world are shut out and we are more private than any country man below the Arctic Circle has ever been. We have many friends—good friends in the city. Sometimes we don't see them for six or eight months and this in no way interferes with our friendship. Any place else this would be resented as neglect. . . .

Everyone at one time or another tries to explain to himself why he likes New York better than any place else. A man who worked for me liked it because if he couldn't sleep he could go to an all-night movie. That's as good a reason as any.

Every once in a while we go away for several months and we always come back with a "Thank God I'm home" feeling. For New York is the world with every vice and blemish and beauty and there's privacy thrown in. What more could you ask?